History of New Testament Research:
From Jonathan Edwards to Rudolf Bultmann

History of New Testament Research

Volume 1
From Deism to Tübingen

Volume 2
From Jonathan Edwards to Rudolf Bultmann

Volume 3
From Biblical Theology to Pluralism
(Forthcoming)

History of
New Testament Research

VOLUME TWO:
FROM JONATHAN EDWARDS TO
RUDOLF BULTMANN

William Baird

FORTRESS PRESS　　　MINNEAPOLIS

HISTORY OF NEW TESTAMENT RESEARCH
Volume Two: From Jonathan Edwards to Rudolf Bultmann

Copyright © 2003 Augsburg Fortress. All rights reserved. Except for brief quotations in critical articles or reviews, no part of this book may be reproduced in any manner without prior written permission from the publisher. Write: Permissions, Augsburg Fortress, Box 1209, Minneapolis, MN 55440.

Scripture quotations are from the New Revised Standard Version Bible, copyright © 1989 by the Division of Christian Education of the National Council of the Churches of Christ in the USA and used by permission.

Volume 2: From Jonathan Edwards to Rudolf Bultmann
ISBN 0-8006-2627-3

The Library of Congress has cataloged volume 1 as follows:

Baird, William,
    History of New Testament research / William Baird.
      p. cm.
    Includes bibliographical references and indexes.
    Contents: v. 1. From deism to Tübingen.
    ISBN 0-8006-2625-5 (v. 1. : alk. paper)
    1. Bible. N.T.—Criticism, interpretation, etc.—History.
I. Title.
BS2350.B35 1992
225'.072—dc20   92-22629

The paper used in this publication meets the minimum requirements of American National Standard for Information Sciences — Permanence of Paper for Printed Library Materials, ANSI Z329.48-1984.

Printed in Canada
07   06   05   04   03   1   2   3   4   5   6   7   8   9   10

For

John Edward Baird
Eric Robb Baird
William Robb Parks

Contents

Acknowledgments   xi

Introduction   xiii

Abbreviations   xvii

Part I
New Testament Research in the Era of Expanding Empire

1. New Testament Research in America during the Nineteenth Century   3

   A Calvinist Precursor: Jonathan Edwards 6
   From Unitarian Biblicism to Transcendental Skepticism:
      Andrews Norton and Theodore Parker 10
   The Maturing of American Scholarship:
      Moses Stuart and Edward Robinson 20
   Classical Orthodoxy at Princeton: Charles Hodge 31
   A Hermeneutical Alternative: Horace Bushnell 37
   History, Piety, and Ecumenism: Philip Schaff 43
   Summary 53

2. The Establishment of Historical Criticism in Great Britain   54

   New Testament Studies before and in the
      Time of the Cambridge Three 55
   The Cambridge Triumvirate:
      Fenton John Anthony Hort, Joseph Barber Lightfoot, and
      Brooke Foss Westcott 60
   Summary 82

3. The Triumph of Liberalism on the Continent   85

The Establishment of Liberalism: Albrecht Ritschl 86
The Reconstruction of Early Christian History:
   Eduard Reuss and Carl Weizsäcker 93
Faith and Historicism: Bernhard Weiss 101
Toward Critical Consensus: Heinrich Holtzmann 111
The Zenith of Liberalism: Adolf von Harnack 122
Summary 135

4. The Return of Skepticism   137

Militant Skepticism: Franz Overbeck 138
Doctrine Conceals History: William Wrede 144
Tradition Transforming History: Julius Wellhausen 151
Criticism contra Skepticism: Adolf Jülicher 156
Heretical Skepticism: Alfred Loisy 163
Summary 172

Part II
New Testament Research in the Era of Global Conflict

5. New Discoveries: Linguistic, Geographical, and Historical Research 177

Words and Their Social and Religious Implications:
   Adolf Deissmann 178
Grammatical and Lexicographical Research: Alexander Buttmann
   and Friedrich Blass; Hermann Cremer and C. L. W. Grimm 184
Linguistic Research in England: J. H. Moulton 186
New Testament Geography, History, and Apologetics:
   William M. Ramsay 189
Linguistic and Cultural Setting of Jesus: Gustaf Dalman 195
The Study of Historical Backgrounds 199
Research in Jewish Backgrounds: Emil Schürer and
   Robert Henry Charles 199
Research in Hellenistic Backgrounds: Paul Wendland,
   Edwin Hatch, and Otto Pfleiderer 209
Summary 220

6. Methodological Developments — 221

History of Religion and Related Methods 222
Thoroughgoing Eschatology: Johannes Weiss, Albert Schweitzer 222
The History of Religion School 238
Jewish Research and the New Testament: Claude G. Montefiore and
    Joseph Klausner 253
Gospel Research in England: William Sanday, B. H. Streeter,
    F. C. Burkitt 261
Form Criticism: Karl Ludwig Schmidt, Martin Dibelius, Rudolf
    Bultmann 269
Summary 286

7. The Advance of American New Testament Research — 288

New Testament Research at Union Theological Seminary:
    Charles Augustus Briggs and James Moffatt 289
New Testament Research at Yale: Benjamin Wisner Bacon 299
The Chicago School: Ernest DeWitt Burton, Shailer Mathews,
    Shirley Jackson Case, Edgar Johnson Goodspeed 305
American Women in New Testament Research 330
Conservative Reaction: Benjamin B. Warfield
    and J. Gresham Machen 341
Summary 359

8. Conservative Alternatives on the Continent — 361

Critics of the History of Religion: Ernst von Dobschütz
    and Paul Feine 362
Conservative Criticism: Theodor Zahn and Adolf Schlatter 367
Roman Catholic Biblical Research: Marie-Joseph Lagrange 384
Summary 393

9. The Refining of Historical Criticism — 396

Continuing Discovery and Research in Text Criticism:
    Hermann Freiherr von Soden, James Rendell Harris,
        and Kirsopp Lake 397
New Testament Grammar and Lexicography:
    Archibald Thomas Robertson and Walter Bauer 412
Research in Jewish Backgrounds:
    Hermann L. Strack, Paul Billerbeck, and George Foot Moore 417

Research in Hellenism: Arthur Darby Nock 428
The History of Early Christianity: Hans Lietzmann,
    Maurice Goguel, and Walter Bauer 433
Mastery of Historical Exegesis: Hans Windisch
    and Ernst Lohmeyer 455
Summary 469

Epilogue 471

Select Bibliography 478

Index of Subjects 538

Index of Names 547

Index of Scripture 562

Acknowledgments

This volume was written during retirement—what I have too optimistically called a "permanent" sabbatical. Consequently, my work has not enjoyed such benefits as student assistants and faculty secretaries. Mundane tasks like building bibliographies, checking references, and retrieving books have been mine alone. Little wonder progress has been slow and the process has consumed a decade! However, my work has been encouraged by Brite Divinity School and Texas Christian University who not only support an excellent health insurance program for seniors, but provide parking places at the library for emeritus faculty. More important, the Mary Couts Burnett Library contains an excellent collection of New Testament material (including the complete ATLA microfiche collection) and an efficient interlibrary loan department. I have also used the fine resources of the Roberts Library at Southwestern Baptist Theological Seminary. Friends and colleagues have offered support and sympathy, and my wife Shirley has respected my preoccupation with research when travel and leisure would have been more enjoyable. The book is dedicated to three men who have been special to me: my brother John, my son Eric, and my grandson Bill.

Introduction

The New Testament is a small book that has provoked an immense amount of research. As a short theme by Paganini inspired variations by Brahms and still more by Rachmaninoff, so the NT has encouraged endless variations. The musical analogy is fitting, since NT research is more an art than a science. To be sure, modern study of the Bible began with the Enlightenment, when the "scientific method" was applied to all disciplines—including the study of the Holy Scriptures. But the Bible, unlike the natural sciences, which deal with objective data, is a collection of historical literature; and neither history nor literature provides the sort of matter that can be analyzed in a laboratory. Scientific knowledge is cumulative; new hypotheses are built on previous, independently confirmed results. In some areas of NT research, too, scholars appropriate earlier work, for instance, the production of critical texts and linguistic tools. However, in regard to matters of exegesis and theology, NT scholars continue to suppose they can produce something new and better.

The reason the NT has provoked such quantity of research is the significance of the book. For millions of Christians, it is the most important book ever written. To be sure, Christians differ as to the nature of that importance—all the way from those who view the NT as the repository of the inerrant words of God to those who see it as a fallible record of Christianity's origins. For some, it is the accurate account of God's revelation in history; for others, it is the authentic witness to human aspiration of the transcendent. Moreover, persons who do not share the biblical faith are awed by the reverence this book has aroused. And those who have perused its pages are impressed by the power of its rhetoric, the impact of its ethic.

The history of research about the NT is indispensable for the serious student. Scholarship in any discipline demands, at a minimum, knowledge of the history of the discipline. Proposals that appear to be innovative may have already been tried, and, in the pursuit of the new, light from the past provides insight and perspective. Some skeptics have charged that historical criticism has failed—as if there were some absolute goal to be attained. The study of literature and history does not seek finality, but understanding, and the quest for understanding is continually embraced anew. Historical criticism, against the passion for the absolute, provides its own corrective.

The history of NT research is important for theologians, church historians, and students of intellectual history. The history of the interpretation of the Bible is a major feature of the history of doctrine. The developing life of the church has been dominated by debate about the authority and interpretation of the NT. Religion has influenced political thought and played a leading role in social and ethical action. An understanding of religious influence is essential to understanding society and culture, and in the Western world, the development of Christianity has been closely allied to the history of the interpretation of the NT.

When, almost twenty years ago, I began work on this project, I imagined the results could be comprised in a single volume. As the work progressed, it became evident that the material was too vast, and that two volumes would be required. Volume 1 (*From Deism to Tübingen*), covering roughly the research from 1700 to 1870, was published in 1992, with the prospect of a second volume to review the period from 1870 to around 1970. However, the amount of material again loomed too large, and the project, like a runaway snowball, kept increasing in size. The current volume, consequently, is largely limited to the period prior to World War II, covering roughly 1870 to 1940. Actually, some of the scholars included continued to live and write after the war, but their major works precede 1940. In an earlier draft, scholars who are on the border, that is, with important works both before and after the war, were included, namely, V. Taylor, F. C. Grant, H. J. Cadbury, William Manson, T. W. Manson, J. de Zwaan, A. Fridrichsen, and C. H. Dodd. These, primarily because of limitations of space, I have relegated to a projected third volume.

Also in the future volume, I intend to investigate the developments in biblical theology. Barth is not included in volume 2, though his *Romans* appeared in 1918. Bultmann is mentioned in volume 2, but only as a practitioner of *religionsgeschichtliche* method and form criticism. Of course, the first volume of his *Theology of the New Testament* did not appear until 1948, and the biblical theology movement, especially in America, is largely a postwar phenomenon. As to volume 2, the subtitle, *From Jonathan Edwards to Rudolf Bultmann,* delineates the chronological frame in terms of significant scholars—Edwards as early America's greatest theologian and Bultmann as the predominant NT scholar of the twentieth century. Bultmann also represents a major turning point: his early research (reviewed in chapter 6 of volume 2) reflects the zenith of the practice of the historical critical method; his later work (to be assessed in volume 3) represents the crucial shift in mid-century from traditional criticism to theological reflection.

All of this indicates that the basic arrangement of the material in volume 2 is, as in volume 1, more or less chronological. The "more or less" is owing to the complexity of the chronological factors—dates of birth and death, dates of major writings. Many of the scholars lived long lives and wrote over an extended period of time. E. J. Goodspeed, for example, lived from 1871 to 1962 and his publications extend over half a century. Other factors considered in the arrangement, therefore, are topical (types of criticism, methods, points of view) and geographical. The opening chapter presents the rise of criticism in America, beginning with Jonathan Edwards, an eighteenth-century precursor, and continuing through the first two-thirds of the nineteenth century. Thus, chronologically, this chapter brings American research parallel to the European research of volume 1. The geographical factor also points to a limitation of the work: the research reviewed here is largely concerned with American, British, and German scholarship, mostly Protestant. A few French are included (Catholics and Protestants), and mention is made of scholars who have worked in Canada, the Netherlands, and Switzerland. Although this limitation is true of most histories of the discipline, the neglect of research in other areas—for example in Scandinavia and southern Europe—is unfortunate.

As in volume 1, the definition of "NT research" includes the whole discipline of the study of the NT, including text criticism, philology, higher criticism, hermeneutics, exegesis, and theology. The research focuses on individual scholars. The scholars included are selected according to their impact on the ongoing history of the discipline, though the decision to include or exclude is subjective. Scholars are presented in one place—in relation to their chronology, country, and type of research. The only exception in this volume is Walter Bauer, who is treated separately as lexicographer and as an early church historian. The scholars are investigated according to their major works. An effort is made to set their research within the larger historical-cultural context, and within their own biographical development and theological perspective. For biographical data, I have used the standard dictionaries and encyclopedias. Of particular help have been *The New Schaff-Herzog Encyclopedia of Religious Knowledge* and the *Dictionary of Biblical Interpretation,* edited by John H. Hayes. These and the other standard works are not cited in the footnotes unless there is a scarcity of biographical resources. In concentrating on the major writings, an effort has been made to present the views of the scholars faithfully—with the hope that if the scholar were to read it, he or she would be able to embrace it as his or her own. Evaluation and criticism is largely restricted to brief summaries (for each scholar and each chapter). This is largely owing to limitations of space, but also to avoid imposing later perspectives and evaluations on the material. The criticisms and assessments intend to address the material in its own right, in its own setting, in order to sharpen the issues, and not on the basis of some omniscient perspective. No doubt I have not been fully successful in this, and have allowed my own presuppositions to invade.

In view of the huge amount of material, review of secondary sources has been limited to major works that relate directly to the subject. I have not, for example, consulted book reviews unless they are major, written by prominent scholars. In regard to the primary sources, the amount of material considered in the text, notes, and bibliography varies. For scholars who have written extensively (for example, Harnack with more than 1,500 items in his bibliography), the works cited represent a selection of only the most important. For scholars who have published little (for example, F. A. J. Hort), the selections of primary and secondary sources are fairly complete. The bibliography is selective; it does not include all the references that are found in the notes, but only items that are important for NT research. To save space, I have (reluctantly) followed the procedure whereby individual citations within a paragraph have been gathered into a single footnote at the end or toward the end of the paragraph. References to previous scholars and their work are noted in the footnotes (from volume 1, abbreviated as *HNTR* 1). Except for general notices (for example, this "anticipates redaction criticism"), detailed references to work in the future are not made.

Where English translations of material are available I have eagerly used them, only occasionally checking the original. The translations of German and French are my own, unless otherwise noted; they tend to be literal. It is unfortunate that limitations of space make printing of the originals prohibitive. English translations of NT texts are from the NRSV unless otherwise noted. To avoid pejorative usage I often refer to the "Old Testament" as the Hebrew Bible (HB), though in some historical contexts OT seemed fitting.

Trained as a NT historian, I have found it daunting to write a survey of a huge amount of material. As a Neutestamentler, I feel compelled to read all the primary sources, leaving no stone unturned—an obvious impossibility. Nevertheless, I have read a large quantity of material and taken copious notes, of which only a small amount has been distilled into the book. This accounts for the ponderous pace at which I have worked, but even more, it reminds me that what actually gets onto the pages is limited, deceptively simple, sometimes superficial. In writing a survey, I am aware, too, that among the readers are scholars who know more about every individual about whom I write than I do. I beg their indulgence, and hope a survey may prove useful in offering an informative overview, and, at the same time, provide stimulus for further investigation of the primary sources.

Abbreviations

AAR	American Academy of Religion
AARDS	American Academy of Religion Dissertation Series
ABRL	Anchor Bible Reference Library
AJP	*American Journal of Philology*
AJT	*American Journal of Theology*
AR	*Archiv für Religionswissenschaft*
ASNU	Acta seminarii neotestamentici upsaliensis
AThR	*Anglican Theological Review*
ATLA	American Theological Library Association
AV	Authorized (King James) Version
AzTh	Arbeiten zur Theologie
BA	*Biblical Archaeologist*
BDF	Blass, F., A. Debrunner, and R. W. Funk. *A Greek Grammar of the New Testament and Other Early Christian Literature* (Chicago: University of Chicago Press, 1961)
BEHE	Bibliothèque de l'École des Hautes Études
BEvT	Beiträge zur evangelischen Theologie
BFCT	Beiträge zur Förderung christlicher Theologie
BGBE	Beiträge zur Geschichte der biblischen Exegese
BHT	Beiträge zur historischen Theologie
Bib	*Biblica*
BITC	*Bible Interpreters of the Twentieth Century: A Selection of Evangelical Voices* (ed. Walter A. Elwell and J. D. Weaver; Grand Rapids, Mich.: Baker, 1999)

BJRL	*Bulletin of the John Rylands University Library of Manchester*
BJS	Brown Judaic Studies
BR	*Biblical Research*
BRev	*Bible Review*
BZ	*Biblische Zeitschrift*
BZAW	Beihefte zur Zeitschrift für die alttestamentliche Wissenschaft
BZNW	Beihefte zur Zeitschrift für die neutestamentliche Wissenschaft
BZRGG	Beihefte zur Zeitschrift für Religions- und Geistesgeschichte
CBQ	*Catholic Biblical Quarterly*
CFTL	Clark's Foreign Theological Library
CH	*Church History*
Chm	*Churchman*
ConBNT	Coniectanea neotestamentica or Coniectanea biblica: New Testament Series
CQR	*Church Quarterly Review*
CSJH	Chicago Studies in the History of Judaism
CTL	Crown Theological Library
DBI	*Dictionary of Biblical Interpretation* (ed. John H. Hayes; 2 vols.; Nashville: Abingdon, 1999)
Ebib	Études bibliques
Enc	*Encounter*
ETR	*Études théologiques et religieuses*
EvT	*Evangelische Theologie*
ExpTim	*Expository Times*
FCBS	Fortress Classics in Biblical Studies
FRLANT	Forschungen zur Religion und Literatur des Alten und Neuen Testaments
GTA	Göttinger theologische Arbeiten
HB	Hebrew Bible
HDR	Harvard Dissertations in Religion
HHMBI	*Historical Handbook of Major Biblical Interpreters* (ed. Donald K. McKim; Downers Grove, Ill.: InterVarsity, 1998)
HibJ	*Hibbert Journal*
HNT	Handbuch zum Neuen Testament
HNTR	*History of New Testament Research: Volume One: From Deism to Tübingen,* William Baird (Minneapolis: Fortress Press, 1992)
HT	Harper Torchbooks
HTCL	Harper Torchbooks/The Cloister Library

HTR	*Harvard Theological Review*
HTS	Harvard Theological Studies
ICC	International Critical Commentary
Int	*Interpretation*
ITL	International Theological Library
JAAR	*Journal of the American Academy of Religion*
JBL	*Journal of Biblical Literature*
JETS	*Journal of the Evangelical Theological Society*
JJS	*Journal of Jewish Studies*
JPH	*Journal of Presbyterian History*
JQR	*Jewish Quarterly Review*
JR	*Journal of Religion*
JRS	*Journal of Roman Studies*
JSNTSup	Journal for the Study of the New Testament: Supplement Series
JSOT	*Journal for the Study of the Old Testament*
JSOTSup	Journal for the Study of the Old Testament: Supplement Series
JSS	*Journal of Semitic Studies*
JTS	*Journal of Theological Studies*
KEK	Kritisch-exegetischer Kommentar über das Neue Testament (Meyer-Kommentar)
KJV	King James (Authorized) Version
KlT	Kleine Texte
KNT	Kommentar zum Neuen Testament
LCL	Loeb Classical Library
LJS	Lives of Jesus Series
MCTA	*Makers of Christian Theology in America* (ed. Mark G. Toulouse and James O. Duke; Nashville: Abingdon, 1997)
MNTC	Moffatt New Testament Commentary
MTS	Marburger theologische Studien
NovT	*Novum Testamentum*
NovTSup	Supplements to Novum Testamentum
NRSV	New Revised Standard Version
NSHERK	*The New Schaff-Herzog Encyclopedia of Religious Knowledge* (ed. Samuel Macauley Jackson; 13 vols.; Grand Rapids, Mich.: Baker, 1949)
NTAbh	Neutestamentliche Abhandlungen
NTOA	Novum Testamentum et Orbis Antiquus
NTS	*New Testament Studies*

NTTS	New Testament Tools and Studies
PSTJ	*Perkins (School of Theology) Journal*
PTMS	Pittsburgh Theological Monograph Series
PW	Pauly-Wissowa, *Real-Encyclopädie der classischen Altertumswissenschaft*
RB	*Revue biblique*
ResQ	*Restoration Quarterly*
RGG	*Religion in Geschichte und Gegenwart*
RGS	*Die Religionswissenschaft der Gegenwart in Selbstdarstellungen* (ed. Erich Stange; 5 vols.; Leipzig: Felix Meiner, 1925–1929)
RHPR	*Revue d'histoire et de philosophie religieuses*
RSPT	*Revue des sciences philosphiques et théologiques*
RSV	Revised Standard Version
RV	Revised Version (1881)
SBL	Society of Biblical Literature
SBLBAC	Society of Biblical Literature The Bible and American Culture
SBLBMI	Society of Biblical Literature The Bible and Its Modern Interpreters
SBLBSNA	Society of Biblical Literature Biblical Scholarship in North America
SBLCP	Society of Biblical Literature Centennial Publications
SBLDS	Society of Biblical Literature Dissertation Series
SBT	Studies in Biblical Theology
SD	Studies and Documents
SG	Sammlung Göschen
SHAW	Sitzungsberichte der heidelberger Akademie der Wissenschaften
SJT	*Scottish Journal of Theology*
SPAW	Sitzungsberichte der preussischen Akademie der Wissenschaften
SR	*Studies in Religion*
ST	*Studia theologica*
StABH	*Studies in American Biblical Hermeneutics*
TDNT	*Theological Dictionary of the New Testament* (edited by G. Kittel and G. Friedrich; trans. G. W. Bromiley; 10 vols.; Grand Rapids, Mich.: Eerdmans, 1964–1976)
ThSt	Theologische Studien
ThTo	*Theology Today*
TLZ	*Theologische Literaturzeitung*

TPNZJ	*Theologen des Protestantismus im 19. und 20. Jahrhundert* (ed. Martin Greschat; 2 vols.; Urban-Taschenbücher 284, 285; Stuttgart: W. Kohlhammer, 1978)
TRE	*Theologische Realenzyklopädie.* Edited by G. Krause and G. Müller
TRu	*Theologische Rundschau*
TS	Texts and Studies
TS	*Theological Studies*
TSK	*Theologische Studien und Kritiken*
TTL	Theological Translation Library
TU	Texte und Untersuchungen
TZ	*Theologische Zeitschrift*
UJEnc	*The Universal Jewish Encyclopedia*
UNT	Untersuchungen zum Neuen Testament
USQR	*Union Seminary Quarterly Review*
VTSup	Vetus Testamentum Supplements
WTJ	*Westminster Theological Journal*
WUNT	Wissenschaftliche Untersuchungen zum Neuen Testament
ZKG	*Zeitschrift für Kirchengeschichte*
ZNW	*Zeitschrift für die neutestamentliche Wissenschaft*
ZRGG	*Zeitschrift für Religions- und Geistesgeschichte*
ZTK	*Zeitschrift für Theologie und Kirche*

Part I

NEW TESTAMENT RESEARCH IN THE ERA OF EXPANDING EMPIRE

1

New Testament Research in America during the Nineteenth Century

The Bible commands a special place in American culture. Presidents take oaths on it. Trial witnesses swear by it. In times of war, soldiers wear it—in metal binding—over their hearts. This prominence of Scripture accords, too, with the American penchant for ordering life according to written documents. Texts such as the Mayflower Compact and the Constitution put into writing principles of faith and practice. From the beginning, America appeared as a site where the vision of the Bible could be realized. There in the primeval wilderness the divine kingdom, the New Jerusalem, could be built. The immigrants to the New World had abandoned the old garden to seek another Eden.

> The world was all before them, where to choose
> Their place of rest, and providence their guide.[1]

And the way to follow Providence was mapped out in the pages of the Bible.

At the same time, America seemed to provide the soil where the new approach to the Bible would flourish. The innovative methods that had emerged in Europe in the eighteenth and nineteenth centuries had been cultivated by the Enlightenment, and America was a nation founded on Enlightenment ideals. The empiricism and rationalism of Bacon and Locke were woven into the fabric of American political thought. Many of the founding fathers were sympathetic to deism, and the majestic beauty of the new land disclosed the truths of natural theology. These truths could be embodied in a political system that, like Newton's universe, functioned according to a rational order of checks and balances. This system cherished freedom, protected individualism, and promoted unbounded optimism.

---

1. John Milton, *Paradise Lost*, Book XII.

To the enlightened reader, the NT seemed to foster these very ideals. Thomas Jefferson, the author of the Declaration of Independence, believed his political philosophy to be in harmony with the ethics of Jesus. An amateur Bible scholar, Jefferson produced an edition of the Gospels in which he attempted to distinguish the gold from the dross—the authentic from the spurious.[2]

Nevertheless, the American view of the Bible remained largely conservative. Rather than accepting the skepticism of deists such as Jefferson and Franklin, American theologians tended to follow Calvin. Blown by the uncertain winds of the New World, they sought sure moorings in the old faith and the old book. This conservatism was reinforced by the persistence of revivalism in American history—the great awakenings of the eighteenth and early nineteenth centuries. Along with the old-time religion, these revivals fostered American individualism, perfectionism, and the spirit of competition. American religion had been pluralistic since the founding of the thirteen colonies, and the continuing waves of immigrants multiplied the ecclesiastical options. As the people expanded to the west, the denominations competed for their souls, citing chapter and verse to prove that theirs was the truth and the way.

Conservatives could not long take their ease in Zion. Along with the immigrants came new ideas such as Arminianism and Unitarianism. A fountain of liberalism that flowed from Harvard flooded much of Boston and forced Calvinists to retreat to higher ground at Andover and build a solid dam at Princeton. The uncompromising Calvinism of Jonathan Edwards was eroded by some of his disciples. Representatives of the New Divinity or New Haven theology such as Nathaniel Taylor of Yale compromised the doctrine of original sin with the notion that humans were to some degree free and responsible. These newer theological movements, like the mediating theology of the European neologians, embraced the values of the Enlightenment. Theology ought to be rational, in harmony with the order of creation, and the herald of human progress. The Bible ought to address the practical needs of people and foresee a millennium in which human aspirations and divine purposes would be fulfilled. From this perspective, the Scriptures confronted the problems of growing industrialization and poverty, and encouraged movements for social reform. During America's greatest tragedy, the bloody Civil War, words of Scripture were fired as lethal ammunition by both sides of the vicious conflict.[3]

---

2. See O. I. A. Roche, ed., *The Jefferson Bible: With the Annotated Commentaries on Religion of Thomas Jefferson* (New York: Clarkson N. Potter, 1964); F. Forrester Church, "Thomas Jefferson's Bible," in *The Bible and Bibles in America*, ed. Ernest S. Frerichs (Atlanta: Scholars Press, 1988), 145–61.

3. See James Brewer Stewart, "Abolitionists, the Bible, and the Challenge of Slavery," in *The Bible and Social Reform*, ed. Ernest R. Sandeen (Philadelphia: Fortress, 1982), 31–57; Theodore

In this context of contention, modern American NT scholarship was born. Although some have supposed that critical biblical research was smuggled into this country by a few itinerant intellectuals who had studied in Germany, American scholarship exhibits characteristics of its own. To be sure, Americans were decades behind in the mechanics of research—text criticism, linguistics, and higher criticism—yet they shaped a scholarship that fit the American pattern. This scholarship was characterized by freedom, individualism, revivalism, sensitivity to religious experience, and perception of the American dream. Above all, American NT scholarship was closely related to the church. Unlike Europe, where biblical research was conducted primarily in the universities, America produced free-standing church-related seminaries such as Andover and Princeton.[4] Even the divinity schools established at Harvard (1819) and Yale (1822) were designed to prepare persons for ministry. NT study, as a result, had a practical and professional purpose.

In this chapter, attention is given to the development of NT scholarship in America in the first three-fourths of the nineteenth century. After an account of the seminal contribution of an eighteenth-century precursor, Jonathan Edwards, consideration is given to the movement from Unitarian biblicism of Andrews Norton to the transcendental skepticism of Theodore Parker. Then, the emergence of a mature NT criticism is traced in the scholarship of Moses Stuart and his ablest student, Edward Robinson. The orthodox reaction to the newer developments is examined in the work of Princeton's stalwart Charles Hodge. Attention is given to an imaginative, new hermeneutic by Horace Bushnell. Finally, the industry of an Americanized European is investigated—the massive production of the indefatigable Philip Schaff.[5]

Dwight Weld, *The Bible against Slavery; or, An Inquiry into the Genius of the Mosaic System, and the Teachings of the Old Testament on the Subject of Human Rights* (Pittsburgh: United Presbyterian Board of Publication, 1864). In an appendix, Weld presents NT teaching against slavery. For the pro-slavery view, see E. W. Warren, *Nellie Norton: or Southern Slavery and the Bible. A Scriptural Refutation of the Principle Arguments upon Which the Abolitionists Rely. A Vindication of Southern Slavery from the Old and New Testaments* (Macon, Ga.: Burke, Boykin, 1864).

4. See Glenn T. Miller, *Piety and Intellect: The Aims and Purposes of Ante-Bellum Theological Education*, Scholars Press Studies in Theological Education (Atlanta: Scholars Press, 1990); Donald Stanley Klaiss, "The History of the Interpretation and Criticism of the New Testament in America" (Ph.D. diss., University of Chicago, 1934), 32–63.

5. Some important American scholars have not been included, for example, Lutheran theologians such as C. F. W. Walther and C. P. Krauth (see Sydney Ahlstrom, "Theology in America: A Historical Survey, in *The Shaping of American Religion*, ed. James Ward Smith and A. Leland Jamison [Princeton: Princeton University Press, 1969], 272–79); the founder of the Disciples of Christ, Alexander Campbell, who produced a significant translation of the NT (see Thomas H. Olbricht, "Alexander Campbell in the Context of American Biblical Studies, 1810–1876," *ResQ* [33]: 13–28).

A CALVINIST PRECURSOR: JONATHAN EDWARDS (1703–58)

"I should not take it amiss, to be called a Calvinist," wrote Edwards, "though I utterly disclaim a dependence on Calvin, or believing the doctrines which I hold, because he believed and taught them."[6] Actually, Edwards belonged to the tradition of the Puritan divines who had brought biblical scholarship with them to the New World. John Cotton, for example, had written commentaries on 1 John and Revelation.[7] Edwards was primarily not a NT scholar, but a theologian. Often maligned for his notorious sermon, "Sinners in the Hands of an Angry God," Edwards was no fiery orator. His power was in his thought—perhaps the greatest philosophical mind America has produced.

Jonathan Edwards was born in East Windsor, Connecticut, the son of a Harvard-educated minister.[8] At thirteen he entered Yale, and a year later came across of copy of Locke's *Essay concerning Human Understanding*. He found more pleasure in reading it, he said, "than the most greedy miser finds when gathering up handfuls of silver and gold from some newly discovered treasure."[9] For several years Edwards was minister of the Congregational Church in Northampton, Massachusetts, but in 1750 was dismissed because he demanded that only those who displayed outward signs of Christian redemption could partake of the Lord's Supper. Leaving Northampton, Edwards retreated to an obscure parish at Stockbridge where he preached to the Native Americans. In 1857, he was elected president of the College of New Jersey (later Princeton), but five weeks after his inauguration died from a smallpox inoculation.

Edwards's theology was shaped by a variety of influences.[10] From Locke he learned that knowledge comes through the senses, and that revelation, both natural and supernatural, is not in conflict with reason. For Edwards, sense experience also involved the sense of the heart—the feelings and

---

6. Jonathan Edwards, *Freedom of the Will*, vol. 1 of *The Works of Jonathan Edwards*, ed. Paul Ramsey (New Haven: Yale University Press, 1957), 131.
7. See Klaiss, "History of Interpretation," 16–31; Olbricht, "Alexander Campbell," 15–16.
8. Studies of the life and work of Edwards are numerous; among the standard and recent works, see Perry Miller, *Jonathan Edwards*, Meridian Books (Cleveland: World, 1959); William J. Scheick, ed., *Critical Essays on Jonathan Edwards* (Boston: G. K. Hall, 1980); Joseph A. Conforti, *Jonathan Edwards, Religious Tradition, and American Culture* (Chapel Hill: University of North Carolina Press, 1995); Iain H. Murray, *Jonathan Edwards: A New Biography* (Edinburgh: Banner of Truth Trust, 1987).
9. Cited in Arthur Cushman McGiffert Jr., *Jonathan Edwards* (New York: Harper & Brothers, 1932), 8.
10. Among the many works on Edwards's thought, see Conrad Cherry, *The Theology of Jonathan Edwards: A Reappraisal* (Gloucester, Mass.: Peter Smith, 1974); John E. Smith, *Jonathan Edwards: Puritan, Preacher, Philosopher* (Notre Dame, Ind.: University of Notre Dame Press, 1992); Michael J. McClymond, *Encounters with God: An Approach to the Theology of Jonathan Edwards* (New York: Oxford University Press, 1998); Leon Chai, *Jonathan Edwards and the Limits of Enlightenment Philosophy* (New York: Oxford University Press, 1998); Sang Hyun Lee and Allen C. Guelzo, eds., *Edwards in Our Time: Jonathan Edwards and the Shaping of American Religion*

emotions that belong to the spiritual sense.[11] With the Scottish commonsense philosophers, Edwards agreed that some fundamental truths are self-evident, for example, the idea of cause and effect. Behind the chain of causes is the uncaused Being who causes: the Absolute Being, or God. Edwards developed a version of the ontological argument. He argued that there is either being or nothing. To say that nothing exists is an absurdity. Therefore, being exists, and if being (not nothing) is everywhere, then Being is absolute and the source of all being. There is an inner harmony in the Being of God expressed in the mutual love of Father, Son, and Holy Spirit, and a harmony between God and the whole creation.

In contrast to Edwards's idea of the glory of God is his view of the depravity of humanity. The goal of humanity, according to Edwards, is virtue, and virtue requires the human will to respond to the goodness of God. The will of humans, however, is not free. In his treatise *The Freedom of the Will* (1754), Edwards contends that all decisions of the mind are caused by previous decisions, and "if the first act in the train, determining and fixing the rest, be not free, none of them all can be free."[12] Moreover, God's foreknowledge, which Edwards accepts as confirmed by fulfilled prophecy, implies necessity, so that what people will and do is predestined by the ultimate cause, that is, by God. Although created righteous, Adam, according to Edwards, sinned and fell into total depravity. Because of the unity of humanity, all people participate in the sin of Adam. Redemption, in Edwards's opinion, is wholly an action of God's irresistible grace. Justification is a divine accomplishment whereby the righteousness of Christ is imputed to humans. According to Edwards, those who receive God's grace are the elect—people predestined to salvation. Faith is the action whereby humans accept the grace of God, but faith is the action of the Spirit, a gift of God. However, Edwards believes that faith is accompanied by the religious affections. This means that faith is a response of the whole person—a religious experience that includes the knowledge of the heart, feelings and emotions, and, above all, love. "The Scriptures," says Edwards, "do represent true religion, as being summarily comprehended in love, the chief of the affections, and the fountain of all other affections."[13]

Edwards believes the theology he articulates is revealed in Scripture.[14] In his view, to communicate belongs to the nature of God. Creation is God's

(Grand Rapids, Mich.: Eerdmans, 1999); John H. Gerstner, *The Rational Biblical Theology of Jonathan Edwards*, 3 vols. (Powhatan, Va.: Berea Publications, 1991).

11. See David Laurence, "Jonathan Edwards, John Locke, and the Canon of Experience," *Early American Literature* 15 (1980): 107–23.

12. Cited in Frank Hugh Foster, *A Genetic History of New England Theology* (New York: Russell & Russell, 1963), 74.

13. Jonathan Edwards, *Religious Affections*, vol. 1 of *The Works of Jonathan Edwards*, ed. John E. Smith (New Haven: Yale University Press, 1959), 106.

14. See Ralph G. Turnbull, "Jonathan Edwards—Bible Interpreter," *Int* 6 (1952): 422–35; Karl Dietrich Pfisterer, *The Prism of Scripture: Studies on History and Historicity in the Work of*

self-communication, but God's special revelation is given in the Bible. In one of his notebooks Edwards writes, "It seems to me that God would have our whole dependence be upon the Scriptures because the greater our dependence is on the Word of God, the more direct and immediate is our dependence on God himself."[15] The Bible is inspired by the Spirit and infallible, although Edwards tends to stress the inspiration of persons more than words. "The prophet has so divine a sense . . . that he sees as immediately that God is there as we perceive one another's presence when we are talking together face to face." The truth of divine revelation is confirmed by miracles, but these supernatural phenomena were restricted to the biblical era. "But since the canon of Scripture has been completed, and the Christian church fully founded and established," writes Edwards, "those extraordinary gifts have ceased."[16] Edwards believes that there are different levels of inspiration; Romans and John are the most important NT books. In the interpretation of Scripture, Edwards basically affirms the plain, rational meaning of the text.[17]

Edwards also believes that Scripture can have more than one meaning. In Luke 11:47-51, Jesus describes the literal building of tombs, but Edwards assumes that his words have spiritual meaning: the saints continue to endure persecution similar to the abuses suffered by prophets. "This is not the only instance," says Edwards, "wherein Christ is to be understood in two different senses when speaking of a thing, the one a literal sense, the other mystical."[18] The spiritual meaning can also be discerned by typology—a method sanctioned by Scripture (Rom. 5:14) that escapes the literal and avoids allegory. Edwards claims, "almost everything that was said or done, that we have recorded in the Scripture from Adam to Christ, was typical of Gospel things."[19]

Edwards produced three types of exegetical writings. First, he kept extensive notebooks. These were called the "Miscellanies" and "Notes on Scripture."[20] He also created the "Blank Bible"—a large notebook with

---

Jonathan Edwards, Anglo-American Forum 1 (Bern; Herbert Lang, 1975); Conrad Cherry, "Symbols of Spiritual Truth: Jonathan Edwards as Biblical Interpreter," *Int* 39 (1985): 263–71.

15. Cited in Stephen J. Stein, "The Quest for the Spiritual Sense: The Biblical Hermeneutics of Jonathan Edwards," *HTR* 70 (1977): 105.

16. Cited in Gerstner, *Rational Biblical Theology* 1:143, 162.

17. Edwards's concern for rational interpretation is disclosed, for example, in his effort to demonstrate the consistency in the various accounts of the resurrection; see Jonathan Edwards, *Notes on Scripture,* vol. 15 in *The Works of Jonathan Edwards,* ed. Stephen J. Stein (New Haven: Yale University Press, 1998), Entry 220, 154–56.

18. Cited in Stein, "Quest for the Spiritual Sense," 111.

19. Cited in Stephen J. Stein, "The Spirit and the Word: Jonathan Edwards and Scriptural Exegesis," in *Jonathan Edwards and the American Experience,* ed. Nathan O. Hatch and Harry S. Stout (New York: Oxford University Press, 1988), 125.

20. Two volumes of *The Miscellanies* have been published: Entry Nos. a–z, aa–zz, 1–500, vol. 13 in *The Works of Jonathan Edwards,* ed. Thomas A. Schafer (New Haven: Yale University Press, 1994); Entry Nos. 501–832, vol. 18 of *Works,* ed. Ava Chamberlain (New Haven: Yale University

pages of the Bible interleaved with pages crammed with notes. Second, Edwards preached sermons that were saturated with biblical texts and imagery. Finally, he published major theological works that draw deeply from the reservoir of biblical ideas.

Edwards never wrote a formal commentary on a biblical book. John Gerstner, however, has searched Edwards's works on the Bible and extracted material so as to construct a commentary on the Epistle to the Hebrews. Regarding critical questions, Edwards argues that Paul is the author, that the letter was written about four years before the destruction of Jerusalem, and that it was addressed to Jewish Christians of Palestine to aid in the conversion of Jews. Edwards's exegesis intends to unlock the theological meaning of the texts, and his hermeneutical key is Christ. According to Edwards, the golden urn that held manna and Aaron's rod that budded (Heb. 9:4) should be interpreted typologically. "Both these represented Christ and . . . that spiritual nourishment . . . and refreshment we have by Him."[21]

Edwards's theological use of the NT is evident in his magnum opus, *Original Sin*. According to Edwards, total human depravity is the consequence of Adam's fall, for the sin of Adam is imputed to all. The second part of Edwards's book offers biblical sanction for this doctrine of original sin. After reviewing Genesis and other texts from the HB, Edwards presents a chapter providing proofs from the NT. For example, he notes the words of Jesus in conversation with Nicodemus, "What is born of the flesh is flesh; and what is born of the Spirit is spirit" (John 3:6). According to Edwards, flesh is totally corrupt, and texts from Romans 7 and 8 and Galatians 5 show that flesh and spirit are absolute opposites. Edwards presents a word study of the Greek terms to prove that "flesh" represents human nature. That humanity is corrupt, Edwards proves by quoting Paul: "I know that nothing good dwells within me, that is, in my flesh" (Rom. 7:18). Edwards concludes: "And so the word 'flesh,' which signifies man, came to be used to signify man as he is in himself, in his natural state, debased, corrupt and ruined."[22]

Edwards was fascinated with the book of Revelation. In 1723, he started to make entries in his "Notes on the Apocalypse"—his only notebook dedicated to a single biblical book.[23] Throughout his career, Edwards added to the "Notes," preached sixty-six sermons on Revelation, and displayed a per-

---

Press, 2000). The *Notes on Scripture*, consisting of more than 500 entries, have been published in vol. 15 in *Works*, ed. Stephen J. Stein (New Haven: Yale University Press, 1998).

21. Gerstner, *Rational Biblical Theology* 1:341.

22. Jonathan Edwards, *Original Sin*, vol. 3 in *Works*, ed. Clyde A. Holbrook (New Haven: Yale University Press, 1970), 279.

23. Jonathan Edwards, *Apocalyptic Writings: "Notes on the Apocalypse"; An Humble Attempt*, vol. 5 in *Works*, ed. Stephen J. Stein (New Haven: Yale University Press, 1977). See Stephen J. Stein, "A Notebook on the Apocalypse of Jonathan Edwards," in *Critical Essays on American Literature*, ed. William J. Scheick (Boston: G. K. Hall, 1980), 166–76.

sistent interest in eschatology and the millennium.[24] For Edwards, the crucial issue in the interpretation of the Apocalypse is the identification of the Antichrist, and for him, the Antichrist is the Roman papacy. Positively, Revelation heralds the redemptive work of Christ in history and the intimate relationship between Christ and the church. Edwards thinks that the Apocalypse predicts the future from the time of the author, the apostle John, until the end of history when God's purposes will be fulfilled. Edwards believes that his own time is the era of the sixth bowl (Rev. 16:12), and that signs of the approaching millennial reign of righteousness are already appearing in America. After the millennium, Christ will return, the dead will be raised to final judgment, and God's purposes for creation and history will be consummated. Edwards is a post-millennialist.

In summary, Edwards's biblical criticism is conservative: he accepts the traditional authorship of the canonical books and he exerts great effort to harmonize the biblical narratives. Nevertheless, he pursues the historical meaning of the text and makes use of philological method and rational analysis in the process. Edwards's primary contribution is in the area of biblical theology. For him, the Bible is the Word of God—the source of truth to be probed and preached. Edwards's interpretation of the NT no doubt betrays his theological bias. Yet, his stern Calvinism is not doctrinaire, but sensitive to the empiricism and rationalism of the Enlightenment. Moreover, Edwards announces themes that will be played in variations by his followers: the Reformed tradition, the importance of the Bible for life and thought, the polemical and apologetic use of the Bible, the providential interpretation of American destiny. Most of all, Edwards sounds the two notes that become dominant themes among his successors: the empiricism and rationalism echoed by Norton, Stuart, Robinson, and Hodge; the emotional, intuitive, and aesthetic sensitivity reflected in Parker and Bushnell. Indeed, the combination of criticism and pietism in the work of Philip Schaff is anticipated in Edwards's brilliant harmonization of these two: the unity of reason and the affections, the religion of the head and of the heart.

FROM UNITARIAN BIBLICISM TO TRANSCENDENTAL SKEPTICISM: ANDREWS NORTON AND THEODORE PARKER

In 1805, Henry Ware, a Unitarian, was appointed Hollis Professor of Divinity at Harvard. Unitarians come in several varieties, but they agree on two basic points: opposition to the doctrine of the Trinity, and denial of the deity of Christ. American Unitarianism was fostered by influences from

---

24. See Stephen J. Stein, "Providence and the Apocalypse in the Early Writings of Jonathan Edwards," *Early American Literature* 13 (1978/79): 250–67; C. C. Goen, "Jonathan Edwards: A New Departure in Eschatology," in *Critical Essays on American Literature*, ed. William J. Scheick (Boston: G. K. Hall, 1980), 151–65.

England.²⁵ British Bible scholars such as William Whiston (1667–1752) and Daniel Whitby (1638–1725)—noted for their anti-Trinitarian sentiments and Arian sympathies—were widely read in the American colonies. Growing dissatisfaction with orthodox Calvinism's inability to cope with the new ideas of the Enlightenment encouraged eighteenth-century New England clergy such as Jonathan Mayhew and Charles Chauncy to embrace liberal doctrines. By the time of Ware's appointment at Harvard, many Boston congregations had moved into the Unitarian camp.

In 1819, William Ellery Channing preached an ordination sermon in Baltimore that became the Magna Carta of American Unitarianism. Channing was a Harvard-trained minister who served the Federal Street Church in Boston. His sermon considered two main issues: the principles of biblical interpretation and the doctrines derived from proper interpretation. In regard to the first point, Channing advocated historical method, and insisted that the meaning of the Bible "be sought in the same manner as that of other books."²⁶ In regard to the second, Channing argued that the NT, interpreted historically, taught the unity of God (not the Trinity), the unity (not the two natures) of Christ, and God's moral perfection (rather than human depravity, election, and substitutionary atonement). "We challenge our opponents," declared Channing, "to adduce one passage in the New Testament where the word God means three persons."²⁷

Andrews Norton (1786–1853)

The effort to advance the cause of Unitarianism by study of the NT was ably exercised by Andrews Norton.²⁸ Norton was born and reared in Hingham, Massachusetts, where Henry Ware had served as minister prior to his Harvard appointment. Norton entered Harvard in 1801, and graduated Phi Beta Kappa in 1804. After additional study with Ware, he served for a time as an instructor at Bowdoin College. When Harvard Divinity School was founded in 1819, Norton was appointed Samuel Dexter Professor of Sacred Literature. Harvard's president, James Walker, remarked that Norton appeared "not as one in the act of seeking after truth, but as one who had found it."²⁹ Norton was married to Catherine Eliot, the daughter of a

---

25. See Conrad Wright, *The Beginnings of Unitarianism in America* (Boston: Star King, 1955).
26. David Robinson, ed., *William Ellery Channing: Selected Writings* (New York: Paulist, 1985), 72; see Eugene Robert Chable, "A Study of the Interpretation of the New Testament in New England Unitarianism" (Ph.D. diss., Columbia University, 1955).
27. Robinson, *Channing*, 79.
28. See Lilian Handlin, "Babylon est delenda—the Young Andrews Norton," in *American Unitarianism: 1805–1865*, ed. Conrad Edick Wright (Boston: Massachusetts Historical Society and Northeastern University Press, 1989), 53–85; James Turner, "Religion et langage dans l'Amérique du XIXᵉ siècle: Le cas étrange de Andrews Norton," *RHR* 110 (1993): 431–62; William Baird, "Andrews Norton (1786–1853)," in *MCTA*, 184–86.
29. Cited in George Huntston Williams, *The Harvard Divinity School: Its Place in Harvard University and in American Culture* (Boston: Beacon, 1954), 1.

prominent merchant. Supported by her wealth, Norton resigned from Harvard in 1830 to devote his career to research and writing.

Although Norton did not like the title "Unitarian," his NT research supported doctrines that the Unitarians espoused. Norton also opposed transcendentalism—the movement that was to transform Unitarianism under the leadership of such thinkers as Ralph Waldo Emerson and Theodore Parker.[30] In contrast to the transcendentalists, Norton believed the Bible to be the infallible revelation of God, confirmed by miracles. "As regards the Apostles," he wrote, "we believe that their minds were enlightened by the Spirit of God, and by direct miraculous communications from him, in regard to the essential truths of Christianity."[31] Nevertheless, the Bible should be interpreted like any other book, that is, by historical method. Because of the limitations of the original auditors (for example, their belief in demons), the message of the NT had to be accommodated to its historical context. Thus, the interpreter must distinguish the great truths of the Bible from its local and temporary expressions. In his inaugural address as Dexter Professor, Norton affirms his devotion to natural theology and a rational understanding of God, while at the same time confessing his faith in special revelation. "But our religious faith rests for its main support on what we believe the declarations of God, communicated by Jesus Christ."[32]

In 1819, Norton published *A Statement of Reasons for Not Believing the Doctrines of the Trinitarians.* This lengthy document asserts that popular opposition to Christianity results from a misunderstanding of the nature of Christianity. A major feature of this misunderstanding is a distorted view of Scripture. "False religion," says Norton, "has thrown its veil over the character, and perverted the meaning, of the books of the Old and New Testaments." After arguing that the doctrine of the Trinity is irrational and the idea of the two natures of Christ self-contradictory, Norton takes up "The Proposition, that Christ is God, proved to be false from the Scriptures." He argues, for example, that texts that have often been used to support the deity of Christ have been misinterpreted. Although John 1:1 says, "the Word was God," it also says that "the word was with God." According to Norton, a being who is *with* God, cannot be identical to God. The title "Son of God," in Norton's opinion, does not mean identity but distinction, and texts such as 1 Cor. 15:24-28, where Paul says that the Son will be subjected to God, prove that the Son is different and subordinate. Even the supernatural conception of Jesus does not confirm his deity. "Though conceived by a mira-

---

30. See Robert D. Habich, "Emerson's Reluctant Foe: Andrews Norton and the Transcendental Controversy," *New England Quarterly* 65 (1991): 208–37.

31. Andrews Norton, *A Statement of Reasons for Not Believing the Doctrines of the Trinitarians, concerning the Nature of God and the Person of Jesus,* 3d ed. (Boston: Walker, Wise, 1859), 412.

32. Andrews Norton, *Inaugural Discourse, Delivered before the University in Cambridge, August 10, 1819* (Cambridge, Mass.: Hilliard and Metcalf, 1819), 12.

cle," writes Norton, "he was born into the world as other men are, and such as other men are."³³ Texts that seem to imply a Trinity, according to Norton, do not actually mean what the Trinitarians imagine. Matthew 28:19, to be sure, admonishes the disciples to baptize in the "name of the Father and of the Son and of the Holy Spirit," but nothing, in Norton's opinion, supports the assumptions of the Trinitarians that the Holy Spirit is a person, or that all three are deities, or that they constitute one divine Being.

Norton's major contribution to NT research is his *Evidences of the Genuineness of the Gospels*. He had begun work on this project in 1819, and published the first volume in 1837. By 1848, the second edition had swelled to three large volumes.³⁴ Norton begins by arguing that the extant canonical Gospels are essentially the same as they were originally written. Speculating about the number of Christians (about three million) and the number of the copies of the Gospels (about one for every fifty Christians), Norton comes to the conclusion that some sixty thousand copies of the Gospels were extant around 200 C.E. Because the random samples of these copies available to Norton are in essential agreement, he assumes that the whole sixty thousand must have been in agreement. "The agreement, then, at the end of the second century, among the numerous copies of the respective Gospels, proves, that an archetype of each Gospel had been faithfully followed by the transcribers."³⁵ Norton also argues that the early Christians were faithful in transmitting the Gospels, and that later interpolations would have been obvious because they would not have fit the linguistic and historical situation of the originals.

Norton proceeds to defend traditional authorship of the four Gospels. He notes that the church fathers, especially Irenaeus, support authenticity. According to Norton, what Justin Martyr describes as "Memoirs of the Apostles" are identical with the four canonical Gospels. In the course of arguing that the agreement among the first three Gospels confirms their authenticity, Norton expresses his opinion on the Synoptic Problem. He reaches three conclusions: (1) The writers of the first three Gospels did not use each other as sources; (2) they were not dependent on common written documents; (3) they did not make use of late oral tradition. According to Norton's own theory, the apostles observed the deeds of Jesus and heard his teachings, and, like rabbinic students, memorized what they had seen and heard—a theory reminiscent of J. C. L. Gieseler.³⁶ Before their mission

---

33. *Statement of Reasons*, 36, 65.
34. Andrews Norton, *The Evidences of the Genuineness of the Gospels*, 2d ed., 3 vols. (Cambridge, Mass.: John Owen, 1846, 1848). An edition that incorporates the material of the three volumes into a single volume has been published: Andrews Norton, *The Evidences of the Genuineness of the Gospels, Abridged Edition* (Boston: American Unitarian Association, 1873).
35. *Genuineness of the Gospels* 1:55.
36. See *HNTR* 1:296–98.

began to expand, the apostles spent time together, reminiscing and correcting their recollections. Thus, the original message of the apostles, according to Norton, was formulated early and faithfully recorded in the Gospels. Verbal agreements are also explained by Norton's hypothesis that the apostles very early preached in Greek—a language he thinks was widely used in Palestine in the time of Jesus. The Gospels, Norton concludes, were written independently, at about the same time, around 60 C.E.

In the second and third volumes of the *Evidences*, Norton observes that the canonical Gospels were used by the Gnostics. Thus, he argues, even the heretics witness to the authenticity of Matthew, Mark, Luke, and John. Norton is convinced that Gnosticism did not appear until the second century, so that the effort—for instance, by F. C. Baur—to detect gnostic influence in the NT is misplaced:

> His [Baur's] work, like those of many of his countrymen, exhibits an incapacity of thinking clearly and consistently, and of presenting a lucid and well-digested exposition of a subject; . . . It belongs to that class of speculative writings, of which Germany has been so fertile, treating of the most important subjects, and promulgating, sometimes with dogmatical phlegm, and sometimes with heartless flippancy, doctrines the most disastrous to faith and morals.[37]

Because *The Evidences of the Genuineness of the Gospels* had dealt primarily with the external evidence, Norton turned to an investigation of the internal data. This work, which was left unfinished at the time of Norton's death, was edited and published as the *Internal Evidences of the Genuineness of the Gospels* in 1855.[38] In Part I, Norton refutes attacks upon the reliability and authenticity of the Gospels, especially D. F. Strauss's notorious *Life of Jesus*.[39] In reaction to Strauss's notion that the Gospels are largely myth or fiction, Norton argues that the accounts are based on reliable witnesses, and that the Gospel picture of Jesus is intrinsically genuine. In Part II, Norton argues that the Gospel narratives are essentially consistent and in harmony with their historical situation. The teachings of Jesus display a system of religion better than all others—a system that Norton believes the Gospel writers were incapable of inventing. Jesus' character, in Norton's opinion, is superior to all other persons in spite of texts that have been misconstrued to imply some qualification. For example, Norton believes that Jesus delayed the healing of the woman's daughter (Matt. 15:21-28; Mark 7:24-30) in order to emphasize it—to correct the disciples who shared the Jewish hostility to the heathen. Besides, the word used for "dogs" is a diminutive. "It properly denotes those little dogs which were kept as playthings."[40] Norton's

---

37. *Genuineness of the Gospels* 2:46–47. On F. C. Baur, see *HNTR* 1:258–69.
38. (Boston: Little, Brown, 1855).
39. See *HNTR* 1:250–55.
40. *Internal Evidences*, 281.

final estimate of Jesus is presented at the end of the third volume of his earlier *Genuineness of the Gospels*:

> The founder of our religion . . . was unquestionably the most wonderful individual who ever appeared on earth. A Jew, a Galilaean, in humble life, poor, without literary culture, without worldly power or influence; teaching but for a short time (probably not more than two years); wandering about the shores of the lake of Galilee and of the Jordan; scarcely entering Jerusalem but to be driven away by persecution, till at last he went thither to perish under it; collecting during his lifetime only a small body of illiterate, and often wavering, followers; addressing men whose incapacity, prejudices, or hatred continually led them to mistake or to pervert his meaning; surrounded, and apparently overpowered, by his unbelieving countrymen, who regarded him as a blasphemer and caused him to suffer the death of the most unpitied of malefactors,—this person has wrought an effect, to which there is nothing parallel, on the opinions and on the condition of the most enlightened portion of our race. The moral civilization of the world, the noblest conceptions which men have entertained of religion, of their nature and of their duties, are to be traced back directly to him.[41]

In sum, Andrews Norton is a child of the Enlightenment. He affirms natural theology, empiricism, and rationalism. He has mastered the skills of historical method, including text criticism and philology. In spite of his critical conservatism, Norton understands himself to be a liberal. On the one hand, he accepts the miracles and special revelation; on the other, he rejects the Trinity and the deity of Christ and stresses the ethics of Jesus. No doubt Norton enlists the historical method in support of his own position. Although the NT does not articulate the understanding of the Trinity and Christology that became orthodox in the fourth century, it implies more on these matters than Norton is willing to admit. For the history of NT research, what seems ironic is the use of a "conservative" criticism in support of a "liberal" theology.

Theodore Parker (1810–60)

Theodore Parker could have been a great Bible scholar, but he was lured by other interests.[42] Henry Steele Commager describes him as "the greatest

---

41. *Genuineness of the Gospels* 3:325–26. The year he died Norton completed a translation of the Gospels that was published two years later: *A Translation of the Gospels with Notes*, 5th ed., 2 vols. (Cambridge, Mass.: John Wilson and Son, 1882). The second volume contains Norton's notes on the text.

42. Among the many works on Parker, see Robert C. Albrecht, *Theodore Parker*, Twayne's United States Authors (New York: Twayne, 1971); John White Chadwick, *Theodore Parker: Preacher and Reformer* (Boston: Houghton, Mifflin, 1901); Henry Steele Commager, *Theodore Parker* (Boston: Beacon, 1947); Octavius Brooks Frothingham, *Theodore Parker: A Biography* (Boston: James R. Osgood, 1874); John Weiss, *Life and Correspondence of Theodore Parker*, 2 vols. (New York: D. Appleton, 1864).

preacher of his day."⁴³ Parker was born in Lexington, Massachusetts, the son of an unprosperous farmer; his grandfather fought in the Revolution.⁴⁴ Because of his intellectual brilliance, Parker was admitted to Harvard, where he completed all the course work, but was denied the degree because he could not afford the fees. In 1843, Parker toured Europe where he met British intellectuals such as Thomas Carlyle and German theologians such as August Tholuck, Heinrich Ewald, and Baur. In 1846, Parker was appointed minister of the Twenty-Eighth Congregational Society of Boston, a Unitarian church of seven thousand members that met in Boston's Music Hall because of the crowds. Lecturing across the country, Parker championed virtually every social cause of the day: antislavery, temperance, education of women, prison reform, better treatment of the Native Americans. In his later years, he fought a continuing battle with illness, and he finally succumbed in Italy. Among his acquaintances in Italy was Elizabeth Barrett Browning, who is reported to have said of Parker, "he believes nothing."⁴⁵

As a transcendentalist, Parker is sometimes compared with Ralph Waldo Emerson.⁴⁶ Although they shared hostility to bibliolatry and orthodox Christology, Emerson abandoned institutional religion whereas Parker stayed with the church. Both were opposed to the rational supernaturalism that characterized the thought of such Unitarians as Norton. Parker's point of view is set forth in his essay "Transcendentalism," written around 1850.⁴⁷ In this essay, Parker contends that there are two main schools of philosophy in contemporary thought: sensationalist and transcendentalist. The former, formulated by Locke, believes that all knowledge comes through the senses. The latter, influenced by romanticism and idealism, believes that the mind has ideas of its own and that truth can be grasped by intuition. In religion, transcendentalism discerns in humanity a religious nature and consciousness of God.

Parker's thought is further clarified in a sermon he preached in Boston in 1841 titled "The Transient and the Permanent in Christianity." Based on Luke 21:33, the sermon asserts that the forms and doctrines by which Christianity is expressed are temporary and transient. The permanent, on the

---

43. Henry Steele Commager, ed., *Theodore Parker: An Anthology* (Boston: Beacon, 1960), 1.
44. On the Battle Green at Lexington stands a stone with the inscription, "Don't fire unless fired on, but if they want to have a war . . . let it begin here," attributed to Captain Parker, Theodore Parker's grandfather.
45. Parker archives, Rare Books and Manuscripts Collection, Boston Public Library.
46. See John Edward Dirks, *The Critical Theology of Theodore Parker,* Columbia Studies in American Culture 19 (New York: Columbia University Press, 1948; repr., Westport, Conn.: Greenwood, 1970); Perry Miller, "Theodore Parker: Apostasy within Liberalism," *HTR* 54 (1961): 275–95.
47. Commager, ed., *Theodore Parker*, 89–97.

other hand, is to be found in the teachings of Jesus. "So the Christianity of Jesus is permanent, though what passes for Christianity with popes and catechisms, with sects and churches, in the first century or in the nineteenth century, prove transient also." According to Parker, the permanent are those great moral and religious truths—the love of God and humans, oneness with God—truths that are perceived intuitively. The doctrine of verbal inspiration, in Parker's opinion, turns the NT into an idol and has no foundation in the Bible itself. "If Christianity were true, we should still think it was so, not because its record was written by infallible pens, nor because it was lived out by an infallible teacher; but that it is true, like the axioms of geometry, because it is true, and is to be tried by the oracle God places in the breast."[48]

Parker's basic approach to the Bible is expressed in his essay "The Relation of the Bible to the Soul." Here Parker asserts that no other book "speaks equally and with the same authority to the lofty and low, the learned and the ignorant."[49] The Bible, however, is not, in Parker's opinion, the master of the human soul, nor the sole foundation of religion. True religion, says Parker, is older than creation—words reminiscent of the deist Matthew Tindal.[50] The Bible is important because it witnesses to the religion of Jesus, but some Christians have understood Christianity better than the writers of the NT, and Parker believes that the biblical message may be superseded. "It is only impious Superstition that dares foreshorten God, and say there is for man no higher revelation than past times can bring, and that Infinity is exhausted."[51]

Parker was widely read in biblical research. His library, which contained more than thirteen thousand books and pamphlets, included works of virtually all the major German NT scholars of the eighteenth and early nineteenth centuries.[52] In 1843, Parker completed work on a translation of W. M. L. de Wette's *Introduction* to the OT. This was not merely a translation, but an enlargement of de Wette's *Einleitung*. Parker added material from the church fathers, an annotated bibliography, and notes of his own. In all of this, Parker displays much erudition and mastery of a vast amount of scholarly material. In the translator's preface, he says, "I intend, at some future day to prepare an Introduction to the New Testament on a similar plan,"[53] and in a letter sent to de Wette in 1845, Parker writes, "I intend also

---

48. Ibid., 43, 51.
49. "The Relation of the Bible to the Soul," *Western Messenger*, vol. 8, no. 8 (December 1840; January 1841): 338.
50. *HNTR* 1:41–43.
51. "Relation of the Bible," 391.
52. The library of Theodore Parker is housed in the Rare Books and Manuscripts Collection, Boston Public Library.
53. *A Critical and Historical Introduction to the Canonical Scriptures of the Old Testament. From the German of Wilhelm Martin Leberecht de Wette. Translated and Enlarged by Theodore Parker*, 2d ed. (Boston: Charles C. Little and James Brown, 1850), x. On de Wette, see *HNTR* 1:221–29.

to prepare, with your *help*, a critical and historical introduction to the New Testament."⁵⁴ Parker's intention was never realized. In 1840, he wrote a review of David Friedrich Strauss's *Life of Jesus* in which he faithfully presents Strauss's argument. In criticizing Strauss, Parker questions Strauss's claim to work without presuppositions and Strauss's denial of the authenticity of the Gospels without adequate source-critical research. In the end, however, Parker is virtually the only American to speak a good word for Strauss's book: "It not only surpasses all its predecessors in learning, acuteness, and thorough investigation, but it is marked by a serious and earnest spirit."⁵⁵

For the history of NT research, Books III and IV of Parker's *Discourse of Matters Pertaining to Religion* are important. Book III is titled "The Relation of the Religious Element to Jesus of Nazareth, or A Discourse of Christianity." In regard to the sources for the life and teachings of Jesus, Parker believes that Matthew is the oldest Gospel, followed by Luke, who used Matthew, and Mark, who used Matthew and Luke. Parker, therefore, adopts a version of the Griesbach hypothesis, and has little patience with the theory proposed by Norton.⁵⁶ Parker writes, "The theory of an oral gospel which the noble men learned by heart and repeated when they wanted to tell about the most remarkable man the world ever saw reduces them to a set of gossiping grannies, and I can't bear it."⁵⁷ According to Parker, "the Synoptics give us in Jesus a very different being from the Christ whom John describes, and all four make such contradictory statements on some points, as to show they were by no means infallibly inspired." The Fourth Gospel, in Parker's opinion, was composed more than a hundred years after the birth of Jesus by an unknown author "who had a controversial and dogmatic purpose in view, not writing to report facts as they were; so he invents actions and doctrines to suit his aim, and ascribes them to Jesus with no authority for so doing."⁵⁸

Parker believes that Jesus began his career as a reformer who "burst the old wine-skins of Judaism." However, Jesus, according to Parker, gradually breaks with Judaism, attacks the religious leaders, and claims to be the Messiah. His religion has no concern for ceremonies, but only for morality—an absolute religion that advocates the love of God and humanity. The authority for this religion is grounded in the truth Jesus proclaims, not in miracles.

---

54. Cited in Weiss, *Theodore Parker* 1:259.
55. "*Das Leben Jesu, Kritisch bearbeitet* von Dr. David Friedrich Strauss (Tübingen, 1837), 2 voll. 8vo; *The Life of Jesus, critically treated*, etc., Second improved edition" (1st ed., 1835; 3d, 1839), *The Christian Examiner and General Review* 28 (third series, vol. 10, no. 3, July 1840): 313.
56. On the Griesbach hypothesis, see *HNTR* 1:143–47.
57. Cited in Dirks, *Critical Theology of Theodore Parker*, 50.
58. *A Discourse of Matters Pertaining to Religion*, ed. Thomas Wentworth Higginson (Boston: American Unitarian Association, 1709), 222, 226.

In Parker's opinion, miracles that transgress God's laws are impossible, and even if Jesus performed what his contemporaries thought to be miracles, that would not authenticate his teachings. According to Parker, Jesus was not the inventor of the truth he taught. "Whatever is consistent with reason, conscience, and the religious faculty, is consistent with the Christianity of Jesus, all else is hostile; whoever obeys these three oracles is essentially a Christian, though he lived ten thousand years before Jesus, or living now, does not own his name." Parker believes Jesus not to be without limitations, for example, his idea of a visible kingdom, his harsh words to opponents; yet, he transcended his limitations.

> [Jesus], a man ridiculed for his lack of knowledge, in this nation of forms, of hypocritical priests and corrupt people, falls back on simple morality, simple religion, unites in himself the sublimest precepts and divinest practices, thus more than realizing the dream of prophets and sages; rises free from so many prejudices of his age, nation, or sect; gives free range to the spirit of God in his breast; sets aside the law, sacred and time-honored as it was, its forms, its sacrifices, its temple and its priests; . . . and pours out doctrines beautiful as the light, sublime as heaven, and true as God.[59]

Book IV of Parker's *Discourse* is titled "The Relation of the Religious Element to the Greatest of Books, or A Discourse of the Bible." Although he has high regard for the Scriptures, Parker believes most efforts to establish the authority of the Bible to be woefully wrong. The attempt to support biblical authority by tradition is confounded by the evidence that tradition is not consistent. Similarly, claims of biblical infallibility, according to Parker, make use of circular argument. In regard to the Hebrew Bible, Parker does not believe that the prophets were able to make miraculous predictions. "But I do not hesitate to say," says Parker, "it has never been shown that there is, in the whole of the Old Testament, one single sentence that in the plain and natural senses of the words foretells the birth, life, or death of Jesus of Nazareth." Turning to the NT, Parker identifies seven of the canonical books he believes not to be authentic: Hebrews (not by Paul), 2 Peter, 2 and 3 John, James, Jude, and Revelation (not by John the Apostle). In regard to the Epistles and the historical books (the Gospels and Acts), Parker claims that nothing in them requires divine inspiration. Parker thinks the Gospels should be subject to searching criticism in order to separate "their mythological and legendary narratives from what is purely a matter of fact." However, proper interpretation of the Bible will disclose its enduring value.

> Take it as other books, we have its beauty, truth, religion, not its deformities, fables, and theology. We shall not believe in ghosts, though Isaiah did; nor in

---

59. Ibid., 228, 259, 268.

devils, though Jesus teach there are such. We shall see the excellence of Paul in his manly character, not in the miracles wrought by his apron; the nobleness of Jesus in the doctrine he taught and the life he lived, not in the walk on the water or the miraculous draughts of fish.[60]

Looking back over the accomplishments of Theodore Parker, one notes that he is a different kind of Unitarian. In contrast to Norton, who accepted the authority of the Bible and used historical criticism to support his Unitarian beliefs, Parker uses historical criticism to demolish the authority of the Bible. Actually, Norton and Parker represent two fundamentally different ways of perception: Norton adopts the method of empiricism, confirming objective truth by material proofs (for example, miracles); Parker advocates the way of imagination, sensing implicit truth by intuition. At the same time, Parker, more than any other American scholar of the nineteenth century, accepts the results of German higher criticism. The resulting tension between empiricism and intuition would continue to occupy American NT research. In any event, Parker's extensive negative criticism—his rejection of inspiration, his attack on miracles and prophecy—owed much to the empirical method. His positive criticism praised the religion of Jesus. However, because this religion was older than Jesus, available to anyone with perceptive intuition, and open to future increments, Parker's Jesus had no permanent place to lay his head. For Parker, the NT provided texts for moving sermons; it offered no unique revelation.

THE MATURING OF AMERICAN SCHOLARSHIP: MOSES STUART AND EDWARD ROBINSON

With Moses Stuart, biblical criticism in America came of age. The way was prepared, however, by others. Among the most important was Joseph Stevens Buckminster (1784–1812), a precocious scholar who studied Latin at four and graduated from Harvard at sixteen. He was influenced by liberal British and German scholarship and supervised an American edition of Griesbach's text. In 1811, Buckminster was appointed Dexter Lecturer on Biblical Criticism at Harvard, but died the next year before he could assume the position. At about this time, American scholars began to migrate to Germany for theological study. Edward Everett went to Göttingen in 1815, and was one of the first Americans to earn a German doctorate. After returning to Harvard to teach classics, Everett left academia for a career in politics. George Bancroft so impressed the Harvard corporation with his brilliance that they sent him to Göttingen, where he earned the doctorate and went on to Berlin for additional study. Like Everett, Bancroft abandoned theology, but he turned to history, and is remembered for his

60. Ibid., 311, 328, 339.

monumental ten-volume history of the United States. These and others who followed in their footsteps were instrumental in introducing the methods and results of German criticism to America.[61]

A base of operations for Stuart's work was provided by Andover Theological Seminary. When Harvard fell to the Unitarians in 1805 with the appointment of Henry Ware, the more orthodox Calvinists reacted by founding a school of their own. Located at Andover, Massachusetts, the "Theological Institute" (nicknamed "Zion's Hill") began in 1808 with two professors and thirty-six students. The faculty were required to pledge loyalty to Scripture and the Westminster Confession, and opposition to atheists, Jews, "Mohametans," Arians, Arminians, Unitarians, and other types of heretics.[62] The Bible held an important place in the curriculum, and the best thing Andover could have done was to appoint a young preacher from New Haven as Professor of Sacred Literature: Moses Stuart.

Moses Stuart (1780–1852)

Stuart was born in Wilton, Connecticut.[63] He entered Yale in 1797, and graduated at the head of his class two years later. While studying law, Stuart served as a tutor at Yale. In 1802, he was converted in a revival that swept the campus under the leadership of Yale's president, Timothy Dwight, the grandson of Jonathan Edwards. Stuart abandoned law for ministry and studied theology with Dwight. In 1806, he was installed as minister of Center Church in New Haven. Called to Andover in 1810, Stuart was responsible for teaching the whole Bible and all the related disciplines. Although he had studied classical Greek at Yale, he largely taught himself Hebrew, Aramaic, Syriac, and Arabic. At the auction of Buckminster's library in 1812, Stuart outbid Everett for a copy of J. G. Eichhorn's *Einleitung in das Alte Testament*, and mastered German. As a teacher, Stuart would identify bright students during their first year, take them under his wing, and invite them to stay on for additional study after their completion of the three-year seminary course. Thus he developed a graduate program in biblical studies that became the forerunner of Ph.D. programs that were to appear in the 1860s.

---

61. See Jerry Wayne Brown, *The Rise of Biblical Criticism in America, 1800–70: The New England Scholars* (Middletown, Conn.: Wesleyan University Press, 1969), 10–44; Chable, "Interpretation of the New Testament," 76–121; Jurgen Herbst, *The German Historical School in American Scholarship: A Study in the Transfer of Culture* (Ithaca, N.Y.: Cornell University Press, 1965), 1–22; 73–97.

62. See John Herbert Giltner, "Moses Stuart: 1780–1852" (Ph.D. diss., Yale University, 1956), 132—38.

63. See John H. Giltner, *Moses Stuart: The Father of Biblical Science in America*, SBLCP (Atlanta: Scholars Press, 1988); R. W. Yarbrough, "Stuart, Moses (1780–1852)," in *HHMBI*, 368–72; William Baird, "Moses Stuart (1780–1852)," in *MCTA*, 115–17. A superb collection of Stuart's papers is housed in the Special Collections of the Franklin Trask Library at Andover Newton Theological School; these include, for example, the handwritten notes of Lectures on Hermeneutics, and a Syriac grammar, written in a small notebook in his own hand.

In 1848, Stuart retired from Andover because of ill health. Stuart's epitaph, inscribed on a monument in the ancient burial ground at Andover, reads in part, "he is justly entitled to be called among the Scholars of his native country, The Father of Biblical Science."

Moses Stuart was essentially a biblical scholar, but his theological viewpoint is evident in his controversial writings. In response to William Channing's famous ordination sermon, Stuart published *Letters to Rev. Wm. E. Channing*. Stuart, at the outset, expresses his fundamental agreement with Channing's methodology. "I must read this book [the Bible], as I do all other books," says Stuart. However, according to Stuart, Channing's view of Trinitarians is a caricature. Trinitarians do not, says Stuart, believe in tritheism, but they do affirm undefinable differences within the Godhead. The NT, in Stuart's reading, recognizes these distinctions and affirms the three persons of the Trinity. In regard to Christology, Stuart detects three types of NT texts. First, there are texts that indicate the divinity of Christ or refer to Christ as "God." John 1:1, for example, affirms the preexistence of Christ and says that the Logos was God. Second, there are texts that present Christ as equal with God. In this class Stuart includes Phil. 2:6-7. He argues that the phrase μορφῇ θεοῦ does not mean mere resemblance of God, but that it describes Christ's divine nature—an interpretation confirmed by Paul's statement that Christ was equal with God. Third, he presents texts that, according to Stuart, prove that Christ embodied divine attributes: omniscience (John 6:46), divine power (Heb. 1:3), and eternity (John 1:1). Stuart concludes that "the New Testament bestows upon Christ the appellation of God" and that "it represents him as the Creator, Preserver, and Governor of the universe; declares his omniscience, his omnipotence, and his eternity . . . and . . . exhibits Christ as the object of prayer and divine worship."[64]

Stuart held a high doctrine of biblical authority and believed in plenary, though not verbal, inspiration. The words of the Bible were not dictated, according to Stuart, for that would deny the integrity of the authors. Nevertheless, "the inspired man ascends an intellectual and moral eminence so high, that his prospect widens almost without bounds, and what is altogether hidden from ordinary men is more or less distinctly within his view."[65] In spite of this lofty doctrine of inspiration, Stuart affirms a form of progressive revelation:

---

64. Moses Stuart, *Letters to Rev. Wm. E. Channing, Containing Remarks on his Sermon, Recently Preached and Published in Baltimore* (Andover: Flagg and Gould, 1819), 53, 112–13. See Bruce M. Stephens, "Breaking the Chains of Literalism: The Christology of Moses Stuart," *Covenant Quarterly* 50 (1992): 34–47.

65. Moses Stuart, *A Commentary on the Apocalypse*, 2 vols. (Andover: Allen, Morrill & Wardwell, 1845) 1:168.

The earlier part of revelation is merely inceptive; not designed as a full and complete development of a perfect religion, but adapted to the earlier state of the world. More of sensible objects are presented in these early communications than in the later periods of revelation, when it was made in a manner more spiritual, & perfect.[66]

Stuart was devoted to the grammatico-historical method. To foster this method, he translated Ernesti's *Institutio interpretis Novi Testamenti*—a classic statement of Enlightenment principles of interpretation.[67] In an effort to make Ernesti's work more useful, Stuart provides a readable translation and adds notes of his own. For instance, where Ernesti discusses tropical or figurative language, Stuart notes that language about God is necessarily metaphorical. Nevertheless, Stuart believes that the message of the Bible is essentially clear and understandable to human common sense.[68] Stuart also adopts the principle, at least as old as the Reformation, that Scripture should be interpreted by Scripture. Stuart refers to this principle as the "analogy of Scripture," which he prefers to "analogy of faith," because the latter imposes an external creed. The analogy of Scripture can function, according to Stuart, because the Bible presents a consistent message. "When I am persuaded that the whole of the [Scriptures] are *one system* of revealed truth, I am at liberty to quote from the whole, in a certain sense as the works of one author, in order to illustrate what is obscure by what is plain."[69] Stuart's method stresses two things: the search for the meaning of words, and the search for the meaning of things. For the former, the exegete must make use of philological and grammatical analysis, and give attention to the customary usage of the terms and their meaning in other contexts. For the latter, the interpreter must view the author and the audience in their historical, geographical, and religious setting.

Stuart's concern for the meaning of words is seen in his linguistic and grammatical works. In 1830, he published *Exegetical Essays on Several Words Relating to Future Punishment*.[70] In this book, Stuart investigates the meaning of NT terms according to their Hebrew and classical background and their use in the NT. For example, in regard to αἰών, Stuart finds ninety-five occurrences in the NT, of which sixty-four refer to time or unlimited time; five of these, he believes, refer to the future judgment. After the analysis of several

---

66. Cited in Brown, *Biblical Criticism in America*, 58.
67. *Elements of Interpretation, Translated from the Latin of J. A. Ernesti and Accompanied by Notes, with an Appendix Containing Extracts from Morus, Beck, and Keil*, by Moses Stuart, 3d ed. (Andover: Mark Newman, 1827). For Ernesti's research, see *HNTR* 1:109–12.
68. See Mark Granquist, "The Role of 'Common Sense' in the Hermeneutics of Moses Stuart," *HTR* 83 (1990): 305–19.
69. Cited in Brown, *Biblical Criticism in America*, 58.
70. (Andover: Flagg and Gould, 1830); repr. (Rosemead, Calif.: The Old Paths Book Club, 1954).

other terms, Stuart concludes that the Bible does indeed teach that there is a place of eternal punishment. Thus, he enlists philology in the service of theology, in particular, in opposition to the doctrine of universalism. As early as 1813, Stuart began to produce grammars and syntactical works on Hebrew and Greek for the use of his students. In 1825, together with his student Edward Robinson, Stuart published a translation of Georg Winer's *Grammatik des neutestamentlichen Sprachidioms*.[71] Stuart's own *A Grammar of the New Testament Dialect* appeared in 1834.[72]

Stuart's critical view of the Gospels is seen in his lengthy review of Norton's *Evidences of the Genuineness of the Gospels*. In this review, Stuart accepts Norton's two major points: that the canonical Gospels are essentially the same as they were originally composed; that the Gospels were written by those to whom they have been traditionally ascribed. Stuart's solution to the Synoptic Problem is essentially the same as Norton's:

> There is nothing strange then in the fact, that those who sat daily at the feet of Jesus for more than three years, should have remembered to a wide extent his sayings and doings; nothing strange in the fact, that when they reduced the account of these things to writing, there should have been so many striking coincidences between different writings.[73]

Stuart's major contribution to NT research is found in his commentaries. In 1825, the Andover trustees recommended that commentaries be produced to demolish the errors of the German critics. Two years later, Stuart responded with his massive two-volume commentary on *Hebrews*. In his preface Stuart states that "to translate, so as to make an author, who has composed in another language, altogether intelligible, and yet preserve all the shades, and colouring, and nice transitions, and (so far as may be) even the idioms themselves of the Original, is the very highest and most difficult work which an interpreter is ever called to perform."[74] The first volume (more than 450 pages) is devoted to critical questions. Stuart believes that Hebrews was an actual epistle, written to Jewish Christians of Palestine who were familiar with the temple cult, probably the members of the church in Caesarea. As to the author, Stuart notes the support of Pauline authorship in the east; he believes opposition in the west resulted from Roman antagonism to the Montanists, who relied on Hebrews. In regard to internal evidence, Stuart detects shreds of data that point to Paul as the writer. For

---

71. *A Greek Grammar of the New Testament, Translated from the German of George Benedict Winer* (Andover: Flagg & Gould, 1825).

72. (Andover: Gould & Newman, 1834).

73. Moses Stuart, "Review of 'The Evidences of the Genuineness of the Gospels,' by Andrews Norton, vol. 1, Boston, 1837," *American Biblical Repository*, vol. 11, no. 35 (April 1838): 327–28.

74. Moses Stuart, *A Commentary on the Epistle to the Hebrews*, 2 vols. (London: John Miller, 1828) 1:xii.

example, he thinks that Heb. 13:18-19 implies that the writer is in prison and expects to be released (as Paul in Phil. 2:24; Philemon 22). Stuart is effective in answering the argument that Hebrews uses a different vocabulary—the argument from *hapax legomena*. According to Stuart's count, there are 112 words in Hebrews that are not found elsewhere in the NT. Stuart shows, however, that 1 Corinthians contains 230 words that are not found elsewhere in the Pauline letters. On an average, Hebrews has twelve *hapax legomena* per page, whereas 1 Corinthians has eighteen. Stuart concludes that Paul is the author.

The second volume of Stuart's *Hebrews* presents the details of exegesis. Beginning with general comments, Stuart states that Hebrews is a letter by a Hebrew Christian (Paul) to Hebrew Christians to urge them not to fall back into Judaism. As to format, Stuart arranges the material in sections and introduces each section with a paragraph in smaller print that presents a summary of the content of the section. Comments are presented verse by verse, with attention to terms and phrases. Twenty excursuses, on especially important or difficult texts, are appended. An example of Stuart's exegesis can be seen in his interpretation of Heb. 2:9, which he translates: "but we see Jesus . . . crowned with glory and honor on account of the suffering of death, after that he had, by the grace of God, tasted of death for all." According to Stuart, the intent of the text is to answer the Jewish objection that Jesus was only human and suffered an ignominious death. In answer, "Paul," as Phil. 2:8-11 also shows, argues that Christ's suffering is the way to his glory. Giving attention to details, Stuart contends that ὅπως in Heb. 2:9 cannot mean "in order that," as it usually does, because to say that Jesus was crowned with glory *in order to* taste death makes no sense. Thus, Stuart argues that ὅπως means "after" in this context, and he cites other NT and classical references in support. Stuart also claims that the verb meaning "to taste" (γεύσηται) in the aorist subjunctive refers to the past. Citing classical references, Stuart says that "to taste" death means to experience it. Thus, Stuart concludes that the text means that *after* Christ had experienced death he was glorified.

In 1832, Stuart published the first edition of his commentary on *Romans*. In the introduction, Stuart argues that the church of Rome was not founded by Peter, but by the people named in chapter 16; it consisted of both Jewish and Gentile members. Stuart argues that Romans is a unity. He believes that the appearance of the doxology at the end of chapters 14 or 16 in the various manuscripts results from Paul's writing over a period of time, and making additions to his own composition. The substance of the Epistle to the Romans is acclaimed in the motto: Christ our justification and sanctification. The format is essentially the same as that of the Hebrews commentary. In regard to the phrase δικαιοσύνη θεοῦ (1:17), Stuart believes the construction is *genitivus actoris*, so that the righteousness of God "is the justification which God bestows, or the justification of which God is the author." Discussing ἱλαστήριον (3:25), Stuart rejects the translation "mercy seat," since it would create an impossible metaphor: Christ the mercy seat sprinkled with his own blood. Besides, the verb προέθετο, "to publicly expose," could not be used for the mercy seat, since the mercy seat is never openly exhibited. In regard to 5:12-21, Stuart believes the intent of the text is to present a comparison of the blessings "Christ has procured for us . . . with the evil consequences which ensued upon the fall of our first ancestor."[75] Stuart believes that ἐφ' ᾧ (v. 12) does not mean "in whom," since there is no antecedent within the immediate context, and the relative construction would instead require ἐν ᾧ. Thus, Stuart thinks the meaning is adverbial: "because" all sinned. Consequently, he rejects the idea that Adam's sin was imputed to all. According to Stuart, the parallel between Adam and Christ in 5:18-19 indicates individual responsibility in sinning just as in receiving grace. Stuart concludes that the consequence of Adam's sin is death, but that the responsibility for sinning belongs to each individual.[76]

Stuart's two-volume commentary on the *Apocalypse* presents a distinctive understanding of the nature and meaning of the Apocalypse. Basically, Stuart understands Revelation to be a type of prophetic literature, similar in form to Ezekiel and Daniel, and to the Jewish apocalyptic books such as Enoch and 2 Esdras. The purpose of Revelation, according to Stuart, is to encourage persecuted Christians by depicting "The final and complete triumph of Christianity over all opposition and all enemies, and the temporal and eternal glory and happiness to which this triumph leads the church." In interpreting the enigmatic symbols of the book, Stuart adopts the heremeneutical principle "that GENERIC, *and not specific and individual, representations*" are to be identified. This means that the interpreter needs to see the big picture—the overall struggle with evil—and not be preoccupied with the identification of each symbol as a particular person or event. On matters of critical introduction, Stuart spends more than 140 pages to argue that the author is John the son of Zebedee, the author of the Fourth Gospel. Stuart contends that at the time of composing the Apocalypse, John had recently moved from Palestine, and was still writing a Hebraic brand of Greek. Stuart concludes, "With all the evidence that is before me from history, and all from diction, style, and course of thought, I feel compelled to believe that *the balance is decidedly in favour of an apostolic origin.*"[77]

---

75. Moses Stuart, *A Commentary on the Epistle to the Romans, with a Translation and Various Excursuses*, 2d ed. (Andover: Gould and Newman, 1835), 62, 199.

76. See Stephen J. Stein, "Stuart and Hodge on Romans 5:12-21: An Exegetical Controversy about Original Sin," *JPH* 47 (1969): 340–58.

77. Moses Stuart, *A Commentary on the Apocalypse*, 2 vols. (Andover: Allen, Morrill & Wardwell, 1845) 1:155, 203, 422.

In the commentary proper (volume 2), Stuart presents his understanding of the arrangement of the book and its relation to the author's conception of history. After an introduction (chs. 1–5), Stuart believes the prophecies of the book describe the on-going triumph of Christianity according to three catastrophes or three general periods. The first catastrophe depicts the overthrow of Jewish persecuting power (chs. 6–11). The "great city . . . called Sodom and Egypt" (11:8), according to Stuart, is Jerusalem. The second catastrophe describes the destruction of the Roman persecuting power (chs. 12–19). In regard to chapter 13, Stuart believes that the beast from the sea (v. 1) represents Roman imperial power, while the beast from the earth (v. 11) symbolizes religious power. Stuart vigorously opposes the notion that the beasts represent the pope and the hierarchy of the Roman Catholic Church. The third catastrophe and its sequel disclose the final triumph over the forces of evil in the distant future (20:1—22:5). Stuart, betraying his generic method, is inclined to take the one thousand years literally. According to Stuart, Christ will not come until after the millennium, and then the resurrection and the judgment will be followed by the appearance of the new heaven and the new earth.

In sum, Stuart contributes four significant points for the interpretation of the Apocalypse: (1) the book must have made sense to the original readers—the main interpretation is historical, and only a small part of the book refers to the distant future; (2) the book must be interpreted according to its literary genre—it is a poetic-prophetic book like the Jewish apocalyptic documents; (3) the method of interpretation is generic—the interpreter should not seek for precise identification of symbols, but their larger meaning; (4) in terms of the larger meaning—the triumph of Christianity over all opposition—the book has continuing relevance.

In retrospect, Moses Stuart towers over American scholars of his time like a tall Redwood above the forest. He made the modern historical-critical method normative for biblical study in America. He embraced German methodology without submitting to its conclusions. His commentaries went through repeated editions in England. Moreover, Stuart tried to resist the temptation to let presuppositions determine his interpretation—with considerable success. Actually, his presuppositions intrude where they are least expected: in his treatment of questions of higher criticism. Although Stuart makes comprehensive and compelling cases for authenticity, he tends to overstate his arguments. The basic presupposition that determines the results is a view of biblical authority that assumes the authenticity of the canon. Although this view may compromise his critical judgments, it also motivates his vigorous study of the Bible—study that exemplifies philological skill, exegetical brilliance, mastery of a huge amount of critical and historical detail, and, above all, devotion to the relevance of the biblical message.

Edward Robinson (1794–1863)

Stuart's most able pupil was Edward Robinson.[78] Although his critical work is tedious, Robinson's creative contribution to the understanding of biblical geography gained him an international reputation. Robinson was born near Southington, Connecticut, the son of a Congregational minister. He was educated at Hamilton College in Clinton, New York (1812–16). On a visit to Andover in 1822, Robinson fell under the spell of Stuart, who persuaded him to study in the seminary. In 1826, Robinson went to Europe, where he studied four years, primarily at Halle and Berlin. Returning to Andover, he was named Professor of Biblical Literature in 1830. In 1837, Robinson was appointed to the faculty of Union Theological Seminary in New York. Union had been founded in 1836 by a group of clergy and laity who wanted to establish a seminary in the city.[79] Although faculty were required to affirm the Bible as the infallible rule of faith and practice and submit to the Westminster Confession, the school was free from ecclesiastical control and open to students of all denominations. In 1841, Robinson took up his position at Union, where he taught Old and New Testament and all the related disciplines.

Robinson's basic approach to the Bible is set forth in his inaugural address at Union. In the address, Robinson declares, "as the Word of God is the corner-stone of all Christian Theology, so the study and interpretation of that Holy Word, must of right be regarded as the first and fundamental branch of all theological education." According to Robinson, comprehension of the Scriptures requires us "to place ourselves in the situation of the Jews; hear as they heard, and understand the language as they understood it." Besides the biblical languages, the student needs to know introduction to the Bible (higher criticism), text criticism, hermeneutics, biblical history, chronology, and geography. Regarding exegetical methodology, Robinson advocates a historical method that seeks the literal meaning. "In short, viewing the subject under every aspect, I must hold that any system of interpretation, which departs from the plain and obvious meaning of the language of Scripture, rests upon a wrong foundation, and is fraught with danger to the mind earnestly seeking after divine truth." At the same time, Robinson

---

78. See Jay G. Williams, *The Times and Life of Edward Robinson: Connecticut Yankee in King Solomon's Court*, SBLBSNA 19 (Atlanta: SBL, 1999); Henry B. Smith and Roswell D. Hitchcock, *The Life, Writings and Character of Edward Robinson*, America and the Holy Land (New York: Arno, 1977); Julius A. Bewer, "Edward Robinson as a Biblical Scholar," *JBL* 58 (1939): 355–63; Philip J. King, "Edward Robinson: Biblical Scholar," *BA* 46 (1983): 230–32; J. Andrew Dearman, "Edward Robinson: Scholar and Presbyterian Educator," *American Presbyterians: Journal of Presbyterian History* 69 (1991): 163–74.

79. See Robert T. Handy, *A History of Union Theological Seminary* (New York: Columbia University Press, 1987); J. A. Sanders, "The Bible at Union: 1835 to the Present," *USQR* 52 (1998): 123–30.

insists that the exegete needs a "spiritual frame of mind"—sensitivity to the spiritual sense of Scripture. Robinson illustrates this point by analogy: the person who has no ear for music cannot understand music.[80]

Edward Robinson's most important contribution to the history of NT research is his pioneering work in biblical geography.[81] In 1838, and again in 1852, Robinson engaged in extensive exploration in the Near East. His original plan had been to present the results of his observations in a scientific work of geography, but his friends persuaded him to write the report in the form of a diary. The result is one of the most fascinating works of biblical scholarship ever written.[82] At Cairo, Robinson organized a caravan that included five camels, three dromedaries, two muskets, and a pair of pistols. With this unwieldy company, Robinson traveled to Suez and on to St. Catherine's monastery, where he attempted to identify Mount Sinai. From Sinai, they traveled to Akabah and on to Jerusalem, where Robinson spent several days and made excursions to Bethel, the Dead Sea, Bethlehem, Gaza, and Hebron. From Jerusalem they journeyed to Galilee, where Robinson visited Nazareth and the Sea of Galilee and rode a mule to the top of Mount Tabor. From Galilee, he traveled to Tyre and Sidon, and completed the Near Eastern trip in Beirut.

The 1852 trip began at Beirut, and Robinson traveled, mostly on horseback, through Galilee and Samaria to Jerusalem, where he stayed for some days. He then returned to Galilee to visit such sites as Bethsaida and Chorazim. Then his route turned northeast to Damascus. From Damascus he traveled west to Beirut, with a visit to majestic Baalbek on the way.

In general, Robinson depicts a vivid account of arduous journeys—a romantic adventure in the storied lands of the Bible. On seeing Jerusalem

---

80. Edward Robinson, *The Bible and Its Literature; An Inaugural Address, Delivered in the Mercer-Street Church, in the City of New York, January 20, 1841. With the Charge by the Rev. William Patton* (New York: Office of the American Biblical Repository, and the America Eclectic, 1841), 16, 23, 34, 43.

81. Robinson also made important contributions to biblical linguistics; see Brown, *Biblical Criticism in America*, 111–24; Bewer, "Robinson as a Biblical Scholar," 355–63. Among these are Robinson's translation (with Stuart) of G. Winer's *Greek Grammar*, and his translation of Philip Buttmann's *Greek Grammar* (see p. 184, below), and his own *Greek and English Lexicon of the New Testament* (1836). See also Robinson's "Philology and Lexicography of the New Testament," *Biblical Repository*, vol. 4, no. 13 (January 1834): 154–82. Robinson also published harmonies of the Gospels: *A Harmony of the Gospels in Greek, in the General Order of Le Clerc and Newcome, with Newcome's Notes. Printed from the Text and with the Various Readings of Knapp. The Whole Revised and the Greek Text Newly Arranged by Edward Robinson* (Andover: Gould and Newman, 1834); *A Harmony of the Four Gospels in Greek, according to the Text of Hahn, Newly Arranged, with Explanatory Notes*, rev. ed. (Boston: Crocker and Brewster, 1853); *A Harmony of the Four Gospels in English, according to the Common Version. Newly Arranged, with Explanatory Notes*, 12th ed. (Boston: Crocker & Brewster, 1866).

82. Edward Robinson, *Biblical Researches in Palestine, and in the Adjacent Regions: A Journal of Travels in the Year 1838, by E. Robinson and E. Smith*, 2 vols. (Boston: Crocker and Brewster, 1856); Edward Robinson, *Later Biblical Researches in Palestine, and in the Adjacent Regions: A Journal of Travels in the Year 1852, by E. Robinson and E. Smith and Others*, 2d ed. (Boston: Crocker and Brewster, 1871).

for the first time, he writes, "From the earliest childhood I had read of and studied the localities of this sacred spot; now I beheld them with my own eyes; and they all seemed familiar to me, as if the realization of a former dream." At Nazareth, Robinson climbs a hill to the west of the city and is moved by the panoramic view:

> In the village below, the Saviour of the world had passed his childhood; and although we have few particulars of his life during those early years, yet there are certain features of nature which meet our eyes now, just as they once met his. He must often have visited the fountain near which we had pitched our tent; his feet must frequently have wandered over the adjacent hills; and his eyes doubtless have gazed upon the splendid prospect from this very spot.

Emotion, however, does not overwhelm Robinson's rationalism. On viewing the precipice where Jesus escaped the angry citizens of Nazareth (Luke 4:29-30), Robinson remarks, "There is here no intimation that his escape was favoured by the exertion of any miraculous power; but he made his way fearlessly through the crowd; and probably eluded their pursuit by availing himself of the narrow and crooked streets of the city."[83]

Before being carried away by rhetoric, the reader needs to recognize Robinson's solid scientific results. He properly identified more than one hundred biblical sites.[84] To identify a site, Robinson frequently considered the modern Arabic name of the place, and then, by means of linguistic cognates, discerned the equivalent name in biblical times. Robinson often rejected traditional identifications. Mount Tabor, for example, he did not believe to be the site of transfiguration, since, according to his reading of the gospel accounts, the location of the transfiguration was north of the Sea of Galilee, not southwest, as at Tabor. About a favorite tourist trap in Bethany, Robinson says, "It is hardly necessary to remark, that there is not the slightest probability of its ever having been the tomb of Lazarus." Robinson expends much effort in identifying sites in Jerusalem. In regard to the place of the crucifixion and burial of Jesus, he concludes, "Thus in every view which I have been able to take of the question, both topographical and historical, I am led irresistibly to the conclusion, that the Golgotha and the tomb now shown in the church of the Holy Sepulchre, are not upon the real places of the crucifixion and resurrection of our Lord."[85] Also in Jerusalem, Robinson identifies the remains of an arch that once supported a bridge from the western wall of the temple area to Mount Zion, known today as "Robinson's Arch." Amazingly, Robinson crawls through Hezekiah's tunnel without identifying it. Sometimes an uncritical reading of the Bible lures Robinson into mistaken identity. For example, he incor-

---

83. *Biblical Researches* 1:221; 2:337, 335.
84. See W. F. Stinespring, "The Critical Faculty of Edward Robinson," *JBL* 58 (1939): 379–87.
85. *Biblical Researches* 1:432, 417.

rectly rejects Tell Hum as the site of Capernaum. His reason is that Mark 6:53 says that after the feeding of the five thousand, Jesus and the disciples crossed the sea and landed at Gennesaret. John 6:17, 24, however, says that on this occasion they sailed to Capernaum. Therefore, concludes Robinson, Capernaum must be in the land of Gennesaret.

In summary, Robinson's work on biblical geography made him the first American biblical scholar to be widely praised in Europe. He was awarded a gold medal from the Royal Geographical Society of London and an honorary degree from Halle. Robinson's vivid narrative of his travels may have done more to promote the study of the Bible than hosts of academic lectures on higher criticism. He carried the NT out of the stuffy classroom into the climate of its original environment, where it came alive.

CLASSICAL ORTHODOXY AT PRINCETON: CHARLES HODGE (1797–1878)

The Unitarians of Harvard and the moderate Calvinists of Yale and Andover met a stalwart foe in Charles Hodge of Princeton. In contrast to Andover, which was founded by a voluntary society, Princeton was established (in 1812) by the action of the General Assembly of the Presbyterian Church. According to the plan adopted by the General Assembly, the purpose of the school was "to form men for the ministry" and foster an education that combined "piety of heart" and "solid learning." Of the two original faculty members, Archibald Alexander and Samuel Miller, Alexander was the more influential. He was steeped in a Calvinist tradition that honored the authority of the Bible and the classical orthodoxy of theologians such as François Turretin. Alexander also owed much to Locke's rationalistic epistemology and Scottish commonsense philosophy. According to the latter, some truths are self-evident, and humans have the facilities of analysis and reason that can grasp reality. In his inaugural address, Alexander promoted two crucial endeavors: "to ascertain that the Scriptures contain the truths of God," and "to ascertain what these truths are." In regard to the first, Alexander declared that the Bible consists of facts recorded by reliable witnesses and confirmed by miracles and fulfilled prophecy. In regard to the second, Alexander advocated a method of interpretation that attended "to the grammatical and literal sense of the words employed, to the force and significance of the figures and allusions used, and to the idiom of the language in which they were written." Beyond this, the student needs "the illumination and assistance of the Holy Spirit."[86]

---

86. Cited in Mark A. Noll, ed., *The Princeton Theology 1812–1921: Scripture, Science, and Theological Method from Archibald Alexander to Benjamin Breckinridge Warfield* (Grand Rapids, Mich.: Baker, 1983), 56, 75, 81, 85.

Sitting in the gallery, enthralled by Alexander's message, was a teenager named Charles Hodge.[87] Born in Philadelphia, Hodge moved to Princeton in 1812 to enter the College of New Jersey (later Princeton). In 1815, he was converted in a campus revival, and decided for the ministry. He entered Princeton Seminary and graduated in 1819. Hodge was appointed assistant teacher in biblical languages in 1820, and two years later named Professor of Oriental and Biblical Literature. Beginning in 1826, he spent two years studying in Europe, primarily at Paris, Halle, and Berlin. Hodge returned to Princeton, and in 1840 moved to the chair of Systematic Theology, although he continued to teach NT. Hodge's fifty years of teaching were celebrated in 1872, with some four hundred former students and dignitaries from across the nation in attendance. In his response to the admiring assembly, Hodge said, "I am not afraid to say that a new idea never originated in this Seminary."[88]

Although Hodge may not have been bursting with new ideas, he expressed the old in new and compelling ways.[89] Hodge's theological edifice is built on three main pillars: Scripture, untainted by the rationalism of European criticism; Calvinist confessionalism, as formulated by the seventeenth-century scholastics; and commonsense philosophy, with its stress on clear, empirical investigation. Hodge believes that theology is a science, committed to two basic tasks: (1) to ascertain and state the facts recorded in the Bible—the duty of the biblical theologian; and (2) to discern the inner relation of these facts and to arrange them in a harmonious order—the work of the systematic theologian. Thus, the Bible scholar works inductively, collecting data from the Bible the way the scientist collects data from nature. "The Bible," says Hodge, "is to the theologian what nature is to the man of science. It is his store-house of facts." In arranging the biblical facts, Hodge believes the systematic theologian should use reason and religious experience, although experience is judged by Scripture. "The true method in theology," writes Hodge, "requires that the facts of religious experience should be accepted as facts, and when duly authenticated by Scripture, be

---

87. Alexander A. Hodge, *The Life of Charles Hodge* (New York: Arno, 1969); W. Andrew Hoffecker, *Piety and the Princeton Theologians: Archibald Alexander, Charles Hodge, and Benjamin Warfield* (Phillipsburg, N.J.: Presbyterian and Reformed Publishing Co., 1981); Noll, *Princeton Theology*, 1–17; James H. Smylie, "Charles Hodge (1797–1878)," in *MCTA*, 153–60.

88. Cited in A. Hodge, *Life of Charles Hodge*, 521.

89. See Ralph John Danhof, *Charles Hodge as a Dogmatician* (Goes, Netherlands: Oosterbaan & Le Cointre, 1929); David F. Wells, "Charles Hodge," in *Reformed Theology in America: A History of Its Modern Development*, ed. David F. Wells (Grand Rapids, Mich.: Eerdmans, 1985), 36–59; repr. in *The Princeton Theology*, ed. David F. Wells (Grand Rapids, Mich.: Baker, 1989), 37–62. For a short summary of Hodge's theology, see Mark A. Noll, ed., *Charles Hodge: The Way of Life* (New York: Paulist, 1987).

allowed to interpret the doctrinal statements of the Word of God."[90] Hodge also believes the facts of Scripture cannot contradict the facts of science. He says that "there is not only no discrepancy between the Mosaic account of creation and the assumed facts of geology, but there is a most marvelous coincidence between them."[91]

Basic to Hodge's NT research is his understanding of revelation and inspiration.[92] He says, "the Bible contains all the extant revelations of God, which He designed to be the rule of faith and practice for his Church; so that nothing can rightfully be imposed on the consciences of men as truth or duty which is not taught directly or by necessary implication in the Holy Scriptures." For Hodge, inspiration is a distinctive, clearly delineated action of God. Hodge says that "inspiration was an influence of the Holy Spirit on the minds of certain select men, which rendered them the organs of God for the infallible communication of his mind and will." Inspiration should not, according to Hodge, be confused with revelation: "The effect of revelation was to render the recipient wiser. The effect of inspiration was to preserve him from error in teaching."[93] According to Hodge, inspiration extends to the whole Bible and includes everything that is in the Bible—historical and geographical details as well as religious and moral teaching. Moreover, inspiration has to do with words, not just concepts—words that display "absolute freedom from error."[94] Although Hodge is sure that apostles were inspired to write Scripture, he denies that they were inspired in everything they did. For example, "Peter erred in conduct at Antioch; but this does not prove that he erred in teaching."[95]

In regard to method of interpretation, Hodge believes some basic rules should be followed. First of all, the words of Scripture should be taken in "their plain historical sense." Second, Scripture should be interpreted by Scripture, as Stuart and a host of others had insisted. For Hodge, this can be called either the analogy of Scripture or the analogy of faith. In the third place, Scripture should be interpreted with the guidance of the Spirit: "As

---

90. Charles Hodge, *Systematic Theology*, 3 vols. (Grand Rapids, Mich.: Eerdmans, 1952) 1:1–2, 16.

91. Cited in Jonathan Wells, *Charles Hodge's Critique of Darwinism: An Historical-Critical Analysis of Concepts Basic to the 19th Century Debate* (Lewiston, N.Y.: Edwin Mellen, 1988), 56.

92. See Thomas H. Olbricht, "Charles Hodge as an American New Testament Interpreter," *JPH* 57 (1979) 117–33; John H. Gerstner, "The Contributions of Charles Hodge, B. B. Warfield, and J. Gresham Machen to the Doctrine of Inspiration," in *Challenges to Inerrancy: A Theological Response*, ed. Gordon R. Lewis and Bruce Demarest (Chicago: Moody, 1984), 347–59; M. A. Noll, "Hodge, Charles (1797–1878)," in *HHMBI*, 325–30.

93. *Systematic Theology* 1:183, 154, 155.

94. "Inspiration," *Biblical and Repertory and Princeton Review* 29 (1857): 682. A facsimile of this essay, which reviews a book on inspiration by William Lee of Dublin, is printed in Mark A. Noll, ed., *The Princeton Defense of Plenary Verbal Inspiration, Fundamentalism in American Religion, 1880–1950* (New York: Garland, 1988).

95. *Systematic Theology* 1:166.

only those who have a moral nature can discern moral truth, so those only who are spiritually minded can truly receive the things of the Spirit."[96]

Hodge's exegetical work is demonstrated in his commentaries on Romans, 1 and 2 Corinthians, and Ephesians—all still in print. Benjamin Warfield, Hodge's most famous student, said of his professor, "He had . . . no taste for the technicalities of Exegesis."[97] Actually, Hodge was sensitive to exegetical issues and was in command of a vast amount of critical material, but his commentaries are, nevertheless, heavily theological. Hodge's *Romans* first appeared in 1835, was later revised, and went through countless reprints. In the introduction, Hodge asserts that Paul's Epistles "are far more logical than ordinary letters."[98] As to format, Hodge orders the material according to chapters and divides the chapters into sections. The material in each section is treated under four heads: Analysis (the structure of the section), Commentary (verse-by-verse comments on Greek terms and phrases), Doctrine (a listing of doctrinal points detected in the text), and Remarks (practical application of the text).

On Rom. 3:21-31, for example, Hodge's "Analysis" notes that the text presents the method of salvation: its nature, ground, object, and results. In the "Commentary," discussing the term ἀπολύτρωσις (v. 24), Hodge says that it has two basic meanings: ransom effected by a payment; or the simple idea of deliverance without payment. Hodge concludes that only the first meaning is possible. "When applied to the work of Christ, as affecting our deliverance from the punishment of sin, it is always taken in its proper sense, *deliverance effected by the payment of a ransom*." On ἱλαστήριον, Hodge, like Stuart, rejects the translation "mercy seat," since this metaphor would not fit the context: one cannot speak of the blood of the mercy seat, but of the blood of the sacrifice. Hodge concludes that the translation should be "propitiatory sacrifice":

> The obvious meaning, therefore, of this important passage is, that God has publicly set forth the Lord Jesus Christ, in the sight of the intelligent universe, as a propitiatory sacrifice for the sins of men. It is the essential idea of such a sacrifice, that it is a satisfaction to justice. It terminates on God. Its primary design is not to produce any subjective change in the offerer, but to appease God.

As to "Doctrine," Hodge summarizes what his "Commentary" has said about justification, mainly that it is not our work but the work of Christ for us. Hodge also claims that the law of God is immutable: "its penalty must be inflicted either on the sinner or his substitute." Under "Remarks," Hodge

---

96. Ibid. 1:187, 188.
97. Cited in A. Hodge, *Life of Charles Hodge*, 589.
98. *Commentary on the Epistle to the Romans*, rev. ed. (Philadelphia: Alfred Martien, 1873), 4.

declares that all preaching is mistaken that does not lead sinners to feel the necessity of receiving Christ.[99]

On Rom. 5:12-21, Hodge's "Analysis" asserts that the design of this text is to present the justification of the sinner on the ground of the righteousness of Christ in contrast to the condemnation of all people on the basis of the sin of Adam. The main arguments, then, are in vv. 12 and 18-19; Hodge takes vv. 13-17 as a parenthesis. In the "Commentary," Hodge allots seventeen pages to v. 12. His main line of argument is the parallel between Adam and Christ: "Adam was the cause of sin in a sense analogous to that in which Christ is the cause of righteousness."[100] On the disputed phrase ἐφ' ᾧ, Hodge argues, mainly from grammar, that the translation should not be "in whom" but "because," so that the meaning is: "All men die *because* all sinned." However, Hodge rejects the arguments that the text means all sinned individually, and he believes the aorist tense indicates a single action in the past. All sinned in Adam, their representative.

Hodge's *Ephesians* was originally published in 1856. In the introduction, he contends that Ephesians was written by Paul from his Roman imprisonment. Although the words "in Ephesus" (1:1) are missing from some manuscripts, Hodge believes the letter was written to the Ephesians, to be shared with neighboring churches. In refuting objections to Pauline authorship, Hodge decries "the German critics, for whom in general, novelty is every thing, the last opinion always being the best." However, in discussing commentaries on Ephesians, Hodge says that "Meyer is, perhaps, the ablest commentator on the New Testament in modern times." In favor of Pauline authorship, Hodge notes that the letter purports to be from Paul, and, in his opinion, the style and doctrine are Pauline. "Finally and mainly," says Hodge, "the epistle reveals itself as the work of the Holy Ghost, as clearly as the stars declare their maker to be God. In no portion of the Sacred Scriptures are the self-evidencing light and power of divine truth more concentrated than they are here."[101]

The comments on Eph. 1:4, to which Hodge devotes six pages, are typical of his theological exegesis. The text says, "he [God] chose us before the foundation of the world." In this verse, "us," in Hodge's opinion, does not mean Paul; it includes believers scattered in many places and times. The force of the text is to make the point that the elect have a covenant union with Christ that precedes their actual union with him.

> There is a federal union with Christ which is antecedent to all actual union, and is the source of it. . . . Their voluntary union with Christ by faith, is not the

---

99. Ibid., 141, 144, 160.
100. Ibid., 228. See Stein, "Stuart and Hodge on Romans 5:12-21," 340–58.
101. *A Commentary on the Epistle to the Ephesians* (Grand Rapids, Mich.: Eerdmans, n.d.), xvi, xx, xv. On H. A. W. Meyer (1800–1873), see *HNTR* 1:365–70.

ground of their federal union, but, on the contrary, their federal union is the ground of their voluntary union. It is, therefore, in Christ, i.e. as united to him in the covenant of redemption, that the people of God are elected to eternal life and to all the blessings therewith connected.

Election is from before the foundation of the world. "From eternity," says Hodge, "the whole scheme of redemption with all its details and in all its results lay matured in the divine mind. Hence every thing is certain. There is no possibility of either failure or of any change of purpose."[102]

Hodge's commentary on *1 Corinthians* appeared in 1857, and his *2 Corinthians* two years later.[103] As to the historical situation addressed in 1 Corinthians, Hodge thinks there were four factions in the church. The Cephas party he identifies as Judaizers and the Christ party as those who claimed an exclusive relation to Christ. Although addressed to particular problems of Corinth, the epistle has a larger meaning. "The cases may never occur again," says Hodge, "but the principles involved in their decision, are of perpetual obligation, and serve as lights to the church in all ages." On Paul's cryptic word "the rock was Christ" (1 Cor. 10:4), Hodge believes the text makes two basic points: (1) the Israelites were constantly provided with water miraculously; (2) Christ was the source of this supply. This metaphorical presentation of Christ as the rock provides Hodge with the occasion for larger christological reflection:

> This passage distinctly asserts not only the preexistence of our Lord, but also that he was the Jehovah of the Old Testament. He who appeared to Moses and announced himself as Jehovah, the God of Abraham, who commissioned him to go to Pharaoh, who delivered the people out of Egypt, who appeared on Horeb, who led the people through the wilderness, who dwelt in the temple, who manifested himself to Isaiah, who was to appear personally in the fullness of time, is the person who was born of a virgin, and manifested himself in the flesh. He is called, therefore, in the Old Testament, an angel, the angel of Jehovah, Jehovah, the Supreme Lord, the Mighty God, the Son of God—one whom God sent—one with him, therefore, as to substance, but a distinct person.[104]

In overview, the thrust of Hodge's work is heavily polemical and apologetic. In the face of what appeared to be a growing infidelity, the moderating theologies of New England, according to Hodge, had compromised the solid Calvinism of Edwards. Hodge countered with a "scientific" biblical theology—a theology based on the factual data of Scripture. The data provided by the Bible, according to this view, were confirmed by a precise doctrine of

---

102. Ibid., 31, 32.
103. Charles Hodge, *An Exposition of the First Epistle to the Corinthians* (New York: A. C. Armstrong & Sons, 1894); Charles Hodge, *An Exposition of the Second Epistle to the Corinthians* (New York: George H. Doran, 1859).
104. *First Corinthians*, xxi, 175.

inspiration. According to this doctrine, the writers of Scripture were protected from error in anything they wrote by means of a distinctive action of God through the Spirit without apparent parallel in the divine economy. To those who did not share this view, Hodge's doctrine of inspiration appeared to be arbitrary, designed to provide an unassailable ground upon which Calvinist orthodoxy could be constructed. In any event, Hodge's doctrine of inerrancy would be refined by his disciples, and continue to play a crucial role in the ongoing study of the NT in America. The ongoing debate would demonstrate, too, how decisive presuppositions are for NT research. If one's fundamental presupposition is that NT writers cannot err, that presupposition seems to restrict historical investigation. One wonders, too, if the concept of inerrancy, with its stress on factual, objective data, adequately appreciates the nature of biblical language and thought—an issue explicit in the research of Horace Bushnell.

A HERMENEUTICAL ALTERNATIVE: HORACE BUSHNELL (1802–1876)

The literary aspects of Scripture that largely eluded Hodge became a prominent feature of Bushnell's thought. For Hodge, theology was a science; for Bushnell, theology was an art. Horace Bushnell, sometimes called the father of American liberalism, was born near Litchfield, Connecticut.[105] He studied at Yale College and Yale Divinity School, where the leading theologian was Nathaniel Taylor—an architect of the moderate Calvinism of the New Divinity or New England Theology. More influential was Josiah Willard Gibbs, the Professor of Sacred Literature, who was intensely interested in the nature of biblical language.[106] Bushnell was ordained and named pastor of the prominent North Church of Hartford in 1833, where he was noted for his eloquent preaching. In 1848, while reading devotional classics, Bushnell emerged from his study, declaring that he had received a revelation. When his wife asked what had been revealed, he said, "the gospel." Later, reflecting on the experience, he said it gave him "a clearer

---

105. See Robert L. Edwards, *Of Singular Genius, Of Singular Grace: A Biography of Horace Bushnell* (Cleveland: Pilgrim, 1992); Mary Bushnell Cheney, *Life and Letters of Horace Bushnell* (New York: Harper & Brothers, 1880); William R. Adamson, *Bushnell Rediscovered* (Philadelphia: United Church Press, 1966); Barbara M. Cross, *Horace Bushnell: Minister to a Changing America* (Chicago: University of Chicago Press, 1958); Howard A. Barnes, *Horace Bushnell and the Virtuous Republic,* ATLA Monograph Series 27 (Metuchen, N.J.: Scarecrow, 1991); George B. Stevens, "Horace Bushnell and Albrecht Ritschl: A Comparison," *AJT* 6 (1902): 35–56.

106. Gibbs had been a student of Moses Stuart. He published a translation of Gesenius's *Lexicon* (1824) and was noted for his avid reading of German scholarship. Influenced by Coleridge, Gibbs emphasized the metaphorical and symbolic nature of biblical language. See Brown, *Biblical Criticism in America,* 171–77; Roland H. Bainton, *Yale and the Ministry: A History of Education for the Christian Ministry at Yale from the Founding in 1701* (New York: Harper & Brothers, 1957), 87–88.

knowledge of God."[107] Unitarians considered Bushnell to be too conservative for a chair at Harvard, while orthodox Congregationalists repeatedly charged him with heresy. Bothered by chronic lung disease, Bushnell resigned from his pulpit in 1859, but continued to travel, lecture, and write until his death in 1876.

Bushnell was not a systematic thinker.[108] He opposed Calvinistic orthodoxy, on the one hand, and the lack of vitality among the liberals, on the other; both, he thought, were too rationalist. Bushnell was influenced by Taylor's moderate Calvinism, but even more by romanticism. He considered Samuel Taylor Coleridge's *Aids to Reflection* the most important book next to the Bible.[109] According to Bushnell's daughter, Mary Bushnell Cheney, the theory of language is "the key to Horace Bushnell, to the whole scheme of his thought, to that peculiar manner of expression which marked his individuality."[110] Like Parker's transcendentalism, Bushnell's understanding of language stands in bold opposition to the empiricism of Locke and the Scottish commonsense philosophy.[111] This understanding is most fully set forth in a *Dissertation on Language*, published in Bushnell's book *God in Christ*—a book that presents Bushnell's 1848 lectures at Yale, Harvard, and Andover.[112]

In the *Dissertation*, Bushnell asserts that there are two kinds of language: physical language—the language that names objects and is grounded in empiricism; and intellectual language—the language of emotion, spirit, poetry, metaphor, and symbol. According to Bushnell, all religious language belongs to the second kind. It is a figurative language that expresses feeling and religious experience. The Bible, when taken literally and subjected to logic, seems absurd; when taken as symbol and poetry, it discloses a higher level of truth. Bushnell believes that the ordering of words into language assumes a universal intelligence, and this constitutes a linguistic argument for the existence of God. Bushnell also believes that no exact correspondence exists between words and objects; words are symbols that merely represent objects. How much more is this true, insists Bushnell, in

---

107. Cited in Cheney, *Life and Letters*, 192.

108. Barnes (*Horace Bushnell*) argues that Bushnell's thought developed in three stages: (1) naturalism, or Congregational Unitarianism (seen in *Christian Nurture*); (2) soft dualism, or Congregational Transcendentalism (seen in *God in Christ*); (3) hard dualism, or Congregationalist (seen in *Nature and the Supernatural* and *Vicarious Sacrifice*).

109. See *HNTR* 1:339–43.

110. *Life and Letters*, 203. See David L. Smith, *Symbolism and Growth: The Religious Thought of Horace Bushnell*, AARDS (Chico, Calif.: Scholars Press, 1981); Conrad Cherry, "The Structure of Organic Thinking: Horace Bushnell's Approach to Language, Nature, and Nation," *JAAR* 40 (1972): 3–20; James O. Duke, *Horace Bushnell: On the Vitality of Biblical Language* (Chico, Calif.: Scholars Press, 1984).

111. See Donald A. Crosby, *Horace Bushnell's Theory of Language: In the Context of Other Nineteenth-Century Philosophies of Language* (The Hague: Mouton, 1975).

112. *God in Christ: Three Discourses Delivered at New Haven, Cambridge and Andover, with a Preliminary Dissertation on Language* (New York: Charles Scribner's Sons, 1910).

regard to intellectual and moral expressions. No language is adequate for the expression of truth, and difficulties arise when the theologian fails to distinguish truth from the form of expression. "A very great share of our theological questions, or disputes," says Bushnell, "originate in the incapacity of the parties to separate truths from their forms, or to see how the same essential truth may clothe itself under forms which are repugnant."[113] Efforts to prove theological doctrine, in Bushnell's opinion, are futile.

On the basis of this theory of language, Bushnell develops his main theological ideas. Revelation, for Bushnell, is not the imparting of data, but God's self-communication. God is both the subject and the object of revelation. "What is Christian truth?" asks Bushnell. "Pre-eminently and principally it is the expression of God—God coming into expression, through histories and rites, through an incarnation, and through language—in one syllable, by the Word."[114] In regard to the Bible, Bushnell insists that its authority cannot be established by external arguments or theories of infallibility. If the Bible were infallible, fallible humans would not be able to appropriate its message. The authority of the Bible is grounded in its intrinsic authority—an authority confirmed by religious experience. According to Bushnell, the Bible is the authoritative expression of the symbols that are crucial to Christianity. In poetry and symbol, it presents the picture of God, with Christ at the center. Although the Bible should be read primarily as literature, Bushnell approves the historical method of interpretation. "We take up the account of Christ, in the New Testament, just as we would any other ancient writing, or as if it were a manuscript just brought to light in some ancient library."[115] But beyond historical reconstruction, beyond analysis of grammar, the interpreter must seek to share the religious experience of the author.

Bushnell produced no major works of criticism or exegesis. However, his main theological writings make use of NT material, and address questions of crucial concern for biblical interpretation. Bushnell's *Nature and the Supernatural*, originally published in 1858, is important for the problem of miracles. What, asks Bushnell, is the supernatural? He answers that "God has, in fact, erected another and higher system, that of spiritual being and government, for which nature exists; a system not under the law of cause and effect, but ruled and marshaled under other kinds of laws and able continually to act upon, or vary the action of the processes of nature." God is not captive to the laws of nature, and God's supernatural action does not counter or suspend the laws of nature. Nature and the supernatural,

---

113. Ibid., 49.
114. Ibid., 74.
115. Horace Bushnell, *Nature and the Supernatural, as Together Constituting the One System of God* (New York: Charles Scribner's Sons, 1889), 277.

according to Bushnell, function harmoniously within the larger system of God's economy. God functions as the "brain of the world." From this perspective, phenomena that are called miracles are to be expected. Actually, Bushnell believes that human sin has made the natural world unnatural, so that miracles—supernatural actions—render the unnatural natural. By way of definition, Bushnell states that a miracle "is a supernatural act, an act, that is, which operates on the chain of cause and effect in nature from without that chain, producing, in the sphere of the senses, some event that moves our wonder, and evinces the presence of more than human power." Bushnell believes that Jesus, as a supernatural being, performed miracles, and that his greatest miracle was changing human lives. Consistent with his own argument, Bushnell claims that miracles continue to his own day; and to make the point, cites modern examples of glossolalia, answered prayer, and faith healings.[116]

Important for his understanding of human nature, and especially for the doctrine of original sin, are Bushnell's works on *Christian Nurture*.[117] The oft-repeated theme of these works is: "That the child is to grow up a Christian, and never know himself as being otherwise."[118] Taken out of context and without regard for Bushnell's other works, this statement is sometimes misconstrued to imply that Bushnell believed children were born good. Although he rejected the idea of imputed sin and total depravity, Bushnell did acknowledge the fall and the universality of sin. What he opposed was the notion that children should be treated as outside the Christian community and reared in a sense of sin until they had experienced a dramatic conversion. Bushnell believed that the child was born into a world of sin, but could be nurtured by the family and the church to love God, exercise discipline, and develop spiritually. This view was proved to be scriptural by infant baptism—a rite that Bushnell believed to be in accord with early Christian practice.

Bushnell's lecture at Yale was titled "*Concio ad clerum*: A Discourse on the Divinity of Christ." In this lecture, Bushnell steered a narrow course between the rocks of orthodoxy and the shallows of Unitarianism. For Bushnell, attempts to define precisely the person and natures of Christ are futile. Although he proposed a Christology from below, he actually sacrifices the humanity of Christ to his divinity:

---

116. Ibid., 38, 253, 337. See William Alexander Johnson, *Nature and the Supernatural in the Theology of Horace Bushnell*, Studia Theologica Lundensia, 15 (Lund: CWK Gleerup, 1963); idem, "Nature and the Supernatural in the Theology of Horace Bushnell," *Enc* 26 (1965): 65–74; Robert Bruce Mullin, "Horace Bushnell and the Question of Miracles," *CH* 58 (1989): 460–73.

117. In 1847, Bushnell published *Discourses on Christian Nurture*, repr. in *Views of Christian Nurture, and of Subjects Adjacent Thereto* (Hartford: Edwin Hunt, 1848); in 1860, the ideas were more fully developed in *Christian Nurture* (New York: Charles Scribner, 1864).

118. *Christian Nurture*, 10.

He differs from us, not in degree, but in kind; as the half divine parentage under which he enters the world most certainly indicates. He is in such a sense God, or God manifested, that the unknown term of his nature, that which we are most in doubt of, and about which we are least capable of any positive affirmation, is the human.[119]

As proofs of Christ's divinity, Bushnell lists his preexistence, his miraculous birth, and his sinlessness. Bushnell also presents texts—mostly from the Fourth Gospel—in which Jesus claims his own divinity. In discussing the incarnation, Bushnell, again erasing the line between the natural and the supernatural, contends that the human can embody the divine. Moreover, the suffering of the divine Christ is the expression of the suffering love of God; Bushnell rejects the classical doctrine of the impassibility of God.

Beginning with his Harvard lecture of 1848, and in subsequent publications, Bushnell addressed a critical issue in American theology and NT interpretation—the doctrine of the atonement.[120] In the main, he rejects the orthodox doctrine of substitutionary atonement with its theory of punishment and satisfaction. In opposition to the orthodox idea, Bushnell raises the moral objection that an innocent one is punished while the guilty are excused. Bushnell also opposes the belief that sinners are abhorrent to God, and that the cry from the cross means that Christ was forsaken by God. Instead, Bushnell believes that the crucifixion displays God's love for sinners and God's participation in the suffering of Christ. In accord with his theory of language, Bushnell believes that much of the misunderstanding of the atonement results from a misreading of the biblical texts. He insists that the OT texts should be read in their historical setting, and when that is done, he believes that the exegete will discover in the Hebrew sacrificial system no emphasis on the suffering or penalty of the victim and no idea of satisfaction or substitution. Against this background, Bushnell believes that the sacrifice of Christ must be seen as figurative. "He is a sacrifice," says Bushnell, "in much the same sense as he is a Lamb. He is not offered upon any altar, not slain by a priest, not burned with fire." In regard to Heb. 9:22 ("without the shedding of blood there is no forgiveness of sins"), Bushnell declares, "It is difficult to speak with due patience of this unhappy text, so long compelled to grind in the mill of expiation; turning out, always, in the slow rotation of centuries, this creak of harsh announcement, that God

---

119. *God in Christ*, 123.
120. The lecture at Harvard Divinity School, "A Discourse on the Atonement," was published in *God in Christ*, 183–275. This was followed by *Vicarious Sacrifice, Grounded in Principles of Universal Obligation* (New York: Charles Scribner, 1866), and then by *Forgiveness and Law, Grounded in Principles Interpreted by Human Analogies* (New York: Scribner, Armstrong, 1874). The two latter books were combined as *The Vicarious Sacrifice, Grounded in Principles Interpreted by Human Analogies*, 2 vols. (New York: Charles Scribner's Sons, 1877).

must have some bloody satisfaction, else he can not let transgression go!"[121]

Bushnell's own view of the atonement has much in common with the "moral influence" theory—the idea that the love of God disclosed in the cross of Christ moves humans to repentance, conversion, and a life of obedience. Thus, Bushnell cites 2 Cor. 5:17-18 to indicate that the world (humanity) is reconciled or changed, not God. The coming of Christ, whose total life and work is vicarious sacrifice, transforms the human situation. "The entering of one such perfect life into the world's history changes, in fact, the consciousness of the race."[122] The coming of Christ also transforms the individual sinner. But, as well as this subjective side, Bushnell believes that atonement has an objective aspect. "Atonement then is a change wrought in us," says Bushnell, "a change by which we are reconciled to God. Propitiation is an objective conception, by which that change, taking place in us, is spoken of as occurring representatively in God." In his later writings, Bushnell emphasizes this objective aspect of atonement—the idea that propitiation involves a change in God. Arguing from human analogy, he observes that when a person forgives another, the one forgiving identifies with the forgiven and pays the cost of forgiveness. In the same way, Bushnell believes that Christ's atoning death fulfills the demand of obedience to God. Nevertheless, what is revealed in the sacrifice of Christ is the eternal truth about God. It is "a revelation in time, of just that love that had been struggling always in God's bosom"—a revelation that "there is a cross in God before the wood is seen upon Calvary."[123]

Looking back over the work of Horace Bushnell, one recognizes a distinctive contribution, reminiscent of Edwards's stress on the affections and imagination. Bushnell's theory of language, with its recognition of the imperfect correspondence between word and object, makes an important contribution to hermeneutics. His conviction that the language of Scripture is figurative is important for biblical exegesis, though his theory could have been more discriminating in view of the variety of literary genres within the NT. Nevertheless, Bushnell raised a crucial question for NT research: how can human words—no matter how accurate or inspired—adequately express the Word of God? Also significant is Bushnell's effort to span the chasm between the natural and the supernatural, attempting to avoid the dualism that has plagued much religious thought. In doing so, Bushnell contributes to the understanding of miracles by refusing to see them as contrary to natural law, and to view them instead in relation to God's creative activity. Finally, Bushnell displays an imaginative spirit that has breathed new life into the old doctrines of Christology and the atonement.

---

121. *Vicarious Sacrifice* 1:473, 515.
122. *God in Christ*, 206.
123. *Vicarious Sacrifice* 1:523; 1:69, 73.

HISTORY, PIETY, AND ECUMENISM: PHILIP SCHAFF (1819–93)

Philip Schaff was fond of saying, "I am a Swiss by birth, a German by education, an American by choice."[124] Much of Schaff's enormous energy was dedicated to building a bridge between the Old World and the New. When he came to America in 1844, the twenty-five-year-old Schaff joined the faculty of the little seminary of the German Reformed Church at Mercersburg, a village nestled in the Cumberland Valley of south-central Pennsylvania. The other professor at the time was John W. Nevin (1803–86). Nevin and Schaff together articulated Mercersburg theology—one of the most creative movements in American religious history.[125] Educated at Union College and Princeton Seminary, Nevin served as Professor of Biblical Literature at Western Theological Seminary, a Presbyterian school near Pittsburgh.[126] When he moved to Mercersburg, Nevin joined the German Reformed Church. In his provocative work *The Anxious Bench* (1843), Nevin attacked the emotionalism of revivalism. His *The Mystical Presence* (1846) recognized the centrality of the Eucharist in Christian worship. The heart of Nevin's theology was the incarnation.

Philip Schaff was born in Chur, Switzerland, an illegitimate child, raised in an orphanage.[127] In 1837, he entered the University of Tübingen, where he was impressed with Baur's erudition, and from Baur, learned to view history as process:

> Dr. Baur filled me with intellectual admiration for his rare genius and scholarship. He had great magnetism as a teacher. . . . He gave me the first idea of historical development, or a constant and progressive flow of thought in the successive ages of the church. He made sad havoc with the literature of the apostolic age. . . . But his bold critical researches stimulated an immense activity in every direction and led to many valuable results.[128]

---

124. Cited in David S. Schaff, *The Life of Philip Schaff: In Part Autobiographical* (New York: Charles Scribner's Sons, 1897), 1.
125. See James Hastings Nichols, *Romanticism in American Theology: Nevin and Schaff at Mercersburg* (Chicago: University of Chicago Press, 1961).
126. See Richard E. Wentz, *John Williamson Nevin: American Theologian* (New York: Oxford University Press, 1997); Sam Hamstra Jr. and Arie J. Griffioen, eds., *Reformed Confessionalism in Nineteenth-Century America: Essays on the Thought of John Williamson Nevin*, ATLA Monograph Series 38 (Lanham, Md.: Scarecrow, 1995).
127. On Schaff's life and work, see D. Schaff, *Life of Philip Schaff*; George Shriver, *Philip Schaff: Christian Scholar and Ecumenical Prophet* (Macon, Ga.: Mercer University Press, 1987); Gary K. Pranger, *Philip Schaff (1819–1893): Portrait of an Immigrant Theologian*, Swiss American Historical Society Publications 11 (New York: Peter Lang, 1997); Stephen R. Graham, *Cosmos in the Chaos: Philip Schaff's Interpretation of Nineteenth-Century American Religion* (Grand Rapids, Mich.: Eerdmans, 1995).
128. Cited in Klaus Penzel, ed., *Philip Schaff: Historian and Ambassador of the Universal Church: Selected Writings* (Macon, Ga.: Mercer University Press, 1991), 26. On F. C. Baur, see *HNTR* 1:258–69.

In 1839, Schaff moved to Halle, where he was influenced by A. Tholuck, and the next year, to Berlin, where he was enamored with A. Neander.[129] When he arrived in Mercersburg, Schaff was welcomed by a crowd of students, townspeople, and the municipal band. His inaugural address, "The Principle of Protestantism," was not so well received. The conservative wing of the German church found the address too sympathetic with Catholicism, and charged Schaff with heresy. He was exonerated, however, by the synod.[130] In 1853–54, Schaff made a trip to Europe, and while in Germany, lectured on America. In these lectures, Schaff envisaged America as the place where Christianity would flourish and Christian unity would be accomplished. "Either humanity has no earthly future and everything is tending to destruction, or this future lies—say not exclusively, but mainly—in America, according to the victorious march of history, with the sun from east to west."[131]

In 1870, Schaff was appointed to the faculty of Union Theological Seminary in New York. During his Union career, Schaff moved from chair to chair: from Theological Encyclopedia and Christian Symbolics, to Hebrew, to Biblical Literature, and finally to Church History. In support of various projects, Schaff made repeated trips to Europe. In 1877, he traveled to Egypt and the Holy Land and published a book of his observations.[132] From 1872 to 1881, Schaff worked tirelessly in support of the British-American project to publish a revision of the authorized version of the Bible,[133] and in 1880, he played a leading role in the organization of the Society of Biblical Literature. In 1888, Schaff founded the American Society of Church History and served as its president until his death in 1893. In that year, he presented a lecture to the World's Parliament of Religions, meeting in Chicago. In this lecture—which, owing to Schaff's failing health, had to be delivered by a friend—he said, "The church must keep pace with civilization, adjust herself to the modern conditions of religious and political freedom, and accept the established results of biblical and historical criticism, and natural science."[134]

Schaff's NT Research

Although most of his publications are in the area of church history, Schaff produced significant biblical studies. His most popular book was *The Person*

---

129. Schaff's notes on lectures of Baur in Tübingen and Neander in Berlin are preserved in the special collections of the Burke Library, Union Theological Seminary, New York. On A. Neander, see *HNTR* 1:235–42.

130. See George H. Shriver, "Philip Schaff: Heresy at Mercersburg," in *American Religious Heretics: Formal and Informal Trials,* ed. George H. Shriver (Nashville: Abingdon, 1966), 18–55.

131. Cited in Penzel, *Philip Schaff,* 178.

132. Philip Schaff, *Through Bible Lands: Notes of Travel in Egypt, the Desert, and Palestine, with an Essay on Egyptology and the Bible, by Edouard Naville* (London: James Nisbet, 1888), 15.

133. See p. 82, below.

134. Cited in Shriver, *Philip Schaff,* 105.

of Christ, originally published in German in 1865, immediately translated into English and then into a host of languages, including Bulgarian and Japanese. The purpose of the book was to present Christ as the central miracle of Christianity and the source of human salvation. The question about Christ, says Schaff, "is a personal question of personal salvation, which can only be obtained through Jesus." In the introduction, Schaff declares that there are two ways to view Christ: from above (as in the prologue of the Fourth Gospel) or from below (as in a historical analysis of his life). Schaff chooses the latter, and moves from the humanity of Jesus to his divinity. Jesus, according to Schaff, developed through all the stages of growth as an ideal expression. "He was the model infant, the model boy, the model youth, and the model man." Schaff believes Jesus' baptism was his messianic inauguration. Throughout his life, according to Schaff, Jesus lived without error. In his crucifixion Jesus suffered innocently for the sin of others and offered forgiveness to his enemies.

> Such was Jesus of Nazareth,—a true man in body, soul, and spirit, yet differing from all men; a character unique and original from tender childhood to ripe manhood, moving in unbroken union with God, overflowing with love to man, free from every sin and error, innocent and holy, devoted to the noblest ends, teaching and practising all virtues in perfect harmony, sealing the purest life with the sublimest death, and ever acknowledged since as the one and only perfect model of goodness and holiness.[135]

Having painted this glowing portrait of Jesus, Schaff proceeds to draw apologetic and polemic implications. Basically, he argues that the character of Jesus displayed in this reconstruction can only be explained by his divinity. Proof of Christ's divinity can be seen, according to Schaff, in Jesus' claims about himself. Jesus refers to himself as "Son of Man"—a title that has its background in Dan. 7:13-14, and in Syriac means "man" in general. Consequently, Schaff believes the title presents Jesus as "the ideal, the universal Man." According to Schaff, Jesus claimed to be the unique Son of God, fully conscious of his own preexistence (John 8:58) and unique unity with God (John 10:30). In the course of answering the theory that the story of Jesus is a poetic fiction, Schaff assails the work of David Friedrich Strauss and Ernest Renan. "Strauss's *Leben Jesu*," says Schaff, "is related to Renan's *Vie de Jésus* as the heavy armor of a medieval knight to the parade uniform of a holiday soldier, as a siege cannon to a popgun, as an iron statue to a tawdry wax figure; but both start essentially from the same naturalistic premises and arrive at the same conclusions."[136] In reaction, Schaff contends that the Gospels are not myth but solid history. Finally, Schaff arrays a whole company of important people who praise Jesus as the greatest of

---

135. *The Person of Christ: His Perfect Humanity as Proof of His Divinity, with Impartial Testimonies to His Character*, rev. ed. (New York: Georg H. Doran, 1913), 7, 17, 73.

136. Ibid., 80, 103. On Strauss and Renan, see *HNTR* 1:246–58, 375–84.

men—people all the way from the centurion at the cross to Napoleon and Goethe. In a later essay, Schaff attempts something that few historians have been willing to hazard: speculation about the physical appearance of Jesus:

> Jesus in the days of his flesh had probably nothing extraordinary or imposing in his personal appearance that would strike the superficial observer, and in his dress and mode of daily life he no doubt conformed to the habits of his countrymen, as well as in his language and even in the peculiarities of the dialect of Galilee. Hence the woman of Samaria at once recognized him as a Jew. Yet we can hardly think of him as a Jew. We cannot associate him with the lineaments of any particular nationality. He is the universal man for universal imitation.[137]

One of Schaff's major contributions to biblical study in America was his supervision of the translation of J. P. Lange's multivolume commentary on the Old and New Testaments.[138] Beginning with his early correspondence with Lange and continuing through his work as general editor, Schaff spent twenty years on this mammoth project. He enlisted the work of fifty collaborators (forty-seven Americans and three British), representing seven denominations, all the way from Episcopal to Baptist. The final edition totaled twenty-five volumes. As well as editing the series, Schaff did the major work on Matthew, John, the first three chapters of Luke, and first six of Romans. Schaff's own comments and notes (printed in brackets) swell the Matthew commentary to one-fourth larger than Lange's original. In the main, Schaff adds details: text-critical information, references to English-speaking commentators, opinions of his own.[139] In commenting on Matt. 16:18, Schaff analyzes the distinction between πέτρος (Peter) and πέτρα (the rock on which the church is to be built). He concludes that although Christ is truly the foundation of the church (1 Cor. 3:11), the rock in this text refers to Peter. This interpretation Schaff believes to be correct, because the text presents the metaphor of Christ as the builder, and to make him the foundation would be to mix metaphors. Besides, Schaff believes there is a sense in which the apostles are the foundation, as Eph. 2:20 indicates.

---

137. "Christ His Own Best Witness: An Apologetic Essay," in Philip Schaff, *Christ and Christianity: Studies on Christology, Creeds and Confessions, Protestantism and Romanism, Reformation Principles, Sunday Observance, Religious Freedom, and Christian Union* (New York: Charles Scribner's Sons, 1885), 36.

138. See *HNTR* 1:370–72. For a survey of the American work on the Lange project, see Jerry Dean Campbell, "Biblical Criticism in America 1858–1892: The Emergence of the Historical Critic" (Ph.D. diss., University of Denver, 1982), 67–130.

139. Schaff's competence in text criticism is demonstrated in his *A Companion to the Greek Testament and the English Version* (New York: Harper & Brothers, 1883). Written in connection with his work on the Revised Version (see p. 82, below), this manual provides a clear and comprehensive introduction to the discipline.

Schaff's contribution to the Romans commentary illustrates his critical and exegetical work. In the preface to the American edition, he asserts that Romans "presents in systematic order the fundamental truths of Christianity," and declares that "it is the bulwark of the evangelical doctrines of sin and grace against the obscuration of the gospel, whether by judaizing bigotry or by paganizing licentiousness." Schaff observes that his own additions will give attention to British and American scholars whose work is ignored by the Germans "as if exegesis had never crossed the English Channel, much less the Atlantic Ocean." On Rom. 3:25, Schaff comments on Lange's presentation of three possible meanings of ἱλαστήριον: (1) expiatory sacrifice; (2) means of propitiation; (3) mercy seat. Schaff concludes that only (1) and (3) are possible, and says that Lange has made the mercy-seat interpretation "more plausible than any other commentator." On Rom. 5:12, Schaff, like Stuart, rejects the interpretation of ἐφ' ᾧ as meaning "in whom" with either "Adam" or "death" as the antecedent. Instead, Schaff construes the phrase as a conjunction meaning "so far as," or "inasmuch as" all sinned. Thus, Schaff, in contrast to Hodge, rejects the idea that Adam's sin is imputed, and believes instead that people are morally responsible for their sinning. Nevertheless, Schaff does think that all humans sinned in Adam "virtually or potentially; in other words, that Adam fell, not as an individual simply, but as the real representative head of the human race, and that his fall vitiated human nature itself, and prospectively his whole posterity."[140]

Schaff, Church History, and the NT

Schaff's contribution to the study of church history was immense. Besides his four-volume *History of the Christian Church*, Schaff published *The Creeds of Christendom* (three volumes) and edited most of the twenty-eight-volume set of the *Nicene and Post-Nicene Fathers*. For NT research, Schaff's works on historiography and the history of the early church are most important. In the early nineteenth century a new historical consciousness emerged that moved beyond the Enlightenment ideas of uniformity and facticity to a concern with meaning. Individual events were seen in relation to the unfolding of a universal idea. From Hegel (via Baur), Schaff learned the universalism of idealism; from romanticism (via Neander), Schaff learned the concern for the individual.[141] In *What Is Church History?*, Schaff contends that church

---

140. J. Lange and F. R. Fay, *The Epistle of Paul to the Romans*, trans. J. G. Hurst, ed. P. Schaff and M. B. Riddle, 2d ed., *A Commentary on the Holy Scriptures; Critical, Doctrinal, and Homiletical* by John Peter Lange, vol. 5 of the New Testament (New York: Scribner, Armstrong, 1875), v, vi, 132, 179.

141. See Klaus Penzel, "Church History in Context: The Case of Philip Schaff," in *Our Common History as Christians: Essays in Honor of Albert C. Outler*, ed. John Deschner, Leroy T. Howe, and Klaus Penzel (New York: Oxford University Press, 1975), 217–60.

history is the story of the process in which revelation is translated into life—the organic development of the body of Christ.[142] This history finds its center and meaning in Jesus Christ. Schaff believes a new day in historiography is about to dawn. This will involve mastery of the sources, understanding of the organic process of history, and imaginative presentation. "The material is prepared; the plan of the edifice too is ready in its main outline; only the master hand is waited for, that shall put the work together, and cause the parts to appear as a complete, magnificent and harmonious whole."[143] Schaff was too modest to claim it, but the master hand was his.

On the basis of this historiography, Schaff produced his works on the history of the early church. Originally written in German, his *History of the Apostolic Church* appeared in English in 1853.[144] In 1858, the first volume of his *History of the Christian Church*, including 140 pages on the apostolic age, was published. In 1882, this first volume was expanded into two, of which the first covered the apostolic age (1–100 C.E.) and totaled 863 pages plus an index.[145] Thus, Schaff's account of the early church is fully presented in his *History of the Apostolic Church* (HAC) and in the 1882 edition of the first volume of his *History of the Christian Church* (HCC). In HCC, Schaff begins the chronicle of the history with a chapter on Jesus; in HAC, the story starts with Pentecost.

In the chapter on Jesus, Schaff detects "no conflict between the historical Jesus of Nazareth and the ideal Christ of faith." The historical Jesus of Schaff's reconstruction is the result of a conservative reading of the Gospels. Jesus was born of a virgin at the time of the census, correctly reported in Luke 2:1. "He knew from the beginning that he was the Messiah of God and the King of Israel." "He announced the founding of a spiritual kingdom which should grow from the smallest seed to a mighty tree, and, working like leaven within, should gradually pervade all nations and countries." Jesus, according to Schaff, performed miracles that served as super-

---

142. *What Is Church History? A Vindication of the Idea of Historical Development* (Philadelphia: J. B. Lippincott, 1846). A facsimile is printed in Charles Yrigoyen Jr. and George M. Bricker, eds., *Reformed and Catholic: Selected Historical and Theological Writings of Philip Schaff* (Pittsburgh: Pickwick, 1979), 17–144.

143. Ibid., 79 (in the 1979 volume). See Klaus Penzel, "The Reformation Goes West: The Notion of Historical Development in the Thought of Philip Schaff," *JR* 62 (1982): 219–41; David W. Johnson, "The Artist Works the Gold: The Vision of Philip Schaff," *ThTo* 50 (1993): 409–16.

144. *History of the Apostolic Church, with a General Introduction to Church History*, trans. Edward E. Yeomans (New York: Scribner, Armstrong, 1874).

145. *History of the Christian Church*, 3d ed., vol. 1, *Apostolic Christianity, A.D. 1–100* (New York: Charles Scribner's Sons, 1904). Schaff's concern with the sources of early church history is illustrated by his research on the recently discovered *Didache*: Philip Schaff, *The Oldest Church Manual, Called the Teaching of the Twelve Apostles: The Didache and Kindred Documents, in the Original, with Translations and Discussions of Post-Apostolic Teaching, Baptism, Worship, and Discipline, with Illustrations and Fac-similies of the Jerusalem Manuscript* (New York: Funk & Wagnalls, 1885).

natural signs to prove his doctrine and his person. Jesus was opposed and condemned by the Jewish hierarchy. In Schaff's opinion, the resurrection "was a re-animation of the dead body of Jesus by a return of his soul from the spirit-world, and a rising of body and soul from the grave to a new life, which after repeated manifestations to believers during the short period of forty days entered into glory by the ascension to heaven." "Truly," says Schaff, "Jesus Christ, the Christ of the Gospels, the Christ of history, the crucified and risen Christ, the divine-human Christ, is the most real, the most certain, the most blessed of all facts."[146]

Although he is critical of Tübingen's portrayal of early Christian history as a battle between Petrine and Pauline Christianity, Schaff's construction owes much to Baur. Schaff depicts the development of early Christian history in three stages: Peter and the conversion of the Jews, Paul and the conversion of the Gentiles, and John and the consolidation of Jewish and Gentile Christianity. In presenting the first period, Schaff closely follows the narrative of Acts. He believes the phenomenon of speaking in tongues on Pentecost not to be ecstatic glossolalia, but a miracle of understanding foreign languages. According to Schaff, the notice that persecution dispersed from Jerusalem "all except the apostles" (Acts 8:1) does not suggest a schism within the church, but merely indicates that the apostles thought they should stay and face the opposition.

In regard to the second stage, Schaff emphasizes the importance of Paul's conversion. Paul, in Schaff's opinion, experienced "a real, objective, personal appearance of Christ from heaven, which was visible to his eyes and audible to his ears, and at the same time a revelation to his mind through the medium of the senses." According to Schaff, Paul's central theological idea—justification by faith—was grounded in his conversion experience. "His whole theology, doctrinal, ethical, and practical, lies, like a germ, in his conversion; but it was actually developed by a sharp conflict with Judaizing teachers who continued to trust in the law for righteousness and salvation, and thus virtually frustrated the grace of God and made Christ's death unnecessary and fruitless." Schaff believes the conflict between Paul and Peter in Antioch resulted from Peter's "impulsive temper, which made him timid or bold according to the nature of the momentary impression." In the earlier book (HAC), Schaff rejected the hypothesis of a second Roman imprisonment for Paul. However, in HCC, Schaff argues in support of the second imprisonment on the ground that the travels presupposed in the Pastoral Epistles fit more readily into the period between two imprisonments.[147]

---

146. HCC 1:101, 157, 105, 175, 111.
147. HCC 1:310, 302–3, 354.

The hero of the third stage of early Christianity is the Apostle John. "He lived to the close of the first century," says Schaff, "that he might erect on the foundation and superstructure of the apostolic age the majestic dome gilded by the light of the new heaven." Schaff imagines that John was both a son of thunder and the apostle of love—two features of his personality reflected, respectively, in his writings: the Apocalypse and the Fourth Gospel. "The Gospel," says Schaff, "is 'the Apocalypse spiritualized,' or idealized. Even the difference in style, which is startling at first sight, disappears on closer inspection." In HAC, Schaff had concluded that John's banishment to Patmos had occurred during the reign of Domitian, but in HCC, he changed his view and argues that Revelation described the Neronian persecution. Schaff also believes that the "Hebrew coloring and fiery vigor of the Apocalypse and the pure Greek of the calm repose of the fourth Gospel" could be more readily explained if the former had been written twenty years earlier. Schaff concludes that John was banished to Patmos under Nero, wrote the Apocalypse shortly after Nero's death, returned to Ephesus to write his Gospel, and died around the end of the century.[148]

After completing his survey of the history of early Christianity, Schaff turns to the life and thought of the apostolic church. He believes Christianity was a potent force for the betterment of society:

> Henceforth we find woman no longer a slave of man and tool of lust, but the pride and joy of her husband, the fond mother training her children to virtue and godliness, the ornament and treasure of the family, the faithful sister, the zealous servant of the congregation in every work of Christian charity, the sister of mercy, the martyr with superhuman courage, the guarding angel of peace, the example of purity, humility, gentleness, patience, love, and fidelity unto death. Such women were unknown before.

In regard to worship, Schaff notes the importance of baptism and the Lord's Supper. Concerning baptism, Schaff believes that the mode was immersion and that children were included. Concerning the Lord's Supper, Schaff bewails the "most unedifying and barren" eucharistic controversies that have plagued the church. In regard to church order, he believes that "presbyters" and "bishops" are two terms for the same office. The doctrine of the episcopacy and apostolic succession cannot, according to Schaff, be traced to the apostolic age. The Jerusalem conference, however, gives "apostolic sanction to the synodical form of government."[149]

Concerning the theology of the early church, Schaff acknowledges a variety of expressions, but finds essential agreement. According to Schaff,

---

148. HCC 1:412, 420, 428.
149. HCC 1:474, 504.

Paul believed salvation was accomplished through Christ, whose atoning sacrifice redeems people and reconciles them to God. Paul, in Schaff's opinion, teaches eternal election and predestination to salvation, but does not deny human freedom and responsibility. "Faith is the free gift of God, and at the same time the highest act of man." Central to John's theology is his idea of the incarnation of the Logos. "The Logos became man—not partially but totally, not apparently but really, not transiently but permanently, not by ceasing to be divine, nor by being changed into a man, but by an abiding, personal union with man."[150]

The final chapter in HCC considers the literature of the NT according to three classes: historical (the Gospels and Acts), didactic (the Epistles), and prophetic (the Apocalypse). As to the Gospels, Schaff observes, "The interrelationship between Matthew, Mark and Luke is, perhaps, the most complicated and perplexing critical problem in the history of literature." In pondering this problem, Schaff rejects the hypotheses that the evangelists used each other's Gospels, or that they were dependent on common written sources. If Matthew and Luke had used Mark, Schaff thinks they would have been guilty of plagiarism. Schaff's own theory, reminiscent of Norton and Stuart, is that the sources of the Gospels were the oral tradition of eyewitness—memorized and formulated early—and some written fragments. "We conclude, then, that the Synoptists prepared their Gospels independently, during the same period (say between A.D. 60 and 69), in different places, chiefly from the living teaching of Christ and the first disciples, and partly from earlier fragmentary documents." Schaff believes the Synoptics were written in canonical order.[151]

Schaff next discusses each Gospel individually. Matthew, he thinks, was written by Matthew the tax collector, formerly called Levi, one of the Twelve. Mark, authored by John Mark, presents "the oral Gospel of his spiritual father and teacher," that is, Peter. Schaff includes a lengthy note on Mark 16:9-20, and argues that although the genuineness cannot be proved, the material rests on apostolic tradition. Luke, in Schaff's opinion, was written by Luke, the travel companion of Paul, a Gentile, probably a Syrian of Antioch. He was a physician, as indicated by "the accuracy of his medical terms and description of diseases." Schaff describes the Gospel of John as "the most original, the most important, the most influential book in all literature." Although he tends to magnify John's agreements with the Synoptics, Schaff admits that the presentation of Jesus' discourses is different. "We must freely admit at the outset that John so reproduced the words of his

---

150. HCC 1:535.
151. HCC 1:590, 605–6.

Master as to mould them unconsciously into his own type of thought and expression."[152]

In regard to the Epistles, Schaff accepts all of the Catholic Letters and the Pastoral Epistles as authentic. From his first Roman imprisonment, according to Schaff, Paul wrote Ephesians (an encyclical letter) and Colossians (which addresses a type of Gnosticism), and Philemon. Hebrews, in Schaff's judgment "is a homily, or rather a theological discourse," written by a member of the Pauline school before the destruction of Jerusalem.[153] Concerning the Apocalypse, Schaff agrees with Stuart that it made sense to the original readers, so that its prophecies have to do mainly with the destruction of Jerusalem and the Roman persecution of the church. In HCC, Schaff presents a final section titled "Faith and Criticism." Although he objects to a negative and destructive criticism, he does not oppose a healthy skepticism or the use of reason. "There is no necessary conflict between faith and criticism any more than between revelation and reason or between faith and philosophy."[154]

In summary, the work of Philip Schaff presents a massive accomplishment. His energy for conceiving and accomplishing scholarly projects seems boundless. In the tradition of the greatest European scholars of the Enlightenment, Schaff displays great erudition and mastery of mountains of primary and secondary material. The tools of historical research—analytical insight, critical discernment, linguistic skills—all are at his command. Most important is Schaff's contribution to historiography—his view of history as dynamic process. This method was especially useful for understanding history as the story of living persons, and for comprehending religious experience at the heart of early Christian history. Schaff's understanding of history was facilitated by idealism—a philosophy that allowed him to be sensitive to the transcendent, spiritual meaning of history, while at the same time concerned with concrete events and persons. This philosophy of history also corresponded to the dual character of Schaff's intellectual life. On the one hand, he was dedicated to critical research; on the other, he was committed to personal piety. Although held together by idealism's dialectic, these two forces sometimes came into conflict. On the one hand, Schaff could analyze the Synoptic Problem; on the other, his pious presuppositions about the Bible and the character of Christ made an objective analysis of the life of Jesus problematic. The result was NT research glowing with religious fervor, but cramped by conservative criticism.

---

152. HCC 1:631, 650, 688, 693.
153. HCC 1:810.
154. HCC 1:863.

SUMMARY

The rise of NT research in America is not widely known or adequately appreciated. From the days of Edwards, it was grounded in two characteristic features of American religion: rational empiricism and personal pietism. The former is seen in Norton's natural theology, in Hodge's idea of theology as a science, and in Robinson's investigation of biblical geography. The latter is evident in Parker's stress on religious experience and ethics, and in Bushnell's understanding of language. The distinctions, however, should not be too sharply drawn. Norton also believes in special revelation, Hodge affirms the experience of the Spirit, and Robinson walked in the footsteps of Jesus; Parker praises German scholarship, and Bushnell recommends historical criticism. Scholars such as Stuart and Schaff try to hold piety and criticism together. Indeed, for all these theologians, criticism is enlisted in the support of their own religious commitments. In any event, the work of these scholars proves that the historical-critical method has been established in America. That the method does not function as an objective science is obvious from the conflicting results: Norton uses historical criticism to deny the divinity of Christ; Hodge uses it to confirm Calvinistic orthodoxy. All of this shows that methodological issues have not been resolved: the role of presuppositions, the relation of personal faith to empirical research, the function of empathy and imagination in exegesis—issues that will continue to attend NT research in the future.

As to the details of research, the Americans have become proficient in text criticism and philology, producing grammatical and lexicographical tools for the use of their students and countrymen. With the exception of Parker, their higher criticism is uniformly conservative. Their analysis of the Synoptic Problem is superficial, and the investigation of questions of authorship and date, though not without rigor, tends to overvalue the tradition. In historical investigation, precision of analysis is compromised by a passion for harmonization. As to theology, all of these scholars hold a high doctrine of biblical authority; all of them confess the importance of Jesus; all of them affirm the relevance of the NT for church and society. Nevertheless, their doctrinal disputes herald the battles of the future—battles about inspiration and inerrancy, Jesus and Christology, sin and atonement—battles in which opposing forces will launch the texts of the NT as guided missiles. America is a country of religious freedom and religious fervor—a land where the NT is continually studied with discord and devotion.

2

The Establishment of Historical Criticism in Great Britain

In the Victorian era, the British empire in NT study was founded by F. J. A. Hort, J. B. Lightfoot, and B. F. Westcott. These three scholars, the famous Cambridge triumvirate, launched a flotilla of research that established English biblical scholarship as a power in the theological world. For Great Britain, it was the best of times. Victoria had been on the throne since 1837, and the nation was at the height of its power. The empire was spreading round the globe, putting crimson patches on the map to mark the areas of British sovereignty. Religion, too, reflected the self-confidence of this prosperous time. Church buildings were being constructed or renovated. The number of active communicants was on the increase. The popular press was fascinated with topics of religious interest. The old song had never seemed so true:

> And guardian angels sung this strain
> —"Rule, Britannia, rule the waves."

In the face of these good times, signs of crisis began to appear.[1] New discoveries in science challenged the assumptions of the old faith. In 1859, Darwin's *Origin of the Species* was published. From Darwin's perspective, natural selection seemed more important for creation than providence. And humanity, rather than molded immediately into the image of God, had evolved from lower forms of life on an earth no longer the center of the

---

1. For useful surveys of religious life and thought in England in the latter half of the nineteenth century, see L. E. Elliott-Binns, *The Development of English Theology in the Later Nineteenth Century* (London: Longmans, Green, 1952); idem, *English Thought, 1860–1900: The Theological Aspect* (Greenwich, Conn.: Seabury, 1956); David L. Edwards, *Christian England*, vol. 3, *From the Eighteenth Century to the First World War* (Grand Rapids, Mich.: Eerdmans, 1984); Otto Pfleiderer, *The Development of Theology in Germany since Kant: and Its Progress in Great Britain since 1825*, trans. J. Frederick Smith, 3d ed. (London: George Allen & Unwin, 1909).

universe. With Herbert Spencer, the theory of evolution was applied to all aspects of human history. For modern persons, heirs and participants in this progressive process, the outmoded norms of past and its scriptural records seemed irrelevant.

On the eastern horizon appeared a cloud no bigger than a human hand—the portent of the storms of radical German theology. Although David Friedrich Strauss's *Life of Jesus* had been brilliantly translated by George Eliot, the work of F. C. Baur and the Tübingen school had largely been ignored in Britain.[2] When in the early 1870s a fellow of an Oxford college was asked if the Tübingen school was much read, he replied, "No, no theology of any school is much read at Oxford."[3] However, the Channel was not wide enough to keep England in splendid isolation. In 1874, two volumes of an anonymous work titled *Supernatural Religion* were published. This work, to which a third volume was appended in 1876, popularized the results of radical German criticism.[4] Actually written by W. R. Cassels, a merchant and amateur scholar, the book leveled a broadside at miracles and supernatural religion in general, and argued that none of the Gospels were authentic. The book was an immediate sensation.

The response of the theological establishment was reactionary: batten down the hatches and ride out the storm! According to the traditionalists, German criticism was too extreme to be taken seriously, and members of the Tübingen school seemed already to be abandoning ship. The Cambridge three, however, set another course. Avoiding the waves of skepticism on the left and the shoals of orthodoxy on the right, they assimilated the results of the new science and embraced the modern methods of historical research. For them, God's truth had been revealed in history—a history that had nothing to fear from rigorous criticism.

NEW TESTAMENT STUDIES BEFORE AND IN THE TIME OF THE CAMBRIDGE THREE

Since the days of the deists, nothing startling had taken place in British biblical studies. NT research in the main had been conservative, resistant to the Enlightenment methods. To be sure, exceptions can be found: Herbert Marsh's intricate solution to the Synoptic Problem, J. J. Tayler's critical analysis of the Fourth Gospel, and the resolve to read the NT like any other book affirmed in *Essays and Reviews*. Coleridge was hailed as a prophet with

---

2. See *HNTR* 1:246–58, 258–78.
3. Cited by C. K. Barrett, "Quomodo historia conscribenda sit," *NTS* 28 (1982): 309.
4. *Supernatural Religion: An Inquiry into the Reality of Divine Revelation,* Popular Edition (London: Watts, 1902)—a shortened (912 pp. + index) revised ed. preserves the main lines of argument in a single volume.

some honor in his own country, but he was poet more than critic, concerned with imagination more than history.⁵ Although they excelled in classical learning and fostered scientific research, the English universities lacked the ardent devotion to universal *Wissenschaft* that characterized the German institutions of higher learning.⁶ Oxford and Cambridge, closely allied to church and state, intended to train Christian leaders for society and nation, rather than aspiring scholars committed to independent research.

Victorian "Lives" of Jesus

British conservatism is evident in the popularity of pious biographies of Jesus. These, too, were provoked by an anonymous best-seller. In 1865, a book titled *Ecce Homo: A Survey of the Life and Work of Jesus Christ* appeared. The second edition (1866), revealed the author to be J. R. Seeley, a professor of Latin at University College, London.⁷ To the dismay of many Britons, Seeley ignored the Christ of religious tradition and focused on the human personality of Jesus and the ethical principles of the kingdom of God. Although the orthodox and evangelicals were scandalized, W. E. Gladstone, sometime prime minister, contended that light on the humanity of Jesus would reflect his true divinity.⁸ Actually, the book was untouched by historical criticism. Seeley accepted all four of the Gospels as authentic and equally reliable as historical records.

In response to Seeley's book, "lives" of Jesus were published in overabundance, the most famous by Frederic W. Farrar (1831–1903).⁹ Educated at Kings College, London, and Trinity at Cambridge, Farrar rose meteorlike from lower ranks of the clergy to become Canon at Westminster and finally Dean of Canterbury. He presented lectureships at both Cambridge and Oxford and was immensely popular as a preacher. Farrar published a

---

5. See *HNTR* 1:31–57, 298–301, 314–18, 358–60, 338–43.
6. See Daniel L. Pals, *The Victorian "Lives" of Jesus*, Trinity University Monograph Series in Religion 7 (San Antonio, Tex.: Trinity University Press, 1982), 125–63; R. Morgan, "Historical Criticism and Christology: England and Germany," in *England and Germany. Studies in Theological Diplomacy*, ed. S. W. Sykes, Studies in the Intercultural History of Christianity 25 (Frankfurt: Peter D. Lang, 1982), 80–108.
7. Everyman's Library, 305 (London: J. M. Dent & Sons, 1908).
8. W. E. Gladstone, *"Ecce Homo"* (London: Strahan, 1868).
9. As well as the work of Farrar, lives of Jesus were written by such authors as William Hanna, J. C. Geikie, James Stalker, A. M. Fairbairn, and W. Robertson Nicoll; see Pals, *Victorian "Lives,"* 59–124. Of special interest is the work of a converted Jew, Alfred Edersheim (1825–89), *The Life and Times of Jesus the Messiah*, 2 vols. (New York: E. R. Herrick, n.d.). A distinctive feature of this huge work (more than 1,300 pages) is the extensive use of Jewish sources, particularly rabbinic, to illuminate the life, customs, and religion of Palestinian Judaism. Edersheim's Jesus, who is presented in stark opposition to his Jewish setting, is a theological phantom, a figure devoid of flesh and blood.

long shelf of books, including significant biblical studies.[10] Of particular interest is his *History of Interpretation*—a chronicle of the development of exegesis from the beginning through the mid-nineteenth century. According to Farrar, this history is largely a tragic story of misinterpretation. Nevertheless, he believed that radical critics had inadvertently confirmed the truth and authority of the Bible: "it is by means of those very investigations that the Bible has triumphed over keen ridicule, over charges of fiction, over naturalist explanations, over mythical theories, over destructive criticism."[11]

Eager to capitalize on the public interest in Jesus, the publishers found in Farrar the ideal author. He was highly regarded as a scholar, and he had written a couple of popular novels. Moreover, he would not disturb the piety of the general reader, for his book would be "avowedly and unconditionally the work of a believer."[12] Offered an advance of five hundred pounds with an additional one hundred pounds to finance a trip to Palestine, Farrar accepted the assignment, toured the Holy Land, and produced the massive *Life of Christ*—a conservative biography, marked by vivid descriptions of the geographical setting and boundless imagination. As to sources, Farrar accepts all four Gospels as historically reliable. "Throughout this book," he says, "it will be seen that I accept unhesitatingly the genuineness of St. John's Gospel."[13] Although he acknowledges that an exact chronological reconstruction is not possible, he essentially presents a harmonization in which the Fourth Gospel provides a framework for arranging the details. Considering Matthew's Sermon on the Mount and Luke's a Sermon on the Plain, Farrar imagines that Jesus descended from one of the peaks of the Horns of Hattin to the high saddle between the two, so that the sermon was, at the same time, on the mountain and on a level place.

Farrar embraces the miracles unashamedly. He contends that anyone who accepts Christ as the Son of the God, who is the author of creation, will not be troubled by miracles. Consequently, Farrar affirms the raisings of the widow's son and Jairus's daughter. As to the reason for the omission of the raising of Lazarus from the Synoptic Gospels, Farrar contends that the first three evangelists, prior to the passion narrative, were concerned exclusively with Galilean events. Farrar does not ignore critical issues completely, and on occasion doffs his hat in the direction of rationalism. The agency

---

10. His books include, for example, *The Bible: Its Meaning and Supremacy* (New York: Longmans, Green, 1897); *The Early Days of Christianity* (New York: Funk & Wagnalls, 1883); *The Life and Work of Paul*, 2 vols. (New York: E. P. Dutton, 1879); *The Witness of History to Christ: Five Sermons Preached before the University of Cambridge: Being the Hulsean Lectures for the Year 1870* (London: Macmillan, 1892); commentaries on Luke and Hebrews in the series "The Cambridge Bible for Schools and Colleges."

11. *History of Interpretation*, Bampton Lectures, 1885 (Grand Rapids, Mich.: Baker, 1961), 424.

12. Frederic W. Farrar, *The Life of Christ*, 2 vols.(London: Cassell, Petter & Galpin, n.d.) 1:vii. Originally published in 1874, the book went through a variety of editions, mostly reprints.

13. Ibid. 1:141 n. 2.

through which Jesus was tempted, says Farrar, may not have been a literal embodiment of Satan, and demon possession may represent a primitive explanation of epilepsy or mental disorder. In a lengthy excursus ("Was the Last Supper an Actual Passover?") Farrar insists that the discrepancy between the Fourth Gospel and the Synoptics cannot be harmonized.[14] He concludes that John is correct: the Last Supper took place on the evening prior to the official Passover observance.

Regardless of critical judgments, readers could not resist Farrar's luxuriant rhetoric. He imagines, for example, a final stroll that Jesus might have taken in Bethany: "The exquisite beauty of the Syrian evening, the tender colours of the spring grass and flowers, the waves around Him paling into solemn grey, the distant hills bathed in the primrose light of sunset, the coolness and balm of the breeze after the burning glare—what must these have been to Him to whose eye the world of Nature was an open book, on every page of which He read His Father's name!" Farrar is convinced that the cross of Jesus was "doubtless taller than the other two." The religion Jesus taught was vastly superior to that of the rabbis whose teaching was "narrow, dogmatic, material . . . cold in manner, frivolous in matter . . . servile to all authority . . . at once erudite and foolish . . . intricate with legal pettiness and labyrinthine system." By way of contrast, the Christianity Jesus founded "has never been proved to be otherwise than perfect and entire."[15]

Farrar's *Life of Christ* was a phenomenal success. It was translated into most European languages, and sold more than a hundred thousand copies within a short time. From a critical perspective, however, Farrar's Jesus does not come into focus. Attempting to harmonize the disparate accounts of the Synoptics and the Fourth Gospel, Farrar presents a blurred picture. The human Jesus is overshadowed by the divine, so that Christ emerges as an unreal, superhuman figure, shrouded in a thin fabric of scholarship.

Samuel Davidson (1807–98)

Although the conservatism of the biographies of Jesus is typical of British scholarship, Samuel Davidson constitutes a notable exception.[16] A Congregationalist, Davidson taught biblical literature and church history at the Lancashire Independent College in Manchester. His critical work on the HB, in which he questioned the Mosaic authorship of the Pentateuch, aroused suspicion of heresy, and finally forced his resignation from the College.[17] Freed from these academic restraints, Davidson read Baur and the

---

14. Ibid. 2:474–83.
15. Ibid. 2:265, 400; 1:266, 270.
16. Most of the "lives" of Jesus were conservative, rationalistic biographies published by such authors as R. D. Hanson (1869) and Thomas Scott (1872); see Pals, *Victorian "Lives,"* 72–77.
17. In 1856, Davidson produced a new edition of the second volume of T. H. Horne's *Introduction to the Critical Study and Knowledge of the Holy Scriptures*; see Anne Jane Davidson, ed., *The*

Tübingen School, and eventually published a massive two-volume *Introduction* to the NT.[18] In this work, he arranges the material chronologically, according to his understanding of the order of composition of the canonical books. Davidson begins with 2 Thessalonians, which he accepts as authentic and written prior to 1 Thessalonians, and ends with 2 Peter, which he considers spurious. He thinks that 2 Corinthians is a unity and Romans 16 a non-Pauline addition. Against Baur, Davidson contends for the authenticity of Colossians and Philippians. His appreciation for Baur, however, is undiminished:

> Only those who are not real critics themselves or dogmatise in orthodox mood, will venture to speak of Baur's dissertation on the epistle [Philippians] as the insanity of hypercriticism. Few critics are insane after the same fashion; none certainly who fling epithets against one that has left the abiding mark of his intellect on the criticism of the New Testament.

Hebrews, according to Davidson, was probably written by Apollos. In Davidson's opinion, John the son of Zebedee is the author of the Apocalypse, but not the Fourth Gospel. The latter is "a Gnostic gospel, in which Alexandrian philosophy and Hellenic culture combine to set forth Christ Jesus in his mysterious relation to the Father and to believers."[19] Davidson considers the hypothesis of a second Roman imprisonment to be a fiction, concocted to salvage the authenticity of the Pastoral Epistles.

In regard to the Synoptic Problem, Davidson surveys the various theories and opts for the Griesbach hypothesis.[20] Davidson denies that any of the Gospels were written by the authors to whom they have been traditionally ascribed. He thinks Matthew was not written before 110, and dates Luke at about 115, and Mark around 120. Skeptical of the historical reliability of Acts, Davidson is convinced that the author was no travel companion of Paul. The "we-sections," according to Davidson, were possibly written by Luke or Timothy, and constitute a source used by the anonymous author. All in all, Davidson has written an impressive historical-critical introduction to the NT—lucid, carefully reasoned, based on extensive research. However, Davidson was like a poor foundling in England's intellectual household. Without connections in the ecclesiastical or academic establishment, he made little impact on British NT research.

Autobiography and Diary of Samuel Davidson (Edinburgh: T. & T. Clark, 1899). After his departure from the Independent College (1857), Davidson published an extensive account of his critical work on the HB: Samuel Davidson, *An Introduction to the Old Testament, Critical, Historical, and Theological*, 3 vols. (London: F. Norgate, 1863).

18. *An Introduction to the Study of the New Testament, Critical, Exegetical, and Theological*, 2 vols. (London: Longmans, Green, 1868). On Baur and the Tübingen school, see *HNTR* 1:258–78.
19. Ibid., 1:202; 2:346.
20. See *HNTR* 1:143–47.

THE CAMBRIDGE TRIUMVIRATE:
FENTON JOHN ANTHONY HORT, JOSEPH BARBER LIGHTFOOT, AND BROOKE FOSS WESTCOTT

The lives and work of Hort, Lightfoot and Westcott are closely intertwined. They all studied and taught at Cambridge. They were all dedicated churchmen. Westcott was the oldest, but he outlived the other two. Westcott also "outpublished" the others. Hort, who published least, made his major contribution in lower criticism. Lightfoot, who died first, was primarily a historian.

Fenton John Anthony Hort (1828–92)

Born in Dublin of English parents, Hort studied at Rugby and Trinity College, Cambridge.[21] At Cambridge he made lifelong friendships with Lightfoot and Westcott. Hort's intellectual prowess was awarded by honors in classics, moral philosophy, and natural science. Early in his academic career, he expressed antipathy toward Teutonic scholarship. "I have hardly ever come into contact with anything belonging to German Theology," he wrote to Westcott, "without being chilled by the way in which it seems almost universally regarded by its warmest cultivators as an interesting scholastic speculation . . . and feeling thankful that we English cannot forget that the Truth is that in which we daily live." In 1872, he began his long teaching career at Cambridge: first as tutorial fellow at Emmanuel College, then as Hulsean Professor (1878), and finally as Lady Margaret's Professor of Divinity (1887). Hort's meager list of publications was owing in part to his fragile health, but also to the distraction of many alluring projects. In 1858, he wrote to the publisher Alexander Macmillan, expressing his hope to publish a grammar, a translation of the NT, and a history of the early church. But, as he said, "The Church History may be only one of my many castles in the air."[22] Perhaps the chief reason for Hort's dearth of publications is disclosed in Westcott's reference to "the standard of perfection which Dr Hort set before himself."[23]

Although remembered primarily as a text critic, Hort was extravagantly described by William Sanday as "Our greatest English theologian of the century."[24] As a theologian, Hort—an accomplished botanist—was open to

---

21. For surveys of the life and work of Hort, see Arthur Fenton Hort, *Life and Letters of Fenton John Anthony Hort*, 2 vols. (London: Macmillan, 1896); Graham A. Patrick, *F. J. A. Hort: Eminent Victorian* (Sheffield: Almond, 1987); idem, "F. J. A. Hort, 1828–1892: A Neglected Theologian," *ExpTim* 90 (1978–79): 77–81; William Sanday, "The Life and Letters of F. J. A. Hort," *AJT* 1 (1897): 95–117; Peter Walker, "Hort Recalled," *Theology* 90 (1987): 281–88.

22. A. F. Hort, *Life and Letters of Hort* 1:223, 393.

23. In "Prefatory Note" to Fenton John Anthony Hort, *The Way the Truth and the Life: The Hulsean Lectures for 1871* (London: Macmillan, 1908), vii–viii. Hort also spent a large amount of time and energy working as a member of the NT revision company of the Revised Version.

24. Sanday, "Life and Letters," 97.

new scientific discoveries. In a letter to Westcott, he wrote, "Have you read Darwin? . . . In spite of difficulties, I am inclined to think it unanswerable." Hort was also open to a more liberal use of criticism than his Cambridge colleagues. In responding to the invitation to participate in a commentary series, he wrote to Lightfoot, "If you make a decided conviction of the absolute infallibility of the N. T. practically a *sine qua non* for co-operation, I fear I could not join you."[25] In answer to Westcott's opinion that changes in the Greek text would be branded as heresy, Hort wrote, "I do not know that I am greatly alarmed at the charge of heresy about the text personally. Nobody in their senses likes it, I suppose: but I can hardly remember when I have felt myself anything else but a predestined heretic in the eyes of others."[26]

Hort's own theological position is stated in his Hulsean Lectures of 1871, titled *The Way the Truth and the Life*, published posthumously.[27] Based on John 14:5-6, these lectures express Hort's central concern with the incarnation. He believes the truth of God is revealed in Christ—a personal revelation that must be received experientially in life, in the world. The truth revealed in Christ is a truth that had been present in history and in nature, but finally and fully revealed in Jesus. The fullest expression of this truth, according to Hort, is recorded in the Gospel of John. To God's truth humans must make a living response, sensitive to the higher, spiritual meaning of life—a combination of ethics and spirituality:

> All our primary knowledge of God is through Him, the true Son of the true Father. All our primary knowledge of Him, the Son, is through His revelation in human flesh and blood under the conditions of earthly life, and through the testimony of those who had conversed with Him by their bodily senses.[28]

Around 1860, the Cambridge three formulated a plan to produce a commentary series for the NT. Lightfoot was to do the Pauline letters, Westcott the Johannine literature, and Hort the Synoptic Gospels and the Catholic Epistles. Although Hort completed nothing, fragments of his critical and exegetical work on 1 Peter, James, and Revelation were collected and published after his death.[29] Hort's critical judgments are consistently conserva-

---

25. A. F. Hort, *Life and Letters of Hort* 1:414, 420. See Graham Neville, "Science and Tradition: F. J. A. Hort and His Critics," *JTS* 50 (1999): 560–82.

26. Cited in Graham A. Patrick, "1881–1981: The Centenary of the Westcott and Hort Text," *ExpTim* 92 (1980–81): 363.

27. (London: Macmillan, 1908); this is a reprint of the 2d ed. (1894); the original was published in 1893. See Ina M. Davies, "Reason in Christian Apologetic: Some Lessons from F. J. A. Hort," *Theology* 69 (1966): 295–302.

28. *The Way the Truth and the Life*, 163.

29. *The First Epistle of St Peter, I.1—II.17: The Greek Text with Introductory Lecture, Commentary and Additional Notes* (London: Macmillan, 1898); *The Epistle of St James: The Greek Text with Introduction, Commentary as far as Chapter IV, Verse 7, and Additional Notes* (1909); repr. in F. J. A. Hort, *Expository and Exegetical Studies: Compendium of Works Formerly Published Separately* (Minneapolis: Klock and Klock, 1980); *The Apocalypse of St John I–III: The Greek Text, with Introduction, Commentary, and Additional Notes* (London: Macmillan, 1908).

tive. He accepts the authenticity of 1 Peter, and dates it during the Neronian persecution. James, according to Hort, was written by the brother of Jesus, addressed to Jewish Christians of Syria to correct their misunderstanding of Paul. Hort believes that Revelation was written during the Neronian persecution by John the son of Zebedee (who later wrote the Fourth Gospel). Hort's critical judgments about Romans and Ephesians, originally presented in lectures, were also published after his death.[30] Hort argues for the integrity of Romans 1–16 and the Pauline authorship of Ephesians, which he takes to be an encyclical epistle. Hort's contribution to church history is set forth in another posthumous publication, *Judaistic Christianity*, based on lectures from the latter part of his academic career.[31] This work traces the history of the church from its beginning to the mid-second century, and for the early period, follows Acts uncritically.

If none of the posthumous publications had appeared, Hort's work on the Greek text would have secured his reputation as a NT scholar. As Elliott-Binns writes, "Westcott and Hort's text of the New Testament was perhaps the greatest single contribution to biblical studies made by English scholars in our period."[32] The plan to produce a revision of the text was conceived when Hort and Westcott, at ages twenty-five and twenty-eight, were taking a walk through the countryside in 1853. Their edition of the text finally appeared in May 1881, five days before the publication of the Revised Version, and their second volume, containing the *Introduction and Appendix*, was published a few months later.[33] Although both volumes were a joint project, Westcott was inclined to tire of the details. He wrote to Hort in 1862, "I cannot express to you the positive dislike—I want a stronger term—with which I look on all details of spelling and breathing and form."[34] In its American edition, the Westcott-Hort text consists of 539 pages in the order: Gospels, Acts, Catholic Epistles, Pauline Epistles, Apocalypse.[35] Alternate readings are noted in the margins and by signs that refer to the appendix of volume 2. At the end of the first volume, a short summary of the text-critical principles, documentary evidence for the text, the

---

30. F. J. A. Hort, *Prolegomena to St Paul's Epistles to the Romans and the Ephesians* (London: Macmillan, 1895).

31. *Judaistic Christianity: A Course of Lectures* (Cambridge: Macmillan, 1894), 56, 64–65. For Hort's work as a church historian, see E. G. Rupp, *Hort and the Cambridge Tradition: An Inaugural Lecture* (Cambridge: Cambridge University Press, 1970). See also Hort's *The Christian Ecclesia: A Course of Lectures on the Early History and Early Conception of the Ecclesia* (1897; repr., Shilling Theological Library; London: Macmillan, 1914).

32. *English Thought*, 173.

33. Brooke Foss Westcott and Fenton John Anthony Hort, *The New Testament in the Original Greek: Introduction and Appendix* (New York: Harper & Brothers, 1882).

34. Arthur Westcott, *Life and Letters of Brooke Foss Westcott*, 2 vols. (London: Macmillan, 1903) 1:281.

35. Brooke Foss Westcott and Fenton John Anthony Hort, *The New Testament in the Original Greek* (New York: American Book Company, n.d.).

system of notation used, a list of the readings discussed in the appendix of the second volume, and a list of the quotations from the OT are included.

Although the *Introduction* represents the thought of both scholars, Hort did the writing. He was reluctant, however, to be given special credit, and only after considerable persuasion, allowed the inclusion of the following statement:

> For the principles, arguments, and conclusions set forth in the Introduction and Appendix both editors are alike responsible. It was however for various reasons expedient that their exposition and illustration should proceed throughout from a single hand; and the writing of this volume and the other accompaniments of the text has devolved on Dr Hort.

At the outset, Hort sets forth the purpose of the project: "This edition is an attempt to present exactly the original words of the New Testament, so far as they can now be determined from surviving documents." Hort continues, "the primary work of textual criticism is merely to discriminate the erroneous variants from the true." Although progress has been made in restoring the text, better methods and "the wealth of documentary evidence now accessible" clamor for a new edition—an edition that would displace the hallowed Textus Receptus on which the AV had been based.[36]

Hort turns next to the methods of textual criticism. He and Westcott advocate a plurality of methods, used in concert. Beginning with the internal evidence, these scholars analyze the text itself, attempting to ascertain the most probable reading. "Intrinsic probability" seeks the reading that may be expected of the author, determined by such considerations as the author's style, grammar, and the larger context. "Transcriptional probability" seeks the reading that may be expected of a copyist, determined by such considerations as probable error and the propensity of copyists to "improve" the text. Most important, Westcott and Hort believe the text critic must analyze the document as a whole to determine how variants are related to the entire document. Crucial for these scholars is the genealogical method whereby individual documents or manuscripts are found to be interrelated. By grouping documents according to their common errors or variants, a family tree of documents can be reconstructed. "The proper method of Genealogy consists . . . in the more or less complete recovery of the texts of successive ancestors by analysis and comparison of the varying texts of their respective descendants, each ancestral text so recovered being in its turn used, in conjunction with other similar texts, for the recovery of the text of a yet earlier ancestor."[37]

Next Hort turns to the application of these methods to the text of the NT. He presents a chronological survey of the documents to be used in tex-

---

36. *Introduction and Appendix*, 18, 1, 3, 14. On the Textus Receptus, see *HNTR* 1:28 n. 71.
37. *Introduction and Appendix*, 57.

tual reconstruction: Greek manuscripts (uncials and cursives), ancient versions (Latin, Syriac, and Egyptian), and quotations from the church fathers. In analyzing this material, Westcott and Hort observed that the great bulk of variants found in the late manuscripts were identical with the readings of Chrysostom, that is, the text of the Antioch church around 400. They took this to mean that "all the important ramifications of transmission preceded the fifth century." The standard fifth-century text that Westcott and Hort called "Syrian" (other scholars, "Byzantine") was shown to display readings posterior and inferior to the other major text families. Hort concludes, "It follows that all distinctively Syrian readings may be set aside at once as certainly originating after the middle of the third century, and therefore, as far as transmission is concerned, corruptions of the apostolic text."[38]

Next Hort discusses the characteristics and history of the major ancient text-types or families. He notes that the Western text—primarily witnessed by D, the old Latin and the old Syriac—is characterized by love of paraphrase and interpolation. The Alexandrian text, according to Hort, is a non-Western, pre-Syrian text, attested by Origen and the Egyptian versions. Besides these two ancient text-types, Westcott and Hort suppose that a third text existed in the second century that they call the Neutral text. This text, attested by the manuscripts Sinaiticus (ℵ) and Vaticanus (B), Westcott and Hort believe to have been virtually free from the corruptions of the Western and the Alexandrian text. Hort concludes, "it is our belief (1) that readings of ℵB should be accepted as the true readings until strong internal evidence is found to the contrary and (2) that no readings of ℵB can safely be rejected absolutely, though it is sometimes right to place them only on an alternative footing, especially where they receive no support from Versions or Fathers."[39] Following these procedures, and relying on their reconstruction of the hypothetical neutral text, Westcott and Hort produce a text of their own—a text they believe to be very close to the apostolic original.

After a final section presenting the mechanical details of the Westcott–Hort edition, Hort presents the appendix that includes "Notes on Selected Readings." These notes, arranged in the order of the NT books, analyze 425 textual variants, classified into four categories: (1) interpolations in the text; (2) rejected readings of special interest; (3) texts where there is reason for discussing alternate readings or punctuation; (4) texts about which Westcott and Hort have not been able to conclude that any reading is certainly correct. For example, Hort presents a note on Matt. 6:13b—the traditional ending of the Lord's Prayer. The variant is noted in

---

38. Ibid., 93, 117.
39. Ibid., 225.

the margin of the NRSV: "For the kingdom and the power and the glory are yours forever. Amen." This variant belongs to Hort's second category, that is, readings that have been rejected but are of special interest. Hort notes that the variant has the support of the Syrian text, but is not found in ℵ or B. He thinks this doxology originated in liturgical use in Syria and eventually found its way into Greek texts of Matthew.[40]

In response to Westcott and Hort's text, not all critics were enthusiastic. Bitter opposition was voiced by John W. Burgon, Dean of Chichester. In a series of articles—primarily aimed at the Revised Version—Burgon attacked the Greek text on which the revision was based. He ridiculed the notion that the true text had been lost for fifteen hundred years and only preserved in Codex Sinaiticus and Codex Vaticanus. Burgon also quoted the renowned text critic F. H. A. Scrivener as saying, "Dr. Hort's System is entirely destitute of historical foundations."[41] From a more distant and less passionate perspective, most scholars praise the enormous contribution of Westcott and Hort to text-critical theory and practice.[42] To be sure, their hypothesis of a neutral text is illusory,[43] and their notion that this hypothetical text betrays "no signs of deliberate falsification of the text for dogmatic purposes" is too sanguine.[44] Since the time of Westcott and Hort, new manuscripts, notably a large quantity of papyri, have been discovered, and new textual methods advanced. Nevertheless, later text critics built on their foundations, and critical texts published more than a century later deviate little from their text .

---

40. An example of Hort's text-critical skill in the service of theology is seen in his essay "*On* ΜΟΝΟΓΕΝΗΣ ΘΕΟΣ *in Scripture and Tradition,*" in his *Two Dissertations* (Cambridge: Macmillan, 1876), 1–29.

41. John William Burgon, *The Revision Revised. Three Articles Reprinted from the Quarterly Review* (London: John Murray, 1883), iv.

42. For modern appraisals of Westcott and Hort's text-critical work, see K. Lake, *The Text of the New Testament*, 6th rev. ed. by Silva New, Oxford Church Text Books (London: Rivingtons, 1949); Graham A. Patrick, "1881–1981: The Centenary of the Westcott and Hort Text," *ExpTim* 92 (1980–81): 359–64; Frank Pack, "One Hundred Years since Westcott and Hort: 1881–1981," *ResQ* 26 (1983): 65–79; Ernest C. Colwell, "Hort Redivivus: A Plea and a Program," in *Transitions in Biblical Scholarship,* ed. J. Coert Rylaarsdam, Essays in Divinity (Chicago: University of Chicago Press, 1968), 131–55.

43. Kurt Aland and Barbara Aland, *The Text of the New Testament: An Introduction to the Critical Editions and to the Theory and Practice of Modern Textual Criticism,* trans. Erroll F. Rhodes (Grand Rapids, Mich.: Eerdmans, 1987), 14: "Actually there is no such thing as a 'neutral' text of the New Testament."

44. *Introduction and Appendix,* 282.

Joseph Barber Lightfoot (1828–89)

Lightfoot was born in Liverpool, apparently unrelated to John Lightfoot, the seventeenth century expert on Judaism.[45] At nineteen, J. B. Lightfoot entered Trinity College, Cambridge, where he read classics with Westcott, and established his friendship with Hort. He was elected fellow of Trinity in 1854, and later, appointed tutor. In 1861, Lightfoot was named Hulsean Professor of Divinity at Cambridge. About his lectures, a student wrote, "But there was something electric in his quick sympathy with the young, in his masculine independence, in his strong practical good sense, in his matchless lucidity of exposition; and these gifts caused his lecture-room to be thronged by eager listeners."[46] From 1870 to 1880, he was a member of the NT company of the revisers of the NT. In 1875, Lightfoot was appointed Lady Margaret's Professor of Divinity at Cambridge. He was elected Bishop of Durham in 1879, where he remained until his death at age sixty-one.

Lightfoot was a historian, not a theologian. However, he adopted a theological view of history as the progressive process in which God is at work. God, according to Lightfoot, is revealed in history, and the supreme action of God is the incarnation—the Logos embodied in Christ. The unique record of God's revelation, in Lightfoot's opinion, is to be found in the Bible. In a series of articles, he answers the arguments of the anonymous author of *Supernatural Religion*.[47] In the course of his answer, Lightfoot defends the authenticity and reliability of the early Christian documents in support of an orthodox interpretation of early Christian history. In the main, Lightfoot took a position between rationalist critics on the left and the uncritical orthodox on the right. He was devoted to careful reading of the original sources in their historical context.

Lightfoot's Commentaries on the Pauline Epistles

Lightfoot's major contribution to NT research is to be found in his commentaries.[48] For the projected series to be undertaken along with Hort and Westcott, Lightfoot agreed to work on the Pauline letters. In time, he com-

---

45. For the life and work of Lightfoot, see Geoffrey R. Treloar, *Lightfoot the Historian: The Nature and Role of History in the Life and Thought of J. B. Lightfoot (1828–1889) as Churchman and Scholar*, WUNT 2.103 (Tübingen: Mohr Siebeck, 1998); J. D. G. Dunn, "Lightfoot, J(oseph) B(arber) (1828–1889)," in *HHMBI*, 336–40; *Bishop Lightfoot: Reprinted from the Quarterly Review, with a Prefatory Note by Brooke Foss Westcott* (London: Macmillan, 1894). See also Bruce N. Kaye, "Lightfoot and Baur on Early Christianity," *NovT* 26 (1984): 193–224; George R. Eden and F. C. MacDonald, eds., *Lightfoot of Durham: Memories and Appreciations* (Cambridge: Cambridge University Press, 1933). On John Lightfoot, see *HNTR* 1:11–17.
46. Cited in *Bishop Lightfoot*, 23.
47. See p. 55, above.
48. See Lightfoot's review essay, "Recent Editions of St Paul's Epistles," *Journal of Classical and Sacred Philology* 3 (1856): 81–121; Paul H. Richards, "The Interpreter at Work: XVI. J. B. Lightfoot as a Biblical Interpreter," *Int* 8 (1954): 50–62.

pleted major commentaries on Galatians, Philippians, and, in one volume, Colossians and Philemon. For Lightfoot's reconstruction of early church history (contra Tübingen), Galatians was crucial. Lightfoot's commentary on this Epistle first appeared in 1865, and went through ten editions by the time of his death.[49] In the introduction, Lightfoot investigates the people and location of the churches addressed. He concludes that they were the ethnic Gauls of north Galatia. As to the date, Lightfoot detects development in Paul's ongoing battle with the Judaizers, and decides that Galatians was written after 2 Corinthians and before Romans. The format of the commentary prints the Greek text (provided by Westcott and Hort) at the top of the page, with Lightfoot's comments by chapter and verse in double columns below. Within the comments, Lightfoot indicates the structure of the letter by introducing each section with a paraphrase. At the end of every chapter, he presents extended notes on major problems of the chapter, and, at the end of the commentary, extensive "dissertations" on important issues.[50]

The character of Lightfoot's exegetical work can be illustrated by one or two examples. Lightfoot understands Gal. 1:15-17 to be an account of Paul's conversion that displays three aspects of his consecration to ministry: predestination to high office, call to apostleship, and fulfilling of the apostolic calling. At the end of his comments on chapter 1, Lightfoot adds a note on Paul's first visit to Jerusalem after his conversion. He believes the differences between Paul's account (Gal. 1:18-24) and Luke's (Acts 9:26-30) can be explained by different perspectives and aims. For example, Lightfoot resolves the discrepancy in regard to Paul's public activity by supposing that Acts describes Paul's preaching to Hellenistic Jews *in Jerusalem*, whereas the Galatians account implies that Paul had to leave town in a hurry, so that he was unknown beyond the city *in the churches of Judea*. "But though the two accounts are not contradictory," says Lightfoot, "the impression left by St Luke's narrative needs correcting by the more precise and authentic statement of St Paul." In commenting on 3:13 ("Christ redeemed us from the curse of the law by becoming a curse for us") Lightfoot makes a case for substitutionary atonement. The verb ἐξηγόρασεν means "redeem" or "ransom," and the idea of substitution Lightfoot believes to be supported by 2 Cor. 5:21. "The victim," he says, "is regarded as bearing the sins of those for whom atonement is made. The curse is transferred from them to it." Insofar as Christ had undergone the punishment of the law, he had, accord-

---

49. *The Epistle of Paul to the Galatians: With Introductions, Notes and Dissertations* (Grand Rapids, Mich.: Zondervan, n.d.).
50. A collection of some of the most important dissertations from Lightfoot's commentaries has been published separately: J. B. Lightfoot, *Dissertations on the Apostolic Age: Reprinted from Editions of St Paul's Epistles* (London: Macmillan, 1892).

ing to Lightfoot, become a curse. However, Lightfoot goes on to say, "He was in no literal sense κατάρατος ὑπὸ θεοῦ (cursed by God), since Paul, in quoting the LXX of Deut. 21:23, omits the words ὑπὸ θεοῦ.[51]

To the end of his *Galatians* Lightfoot appends a "dissertation" on "St Paul and the Three"—an essay that presents Lightfoot's reconstruction of the history of the apostolic age. He notes that after the resurrection only three of the immediate disciples of Jesus continue in the tradition: Peter, John, and James, the brother of the Lord. Lightfoot traces the relation of Paul to these three leaders according to three periods of early Christian history. In the first, Lightfoot notes the extension of the church to the Gentiles—a move in which he believes Peter played a major role. In the second period, the decisive event, according to Lightfoot, was the Jerusalem Council. Lightfoot believes the Council settled the disputed points between the Jewish and Pauline churches, and affirmed Paul's Gentile mission. Paul, however, continued to encounter bitter opposition from Jewish extremists, but not, according to Lightfoot, from mainline Jewish Christianity as represented by James, Peter, and John.

> Henceforth St Paul's career was one of life-long conflict with Judaizing antagonists. Setting aside the Epistles to the Thessalonians, which were written too early to be affected by this struggle, all his letters addressed to churches, with but one exception [Ephesians], refer more or less directly to such opposition. . . . The systematic hatred of St Paul is an important fact, which we are too apt to overlook, but without which the whole history of the Apostolic ages will be misread and misunderstood.[52]

In the third period, Lightfoot believes the churches were freed from their connection with Judaism. The main line of Jewish Christianity, even in Jerusalem, became increasingly united with the Gentile believers. According to Lightfoot, this harmony is faithfully described in the Acts of the Apostles, which is not an unhistorical harmonization of Peter and Paul (as Baur supposed), but a reliable historical document confirmed by Paul's Epistles.

Lightfoot's *Philippians* first appeared in 1868 and went through a number of editions, mostly reprints.[53] In the introduction, Lightfoot recounts the history of Paul at Rome—a history that he thinks involved two imprisonments. Again detecting development in Paul's thought, Lightfoot infers that Philippians was written between Paul's earlier letters (Galatians and Romans) and his later letters (Colossians and Ephesians), and thus, during the early part of his first Roman imprisonment. Lightfoot concludes, "The

---

51. *Galatians*, 92, 139, 140.
52. Ibid., 311.
53. J. B. Lightfoot, *Saint Paul's Epistle to the Philippians: A Revised Text with Introduction, Notes, and Dissertations* (London: Macmillan, 1927). The twelfth edition, cited in reprint here, was published posthumously, and includes in its preface statements Lightfoot had made in regard to the apostolic origin of the threefold ministry, including an address of 1888.

Epistle to the Philippians is not only the noblest reflexion of St Paul's personal character and spiritual illumination, his large sympathies, his womanly tenderness, his delicate courtesy, his frank independence, his entire devotion to the Master's service; but as a monument of the power of the Gospel it yields in importance to none of the apostolic writings."[54] The format is essentially the same as Lightfoot's *Galatians*. His exegesis follows the pattern of careful attention to philological and historical details. For example, in commenting on 1:1, Lightfoot investigates the unique address to "the bishops and deacons." He believes Paul mentions these leaders because a contribution had been sent to him (4:18), probably in the name of the church's officers. In 1:1, the term ἐπίσκοπος, according to Lightfoot, describes the same office as πρεσβύτερος, for the two terms are used interchangeably elsewhere in the NT. In discussing 2:6, Lightfoot employs linguistics in the service of theology: the phrase ἐν μορφῇ θεοῦ refers to Christ's existence prior to the incarnation and indicates that he participated in the essence of God.

To his *Philippians*, Lightfoot appends a dissertation "The Christian Ministry"—one of his most important works.[55] At the outset, Lightfoot writes, "Every member of the human family was potentially a member of the Church, and, as such, a priest of God." Nevertheless, the ordering of the life of the church made offices necessary. Although every one acknowledges that a threefold order had developed by the mid-second century, scholars debate about the date of this development. "In this clamour of antagonistic opinions," says Lightfoot, "history is obviously the sole upright, impartial referee; and the historical mode of treatment will therefore be strictly adhered to in the following investigation." Lightfoot proceeds to trace the development of the three offices. He believes the order of deacon was established by the selection of the seven of Acts 6:3-6. The order of presbyter, Lightfoot thinks, was borrowed from the synagogue and first appeared in the Jerusalem church. However, in the Gentile churches, the term ἐπίσκοπος was increasingly used for this same office. The office of bishop as a separate order did not, in Lightfoot's opinion, appear prior to 70; the bishop originally was a local official, not a substitute for an apostle. "In other words, the episcopate was formed not out of the apostolic order by localisation but out of the presbyterial by elevation; and the title, which originally was common to all, came at length to be appropriated to the chief among them." This development, according to Lightfoot, had occurred within the apostolic age. However, the bishop in this period did

---

54. Ibid., 72.
55. This dissertation has been published separately as a monograph: J. B. Lightfoot, *The Christian Ministry* (London: Macmillan, 1901).

not exercise sacerdotal functions—functions later added by Gentile churches under the influence of the mystic rites of Hellenistic religion.[56]

The same sort of historical criticism characterizes Lightfoot's commentary on *Colossians and Philemon*.[57] First published in 1875, this commentary purports to explicate "the theological conception of the Person of Christ, which underlies the Epistle to the Colossians."[58] In the introduction, Lightfoot argues that Colossians was written late in Paul's first Roman imprisonment (around 63). The heresy that troubled the church, in Lightfoot's opinion, was similar to the religion of the Essenes—a religion that combined Gnosticism and Judaism, preoccupied with cosmogony and asceticism. In response, Paul presents a Christology that affirms Christ's relation to God and to the universe. This Christology is expressed, in particular, in Col. 1:15-17. In Lightfoot's opinion, the idea of the Logos (though the term is not used) underlies the Christology of this text. In relation to Christ, the meaning is twofold: the "Word" is a divine person; the "Word" became incarnate in Jesus. In the phrase "He is the image of God," the crucial term, according to Lightfoot, is εἰκών (image). Philo uses this word to depict the Logos, and Wisdom of Solomon uses it to describe the divine Sophia. Although the obvious meaning is "likeness," Lightfoot detects two related meanings: representation, that is, a copy of an archetype; and manifestation, that is, the disclosure of the hidden. Paul's declaration that Christ is "the first-born of all creation" employs the term πρωτότοκος. This word is used not only in Alexandrian thought, but also in Palestinian messianic reflection, where, in Lightfoot's opinion, it depicts God's firstborn as higher than the kings of the earth (LXX of Ps. 89[88]:27). In Pauline usage, Lightfoot discerns two meanings: (1) priority: the firstborn is not the first creation, but existed before creation; (2) sovereignty: Christ is Lord of creation by primogeniture.[59]

Lightfoot's Research in Early Church History

Lightfoot's most enduring contribution is in the area of early church history. This is already apparent in *Historical Essays*, a collection of lectures Lightfoot had delivered prior to his appointment as Bishop of Durham.[60]

---

56. *Philippians*, 183, 187, 196.
57. *Saint Paul's Epistles to the Colossians and to Philemon: A Revised Text with Introductions, Notes, and Dissertations*, 3d ed. The Epistles of St Paul. III. The First Roman Captivity. 2. Epistle to the Colosssians. 3. Epistle to Philemon (London: Macmillan, 1879).
58. Ibid., viii.
59. Further examples of Lightfoot's critical and exegetical work can be seen in collections of his writings published posthumously: *Notes on the Epistles of St Paul (I and II Thessalonians, I Corinthians 1–7, Romans 1–7, Ephesians 1:1-14): Based on the Greek Text from Previous Unpublished Commentaries*, Classic Commentary Library (Grand Rapids, Mich.: Zondervan, 1957); *Biblical Essays* (London: Macmillan, 1893). The first three lectures in the latter work are dedicated to defending the authenticity of the Gospel of John.
60. (London: Macmillan, 1896).

The collection includes a lengthy lecture titled "Christian Life in the Second and Third Centuries." Here Lightfoot, anticipating NT scholarship's later concern with sociological research, discusses the relation of Christians to society and state, and describes the inner life of the church, especially its worship. However, Lightfoot's magnum opus is his two-part, five-volume *The Apostolic Fathers*.[61] The great Adolf Harnack, who was not accustomed to floating accolades across the English channel, said that "this work is the most learned and careful Patristic monograph which has appeared in the nineteenth century."[62] Lightfoot's research is characterized by clarity and precision, and a historical sense that sees the details within the larger movement of history.[63]

Lightfoot's *Apostolic Fathers* undermined the foundations of the Tübingen school's reconstruction of second-century Christianity.[64] According to Baur, the bitter Petrine–Pauline conflict continued into the latter half of the century. Lightfoot's interpretation of Clement and Ignatius, however, presents a picture of the church at the beginning of the century untainted by Jewish-Gentile antagonism. To be sure, Lightfoot acknowledges conflict within the apostolic age, but he ascribed the cause of this conflict to Judaizers, not to Peter and the Jewish-Christian apostles.[65] In entering into the scholarly debate, Lightfoot observes, "I have been reproached by my friends for allowing myself to be diverted from the more congenial task of commenting on S. Paul's Epistles."[66] However, Lightfoot considered the "diversion" to be of utmost importance for the understanding of early Christianity.

A short summary can scarcely do justice to Lightfoot's *Apostolic Fathers*. Part I is devoted to the discussion of Clement of Rome. At the beginning of the first volume, Lightfoot presents a general introduction to the Apostolic Fathers. He defines the Apostolic Fathers as those who were historically associated with the apostles. Thus, only the works of Clement, Ignatius, and Polycarp can properly be classified as belonging to the Apostolic Fathers. A chapter on "Clement the Doctor" surveys the life and work of Clement of Rome. Next, Lightfoot presents a critical evaluation of the manuscript and versions of Clement's writings and the writings attributed to him. He

---

61. *The Apostolic Fathers. Part I. S. Clement of Rome: A Revised Text with Introductions, Notes, Dissertations, and Translations*, 2 vols. (London: Macmillan, 1890); *The Apostolic Fathers. Part II. S. Ignatius. S. Polycarp: Revised Texts with Introductions, Notes, Dissertations, and Translations*, 3 vols., 2d ed. (London: Macmillan, 1889).
62. Cited in *Bishop Lightfoot*, 36.
63. See L. W. Barnard, "Bishop Lightfoot and the Apostolic Fathers," *CQR* 161 (1960): 423–35.
64. See *HNTR* 1:258–69.
65. See Kaye, "Lightfoot and Baur," 193–224. Barrett ("Quomodo historia," 303–20) understates the differences between Lightfoot and Baur when he says that the former merely destroyed the chronology of the latter.
66. *Apostolic Fathers*, Part II, 1:xv.

concludes that 1 Clement was written around 95 or 96. In volume 2, Lightfoot presents the Greek text of 1 Clement at the top of the page with his notes in double columns beneath. This is followed by an introduction to the so-called Second Epistle of Clement. Lightfoot contends that this document was neither an epistle nor a writing of Clement; it was, in his opinion, "An Ancient Homily," composed around 120–40. After presenting an annotated text of this pseudonymous work, Lightfoot offers English translations of 1 Clement and the "Ancient Homily."

Part II is devoted to the discussion of Ignatius and Polycarp. In the preface of the first volume, Lightfoot highlights the importance of Ignatius for the debate about second-century Christianity. "To the disciples of Baur," he declares, "the rejection of the Ignatian Epistles is an absolute necessity of their theological position. The ground would otherwise be withdrawn from under them, and their reconstructions of early Christian history would fall in ruins on their heads."[67] After an introductory chapter on "Ignatius the Martyr," Lightfoot analyzes the manuscripts and versions of the epistles of Ignatius, and examines the quotations and references to Ignatius in other patristic writings. In discussing "spurious and interpolated epistles," Lightfoot investigates the three main recensions of the Ignatian writings: the long (Latin) recension of thirteen epistles, the middle (Greek) recension of seven letters, and the short (Syriac) recension of three letters. With incisive argument from external and internal evidence, Lightfoot concludes that the seven letters of the middle recension are authentic. The rest of this massive volume (more than 720 pages) is devoted to Polycarp. After a survey of his life and work, Lightfoot analyzes the manuscripts and versions of Polycarp's epistle, and examines references to Polycarp in other patristic authors. He concludes that Polycarp's letter to the Philippians is authentic. Lightfoot also believes that the Martyrdom of Polycarp, which he dubs the "Letter of the Smyrnaeans," is an authentic letter from the church of Smyrna to the church of Philomelium, written at the time of Polycarp's martyrdom.

Volume 2 of Part II includes an introduction, texts, notes, and translations of the seven Epistles of Ignatius and the Acts of Martyrdom of Ignatius. The third and final volume presents additional material on Ignatius and Polycarp. This includes the texts of the Latin, Syriac, and Greek recensions of the Ignatian epistles; the texts, notes, and translations of Polycarp's Epistle to the Philippians and the letter of the Smyrnaeans. In mass, the five volumes comprise a staggering display of scholarly erudition. Lightfoot shows himself to be master of linguistic detail, text criticism, and an enormous amount of historical information. All of this is presented in vigorous, lucid prose—a joy to read and a model of historical research.

---

67. Ibid., Part II, 1:xi–xii.

Brooke Foss Westcott (1825-1901)

Westcott was born in Birmingham, the son of a manufacturer.[68] At the age of nineteen, he went to Cambridge, where he studied at Trinity College, received academic honors, and became an instructor of students such as Hort and Lightfoot. From 1852 to 1870, Westcott served as an assistant master at the prestigious Harrow School, where his colleagues viewed him as "a man of genius, a really great scholar, an original thinker, a rising and genuine theologian."[69] From 1870 to 1890, Westcott served as Regius Professor of Divinity at Cambridge. In spite of his weak, high-pitched voice, Westcott was named select preacher at Oxford and appointed Canon of Westminster. In 1890, Westcott succeeded Lightfoot as Bishop of Durham, a post he held until is death in 1901.

Westcott's Theology

Westcott was highly regarded as a theologian.[70] Actually, his thought was eclectic, displaying influences of Platonism, idealism, and even positivism.[71] Westcott reveled in paradox and his thinking was imprecise. One day when a dense fog descended on London, Professor H. P. Liddon of Oxford was said to have remarked that the cause was "Dr Westcott having opened his study window in Westminster."[72] A summary of Westcott's theology is presented in *The Gospel of Life*, a book based on lectures he delivered to students at Cambridge.[73] In brief, Westcott contends that theology is concerned with problems of life, and Christian revelation provides a final solution to these problems. Westcott believes the central theological truth is embodied in the incarnation. "All earlier history leads up to the Incarna-

---

68. For Westcott's life and work, see Joseph Clayton, *Bishop Westcott,* Leaders of the Church, 1800–1900; ed. George W. E. Russell (London: A. R. Mowbray, 1906); Arthur Westcott, *Life and Letters of Brooke Foss Westcott,* 2 vols. (London: Macmillan, 1903).

69. Cited in A. Westcott, *Life and Letters* 1:273.

70. See Folke Olofsson, *Christus Redemptor et Consummator: A Study in the Theology of B. F. Westcott,* Acta Universitatis Upsaliensis: Studia Doctrinae Christianae Upsaliensia 19 (Uppsala: Uppsala University, 1979).

71. See David Newsome, *Bishop Westcott and the Platonic Tradition: The Bishop Westcott Memorial Lecture, 1968* (Cambridge: Cambridge University Press, 1969); Brooke Foss Westcott, *Essays in the History of Religious Thought in the West* (London: Macmillan, 1891), 49: "Plato is an unconscious prophet of the Gospel. The Life of Christ is, in form no less than in substance, the Divine reality of which the Myths were an instructive foreshadowing." See the appendix, "Aspects of Positivism in Relation to Christianity," in Westcott's *The Gospel of the Resurrection: Thoughts on Its Relation to Reason and History* (London: Macmillan, 1906), 211–34.

72. Cited in Henry Chadwick, *The Vindication of Christianity in Westcott's Thought: The Bishop Westcott Memorial Lecture, 1960* (Cambridge: Cambridge University Press, 1961), 4.

73. *The Gospel of Life: Thoughts Introductory to the Study of Christian Doctrine* (London: Macmillan, 1892).

tion: all later history has contributed to the interpretation of it."[74] Thus, Christ, who came in the fullness of time, is the goal of God's progressive revelation in history. In Wescott's opinion, "Christianity is the only historical religion," because its essence—the incarnation—is historical.[75]

Westcott believes the resurrection of Christ to be crucial to Christianity: "If the Resurrection be not true, the basis of Christian morality, no less than the basis of Christian theology, is gone." In resurrection "we see the whole of man, his body and soul, raised together from the grave." Westcott acknowledges that it is belief in the resurrection, and not the fact of the resurrection, on which the church is based. However, he thinks this belief is confirmed by action, and he concludes, "it is not too much to say that there is no single historic incident better or more variously supported than the Resurrection of Christ."[76]

According to Westcott, God's action in history is recorded in the Bible. The Bible also witnesses to the progressive character of revelation. "Thus in the main the Bible is the continuous unfolding in many parts and many ways of the spiritual progress of mankind." Most important, the Bible is a historical document. "This Catholicity of the Bible," says Westcott, "is made more impressive by the fact that the Bible is in a large degree historical. It has pleased God to reveal Himself in and through life; and the record of the revelation is literary and not dogmatic."[77] In a letter to Hort, Westcott confirms his commitment to the Bible's authority: "All I hold is, that the more I learn, the more I am convinced that fresh doubts come from my own ignorance, and that at present I find the presumption in favour of the absolute truth—I reject the word infallibility—of Holy Scripture overwhelming."[78] Although the Bible is historical, it is also unique: "I have always tried to read it like any other book, and because I have done so I have come to the conclusion that it is utterly unlike any other book in the world."[79]

Westcott's Research on the Gospels and the Canon

In contrast to Hort, who found it difficult to publish anything, Westcott seemed to believe that every thought that entered his head was worth writing down and mailing off to Mr. Macmillan. In any event, Westcott made important contributions to NT research, not the least of which was his brilliant work with Hort on the Greek text. In 1850 when Westcott was only twenty-five, he won a prize for an essay titled "On the Alleged Historical

---

74. Ibid., xxii. See Brooke Foss Westcott, *Christus Consummator: Some Aspects of the Work and Person of Christ in Relation to Modern Thought* (London: Macmillan, 1887).
75. *Gospel of Life*, 254–55.
76. *Gospel of the Resurrection*, 6, 139, 115.
77. Brooke Foss Westcott, *The Epistles of St John: The Greek Text with Notes and Essays*, 2d ed. (Cambridge: Macmillan, 1886), viii, vii.
78. A. Westcott, *Life and Letters of Westcott* 1:207.
79. Cited in Clayton, *Bishop Westcott*, 153.

Contradictions of the Gospels." This was expanded into a book, *The Elements of the Gospel Harmony* (1851), in its second (1860) and later editions titled *An Introduction to the Study of the Gospels*. In the introduction, Westcott discusses inspiration and interpretation. He finds two theories of inspiration to be erroneous: the view that the words of Scripture were given by divine dictation, and the view that inspiration is nothing more than human insight. Westcott believes inspiration combines divine influence and human expression. "Mere mechanical infallibility is but a poor substitute for a plenary Inspiration, which finds its expression in the right relation between partial human knowledge and absolute Divine truth."[80] Westcott's concern to find the literal sense of Scripture is expressed in the introduction to his commentary on the Epistles of John:

> It has been my main desire to call attention to the minutest points of language, construction, order, as serving to illustrate the meaning of St John. . . . The exact words are for us the decisive expression of the Apostle's thought. I have therefore . . . begun by interpreting the Epistles as I should 'interpret any other book', neglecting nothing which might contribute to a right apprehension of its full meaning. I do not feel at liberty to set aside the letter of a document till it has been found to be untenable.[81]

However, this passion for the literal does not exclude the quest for the spiritual meaning. "Whoever has watched attentively the workings of his own mind will feel that in criticism and philology there is still room for the operation of that Spirit of God which is promised to the Christian scholar."[82]

After these introductory issues, Westcott discusses the historical background of the Gospels. In investigating the origin of the Gospels, Westcott accepts the tradition of Papias that Mark preserved the preaching of Peter, and that Matthew wrote a gospel in Hebrew. To explain the agreements and variations among the Gospels, Westcott considers three main hypotheses: the theory of mutual dependence, the hypothesis of a common written source or sources, and the idea that each Gospel is independently based on the oral gospel. Westcott opts for the third hypothesis. In an argument that is reminiscent of J. C. L. Gieseler, he contends that the apostles, over a period of twenty years together, ordered, formulated, and largely memorized the oral gospel that later was written in the individual Gospels.[83] "In their common features they seem to be that which the earliest history declares they are, the summary of the Apostolic preaching, the historic

---

80. *An Introduction to the Study of the Gospels*, 7th ed. (London: Macmillan, 1888), 41.
81. *Epistles of St John*, v.
82. *Study of the Gospels*, 44.
83. On Gieseler, see *HNTR* 1:296–98.

groundwork of the Church."[84] Turning to the Gospels individually, Westcott concludes that Matthew was written by the tax collector whom Mark and Luke call Levi, probably in Judea; Mark was written by John Mark, probably in Italy; Luke was written by Luke, the travel companion of Paul, probably in Greece.

Westcott's book on the history of the NT canon first appeared in 1855; it was substantially revised in a second edition of 1866 and reprinted in subsequent editions.[85] In Westcott's opinion, the history of the canon is a crucial ingredient of the history of the church. The apologetic purpose of Westcott's *History* is expressed in a single sentence of the introduction:

> But if it can be shewn that the Epistles were first recognized exactly in those districts in which they would naturally be first known; . . . that the Canon as we receive it now was fixed in a period of strife and controversy; that it was generally received on all sides; that even those who separated from the Church and cast aside the authority of the New Testament Scriptures did not deny their authenticity: if it can be shewn that the four Gospels include . . . all that has been preserved of the Life and Teaching of Christ, and that they adequately explain what is known of the other forms in which these were represented: if it can be shewn that the first references to the Canonical Books are perfectly accordant with the express decisions of a later period; and that there is no trace of the general reception of any other books: if it can be shewn that the earliest forms of Christian doctrine and phraseology exactly correspond with the different elements preserved in the New Testament; it will surely follow that a belief in the authority of the books of the New Testament so widely spread throughout the Christian body, so deeply rooted in the inmost consciousness of the Christian Church, so perfectly accordant with all the facts which we do know, can only be explained by admitting that they are genuine and Apostolic, a written Rule of Christian Faith and Life.[86]

The rest of the book simply fills in the details that support this conclusion.

Although he traces the history of the canon from the beginning to the end of the fourth century, Westcott's account of the early period (70–170) is most important. This period includes the age of the Apostolic Fathers (70–120) and the age of the Greek apologists (120–70). In discussing the Fathers, Westcott strains to find evidence that Clement, Ignatius, and Polycarp knew and used the NT writings as authoritative. He surely goes too far when he claims, "Papias affirmed the exact accuracy of the Gospel of Mark." Westcott believes that the writings of the Apostolic Fathers "prove that Christianity was Catholic from the very first, uniting a variety of forms in

---

84. *Study of the Gospels*, 209.
85. *A General Survey of the History of the Canon of the New Testament*, 7th ed. (London: Macmillan, 1896). For a nontechnical treatment of the same subject, see Westcott's *The Bible in the Church: A Popular Account of the Collection and Reception of the Holy Scriptures in the Christian Churches* (London: Macmillan, 1879).
86. *History of the Canon*, 14.

one faith. They shew that the great facts of the Gospel-narrative and the substance of the Apostolic letters formed the basis and moulded the expression of the common creed." In a way analogous with the inspiration of Scripture, Westcott thinks God guided the historical process that produced the canon. "The same Divine Power which watched over the fragmentary recital of the acts and words of the Lord and His disciples, so that nothing should be wanting which it concerns us to know, acted (as far as we can see) in like manner in preserving for our perpetual instruction those among the writings of the Apostles which had an abiding significance."[87]

Regarding the apologists, Westcott attends primarily to Justin Martyr. He argues that what Justin describes as the "Memoirs of the Apostles" is a collection of the first three canonical Gospels. Justin's quotations, he says, "afford no ground for the belief that the Memoirs were anything but the Synoptic Gospels which we have, and they exhibit no trace of the use of any other Evangelic records. Justin lived at a period of transition from a traditional to a written Gospel, and his testimony is exactly fitted to the position which he held."[88] Westcott also believes that the Muratorian fragment presents the canon of the western church shortly after the middle of the second century—a canon largely confirmed by the Old Syriac and Old Latin versions and even by heretics. Thus, with the exception of a very few books, the NT canon was recognized in east and west by 170. In presenting the later history, Westcott investigates the canonicity of the disputed books, and concludes that only 2 Peter remains questionable.[89]

Westcott's NT Commentaries

Westcott's major contribution to NT research is presented in his commentaries.[90] He had been at work on the Gospel of John since around 1860 when he accepted it as part of his assignment for the series with Hort and Lightfoot. His intention had been to publish a commentary on the Greek text, but in 1881 he contributed the section on the Fourth Gospel to the

---

87. Ibid., 47, 59, 42–43.
88. Ibid., 168.
89. Besides his work on the canon, Westcott published two other general works: *A General View of the History of the English Bible*, 3d ed. by William Aldis Wright (New York: Macmillan, 1922), which traces the history of translation from Tyndale to the Authorized Version; and "New Testament," an article in *A Dictionary of the Bible*, 3d ed. William Smith, 3 vols. (London: John Murray, 1863) 2:506–34, which presents a history of the NT text criticism.
90. For an appraisal of Westcott's exegetical work, see Howard Tillman Kuist, "The Interpreter at Work: XV. Brooke Foss Westcott (1825–1901)," *Int* 7 (1953): 442–52; C. K. Barrett, *Westcott as Commentator: The Bishop Westcott Memorial Lecture, 1958* (Cambridge: Cambridge University Press, 1959); Edwyn Clement Hoskyns, *The Fourth Gospel*, ed. Francis Noel Davey (London: Faber and Faber, 1947), 41–44.

Speaker's Commentary series, which was issued later as a separate volume.[91] After Westcott's death, his son published a commentary on the Greek text making use of his father's notes, but the introduction and substance of the earlier commentary remain unchanged.[92]

In the introduction, Westcott gives primary attention to the question of authorship. He argues that the author is a Jew, as evidenced, among other things, by his knowledge of the OT. Although his quotations sometimes agree with the Hebrew text and sometimes with the LXX, "there is no case where a quotation agrees with the LXX against the Hebrew."[93] Wescott also argues that the author is a Palestinian (implied by his knowledge of topographical details), an eyewitness (implied by the vividness of his narrative), and an apostle (implied by his knowledge of intimate information). This apostle, according to Westcott, was John the son of Zebedee whose mother was Salome, the sister of the mother of Jesus.[94] Westcott believes that the Fourth Gospel was written from Ephesus in the last decade of the first century. According to Westcott, John wrote not to supplement the other Gospels, but to interpret the meaning of the historical tradition:

> Christian doctrine is history, and this is above all things the lesson of the fourth Gospel. The Synoptic narratives are implicit dogmas, no less truly than St John's dogmas are concrete facts. The real difference is that the earliest Gospel contained the fundamental facts and the words which experience afterwards interpreted, while the latest Gospel reviews the facts in the light of their interpretation. Christian doctrine is history, and this is above all things the lesson of the fourth Gospel. The Synoptic narratives are implicit dogmas, no less truly than St John's dogmas are concrete facts. The real difference is that the earliest Gospel contained the fundamental facts and the words which experience afterwards interpreted, while the latest Gospel reviews the facts in the light of their interpretation.[95]

---

91. B. F. Westcott, *The Gospel According to St John: The Authorized Version with Introduction and Notes* (London: John Murray, 1894). For a thorough analysis and assessment of Westcott's interpretation of the Fourth Gospel, see Tord Larsson, *God in the Fourth Gospel: A Hermeneutical Study of the History of Interpretations*, ConBNT Series 35 (Stockholm: Almqvist & Wiksell, 2001), 98–140.

92. Brooke Foss Westcott, *The Gospel According to St. John: The Greek Text with Introduction and Notes*, ed. A. Westcott, 2 vols. (Grand Rapids, Mich.: Eerdmans, 1954). Besides his commentaries on the Johannine literature, Westcott presented popular lectures on major themes from the Fourth Gospel: Brooke Foss Westcott, *The Revelation of the Father: Short Lectures on the Titles of the Lord in the Gospel of St. John* (London: Macmillan, 1887).

93. *Gospel of John: AV*, xiv.

94. Westcott's argument: according to John 19:25, the sister of the mother of Jesus was present at the crucifixion; according to Mark 15:40, the women at the cross were Mary Magdalene, Mary the mother of James and Joses, and Salome; according to Matt. 27:56, the women beholding the crucifixion were Mary Magdalene, Mary the mother of James and Joses, and "the mother of the sons of Zebedee"; thus Salome must be the mother of John and the sister of the mother of Jesus; John and Jesus were cousins.

95. *Gospel of John: AV*, xli.

John, in Westcott's opinion, also wrote the Apocalypse; the differences are explained by the different times of writing—the Apocalypse written before the destruction of Jerusalem, the Gospel, in the last decade of the first century.

As to format, the text in the AV is printed at the top of the page.[96] The notes are in double columns below the text, and are ordered according to Westcott's outline of the content of the Gospel. Additional notes are added at the end of chapters. Westcott's exegesis of the prologue (John 1:1-18) is typical. At the outset, he presents the structure of the whole passage: verse 1 is an introduction; vv. 2-18 are divided into three subsections. Concerning v. 1, Westcott notes the parallel in Gen. 1:1. He argues that the background of the Logos is not to be found in Alexandria, but in the *Memra* of the Aramaic Targums. The first subsection (1:2-5) presents the essential facts about the Logos. The statement, "All things came into being through him," indicates that God is the source, the Logos the mediate agent. Westcott argues that the text makes two distinct points: the act of creation by the Word; the continuation of creation (life) in him. On v. 5, Westcott rejects the AV's "the darkness comprehended it not." According to Westcott, the translation should state that the darkness, which represents the human fall, did not "overcome" the light. The second section of the prologue (1:6-13) describes the historical manifestation of the Word in a general way, and the third (1:14-18) presents the incarnation specifically. In commenting on v. 9, Westcott investigates the ambiguity of the participle ἐρχόμενον: is it to be construed with "light" or with "everyone"? Westcott believes the participle goes with "light"; he translates: "There was the light, the true light which lighteth every man, coming into the world."[97] Westcott believes this translation properly presents the continual coming of the light—the progressive, universal revelation that reaches fulfillment in Christ. For Westcott, v. 14 is crucial. He believes it picks up the statement of v. 1, so that two main points are made in the prologue: the Word was God; the Word became flesh. Although one cannot know how the Word became flesh, Westcott is convinced that miraculous conception is "necessarily implied."[98] He also believes the text indicates that the person of Christ was divine before and after the incarnation, although "His Humanity is real and complete."[99] Westcott argues that the text of v. 18 should read μονογενὴς θεός (only begotten God) rather than μονογενὴς υἱός (only begotten Son). This, in Westcott's judgment, is supported by textual evidence, and context: just as the Word is called θεός in v. 1, so the Word can be called μονογενὴς θεός in v. 18.

---

96. In the commentary on the Greek text, the Greek text is printed on the left-hand page, the RV on the right.
97. *Gospel of John: Greek*, 11.
98. *Gospel of John: AV*, 10.
99. Ibid., 11.

According to Westcott, the signs of the Fourth Gospel represent both literal miracles and deeper spiritual truth. In discussing the resurrection of Christ, Westcott acknowledges differences in the various Gospel accounts, but he believes they agree on the main points: that the appearances occurred only to believers and that the first was to Mary Magdalene. Westcott presents a fascinating, provisional chronology of the events of Easter day. For example, at around 5:00 A.M., Mary Magdalene and the other women set out for the tomb. Mary gets there first, and goes to report to Peter and John before the other women arrive (John 20:1-2). About 6:30, Peter and John visit the sepulcher and leave (John 20:3-10). Around 7:00, the Lord reveals himself to Mary Magdalene, who had returned to the tomb (John 20:14-18). This sort of reconstruction demonstrates Westcott's stress on the facticity of the resurrection, although he affirms the necessity of the eyes of faith. "We see that only which we have the inward power of seeing. Till Mary was placed in something of spiritual harmony with the Lord she could not recognise Him."[100]

Westcott's commentary on the *Epistles of John* first appeared in 1883. In the introduction, Westcott contends that all three Epistles were written by the apostle John from Ephesus during the last decade of the first century. First John, despite its lack of an epistolary beginning and ending, is, according to Westcott, a genuine epistle. Westcott's concern with grammatical details can be seen in his exegesis of 1 John 1:1. He notes that in the phrase "what was from the beginning" the verb $\mathring{\eta}\nu$ is in the imperfect tense, referring to that which was continually from the beginning; in the phrase "what we have heard" the verb $\dot{\alpha}\kappa\eta\kappa\acute{o}\alpha\mu\epsilon\nu$ is in the perfect tense, indicating the present result of past action—the presence of Christ in the church; in the phrase "what we have seen" the verb $\dot{\epsilon}\theta\epsilon\alpha\sigma\acute{\alpha}\mu\epsilon\theta\alpha$ is in the aorist tense, referring to the past event when John and the apostles saw Jesus.

Westcott was fascinated by the Epistle to the Hebrews. "No work in which I have ever been allowed to spend many years of continuous labour," he writes, "has had for me the same intense human interest as the study of the Epistle to the Hebrews." In the introduction to his commentary, Westcott argues that the original language of Hebrews was Greek, and that it was addressed to a congregation of Jewish Christians in or near Jerusalem. Since no mention is made of the catastrophic destruction of Jerusalem, Westcott is confident that Hebrews was written prior to A.D. 70. According to Westcott, "The language of the Epistle is both in vocabulary and style purer and more vigorous than that of any other book of the N.T." In discussing authorship, Westcott reviews the internal and external evidence and concludes that Paul was not the author. Westcott proceeds to review other possible candidates, and concludes that Hebrews must be considered

---

100. Ibid., 291.

anonymous. Westcott says, "we confess that the wealth of spiritual power was so great in the early Church that he who was empowered to commit to writing this view of the fulness of Truth has not by that conspicuous service even left his name for the grateful reverence of later ages."[101] Thus, Westcott expresses a surprising opinion: an anonymous document can be canonical.

The commentary (about five hundred pages in length) displays his typical concern with textual, linguistic, and historical details in the service of theology and practical Christianity. An example of his exegesis is seen in the comments on 8:1-6—a passage that Westcott considers crucial to the author's central theme. These verses are titled "The new Sanctuary" and are part of a section titled "A general view of the scene and conditions of Christ's high priestly work" (chapter 8). Westcott thinks vv. 1-2 present a general view of Christ's work as high priest: the session at the right hand of the throne; the ministry in the sanctuary. The sanctuary in which Christ serves is the "true tent," that is, the heavenly or ideal tabernacle of which the earthly was but a symbol. Verses 3-4 describe the scene of Christ's work. When the text says, "if he were on earth, he would not be a priest at all" (v. 4), Westcott thinks the author is contending that Christ's service has to be in heaven, in contrast to the earthly Levitical priesthood. Westcott thinks vv. 5-6 indicate that Levitical worship points toward a ministry that mediates a better covenant. "The Mosaic system," he says, "was not complete in itself, original and independent: it was a copy of an archetype. It had no spiritual substance: it was only a shadow." Verse 6 assumes that a covenant requires a mediator. According to Wescott, Christ as mediator combines the office of Moses (the lawgiver) and Aaron (the priest). "Thus the Gospel itself, though in one sense opposed to the Law, was not only the fulfilment of the Law; but in itself the 'perfect Law.'"[102]

Westcott's commentary on Hebrews includes forty-two additional notes, appended to the end of the chapters. Westcott's longest note is on the topic "The pre-Christian idea of Sacrifice." In this note, Westcott points out the variety of practices, the importance of the covenant motif, and the lack of emphasis on the suffering of the victim. With this background established, Westcott turns to "Aspects of Christ's Sacrifice." Here he understands Christ's sacrifice as representative of the two main aspects of his work: the restoration of right relation to God, and the realization of the divine image in humanity. In his note "The Christology of the Epistle," Westcott emphasizes two main points: the divine nature of the Son, and the work of the

---

101. Brooke Foss Westcott, *The Epistle to the Hebrews: The Greek Text with Notes and Essays* (London: Macmillan, 1889), ix, xliv, lxxix.
102. Ibid., 216, 218. Besides his commentaries on the Johannine literature and Hebrews, Westcott, at his death, left an unfinished commentary that was later edited by J. M. Schulhof and published: Brooke Foss Westcott, *Saint Paul's Epistle to the Ephesians: The Greek Text with Notes and Addenda* (Grand Rapids, Mich.: Eerdmans, 1950).

incarnate Christ. On the former point, he says, "In Christ the essence of God is made distinct: in Christ the revelation of God's character is seen." On the latter, he stresses the humanity of Christ without abandoning his divinity. "In this union of two Natures in the one Person of Christ, Whose Personality is Divine, to use the technical language of Theology, we recognise the foundation-fact of a true fellowship of God and man."[103]

This survey of the work of Hort, Lightfoot, Westcott can be concluded by reference to a project in which all three participated: the Revised Version of the NT.[104] The translation was launched at the Canterbury Convocation of the Church of England in 1870. This meeting appointed a committee that established principles and invited the participation of other scholars. The scholars were organized into OT and NT companies. Among those invited to participate in the NT company were Hort, Lightfoot, and Westcott—a total of twenty-four scholars, mostly from Oxford and Cambridge. Work was begun the same year, with meetings four days a month over a decade. Also in 1870, the cooperation of American scholars was secured, and under the leadership of Philip Schaff, OT and NT companies were appointed in America.[105] The revision of the NT was published in England in 1881. At the same time, an American edition appeared with an appendix listing some three hundred disagreements with the British edition. The RV displayed some thirty-six thousand departures from the AV. More than three million copies were sold in Great Britain and the United States within less than a year, and the *New York Observer* of May 26, 1881, declared, "No event of modern times has excited more universal interest among the English-speaking nations than the publication of the Revised New Testament."[106]

SUMMARY

In summary, the Cambridge three made a large contribution to the history of NT research. Hort, Lightfoot, and Westcott were scholars of immense erudition. They possessed linguistic and analytical skills; they displayed his-

---

103. *Hebrews*, 425, 427.
104. See J. B. Lightfoot, *On a Fresh Revision of the English New Testament* (London: Macmillan, 1871); B. F. Westcott, *History of the English Bible*, 320–32; Klaus Penzel, ed., *Philip Schaff: Historian and Ambassador of the Universal Church: Selected Writings* (Macon, Ga.: Mercer University Press, 1991), 251–71; Philip Schaff, *A Companion to the Greek Testament and the English Version* (New York: Harper & Brothers, 1883), 371–494; J. B. Lightfoot, Richard Chenevix Trench, and J. C. Ellicott, *The Revision of the English Version of the New Testament. With an Introduction by Philip Schaff* (New York: Harper & Brothers, 1873); Frederick C. Grant, *Translating the Bible* (Greenwich, Conn.: Seabury, 1961), 83–93.
105. See p. 44, above.
106. Cited by Schaff in Lightfoot, *Revision of the English Version*, 410. Attacks on the new translation, for example, by J. W. Burgon (*Revision Revised*), were answered by Westcott, *Some Lessons of the Revised Version of the New Testament* (London: Hodder and Stoughton, 1898).

torical and theological sensitivity. They had mastered a huge amount of historical data, especially in classical and patristic studies. As they entered the Canaan of biblical research, they were not like grasshoppers, but giants in their own right—equal in stature to the tallest of the Germans. Moreover, these British scholars were servants of the church, dedicated to the relevance of the Bible for faith and life. To be sure, their work lacked excitement, and they were inclined to turn the land of milk and honey into an arid region. Their theology also lacked precision. Their doctrine of inspiration, for example, assumed a vague notion of divine-human cooperation; they accepted most everything as reliable, but were reluctant to talk of infallibility.

Nevertheless, Hort, Lightfoot, and Westcott understood the intimate relation between historical theology and biblical research. For them, the central truth of Christianity was the incarnation. This meant that God had acted in history to reveal divine truth—a truth not distilled into doctrine, but embodied in human life. History, therefore, was crucial, and the study of history was of utmost importance. In this study, attention had to be given to the literal meaning of the text, requiring rigorous attention to linguistic and grammatical detail. The literal, historical exegesis, however, did not exhaust the meaning of the text. As Westcott's dull but instructive commentary on John shows, the interpreter must move from the historical record to the theological meaning the evangelist intended to convey. With the Cambridge triumvirate, this kind of historical-critical research was established in England. In 1860, authors of the *Essays and Reviews* were charged with heresy for reading the NT like any other book;[107] in 1889, the writers of *Lux Mundi* could assume the historical method as axiomatic.[108] The Lambeth Conference of 1897 affirmed the right and duty of theologians to use critical methods in the study of the Bible. The change resulted, more than anything else, from the efforts of Hort, Lightfoot, and Westcott.

In substance, the major contribution was Westcott and Hort's critical text. Besides this, the Cambridge three left a stack of NT commentaries that can be read with profit today. Their reconstruction of early Christian history—especially Lightfoot's work on the Apostolic Fathers—provided a viable alternative to Tübingen's tottering edifice. To be sure, their critical

---

107. *HNTR* 1:358–60.
108. Charles Gore, ed., *Lux Mundi: A Series of Studies in the Religion of the Incarnation* (London: John Murray, 1889). Written by highly regarded church leaders (all Oxford men), this work assesses the religious situation at the time. The authors stress the doctrine of the incarnation and embrace the new developments in science, including the theory of evolution. No essay deals directly with the Bible, though Gore's contribution, "The Holy Spirit and Inspiration," asserts that historical criticism is not to be feared: "In the case of the New Testament certainly we are justified in feeling that modern investigation has resulted in immensely augmenting our understanding of the different books, and has distinctly fortified and enriched our sense of their inspiration" (361).

judgments on matters of canonicity and authenticity were excessively conservative. Above all, the major flaw in the work of the Cambridge three was the lack of comprehensive, rigorous criticism of the Gospels. Their devotion to the Fourth Gospel is understandable in light of their preoccupation with the incarnation, but their attempt to harmonize John and the Synoptics, like that of the authors of the Victorian lives of Jesus, resulted in an indistinct image. The study of the Synoptics—except for Westcott's premature work—was virtually ignored. Critical research on the Synoptic Gospels would await a later generation of British scholarship.

3

The Triumph of Liberalism on the Continent

In the last decades of the nineteenth century as Britain was expanding its empire, the German states were consolidating into a single nation. Germany had been a weak coalition of small countries, but under the suzerainty of Prussia it became a powerful nation, indeed, an empire. This result was achieved largely by the Machiavellian efforts of a skillful diplomat, Otto von Bismarck. To accomplish his goal, Bismarck manipulated the southern German states, which had resisted unification, into enlisting with Prussia against France, the common enemy. Armed with the new rapid-firing rifle, the German troops marched all the way to Paris. The Franco-Prussian War (1870–71) not only humiliated the French, it effected German unity and the accession of territory beyond the Rhine. After Bismarck, the same sort of nationalism and militarism that marked his government was promoted by his successors. The German Wehrmacht was supported by a burgeoning industrialism that outdistanced the British. Germany established colonies in Africa. German population increased and German cities expanded. Most of all, Germany enjoyed an era of growing success, wealth, and boundless self-confidence.

It was also a time of rapid intellectual advance. Science or *Wissenschaft*, which was becoming a religious cult, became enshrined in the cathedrals of higher learning. The universities, especially Berlin, increased in size and prestige. Confident in the course of human progress, the German *Volk* evolved a culture that honored intellectual achievement. Moreover, the new political and cultural nationalism had its roots in the deep soil of German tradition—a tradition articulated in the language of Luther and his Bible. The empire, indeed, was militantly Protestant. Recent reverberations from Rome, such as the Vatican Council's dogma of papal infallibility (1870), reminded the people of battles of other days—battles in which

Germans had prevailed. This tradition of anti-Catholicism came to expression in Bismarck's *Kulturkampf* (struggle for civilization). To Bismarck, the Roman clergy, clothed in arcane vestments, looked like foreign agents, a threat to the goals of the German empire. Although Bismarck's efforts to suppress the Roman Catholic Church largely failed, the dominance of Protestant Christianity remained uncontested.

Although political and social liberalism was in decline, theological liberalism ascended in triumph. This is not to say that all religious leaders became liberals. On the contrary, much of the ecclesiastical establishment and many laypersons remained loyal to Lutheran orthodoxy. Nevertheless, the future was on the side of the theological progressives. Their dedication to *Wissenschaft* won them a place in the universities, and the universities were a dominant force in German culture. Along with their affirmation of the freedom of inquiry and the scientific method, the liberals were opposed to every kind of orthodoxy. They detested dogma in general, and opposed a host of traditional doctrines: the preexistence and deity of Christ, the virgin birth of Jesus, the bodily resurrection, substitutionary atonement. Noted for their rationalism and skepticism, the liberals were suspicious of the supernatural, the miraculous, and the mystical. They were not citizens of the heavenly city, but at home in this world, wedded to its culture, celebrating its secularism.

In regard to the Bible, the liberal scholars abandoned the orthodox doctrine of inspiration and rejected the idea of infallibility. They adopted the Enlightenment method of scientific, historical criticism. Although many members of the Tübingen school had become truant, the liberals maintained the historicism of Baur with its belief in uninhibited criticism and historical development.[1] Most of all, the liberal theologians had unlimited confidence in human ability to master the data and resolve all the historical and exegetical problems. Having eaten of the tree of *Wissenschaft*, they had become like God, knowing the difference between fact and fable.

THE ESTABLISHMENT OF LIBERALISM:
ALBRECHT RITSCHL

Although the cornerstone had been laid by Schleiermacher, Ritschl is the architect of modern liberalism. Albrecht Ritschl (1822–89) was born in Berlin, the son of a pastor who was later appointed bishop of the church in Pomerania.[2] Ritschl began his university studies in 1839 at Bonn and transferred to Halle two years later. After brief stints at Berlin and Heidelberg,

---
1. See *HNTR* 1:258–78.
2. See Otto Ritschl, *Albrecht Ritschls Leben*, vol. 1, *1822–1864*, vol. 2, *1864–1889* (Freiburg i. Br.: J. C. B. Mohr [Paul Siebeck], 1892, 1896); Robert Mackintosh, *Albrecht Ritschl and His School*, Great Christian Theologies (London: Chapman and Hall, 1915).

Ritschl moved to Tübingen, where he fell temporarily under the spell of F. C. Baur. Ritschl began his teaching career at Bonn in 1846, where in 1852 he was advanced to full professor. Ritschl's teaching at Bonn concentrated on the NT, but he increasingly turned to history of doctrine, systematic theology, and ethics. In 1864, he was invited to the faculty at Göttingen where he remained for the rest of his career. Among his important students were William Wrede and Johannes Weiss.[3] According to Adolf von Harnack, "no theologian has arisen in the last generation who equals him in significance, and as those who knew him personally will never forget the steadfast man and true friend, so also will theological scholarship hold the great teacher powerfully in memory; just as he himself has left in his works an immortal monument."[4]

Ritschl's Theology

Ritschl was influenced by Luther's stress on faith in Christ as the means of salvation, but he opposed Lutheran orthodoxy's transformation of the dynamic message of the Reformation into dogma.[5] From Schleiermacher, Ritschl inherited the concern for religious consciousness, but, influenced by Kant, he emphasized ethics more than feeling.[6] Ritschl opposed metaphysics because metaphysics focused on nature and the cosmos rather than on the transcendent God.[7] For his own part, Ritschl approaches theology from the perspective of history. He believes the essence of Christianity is to be found in Jesus, the founder of the church, and in the apostles, its first representatives. According to Ritschl, God cannot be known as an abstract Absolute, but only in God's revelation in history, supremely in Jesus.[8]

---

3. See pp. 144–51, 223–29 below.

4. *Albrecht Ritschl, 1846–1864: Rede, am 30. April 1922 zum hundertsten Geburtstag, Gedenkfeiern der Universität Bonn für einstige Mitglieder* (Bonn: Ludwig Röhrscheid, 1922), 16.

5. Among the many works on Ritschl's theology, see Albert Temple Swing, *The Theology of Albrecht Ritschl, together with Instruction in the Christian Religion, by Albrecht Ritschl*, trans. from 4th ed. by Alice Mead Swing (New York: Longman's Green, 1901); Rolf Schäfer, *Ritschl: Grundlinien eines fast verschollenen dogmatischen Systems*, BHT 41 (Tübingen: J. C. B. Mohr [Paul Siebeck], 1968); Alfred E. Garvie, *The Ritschlian Theology: Critical and Constructive: An Exposition and an Estimate*, 2d ed. (Edinburgh: T. & T. Clark, 1902); David L. Mueller, *An Introduction to the Theology of Albrecht Ritschl* (Philadelphia: Westminster, 1969); James Richmond, *Ritschl: A Reappraisal: A Study in Systematic Theology* (London: Collins, 1978); Stephan Weyer-Menkhoff, *Aufklärung und Offenbarung: Zur Systematik Theologie Albrecht Ritschls*, GTA 37 (Göttingen: Vandenhoeck & Ruprecht, 1988); David W. Lotz, "Ritschl in His Nineteenth-Century Setting," in *Ritschl in Retrospect: History, Community, and Science*, ed. Darrell Jodock (Minneapolis: Fortress, 1995), 8–27.

6. On Schleiermacher, see *HNTR* 1:208–20.

7. See "Theology and Metaphysics: Toward Rapprochement and Defense," in Albrecht Ritschl, *Three Essays: Theology and Metaphysics; "Prolegomena" to The History of Pietism; Instruction in the Christian Religion*, trans. Philip Hefner (Philadelphia: Fortress, 1972), 151–217.

8. See Daniel L. Deegan, "Albrecht Ritschl on the Historical Jesus," *SJT* 15 (1962): 133–50. See also Dietz Lange, "Das Verständnis von 'Offenbarung' bei Albrecht Ritschl und Karl Barth," in *Gottes Reich und menschliche Freiheit: Ritschl-Kolloquium (Göttingen, 1989)*, ed. Joachim Ringleben, GTA 46 (Göttingen: Vandenhoeck & Ruprecht, 1990), 40–59.

Ritschl's theology is Christocentric, but his Christology is a Christology from below. Ritschl is not concerned with the traditional doctrine of the two natures of Christ, but with Christ's work. The proof of Christ's divinity is the quality of his obedience, his fulfillment of God's goal for humanity:

> Thus must the divinity or lordship of Christ over the world be grasped in the definite features of his historical life as an attribute of his temporal existence. For what Christ is according to his eternal determination and what he effects in us according to his exaltation to God would not be knowable at all for us if it were not effective also in his temporal-historical existence.[9]

Ritschl's major theological work on justification and reconciliation contends that sin (failure to acknowledge God) is overcome by God's love disclosed in Christ, resulting in communion with God and community with believers. According to Ritschl, justification overcomes guilt; reconciliation overcomes alienation.

Although Ritschl is usually viewed as a systematic theologian, he considered himself to be a biblical theologian.[10] Ritschl held a high view of biblical authority:

> It stands as the foundation-principle of the Evangelical Church that Christian doctrine is to be obtained from the Bible alone. This principle has direct reference to the original documents of Christianity gathered together in the New Testament.... These books are the foundation of a right understanding of the Christian religion from the point of view of the community, for the reason that the Gospels set forth in the work of its Founder the immediate cause and final end of the common religion, and the Epistles make known the original state of the common faith in the community, and moreover in a form not yet affected by the influences which as early as the second century had stamped Christianity as Catholic.[11]

Ritschl rejected the orthodox doctrine of inspiration, but was conservative on critical issues. He believed that both the Fourth Gospel and the Apocalypse were written by John; he accepted all the epistles attributed to Paul as authentic except 1 Timothy. Nevertheless, Ritschl employed the historical-critical method, informed by faith and in the context of the believing community.

---

9. Quoted by William R. Barnett, "Historical Understanding and Theological Commitment: The Dilemma of Ritschl's Christology," *JR* 59 (1979): 205. See Gerald W. McCulloh, *Christ's Person and Life-Work in the Theology of Albrecht Ritschl with Special Attention to Munus Triplex* (Lanham, Md.: University Press of America, 1990).

10. See Clive Marsh, *Albrecht Ritschl and the Problem of the Historical Jesus* (San Francisco: Mellen Research University Press, 1992); Otto Ritschl, *Albrecht Ritschls Leben*, vol. 2, *1864–1889* (Freiburg i. Br.: J. C. B. Mohr [Paul Siebeck], 1896), 168–78; Gerald W. McCulloh, "A Historical Bible, A Reasonable Faith, A Conscientious Action: The Theological Legacy of Albrecht Ritschl," in Lotz, *Ritschl in Retrospect*, 31–50.

11. Ritschl, *Instruction in the Christian Religion*, 172.

Ritschl's NT Research

Ritschl produced significant work on the Gospels and Jesus. In one of his earliest publications, *Das Evangelium Marcions und das kanonische Evangelium des Lucas* (1846), Ritschl supported Baur's hypothesis that the canonical Gospel of Luke was dependent on the earlier Lucan gospel of Marcion's canon.[12] This view Ritschl abandoned in an essay reviewing current criticism of the Synoptic Gospels, published in 1851.[13] In this essay, Ritschl argues that Luke used Mark, the earliest Gospel, as a primary source. In Ritschl's opinion, Mark is not tainted by theological tendencies, but presents reliable history. Ritschl made a contribution to Johannine research with an essay on the prologue of the Fourth Gospel.[14] Observing that the introduction of John the Baptist in v. 6 appears to interrupt the flow of the narrative, Ritschl attempts to restore the original order of the prologue. He believes that the text presents three stages of revelation: in the first, the evangelist describes revelation in creation; in the second, revelation to the people of God; and in the third, revelation in the historical person of Jesus. On the basis of his study of the Gospels, Ritschl arrives at his understanding of Jesus. Mark is accepted as the most reliable historical source, but Ritschl also uses John, and presents Jesus according to six main categories: as Son of God, as teacher, as Lord, as the obedient one, as founder of the kingdom, as prophet and Messiah.[15]

Ritschl's break with Baur is evident in his research on the history of early Christianity.[16] Ritschl's opposition to Baur is explicit in his essay on historical method in research about early Christianity.[17] Although Baur purports to employ the critical method, Ritschl charges that his research is dominated by his philosophical presuppositions. As to the substance of Baur's reconstruction, Ritschl believes Baur's notion that Christianity is the product of a synthesis of Jewish and Gentile Christians represents a misreading of the sources. Ritschl's own reconstruction of early Christianity is presented in his book on the origin of the ancient catholic church. Ritschl's thesis is that "catholic Christianity did not arise out of a reconciliation

---

12. (Tübingen: Osiander, 1846).
13. "Über den gegenwärtigen Stand der Kritik der synoptischen Evangelien," in *Gesammelte Aufsätze* (Freiburg i. Br.: J. C. B. Mohr [Paul Siebeck], 1893), 1–51; reprinted from *Tübinger Theologische Jahrbücher* 10 (1851): 480–538.
14. "Zum Verständnis des Prologs des johanneischen Evangeliums. Ein Vorschlag," *TSK* 48 (1875): 576–82.
15. See Marsn, *Ritschl*, 43–190.
16. See Philip Hefner, "The Role of Church History in the Theology of Albrecht Ritschl," *CH* 33 (1964): 338–55; idem, "Baur Versus Ritschl on Early Christianity," *CH* 31 (1962): 255–78.
17. "Ueber geschichtliche Methode in der Erforschung des Urchristenthums," *Jahrbücher für Deutsche Theologie* 1 (1861): 429–59; repr. in Ferdinand Christian Baur, *Ausgewählte Werke in Einzelausgaben*, ed. Klaus Scholder, vol. 5, *Für und wider die Tübinger Schule* (Stuttgart-Bad Cannstatt: Friedrich Frommann [Günther Holzboog], 1975), 469–99.

between Jewish and Gentile Christians, but that it is a stage of Gentile Christianity alone." In the first part of the book, Ritschl investigates the emergence of Christianity from Judaism and the relation of Jesus to the Mosaic Law. He argues that Jesus rejected external requirements and stressed matters of the human heart. According to Ritschl's Jesus, the will of God is epitomized in the commands to love God and neighbor. "The complete development of the highest purpose of love, which the law itself expresses, can itself only be accomplished through the annulling of the decrees and devices of the law, which do not serve this but other purposes." In regard to Paul, Ritschl rejects the idea of a contradiction with the other apostles, and affirms both "the originality of Paul" and "his continuity with the early apostles."[18] According to Ritschl, Paul's doctrine of justification by faith is mainly concerned with ethics and the divine-human relationship. In Ritschl's opinion, Paul does not understand the sacrifice of Christ as a penalty or appeasement, but as an act of divine-human reconciliation. The death of Christ is not a ransom paid to anyone, let alone the devil. Redemption, according to Ritschl, is inward, resulting in a new relation with God and a new quality of life in response.

Next, Ritschl discusses Jewish Christianity in the apostolic age. In reviewing the sources, Ritschl contends that the Epistle of James was written by James the brother of Jesus, 1 Peter by Simon Peter, and the Apocalypse by John the son of Zebedee. All three of these apostles, in Ritschl's judgment, stress the importance of ethical obedience. However, beside these apostles and their followers, Ritschl detects another group of Jewish Christians, the *Judenchristen*. At the Jerusalem conference, the apostles agreed that Gentile converts need not keep the law, but that they should conform to the requirements of the apostolic decree (Acts 15:23-29). The *Judenchristen*, according to Ritschl, did not accept this compromise, but insisted that membership in the covenant people required circumcision. "Therefore, they deny the apostolic call of Paul, which the early apostles explicitly recognize."[19] In tracing the ongoing history of early Christianity, Ritschl argues that the sect of the Ebionites carries on the beliefs and practices of the *Judenchristen*. Ritschl believes that the Epistle to the Hebrews, authored by a Jewish Christian of the Pauline school, opposes the Ebionites and proclaims a message like that of the Jerusalem apostles.

In contrast to these varieties of Jewish Christianity, Gentile Christianity, in Ritschl's opinion, gradually deviated from the religion of Paul, and, in reaction to such heresies as Gnosticism, became increasingly legalistic, and eventuated in the ancient catholic church. Thus, in contrast to Baur's Jew-

---

18. *Die Entstehung der altkatholischen Kirche: Eine kirchen- und dogmengeschichtliche Monographie*, 2d ed. (Bonn: Adolph Marcus, 1857), 23, 45, 52.

19. Ibid., 147.

ish (Petrine) Christianity versus Gentile (Pauline) Christianity, synthesized in the second century as early catholicism, Ritschl presents (1) a Jewish Christianity of the early apostles (sympathetic to Paul and the Gentile mission), (2) a Jewish Christianity (*Judenchristen*) opposed to Paul and the Gentile mission, (3) and Pauline Christianity, originally sympathetic to Jewish Christianity, eventually deviating from the true understanding of Paul and becoming increasingly legalistic and Hellenized, finally transformed into early catholic Christianity.

Ritschl's main contribution to NT research is found in the second volume of his massive three-volume work on *The Christian Doctrine of Justification and Reconciliation*.[20] This second volume—a significant work of biblical theology—has never been translated into English; a simple survey cannot do it justice. Ritschl begins with a discussion of the idea of the forgiveness of sins in the teachings of Jesus. The center of Jesus' teaching is his idea of the kingdom of God. According to Ritschl, the kingdom is not a political or eschatological concept, but a spiritual and ethical reality. The kingdom is the rule of God, which Ritschl finds already present in the life and ministry of Jesus; the kingdom involves God's initiative and human response.[21]

Ritschl discusses the relation of the biblical idea of God to the understanding of forgiveness of sins and reconciliation. He argues that the NT makes a shift in emphasis. "In so far as the holiness of God as the theme of the covenantal life defined the content of the Mosaic Law, it is replaced in the New Testament by the love of God." Neither the HB nor the NT, in Ritschl's view, understand justification as punitive justice. In the prophets, the idea of righteousness is ethical, involving a relation to God. Ritschl argues that the OT expression of the wrath of God does not refer to the character of God, but depicts God's reaction against human opposition to divine holiness. In the NT, Ritschl believes the wrath of God refers primarily to the future judgment. Ritschl concludes, "the conception of the emotion of wrath *[Zornaffect]* of God has no religious value for Christians."[22]

In investigating the meaning of Christ's death for the forgiveness of sins, Ritschl denies that the sacrifice of Christ involved a penal substitution. He thinks the reference to blood does not imply some intrinsic efficacy of blood as sacrifice; rather, it provides a graphic description of Christ's death as the fulfillment of his vocation—the sacrificial significance of his whole life. Ritschl says that "not the necessity of the death, but the voluntary

---

20. *Die christliche Lehre von der Rechtfertigung und Versöhnung: Zweiter Band: Der biblische Stoff der Lehre* (Bonn: Adolf Marcus, 1874).
21. See Hans Schwarz, "The Centrality and Bipolar Focus of the Kingdom: Ritschl's Theological Import for the Twentieth Century," in Lotz, *Ritschl in Retrospect*, 104–22; Stephan Weyer-Menkhoff, "'Reich Gottes'—Zur Doppeldeutigkeit der Theologie Albrecht Ritschls," in Ringleben, *Gottes Reich und menschliche Freiheit*, 60–68.
22. *Rechtfertigung und Versöhnung* 2:100, 154.

acceptance of it in the course of full obedience to vocation is the value of the death of Christ as saving event."[23] Dealing with exegetical details, Ritschl insists, for example, that the preposition ὑπέρ in such phrases as "one died for all" (2 Cor. 5:14) means "for the benefit of," not "in place of."

Ritschl contends that the effort to found the orthodox doctrine of substitutionary atonement on Pauline texts is groundless. Paul, in Ritschl's judgment, does not say that the wrath of God is propitiated by the death of Christ. The term ἱλαστήριον (Rom. 3:25) means "mercy seat," and expresses the forgiving grace of God. Ritschl thinks Paul's distinctive doctrine is determined by his polemical situation. In his dispute with Pharisaic Judaism, Paul, according to Ritschl, borrowed terms from his opponents, giving the false impression that he was concerned with legal and ceremonial matters. Ritschl thinks that Paul, like Jesus, understood righteousness as the fulfilling of the law—an ethical righteousness made possible by the new relation to God and empowered by the Spirit. Paul understands Christ as both the bearer of God's righteousness and the model for human righteousness. Throughout the NT, Ritschl finds the basic idea of God's justification in Christ and the human response in faith resulting in reconciliation. He thinks the Epistle to the Hebrews and the Epistle of James both stress the idea of ethical obedience grounded in faith and fulfilling the will of God. For Ritschl, the unity of religion and ethics finds its lofty expression in the work of John. Especially in the First Epistle, the practice of love responds to the action and character of God as love. God is light, and believers walk in the light through fellowship with God and in the community of love.

In summary, Ritschl shows himself to be a skillful and sensitive interpreter. He makes use of grammatical-historical exegesis. He probes the depths of theological meaning. Although he holds a high doctrine of biblical authority, he adopts a canon within the canon, made up primarily of the prophets and the Gospels. He is largely oblivious to the hermeneutical problem, and simply assumes that ancient biblical teaching can be applied directly to the problems of his own day. Ritschl's reconstruction of early Christianity, with its recognition of variety within Judaism, is an improvement on Baur, though his penchant to harmonize tends to erase the conflicts that Baur recognizes. Although he does not ignore texts problematic to his position, Ritschl is captive to his own presuppositions. Although he claims that unbiased historical investigation will provide the criterion, his picture of Jesus is actually a harmonization of the Christologies of the four Gospels. Ritschl is virtually blind to the blazing colors of early Christian apocalyptic. Nevertheless, he offers an ardent, often convincing, alternative to the orthodox reading of the NT. He provides the inspiration for a liberal theology that has continued to influence Christian thought.

---

23. Ibid., 163.

THE RECONSTRUCTION OF EARLY CHRISTIAN HISTORY: EDUARD REUSS AND CARL WEIZSÄCKER

Eduard Reuss (1804–91)

Reuss, like Ritschl, viewed the history of early Christianity from a liberal perspective. Recognized as the founder of the Strasbourg school, Reuss, with a foot on each side of the Rhine, was a mediator between German and French scholarship. He is best known for his work on the Pentateuch, but his contribution to NT research is significant. Born in Strasbourg in 1804, Reuss attended the university there (1821–25).[24] Considering his training at Strasbourg to be inadequate, he also studied at Göttingen, Halle, and Paris. Reuss began teaching at Strasbourg in 1828, and ten years later was promoted to full professor.

Reuss considered himself a rationalist, though he believed reason should be combined with faith. He was opposed to orthodoxy, sympathetic to moderate liberalism, and wary of radicalism. His theology, which was influenced by Kant, Schleiermacher, and romanticism, has been called "rational mysticism." Reuss affirmed the importance of the Bible for theology, but denounced biblicism. In a letter to a former student, he wrote, "The books of 'the' Bible can lose their external value; the ideas belong to humanity, and where they are recognized as true, they are of divine origin, even if they had never been written. The old literal orthodoxy is irretrievably vanquished; only imbeciles need it."[25] Nevertheless, Reuss believed that the Bible presented divine revelation in history; the high points in that historical disclosure were Moses and Jesus. For Reuss, Jesus was a model of the aspiration of humans—to be perfect like God.

Reuss produced a variety of works related to the study of the NT. His monumental multivolume *La Bible, traduction nouvelle avec introductions et commentaires* presents, as the titles indicates, a new translation of the Bible into French with critical introductions and grammatico-historical interpretation.[26] For example, the more than seven-hundred-page volume on the first three Gospels presents a lengthy introduction (112 pages) that includes a detailed analysis of the Synoptic Problem. Reuss also made important contributions to text criticism. His *Bibliotheca Novi Testamenti Graeci* offers an investigation of more than 580 printed texts of the NT from

---

24. See Jean Marcel Vincent, *Leben und Werk des frühen Eduard Reuss: Ein Beitrag zu den geistesgeschichtlichen Voraussetzungen der Bibelkritik im zweiten Viertel des 19. Jahrhunderts,* BEvT 106 (Munich: Ch. Kaiser, 1990); idem, "Le 'Rationalisme Mystique' d'Édouard Reuss et ses incidences sur La Bible, *RHPR* 74 (1944): 43–66; Ed. Jacob, "Édouard Reuss, un théologien indépendant," *RHPR* 71 (1991): 427–35; André Caquot, "Reuss et Renan," *RHPR* 71 (1991): 437–42.

25. Quoted in Vincent, *Eduard Reuss*, 316.

26. (Paris: Sandoz et Fischbacker, 1876). See A. Causse, "La Bible de Reuss et la Renaissance des études d'histoire religieuse en France, *RHPR* 9 (1929): 1–31.

the Complutensian Polyglot (1514) to the edition of A. Hahn (1861).[27] Reuss had a special interest in the Gospel of John.[28] According to Reuss, the Gospel of John is the only document that combines eyewitness information and profound religious understanding of the personality of Jesus. Thus, Reuss thinks that it was Jesus himself, faithfully represented by the apostle John, who eliminated Jewish eschatology; it was Jesus himself who perceived the spiritual significance of the miracles. In comparing the Synoptic Gospels with John, Reuss writes, "There according to the Synoptics 'the teaching of Jesus' as ethical sensitivity is presented, here faith is awakened; . . . there is the invitation to Love, here the believing soul is identified with eternal life itself; there is law, here gospel."[29]

Reuss published two major works on the NT: *History of the Sacred Scriptures of the New Testament* and *History of Christian Theology in the Apostolic Age*.[30] Originally written in German and first published in 1842, the former book presents a critical introduction to early Christian literature. The distinctive feature of Reuss's work is his presentation of the documents in relation to the history of early Christianity, and his inclusion of writings not contained in the NT canon. Reuss organizes his presentation into five books.

In the first book, which is essentially a critical introduction to the literature of the NT, Reuss begins with a survey of the history that produced the early Christian documents. In discussing the life and teachings of Jesus, Reuss declares that Jesus' contribution "was the holy activity of his life and the free sacrifice of his death, an imperishable example for his disciples and an inexhaustible fountain of salvation for all mankind." In regard to Paul, Reuss writes, "Thus exalting, in the light of revelation, his own personal experience into universal history, he more than sufficiently filled up the gaps which his view of the Law found in the religious ideas of the time with a pure Mysticism, far removed from all idle dreaming."[31] Reuss thinks this "mysticism" is the most important element in the teaching of Paul. He also thinks Paul's theology underwent development in which his earlier preoccupation with Jewish messianism was progressively replaced by a concern for spiritual matters.

Turning to an investigation of the NT documents, Reuss begins with the Pauline letters. He notes Paul's distinctive style: "Broken sentences, ellipses, parentheses, leaps in the argument, allegories, rhetorical figures, express,

---

27. (Brunsvigae: C. A. Schwetschke et Filium [M. Bruhn], 1872).
28. "Die johanneische Theologie, eine exegetische Studie," *Beiträge zu den theologischen Wissenschaften* 1 (1847): 1–84, summarized by Vincent, *Édouard Reuss*, 327–33.
29. Quoted in Vincent, *Édouard Reuss*, 332.
30. Eduard (Wilhelm Eugen) Reuss, *History of the Sacred Scriptures of the New Testament*, trans. from 5th ed. by Edward L. Houghton, 2 vols. (Boston: Houghton Mifflin, 1884); Eduard Reuss, *History of Christian Theology in the Apostolic Age*, trans. from 3d ed. by Annie Harwood, with preface and notes by R. W. Dale, 2 vols. (London: Hodder and Stoughton, 1872, 1874).
31. *History of the Sacred Scriptures* 1:18, 50.

in an inimitable way, all the moods of an active and cultivated mind, all the affections of a rich and deep soul, and everywhere betray a pen at once keen and yet too slow for the thought." In regard to the Corinthian correspondence, Reuss identifies the "Christ party" as Judaizers, and those who deny the resurrection as Gnostics. Reuss thinks that during Paul's three-year ministry in Ephesus, he traveled to Crete and Illyria, making it possible to fit the composition of 1 Timothy and Titus into the career of Paul, prior to his Roman imprisonment. Reuss believes Ephesians (an encyclical), Colossians, and Philemon were written from Caesarea; Philippians and 2 Timothy from Rome. In regard to the other NT Epistles, Reuss notes difficulties, but accepts the authenticity of 1 Peter and James. His view of the latter is striking: "In reality the Epistle of James contains in itself alone more verbal reminiscences of the discourses of Jesus than all the other apostolic writings taken together."[32] Reuss believes Hebrews was written by a Jewish Christian, possibly Apollos. The Apocalypse, in Reuss's view, reflects the anxiety provoked by the Neronian persecution. John the apostle might have been its author, but the same writer, according to Reuss, could not have composed the Fourth Gospel.

As to Gospel criticism, Reuss believes that the Synoptic Problem defies definitive resolution. Nevertheless, he adopts a version of the two-document hypothesis: a collection of sayings written in Hebrew by Matthew, and a primitive gospel composed by Mark on the basis of recollections of Peter (an *Urmarcus*) serve as the two main sources for the Synoptics. According to Reuss, canonical Mark is the earliest written Gospel; the author of Matthew (who was not an eyewitness) used the sayings source and *Urmarcus*; Luke used *Urmarcus* and two or three other sources, but not the sayings source. Reuss completes his critical introduction to early Christian literature with a discussion of postapostolic books and pseudepigraphic literature. For example, he argues that neither Jude nor 2 Peter is authentic.

In the second book of his *History of the Sacred Scriptures of the New Testament*, Reuss presents a history of the canon. Reuss also published *Histoire du canon des saintes-écritures dans l'église chrétienne*—a more extensive study that provides additional details.[33] Reuss believes that impetus to canonization was provoked by the Gnostics, but he denies that Marcion was the first to formulate a NT canon. In discussing the development of the canon in the late second century, Reuss observes, "the formation of the sacred collection was a matter of local custom, unconscious tradition, practical needs, relations more or less intimate, more or less accidental between the various

---

32. Ibid. 1:68, 140.
33. Second ed. (Strasbourg: Treuttel et Wurtz, 1863); Eng. trans.: Eduard Reuss, *History of the Canon of the Holy Scriptures*, trans. from 2d ed. by David Hunter (Edinburgh: James Gemmell, 1884).

churches." Reuss considers the efforts by Eusebius to provide a rationale for the canon to be arbitrary: "And, when all is done, the most positive result to which he comes is still uncertainty, and an uncertainty so great that he gets confused while making a statement of it."[34] In the main, Reuss is suspicious of the process of canonization; he thinks it depended more on ecclesiastical custom than on historical understanding.

The third, fourth, and fifth books of the *History of the Sacred Scriptures* are dedicated to the study of text criticism, the history of translation, and the history of interpretation. In regard to the text, Reuss notes the difficulty of grouping the manuscripts into families, but believes three text-types can be identified: Alexandrian, Constantinopolitan, and Occidental. Reuss reviews the work of text critics from J. Mill to C. Tischendorf, applauding the abandonment of the Received Text. In regard to translation, Reuss traces the history of versions of the NT from earliest times to the present, from ancient Syriac to modern French. In regard to interpretation, he presents a history from the beginnings until his own time. After investigating patristic exegesis and observing the decline of the study of the Bible in the Middle Ages, Reuss hails the revival of biblical exegesis in the Reformation. In the modern period, he sees a gradual revolution in the philological work of J. A. Ernesti and the historical research of J. S. Semler. He resonates, however, to the poetic sensitivity of J. G. Herder.[35] Reuss is less than sanguine about the victory of the grammatico-historical method. "In reality it was chiefly a rationalism in philological matters not always conscientious, in historical questions not always unprejudiced, and either thrusting religious things into the background or emptying them of their meaning." He continues: "It is a sign of the times that controversy can be carried on now over rules of syntax with equal vehemence and in relation to the same passages over which our fathers were concerned for the salvation of their souls."[36]

Reuss's second major work on the NT, *History of Christian Theology in the Apostolic Age,* originally appeared in French in 1852.[37] In the introduction, Reuss defines theology as the science of the relation of God to humanity. Like philosophy, it uses reason; unlike philosophy, it presumes revelation. According to Reuss, "Biblical theology is then a historical science. It does not demonstrate, it narrates. It is the first chapter in the history of Christian doctrine." Reuss claims adherence to strict historical-critical method. "The fidelity to fact is regarded as the first duty of the historian."[38] He arranges his work in seven books.

---

34. *History of the Canon*, 147, 149.
35. See *HNTR* 1:108–14, 117–27, 174–77, 177–83.
36. *History of the Sacred Scriptures* 2:601, 615.
37. Trans. from 3d ed. by Annie Harwood, with preface and notes by R. W. Dale, 2 vols. (London: Hodder and Stoughton, 1872, 1874).
38. Ibid. 1:10, 15.

After a discussion of the theology of Judaism (book 1), book 2 discusses the "Gospel," that is, the teaching of Jesus as the foundation of Christian theology. Reuss believes that Jesus replaced the Jewish idea of political theocracy with his understanding of the kingdom of God as the ethical and spiritual rule of God, already present in his words and deeds. "The kingdom is indeed advancing slowly and insensibly towards a glorious perfection in a heavenly order of things." Reuss believes that Jesus called individuals to repent and obey an inward ethic of love toward neighbor and enemy—a universal ethic. Jesus adopted the title "Son of Man" as his distinctive messianic self-designation—a title which, according to Reuss, describes Jesus as the model human, "the realization of the moral ideal in the person of Him who assumed such a name."[39] Reuss is troubled by the apocalyptic language and references to the imminent eschaton that the evangelists ascribe to Jesus. He asks, "Can His religion, else so pure, so spiritual, so essentially free from all alloy of earth, have been consummated by an eschatology so grossly material?"[40] In reply, he contends that John, the eyewitness, does not attribute such sayings to Jesus, and that even the Synoptics stress the kingdom as coming with gradual growth, not revolution. Whatever apocalyptic imagery Jesus may have used should not, according to Reuss, be taken literally.

The third book of the *History of Christian Theology* presents Reuss's picture of the apostolic church. For this community, the memory of Jesus was alive and compelling. It "had been instructed by His sermons, edified by His example, comforted by His very presence; it had sat at His table, lodged beneath His roof, had walked, suffered, prayed with Him."[41] Reuss thinks the controversy between the Jewish and Gentile believers was resolved at the Jerusalem Council. According to the compromise, Gentile converts were not compelled to keep the law, but were required to observe the prescriptions of the apostolic decree (Acts 15:23-29) in order to maintain social intercourse with the Jewish Christians. Reuss believes the Jerusalem apostles continued to maintain the Jerusalem compromise, whereas the Pharisaic Jewish Christians, the Judaizers, insisted on circumcision and the whole law. The latter, not the apostles, were the foes of Paul in Galatia and Corinth.[42]

After a discussion of Jewish Christian theology (book 4) that takes the Apocalypse and James as major sources, Reuss turns, in his fifth book, to the

---

39. Ibid. 1:157, 199.
40. Ibid. 1:215.
41. Ibid. 1:236.
42. Reuss was more sympathetic with Baur than many of his contemporaries. He recognized conflicting tendencies in the early church, although he did not adopt Baur's view of primitive Christianity as essentially a conflict between Petrine and Pauline factions. See Jean Marcel Vincent, "Die Stellung Eduard Reuss' zur Baurschen Tendenzkritik," *TZ* 50 (1994): 1–8.

theology of Paul. As sources, Reuss uses all thirteen letters attributed to Paul, but understands Romans to be foundational. He rejects the orthodox doctrine of original sin, but believes Paul considered all humans to be sinners, standing under the judgment of God. In Reuss's understanding of the Pauline process of salvation, God is the author, Christ the mediator, and humans the heirs. In explicating Paul's idea of redemption, Reuss contends that Paul's sacrificial language is symbolic. "It is . . . a fact that in the theology of Paul it is not the death of Christ, but the faith of man, which is the main thing, the pivot of the whole system; and this faith does not relate exclusively to the fact of the death of Christ, but also to the fact of His life." "Justification is the declaration of God, by which remission of sins is granted to the man who is a sinner, in consideration of his faith." "Faith, then, according to Paul, is at once an act of the reason or conviction, an act of the heart or trust, an act of the will or self-surrender."[43]

Reuss's sixth book of the *History of Christian Theology* discusses other epistles and historical writings. In regard to the literature of the Pauline school, Reuss thinks that Hebrews is not an epistle, but "a treatise on transcendental theology." He believes 1 Peter to be a homiletical treatise that expresses Pauline ideas. Among the historical books, he views Acts as an apologetic and polemical work, designed to present a universal Christianity. "If we were called upon distinctively to characterize the theology of the Acts," writes Reuss, "we should say that it bases salvation, not upon the mystical fact of regeneration, as does Paul, but upon the eschatological fact of the fulfillment of the prophecies, as does Judaeo-Christianity."[44] In regard to the Synoptics, Reuss contends that they are more concerned with history than theology. Matthew, according to Reuss, is not exclusively engrossed in Jewish Christianity, and Luke is not primarily a proponent of Paulinism.

In his seventh book Reuss presents the theology of John, using the Fourth Gospel and 1 John as primary sources. With John, "History is transmuted into doctrine," resulting in "essentially a mystical theology"—a procedure that Reuss heartily approves. According to Reuss's interpretation, John presents three attributes of the transcendent God: God is light (omniscient and holy); God is love (related to all living beings); God is life (the life-giving Creator). The Word, who is both one with God and subordinate to God, embodies these three attributes. Reuss rejects the notion that incarnation involves humiliation. "That the Word should have taken flesh, that He should have become man, does not degrade the Word, but exalts humanity."[45] The response to God's saving action in the Word is faith, according to Reuss, an act of thought, will, and feeling. In his final conclu-

---

43. *History of Christian Theology* 2:154, 155; 2:90.
44. Ibid. 2:255, 305.
45. Ibid. 2:346, 376, 408.

sion, Reuss confesses that his concern to present the theology of the first century rests on his commitment to the authority of the apostles. He believes that he has demonstrated the originality and truth of the gospel—the gospel that provides the permanent model and norm for Christian teaching. After the era of the apostles, Reuss believes, this vital, mystical theology was turned into dogmatic systems. "The life which comes from God, so soon as it passes into the hands of men, is transformed into dogmas, cast into the mould of formularies, and thus we had almost said extinguishes its own vitality."[46]

Looking back over the work of Eduard Reuss, the observer is impressed with his erudition—his mastery of the material, his skill in multiple areas of NT research. Of major importance is his role in disseminating the results of German biblical criticism in France. Like Ritschl, conservative on many critical issues, Reuss joins the advancing parade of liberal criticism and displays its major features. He opposes metaphysics and dogmatic orthodoxy. He embraces the method of historical criticism, and, among other things, affirms the priority of Mark. Reuss confesses the centrality and normative character of the Jesus of history, and, like Ritschl, detects the center of the historical Jesus in his idea of the kingdom of God. Like the other liberals, Reuss is eager to divest Jesus of every shred of apocalyptic. Reuss's distinctive way to accomplish this critical move is via the Fourth Gospel—the Gospel written, according to Reuss, by an apostle who knew firsthand that Jesus eschewed Jewish eschatology. In Reuss's view, it was later followers of Jesus who sold the spiritual message of the kingdom for a mess of apocalyptic pottage. Nevertheless, Reuss detects a continuity in early Christian history in place of the dialectic conflict depicted by Baur—a continuity that comes to expression in the mysticism of Paul and the mystical theology of John. Like Narcissus, Reuss peers into the Pauline Epistles and the Fourth Gospel and sees the reflection of his own theological image.

Carl Weizsäcker (1822–99)

Standing in a position close to Reuss, though somewhat to the left, is Carl Weizsäcker.[47] Born in Oehringen, near Stuttgart, Weizsäcker studied at Tübingen, where, in 1861, he had the unenviable distinction of succeeding F. C. Baur. Weizsäcker was essentially a historian who assumed a mediating position between orthodoxy and the hypercriticism of Baur. He published two works of major importance for the history of NT research: a book on the gospel tradition, and a large work on the history of the apostolic age.

Originally published in 1864, Weizsäcker's *Untersuchungen über die evangelische Geschichte* is an investigation of the sources used in reconstructing

---

46. Ibid. 2:534.
47. For a summary of Weizsäcker's life and thought, see Alfred Hegler, *Zur Erinnerung an Carl Weizsäcker*, Hefte zur "Christlichen Welt" 45 (Tübingen: J. C. B. Mohr [Paul Siebeck], 1900).

the history of Jesus.[48] In regard to the Synoptic Gospels, Weizsäcker advocates a version of the two-document hypothesis. According to this hypothesis, Matthew, Mark, and Luke depend on a primitive narrative source, an *Urmarcus*, which is most closely followed by Mark. Matthew and Luke, according to Weizsäcker, also used a second source, a collection of sayings of Jesus, a document that Weizsäcker thinks fits the description of the Logia attributed to Matthew by Papias. *Urmarcus*, in Weizsäcker's opinion, is a reliable historical witness, written in Palestine prior to the destruction of Jerusalem. Besides these two main sources of the Synoptics, Weizsäcker designates a third major source for the history of Jesus: the Gospel of John. According to Weizsäcker, this gospel was written by a disciple of the apostle John who witnesses to reliable apostolic tradition.

On the basis of these sources, Weizsäcker offers his reconstruction of the history of Jesus. Weizsäcker interprets the baptism as a religious experience in which Jesus receives his messianic vocation. Jesus' primary activity, according to Weizsäcker, is the proclamation of the kingdom of God—a spiritual reality, already present in the ministry of Jesus. Weizsäcker believes the later Galilean ministry was marked by two turning points: the attempt at the feeding of the multitude to make Jesus king, and the confession of Peter. After these events, Jesus, according to Weizsäcker, more fully instructed the disciples in the meaning of his messiahship. Weizsäcker relies heavily on the Fourth Gospel for his reconstruction of the passion narrative. The resurrection, in his opinion, was no subjective vision, but a miracle in the sense that the whole life of Jesus was a miracle. "The true greatness and miracle of his life consists in this, that his gospel is the gospel of his person, that the divine kingdom which he preached, he founded on this alone, and that the authority of his action he obtained out of the certainty of his unique relation to God."[49]

Weizsäcker's second important book, *The Apostolic Age of the Christian Church*, was originally published in 1886.[50] Following in the footsteps of his predecessor, Weizsäcker finds Acts to be largely unreliable—providing little solid information about the beginnings of the church in Jerusalem, and sometimes contradicting the data from the Pauline Letters. As to Paul, Weizsäcker believes his conversion also involved a call to mission and his Christology lacked interest in the historical Jesus. According to Weizsäcker, Paul did not understand the death of Christ as a penalty or substitution, but

---

48. *Untersuchungen über die evangelische Geschichte: ihre Quellen und den Gang ihrer Entwicklung*, 2d ed. (Tübingen: J. C. B. Mohr [Paul Siebeck], 1901).
49. Ibid., 369.
50. *Das apostolische Zeitalter der christlichen Kirche*, 2d ed. (Freiburg i. Br.: J. C. B. Mohr [Paul Siebeck], 1892); Eng. trans.: Carl von Weizsäcker, *The Apostolic Age of the Christian Church*, trans. from 2d. rev. ed. by James Millar, 2 vols., TTL (London: Williams & Norgate, 1907).

as a divine action in which the flesh was defeated and spiritual power triumphed. Paul's doctrine of righteousness, in Weizsäcker's opinion, is primarily ethical. Weizsäcker finds the account of the Jerusalem Council in Acts 15 to be misleading, since it presents the apostolic decree, which he believes was composed much later, as a pronouncement of the Council.

Turning to later developments, Weizsäcker argues that the Roman church was predominantly Gentile, and that Paul wrote to preclude the future threat of Judaizers. Weizsäcker thinks Romans 16 was originally a separate letter sent to Ephesus. He rejects the hypothesis of a second Roman imprisonment. Weizsäcker locates the Johannine school in Ephesus, where followers of John produced the Fourth Gospel and the Apocalypse. The latter, according to Weizsäcker, does not report actual visions, but is essentially a literary composition. The background of the Logos idea Weizsäcker discovers in Alexandrian Judaism. The understanding of the Logos as incarnate person, however, goes back to the experience of the apostle John, who is the source of the tradition recorded in the Fourth Gospel.

> We can observe in all this the double motive: the new knowledge which has outgrown primitive Christianity and the primitive Apostolic tradition are confirmed and attested from the lips of Jesus; the connection is, however, to be maintained, the authority of the original Apostles to be preserved. . . . Therefore, the present, the new Gospel, only gave the key to the right understanding of the older tradition.[51]

Weizsäcker concludes with a discussion of the developments in worship and the emergence of orders of leadership in the early church. Basic to the life of the church, according to Weizsäcker, was a concern with ethics.

FAITH AND HISTORICISM:
BERNHARD WEISS (1827–1918)

Like a horse and buggy in the age of the locomotive, Bernhard Weiss looks out of place in a survey of liberalism. Albert Schweitzer, however, classifies Weiss's biography of Jesus among the liberal lives, and, in face of orthodox opposition, Weiss supported the appointment of Harnack to the Berlin faculty.[52] Born in Königsberg, Weiss was educated at Königsberg, Halle, and Berlin.[53] He began his teaching career at Königsberg at the age of twenty-five. From 1863 to 1877, he served on the faculty at Kiel, and from 1877 to 1908, as professor of NT at Berlin. Weiss is usually characterized as a

---

51. *Apostolic Age* 2:213.
52. Albert Schweitzer, *The Quest of the Historical Jesus: A Critical Study of Its Progress from Reimarus to Wrede*, trans. W. Montgomery (New York: Macmillan, 1957), 217; see p. 123, below.
53. For Weiss's life and work, see Caspar René Gregory, "Bernhard Weiss and the New Testament," *AJT* 1 (1897): 16–37.

mediating theologian. Indeed, Emanuel Hirsch describes him as "the most distinguished representative of this half-critical half-traditional view."[54] Like the Rock of Gibraltar, Weiss stood against currents from many directions: he rejected the old orthodoxy, while affirming the Reformation faith; he opposed the Tübingen school, while employing the critical method; he decried rationalism, while erecting reasonable arguments. Above all, he believed theological truth to be historically grounded and recorded in the Bible. According to Weiss, what the Bible says, historically interpreted, is the truth—a historicism permeated by profound religious faith.

Criticism and Commentaries

As the German factories were pouring out huge quantities of manufactured goods, so Weiss produced an enormous amount of biblical scholarship. With tireless intellectual energy, he contributed to the major areas of NT research: higher criticism, exegesis, theology, and text criticism. Weiss maintained an interest in the study of the Synoptic Gospels throughout his career. In 1872, he published a book on the Gospel of Mark and its parallels.[55] In this book, Weiss argues that Matthew and Mark are dependent on an old apostolic source that he identifies with the Logia attributed to Matthew by Papias. Weiss thinks Mark shaped this source into a narrative by use of reminiscences he had learned from Peter. Four years later, Weiss published a similar book on the Gospel of Matthew.[56] In the introduction, he contends that the writer of Matthew used both the Logia—which Weiss thinks includes narrative as well as teaching material—and Mark as sources. Since the author of Matthew uses Mark, a nonapostolic source, he cannot, in Weiss's opinion, be the apostle Matthew. Later in his career, Weiss produced a similar work on Luke.[57] Here he notes that the sayings source (the Logia) has come to be called "Q" (for *Quelle*, or "source"). As well as Q and Mark, Luke has employed a third source that Weiss calls "L." In 1908, Weiss published a book on the sources of the Synoptic tradition in which he presents his reconstruction of the texts of Q and L.[58] In 1905, Weiss published a book on the historicity of the Gospel of Mark.[59] Here he defends the tradition that Mark records the reminiscences of Peter, and rejects Wrede's

---

54. Emanuel Hirsch, *Geschichte der neuern evangelischen Theologie* (Gütersloh: C. Bertelsmann, 1954) 5:557.
55. *Das Marcusevangelium und seine synoptischen Parallelen* (Berlin: Wilhelm Hertz, 1872).
56. *Das Matthäusevangelium und seine Lucas-Parallelen* (Halle: Buchhandlung des Waisenhauses, 1876).
57. *Die Quellen des Lukasevangeliums* (Stuttgart: J. G. Cotta, 1907).
58. *Die Quellen der Synoptischen Überlieferung*, TU 32, 3d Reihe, 2/3 (Leipzig: J. C. Hinrichs, 1908).
59. *Die Geschichtlichkeit des Markusevangeliums*, Biblische Zeit- und Streitfragen (Lichterfelde-Berlin: Edwin Runge, 1905).

contention that Mark is a dogmatic rather than a historical account.[60] According to Weiss, the "messianic secret" does not represent a theological fabrication of Mark, but a historical fact—Jesus' concern to avoid the mistaken messianic expectation of the masses.

A comprehensive view of Weiss's historical criticism is provided by his massive *Lehrbuch der Einleitung in das Neue Testament,* published in 1886, and translated into English three years later.[61] After a section on the history of the NT canon, Weiss presents critical introductions to the books of the NT according to his understanding of their chronological order. Beginning with the Pauline Epistles, Weiss finds all thirteen letters attributed to Paul to be authentic. He believes Paul's doctrine of justification was formulated in response to the Judaizers. "We only know as a matter of history that his peculiar doctrine of salvation first emerged with the clearness of a principle and with full certainty, in the Epistle to the Galatians, that it was in the struggle with Judaism that he forged his sharpest weapons."[62] In regard to 1 Corinthians, Weiss thinks the Christ-party represented Judaizers, and the factions at the Lord's Supper were socioeconomic. According to Weiss, Romans 16 was originally addressed to Ephesus. He thinks Colossians, Philemon, and Ephesians were written from the Caesarean imprisonment, Philippians from Rome. In regard to the Pastoral Epistles, Weiss adopts the hypothesis of a second Roman imprisonment. Weiss is convinced that Paul is not the author of Hebrews, and of the various possible candidates, he thinks Barnabas is more likely than most.

Weiss's discussion of Revelation and the Catholic Epistles is traditional. He believes the Apocalypse was written by John the Apostle from Ephesus around 69–70. In regard to the Catholic letters, Weiss argues that Jesus had real brothers, children of Mary. Among these were James, who wrote the Epistle of James, and Jude, who wrote the Epistle of Jude. Weiss believes Peter wrote 1 Peter from Babylon (not Rome) to Jewish Christians in Asia Minor around 50. Second Peter, he thinks, was written by Peter to Gentile Christians of the same area about ten years later. Weiss contends that 1 John is a real letter, not a treatise or homily, written by John, the author of the Apocalypse, whose style had improved during the intervening twenty years.

The final section of Weiss's *Introduction* is dedicated to the historical books. Weiss rehearses his solution to the Synoptic Problem as developed in his books on the Gospels, namely, that the two basic sources are Mark and Q. In regard to Mark, he thinks the author was John Mark, the nude youth of 14:51-52. Matthew, according to Weiss, was written by a Jewish Christian

---

60. See pp. 147–49, below.
61. *A Manual of Introduction to the New Testament,* trans. A. J. K. Davidson, 2 vols., Foreign Biblical Library (New York: Funk & Wagnalls, 1889).
62. Ibid. 1:241.

of the diaspora. Weiss believes that Luke was the author of the third Gospel and the Acts of the Apostles; the "we-sections" in Acts recount events in which Luke himself participated. The Fourth Gospel, according to Weiss, was written by John the Apostle, who consciously corrected the accounts of the Synoptics. "In truth all unbiased criticism teaches that in every important point in which he deviates, he has historical probability in his favour."[63]

Employing his critical and exegetical skill, Weiss published a full shelf of commentaries. An early example is his work on Philippians.[64] In this work, Weiss presents the critical and exegetical details according to the history of research. However, his commentary on Philippians was a mere warm-up for more energetic exercises to come. In 1878, Weiss made his first contribution to the famous Meyer series—a collection of commentaries, recognized from its beginning until today as a model of historical-critical exegesis.[65] To various editions of this series, Weiss contributed commentaries on Matthew, Mark, Luke, John, Romans, the Pastoral Epistles, Hebrews, and the Johannine Epistles. Two of these volumes can serve as samples.

In his commentary on *Matthew*, Weiss orders his comments according to Matthew's chapters, grouping verses together in smaller sections.[66] Footnotes refer to text-critical matters, secondary arguments, and references to the work of other scholars. To some sections, Weiss adds additional notes. An example of his exegetical work can be seen in his comments on the confession of Peter (Matt. 16:13-20). The source for the account Weiss finds in Mark. The phrase "Son of Man" in this text is not, in Weiss's opinion, a messianic title, but represents the Aramaic manner of self-designation ("I," as in Mark 8:27). Weiss believes the whole text should be interpreted according to the metaphor of building. Thus, Peter, insofar as his confession represents his rock-like character, symbolizes the foundation of the church. The reference to Hades carries on the building metaphor: Hades is like a fortress with solid doors. The reference to keys also maintains the metaphor: the church is like a house with doors that can be locked or unlocked. The mention of Peter, in connection with the keys, shifts his function as foundation of the building to the role of steward—the leader who orders the life within the house.

Weiss's commentary on *Romans* follows the same pattern.[67] According to Weiss, Paul "wrote to the Gentile church of the capital city this letter, which intended to explain his new law-free doctrine of salvation in relation to the

---

63. Ibid. 2:370.
64. *Der Philipper-Brief ausgelegt und die Geschichte seiner Auslegung kritisch dargestellt* (Berlin: Wilhelm Hertz, 1859).
65. See *HNTR* 1:365–70.
66. *Das Matthäus-Evangelium*, 9th ed., KEK (Göttingen: Vandenhoeck & Ruprecht, 1898).
67. *Kritisch-Exegetisches Handbuch über den Brief des Paulus an die Römer*, 7th ed., KEK (Göttingen: Vandenhoeck & Ruprecht, 1886).

divine revelation of the Old Testament and the salvation-historical claims of Israel." In commenting on 3:25, Weiss argues that ἱλαστήριον does not mean "mercy seat," because the mercy seat would refer to a sacrifice offered in the secret holy of holies, whereas Paul is speaking of the one "whom God put forward" openly. Considering grammatical details, and arguing from context, Weiss attempts to unravel the interrelation of the phrases. For instance, he argues that διὰ τῆς πίστεως ("through faith") does not go with προέθετο ("put forward"), nor with ἐν τῷ αὐτοῦ αἵματι ("in his blood"). Instead, Weiss believes the phrase goes with ἱλαστήριον ("sacrifice of atonement"), since salvation is accomplished by the divine act of sacrifice, not human faith; and blood is not the object of faith, since it merely describes the sacrifice as a means of God's action. The object of faith is God's saving action in Christ. Thus, "through faith" explains how ἱλαστήριον becomes subjectively effective. "God set forth in his blood Christ as a means of expiation, effective through faith, that is, that in the violent death, his blood had to be poured out, in which the power and operation of that means of expiation should be objectively based."[68]

Weiss's Jesus

Mustering all his critical and exegetical power, Weiss produced a widely read life of Jesus. Originally published in 1882 in two volumes, the English three-volume edition appeared in 1894.[69] Commenting on his accomplishment, Weiss wraps himself in a mantel of unabashed self-confidence: "I forced my way to perfect clearness regarding the history and character of our evangelical tradition." Although Weiss acknowledges that faith "must remain independent of the results of historical investigation," he thinks historical investigation can demonstrate that faith responds to reliable history. "Christianity," says Weiss, "is not a sum of new religious or ethical ideas, but a belief in the religious significance of historical facts." "I trust to be able to prove that honourable scientific endeavour can go hand in hand with orthodox faith."[70]

In a long introductory section, Weiss investigates the sources for reconstructing the life of Jesus. He repeats his solution to the Synoptic Problem with an assault on the Griesbach hypothesis—"the sole instance of a pure blunder" in the history of the problem. Regarding the second Gospel, Weiss writes, "The Mark-document . . . always remains a source of the first rank, because it reflects with perfect directness the impression produced by the

---

68. Ibid., 36, 180. Besides his extensive contribution to the Meyer series, Weiss published a two-volume commentary on the NT, which has been translated into four volumes in the English edition: *A Commentary on the New Testament* (New York: Funk & Wagnalls, 1906).

69. *The Life of Christ*, trans. J. W. Hope and M. G. Hope, 3 vols., Foreign Theological Library (Edinburgh: T. &. T. Clark, 1894).

70. Ibid. 1:vii, ix, xi.

narratives of the eye-witness of the life of Jesus." Weiss argues at length (more than forty pages) that John the Apostle is the author of the Fourth Gospel. He thinks "the son of thunder of the Apocalypse became, through the training of the Spirit and divine guidance, refined and matured into a mystic in whom the flames of youth had died down into the glow of a holy love." Although the Gospels must be interpreted by historical criticism, Weiss insists that a valid account of the life of Jesus requires sensitivity to the gospel message. "The Gentile or Jew, or he who has broken with the Christian religion, could as little write a history of Jesus, which in its deepest essence shall be a just one, as a blind man could write a history of painting, or a deaf man a history of music."[71]

In presenting the life of Jesus, Weiss orders the narrative into six sections. The first is titled the "Preparation," and includes material from the birth stories to the miracle at Cana. As Jesus grew up, Weiss believes he was immune to the influence of the Jewish sects. "We must, accordingly, come to the conclusion that Jesus received no impulses from any of the peculiar religious tendencies that were current among the people, that He grew up spiritually as a child of His nation under the influences of His pious parents' home, and of the free, active, natural life around Him."[72]

The second period of Jesus' life Weiss calls the "Seed Time." This period includes the early public ministry of Jesus, and begins with the cleansing of the temple. According to Weiss, only one cleansing took place, and John, in contrast to the Synoptics, locates it correctly. According to Weiss, Jesus understands the kingdom of God as the rule of righteousness; it is essentially an ethical concept. Regarding the miracles, Weiss says, "The ultimate cause can only be found in the unique character of His person, and—as this consisted more especially in His prefect sinlessness—in a forcibleness inherent in His corporeal organism, and resting on the unconditioned sway His spirit wielded over His body, enabling Him to convey by a touch to others the health that was peculiarly His own."[73]

The third stage in the life of Jesus Weiss calls the "Period of Conflicts." Weiss sees the beginning of the failure of the public ministry in the account of the exorcism of the demoniac in which the Gerasenes order Jesus to get out of their neighborhood. Weiss thinks there was only one demoniac (as in Mark 5:2, rather than Matt. 8:28), and doubts that the evil spirits actually entered the swine. He says, "the fact of the matter must therefore be that the lunatic, when in the last paroxysm which usually attended recovery, flung himself into the herd, and drove them down" into the sea. Faced with the increasing opposition, Jesus turned his attention more to the future consummation of the kingdom. "This is the same king-

---

71. Ibid. 1:41, 52, 107, 193. On the Griesbach hypothesis, see *HNTR* 1: 143–47.
72. Ibid. 1:290.
73. Ibid. 2:96.

dom of God which here begins to be realized, but there is perfected."⁷⁴

In the fourth period, the "Crisis," Weiss sees the turning point in the feeding of the multitude. He believes there was only one feeding, as reported in the old apostolic source (the Logia). Mark, who used the source, also heard about a feeding from Peter, and assumed there were two. In any case, John correctly reports the crucial detail: the crowd wants to make Jesus king, that is, they want to force him into their nationalistic mold of messiahship. Jesus rejects this temptation.

> By choosing to describe Himself as Son of man in order to lead away from the conception of a temporal regal majesty, which the people, without exception, connected with the idea of the Messiah, Jesus shows distinctly that He can only be the Mediator of salvation and deliverance for the people when He is believingly received as He presents Himself in the form of a simple, if yet unique, Son of man, and when they shall give up all demands for the appearance of the Messiah in a dazzling regal form.⁷⁵

Deciding to terminate his Galilean ministry, Jesus travels to the north. At Caesarea Philippi, the disciples confess openly what the crowd had denied, and Jesus for the first time predicts his passion.

> God's grace had been manifested in the sending of the Messiah; and if He permitted this enormity to happen, it could only be in order to procure an atonement sufficient for the sins of the whole world. Thus Jesus was to be the propitiatory sacrifice, purifying the sin-stained people with His blood, and enabling them to enter into a new covenant relationship with God (Mark xiv. 24); His blood was to be shed for many for the remission of sins (Matt. xxvi. 28).⁷⁶

Weiss thinks that Jesus also predicted his resurrection and his second coming.

During the fifth or "Jerusalem Period," Jesus raised Lazarus. Weiss believes the Synoptics do not mention this miracle, because they do not intend to narrate events after the departure from Galilee and prior to the final visit to Jerusalem. Also in the Jerusalem period, Weiss includes the story of the woman caught in adultery (John 7:53—8:11)—a story that he believes recalls an unknown, authentic tradition. Also in Jerusalem was the last period of Jesus' life, the "Time of Suffering." Following John, Weiss believes Jesus celebrated the Passover meal a day early, so that his execution coincided with the slaughter of the Passover lamb. Weiss affirms the bodily resurrection, but notes that a transformation occurred: "But the fact is apparent that even the disciples did not infer from this that Jesus had returned to earthly existence, for certain traits in His appearances showed that to be impossible; they believe in His resurrection to celestial life, which

---

74. Ibid. 2:228, 369.
75. Ibid. 3:7.
76. Ibid. 3:74–75.

does not presuppose the resumption of an earthly body, but the transformation of it into a glorified one."[77]

NT Theology

Early in his career, Weiss produced monographs on the theology of Peter and the theology of John.[78] However, a comprehensive presentation of NT theology is found in his *Biblical Theology of the New Testament*, originally published in 1868; the English edition is based on the third revised edition of 1880.[79] In the introduction, Weiss contends that biblical theology is a historical discipline that assumes God's revelation in history. "The revelation of God in Christ has been effected, not by the communication of certain ideas and doctrines, but by the historical fact of the manifestation of Christ upon earth, which has brought to the lost, sinful world a salvation whose God-given commencement has guaranteed its completion." Since NT theology is a historical discipline, Weiss believes the material must be arranged chronologically, and studied by grammatico-historical exegesis. "Now it is a fundamental hermeneutical principle of methodical exegesis not to explain the Scriptures by means of a dogmatic or philosophical system of doctrine . . . but to explain each writer by means of himself, so that we may understand every individual word from out of the whole circle of ideas from which it is written."[80] According to Weiss, NT theology does not begin with the teachings of Jesus, but with the doctrine of the apostles who presuppose the life and teaching of Jesus. Weiss attempts to reconstruct this doctrine on the basis of three main sources: the speeches of Acts, 1 Peter, and the Epistle of James. According to Weiss, the speeches in Acts proclaim Jesus as the fulfillment of the OT; Peter focuses on the suffering of Christ; and James understands Christianity as the perfect law.

Turning to Paul, Weiss argues that Pauline theology shows a development from the earliest preaching (the Areopagus speech of Acts and the Thessalonian correspondence), through his four major letters, to the imprisonment Epistles, and finally into the Pastoral Epistles. In the earliest period, Weiss discovers an emphasis on apocalyptic eschatology. In the four main letters (Romans, 1 and 2 Corinthians, and Galatians), Weiss discovers Paul's basic understanding of sin and salvation. According to Weiss, Paul seems to suppose that sin is a sexually transmitted disease. "But since it is only by the process of procreation that Adam stands in a living connection with the whole race, this being also the reason why it is he that is named

---

77. Ibid. 3:391.
78. *Der Petrinische Lehrbegriff: Beiträge zur biblischen Theologie, sowie zur Kritik und Exegese des ersten Briefes Petri und der petrinischen Reden* (Berlin: Wilhelm Schultze, 1855); idem, *Der Johanneische Lehrbegriff in seinen Grundzügen untersucht* (Berlin: Wilhelm Hertz, 1862).
79. 2 vols., CFTL (Edinburgh: T. & T. Clark, 1882–83).
80. Ibid. 1:4, 17.

throughout Rom v., although it was really Eve that sinned first, it is in the highest degree probable that . . . he [Paul] has conceived of that influence as being brought about by sexual procreation." Weiss believes Paul viewed Christ as the preexistent being through whose vicarious and substitutionary death redemption was accomplished. In the imprisonment Epistles, Weiss observes that Christ is viewed as the mediator of creation in whom the essence of the cosmos is summed up. "In the Pastoral Epistles, Christianity is regarded as essentially the doctrine of truth, on a believing knowledge of which salvation depends."[81]

After a discussion of the doctrine of the post-Pauline period (including Hebrews, 2 Peter, Jude, the Apocalypse, and the Synoptics), Weiss turns to the apex of NT theology in John—"the final result of Biblical theology in the deepest conception and the highest glory."[82] According to Weiss, John presents a mystical, spiritual gospel. Weiss thinks that Christ's knowledge of God goes back to his prehistorical existence with God. According to Weiss, John's use of the title "Son of Man" has its background in Daniel, and describes Christ's heavenly origin. Through his atoning death, Christ brings eternal life that is already present. The condition for receiving salvation is faith, that is, belief that Jesus is the Son of God. The believer has continuing fellowship with Christ through the Spirit, the Paraclete. Weiss believes John shares the common view of the NT that the return of Christ is imminent.[83]

Text Criticism

Although text criticism is usually viewed as a preliminary discipline, Weiss's publications on the text of the NT belong to his later years. Consequently, Weiss brought to the discipline the skill of a mature scholar whose experience as an exegete informed his text-critical research. Beginning in 1891, Weiss produced a series of works on the Greek text of the NT. His basic approach is inductive: he concentrates on a section of the NT, analyzes and evaluates the variants found in the major uncial manuscripts, and finally produces a critical text. In 1891, Weiss published his work on the text of the Apocalypse.[84] Beginning with an analysis of the more recent (eighth and ninth century) manuscripts, Weiss contends that most of the variants have resulted from an earlier, systematic emendation of the text. In regard to the older texts, Weiss argues that ℵ, A, and C represent a stage in the

---

81. Ibid. 1:336–37, 125.
82. Ibid. 2:315.
83. In his late seventies, Weiss offered another exposition of NT theology: *The Religion of the New Testament*, trans. George H. Schodde (New York: Funk & Wagnalls, 1905). Written for the laity, this book presents the religion of the NT topically, rather than historically.
84. Bernhard Weiss, *Die Johannes-Apocalypse: Textkritische Untersuchungen und Textherstellung*, TU 7/1 (Leipzig: J. C. Hinrichs, 1891).

development of the text before the emendation process was complete. None of these uncials faithfully represents the older, unemended text, though Weiss thinks that ℵ (Sinaiticus) is the least, and A (Alexandrinus) the most reliable. Finally, on the basis of his analysis, Weiss presents his reconstructed text. In the next year, he published as similar work on the Catholic Epistles, and in 1896, a similar study of the text of the Pauline Epistles.[85] In the former, Weiss gives special attention to Codex Vaticanus, which he believes to be the most valuable witness to the text of the Catholic letters. In the work on the Pauline Epistles, Weiss analyzes the textual variants according to categories: exchanges of words, omissions and additions, changes in word order, orthographic variants. Weiss also published two monographs on the text of Acts. In the first, he analyzes the variants according to the same categories he used for the Pauline Letters.[86] The second assesses the value of Codex D for the reconstruction of the text of Acts.[87] In investigating the variants, Weiss detects careless and intentional alterations, and concludes that D is inferior to the other major uncial MSS. In 1900, Weiss published a text-critical study of the four Gospels in which he concludes that the longer ending of Mark (16:9-20) is spurious and that John 21 is an appendix, added by a later hand.[88]

These various text-critical studies were collected and published under the title *Das Neue Testament: Textkritische Untersuchungen und Textherstellung*.[89] Weiss's own reconstruction of the Greek NT has been published in a three-volume edition with short critical introductions to the NT books and notes on the various sections of the NT.[90] The importance of Weiss's edition of the text is widely recognized.[91] After 1901, the editions of the widely used Nestle text of the NT were essentially a composite of three editions of the Greek text: those of Tischendorf, Westcott and Hort, and

---

85. *Die Katholischen Briefe: Textkritische Untersuchungen und Textherstellung*, TU 8/3 (Leipzig: J. C. Hinrichs, 1892); idem, *Textkritik der Paulinischen Briefe*, TU 14/3 (Leipzig: J. C. Hinrichs, 1896).
86. *Die Apostelgeschichte: Textkritische Untersuchungen und Textherstellung*, TU 8/3 (Leipzig: J. C. Hinrichs, 1893).
87. *Der Codex D in der Apostelgeschichte: Textkritische Untersuchung*, TU, n.F. 2/1 (Leipzig: J. C. Hinrichs, 1897).
88. *Die Vier Evangelien im berichtigten Text, mit kurzer Erläuterung zum Handgebrauch bei der Schriftlektüre* (Leipzig: J. C. Hinrichs, 1900).
89. 3 vols. (Leipzig: J. C. Hinrichs, 1894–1900).
90. *Das Neue Testament: Handausgabe des Griechischen Textes*, 3 vols. (Leipzig: J. C. Hinrichs, 1896–1905).
91. See Bruce M. Metzger, *The Text of the New Testament: Its Transmission, Corruption, and Restoration*, 3d ed. (New York: Oxford University Press, 1992), 137–38; Caspar René Gregory, *Canon and Text of the New Testament*, ITL (New York: Charles Scribner's Sons, 1924), 464.

Weiss. Where two of these editions agreed, the reading was adopted in the Nestle text.[92]

In summary, the importance of Bernhard Weiss is affirmed by the sheer magnitude of his work. Moreover, several of his major works were translated into English, so that his influence reached Great Britain and America, where readers of the Bible were ready to hear a reassuring German voice. In contrast to the skepticism of Tübingen, here was a scholar who believed something—and what a scholar he was: skilled in all points of biblical research, yet without major sin. To be sure, Weiss explicitly rejected biblicism, yet he affirmed the miracles of Jesus, supported substitutionary atonement, and accepted the traditional authorship of every book of the NT except Hebrews. Although Weiss attends to the Synoptic Problem, his solution is not crucial to his work, since he considers accounts of all the Gospels to be essentially reliable. With Ritschl and his followers, Weiss understands the kingdom as essentially spiritual and ethical. Weiss's picture of Jesus tends to assume a suprahistorical aura, since it is filtered through his vision of the Christ of the Fourth Gospel. Weiss's portrait of Paul also lacks clarity, since it attempts to encompass in a single continuum developments from 1 Thessalonians to the Pastoral Epistles. Although Weiss claims objective, nondogmatic exegesis, he confesses the necessity of faith for understanding, and faith, for Weiss, carries a lot of dogmatic baggage. Nevertheless, with an irenic spirit, Weiss practices rigorous criticism, faces all the questions openly, and offers compelling answers.

TOWARD CRITICAL CONSENSUS: HEINRICH HOLTZMANN (1832–1910)

In the wake of the radical criticism of Tübingen, and against the tide of the conservative criticism of Bernhard Weiss, a kind of criticism emerged that was to dominate liberal NT research for generations to come. This criticism was articulated in the work of Heinrich Holtzmann. Born in Karlsruhe, Holtzmann was the son of a pastor.[93] Most of his study was done at Heidelberg, though he spent a year in Berlin (1851–52). Holtzmann began his teaching career at Heidelberg, where he moved through the ranks from

---

92. During the latter part of his life, Weiss engaged in rearguard action against the advancing forces of criticism; see his *The Present Status of the Inquiry concerning the Genuineness of the Pauline Epistles* (Chicago: University of Chicago Press, 1897); *Der Jakobsbrief und die neuere Kritik* (Leipzig: A. Deichert [Georg Böhme], 1904); *Der erste Petrusbrief und die neuere Kritik*, Biblischen Zeit- und Streitfragen 2/9 (Lichterfelde-Berlin: Edwin Runge, 1906); *Das Johannesevangelium als einheitliches Werk geschichtlich erklärt* (Berlin: Trowitzsch & Sohn, 1912).

93. For a summary of Holtzmann's life and work, see Walter Bauer, "Heinrich Julius Holtzmann: Ein Lebensbild," in *Aufsätze und kleine Schriften*, ed. Georg Strecker (Tübingen: J. C. B. Mohr [Paul Siebeck], 1967), 285–341; Hans Rollmann, "Holtzmann, von Hügel and Modernism - I," *Downside Review* 97 (1979): 128–43; Étienne Trocmé, "Le Nouveau Testament à la faculté de théologie protestante de 1870 à 1956," *RHPR* 68 (1988): 113–120.

instructor to full professor (1858–65). In 1874, Holtzmann was appointed professor of NT at Strasbourg. Just as Alsace had fallen in the Franco-Prussian War, so the Strasbourg school surrendered to the potent German scholarship of Holtzmann.[94] He brought with him a reputation for effective teaching. One of his former Heidelberg students wrote:

> How much I owe to these lectures for my whole life and calling, especially for preaching, I cannot easily say. . . . Here we learned that there was no conflict between scientific and practical exegesis for the conscientious preacher, but that only the most intimate connection of the two would lead to the goal. . . . Here Holtzmann the human being opened his heart to us, while the theologian opened to us the text.[95]

Among his students at Strasbourg was Albert Schweitzer.[96] Holtzmann, a scholar of broad learning, contributed articles on a variety of subjects for a theological encyclopedia.[97] He was fluent in Italian, visited Rome frequently, and reviewed with appreciation the works of Italian and French Roman Catholic scholars.

Although he is usually identified as a mediating theologian, Holtzmann advocated views of the advancing liberalism: stress on the religious consciousness of Jesus, understanding the kingdom of God as spiritual and ethical, emphasis on the universality of Christianity. Holtzmann considered himself an objective historian and exegete, guarding against dogmatic presuppositions. Nevertheless, he affirmed revelation in history, primarily God's action in Christ.[98] The Bible, the record of historical revelation, was of crucial importance to Holtzmann. He believed the religion of Jesus and the faith of the apostles to be normative for Christian thought. He contributed to many areas of NT study: history, higher criticism, exegesis, and NT theology.

---

94. See David Barrett Peabody, "H. J. Holtzmann and His European Colleagues: Aspects of the Nineteenth Century European Discussion of Gospel Origins," in *Biblical Studies and the Shifting of Paradigms, 1850–1914*, ed. Henning Graf Reventlow and William Farmer, JSOTSup 192 (Sheffield: Sheffield Academic Press, 1995), 50–131. On political aspects of Holtzmann's appointment to Strasbourg, see David Laird Dungan, *A History of the Synoptic Problem: The Canon, the Text, the Composition, and the Interpretation of the Gospels*, ABRL (New York: Doubleday, 1999), 326–29.

95. E. Simons in the foreword to Heinrich Holtzmann, *Praktische Erklärung des I. Thessalonicherbriefes*, ed. Eduard Simons (Tübingen: J. C. B. Mohr [Paul Siebeck], 1911), v–vi.

96. See Jean Héring, "De H. J. Holtzmann à Albert Schweitzer," in *Ehrfurcht vor dem Leben: Albert Schweitzer: Eine Freundesgabe zu seinem 80. Geburtstag*, ed. Fritz Buri (Bern: Paul Haupt, 1954), 21–29.

97. H. Holtzmann and R. Zöpffel, *Lexikon für Theologie und Kirchenwesen: Lehre, Geschichte und Kultus, Verfassung, Feste, Sekten und Orden der christlichen Kirche; das Wichtigste bezüglich der übrigen Religionsgemeinschaften*, 2d ed. (Braunschweig: C. A. Schwetschke und Sohn, 1888).

98. See Karl Gerhard Steck, "Heinrich Julius Holtzmanns Beitrag zur Kontroverse über Schrift und Tradition," in *Hören und Handeln: Festschrift für Ernst Wolf zum 60. Geburtstag*, ed. Helmut Gollwitzer und Hellmut Traub (Munich: Chr. Kaiser, 1962), 372–87.

NT History and Higher Criticism

Sensitive to the growing interest in the religious context and the continuing importance of the development of early Christianity, Holtzmann published a large work (more than eight hundred pages) on the history of Judaism and Christianity in the NT era. The book presents the history of Judaism from the Maccabean period through the Bar Kochba revolt, and the history of Christianity from the beginning into the second century. In discussing the significance of Jesus within this history of Judaism, Holtzmann says, "The teaching of Jesus . . . is the foundation and presupposition of everything that belongs to the historical development of Christian consciousness; it is not, like the teaching of Paul or John, theology, it is religion, it is the religion itself."[99]

In response to Jesus, a community arose. In time, this community broke with Judaism, incorporated Gentiles, and understood Christianity to be universal. Crucial for this development is the life and thought of Paul. Paul's universal message, Holtzmann thinks, stands in continuity with the teaching of Jesus:

> If the expressions of Jesus about himself are mainly attached to his sayings about the kingdom of God, so the main weight of the Pauline proclamation falls on the person of the Messiah. The fundamental question is not how Jesus through word and deed led people to the kingdom of God, but what he suffered in order to become their redeemer, how he through resurrection, exaltation, and heavenly activity showed himself as redeemer. Paulinism is thus essentially doctrine.[100]

Turning to what he calls "Alexandrian Christianity," Holtzmann discusses the Epistle to the Hebrews and the Gospel of John. He also notes the rise of church consciousness and the eventual emergence of the ancient catholic church. In tracing the development of early Christian literature, Holtzmann observes the first examples in the occasional letters of Paul, and the eventual appearance of the Gospels. Holtzmann believes Acts recounts the transition from Palestinian origins to the universal vision of Paul. In a final section, Holtzmann traces the spread of Christianity in the Roman Empire, presenting the development of the church in various geographical locations: Jerusalem and Syria, Asia Minor, Macedonia, Corinth, and Rome.

The sum of Holtzmann's higher critical opinions is contained in his massive *Introduction to the NT*.[101] After an introductory section on the history of the discipline, Holtzmann presents what he calls the "general part" of his

---

99. *Judenthum und Christenthum im Zeitalter der apokryphischen und neutestamentlichen Literatur,* vol. 2 of *Geschichte des Volkes Israel und der Entstehung des Christenthums,* by Georg Weber and Heinrich Holtzmann (Leipzig: Wilhelm Engelmann, 1867), 381.
100. Ibid., 576–77.
101. *Lehrbuch der historisch-kritischen Einleitung in das Neue Testament,* 2d ed., Theologischer Lehrbücher (Freiburg i. Br.: J. C. B. Mohr [Paul Siebeck], 1886).

Introduction. This part reviews the nature and history of text criticism, and presents a history of the development of the NT canon. In the "special part," Holtzmann presents critical introductions to the NT documents in the order of his chronological reconstruction. Beginning with the Pauline Letters, Holtzmann rejects 2 Thessalonians because he thinks it presents a non-Pauline eschatology. Second Corinthians 10–13 is not, in Holtzmann's opinion, a separate letter, but Paul's final blow against Judaizing opponents in Corinth. Holtzmann believes Paul's purpose in writing Romans was to inoculate the church against the disease of the Judaizers who might infect Rome in the future.

In regard to Colossians and Ephesians, Holtzmann's *Introduction* presents a summary of the position he had taken earlier in a lengthy monograph (more than three hundred pages).[102] In that monograph, Holtzmann begins by noting arguments against the authenticity of Ephesians. He then proceeds to analyze literary parallels between Ephesians and Colossians, discovering, to his own satisfaction, that sometimes the former, sometimes the latter has the more original expression. Turning to philological analysis, Holtzmann observes that both letters have many non-Pauline terms, and that they have much of this non-Pauline vocabulary in common. On the basis of literary and philological analysis, Holtzmann concludes that Colossians contains both original Pauline material and material produced by the pseudonymous writer of Ephesians. He formulates the hypothesis that canonical Colossians incorporates an original short letter of Paul to which the author of Ephesians has added interpolations. In regard to the historical situation, Holtzmann concludes that the original, noninterpolated Colossians was written from Paul's Roman imprisonment between 62 and 64. Ephesians and canonical Colossians, according to Holtzmann, were written in the postapostolic age by a Jewish Christian author who applies Paul's attack on the Colossian false teachers to the Gnostics of his own time.

In discussing 1 and 2 Timothy and Titus in his *Introduction*, Holtzmann presents a summary of the critical judgments he had formulated in a separate work on the Pastoral Epistles.[103] In the earlier work, Holtzmann begins by presenting arguments against the authenticity of the Pastorals. He contends that it is impossible to fit these Epistles into Paul's life prior to his Roman imprisonment, and argues that the hypothesis of a second Roman imprisonment is a fabrication created to salvage the authenticity of the Pastorals. Gathering evidence from style and vocabulary, Holtzmann notes the abundance of non-Pauline terms and the dearth of typical Pauline expressions. Holtzmann believes the heresy opposed by the Pastorals is a Jewish

---

102. *Kritik Epheser- und Kolosserbriefe: Auf Grund einer Analyse ihres Verwandtschaftsverhältnisses* (Leipzig: Wilhelm Engelmann, 1872).

103. *Die Pastoralbriefe, kritisch und exegetisch behandelt* (Leipzig: Wilhelm Engelmann, 1880).

Gnosticism. The theology of the author is a developed Paulinism that understands faith and love as virtues, the gospel as the standard of truth. Holtzmann thinks the Pastorals were written in the time of Trajan or Hadrian by a Gentile Christian, probably in Rome. Also in his *Introduction*, Holtzmann discusses the Epistle to the Hebrews. Noting the differences in style and thought from the Pauline letters, he concludes that the author is an unidentified Christian of Alexandria. The epistle, he believes, was written after the destruction of Jerusalem, addressed to Jewish Christians in Rome, urging them not to relapse into Judaism.

Turning to the historical books, Holtzmann takes up the Synoptic Gospels and rehearses, with significant variations, results of his five-hundred-page work on the Synoptics, written in 1863. After reviewing the history of the Synoptic Problem, Holtzmann begins his own work with an analysis of Mark. In this earlier book, he finds evidence that Mark used a primitive source, an *Urmarcus*, which he calls Source A. Holtzmann believes all three Gospel writers used this source, but Mark, he thinks, follows it more faithfully. Besides Source A, Holtzmann identifies a second source, made up of discourse material, which he names Source L (Λ, Logia). Holtzmann believes Matthew and Luke used this source independently, though Luke follows it more faithfully. Holtzmann concludes, "We bring together the divergent assertions . . . into a very simple result: we posit an Ur-Matthew in the form of L to precede Matthew, and an Ur-Marcus in the form of A to precede Mark; all further intermediate members are superfluous and would appear only as unknown doublets of known sources and gospels; they are the product of critical double-vision and other hallucinations."[104]

After adopting this solution as a working hypothesis, Holtzmann presents a lengthy chapter (more than one hundred pages) titled *Proben*, that is, tests that he believes support his hypothesis. Most important is Holtzmann's analysis of the linguistic characteristics of each of the Synoptics and the sources. By investigating parallel texts, Holtzmann attempts to delineate the respective styles of Matthew, Mark, Luke, A, and L. This stylistic analysis, he believes, confirms his version of the two-document (A and L) hypothesis. As to the historical reliability of the sources, Holtzmann believes Source L is the Logia that Papias attributes to the apostle Matthew. In regards to the Gospel of Mark, Holtzmann argues that its only written source, Source A, can be identified as the reminiscences of Peter, recorded by John Mark. Thus, all three of the Synoptics use sources that preserve

---

104. *Die synoptischen Evangelien: Ihr Ursprung und geschichtlicher Character* (Leipzig: Wilhelm Engelmann, 1863), 1, 168. For an analysis and critique of Holtzmann's research on the Synoptic Problem, see Hans-Herbert Stoldt, *History and Criticism of the Marcan Hypothesis*, trans. and ed. Donald L. Niewyk (Macon, Ga.: Mercer University Press, 1977), 69–93; John S. Kloppenborg Verbin, *Excavating Q: The History and Setting of the Sayings Gospel* (Edinburgh: T. & T. Clark, 2000), 300–309; Bo Reicke, "From Strauss to Holtzmann and Meijboom: Synoptic Theories Advanced during the Consolidation of Germany, 1830–70," *NovT* 29 (1987): 1–21.

reliable, apostolic tradition. Holtzmann says, "we have found in Source A a historical narrative in whose vivid and essential character the earliest reminiscences of the disciples is made known."[105]

On the basis of this understanding of the sources, Holtzmann believes the historical life of Jesus can be reconstructed. "We may perhaps designate as the most valuable gain of our research that we are thereby put in a position to give a rather definite picture of the historical character of the person of Jesus and of the content that fills the framework of his life." Following Mark, which most faithfully represents Source A, Holtzmann detects an outline of the main events in the life of Jesus. The ordering principle, which Holtzmann believes to be historically correct, is the development of the life of Jesus, marked by his increasing comprehension of his messianic vocation. The turning point in this development, according to Holtzmann, is reached at Caesarea Philippi with Peter's confession. Prior to this time, Jesus had silenced recognition of his messiahship; after the confession, the acknowledgment of his messianic calling—with its crucial role of suffering—becomes public. This messianic claim provokes the bitter opposition that leads rapidly to Jesus' execution. "Thus the career of Jesus comes quickly to its tragic end, an end that by Jesus himself had been foreseen and predicted with ever increasing clarity to be the only possible, the only end worthy of him, as the divine necessity."[106]

In his *Introduction*, Holtzmann acknowledges how his mind has changed since the writing of the earlier work on the Synoptics. For one thing, he no longer affirms the existence of Source A. This change, on the one hand, provides Holtzmann with the advantage of dispensing with a hypothetical document, but, on the other, it erases his earlier argument that an *Urmarcus* could account for the agreements of Matthew and Luke against Mark. Although he has abandoned *Urmarcus*, Holtzmann is inclined to believe that the Gospel of Mark presents Petrine tradition. Holtzmann has also come to the conclusion that Luke used Matthew. This change, of course, makes the hypothesis of Source L (or Q) unnecessary, yet Holtzmann continues to declare that Matthew and Luke used the Logia source. "In any case," he concludes, "the two-document hypothesis offers the truest solution to the Synoptic Problem."[107]

Holtzmann's onslaught on traditional criticism is evident in his *Introduction*'s treatment of the rest of the books of the NT. In regard to Acts, Holtzmann identifies the "we-sections" as a travel report written by a participant in the events reported, probably Luke, but he doubts that the author of the report is the author of Acts. Betraying the continuing influence of Tübin-

---

105. *Die synoptischen Evangelien*, 450.
106. Ibid., 468, 485.
107. *Einleitung in das NT*, 376.

gen, Holtzmann notes the author's effort to record harmonious relationships within the early church: Peter is Paulinized, and Paul is Judaized. As to the Fourth Gospel, Holtzmann senses a combination of historical tradition and theological reflection. "This wavering and shifting between sheer materialism (11:39) and spiritualizing allegory (11:25, 26) constitutes not simply the striking manner of the presentation, but depends directly on the essence of the whole, the combining of the Logos-idea with the definite, historical human form." Holtzmann finds it difficult to believe that a Palestinian Jew of the apostolic circle could have written this document. "If the old tradition that identifies the pillar-apostle with the writer of the Apocalypse should indeed be correct, then the composition of the Fourth Gospel through the Apostle would be even more unthinkable."[108] In regard to the Catholic Epistles, Holtzmann finds the traditional view of the authorship of all these documents to be problematic. For example, he thinks that 2 Peter, which Holtzmann believes to be dependent on nonauthentic Jude, can scarcely come from the pen of the Galilean fisherman. First Peter, with its lofty Greek style and deviation from the Synoptic tradition, was written not by Peter, according to Holtzmann, but by a follower of Paul.

Jesus and Exegesis

Crucial for Holtzmann's thought is his understanding of the historical Jesus, and essential to that understanding is his theory of the development of Jesus' religious consciousness. Consequently, Holtzmann's book *The Messianic Consciousness of Jesus* is of utmost importance.[109] Written after the publication of Wrede's theory of the messianic secret,[110] the burden of Holtzmann's book is to prove by the exegesis of crucial texts that Jesus understood himself to be the Messiah. For example, Holtzmann believes that Jesus' word about the Son of David (Mark 12:35-37) indicates his rejection of the political understanding of messiahship, just as his response to Peter's confession (Mark 8:31) attests to his acceptance of the role of suffering Messiah. The whole process of the trial and execution of Jesus, Holtzmann thinks, cannot be explained apart from Jesus' messianic claim. Holtzmann maintains that "the historian must by all means hold fast to the verdict: Jesus confessed himself as Messiah, he was condemned as false messiah and was executed as messianic pretender."[111] Holtzmann thinks Jesus used the title "Son of Man" to express his special understanding of his own messiahship—a title that has its source in Daniel, but with Jesus takes on universal meaning. The Son of Man, according to Holtzmann, is the true, suffering representative of humanity.

108. Ibid., 461, 471.
109. *Das messianische Bewusstsein Jesu: Ein Beitrag zur Leben-Jesu-Forschung* (Tübingen: J. C. B. Mohr [Paul Siebeck], 1907).
110. See pp. 147–49, below.
111. *Messianische Bewusstsein Jesu*, 35–36.

Combining his critical and exegetical skills, Holtzmann produced significant commentaries. An early example can be seen in his book on the Pastorals.[112] In this book, texts are analyzed verse by verse with attention to Greek terms and phrases, text-critical details, parallels in the LXX and the NT, and the exegesis of patristic and modern scholars. Holtzmann's treatment of 1 Tim. 2:8-15, titled "The Place of Men and Women in the Assembly of the Congregation," may serve as an example. Holtzmann thinks the implication that only men can pray in public reflects the author's dependence on 1 Cor. 14:34-35. This is also indicated, according to Holtzmann, by the use of ἐπιτρέπω ("to permit") in both texts—a term found only here in the Pastorals. Holtzmann believes the instruction on how women are to be saved (v. 15) responds to the description of Eve as a "transgressor" (v. 14). Since "faith and love and holiness" are mentioned, Holtzmann concludes that the author does not intend to suggest that mere "childbearing" is sufficient for salvation.

Holtzmann participated (along with R. A. Lipsius, P. W. Schmiedel, and H. v. Soden) in editing the commentary series *Hand-commentar zum Neuen Testament*. His own contribution includes commentaries on the Synoptic Gospels, Acts, John, the Johannine Epistles, and Revelation. An example of Holtzmann's exegesis and his commentaries on the Johannine literature are combined in a single volume.[113] In the introduction to the section on John, Holtzmann presents his basic understanding of the Fourth Gospel: the form is history; the content is doctrine. In interpreting the prologue, Holtzmann argues that the phrase "in the beginning," and the combination of "word" and "light," reflect Gen. 1:1, 3. However, Holtzmann believes the development of the Logos idea employs concepts drawn from Alexandrian thought. Holtzmann attends to grammatical details. For example, he discusses the question as to whether ὁ γέγονεν goes with the ending of v. 3 or the beginning of v. 4; that is, whether the text should read: "without him not one thing came into being. What has come into being in him is life" (NRSV); or "without him not one thing came into being that has come into being" (NRSV, footnote). Holtzmann opts for the latter on the basis of text, grammar, context, and Johannine thought. On the Christology of the author, Holtzmann concludes, "The singularity and uniqueness of the person of Jesus consists according to him no longer in the fact that Jesus is the

---

112. *Die Pastoralbriefe*.
113. H. J. Holtzmann, *Evangelium, Briefe und Offenbarung des Johannes*, Hand-Commentar zum Neuen Testament 4 (Freiburg i. Br.: J. C. B. Mohr [Paul Siebeck], 1891). In 1908, a third edition, edited by Walter Bauer, printed John in one volume, the Epistles and Revelation in another. For a thoughtful analysis of Holtzmann's exegesis of the Fourth Gospel, see Tord Larsson, *God in the Fourth Gospel: A Hermeneutical Study of the History of Interpretations*, ConBNT Series 35 (Stockholm: Almqvist & Wiksell, 2001), 141–67.

Messiah of the Jews or that he is the prototype of humanity, but that he represents directly the deity on earth in the flesh."[114]

NT Theology

The crown of Holtzmann's scholarly achievement is his monumental two-volume *NT Theology*, originally published in 1896–97.[115] In the introduction, Holtzmann defines NT theology as the scientific presentation of the religious and ethical ideas of the NT. The first part of the book presents the religious ideas of Jesus and the earliest Christians—ideas that must be interpreted within the context of Judaism. Holtzmann understands Jesus to be a unique religious genius who had an acute sense of the reality of God. In contrast to the Jewish concern with ritual and legal piety, Holtzmann believes Jesus proclaimed an inward, ethical religion. According to Holtzmann, Jesus viewed the kingdom as both present and future. Holtzmann thinks the parables of growth describe the "now" of planting and the future of harvesting, so that the kingdom develops gradually. Detecting a shift from the teaching *of* Jesus to the teaching *about* Jesus, Holtzmann discusses the titles attributed to Jesus. He believes Jesus rejected the national, political messiahship implicit in the title "Son of David," and adopted the title "Son of Man" to express his messianic identity. "As it is the virtue of his self-designation as Son of Man that in this title man and Messiah meet, so the religious and theocratic Messiah is found in the Son of God, so that both lines are held in correlation."[116]

Holtzmann turns to the development of theology in early Christianity apart from Paul. He notes the importance of the resurrection faith for shaping the life and thought of the earliest Christians. Baptism became a rite of initiation into the messianic community, and the Lord's Supper remembered Christ's presence. According to Holtzmann, Christianity was a social movement that destroyed humanity's egocentric distinctions and "bridged the gulf between deity and humanity."[117] Holtzmann describes the expansion of Christianity in the Gentile world under the leadership of Stephen and the Hellenists. Under the influence of syncretistic Gnosticism, the original gospel story, according to Holtzmann, was mythologized and dogmatized. He believes each of the Synoptics shaped the gospel tradition according to its own theological perspective. Holtzmann concludes this part of his work with accounts of the apocalyptic theology of Revelation, the

---

114. *Evangelium, Briefe und Offenbarung des Johannes* (1891), 36. Besides his technical commentaries, Holtzmann also published *Praktische Erklärung des I. Thessalonicherbriefes*, 119)—a brief (163-page) commentary, designed to facilitate practical application and use of the text in preaching.

115. *Lehrbuch der neutestamentlichen Theologie*, 2 vols., 2d ed., ed. A. Jülicher und W. Bauer, Sammlung theologischer Lehrbücher (Tübingen: J. C. B. Mohr [Paul Siebeck], 1911).

116. Ibid. 1:352.

117. Ibid. 1:463.

influence of Gnosticism in the Deutero-Pauline letters, and the emergence of the old catholic church.

In the second part of his *NT Theology*, Holtzmann presents the theologies of Paul and the postapostolic writers. The point of departure for understanding Paul, according to Holtzmann, is anthropology. In his view of humanity, Paul is concerned with the inner and outer human being—an ethical, not a metaphysical, dualism. Holtzmann thinks Paul's doctrine of sin shows the dual influence of the HB and Hellenistic thought. On the one hand, sin is inherited from Adam, punished by death; on the other, sin is latent in human nature, and death belongs to the human situation. Holtzmann thinks Paul's understanding of deliverance from this situation is grounded in his own conversion experience—an experience involving a Christophany in which the Hellenistic heavenly man appeared as Messiah. "If the conversion negatively meant break with the law, abandonment of legal justification, so positively it must have meant the universal character of the Pauline missionary preaching."[118]

Holtzmann recognizes the importance of Paul for the development of Christology, soteriology, and ethics. "Paul is the creator of Christology. In place of the doctrine of Jesus stands the doctrine about Christ." Holtzmann believes this Christology also embodies a duality: Christ came in the likeness of sinful flesh, sharing human nature; Christ came as the second Adam, transformed into spiritual reality by his resurrection. In investigating Paul's idea of reconciliation through Christ, Holtzmann again perceives a dual emphasis: on the one hand, Paul describes justification according to Jewish legal concepts; on the other, he depicts reconciliation according to the mystical idea of unity with the dying and rising Christ. "In place of the Jewish legal ideas the intuitions of an ethically oriented mysticism come increasingly into view, which makes out of the singular event a general experience of all believers, and shapes the background of the whole Pauline ethic." Holtzmann believes Paul's ethical imperatives are grounded in the new life; he articulates an ethic of indicative and imperative: "Werde was du bist!" (Become what you are!) Although Paul stresses human freedom, he affirms the ultimate accomplishment of God's purposes.

> Also here it is apparent that righteousness and wrath do not constitute the final purpose, nor power and sovereignty the highest attribute of God, but in both relations love stands above, love claims the field. The last end, since the lost people no longer come into view, is unified and will allow only the purpose of love to be recognized as realized.

Holtzmann admits that Paul uses apocalyptic expressions and expects the imminent return of Christ. However, he believes that Paul's eschatology displays development, becoming increasingly spiritualized; Paul believes the

---

118. Ibid. 2:70.

new life is already present, and in the future fulfillment, "flesh and blood cannot inherit the kingdom of God" (1 Cor. 15:50).[119]

After a discussion of Deutero-Paulinism, Holtzmann presents his understanding of Johannine theology. He believes the author of the Fourth Gospel adopts a Hellenistic worldview. "Indeed, the whole atmosphere that lies over the Johannine conceptual world is Alexandrian, the final development of ancient thinking in general from Plato on, but especially the duality that dominates the Philonic worldview of the ideal world and the natural, the spiritual cosmos and material existence, heaven and earth." Holtzmann arranges his analysis of Johannine thought in two parts: the "theological hemisphere" and the "soteriological hemisphere." In the first, he notes the understanding of God as the invisible, distant Being. The Logos Christology stresses preexistence and God's revelation in history. According to Holtzmann, the Johannine Logos became flesh by means of his birth through human parents, Mary and Joseph. The description of the Logos as the only begotten Son of God affirms the unique sonship of Christ, and expresses his divine nature and unity with the essence of God—a unity that is ethical as well as metaphysical. Holtzmann notes the importance of John's idea of the Spirit—the Doppelgänger of the Logos. "As the Logos is a second mode of the being of God, so is the coming of the Paraclete a coming of the Son, though in a different modality." In regard to the "soteriological hemisphere," Holtzmann believes the Gospel of John stresses God's action in Christ to free people from the power of sin. The response to God's saving action is faith, and, for the author, the object of faith is God or Christ. The life of the believer involves a unity with God who is one with Christ. Holtzmann believes the Fourth Gospel has abandoned apocalyptic eschatology, seeing the future expectation fulfilled with the presence of the Spirit; judgment occurs at the moment of belief, eternal life is already realized.[120]

To summarize: Holtzmann appears to be the consummate nineteenth-century biblical scholar: brilliant linguist, competent historian, endowed with analytical skill and theological sensitivity, master of an enormous quantity of primary and secondary sources. Most important, he articulated an emerging critical consensus that was to prevail among liberal scholars for a century: the two-document hypothesis; the pseudonymity of Ephesians and the Pastoral Epistles; the questionable reliability of Acts; the problematic authorship of the Catholic Epistles; the theological, rather than historical, character of the Fourth Gospel; the importance of Hellenistic backgrounds for the understanding of Paul and John. Moreover, the summary presented here does not adequately disclose the meticulous complexity of Holtzmann's research—a complexity that contributes to the increasing scholarly captivity of the Bible.

119. Ibid. 2:73, 131, 167, 191.
120. Ibid. 2:416, 516.

Holtzmann's solution to the Synoptic Problem has been widely acclaimed. W. G. Kümmel, for instance, says that "Holtzmann grounded the two source hypothesis so carefully that the study of Jesus henceforth could not again dispense with this firm base."[121] Nevertheless, voices have been raised that question Holtzmann's method and results, in particular his linguistic argument.[122] In any case, the two-document hypothesis was for Holtzmann a conservative effort to ground the tradition of Jesus on reliable, apostolic sources. Yet, at the same time, Holtzmann's historical Jesus reflected the portrait of the Jesus of liberalism, the Jesus of nineteenth-century religious culture. In Holtzmann's reconstruction, the old legalism of Judaism had been cast aside like some tattered garment. In its place was the religious experience of Jesus, clothed in the mysticism of Paul, and woven into the seamless robe of Johannine universalism.

THE ZENITH OF LIBERALISM:
ADOLF VON HARNACK (1851–1930)

Life and Thought

The liberalism founded by Ritschl, supported by the historical studies of Reuss and Weizsäcker, and enhanced by the critical research of Weiss and Holtzmann reached its high point in Harnack.[123] Adolf von Harnack was born in Dorpat (Estonia), the son of Theodosius Harnack, an orthodox

---

121. Werner Georg Kümmel, *The New Testament: The History of the Investigation of Its Problems,* trans. S. McLean Gilmour and Howard C. Kee (Nashville: Abingdon, 1972), 151. See also Schweitzer, *Quest of the Historical Jesus,* 151.

122. See Stoldt, *Marcan Hypothesis,* 69–93. David B. Peabody ("Chapters in the History of the Linguistic Argument for Solving the Synoptic Problem: The Nineteenth Century in Context," in *Jesus, the Gospels, and the Church,* ed. E. P. Sanders [Macon, Ga.: Mercer University Press, 1987], 47–68) investigates Holtzmann's dependence on the work of C. G. Wilke and Christoph Adolf Hasert. He also presents E. Zeller's version of the linguistic argument, which, in contrast to Wilke, supports the Griesbach hypothesis.

123. For summaries of Harnack's life and thought, see Agnes von Zahn-Harnack, *Adolf von Harnack,* 2d ed. (Berlin: Walter de Gruyter, 1951); G. Wayne Glick, *The Reality of Christianity: A Study of Adolf von Harnack as Historian and Theologian,* Makers of Modern Theology (New York: Harper & Row, 1967), 16–19; Wilhelm Pauck, *Harnack and Troeltsch: Two Historical Theologians* (New York: Oxford University Press, 1968); Carl-Jürgen Kaltenborn, *Adolf von Harnack als Lehrer Dietrich Bonhoeffers,* Theologische Arbeiten 31 (Berlin: Evangelische Verlagsanstalt, 1973); William A. Mueller, "Adolf von Harnack, Church Historian and Theologian," in *The Teacher's Yoke: Studies in Memory of Henry Trantham,* ed. E. Jerry Vardaman and James Leo Garrett Jr. (Waco, Tex.: Baylor University Press, 1964), 287–97; Martin Rumscheidt, ed., *Adolf von Harnack: Liberal Theology at Its Height* (London: Collins, 1989), 9–41; Marceline Donaldson, "Harnack and Schüssler-Fiorenza: A Comparative Analysis," in *Church Divinity 1985,* ed. John H. Morgan, Church Divinity Monograph Series (Bristol, Ind.: Wyndham Hall, 1985), 1–23; Winfried Döbertin, *Adolf von Harnack: Theologe, Pädagoge, Wissenschaftspolitiker,* European University Studies; Series XXIII: Theology, vol. 258 (Frankfurt am Main: Peter Lang, 1985). For a recent bibliographical summary and assessment of the life and work of Harnack, see Wolfram Kinzig, "Harnack heute. Neuere Forschungen zu seiner Biographie und dem 'Wesen des Christentums'," *TLZ* 126 (2001): 473–500.

theologian who taught at Dorpat and Erlangen. He began his university studies at Dorpat, but transferred to Leipzig, where he passed his doctoral examinations and wrote a dissertation on the history of Gnosticism. Harnack began his teaching career at Leipzig in 1874, and in 1879 was appointed professor at Giessen. During his time at Giessen, Harnack published the first volume of his *History of Dogma*—a book that finalized the theological break with his father. In a letter to his son Adolf, Theodosius Harnack wrote, "Anyone . . . who takes the position that you do on the fact of the resurrection—such a person is in my eyes no longer a Christian theologian."[124]

In 1886, Harnack accepted a faculty position at Marburg, and in 1888, after nine months of bitter controversy, he was appointed Professor of Church History at Berlin. The appointment had been contested by officials of the Prussian church who were shocked by Harnack's skepticism concerning the miracles and the virgin birth. The appointment was supported by Bismarck, and finally confirmed by Kaiser Wilhelm II. During his tenure at Berlin, Harnack taught a host of students, including Adolf Jülicher and Karl Barth, and Americans such as S. J. Case and E. J. Goodspeed. His students praised Harnack for his "animated way of teaching," his "strict scholarly passion for truth and religious ardor," his "humor, wit, and presence of mind of a magic kind."[125] In Berlin, though continually shunned by the ecclesiastical hierarchy, Harnack was active in German cultural and political life. In 1905, he was appointed Director of the Royal Library, a position he held until 1921. Harnack was elevated to the nobility in 1914, the last academic scholar upon whom this honor was conferred.

Harnack was a prodigious worker. To accomplish all he did, he must have been an academic Briareus—the mythological giant with a hundred arms and fifty heads. Harnack had a phenomenal memory and worked rapidly; his bibliography numbers more than fifteen hundred items. He wrote, "My pen is cleverer than I am."[126] Among the factors shaping Harnack's theology was the Lutheran orthodoxy of his father, reflected in Harnack's personal religious piety.[127] Harnack was also influenced by Baur and the Tübingen school.[128] From Baur, Harnack inherited the idea of historical development, and the conviction that Christianity is a historical phenome-

---

124. Quoted by Mueller, "Adolf von Harnack," 295.
125. Quoted by Glick, *Reality of Christianity*, 36. See also K. Aland, W. Elliger, and O. Dibelius, *Adolf Harnack: in memoriam: Reden zum 100. Geburtstag am 7. Mai 1951 gehalten bei der Gedenkfeier der Theologischen Fakultät der Humboldt-Universität Berlin* (Berlin: Evangelische Verlagsanstalt, n.d.).
126. Quoted by J. C. O'Neill, *The Bible's Authority: A Portrait Gallery of Thinkers from Lessing to Bultmann* (Edinburgh: T. &T. Clark, 1991), 216.
127. See G. Wayne Glick, "Nineteenth Century Theological and Cultural Influences on Adolf Harnack," *CH* 29 (1959): 157–82; Adolf von Harnack, *A Scholar's Testament: Meditations by Adolf von Harnack*, trans. Olive Wyon (London: Ivor Nicholson & Watson, 1933).
128. See *HNTR* 1:258–78.

non, to be studied by critical method. Harnack came increasingly under the influence of Ritschl, whom he had met as a youth. In sending Ritschl a copy of the first volume of his *Dogmengeschichte*, Harnack wrote:

> As I put this volume into your hands, it is necessary for me to express to you once more my thanks for everything I have received from you. With the study of your *Entstehung der altkatholischen Kirche* seventeen years ago, I began my theological work, and since then scarcely a quarter year has passed in which I have not learned more from you. The present book is a kind of conclusion of long-standing studies: without the foundation that you laid, it would probably never have been written, as inadequate as it is.[129]

Like Ritschl, Harnack rejected metaphysics and philosophical speculation; his theology was anthropocentric and Christocentric.

Fundamental to Harnack's theology is his view of history.[130] According to Harnack, the study of history demands rigorous collection and analysis of data, but also the wisdom to order the events and discern the meaning of the whole. Harnack believes history is *Geisteswissenschaft*, that is, the history of the spirit or mind. In the study of history, he insists that attention be given to the importance of individual persons, and to the impact of the great events. "The epoch-making events, the knowledge of the monuments, and the investigation of the institutions constitute the backbone of history."[131] According to Harnack, history is the key for understanding reality, the moving force for action. "We study history in order to intervene in the course of history, and we have a right and duty to do so." For Harnack, history is the realm of God's revelation, and the apex of that revelation is Jesus Christ. "The peculiar character of the Christian religion is conditioned by the fact that every reference to God is at the same time a reference to Jesus Christ and vice-versa."[132] Harnack rejected the two-natures doctrine and affirmed the humanity of Jesus.[133] For Harnack, the concern is not the nature of Christ, but his redemptive work. Following Ritschl, Harnack abandoned the doctrine of substitutionary atonement and embraced a moral theory that stressed Jesus as example:

---

129. Zahn-Harnack, *Adolf von Harnack*, 98. See E. P. Meijering, *Theologische Urteil über die Dogmengeschichte: Ritschls Einfluss auf von Harnack*, BZRGG 20 (Leiden: E. J. Brill, 1978).

130. "Über die Sicherheit und die Grenzen geschichtlicher Erkenntnis: Ein Vortrag," in *Erforschtes und Erlebtes, Reden und Aufsätze*, Neue Folge 4 (Giessen: Alfred Töpelmann, 1923), 3–23; see Wilhelm Pauck, "The Significance of Adolf von Harnack's Interpretation of Church History," *USQR* (January 1954): 13–24; Johanna Jantsch, *Die Entstehung des Christentums bei Adolf von Harnack und Eduard Meyer*, Habelts Dissertationsdrucke: Reihe alte Geschichte (Bonn: Rudolf Habelt, 1990).

131. "Sicherheit und Grenzen," 15.

132. Quoted by Glick, *Reality of Christianity*, 108, 145.

133. See Ernst Bammel, "The Jesus of History in the Theology of Adolf v. Harnack," *Modern Churchman* 19 (1976): 90–112.

The reconciler . . . is Christ, since he redeems humans from the law of sin to which they have fallen. . . . How does he redeem? Only through this, that his word, his life, his death, that is, he himself, becomes the experience of the soul, and in this experience, it is freed from the force of the law of sin, from this most unnatural law of nature.[134]

The religion Jesus founded is the supreme religion. Harnack says that "Christianity in its pure form is not a religion beside others, but it is *the* religion. And it is the religion because Jesus Christ is not one master beside others, but because he is the Master, and because his Gospel corresponds to the innate purpose of humanity as history reveals it."[135]

Harnack's Christology is really a "Jesusology." He believes Christianity is founded on the unique person Jesus Christ, and especially his teachings. Although the details cannot be known, Harnack believes that the reports about Jesus provide a reliable picture—a picture that can be reclaimed by historical research. Yet, in spite of his historicism, Harnack is reluctant to agree that faith depends on the results of criticism. "Let the plain Bible-reader continue to read his Gospels as he has hitherto read them; for in the end the critic cannot read them otherwise. What the one regards as their true gist and meaning, the other must acknowledge to be such."[136] Thus, Harnack seems to perceive a self-evident truth in Jesus that transcends historical limits and is available in all times to a universal religious experience. Harnack, who wrote hundreds of pages concerning the details of doctrine and the minutia of criticism, could sum up the *Wesen* (the essence) of Christianity in three principles: "Firstly, the kingdom of God and its coming. Secondly, God the Father and the infinite value of the human soul. Thirdly, the higher righteousness and the commandment of love."[137]

Harnack's Historical Works

Harnack's major work is his massive three-volume (seven in English translation) *Lehrbuch der Dogmengeschichte*, published, 1886–90.[138] A shorter version, *Grundriss der Dogmengeschichte*, appeared in 1889. Much of the same material in an abbreviated form is presented in a series of lectures late in Harnack's career on the *Origin of Christian Theology and Ecclesiastical*

---

134. "Christus als Erlöser," in *Aus Wissenschaft und Leben, Reden und Aufsätze,* Neue Folge 2 (Giessen: Alfred Töpelmann, 1911), 92.
135. Quoted by Glick, *Reality of Christianity,* 210.
136. Adolf Harnack, *Christianity and History,* trans. Thomas Bailey Saunders (London: Adam & Charles Black, 1896), 58.
137. Adolf von Harnack, *What Is Christianity?* trans. Thomas Bailey Saunders, HTCL (New York: Harper & Brothers, 1957), 51.
138. Important for NT research, *Lehrbuch der Dogmengeschichte,* vol. 1, *Die Entstehung des kirchlichen Dogmas,* Sammlung Theologischer Lehrbücher (Freiburg i. Br.: J. C. B. Mohr [Paul Siebeck], 1886); Eng. trans.: *History of Dogma,* vol. 1, trans. from 3d ed. by Neil Buchanan (New York: Russell & Russell, 1958).

Dogma.[139] For the purposes of the history of NT research, the English translation of the shorter work, *Outlines of the History of Dogma*, provides an overview.[140] For details of Harnack's discussion of the NT period, the first volume of the English translation of the larger work, *History of Dogma*, provides the primary data, supplemented by material from the lecture series. In the prolegomena to the *Outlines*, Harnack asserts that the study of the history of Christian doctrine can prescribe the antidote for all that ails Christianity:

> The history of dogma, in that it sets forth the process of the origin and development of the dogma, offers the very best means and methods of freeing the Church from dogmatic Christianity, and hastening the inevitable process of emancipation, which began with Augustine. But the history of dogma testifies also to the unity and continuity of the Christian faith in the progress of its history, in so far as it proves that certain fundamental ideas of the Gospel have never been lost and have defied all attacks.[141]

In the larger *History*, Harnack discusses the presuppositions of the history of dogma: the preaching of Jesus, the teaching of Paul, and the theology of John. According to Harnack, Jesus declared that he was himself the Messiah, the unique revealer of God. However, elsewhere Harnack insists, "The Gospel, as Jesus proclaimed it, has to do with the Father only and not with the Son."[142] According to Harnack, the main subject of Jesus' preaching is the kingdom of God—the rule of God to be consummated in the future, but already present for those who accept the message of Jesus. In Harnack's opinion, the separation of the church from Judaism was decisive—an event in which Paul played a leading role. Paul also played a role, according to Harnack, in the shift from religion to theology. "The crucified and risen Christ became the central point of his theology, and not only the central point, but the one source and ruling principle." Harnack, nevertheless, hails the importance of Paul:

> Paulinism is a religious and Christocentric doctrine, more inward and more powerful than any other which has ever appeared in the Church. It stands in the clearest opposition to all merely natural moralism, all righteousness of works, all religious ceremonialism, all Christianity without Christ. . . . One might write a history of dogma as a history of the Pauline reactions in the Church, and in doing so would touch on all the turning points of the history.[143]

---

139. *Die Entstehung der christlichen Theologie und des kirchlichen Dogmas: Sechs Vorlesungen*, Bücherei der christlichen Welt (Gotha: Leopold Plotz, 1927).
140. *Outlines of the History of Dogma*, trans. Edwin Knox Mitchell, with an Introduction by Philip Rieff (Boston: Beacon Press, 1957).
141. Ibid., 7–8.
142. *What Is Christianity?* 144.
143. *History of Dogma* 1:92, 135–36.

With John, Christianity tilted toward Hellenistic thought, although Harnack denies that the background of Johannine theology is Hellenic. "Johannine theology is Christian mysticism; its native soil, however, is not Greek philosophy of religion, but late Jewish piety and mysticism."[144] Harnack thinks the Christ of John to be "far more human than the Christ of Paul and yet far more Divine"; also for John, "history and doctrine are surrounded by a bright cloud of the suprahistorical."[145]

In tracing the genesis of ecclesiastical dogma, Harnack highlights the influence of Gnosticism and Marcion. According to Harnack, "the Gnostic systems represent the acute secularizing or hellenizing of Christianity." Gnosticism's greatest threat, according to Harnack, was not the content of its doctrine, but its conspiracy to change religion into dogma. "The decisive thing is the conversion of the Gospel into a doctrine, into an absolute philosophy of religion, the transforming of the *disciplina Evangelii* into an asceticism based on a dualistic conception, and into a practice of mysteries."[146] Marcion, in his effort to enlist Paul in his rejection of the God of the OT, formulated a canon composed of a collection of Pauline letters and a version of the Gospel of Luke.[147] According to Harnack, Marcion "deserves the credit for having first grasped and actualized the idea of a canonical collection of Christian writings."[148] Harnack imagines that "Marcion was the only Gentile Christian who understood Paul, and even he misunderstood him."[149] Nevertheless, Harnack is sympathetic with Marcion's attempt to reform Christianity in terms of Paul—an attempt also made by Harnack's two other heroes of the history of dogma, Augustine and Luther. Marcion betters them both: he accomplished in the second century what Harnack believed should be done in the nineteenth: the decanonizing of the OT. He writes, "the rejection of the Old Testament in the second century was a mistake which the great Church rightly avoided; to retain it in the sixteenth century was a fate from which the Reformation was not yet able to escape; but still to preserve it in Protestantism as a canonical document since the nineteenth century is the consequence of a religious and ecclesiastical crippling."[150]

In response to Marcion and the Gnostics, the church in the second century took what Harnack believes to be the disastrous steps toward ecclesias-

---

144. *Entstehung der christlichen Theologie*, 59.
145. *History of Dogma* 1:97.
146. Ibid. 1:226, 252.
147. See Adolf von Harnack, *Marcion: Das Evangelium vom fremden Gott: Eine Monographie zur Geschichte der Grundlegung der katholischen Kirche*, 2d ed., TU 45 (Leipzig: J. C. Hinrichs, 1924); Eng. trans.: *Marcion: The Gospel of the Alien God*, trans. John E. Steely and Lyle D. Bierma (Durham, N.C.: Labyrinth, 1990). The English edition omits the lengthy appendix that includes additional discussion of the text and canon of Marcion.
148. *Marcion* (Eng. trans.), 132.
149. *History of Dogma* 1:89.
150. *Marcion* (Eng. trans.), 134.

tical dogma. Although he acknowledges the process of canonization to be a foundation in support of this unfortunate development, he believes the witness of the literature of the NT to the original, dynamic gospel remained a positive force in the continuing history of Christianity. "Therefore the creation of the New Testament after the apostolic age and until today is the greatest and most beneficial fact of church history."[151] Along with the heresies of Marcion and the Gnostics, Harnack believes the spiritual excesses of the Montanists also provoked the church to crystallize the apostolic gospel into the rigid Christianity of creed, canon, and episcopacy. The fatal step, according to Harnack, was taken by the apologists who secularized the gospel and degraded Christianity into dogma. Their Logos Christology, according to Harnack, transformed Jesus into a cosmic essence.

> It signified the transformation of the faith into a system of beliefs with an Hellenic-philosophical cast; . . . it put back of the Christ of history a conceivable Christ, a principle, and reduced the historical figure to a mere appearance; it referred the Christian to "natures" and naturalistic magnitudes, instead of to the Person and to the ethical.[152]

In short, Harnack sees the whole saga of early Christian history as a story of tragic decline.

Harnack's *The Mission and Expansion of Christianity in the First Three Centuries* was originally published in 1906.[153] According to Harnack, the road to Christian mission was paved by the missionary activity of Judaism.[154] Conditions that fostered the expansion of Christianity include the common culture and the political unity of the Roman Empire. Harnack believes the Christian mission had its first impetus in Jesus, who presented an "implicit universalism." Paul, who believed the law had been abolished in Christ, became the leader of the Gentile mission. Harnack identifies features that fostered the propagation of Christianity: monotheism, a hope for the future, an ethic of self-control, a message of love that created community and promoted social welfare. Harnack understands Christianity as "syncretistic"—"a religion which embraces everything." And why, asks Harnack, did Christianity triumph over its rivals?

> The reason was, that Christianity, viewed in its essence, was something simple, something which could blend with coefficients of the most diverse nature,

---

151. *Entstehung der christlichen Theologie*, 73.
152. *Outlines*, 167.
153. *Die Mission und Ausbreitung des Christentums in den ersten drei Jahrhunderten*, 2d ed., 2 vols. (Leipzig: J. C. Hinrichs, 1906); Eng. trans.: *The Mission and Expansion of Christianity in the First Three Centuries*, trans. James Moffatt, HTCL (New York: Harper & Brothers, 1961).
154. That Harnack's understanding of a Jewish mission is historically problematic and motivated by anti-Judaism is demonstrated by Shaye J. D. Cohen, in *The Future of Early Christianity: Essays in Honor of Helmut Koester*, ed. Birger Pearson (Minneapolis: Fortress, 1991), 163–69.

something which, in fact, sought out all such coefficients. For Christianity, in its simplest terms, meant God as the Father, the Judge and the Redeemer of men, revealed in and through Jesus Christ.[155]

Harnack presents the history of the development of church order in his *The Constitution and Law of the Church in the First Two Centuries*.[156] In the earliest Jewish Christian community, Harnack detects a multiplicity of authorities from which a threefold leadership emerged: apostles, prophets, and teachers. In the Gentile churches Harnack believes the earlier charismatic leaders were increasingly replaced by elected officials. Harnack notes that 1 Peter and the Johannine letters recognize the importance of presbyters or elders. According to Harnack, the "bishops" and "presbyters" of the Pastoral Epistles probably represent the same office. In the second century, Harnack reviews the rise of the monarchical bishop and the confirmation of the authority of the bishops by the theory of apostolic succession. In an appendix, he argues against the thesis of Rudolf Sohm that catholic Christianity was the inevitable outcome of early Christianity. Harnack, on the contrary, contends that the development was a distortion, and that catholicism consummated the hellenizing of Christianity.[157]

Harnack's Research on the NT

Harnack made significant contributions in a variety of areas. Several of his essays in text criticism have been collected into a single volume.[158] In an essay on the "Apostolic Decree," Harnack discusses the textual variants in Acts 15:29, in particular, the omission of πνικτῶν ("what is strangled"). He argues that the Eastern text (which includes this term), adopted by most modern editors, represents the original. Harnack discusses the conflict between the decree and Paul's account of the Jerusalem Council in Galatians 2, where Paul insists that no requirement was placed upon him. Noting the later reference to the decree in Acts 21:25, Harnack concludes that the decree was composed after the Council, so that it was not known to Paul until his final visit to Jerusalem. Harnack thinks the corrector of Acts 15:29 (the editor of the Western text) had attempted to harmonize Paul and Luke by removing the reference to "what is strangled," that is, by trans-

---

155. *Mission and Expansion*, 312–13, 513.
156. *Entstehung und Entwickelung der Kirchenverfassung und des Kirchenrechts in den zwei ersten Jahrhunderten* (Leipzig: J. C. Hinrichs, 1910), trans. F. L. Pogson, ed. H. D. A. Major, CTL 31 (London: Williams & Norgate, 1910).
157. In regard to the history of early Christian literature, Harnack published (1893 to 1904) *Geschichte der altchristlichen Literatur bis Eusebius*, 2d ed. Kurt Aland, 2 vols. in 4 (Leipzig: J. C. Hinrichs, 1958)—a book that presents critical introductions to early Christian apocryphal documents. Harnack had a special interest in the Didache; see his *Die Lehre der Zwölf Apostel, nebst Untersuchungen zur ältesten Geschichte der Kirchenverfassung und des Kirchenrechts*, TU 2 (1886) 1, 2 (Leipzig: J. C. Hinrichs, 1884); idem, *Die Apostellehre und die jüdischen beiden Wege*, 2d ed. (Leipzig: J. C. Hinrichs, 1896).
158. *Studien zur Geschichte des Neuen Testaments und der alten Kirche: I Zur neutestamentlichen Textkritik*, Arbeiten zur Kirchengeschichte (Berlin: Walter de Gruyter, 1931).

forming the decree into a moral admonition rather than a ritual requirement. In his later work on Acts, Harnack abandoned this position.[159]

A number of Harnack's works in historical criticism have been collected and published under the general title *Beiträge zur Einleitung in das Neue Testament*. These have been translated and published as a series titled *New Testament Studies*. In the first volume, *Luke the Physician*, Harnack argues that the tradition about the authorship of Luke and Acts is correct.[160] Harnack thinks the prologue of Luke originally included the name of the author, but that the name was suppressed so as to conform to the pattern of the anonymity of the Gospels. On the basis of shreds of evidence from the NT, Harnack surmises information about Luke: he was a Greek by birth, a person of culture, and a native of Antioch. Harnack presents a detailed linguistic analysis by which he attempts to prove that the "we-sections" employ the same vocabulary and style as the rest of Acts. As to the troubling discrepancies between Acts and the Pauline Epistles, Harnack points out that much of the narrative describes events in which Luke was not present. Harnack also charges that Luke, like so many other ancient theologians, was a Paulinist who did not really understand Paul. In an appendix, Harnack contends that Luke was indeed a physician—an identification supposedly confirmed by the use of "medical" language. Among several examples, Harnack notes the account of the healing of the lame man at the temple gate (Acts 3:7) in which "Dr. Luke" uses the rare word σφυδρά (ankles)—a technical term for the condyles of the leg bones.

The second volume of the *New Testament Studies* discusses *The Sayings of Jesus*. Essentially, this is an analysis of the discourse source used by Matthew and Luke, that is, the "Q" document. Harnack begins with a meticulous stylistic analysis of the non-Marcan texts that Matthew and Luke have in common, and concludes that Matthew more faithfully represents Q. Primarily following Matthew, Harnack produces a reconstruction of Q. He proceeds to analyze the reconstructed document in order to demonstrate that Q has a distinctive and homogeneous vocabulary and style. Discussing the characteristics and subject matter of the reconstructed Q, Harnack concludes that "Q is a compilation of discourses and sayings of our Lord, the arrangement of which has no reference to the Passion, with an horizon which is as good as absolutely bounded by Galilee, without any clearly discernible bias, whether apologetic, didactic, ecclesiastical, national or anti-national." Harnack believes that Q represents early, authentic tradition, and that it is probably earlier and often more reliable than Mark. Harnack believes Q was originally written in Aramaic in Palestine before 70, probably by

---

159. See p. 131, below.
160. *New Testament Studies: I Luke the Physician: The Author of the Third Gospel and the Acts of the Apostles*, trans. J. R. Wilkinson, 2d ed., CTL (London: Williams & Norgate, 1909).

Matthew. Taken together, Harnack, like Holtzmann, believes Q and Mark provide a solid foundation for reconstructing the teachings and life of the historical Jesus.

> Our knowledge of the teaching and the history of our Lord, in their main features at least, thus depends upon two authorities independent of one another, yet composed at nearly the same time. Where they agree their testimony is strong, and they agree often and on important points. On the rock of their united testimony the assault of destructive critical views, however necessary these are to easily self-satisfied research, will ever be shattered to pieces.[161]

In the third of the *New Testament Studies*, Harnack returns to one of his favorite documents, *The Acts of the Apostles*. "To the sacred history of Jesus was now added a second part of this history, and side by side with the Gospel narrative style, which already possessed a fixed type, there was now established the type of this new history!" Harnack believes the author not only created a genre, he also contributed to the whole idea of NT canonicity. "Accordingly St. Luke is really the creator of the New Testament, and in the same sense the creator of the Apostolic, side by side with the Evangelic tradition."[162] Of special importance is Harnack's discussion of the sources of Acts. The "we-sections," he believes, are made up of written notes from Luke's diary. Chapter 1, chapter 2, and 5:17-42 Harnack attributes to a source he names "Jerusalem B"—unwritten, unreliable tradition, probably drawn from Hellenistic circles. "Jerusalem A," or the Jerusalem-Caesarean source (evident in 3:1—5:6; 8:5-40; 9:31—11:18; and 12:1-23) Harnack believes to be more reliable; it originated with Philip (and perhaps his daughters) and is partly written (in Aramaic) and partly oral. The "Jerusalem-Antiochean" source (6:1—8:4; 11:19-30; 12:25—15:35), according to Harnack, is characterized by vivid narrative, and is highly reliable. Also in this volume, Harnack notes how his position has changed in regard to the apostolic decree.[163] He now reads the text and its terms as offering purely moral instruction, so that no tension exists between the decree and Paul's account of the Jerusalem Council or his instruction to the Corinthians regarding meat offered to idols. Thus, Harnack adopts the very harmonization he had earlier charged to the editor of the Western text.

The fourth of the *New Testament Studies* considers *The Date of the Acts and of the Synoptic Gospels*. In regard to Luke's presentation of the Jewishness of

---

161. *New Testament Studies II: The Sayings of Jesus: The Second Source of St. Matthew and St. Luke*, trans. J. R. Wilkinson, CTL (New York: G. P. Putnam's Sons, 1908), 171, 251.

162. *New Testament Studies III: The Acts of the Apostles*, trans. J. R. Wilkinson; CTL 27 (New York: G. P. Putnam's Sons, 1909), xvi, 301. For a review and positive appraisal of Harnack's work on Acts, see W. Ward Gasque, *A History of the Interpretation of the Acts of the Apostles* (Peabody, Mass.: Hendrickson, 1989), 146–55. More critical, especially in regard to Harnack's anti-Judaism, is Joseph B. Tyson, *Luke, Judaism, and the Scholars: Critical Approaches to Luke-Acts* (Columbia, S.C.: University of South Carolina Press, 1999), 30–42.

163. See pp. 129–30, above.

Paul, Harnack finds nothing incongruous in Paul's participation in a Nazarite vow (Acts 21:22-26) or in the report of his behavior before the Sanhedrin (Acts 23:1-10). "Both from the Pauline epistles and from the Acts of the Apostles we learn that the Apostle came into direct conflict with Judaism *just because he conceded too much to Judaism.* His Jewish limitations were his ruin!" Taking up his earlier argument that Paul left Rome after a first imprisonment to engage in further ministry, Harnack contends that Acts was written shortly after that time, that is, in the early 60s. Having pushed the date of Acts back before 64, Harnack is forced to adopt an early date for the Synoptics. In regard to Mark, Harnack believes that he had written an early version of his Gospel in the 50s, and showed a copy of it to Luke in Rome around 60—a copy that Luke used in writing is own Gospel at about this time. Mark, according the Harnack, later revised his Gospel, which was used by the author of Matthew, writing around 70. In support of these early dates, Harnack answers the objection that legendary material in the Gospels represents later tradition. For example, Harnack argues that Matthew's story of the virgin birth did not have its source in Hellenistic mythology, but that it arose when Isa. 7:14 was interpreted messianically. Thus, he thinks that the idea of a supernatural birth of the Messiah was already present in Judaism, and that it appeared early in Christianity. "Our conclusion from this survey is therefore: that we have found nothing to upset the verdict, to which we have been led by critical investigation of the Acts of the Apostles, that the second and third gospels, as well as the Acts, were composed while St Paul was still alive, and that the first gospel came into being only a few years later."[164]

The last two volumes of the *New Testament Studies* provide striking examples of Harnack's scholarly creativity. In *Bible Reading in the Early Church*, he musters evidence to argue that the early Christians—like the pious Jews before them—read the Bible at home.[165] In *The Origin of the New Testament and the Most Important Consequences of the New Creation*, Harnack transcends the conventional history of canon to ask questions about the purpose and meaning of collecting the NT books.[166] For example, he asks why the church created a second collection of sacred writings to be placed beside the OT Scriptures. He answers: the concern to hallow the life and teachings of Jesus, the need to make an authoritative selection from the great variety of early Christian writings, the intent to counter the canon of Marcion and the Gnostics, and the desire to restrict authoritative revelation to the apostolic

---

164. *New Testament Studies IV: The Date of the Acts and of the Synoptic Gospels,* trans. J. R. Wilkinson, CTL 33 (London: Williams & Norgate, 1911), 88, 162.

165. *New Testament Studies V: Bible Reading in the Early Church,* trans. J. R. Wilkinson, CTL 36 (London: Williams & Norgate,1912).

166. *New Testament Studies VI: The Origin of the New Testament and the Most Important Consequences of the New Creation,* trans. J. R. Wilkinson, CTL 45 (London: Williams & Norgate, 1925).

witness in face of the Montanist claim to new disclosures of the Spirit. Harnack also asks why the NT contains four Gospels rather than one. In answer, he argues that the selection was a compromise among dominant churches, each of which had adopted at particular Gospel: Jerusalem, Matthew; Rome, Mark; Corinth, Luke; Ephesus, John. The four were kept separate, rather than being merged into one, according to Harnack, because they were believed to represent four distinct witnesses to apostolic tradition.

In general, Harnack believes the formation of the canon was a mixed blessing. For one thing, the process of canonization relegated some documents to oblivion and thereby obscured the history of the origin of early Christian literature. Also, when the authority of the NT was formalized, Christianity ran the risk of becoming a religion of the book, encouraging the distortion of the vital message into dogma. Although canonization brought an end to the multiplying of legends about Christian origins, Harnack believes it provided sources for an exegesis that could spin out new theological myths—fantasies about Christology and the Trinity. On the other hand, he believes the existence of concrete documents encouraged empirical investigation. Also, canonization raised Pauline Christianity to place of honor—a kind of Christianity that could provide the ferment for repeated reformation within the church. Best of all, according to Harnack, the NT fostered a simple, vital religion that prevented Christian doctrine from deteriorating into philosophy of religion.[167]

Harnack made significant contributions to the study of the Pauline Epistles. Among the most important is his monograph on the collecting of the letters. Harnack believes a collection of ten epistles was made in the last quarter of the first century, and expanded to thirteen by the end of that period. He thinks the collection was probably made first at Corinth, and began with 1 Corinthians; the later collection, including the Pastorals, Harnack believes was probably made in Asia. He is inclined to accept all thirteen letters as authentic, though he is cautious about the Pastorals. "Apart from an arbitrary critical decision, one can therefore assert neither the genuineness nor the ingenuineness of these letters as they exist."[168] Harnack believes the first recognition of the Pauline Letters as canonical was by Marcion. This was true of the larger church by 200, according to Harnack, when

---

167. Besides the *New Testament Studies*, Harnack published many short writings (articles, reviews, letters, lectures, etc.) that have been collected into seven volumes, under the general title *Reden und Aufsätze* (1906–30). A small volume of selections from these collections was published in 1951: Adolf von Harnack, *Ausgewählte Reden und Aufsätze*, ed. Agnes von Zahn-Harnack and Axel von Harnack (Berlin: Walter de Gruyter, 1951).

168. *Die Briefsammlung des Apostels Paulus und die anderen vorkonstantinischen christlichen Briefsammlungen: Sechs Vorlesungen aus der altkirchlichen Literaturgeschichte* (Leipzig: J. C. Hinrichs, 1926), 14–15. In his essay "Die Adresse des Epheserbriefs des Paulus," SPAW 37 (1910): 696–709, Harnack argues that Ephesians was originally sent to Laodicea; the words "in Ephesus," were added, he thinks, when the collection of the thirteen epistles was made there.

Romans was placed at the beginning, references to Rome were omitted, and a non-Pauline doxology (16:25-27) was added.

Another example of Harnack's creative historical imagination can be seen in his essay on the Transfiguration and Paul's report of the resurrection appearances.[169] In this essay, Harnack analyzes the early tradition about the resurrection of Christ recorded in 1 Cor. 15:3-8. On the basis of a meticulous investigation of terms and grammatical structure, he concludes that the original tradition had two parts: "Christ died for our sins according to the Scriptures and was buried; Christ was raised according to the Scriptures and was seen by Cephas." To this earliest form, Harnack believes the words "then by the Twelve" were added. The developing tradition, Harnack thinks, displayed two parallels: "he appeared to Cephas, then to the Twelve; he appeared to James, then to all the Apostles." Harnack thinks "the Twelve" and "all the Apostles" refer to one and the same group. Thus, he surmises, two separate traditions have been combined: the first, a Galilean tradition followed by Mark and Matthew; the second, a Jerusalem tradition followed by Luke and John. In a fascinating excursus, Harnack presents what he takes to be the suppression of Peter's role as the first witness of the resurrection. Although the priority of Peter is confirmed by Paul and Mark, Harnack believes Luke and John diminish the role of Peter in their accounts of the resurrection.[170]

In an intriguing article, Harnack argues that Prisca is probably the author of Hebrews. He begins by analysis of hints about authorship detected in the document. For example, the use of "we" indicates that the author was once a teacher of the group addressed (which Harnack takes to be a house church in Rome). The use of "we" sometimes indicates a plural authorship, but the alternate use of "I" suggests a primary writer. The data also indicate that the author belonged to the circle of Paul, and had been associated with Timothy. Harnack believes Prisca meets all of these qualifications. Harnack thinks Prisca's authorship was suppressed because she was a woman. "But he who takes offense that a woman wrote an epistle that stands in the 'New Testament' may also take offense that Paul named her a colleague and said in praising her that 'all churches of the Gentiles' should be obliged to thank her; he may also find it offensive that she as teacher reclaimed Apollos."[171]

---

169. "Die Verklärungsgeschichte Jesu, der Bericht des Paulus (I. Kor. 15,3ff.) und die beiden Christusvisionen des Petrus," SPAW 7 (1922): 62–80 (repr., Berlin: Akademie der Wissenschaften [Walter de Gruyter], 1922).

170. For another contribution to the study of the tradition about Peter, see Adolf von Harnack, *Petrus im Urteil der Kirchenfeinde des Altertums*, Aus der Festgabe für Karl Müller zum siebzigsten Geburtstag (Tübingen: J. C. B. Mohr [Paul Siebeck], 1922).

171. "Probabilia über die Adresse und den Verfasser des Hebräerbriefs," *ZNW* 1 (1900): 40–41. Harnack's recognition of the importance of women in the early Christian tradition is underscored in his *Meditations*; two of these are based on Matt. 15:22-28 (*Scholar's Testament*,

Looking back over Harnack's work is like viewing the Grand Canyon—one is overwhelmed by the sheer magnitude and dazzled by the variegated details. In regard to the critical issues, Harnack made some distinctive contributions: analysis of the sources of Acts, authorship of Hebrews by Prisca. Although some of his critical judgments seem conservative, they largely serve his liberal agenda. Central to Harnack's theology is the teaching of Jesus in which the kingdom of God is construed as ethical. Thus, he dates Q early and attributes it to apostolic authorship. All three of the Synoptics, he thinks, antedate 70, and provide a reliable record of Jesus' religious life. This supreme religion of Jesus Harnack finds continued by Paul—the Paul who opposes Jewish legalism and affirms a universal religion. After this high point in religious history, Harnack detects a decline—the Hellenizing influence of Gnosticism, the metaphysical concerns of the apologists, the ecclesiastical rigidity of early catholicism. A surprising hero appears in the figure of Marcion, who emulated Paul, abandoned the Hebrew Bible, and created the NT canon. The fixing of the canon Harnack views as a mixed blessing, since, on the one hand, it preserves the record of the religion of Jesus, and, on the other, it provided orthodoxy with quarry for dogma. Yet, for all this complex reconstruction, this dedication to meticulous criticism, Harnack's religious piety prevails: his Jesus is the simple Jesus; his religion is ethics; his God is created in his own image.

SUMMARY

The NT research reviewed in this chapter represents the triumph of liberalism—the realization of the ideal of the Enlightenment. According to this ideal, knowledge is to be acquired by empirical investigation and rational assessment; truth is to be discovered by scientific investigation. Religious liberals, though they concentrate on this world, do not ignore the transcendent; they believe in the God who created the world, who functions in human history. The scholars described in this chapter, from Ritschl to Harnack, believe a human, fallible record of God's work in history is to be found in the Bible. The high point of biblical revelation, according to this view, is Jesus—not perceived as a metaphysical member of the Trinity—but as a person of unique religious experience. The liberal Jesus thought

---

81–82; 192–98). Harnack was also concerned with the application of NT teaching to other social issues and the problem of war; see Adolf Harnack and Wilhelm Herrmann, *Essays on the Social Gospel*, trans. G. M. Craik, ed. Maurice A. Canney, CTL 18 (London: Williams & Norgate, 1907); Adolf von Harnack, *Militia Christi: Die christliche Religion und der Soldatenstand in den ersten drei Jahrhunderten* (Darmstadt: Wissenschaftliche Buchgesellschaft, 1963); Eng. trans.: *Militia Christi: The Christian Religion and the Military in the First Three Centuries*, trans. David McInnes Gracie (Philadelphia: Fortress, 1981).

himself to be the Messiah, but in a non-Jewish, spiritual way; the liberal Jesus proclaimed the kingdom of God, but in a nonapocalyptic, ethical way. Moreover, some of the early disciples of Jesus, despite their ethnic and religious limitations, understood and perpetuated the spiritual and ethical religion of Jesus. Although they expressed this religion in different ways, they were thought to be in essential agreement. According to this view, Paul was not in real conflict with Peter, though Paul more clearly articulated the universal religion of Christianity.

So important was the study of this religion that the scholars perfected their linguistic and analytical skills, and advanced in all the disciplines of NT research: text criticism (especially B. Weiss), higher criticism (especially Holtzmann), source criticism (especially Harnack). In regard to the Gospels, these scholars affirmed the reliable tradition about Jesus by adopting the two-document hypothesis—Mark as witness of Peter, and Q as an early sayings source, perhaps written by Matthew. The Gospel of John remained a point of contention: Ritschl, Reuss, Weizsäcker, and Weiss affirming its historical reliability; Holtzmann and Harnack identifying its theological intent and mystical character. The Acts of the Apostles, once viewed as a theological fiction by Tübingen, had been rehabilitated, ascribed to a participant in the events, and dated early, especially by Harnack. The claim of authenticity for the Pauline Letters had been facilitated by theories of development in Pauline thought—notably by Reuss and Weiss—a development that allowed Paul to escape from Jewish apocalypticism into universal religion (Holtzmann). Holtzmann, however, rode the wave of the future, designating the Pastorals and Ephesians as pseudonymous. The scholars debated, too, about historical backgrounds, hoping to avoid the taint of Hellenism (Harnack) while trying to preserve continuity with the HB, unscathed by Jewish legalism (Ritschl, Holtzmann). Most important, all of these scholars had unswerving devotion to the historical-critical method. Where results differed, they supposed presuppositions had intruded, or that the method had not been applied with sufficient rigor. Yet from the perspective of distance, how inadequate the method appeared to be—depicting a Jesus who looked out of place in ancient Galilee, but quite at home in nineteenth-century Berlin!

4

The Return of Skepticism

Europe at the turn of the nineteenth century was on a collision course with crisis. The strident nationalism and imperialism of the preceding generation had advanced, supported by larger armies with bigger weapons. The nations lived in the tension of an uneasy balance of power. The Triple Alliance of Germany, Austria, and Italy was countered by the Triple Entente of France, Russia, and England. The British, once at ease in isolation, had embraced their continental allies, alarmed by the expanding power of the German navy. These political tensions were sustained by scientific and industrial development. Science moved out of the laboratory into the public forum, applying theory to practical problems. The resulting technologies could build monuments to human achievement, such as the sturdy Eiffel Tower, standing 984 feet above the Paris landscape. Formerly the domain of the experts, science became popular with the masses. The fiction of H. G. Wells, reminiscent of the fancies of Jules Verne, was widely read. Yet, utopia, envisioned by social Darwinism, had not appeared. Poverty and social evils, like the phantom of the opera, were hidden, but not unheard, beneath the streets of the city.

The democratizing of science paralleled developments in political and social progress. Education advanced. Literacy increased. New means of communication and transportation—the wireless, the extending railways—provided a new freedom of information and movement. In contrast to the massive powers of nation and empire, a proud individualism arose. Individual persons, confident in their own knowledge, began to question the old forms and formulas, the hierarchies and traditional powers. In France, the injustice exposed in the Dreyfus affair made citizens suspicious of the government. Also in France, anticlericalism, together with increasing resistance to papal influence, led to the separation of church and state in 1905.

Culture, too, was showing signs of crisis. In philosophy and religion, the older idealism and supernaturalism were eroding. A new humanism emerged in Ludwig Feuerbach's substitution of anthropology for theology. Auguste Comte, abandoning traditional metaphysics, embraced a positivism of science. Nature, not the supernatural, became the primary concern. Pragmatism, like technology, claimed that what worked was true. According to Friedrich Nietzsche, virtually everything that culture had produced, including God, was dead. In literature and the visual arts, the old conventions were betrayed. Émile Zola's novels displayed a blatant naturalism, and impressionist paintings blurred the conventional images. For Claude Monet, the Rouen cathedral took many shapes, none of them in realistic focus. Defying harmonic tradition, Igor Stravinsky's *Rite of Spring*, with its crashing dissonance, provoked a riot when it was performed in Paris in 1913.

NT research was not untouched by these movements. To be sure, confidence in the worldview of the Enlightenment and the reliability of historical criticism remained unshaken. Yet, refinement and rigorous application of the critical method—in the service of secular presuppositions—led to a skepticism reminiscent of Reimarus.[1] Could the orthodox tradition that confirmed the NT canon be trusted? Could the late and fragmentary sources of the Gospels provide the basis for a biography of Jesus? For many observers, the liberal Jesus of the nineteenth century appeared to be dead. Could some feature of his personality or teaching be resurrected? Had the Fourth Gospel transformed him into the gnostic savior of a Hellenistic Christian cult? And what of Paul? Was he, rather than Jesus, the real founder of Christianity?

MILITANT SKEPTICISM:
FRANZ OVERBECK (1837–1905)

Life and Thought

Like an unconscious sleepwalker, Overbeck awoke in mid-career to find himself in theology; he was never quite sure how he got there.[2] Born in St. Petersburg, Overbeck, with his German Lutheran father and French Catholic mother, moved to Dresden in 1849. He began his university education at Leipzig in 1856, and later studied at Göttingen and Berlin. Over-

---

1. *HNTR* 1:170–77.
2. See Martin Henry, *Franz Overbeck: Theologian? Religion and History in the Thought of Franz Overbeck* (Frankfurt am Main: Peter Lang, 1995); Walter Nigg, *Franz Overbeck: Versuch einer Würdigung* (Munich: C. H. Beck, 1931); Arnold Pfeiffer, *Franz Overbeck's Kritik des Christentums*, Studien zur Theologie und Geistesgeschichte des Neunzehnten Jahrhunderts 15 (Göttingen: Vandenhoeck & Ruprecht, 1975); Hermann-Peter Eberlein, *Theologie als Scheitern? Franz Overbecks Geschichte mit der Geschichte*, Theologie in der Blauen Eule 3 (Essen: Die Blaue Eule, 1989).

beck began his teaching career at Jena (1864), but in 1870 moved to Basel, where students had petitioned for a freethinker to be named to the faculty. Overbeck fit the bill, but tempered his radicalism. "As a professor of theology I have kept my basic unbelief to myself, both on the rostrum and in all my relationships with the students committed to my care."[3] At Basel, Overbeck made a lasting friendship with Nietzsche. They lived in the same rooming house for a time, and when Nietzsche suffered an emotional collapse in Italy, Overbeck rushed to his side and brought him back to Basel for treatment. Overbeck shared Nietzsche's agnosticism and disdain of Christianity and modern culture. "I am no theologian and therefore no Christian," he wrote. "I may indeed say that Christianity has cost me my life. Insofar as I never possessed it and only through 'misunderstanding' became a theologian, I have used my life in order to become completely free from it."[4]

In point of view, Overbeck considered himself a member of the Tübingen school without the Hegelian framework. He was agnostic about metaphysical matters, but adopted an ontology of history.[5] For Overbeck, history displays an ontological uniformity and a closed system of reality. Thus miracles, assuming a supernatural cause, are for Overbeck impossible. Nevertheless, he sees history as a developing process; in analogy with biology, it flourishes and dies. A Christianity that claims to be eternal and unchanging, according to Overbeck, is dead. When Christianity at its origin was alive, it was, in Overbeck's opinion, a world-denying religion. Efforts by theologians to accommodate it to the developing culture have utterly destroyed it.[6] In his inaugural address at Basel, Overbeck took an independent stance: against the orthodox, he affirmed historical criticism, but he refused to endorse liberal Christianity.[7] For Overbeck, the basic problem is the historical understanding of early Christianity. In the early church, Overbeck finds a failure to understand the primitive church historically.

---

3. Quoted in Werner Georg Kümmel, *The New Testament: The History of the Investigation of Its Problems*, trans. S. McLean Gilmour and Howard C. Kee (New York: Abingdon, 1972), 203.

4. "Christenthum (mein)," in Franz Overbeck, *Werke und Nachlass: IV Kirchenlexicon Texte Ausgewählte Artikel A-I*, ed. Barbara von Reibnitz (Stuttgart: J. B. Metzler, 1995), 220, 223. See John Elbert Wilson, "Die Zweideutigkeit in Franz Overbecks Aussagen über seinen Unglauben," *TZ* 40 (1984): 211–20.

5. See Johann-Christoph Emmelius, *Tendenzkritik und Formengeschichte: Der Beitrag Franz Overbecks zur Auslegung der Apostelgeschichte im 19. Jahrhundert*, Forschungen zur Kirchen- und Dogmengeschichte 27 (Göttingen: Vandenhoeck & Ruprecht, 1975), 19–52.

6. See Carl Albrecht Bernoulli's foreword in Franz Overbeck, *Christentum und Kultur: Gedanken und Anmerkungen zur modernen Theologie*, ed. Carl Albrecht Bernoulli (1919, repr., Darmstadt: Wissenschaftliche Buchgesellschaft, 1963), vii–xxxviii; new ed.: *Werke und Nachlass: Kirchenlexicon Materialien: Christentum und Kultur* 6/1, ed. Barbara von Reibnitz (Stuttgart: J. B. Metzler, 1996), 3–31.

7. "Über Entstehung und Recht einer rein historischen Betrachtung der Neutestamentlichen Schriften in der Theologie," in *Werke und Nachlass: I Schriften bis 1873*, ed. Ekkehard W. Stegemann und Niklaus Peter (Stuttgart: J. B. Metzler, 1994), 75–106.

Instead, the patristic writers, in their passion to canonize, retreated into allegory and paid homage to dogma. In the Reformation, Overbeck believes historical concern was subverted to a dogmatic understanding of Scripture. Within the nineteenth century, he finds a proper concern with history, and with F. C. Baur, the proper practice of a "pure" historical method.[8] According to Overbeck, "pure" historical method is research free from dogmatic and subjective presuppositions.

Overbeck's skepticism reaches a point of no return in his essay "On the Christianity of Contemporary Theology."[9] Basically an attack on the theology of his day, this essay raises the question, What can properly be called "Christian"? By means of historical investigation, Overbeck discerns that the original, authentic Christianity was eschatological and world-denying. In the later struggle between faith and knowledge, the early theologians of the church borrowed from Greek philosophy and rhetoric to develop an apologetic. The results, in Overbeck's opinion, were the secularization and dissolution of Christianity—a process that he believes has been going on ever since. "It could be said that Christianity is the embalmed form in which Antiquity has come into our own time."[10] Turning to contemporary theology, Overbeck rebukes the futile effort of apologetic theology to defend myths and dogmas. Theologians of this persuasion, he thinks, live in a *Wolkskuckucksheim*—a cloudy cuckoo land. As to the liberals, their concern to found Christianity on the ethical teaching of Jesus is confounded by the apocalyptic and ascetic character of primitive Christianity. In sum, Overbeck concludes that none of the contemporary theologies can be properly called Christian: they miss or distort the original vitality of the Christian religion.

Overbeck's NT Research

Overbeck's major NT work is on the Acts of the Apostles.[11] In 1870, he published the fourth edition of de Wette's commentary on Acts, adding a new introduction and expanding the commentary to triple its size.[12] The intro-

---

8. *HNTR* 1:258–69.
9. "Über die Christlichkeit unserer heutigen Theologie," in *Werke und Nachlass: I*, 167–318.
10. Quoted in Robert B. Luehrs, "Franz Overbeck and the Theologian as Antichrist," *Katallagete* 4 (1973): 18.
11. For a survey of Overbeck's NT research, see Philipp Vielhauer, "Franz Overbeck und die neutestamentliche Wissenschaft," in *Aufsätze zum Neuen Testament*, Theologische Bücherei 31 (Munich: Chr. Kaiser, 1965), 235–52; originally published in *EvT* 10 (1950/51): 193–207; differing from Vielhauer at many points: Martin Rese, "Fruchtbare Missverständnisse: Franz Overbeck und die neutestamentliche Wissenschaft," in *Franz Overbecks unerledigte Anfragen an das Christentum*, ed. Rudolf Brändle and Ekkehard W. Stegemann (Munich: Chr. Kaiser, 1988), 211–26.
12. *Kurze Erklärung der Apostelgeschichte von Dr. W. M. L. DeWette, vierte Auflage bearbeitet und stark erweitert von F. O.* (Leipzig, 1870). See Emmelius, *Tendenzkritik und Formengeschichte;* W. Ward Gasque, *A History of the Interpretation of the Acts of the Apostles* (Peabody, Mass.: Hendrickson, 1989), 80–86.

duction is available to the English reader as the introduction to the translation of Zeller's commentary on Acts.[13] Overbeck begins with his understanding of the plan and purpose of the document. Acts does not, in Overbeck's opinion, offer a reliable chronology. "Hence it follows, as a matter of course, that every attempt to draw up the narrative of the Acts under a complete chronological system is not simply hopeless, but even does violence to the nature of this narrative, and imposes on it a burden foreign to the whole drift of it." The purpose of Acts, according to Overbeck, is to be understood in relation to conflicts in the early church, although not in terms of Tübingen's reconstruction. Overbeck believes the purpose is to defend the author's Judaized Gentile Christianity by presenting Paul (whose true Gentile Christianity has been forgotten) as an advocate of Jewish ideas and practices. According to Overbeck, "the peculiar Gospel of Paul is not presupposed but annihilated."[14]

In regard to sources, Overbeck believes the "we-sections" represent a source used by the author. Although Luke may have been the author of this "memoir," Overbeck believes the use of the first person probably betrays the author's attempt to pose as a travel companion of Paul. Given the freedom with which the author bends the material to fit his purpose, a highly reliable history, according to Overbeck, is not to be expected. The date of Acts, indicated by the development of church order and opposition to Gnosticism, Overbeck puts between 120 and 140. The author, Overbeck thinks, is an unnamed Gentile Christian, probably writing from Asia Minor. In his commentary, Overbeck sees the early chapters as loaded with myth and legend. Later in Acts, he believes Paul's mission is apologetically presented. Overbeck detects the Judaizing of Paul in the narratives that present him in parallel with Peter. According to Overbeck, the author is anti-Jewish, but devoted to a Judaized Gentile Christianity.

Overbeck's distinctive view of early Christianity is developed in his seminal essay "On the Beginnings of Patristic Literature."[15] In this work, Overbeck presents a sharp distinction between *Urliteratur* (primitive literature) and patristic literature. The writings of the NT and the apostolic fathers constitute, according to Overbeck, *Urliteratur*. Overbeck believes this literature has its own distinctive forms: Gospels, acts, apocalypses—although he thinks only the Gospel genre to be a Christian creation. For Overbeck, *Urliteratur* has purely religious interests, and is not addressed to the outside

---

13. "Introduction to the Acts of the Apostles," in *The Contents and Origin of the Acts of the Apostles, Critically Investigated, by Edward Zeller,* trans. Joseph Dare, Theological Translation Fund (London: Williams & Norgate, 1875) 1:2–81.
14. Ibid. 1:12, 28–29.
15. "Über die Anfänge der patristischen Literatur," *Historische Zeitschrift* 48 (1882; repr., Darmstadt: Wissenschaftliche Buchgesellschaft, 1954); summarized by Emmelius, *Tendenzkritik und Formengeschichte,* 163–71.

world. He thinks the formalizing of the canon (around 150–80) brought an end to *Urliteratur;* after that time, no Christian Gospels or epistles could be written. Patristic literature, according to Overbeck's scheme, begins with the apologists. He thinks this literature addresses the heathen world and borrows forms from secular culture; it is superficial; it does not express original, authentic Christianity. By way of contrast, Overbeck believes *Urliteratur* belongs to *Urgeschichte*—the era of original Christianity, characterized by originality and intensity of religious experience. *Urliteratur,* then, is *Gegenwartsgeschichte*—the story of the present, the immediate. This original, vital religious experience, in Overbeck's opinion, should not be intellectualized.[16]

Overbeck's hostility to patristic exegesis is apparent in a university address (1877) on the theme "The Conflict between Paul and Peter in Antioch." According to Overbeck, the text in Galatians 2 does not present the full account of what happened. It concludes with Paul's rebuke of Peter, but does not report the outcome of the conflict. Overbeck thinks this abbreviated account has opened the door to patristic apologetic, namely, to misconstrue the supposed silence of Peter as acquiescence to the opinion of Paul and proof of a Petrine–Pauline compromise. "On the basis of this flimsy foundation, the church fathers with prejudice have erected the peculiar exegetical structure with which they have defended their view of the inner harmony of the canon and the agreement of the apostles with each other in opposition to the narrative of Paul about his conflict with Peter in Antioch."[17] According to Overbeck, the sins of the fathers have been visited upon the children: the same sort of apologetic harmonizing is practiced in his day.

Variations on the theme can be heard in Overbeck's writings on the *History of the Canon.* He published two essays on the canon, a first on the canonization of the Epistle to the Hebrews, a second on the Muratorian canon. In the former, Overbeck contends that the process of canonization has obliterated true historical understanding. At the outset, he notes that Hebrews was used by 1 Clement without identification of the author. Also, the superscription over the canonical edition of the document reads "to the Hebrews"—a designation that the content of the letter belies. According to Overbeck's reconstruction, the epistle was included in the canon without its original introduction, which, he thinks, had been suppressed in order to conceal the true historical setting. Also, he believes an ending had been added to the original that was contrived to make Hebrews appear to be an epistle of Paul. In the history of canonization, the epistle was early accepted as Pauline in the east, but in the west, it was not accepted as Pauline until

---

16. See Henry, *Overbeck,* 184–203.
17. "Über die Auffassung des Streits des Paulus mit Petrus in Antiochien (Gal. 2,11ff.) bei den Kirchenvätern," in *Werke und Nachlass: II Schriften bis 1880,* ed. Ekkehard W. Stegemann and Rudolf Brändle (Stuttgart: J. B. Metzler, 1994) 2:236.

the fourth century. "This history of the reception of Hebrews by the ancient church clearly shows how the complete eclipse of the knowledge of its origin made possible its canonization." In short, Overbeck believes Hebrews was canonized as what it was not; it was neither addressed to the Hebrews nor written by Paul.[18]

At Overbeck's death in 1905, he left a legacy of correspondence and scholarly writings—some twenty thousand pages of material that he called the *Kirchenlexicon*. This consisted of a collection of remarks, notes, and references that Overbeck kept in file boxes, arranged according to various topics, titles, and names.[19] Before his death, Overbeck turned these over to his former student and friend, Carl Albrecht Bernoulli. In the course of time, Bernoulli sorted through this material, arranged it under particular topics, edited it extensively, and produced book-length publications. Among these is an extensive work (more than five hundred pages) on the Fourth Gospel. The book begins with a survey of recent research, devoting a chapter to Baur. Next, Bernoulli presents Overbeck's material on the Johannine tradition. In Overbeck's opinion, the tradition of John's residence in Asia Minor and the development of the Johannine school represents a fictitious effort to promote apostolic authorship. "In short, the 'school of John' is the perfect example of a fantasy." Regarding authorship, Overbeck believes the attention to the "beloved disciple" betrays a conscious effort of the author to present himself as the apostle John. "The pseudonymity of the Gospel belongs to its essential nature, that is, it is a result of its fundamental character, namely, a consequence of the fact that the Fourth Gospel, in contrast to the other Gospels, is a literary creation." Overbeck continues, "The Fourth Gospel can in no way be an eyewitness report of the gospel story, and for the present that is the cornerstone of the criticism of the Gospel." According to Overbeck, John is not a supplementary Gospel. "The Fourth Gospel is indeed a complete Gospel (20:31) that is dependent on and uses the Synoptics; but in doing so it has no other purpose than to transform and raise their tradition to a higher form of the gospel story."[20]

Another of Bernoulli's creations, *Christentum und Kultur*, covers everything from ancient history to modern culture and includes a chapter on early Christianity. In a section on Jesus, Overbeck compares the Galilean to St. Francis, who, according to Overbeck, actually surpassed Jesus in commending the message of peace. However, in comparison with Paul, Overbeck

---

18. "Zur Geschichte des Kanons: Zwei Abhandlungen," in ibid., 459.
19. For a new edition of this material, collected and arranged alphabetically, see Franz Overbeck, *Werke und Nachlass: IV Kirchenlexicon Texte Ausgewählte Artikel A–I; V Kirchenlexicon Texte Ausgwählte Artikel J–Z*, ed. Barbara von Reibnitz (Stuttgart: J. B. Metzler, 1995). Among the entries, many are of interest for NT research, for example, "Apokalyptik," "Exegese."
20. Franz Overbeck, *Das Johannesevangelium: Studien zur Kritik seiner Erforschung*, ed. Carl Albrecht Bernoulli (Tübingen: J. C. B. Mohr [Paul Siebeck], 1911), 206, 236, 249.

thinks Jesus comes out ahead. "All the beautiful sides of Christianity are connected with Jesus, all the ugly with Paul." Overbeck confirms Wrede's judgment that Paul is the second founder of Christianity. "In a certain sense, one cannot avoid recognizing Paul as participant in the foundation of Christianity. It is clear that Christianity, in order to come to life, took a double beginning. The first in Christ, the second in Paul, and the faith of Paul that continued after the death of Jesus is no lesser wonder than the faith in Jesus himself."[21]

Like the apocalyptic beast rising out of the sea, Overbeck made war on the saints. He viewed the whole history of Christendom from patristic to modern times as a chronicle of deception. Exposing the ancient documents to the searing light of "pure" historical research, he accused the formulators of the canon with conspiracy. They had, he believed, manipulated the original sources to make them appear apostolic, and then concealed the clues of their crime. And, even worse, modern theologians who possessed the weapons to bring them to justice joined the conspiracy. Overbeck himself, applying the historical method rigorously, tried to reconstruct the history of primitive Christianity. Yet, what he found—his version of original, authentic Christianity—offered a risky basis for faith. The apocalyptic, otherworldly shell of the liberals had become Overbeck's kernel.

Overbeck's critique is not without substance. The strange world of the Bible is distant from modern culture, and the literature of the NT has a distinctive character. The conflicts in the early church should not be glossed over, and the fallibility of the canonizers of the Bible should be acknowledged. Yet, although the presuppositions of the guardians of tradition must be exposed, so also must be those of the foes of tradition. Overbeck's notion of a "pure" historical method is pure fantasy. Overbeck uncritically presupposes the naturalism and rationalism of the Enlightenment in a way inconsistent with his own romantic view of religious origins. Yet what puts his results under a shadow is not Overbeck's presuppositions, but his failure to recognize that they exist.

DOCTRINE CONCEALS HISTORY:
WILLIAM WREDE (1859–1906)

William Wrede made his reputation by disclosing the "messianic secret." Indeed, his book by that title caused the greatest tremor that NT research had felt since Strauss's *Life of Jesus*.[22] Born in Bücken, Hannover, the son of

---

21. *Christentum und Kultur,* in *Werke und Nachlass* 6/1:88, 95. Early in his career, Overbeck published a critical essay on Paul that employed careful linguistic and exegetical research in the service of theological interpretation: "Über ἐν οἰώματι σαρκὸς ἁμαρτίας Röm. 8,3," in *Werke und Nachlass: I,* 39–73.

22. *HNTR* 1:250–55.

a Lutheran pastor, Wrede studied at Leipzig (where he was influenced by Harnack) and at Göttingen (where he was influenced by Ritschl).[23] After serving as a pastor (1886–89), he was appointed instructor at Göttingen, where he became associated with the scholars of the history of religion school.[24] In 1892 he was called to the faculty at Breslau. Wrede was a master teacher and a talented musician. At age forty-six, he was struck down by a heart ailment.

Wrede was a historian and NT critic, not a systematic theologian. He was suspicious of tradition and dogma, and promoted historical research, free of theological presuppositions.[25] Wrede's point of view is reflected in his book *The Nature of New Testament Theology*.[26] At the outset, Wrede affirms J. P. Gabler's distinction between biblical and dogmatic theology.[27] NT theology, according to Wrede, is a strictly historical discipline, independent of dogmatics in method and results. The dogmatician, in turn, builds his theology upon the results offered by New Testament criticism. "How the systematic theologian gets on with its results and deals with them—that is his own affair." Wrede rejects the method whereby NT theology is ordered according to doctrinal concepts (*Lehrbegriffe*). Such a method assumes that the NT mainly contains doctrine, whereas, in Wrede's view, it actually offers practical instruction and expressions of faith. Rather than imposing doctrinal topics upon the NT, Wrede believes the biblical theologian should organize the material around NT themes: the preaching of Jesus, the faith of the early church, the religion that flourished on Gentile soil. Attention should be given to Paul and how his Pharisaic-Jewish theology was shaped by his conversion. In interpreting the Fourth Gospel, Wrede believes the historical theologian must recognize that the author presents theology in the gospel form. Finally, Wrede rejects the title "New Testament Theology." "The appropriate name for the subject-matter is: early Christian history or religion, or rather: the history of early Christian religion and theology."[28]

---

23. See Hans Rollmann, "Wrede, William (1859–1906)," in *HHMBI*, 394–98.

24. See pp. 222, 238–53, below. For Wrede's appreciation of the school, see W. Wrede, "Das theologische Studium und die Religionsgeschichte," in *Vorträge und Studien* (Tübingen: J. C. B. Mohr [Paul Siebeck], 1907), 64–83.

25. See Hans Rollmann, "From Baur to Wrede: The Quest for a Historical Method," *SR* 17 (1988): 443–54.

26. *Über Aufgabe und Methode der sogenannten Neutestamentlichen Theologie* (Göttingen: Vandenhoeck & Ruprecht, 1897); Eng. trans.: "The Task and Methods of 'New Testament Theology,'" in Robert Morgan, ed., *The Nature of New Testament Theology: The Contribution of William Wrede and Adolf Schlatter*, SBT, Second Series 25 (Naperville, Ill.: Alec R. Allenson, 1973), 68–116.

27. *HNTR* 1:184–87.

28. *Nature of NT Theology*, 69, 116. Wrede's view of the importance of historical-critical research for faith is also seen in his lecture "Die biblische Kritik innerhalb des theologischen Studiums," in *Vorträge und Studien* (Tübingen: J. C. B. Mohr [Paul Siebeck], 1907), 40–63. See also Robert Morgan, "Re-Reading Wrede," *ExpTim* 108 (1997): 207–10.

Wrede offers a nontechnical summary of his NT research in *The Origin of the New Testament*.[29] Originally presented as lectures to a church assembly in 1904, this work begins with a denial of the orthodox doctrine of inspiration. "No," says Wrede, "the books of the New Testament were not . . . literally dictated to the human authors by God Himself; rather were they written by men in a way entirely human." Moreover, "the question as to the origin of the New Testament is a historical, and a purely historical question." Assuming this historical approach, Wrede discusses the NT books in chronological order, beginning with the Pauline Epistles. "Each genuine epistle is the product of a definite time, and designed for a single purpose such as never repeats itself; it has a definite situation of the recipient before the eye of the author."[30] As to critical matters, Wrede considers 2 Thessalonians, Ephesians, and the Pastorals to be non-Pauline.[31] He thinks that Romans 16 was originally addressed to Ephesus, and that Philippians was written from the Roman imprisonment.

In regard to the Gospels, Wrede adopts the two-document hypothesis, but believes a final solution to the Synoptic Problem to be illusive. Anticipating form criticism, Wrede believes the Gospels constitute a new type of literary composition whose writers present collections of small units of tradition.[32] "In the main," he says, "they hand down what they have received. But they themselves shape the tradition variously, make additions, abridgments, and unite according to their own judgment one source with the other." In spite of inaccuracies and shifts in the tradition, Wrede believes a reliable picture of Jesus shines through: "a wholly definite image, which cannot be confused with any other, the image of a real personality not recognizable in every feature, but still speaking to us with the force of reality, exalted, majestic, subduing, great and pure, deep and clear, serious and loving, strong and mild, stands before us."[33] With the Gospel of John, however, "The human personality of Jesus has almost quite disappeared; a divine

---

29. *Die Entstehung der Schriften des Neuen Testaments*, Lebensfragen: Schriften und Leben 18 (Tübingen: J. C. B. Mohr [Paul Siebeck], 1907); Eng. trans.: *The Origin of the New Testament*, trans. James S. Hill, Harper's Library of Living Thought (London: Harper & Brothers, 1909). For an overview of Wrede's major works, see Georg Strecker, "William Wrede: Zur hundertsten Wiederkehr seines Geburtstages," *ZTK* 57 (1960): 67–91; repr. in Georg Strecker, *Eschaton und Historie* (Göttingen: Vandenhoeck & Ruprecht, 1979), 335–59; Hans Rollmann, "William Wrede, Albert Eichhorn, and the 'Old Quest' of the Historical Jesus," in *Self-Definition and Self-Discovery in Early Christianity: A Study in Changing Horizons*, ed. David J. Hawkin and Tom Robinson, Studies in the Bible and Early Christianity 26 (Lewiston: Edwin Mellen, 1990), 79–99.

30. *Origin of the New Testament*, 3, 10.

31. Wrede presents a fuller discussion of the authenticity of 2 Thessalonians in his monograph *Die Echtheit des zweiten Thessalonicherbriefs*, TU, Neue Folge, 9/2 (Leipzig: J. C. Hinrichs, 1903).

32. See pp. 269–86, below.

33. *Origin of the New Testament*, 64, 75. In his essay "Die Predigt Jesu vom Reiche Gottes," in *Vorträge und Studien*, 84–126, Wrede insists on the study of Jesus in his Jewish setting, but stresses the unique person of Jesus and his ethical teaching.

being stands before us, who has existed from the beginning, and who has at its disposal the attributes of omnipotence and omniscience like God Himself."[34]

Wrede turns to the remaining books of the NT. He denies that Acts was written to reconcile the Jewish and Gentile wings of the church. According to Wrede the "we-sections" represent a travel diary used as a source by the author. The last part of Acts he finds to be more reliable than the first. "For instance, the description of the voyage of Paul and of the shipwreck before his arrival in Rome is a real masterpiece of exact description, connecting fact with fact, and giving evidence in every detail of personal observation." Wrede believes the Catholic Epistles to be treatises, not letters, none of them authentic. A chapter on the history of the canon declares that "it is the Church which created the New Testament." According to Wrede, historical criticism "makes the writings of the New Testament anew interesting and fresh, for it teaches us how to understand them as products of actual religious history, as documents in which the actual life, faith, and thought of the first Christian generations are deposited."[35]

Messianic Secret

After the publication of Wrede's *Messianic Secret*, study of the life of Jesus could never be the same.[36] Wrede, however, was anxious that his work not be read as negative criticism:

> If anyone wishes to call my criticism radical on this account, then I have nothing against it. I rely on the fact that things themselves are sometimes most radical and that one can therefore hardly be legitimately reproached for depicting them as they are. On the other hand, I reject the charge of offering a 'negative' criticism in the one reasonable sense the word can have: my entire endeavour has at least been the very positive one of illuminating a small but, as I believe, important portion of descriptive history as well as I could.[37]

---

34. *Origin of the New Testament*, 82. In a more extensive work, Wrede argues that the Fourth Gospel presents apologetic theology, not history: *Charakter und Tendenz des Johannesevangeliums*, 2d ed., Sammlung gemeinverständlicher Vorträge und Schriften aus dem Gebiet der Theologie und Religionsgeschichte 37 (Tübingen: J. C. B. Mohr [Paul Siebeck], 1933), originally published in 1903, in V*orträge und Studien*, 178–231.

35. *Origin of the New Testament*, 101, 140. In his monograph *Das literarische Rätsel des Hebräerbriefs*, FRLANT 8 (Göttingen: Vandenhoeck & Ruprecht, 1906), Wrede argues that Hebrews is not a letter but a treatise, and that its ending was added to make it appear to be a Pauline Epistle.

36. *Das Messiasgeheimnis in den Evangelien: Zugleich ein Beitrag zum Verständnis des Markusevangeliums* (Göttingen: Vandenhoeck & Ruprecht, 1901); Eng. trans.: *The Messianic Secret*, trans. J. C. G. Greig, Library of Theological Translations (Cambridge: James Clarke, 1971). For summaries and critiques, see Albert Schweitzer, *The Quest of the Historical Jesus: A Critical Study of Its Progress from Reimarus to Wrede*, trans. W. Montgomery (New York: Macmillan, 1957), 330–97; William C. Robinson Jr., "The Quest for Wrede's Secret Messiah," *Int* 27 (1973): 10–30; Vincent Taylor, "Important and Influential Foreign Books: W. Wrede's The Messianic Secret in the Gospels," *ExpTim* 65 (1953–54): 246–50; Christopher Tuckett, ed., *The Messianic Secret*, Issues in Religion and Theology 1 (Philadelphia: Fortress, 1983).

37. *Messianic Secret*, 2.

Beginning with an analysis of the Gospel of Mark, Wrede attacks the popular notion that the author presents a reliable account of the development of Jesus' messianic consciousness, with the confession of Peter as the decisive turning point. Instead, Wrede believes Mark intentionally presents Jesus as concealing his messiahship. "According to Mark's account Jesus strictly and of set purpose kept his messianic dignity secret even after the disciples' confession, into his very last period." The reports that the demons recognize Jesus as Messiah is, according to Wrede, an invention of Mark to show that supernatural beings recognize the supernatural in Jesus. Similarly, Jesus' command to silence, in Wrede's view, is a Marcan fabrication. Wrede also detected the fabricated secret in the erroneous explanation of the parables as intended to conceal (Mark 4:11). The motif of the secret, according to Wrede, is not history, but theology. "I would go further and assert that *a historical motive is really absolutely out of the question; or to put it positively, that the idea of the messianic secret is a theological idea.*"[38] According to Mark's theological construction, no one except Jesus' inner circle knew of his messiahship during his lifetime; only after the resurrection was it disclosed. But what is to be made of the apparent contradiction that those charged with secrecy broadcast Jesus' messiahship across the land? Wrede's answer: contradiction belongs to the essence of Mark's theological construct—there must be both secrecy and disclosure. "For this reason both are always important—the enunciation of the great truth and the prohibition of its enunciation." In any case, Wrede concludes that those who construct a historical Jesus on Mark, build on sand. "It must frankly be said that Mark no longer has a real view of the historical life of Jesus." Rather than being a history of Jesus, the "Gospel of Mark belongs to the history of dogma."[39]

According to Wrede, the author of Mark did not invent the messianic secret; he found it already in the tradition before him. In the tradition that developed after Mark, the messianic secret is diminished in both Matthew and Luke. Wrede, however, finds a parallel in John. Here, too, the pattern is repeated: both secret and disclosure are offered; what is hidden in the present will be revealed when the Paraclete comes. In tracing the actual history of the messianic idea, Wrede notes texts (Peter's speech in Acts 2; Paul's confession in Romans 1) where Jesus *becomes* Messiah at the resurrection. Only in the later tradition, according to Wrede, did the idea arise that Jesus was Messiah during his lifetime. In Wrede's opinion, the tradition could not have developed in this way if Jesus had actually claimed to be the Messiah. "If our view could only arise where nothing is known of an open messianic claim on Jesus' part, then we would seem to have in it a positive historical testimony for the idea that Jesus actually did not give himself out

---

38. Ibid., 24, 67.
39. Ibid., 128, 129, 131.

as messiah."[40] Above all, the crucial character of the resurrection faith for the early Christian understanding of Jesus is apparent. If Wrede is right, Mark's Jesus is a fiction—and the nineteenth-century lives of Jesus are fictitious as well.

Paul

The theological world had scarcely recovered from the tremor caused by Wrede's *Messianic Secret* when it was hit by the aftershock: Wrede's book on *Paul*.[41] Actually, the book was a widely acclaimed popular work, noted for its nontechnical, readable style.[42] In the first chapter, Wrede considers Paul the man. He sees Paul as a complex personality—plagued by epilepsy, moved by religious zeal. "Pertinacious and impulsive, turbulent and stable, inconsiderate and tender, in his intolerance bitter to the point of hardness and acrimony, and yet a man of soft sensibility; unyielding and yet pliant; all enthusiasm and glow, all sober prudence; a thinker, a mediator, and yet even more a restless toiler—no scheme will suffice to comprehend the whole man." In Wrede's opinion, Paul was a dynamic speaker who addressed the world's yearning for redemption. As to the Epistles, "They supply the place of Paul's personal presence, prepare the way for his visits, and whether rapidly written, or more deliberately laboured, they enter directly into the active questions of the life of the community." Throughout his career, Paul suffered attacks from the Judaizers, but maintained community with the Jewish Christians; he collected an offering for the Jerusalem church, and, according to Wrede, he had Timothy circumcised, and also observed a Nazarite vow.[43]

Although Paul was not a systematic theologian, "The religion of the apostle is theological through and through: his theology is his religion." Paul's theology is Christocentric: "the whole Pauline doctrine is a doctrine of

---

40. Ibid., 230. Later, in a letter to Harnack (1905), Wrede appears less skeptical, "I am more inclined than ever before to believe that Jesus considered himself chosen as Messiah" (quoted by Rollmann, "Wrede and the 'Old Quest,'" 98). Related to Wrede's discussion of the tradition about Jesus as Messiah is his essay "Jesus als Davidssohn," in *Vorträge und Studien*, 147–77. Here Wrede traces the development of the use of the title Son of David to present Jesus as Messiah. Wrede does not believe Mark 12:35-37 represents an authentic saying of Jesus, but a later tradition in which "Son of David" is being replaced by "Son of God."
41. William Wrede. *Paulus*, 2d ed., Religionsgeschichtliche Volksbücher, 1. Reihe, 5/6. Heft (Tübingen: J. C. B. Mohr [Paul Siebeck], 1907). Eng. trans.: *Paul*, trans. Edward Lummis (1908; repr., Lexington, Ky.: American Theological Library Association, 1962). For a summary and critique, see Hans Rollmann, "Paulus alienus: William Wrede on Comparing Jesus and Paul," in *From Jesus to Paul: Studies in Honour of Francis Wright Beare*, ed. Peter Richardson and John C. Hurd (Waterloo: Wilfrid Laurier University Press, 1984), 23–45; Wolfgang Wiefel, "Zur Würdigung William Wredes," *ZRGG* 23 (1971): 60–83.
42. Albert Schweitzer, *Paul and His Interpreters: A Critical History*, trans. W. Montgomery (1911; repr., New York: Schocken Books, 1964), 168: "Of the value and remarkable literary beauty of the book it is impossible to say too much. It belongs, not to theology, but to the literature of the world."
43. *Paul*, 39–40, 62.

Christ and his work; that is its essence." Christ, according to Paul, was a preexistent, divine being who came in human form to accomplish redemption. In Wrede's opinion, the doctrine of justification by faith was not central to Paul's thought, but only developed in response to Paul's conflict with Judaism.

> In fact the whole Pauline religion can be expounded without a word being said about this doctrine. . . . It would be extraordinary if what was intended to be the chief doctrine were referred to only in a minority of the epistles. That is the case with this doctrine: it only appears where Paul is dealing with strife against Judaism.

According to Wrede, Paul's thought finds its primary background in apocalyptic Judaism.[44]

Most striking is Wrede's view of Paul's place in the history of Christian origins. Wrede perceives a broad chasm between Paul and Jesus. Jesus teaches in simple language; Paul instructs in intellectual, metaphysical terms. Jesus presents ethical teaching to individuals; Paul proclaims redemption to the world. Paul, says Wrede, "stands farther away from Jesus than Jesus himself stands from the noblest figures of Jewish piety." In regard to Christology, Wrede thinks Paul's successor is the writer of the Fourth Gospel.

> When the Johannine Christ recounts how he was with the Father before he became flesh, it is Paul himself who is speaking to us; and when in this gospel John the Baptist extols Jesus as the Lamb of God, that takes away the sins of the world, the voice again is that of Paul. . . . The Pauline Son of God could now be shown in the flesh. In fact, the Pauline doctrine of Christ was, in John, poured into the mould of an image of the earthly life, and in this way won a new charm and new power over our hearts.

Wrede summarizes Paul's enduring influence in three points: (1) he moved Christianity from the sphere of Judaism to the Greco-Roman world; (2) he "gave the Christian community for the first time the consciousness of being a new religion"; (3) he was the first Christian theologian. "It follows then conclusively for all this that Paul is to be regarded as *the second founder of Christianity*." Paul, however, was inferior to Jesus. "This second founder of Christianity has even, compared with the first, exercised beyond all doubt the stronger—not the better—influence." Still worse, the effect of the Christ of Paul is to "crush out the man Jesus."[45]

In overview, Wrede's skepticism seemed more threatening than Overbeck's, since he considered himself a believer, committed to the religion of Jesus. Nevertheless, Wrede tended to derail the quest of the historical Jesus by contending that Mark, the primary source that the quest followed, was

---

44. Ibid., 76, 86, 132.
45. Ibid., 165, 171–72, 175, 179, 180, 182.

not historically reliable. Yet, by his own critical reading of that source, Wrede discovered a Jesus unfriendly to both conservatives and liberals—a Jesus who was not considered by his associates or by himself to be the Messiah. Moreover, the first theologian of the church—who did understand Jesus to be the Messiah—replaced the person and religion of Jesus with a supernatural figure—the preexistent, risen Christ. By this misguided move, Paul became the second founder of the Christianity that was to persist—a Christianity inferior to the religion of the first founder, Jesus. In any event, the attempt to penetrate behind the theological Mark to the historical tradition about Jesus was to become a prominent feature of future research. In the meantime, scholars would continue to raise questions with Wrede's reading of the texts: Was the secret really pre-Marcan? Could the execution of Jesus be explained apart from some sort of messianic identification? Was Paul really so ignorant of, and unconcerned with, the life and teaching of Jesus? Behind these stand the larger hermeneutical questions: how and to what extent did the theology (or religion) of the early Christians confirm or transform the tradition about Jesus? Regardless of the answers, Wrede remains a figure of immense importance; his brilliant insights and daring proposals changed the course of the history of NT research.

TRADITION TRANSFORMING HISTORY: JULIUS WELLHAUSEN (1844–1918)

Famous for his work on the documentary hypothesis concerning the Pentateuch, Julius Wellhausen devoted the latter part of his career to the study of the NT. Born in Hameln (of Pied Piper fame), he was the son of a Lutheran pastor.[46] After working as an instructor at Göttingen, Wellhausen was appointed to the theological faculty at Greifswald. He served there for ten years, but, struggling with his conscience, he finally resigned. "It strikes me as a lie," he said, "that I should be educating ministers of an Evangelical Church to which in my heart I do not belong."[47] Consequently, in 1882, Wellhausen moved to Halle, where he was named lecturer in Semitic languages. He was appointed to a similar position at Marburg three years later. In 1892, he was called to the philosophical faculty at Göttingen, teaching courses in Semitic philology and Assyriology.

---

46. See Rudolf Smend, "Wellhausen in Greifswald," *ZTK* 78 (1981): 141–76; idem, "Wellhausen in Göttingen," in *Theologie in Göttingen: Ein Vorlesungsreihe*, ed. Bernd Moeller, Göttinger Universitätsschrifte, A, 1 (Göttingen: Vandenhoeck & Ruprecht, 1987), 307–24; idem, "William Robertson Smith and Julius Wellhausen," in *William Robertson Smith: Essays in Reassessment*, ed. William Johnstone, JOSTSup 189 (Sheffield: Sheffield Academic Press, 1995), 226–42; idem, "Wellhausen und die Kirche," in *Wissenschaft und Kirche: Festschrift für Eduard Lohse*, ed. Kurt Aland and Siegfried Meurer, Texte und Arbeiten zur Bibel 4 (Bielefeld: Luther, 1989), 225–31.

47. Quoted by J. C. O'Neill, *The Bible's Authority: A Portrait Gallery of Thinkers from Lessing to Bultmann* (Edinburgh: T. & T. Clark, 1991), 201.

Since he viewed history as an evolutionary process, Wellhausen has been identified as a Hegelian. Actually, he was opposed to imposing philosophical patterns upon history, and called for a strictly objective investigation of the sources. "Generally, one has no right to establish a priori any privileged points of view. . . . One must rather proceed from certain impulses furnished by exegesis itself."[48] On the basis of this kind of research, Wellhausen traces the evolution of religion from its primitive beginnings to its apex in the teachings of Jesus. Thus, in the 1894 edition of his *Israelite and Jewish History,* Wellhausen's ultimate chapter is "the Gospel." In this chapter, Wellhausen observes that Jesus preached that the rule of God was at hand. For Wellhausen, this was a call to individual responsibility, not an apocalyptic proclamation. "What then is the kingdom that is already present and consummated only in the future?" asks Wellhausen. "It is nothing other than the community of the souls that strive for God. Self-denial is the means, and community of the souls with God is the result." After the crucifixion, Wellhausen believes the personal impression Jesus had made upon the disciples was so strong that they had visions of him alive. Paul, in Wellhausen's view, was misled by his Jewish heritage so as to formulate the doctrine of justification by faith, yet as his letters to Corinth and Philippi indicate, Paul's major emphasis was on the inner spiritual and ethical life. In any case, Wellhausen finds the truth of Christianity in the religion of Jesus. "Jesus did not found the church, and he pronounced judgment against the Jewish theocracy. The gospel is only the salt of the earth; where it wants to be more, it is less. It proclaims the highest individualism, the freedom of the children of God."[49]

Already in 1874, Wellhausen had published a book on the Pharisees and Sadducees that was important for the historical understanding of the NT.[50] However, in 1902, he wrote to a friend, "During the Christmas holidays I stuck my nose into the Gospels."[51] In effect, Wellhausen began to apply to the study of the NT the skills of literary analysis that he had honed in the investigation of the tradition of Israel.[52] Three years later, Wellhausen pub-

---

48. Quoted by Grégoire Rouiller, "Julius Wellhausen: His Historical and Critical Method," in *Exegesis: Problems of Method and Exercises in Reading (Genesis 22 and Luke 15): Studies Published under the Direction of François Bovon and Grégoire Rouiller,* trans. Donald G. Miller, PTMS 21 (Pittsburgh: Pickwick, 1978), 100. See Lothar Perlitt, *Vatke und Wellhausen: Geschichtsphilosophische Voraussetzungen und historische Motive für die Darstellung der Religion und Geschichte Israels durch Wilhelm Vatke und Julius Wellhausen,* BZAW 94 (Berlin: Alfred Töpelmann, 1965).
49. *Israelitische und Jüdische Geschichte,* 9th ed. (Berlin: Walter de Gruyter, 1958), 365, 371.
50. *Die Pharisäer und die Sadducäer: Eine Untersuchung zur inneren jüdischen Geschichte* (Greifswald: L. Bamberg, 1874).
51. Quoted by Smend, "Wellhausen in Göttingen," 321.
52. See Nils A. Dahl, "Wellhausen on the New Testament," in *Julius Wellhausen and His Prolegomena to the History of Israel,* ed. Douglas A. Knight, *Semeia* 25 (1983): 89–110; Ernst Bammel, "Hirsch und Wellhausen," in *Christentumsgeschichte und Wahrheitsbewusstsein: Studien zur Theologie Emanuel Hirschs,* ed. Joachim Ringleben (Berlin: Walter de Gruyter, 1991).

lished his most important work on the NT, an *Introduction to the Synoptic Gospels*.⁵³ In this book, Wellhausen observes that the earliest gospel tradition was transmitted in Aramaic. Turning to literary considerations, Wellhausen adopts the two-document hypothesis. He believes Mark presents the original order of the gospel narrative. The common non-Marcan material found in Matthew and Luke comes from Q, and agreements in linguistic detail convince Wellhausen that Matthew and Luke used Q in Greek translation. Wellhausen believes Mark to be older and closer to the original tradition than Q. For Wellhausen, the criterion for discerning later tradition is the ecclesiasticizing of the material, that is, the transformation of the original tradition to accommodate concerns of the developing church.

According to his analysis of the tradition, Wellhausen believes the idea of the suffering Messiah to be post-resurrection. However, Wellhausen thinks Jesus must have been recognized as Messiah earlier, since he was executed as king of the Jews. Jesus, according to Wellhausen, intended to reform Judaism, not found a new faith. "Jesus was not a Christian but a Jew."⁵⁴ In Wellhausen's opinion, the personality of Jesus was more important than his teaching. "His person, whose association they were able to enjoy in daily life," says Wellhausen, "had worked more strongly on his disciples than his teaching. That they held him to be the Messiah depended not on his assertion that he was, but on the impression of his person."⁵⁵ To the second edition of his Introduction, Wellhausen adds notes on various topics. For example, on the "Son of Man" he argues that the phrase in Aramaic refers simply to a human being; its use as a messianic title is created by the later gospel tradition. In a note, "The Gospel and Christianity," Wellhausen observes that in early Christian preaching the role of Jesus is changed: from the bearer of the gospel to the content of the gospel. In discussing "The Gospel Narrative Material," Wellhausen argues that the Papias tradition about Mark and Matthew is unreliable. He concludes that the quest for the historical Jesus is fraught with difficulties. "We must resist curiosity about the historical Jesus; we must be satisfied that a series of documents from the time of Christian beginnings is available to us which are cut off by a dark chasm from the later ecclesiastical literature."⁵⁶

After the publication of his Introduction to the Synoptics, Wellhausen published commentaries on the individual Gospels. In his commentary on

---

53. *Einleitung in die drei ersten Evangelien* (Berlin: Georg Reimer, 1905); 2d rev. ed. is reprinted in Julius Wellhausen, *Evangelienkommentare* (Berlin: Walter de Gruyter, 1987), 1–104. For a review and critique, see John Timmer, *Julius Wellhausen and the Synoptic Gospels: A Study in Tradition Growth*, Academisch Proefschrift, University of Amsterdam (Rotterdam: Bonder-Offset N.V., 1970).

54. *Einleitung*, 113. See Hans Dieter Betz, "Wellhausen's Dictum 'Jesus was not a Christian, but a Jew' in Light of Present Scholarship," *ST* 45 (1991): 83–110.

55. *Einleitung*, 114.

56. *Evangelienkommentare*, 170.

Mark, he orders the pericopes according to his understanding of Mark's arrangement. Wellhausen's discussion of the confession of Peter provides an example. He believes Mark presents the confession as a turning point in Jesus' ministry. According to Mark, Jesus at this point acknowledges himself to be the Messiah.

> He is not the Messiah who will establish again the kingdom of Israel, but an entirely different one. He does not go to Jerusalem to set up the kingdom, but in order to be crucified. Through suffering and death he enters into glory, and only in this way can others enter. The kingdom of God is no Jewish kingdom, it is only designated for a few chosen individuals, for the disciples.[57]

As to details, Wellhausen contends that Jesus' question "Who do people say that I am?" (8:27) would make no sense if he had previously declared himself to be Messiah. In regard to 8:33, Wellhausen contends that the words addressed to Peter use the same Semitic idiom as those directed to Satan in Matt. 4:10.

Wellhausen's commentaries on *Matthew* and *Luke* ignore the infancy narratives.[58] In his discussion of the temptation, he argues that the narrative is based on Q, and that Q must have included an account of the baptism, since the temptation narrative presupposes it. The mention of forty days is found in Mark, but Q has heightened the story by saying that Jesus fasted throughout the whole period. In commenting on the temptation to leap from the temple, Wellhausen recalls that Simon Magus had attempted to prove his messiahship by flying through the air. In the *Luke* commentary, Wellhausen argues that the genealogy contradicts the account of the supernatural birth of Jesus; he sees the parenthetical phrase of 3:23 as an effort at harmonizing: "He was the son (as was thought) of Joseph." Wellhausen's comments on the parable of the prodigal son are typical.[59] He thinks the point of the first part of the parable is obvious: the repentant sinner who returns is forgiven and joyously received. Displaying his liberal sympathies, Wellhausen claims that the parable denies the doctrine of original sin: the younger son was not sinful by nature. The meaning of the parable is religious, confirming Wellhausen's stress on the importance of the individual. Wellhausen believes that the second part of the parable is not authentic, that it has been added later.

Wellhausen's commentary on *John* had been preceded by a short critical work regarding what Wellhausen takes to be expansions and changes in the

---

57. *Das Evangelium Marci übersetzt und erklärt*, 2d ed. (Berlin: George Reimer, 1909), 63; repr., *Evangelienkommentare*, 383.
58. *Das Evangelium Matthaei übersetzt und erklärt*, 2d ed. (Berlin: Georg Reimer, 1914); repr., *Evangelienkommentare*, 177–320; idem, *Das Evangelium Lucae übersetzt und erklärt* (Berlin: Georg Reimer, 1904); repr., *Evangelienkommentare*, 459–600.
59. *Evangelienkommentare*, 539–43. See François Bovon, "Julius Wellhausen's Exegesis of Luke 15:11-32," in *Exegesis: Problems of Method and Exercises in Reading (Genesis 22 and Luke 15)*, 118–23.

Fourth Gospel.⁶⁰ For example, his analysis of 14:1—18:1 begins by noting parallels between Mark 14:42-43 ("Get up, let us be going. . . . while he was speaking, Judas arrived") and John 14:30-31 ("the ruler of this world is coming. . . . Rise, let us be on our way"). The "ruler of this world," according to Wellhausen, is Satan incarnate in Judas. Wellhausen believes this narrative in John 14:30-31 is continued in 18:1-3 where Jesus finishes his words, goes to the garden, and Judas comes. Thus, Wellhausen believes the three intervening chapters were added by a later editor. The commentary is devoted to the same sort of literary analysis, attempting to demonstrate that the original gospel was subject to editorial reworking.

> The whole, therefore, like a greater part of Jewish and early Christian literature, is the product of a literary process that had several prior stages. The basic text constitutes only the warp, and is far exceeded in extent by the woof. It can therefore not be viewed as the real Johannine Gospel, but only as an ingredient of it. It is not at all preserved intact or complete. One can distinguish neither it nor the different stages of revision with certainty.⁶¹

For example, Wellhausen believes the narrative of Jesus' encounter with the Samaritan woman displays redactional revision. According to Wellhausen, the original text (4:35-36) presented sowing and reaping as simultaneous, whereas the later revision (4:37-38) presents the two actions as separate. In summarizing the results, Wellhausen identifies an original text (*Grundschrift*) as "A," and redactional work (which took place in several stages) as "B." Wellhausen thinks the Jesus of A is a human being who does not make messianic claims, whereas in B, Christ is hailed as the Son of God whose passion is not suffering, but triumph.⁶²

In sum, Wellhausen's major contribution to NT research is his demonstration that meticulous literary analysis is indispensable for the investigation of the history of early Christian tradition. Wellhausen's actual reconstruction of the tradition by means of this method, however, is not entirely convincing. At the source of the tradition he detects a historical base, which, although difficult to recover, is crucial. For Wellhausen, that historical base is the person of Jesus—an individual who epitomizes authen-

---

60. *Erweiterungen und Änderungen im vierten Evangelium* (Berlin: Georg Reimer, 1907).
61. J. Wellhausen, *Das Evangelium Johannis* (Berlin: George Reimer, 1908); repr., *Evangelienkommentare*, 606–746.
62. Wellhausen's research on Revelation and Acts pursues the same sort of literary analysis. For example, in his *Analyse der Offenbarung Johannis,* Abhandlungen der königlichen Gesellschaft der Wissenschaften zu Göttingen, Philologisch-Historische Klasse, n.f. 9/4 (Berlin: Weidmann, 1907), Wellhausen claims that the compilation of the Apocalypse took place in three stages: (1) sources with references to Nero, written around 70; (2) composition by the author at the time of Domitian; (3) redaction by a later editor to present the document as the work of the author of the Fourth Gospel. In his *Kritische Analyse der Apostelgeschichte,* Abhandlungen der königlichen Gesellschaft der Wissenschaften zu Göttingen, Philologisch-Historische Klasse, n.f. 15/2 (Berlin: Weidmann, 1914), Wellhausen finds abundant evidence of redaction; for example, he thinks the speeches were added by a later editor.

tic religion. Wellhausen believes that Mark, the earliest extant account of the tradition, presents fragments of reliable history. However, he thinks the developing literary expression of the tradition—from Q through Matthew and Luke to John—is dominated by ecclesiastical prejudice; it moves from the historical Jesus to the theological Christ. Yet, for all of his allegiance to objectivity, Wellhausen's results, like those of Overbeck and Wrede, are predetermined by his presuppositions. His antidogmatic, antiecclesiastical bias is fostered by his liberalism, and his praise of the person of Jesus is not untouched by a lingering pietism. Why, one may ask, did the evolution of religion stop with Jesus? But, of course, for Wellhausen it really didn't—it continued in the evolving image of Jesus, reflected in the freedom and individualism of nineteenth-century humanism.

CRITICISM CONTRA SKEPTICISM: ADOLF JÜLICHER (1857–1938)

Ernst Troeltsch described Adolf Jülicher as an "aristocrat of pure scholarship."[63] Born in Falkenberg near Berlin, Adolf Jülicher was the son of a pious Lutheran layman. Jülicher compensated for his physical limitation—he had been born with a defective foot—by excelling in intellectual activity. In 1875, he entered university at Berlin where he studied NT with Otto Pfleiderer, whose work on Paul aroused his excitement.[64] Jülicher, however, found Bernhard Weiss's lectures boring, although he appreciated his commentaries.[65] In 1888, Jülicher was called to the faculty at Marburg, and after two years, was promoted to full professor. He decided to retire in 1923, with plans for extensive research. However, frail health and fading eyesight hindered his work.

Jülicher was primarily a historian and NT critic. He assumed the worldview of the Enlightenment with its empiricism and rationalism. He presupposed the orderly and uniform character of nature, and was leery of the supernatural. In method, Jülicher was dedicated to the rigorous, objective criticism. Jülicher's comprehensive view of Christianity can be seen in a chapter he wrote on the topic "The Religion of Jesus and the Beginnings of

---

63. Quoted by Hans-Josef Klauck, "Adolf Jülicher—Leben, Werk und Wirkung," in *Historische Kritik in der Theologie: Beiträge zu ihrer Geschichte*, ed. Georg Schwaiger, Studien zur Theologie und Geistesgeschichte des Neunzehnten Jahrhunderts 32 (Göttingen: Vandenhoeck & Ruprecht, 1980), 99. See "Adolf Jülicher," in *RGS* :1:159–200; Jochen-Christoph Kaiser, "Adolf Jülicher als Zeitgenosse: Eine biographische Skizze," in *Die Gleichnisreden Jesu 1899–1999: Beiträge zum Dialog mit Adolf Jülicher*, ed. Ulrich Mell; BZNW 103 (Berlin: Walter de Gruyter, 1999), 257–86; Werner Georg Kümmel, "Adolf Jülicher (1857–1938): Theologe, Neutestamentler und Kirchenhistoriker," in *Heilsgeschehen und Geschichte: Vol. 2 Gesammelte Aufsätze 1965–1977*, ed. Erich Grässer and Otto Merk; MTS 16 (Marburg: N. G. Elwert, 1978), 232–44.
64. See pp. 213–20, below.
65. See pp. 101–11, above.

Christianity" for a popular volume on the *History of Christianity*.[66] As to the sources of the life and teaching of Jesus, Jülicher writes, "The Gospels are indeed not historical books, but teaching and propaganda documents." Although they display many defects, "the three Gospels remain a valuable source not only for the history of the church in which the Christ-ideal is deposited, but indeed to a higher degree for the history of Jesus." According to Jülicher, Jesus is a "unique personality . . . a human being of mysterious greatness." According to Jülicher, Jesus saw himself as playing a messianic role in relation to the kingdom, but not as a Jewish Messiah. "Jesus ascribed to himself—next to God—the most important role." According to Jülicher, the future kingdom—the ordering of the world according to God's will—was already present in the person of Jesus; his teaching united the religious and the ethical.[67] In a monograph on recent trends in gospel research, Jülicher disputes Wrede's skepticism concerning the gospel tradition, and argues that Jesus was recognized as Messiah by his disciples prior to his death.[68]

Jülicher believes the early church arose in response to the resurrection faith. This faith was based on the experience of Peter who was convinced he had seen the living Christ. With the arrival of Paul, Jülicher thinks the Christian movement received new vitality, but not a new foundation. In his *Paulus und Jesus*, Jülicher contends, contra Wrede, for a continuity between Paul and Jesus.[69] Jülicher believes Christ crucified was the center of Paul's theology, and he insists that Paul's doctrine of grace and faith does not cut the ethical nerve. "The 'sola fide' of Paul, still miserably misunderstood today as a pillow for ethical slumber, is in truth the triumphant declaration of the alliance between religion and morality."[70] Jülicher believes the author of the Fourth Gospel presents a unique formulation of the Christian message. Making use of the Synoptic Gospels and Paul, and breathing the atmosphere of Greek culture, this author develops a Christ-mysticism. "John immersed the life of Jesus in a radiant sea in which we can scarcely recognize any vestige of the sketch of the actual Jesus." After John, Jülicher views the history of the church as the stone of Sisyphus, always rolling downhill. "But the breadth of the distance between the ideal of religion that Jesus embodied, and the reality, which the fathers around 325 commended as ideal, is immense, and since a value judgment is unavoidable here, one can

---

66. "Die Religion Jesu und die Anfänge des Christentums bis zum Nicaenum (325)," in J. Wellhausen, A. Jülicher, et al., *Die Christliche Religion. I Hälfte: Geschichte der christlichen Religion*, Die Kultur der Gegenwart, Teil I, Abteilung IV (Berlin: B. G. Teubner, 1906), 41–128.

67. *Geschichte der christlichen Religion*, 43, 45, 45–46, 55.

68. *Neue Linien in der Kritik der evangelischen Überlieferung*, Vorträge des Hessischen und Nassauischen theologischen Ferienkurses 3 (Giessen: Alfred Töpelmann, 1906).

69. Religionsgeschichtliche Volksbücher, 1. Reihe, 14. Heft (Tübingen: J. C. B. Mohr [Paul Siebeck], 1907).

70. *Geschichte der christlichen Religion*, 86.

only confirm a progressive religious impoverishment." To reverse this decline, Jülicher recommends a return to the gospel: from Nicea through John to Paul. Once that has been accomplished, a final action is required: "the step from Paul back to the religion of Jesus."[71]

Jülicher on the Parables

The first part of Jülicher's work on the parables originally appeared in 1886.[72] When he published the second part (1899) he brought out a revised edition of Part I. An edition of 1910 binds the two parts into a single volume.[73] The first part (328 pages) presents Jülicher's parable theory; the second (643 pages) applies the theory to the parables of the Gospels. In the first part, Jülicher begins with the question of the genuineness of the parables. Although their authenticity cannot be certainly established, the parables, in Jülicher's opinion, represent the most reliable element of the tradition of the teachings of Jesus. In essence, Jülicher sees the parables as simple comparisons, intended to provide clarity of understanding. They express abstract ideas by concrete comparisons that convey essentially a single meaning. However, Jülicher believes the gospel writers and the ongoing tradition have misconstrued the parables as allegories. "According to the theory of the evangelists the παραβολαί are allegories, therefore, figurative speech, that is, speech in need of translation; in reality they are—that is, they were before they fell into the hands of a zealous revisers—truly distinctive things, comparisons, fables, example stories, but always literal speech." Jülicher defines the parable as "that figure of speech in which the function of an expression (concept) should be ascertained by being placed beside a similar functioning expression from another domain."[74]

Regarding the purpose of the parables, Jülicher rejects the thesis of Mark 4:11-12 that Jesus addressed parables to the outsiders in order to prevent them from understanding the secrets of the kingdom. Jülicher believes this contradicts the intent of Jesus who used parables not to conceal but to reveal. "Jesus employed the parable for all the possible objectives of his speaking, in solemn preaching as in daily communication, for all possible hearers, enemies, the undecided, the ardent admirers, since he discovered

---

71. Ibid., 97, 123, 124.
72. See Mell, *Gleichnisreden Jesu 1899–1999;* Wolfgang Harnisch, ed., *Gleichnisse Jesu: Positionen der Auslegung von Adolf Jülicher bis zur Formgeschichte,* Wege der Forschung 366 (Darmstadt: Wissenschaftliche Buchgesellschaft, 1982).
73. *Die Gleichnisreden Jesu. Erster Teil: Die Gleichnisreden Jesu im Allgemeinen,* 2d ed.; *Die Gleichnisreden Jesu. Zweiter Teil: Auslegung der Gleichnisreden der drei ersten Evangelien* (Tübingen: J. C. B. Mohr [Paul Siebeck], 1910). A summary of Jülicher's interpretation of the parables can be seen in his article "Parables," in *Encyclopaedia Biblica: A Critical Dictionary of the Literary Political and Religious History, the Archaeology Geography and Natural History of the Bible,* ed. T. K. Cheyne and J. Sutherland Black (London: Adam and Charles Black, 1902) 3:3563–67.
74. *Gleichnisreden Jesu. Erster Teil,* 49, 80.

how this form was especially suitable for heightening the clarity and persuasive power of his thoughts."[75] In the subsequent development of the tradition, according to Jülicher, details and allegorical explanations were added. Jülicher believes the evangelists found it difficult to imagine that the one they confessed as Messiah had merely presented clear, simple instruction.

In Part II, Jülicher presents his analysis and interpretation of the parables of Jesus. He includes a total of fifty-three parables, classified in three types: A. Comparisons *(Gleichnisse)* or similes—a total of twenty-eight; B. Narrative parables—a total of twenty-one; C. Example stories—a total of four, all from Luke. An example of type A can be seen in Jülicher's interpretation of the parable of the fig tree (Matt. 24:32-33; Mark 13:28-29; Luke 21:29-31). Jülicher believes Mark is the source used by Matthew and Luke. The meaning of the parable, he thinks, is clear: as one recognizes in the sprouting twigs of the tree the nearness of summer, so one must recognize in current happenings the nearness of the parousia. Among type B, Jülicher classifies the parable of the prodigal son (Luke 15:11-32). He observes that this is a gem among parables, even though devotees of the doctrine of justification by faith tend to devalue it. In regard to details, Jülicher notes the frequent use of καί as evidence of Semitic style; he presents information about inheritance practices in first-century Palestine; he deals with text-critical problems. Jülicher also argues, in contrast to Wellhausen, that the second part of the narrative belongs to the original parable of Jesus. He insists that the interpreter should not suppose that the Father represents God or the older son Judaism. According to Jülicher, the meaning is seen "in the example of a father, who lovingly receives a son who is burdened with guilt, but returns home in penitence, and that the father's joy in contrast to the wrath of the older son . . . is justified; so should Jesus, who accepts publicans and sinners, be justified even though the Pharisees and Scribes murmur."[76] In regard to the parable of the Good Samaritan (Luke 10:29-37), an example of type C, Jülicher notes the inconsistency between v. 29 ("who is my neighbor") and v. 36 ("which of these . . . was a neighbor"). He contends that the author of Luke has inserted the parable into a foreign setting, illustrating the point that the settings are often invented by the evangelists. Again, Jülicher thinks the meaning is clear:

> The sacrificial practice of love finds in the eyes of God and humans the highest value that no prerogative of office or birth can provide. The merciful person, even if he is a Samaritan, deserves salvation rather than the Jewish temple official who is enslaved to selfishness (cf. Rom. 2:14ff.)[77]

---

75. Ibid., 146.
76. *Gleichnisreden Jesu. Zweiter Teil*, 359.
77. Ibid., 596. See Ulrich Mell, "Der barmherzige Samaritaner und Gottes Gerechtigkeit: Eine Auslegung von Lk 10,30-35 in Anknüpfung an Adolf Jülicher," in *Gleichnisreden Jesu 1899–1999*, 113–48.

Jülicher's Introduction

Jülicher's *Introduction to the New Testament* summarized German criticism at the end of the nineteenth century, and became the standard textbook for theological students.[78] To the criticism that his first edition (1894) was not sufficiently theological, Jülicher retorts, "It is not for me, however, to trespass on the domain of another science, that of New Testament theology. . . . I have never allowed myself to be driven on to a false road by the special interests of theology, or the preconceptions of the theological 'Docent'!" In the prolegomena, Jülicher defines NT introduction as "that branch of the science of history—or more accurately, of the history of literature—which treats of the New Testament." In reviewing the history of the discipline, Jülicher hails the revolutionary advance of the Tübingen school whereby the origin and history of NT literature was understood in relation to the historical developments of early Christianity.[79]

The first part of Jülicher's *Introduction* presents the history of the individual books of the NT. In regard to the problem of pseudonymity, Jülicher observes "that believers frequently borrowed from the books of other believers, or of unbelievers, without mentioning any source, and without considering themselves in any way as thieves; and that with the best intentions and the cleanest consciences they put such words into the mouth of a revered Apostle as they wished to hear enunciated with Apostolic authority to their contemporaries, while yet they did not regard themselves in the smallest degree as liars and deceivers." As to the Pauline Epistles, Jülicher defends the authenticity of 2 Thessalonians. He believes the letter to the Galatians was addressed to Christians of the original Galatian territory of central Asia Minor. He identifies the Christ party of the Corinthian church as Judaizers. Jülicher considers 2 Corinthians "the most problematical of all the Pauline Epistles," but also "the most personal of the extant Epistles of Paul." He believes it was a unified, not a composite composition. Romans, on the other hand, circulated in two editions; 16:1-20 was originally, according to Jülicher, a letter recommending Phoebe to the Ephesians. Jülicher defends the authenticity of Colossians, and vacillates about Ephesians. "Although, then, Ephesians may not belong to our unquestioned Pauline heritage, it would yet be equally impossible to deny the Apostle's authorship with any confidence." As to the Deutero-Pauline Letters, Jülicher considers Hebrews to be a real epistle, different in vocabulary, style, and theology from the Pauline Letters. It was not, according to Jülicher, written to Jewish Christians, but to the whole church of Rome, sometime around 85. Jülicher believes attributing the Pastoral Epistles to Paul insults Paul's

---

78. *Einleitung in das Neue Testament*, Grundriss der theologischen Wissenschaft 3/1, 3d and 4th ed. (Tübingen: J. C. B. Mohr [Paul Siebeck], 1901); Eng. trans.: *An Introduction to the New Testament*, trans. Janet Penrose Ward (New York: G. P. Putnam's Sons, 1904).

79. *Introduction*, viii, 2.

coworkers as "miserly, timid, self-seeking and small-minded men. . . . We must judge Paul by his disciples, for he had ten years in which to train them; if they were so immature as would appear from the Pastoral Epistles, he certainly had not finished his course of instruction!"[80]

According to Jülicher, none of the Catholic Epistles is authentic. First Peter, he thinks, presents Pauline theology, and was written by a Roman Christian around 100. "In no New Testament writing can pseudonymity be so abundantly proved as in 2. Peter, and in none has it been recognized by so many scholars who in other matters hold the most conservative views." As to the Johannine literature, Jülicher believes that 1 John is not an epistle, but a manifesto, written by the same author as the writer of the Fourth Gospel. Jülicher considers Revelation to be a literary composition. "The Apocalypse of John is, moreover, the artificial product of study and reflection; its ecstatic visions are merely literary trappings, not actual experiences." Jülicher believes that "it is one of the most assured results of New Testament criticism that not another line from the hand of the writer of the Apocalypse has been preserved to us in the New Testament, least of all in the Gospel of John; for if the Apocalypse is the most Jewish book of the New Testament, the Fourth Gospel is certainly the most anti-Jewish."[81]

Jülicher turns to the historical books. In regard to the Synoptic Problem he adopts the two-document hypothesis. He believes Q was written between 60 and 70, and was used by Mark. Jülicher is sympathetic to the tradition of Papias that Matthew was the author of the Logia (Q) and Mark the interpreter of Peter. Mark, according to Jülicher, was written after 70, and the original ending was cut off, probably to suppress a resurrection appearance to Peter in Galilee. The Gospel of Matthew that exerted "enormous influence upon the Church" was written about 100. Although the Synoptics include legendary material and heighten the miraculous, Jülicher thinks they provide tradition that goes back to the historical Jesus. Jülicher believes the author of the Fourth Gospel used the Synoptic Gospels, and was not an eyewitness. "It is, in fact, the one unassailable proposition which criticism, dealing solely with the internal evidence, can set up concerning the Fourth Gospel, that its author was not 'the disciple whom Jesus loved.'" Jülicher rejects the idea that Acts was written by a travel companion of Paul. He also denies that the author was attempting to harmonize Petrine and Pauline Christianity. "Paul was not Judaised nor Peter Paulinised, but both Paul and Peter were 'Lucanised.'" As to historical value of Acts, Jülicher discovers "the strangest mixture of materials of faultless excellence with others which are almost useless."[82]

---

80. Ibid., 52, 86, 88, 147, 188.
81. Ibid., 236, 266, 280–81.
82. Ibid., 314, 415, 438, 441.

Parts II and III of Jülicher's *Introduction* are devoted to canon and text.[83] He reviews the history of canonization as a gradual process. "The New Testament Canon, in its foundation as in its final form, is the work of the Catholic Church; and since the Church existed only in men, and acted only through men, this meant the bishops and theologians of the second, third and fourth centuries." In regard to the text, Jülicher believes its history is "the history of its corruption." In the effort to restore the original text, Jülicher considers the patristic material to have primary importance. "The first place must here be given to the quotations from the New Testament in the works of ecclesiastical writers, because some of these have the advantage of a higher antiquity than any of the preserved manuscripts, and in their case we may generally be certain to what part of the world the quoted texts belonged."[84]

In contrast to Overbeck, Wrede, and Wellhausen, Jülicher uses criticism to counter skepticism. By means of the historical-critical method, he defends the essential reliability of the gospel tradition, the messianic consciousness of Jesus, and the continuity between Paul and Jesus. This apologetic rests on Jülicher's liberal presuppositions: the line of continuity from Jesus to Paul is a line of religion and ethics; the messiahship of Jesus is a non-Jewish messiahship of religious insight. Similarly, Jülicher's *Introduction*, reminiscent of Holtzmann, represents the growing liberal consensus on critical details.[85] Jülicher's main contribution to the history of NT research is his work on the parables. With Jülicher, the old allegorical method of interpretation was totally discredited. To be sure, he was not, nor did he claim to be, the first to propose the idea that the parables have a single point of application. However, the rigor and extent of his argument produced a monumental and enduring achievement. In the ongoing discussion, of course, flaws in Jülicher's interpretation would become apparent: failure to recognize the eschatological setting, lack of knowledge of rabbinic parallels, a simplistic view of the parables as literal language, blind to the poetic and metaphorical meaning of parabolic expression.[86] Nevertheless, Jülicher is correct in detecting the allegorizing tendency in the early tradition, identifying a significant tool for the study of Christian origins.

83. For a short summary of Jülicher's understanding of canon and text, see also his "Die Geschichte des Neuen Testaments," in *Die Schriften des Neuen Testaments: neu übersetzt und für Gegenwart erklärt*, ed. W. Bousset and W. Heitmüller, 3d ed., 1. Halbband (Göttingen: Vandenhoeck & Ruprecht, 1916), 1–30.
84. Introduction, 503, 588, 599.
85. See pp. 111–22, above.
86. See Kurt Erlemann, "Adolf Jülicher in der Gleichnisforschung des 20. Jahrhunderts," in *Gleichnisreden Jesu 1899–1999* (ed. Mell), 5–37; Paul Fiebig, "Die Widerlegung der Gleichnistheorie Jülichers," in Harnisch, *Gleichnisse Jesu: Positionen der Auslegung von Adolf Jülicher*, 70–82; Johannes Weiss, "Jülichers 'Gleichnisreden Jesu,'" *TRu* 4 (1901): 1–11, repr. in Harnisch, *Gleichnisse Jesu: Positionen der Auslegung von Adolf Jülicher*, 11–19.

HERETICAL SKEPTICISM: ALFRED LOISY (1857–1940)

Alfred Loisy's contribution to NT research is difficult to assess. His biblical criticism is intertwined in his struggle with the Roman Catholic Church; he produced a huge number of publications; his thought is flexible, frequently changing. As to the church, Loisy was a leader of the movement called Catholic modernism.[87] This movement, which flourished from 1890 to 1907, did not have a formal organization; it was a loose collection of individuals who advocated reform to bring the Church into conversation with the modern world. Earlier in the nineteenth century, liberal voices had spoken out in Germany and in England. In reaction, Pius IX issued the Syllabus of Errors (1864), and denied that the papacy should accommodate to modern thought. In 1870, the First Vatican Council declared the doctrine of papal infallibility. However, Leo XIII (1878–1903) took a more moderate position, and his encyclical *Providentissimus Deus* seemed to allow some room for biblical criticism.

France became the center of Roman Catholic modernism. Louis Duchêsne, who taught church history at the Catholic Institute in Paris, adopted the historical-critical method. Loisy, who had studied with Duchêsne, became the ostensible leader. In England, modernism was represented by George Tyrrell (an Irish Jesuit) and Baron Friedrich von Hügel (an Anglicized Austrian). Modernism in France was also represented by the philosopher Maurice Blondel, and in Italy by the biblical scholars Giovanni Semeria and Salvatore Minocchi. With Pius X, the papacy reverted to reaction. His decree *Lamentabili sane exitu* (1907) listed sixty-five objectionable propositions attributed to the modernists, and his encyclical *Pascendi dominici gregis* (1907) rejected modernist biblical research and condemned modernism as an insidious heresy. After this, Roman Catholic modernism was virtually dead.

Loisy's Life and Thought

Alfred Loisy was born in Ambrières in the Marne Valley.[88] If he had not been frail in health, he would probably have become a farmer like his father. Instead, Loisy decided for the priesthood, and attended the seminary at

---

87. See Bernard M. G. Reardon, ed., *Roman Catholic Modernism*, Library of Modern Religious Thought (Stanford, Calif.: Stanford University Press, 1970); John Ratté, *Three Modernists: Alfred Loisy, George Tyrrell, William L. Sullivan* (New York: Sheed and Ward, 1967); Joseph G. Prior, *The Historical Critical Method in Catholic Exegesis*, Tesi Gregoriana, Serie Teologia 50 (Rome: Gregorian University Press, 1999).

88. See Alfred Loisy, *Choses passées* (Paris: Émile Nourry, 1913); Eng. trans.: *My Duel with the Vatican: The Autobiography of a Catholic Modernist*, trans. Richard Wilson Boynton (New York: E. P. Dutton, 1924); idem, *Mémoires: pour servir à l'histoire religieuse de notre temps*, 3 vols. (Paris: Émile Nourry, 1930–31); Albert Houtin and Félix Sartiaux, *Alfred Loisy: Sa vie, son œuvre*, ed. Émile Poulat (Paris: Éditions du Centre National de la Recherche Scientifique, 1960); Friedrich Heiler, *Alfred Loisy (1857–1940): Der Vater des katholischen Modernismus* (Munich: Erasmus, 1948).

Châlons-sur-Marne. He also studied at the Catholic Institute in Paris where he was appointed to the faculty in 1881. While in this position, he attended the lectures of Renan at the Collège de France, and later wrote, "My ambition was some day to vanquish Ernest Renan with his own weapons—using against him the very principles of criticism that I was learning there at his feet."[89] Because of his critical views, Loisy was dismissed from the Institute, and served from 1893 to 1899 as chaplain for a convent of Dominican nuns.

From 1900 to 1904, Loisy lectured at the Sorbonne in Paris. During this period, he reflected on his concern "to adapt the theory of Catholicism to the facts of history, and the practice of Catholicism to the realities of contemporary life." In 1903, five of Loisy's books were placed on the Index of forbidden books, including his studies on the Gospels and his book on the Gospel of John. In response, he swore that he would submit to the discipline of the Vatican, but wrote, "I reserve the right of my own conscience, and I do not intend . . . either to abandon or to retract the opinions which I have uttered in my capacity of historian and of critical exegete."[90] To Pius X he wrote, "I wish to live and die in the communion of the Catholic Church."[91] In 1904, Loisy resigned from his chair at the Sorbonne and moved to a cottage in Garnay, and later to his sister's house in Ceffonds. Despite his dedication to the church, he was excommunicated in 1908. From 1909 to 1931, he occupied the chair of history of religions at the Collège de France—the chair once held by Renan. Loisy died in 1940 as the armored tanks of the Third Reich rolled into France.

Loisy's theological thought evolved in the context of his relation with the church.[92] A summary of Loisy's view of Christianity can be seen in his widely read *The Gospel and the Church*.[93] Ironically, this book, although directed against Protestant liberalism,[94] was among those placed on the Catholic Index. For Loisy, Harnack's attempt to reduce Christianity to an abstract essence was wrongheaded; instead, the truth of Christianity should be seen

---

89. *My Duel with the Vatican*, 94.
90. Ibid., 224, 251.
91. Quoted in Alfred Loisy, *The Gospel and the Church*, trans. Christopher Home, Introduction by Bernard B. Scott, LJS (Philadelphia: Fortress, 1976), xxvi.
92. See Ronald Burke, "Loisy's Faith: Landshift in Catholic Thought," *JR* 60 (1980): 138–64; Valentine G. Moran, "Loisy's Theological Development," *TS* 40 (1979): 411–52; Harvey Hill, "La Science Catholique: Alfred Loisy's Program of Historical Theology," *Zeitschrift für neuere Theologiegeschichte/Journal for the History of Modern Theology* 3 (1996): 39–59; C. J. T. Talar, *Metaphor and Modernist: The Polarization of Alfred Loisy and His Neo-Thomist Critics* (Lanham, Md.: University Press of America, 1987); idem, *(Re)reading, Reception, and Rhetoric: Approaches to Roman Catholic Modernism*, American University Studies 7, Theology and Religion 206 (New York: Peter Lang, 1999); Francesco Turvasi, *The Condemnation of Alfred Loisy and the Historical Method*, Uomini e Dottrine 24 (Rome: Edizioni de Storia e Letteratura, 1979).
93. *L'Évangile et l'Église* (Paris: Alphonse Picard et Fils, 1902); Eng. trans.: *The Gospel and the Church*.
94. See Wendell S. Dietrich, "Loisy and the Liberal Protestants," *SR* 14 (1985): 303–11.

in its fullness, in its historical tradition and ongoing life.[95] In making this case, Loisy charges that Harnack had imposed modern views on ancient Christianity. In regard to the sources, Loisy understands the Gospels as literary compositions that present Jesus as Messiah. As to Jesus' proclamation of the kingdom of God, Loisy argued that the message was essentially eschatological, not instruction about inner religious experience. "The historian," writes Loisy, "must resist the temptation to modernize the conception of the kingdom." In response to Harnack's understanding of Jesus as Son of God in terms of his God-consciousness, Loisy replies, "the title of Son of God belongs . . . to Jesus not because of His inner disposition and His religious experiences, but because of His Providential function as the sole maker of the kingdom of Heaven." In regard to the church, Loisy denounced Harnack's idea that the true community of Christians was invisible. According to Loisy, the disciples constituted a visible congregation from the beginning; the visible church was necessary for the preservation of the gospel. The church, Loisy thinks, arose in response to the preaching of Jesus. "Jesus foretold the kingdom, and it was the Church that came." To Harnack's charge that the sacraments represented a Hellenizing of Christian worship, Loisy responded that the rituals of the church had their origin in the practices of the primitive community, and naturally assimilated symbols from Greek culture as the church moved into the Greco-Roman world.[96] In his later work, Loisy displays the influence of the history of religion method, but he resists the conclusion that early Christianity was a syncretistic religion.[97]

Loisy's NT Research

Félix Sartiaux analyzes Loisy's research according to three main periods: (1) prior to 1911, when Loisy is attempting to maintain relations with the church; (2) 1911–25, when he is influenced by the history of religion school; (3) 1926–33, when he presents his mature understanding of early Christianity.[98] In the early period, Loisy published a book on the canon of the NT, a collection of biblical studies, and a collection of essays on the Gospels. In his *Histoire du canon du Nouveau Testament* (1891) Loisy argues that the basic formulation of the canon was accomplished by the year 220.[99] The Council of Trent, in Loisy's opinion, affirmed canonicity but left the

---

95. See pp. 122–25, above.
96. *Gospel and Church*, 73, 105, 166.
97. See 238–53, below. Loisy's major contribution to the discussion is his *Les mystères païens et le mystère chrétien* (Paris: Émile Nourry, 1914).
98. Houtin and Sartiaux, *Loisy*, 199–224; See Alan H. Jones, *Independence and Exegesis: The Study of Early Christianity in the Work of Alfred Loisy (1857–1940), Charles Guignebert (1857–1939) and Maurice Goguel (1880–1955)*, BGBE 26 (Tübingen: J. C. B. Mohr [Paul Siebeck], 1983.
99. Repr., Frankfurt: Minerva, 1971.

question of authenticity open. In a general essay on biblical criticism, Loisy writes, "We should criticize the Bible with the same exactitude that one brings nowadays to the examination of the documents of secular antiquity."[100] In an essay titled "The Biblical Question and the Inspiration of the Scriptures," Loisy contends that the question of the infallibility of the Bible is a historical question, and when it is answered historically, the Bible is seen to contain errors. Among Loisy's essays on the Gospels is an article that applauds Jülicher's work on the parables. "The gospel parable," writes Loisy, "was a simple story that had for its object of application the kingdom of God; it was to be taken literally; it was perfectly clear, able to make the religion of Jesus intelligible for the masses of the people."[101]

Loisy's major work from the early period is his massive, two-volume study of the Synoptic Gospels. The first volume, which contains more than one thousand pages, presents an extensive (268-page) critical introduction. Loisy is skeptical of the ecclesiastical tradition, and believes the process of canonization largely ignored the question of the historical origin of the books. "Matthew," he says, "is not the gospel of Matthew; Mark is not the gospel of Peter; Luke is not the gospel of Paul. Nothing or almost nothing of the accounts conceived by the tradition survives criticism."[102] According to Loisy, the author of Mark used the Logia (Q) and an early narrative source, written prior to the deaths of Peter and Paul. Loisy believes the Gospel of Mark went through two redactions. The author of Matthew, according to Loisy, used a Greek translation of the Logia—a document that Loisy believed to have been composed between 60 and 70 in Aramaic. Matthew and Luke were written around 100, and in Loisy's judgment, are of less historical value than Mark. The tradition behind the Gospels had its origin in the early Christian proclamation of Jesus as the Christ. As the tradition developed, Loisy believes details such as the miracle stories were added to enhance the picture of Jesus.

On the basis of his analysis of the gospel tradition, Loisy presents his understanding of the life and teachings of Jesus. Largely following the outline of Mark, Loisy accepts the confession of Peter as a historical turning point. Although Loisy believes Jesus' message of the kingdom was eschatological, he does not think it was political, but spiritual and moral.

> The career and teaching of Jesus was the grain of mustard that became a tree, the piece of leaven that fermented the whole lump of dough. Nothing is more insignificant in appearance: a village artisan, naive and enthusiastic, who

---

100. *Études bibliques*, 3d ed. (Paris: Alphonse Picard et Fils, 1903), 119. Loisy's overview of NT criticism is seen in his *Les Livres du Nouveau Testament, traduits du grec en français avec introduction général et notices* (Paris: Émile Nourry, 1922)—a work of more than seven hundred pages that presents translation of the books of the NT with critical introductory notes.

101. *Études évangéliques* (Paris: Alphonse Picard et Fils, 1902), 70.

102. *Les évangiles synoptiques*, 2 vols. (Ceffonds: the Author, 1907–8) 1:58.

believed in the approaching end of the world, the inauguration of a reign of justice, the coming of God on the earth, and who, relying on this first illusion, attributed to himself the principal role in the organization of this unrealizable city; who set himself to prophesying, inviting all of his compatriots to repent of their sins, so as to be reconciled to the great Judge whose coming is imminent and will be sudden like that of a thief; who had to be arrested promptly, which was done by the established powers; who was unable to escape a violent death and who suffered it.[103]

This understanding of the career and teaching of Jesus is expanded in Loisy's *Jésus et la tradition évangélique*—a book addressed to the general reader. In it, Loisy acknowledges the impossibility of producing a biography: "It is now necessary to abandon the writing of the life of Jesus."[104]

The balance of volume 1 and all of volume 2 (almost eight hundred pages) of the Synoptic commentary is devoted to exegesis. The material is presented according to pericopes, and where parallels exist, the texts (in French translation) are printed in parallel columns. Loisy's interpretation of the temptation can serve as an example. In the gospel tradition, Loisy believes this narrative has its meaning in relation to Jesus' messianic consecration at baptism, and is designed to show that Satan is defeated at the beginning of the ministry. Loisy notes that Matthew concludes the account with a reference to the ministering angels (4:11), while Luke says that Satan departed "until an opportune time" (4:13); that time, according to Loisy, is the time of Gethsemane where Luke's account adds a ministering angel (22:43). As to historicity, Loisy believes the temptation narrative is neither true history nor pure myth. Jesus no doubt wrestled with his vocation prior to beginning his ministry in Galilee, but Loisy believes the tradition has shaped the account from the perspective of the end of the ministry, supplying details from the HB.

Later, Loisy published separate, less technical commentaries on *Mark* and *Luke*. In the Marcan commentary, the material is investigated according to pericopes; the text in French is printed at the top of the page with comments in paragraph form below.[105] For example, in regard to the feeding of the four thousand (8:1-10), Loisy thinks the author of Mark found two written accounts of miraculous feedings in his sources, but that they depend on an earlier single tradition. The author, according to Loisy, has used the two accounts for his own purpose, for instance, the mention of the seven baskets of fragments corresponds to the number of table servers appointed in the early church (Acts 6:3). Written a decade and half after the Synoptic commentary, the commentary on *Luke* reveals development in

---

103. Ibid. 1:252.
104. *Jésus et la tradition évangélique* (Paris, 1910; repr., Frankfurt: Minerva, 1971), 5.
105. *L'Évangile selon Marc* (Paris: Émile Nourry, 1912); see Nadia M. Lahutsky, "Paris and Jerusalem: Alfred Loisy and Père Lagrange on the Gospel of Mark," *CBQ* 52 (1990): 444–64.

Loisy's criticism.[106] He notes the recent work of Bultmann and Dibelius on form criticism.[107] He adopts Eduard Norden's thesis that an original gospel written by Luke to Theophilus was later extensively edited. Loisy believes the original gospel differed at both the beginning and the end; the redactor added birth stories and an account of the ascension. According to Loisy, the book to Theophilus was written around 80, and the final, canonical edition was completed at Rome, around 125 to 150.[108]

In the middle period, Loisy published books on Acts, the Fourth Gospel, and Revelation. In the critical introduction to the Acts commentary, Loisy, as in his work on Luke, follows Norden's theory of composition. According to this theory, the original document, the "second book to Theophilus," was written by Luke, the travel companion of Paul. Loisy thinks this original document included the major events narrated in canonical Acts. However, Loisy believes its original ending, which he thinks included an account of the trial, condemnation, and execution of Paul, was excised by the redactor. Loisy thinks the redactor also mutilated the prologue, which he thinks contained an account of Galilean resurrection appearances. The purpose of the redactor, according to Loisy, is to present Christianity as the true Judaism, and to this end, he Judaizes Paul and Hellenizes Peter. After this extensive introduction (more than 120 pages), Loisy presents more than eight hundred pages of commentary. In regard to the ascension (Acts 1:9-11), for example, Loisy believes this text to be the work of the redactor. As to details, he notes the significance of the cloud: it is reminiscent of the cloud of the transfiguration narrative and symbolizes communication between heaven and earth. The story of the ascension, Loisy believes, was created to replace the hope in the imminent parousia; it affirms that though Christ will appear in the future, the work of Christ is now to be accomplished on earth. "The ascension shares in the system of fictions, carefully contrived and arranged, by which the historical relation of Luke was transformed into a legendary apologetic of primitive Christianity."[109]

Loisy's work on the Fourth Gospel is a revision of an earlier book (1903) that was among those placed on the Index. In the new edition, he has revised his theory of composition, and added his analysis of the Johannine Epistles.[110] In the critical introduction (eighty pages), Loisy notes that five documents—the Fourth Gospel, the three Johannine Epistles, and the

---

106. *L'Évangile selon Luc* (Paris: Émile Nourry, 1924).
107. See pp. 269–86, below.
108. Also in this period Loisy published *L'Épître aux Galates* (Paris: Émile Nourry, 1916), a short commentary on Galatians in which he argues that the figure behind the Judaizing opposition in Galatia is James, the brother of the Lord. Loisy also thinks Paul betrays inconsistencies: he claims authority from God, but seeks the approval of the Jerusalem leaders; his mysticism leads him into fanciful arguments in defense of justification by faith.
109. *Les Actes des Apôtres* (Paris: Émile Nourry, 1920), 163.
110. *Le quatrième évangile*, 2d ed.; *Les épîtres dites de Jean* (Paris: Émile Nourry, 1921).

Apocalypse—have all been attributed to the apostle John. After reviewing the history of critical research from the eighteenth century to his own time, Loisy presents his conclusion: the apostle John had nothing to do with the writing of any of these documents. As to the composition of the Gospel of John, Loisy believes an original gospel, composed by a Gentile mystic who shared the Hellenistic ideas of the Gnostics, was written in the last quarter of the first century. The redaction, which involved at least two stages, was designed, according to Loisy, to bring the original mystical gospel into harmony with the Synoptic tradition. The first redaction was made in the early second century, and the second (which added chapter 21) some twenty or thirty years later. As to the commentary (more than five hundred pages), Loisy's analysis of the resurrection of Lazarus is typical. He thinks the original gospel, taking up and expanding the earlier tradition of raisings, included an account of this miracle. The original account, Loisy thinks, described only one sister; Mary and Martha are presented in the redaction according to their behavior as recorded in Luke 10:38-42. The presentation of Martha as resisting the opening of the tomb (because of the stench) represents, according to Loisy, the redactor's concern to emphasize the physical resurrection. Loisy believes the whole story illustrates the saying, "I am the resurrection and the life" (John 11:25).

In his commentary on the *Apocalypse*, Loisy observes its importance for understanding the eschatological beliefs of the early Christians.[111] He believes an original author, using Jewish material, wrote the basic book during the reign of Domitian. A later redactor, writing between 120 and 140, edited the original work in order to present it as apostolic and part of the Johannine collection. Loisy believes the author of the original was a prophet named John who had migrated from Palestine to Asia Minor. He believes the picture of Christ throughout the Apocalypse is not consistent: in the opening chapters he is the revealer; later he becomes the object of the visions. Loisy also notes the problem of a beast with seven heads and ten horns. He thinks the second beast, in distinction from the first (which had its source in Daniel), was a creation of the author. Loisy believes this second beast may represent the archheretic, Simon Magus.

In the 1930s Loisy made his final contributions to NT research. His *The Birth of the Christian Religion* summarizes his earlier work on the NT.[112] He acknowledges that Christianity has presented Jesus as a myth, but he believes a historical person stands behind the myth:

> While the Christian religion was not created by myth alone, so, certainly, it was not created by Jesus alone; its creator was neither Jesus without the myth,

---

111. *L'Apocalypse de Jean* (Paris: Émile Nourry, 1923).
112. *La naissance du christianisme* (Paris: Émile Nourry, 1933); Eng. trans.: *The Birth of the Christian Religion,* trans. L. P. Jacks (London: George Allen & Unwin, 1948).

nor the myth without Jesus. Jesus the Nazorean is at once an historical person and a mythical being who, supporting the myth and supported by it, was finally made by it into the Christ, Lord and God, for the faith which so acknowledged him.

In discussing the sources, Loisy presents his understanding of NT introduction at this point in his career. In the main, he has become more skeptical of the tradition, and inclined to date NT documents later. For example, he says that Matthew cannot have been written much before 125. "To sum the matter up in a sentence, all the difficulties and gropings in the dark which the interpretation of these documents imposes on the impartial historian proceed from the fact that the documents he is interpreting are something other than history."[113]

Loisy's assessment of the life and teaching of Jesus has also moved a little farther to the left. "Let us then recognize the simple fact that the oldest tradition now perceptible about the death of Jesus, like that about his ministry, has already become a liturgical legend, the evolution of which in the gospel literature preserves throughout the same ritual character, complicated by apologetic interests." He believes the idea of the resurrection of Jesus was produced by faith:

> Faith raised Jesus into the glory he expected; faith declared him living for ever because faith itself was determined never to die. Quickened by the ordeal, faith produced out of itself visions that brought balm to its anguish and strength to its affirmations. With the fragments of a shattered hope, and building on the death of Jesus, which might well have killed their faith outright, the disciples founded the religion of Jesus the Christ.[114]

At this point in his career, Loisy interprets the later literature of the NT as evidence for the transformation of the primitive community into the "Christian Mystery."[115] The disciples believed that Christ had been exalted to the right hand of God; they gave him the title "Lord," making him, in Loisy's opinion, the deity of a cult.

In regard to the Epistle to the Romans, Loisy believes that the complex discussion of the law has been woven into the text by a non-Jewish redactor who presents sin as "a fearful and monstrous abstraction."

> The idea of grace is not less ponderous, nor that of redemption less artificial. Sin, the capital evil of humanity, innate in the flesh—though we are not told how—is suddenly annihilated because the Christ, having taken flesh, takes sin upon him also, but without being defiled by it, and then, by the destruction of his own flesh effects the destruction of sin in humanity at large. . . . Childish

---

113. *Birth of the Christian Religion*, 11, 60.
114. Ibid., 79, 85.
115. Loisy had earlier moved in this direction; see his essay "The Christian Mystery," *HibJ* 10 (1911): 45–64.

dreams worked up into a theological nightmare and adapted, by hook or crook, to a lofty moral conception![116]

This mystical move in the Pauline and Deutero-Pauline Letters reaches a high point in the Fourth Gospel. "Here is mysticism at once profound and luminous; a scheme of salvation purely spiritual and yet throbbing with life; a transcendent Christology penetrated through and through by human tenderness and a unique mode of speech which one might think had been created for the lofty use here made of it." In the struggle with Gnosticism, the church, in Loisy's opinion, became virtually a gnostic cult. "Thus Christianity, it its own way, was a gnosis, and so it has always remained."[117]

Loisy's last word about the NT is found in his *The Origins of the New Testament*.[118] In this book Loisy presents the evolution of Christianity from the earliest eschatological message of Jesus to the apologetic catechesis of the catholic church. The development can be seen in the Synoptic Gospels, where the tradition about Jesus is adapted to catechetical and apologetic purposes. Paul, who emphasizes both eschatology and mysticism, provides a turning point in the transition. With the final editions of Acts, John, and the Pastoral Epistles, the apologetic purpose is accomplished. Loisy presents his final estimate of the NT:

> Putting aside all considerations of supernatural magic, and paying no heed to the narrow prejudice of rationalism, which leads to the denial of all human value in whatever is mingled with historical or literary fiction, dismissing all this, it still remains true that the collection of the New Testament, incomplete and incoherent as it may be in many respects, is the everliving witness, to those who have ears to hear, of an extraordinary spiritual movement.[119]

With Loisy, radical criticism had moved from Tübingen to Paris—and the farther he moved from the Church, the more radical his criticism had become. Because of his Catholic background and his prestige as an educator and savant, his impact on French intellectual life was significant. Much of his criticism, to be sure, was borrowed from others—especially the Germans. Yet, he was a scholar of immense comprehension and mastery of detail with exceptional powers of analysis and literary expression. Like other scholars of this chapter, Loisy was skeptical of the developing early

---

116. *Birth of the Christian Religion*, 257, 271. In 1935, Loisy published a collection of studies on the NT epistles: *Remarques sur la littérature épistolaire du Nouveau Testament* (Paris: Émile Nourry, 1935). In three of these, he presents his belief that the Pauline Letters present two theories of salvation, indeed, two personalities of Paul. For example, in Rom. 3:27—4:25, the eschatological idea of salvation is declared, but in 1 Cor. 2:6-13 and in 2 Corinthians 12 the mystical Paul appears.
117. *Birth of the Christian Religion*, 295–96.
118. *Les origines du Nouveau Testament* (Paris, 1936; repr., Frankfurt: Minerva, 1971); Eng. trans.: *The Origins of the New Testament*, trans. L. P. Jacks (New York: Macmillan, 1950).
119. *Origins of the New Testament*, 329.

tradition—even though he honored the total tradition more than many of his Protestant opponents. He also gave major attention to the process of the redaction of early Christian literature. Like many of his contemporaries and successors, he denied the possibility of a biography of Jesus. In regard to Jesus' idea of the kingdom, he sided with the eschatologists rather than the liberals. As to Paul, Loisy, in contrast to most Protestants, disparaged the apostle's life and thought. On critical questions in general, Loisy had moved to the left of the other scholars of this chapter.

SUMMARY

The scholars of this chapter reveal some significant agreements. All of them assume the reliability of the historical-critical method, and are largely oblivious of its presuppositions. They accept the Enlightenment worldview uncritically, and assume an ontology of history whereby what is discerned historically is thought to be true. They are essentially hostile to metaphysics and dogma, especially in their orthodox ecclesiastical expression. However, they are sensitive to the tension between faith and history, for example, the conflict between Catholicism and criticism (Loisy). Overbeck is reluctant to disturb his students' faith; Wellhausen resigns from the theological faculty. Jülicher supposes criticism can retard skepticism, but his results are far from orthodox. These scholars also agree in rejecting the traditional doctrine of inspiration and infallibility. However, some notion of biblical authority seems implicit in their tireless dedication to biblical research, and perhaps in assumptions about revelation in history, or in some idea of the vitality or self-evident authenticity of religious origins.

Among these scholars, an emerging consensus can be seen on some issues: the two-document hypothesis, the unauthenticity of the Pastoral Epistles, the non-Pauline character of Hebrews, the problematic authorship of the Johannine literature and the Catholic Epistles. Jülicher's understanding of the parables as having one essential point of comparison is widely accepted. These scholars are particularly concerned with literary analysis, source criticism, and redaction. They deny that a biography of Jesus is possible, but most of them find some special significance in the life and teachings of Jesus. In regard to the teachings, the scholars differ on a basic question: is Jesus' message of the kingdom of God primarily eschatological or ethical? In the effort to answer this and other questions related to the historical Jesus, these critics, especially Wrede and Loisy, underscore the problem of the Gospels as historical sources. The old distinction between John and the Synoptics has collapsed: Mark, the historical bedrock of the two-document hypothesis, is also acknowledged to be a theological document. What of the tradition behind Mark and Q; is it reliable or is it dominated by theological and apologetic concerns? What are the methods and criteria for evaluating the developing tradition?

These scholars are concerned with ongoing tradition after Jesus. Although only Overbeck, Wrede, and Loisy see Paul as a second founder, the others, betraying a persistent liberalism, are inclined to disparage or ethicize him—relegating the doctrine of justification by faith to a secondary role. Does Paul represent a theologizing or Hellenizing of the original message of Jesus? How reliable is the Acts of the Apostles as a historical document? And what of Christianity of the postapostolic age? Does it represent a developing tradition of ecclesiasticizing and canonizing—an interpolating and redacting—that eclipses the history of early Christianity and its literature? And what of the skepticism of the skeptics? Although suspicion is an essential element of criticism, are all of the bearers of tradition to be viewed as traitors? Is it possible that some of the early traditioners might have been as faithful to the religion and ethics of Jesus as the later "pure" historians? In any case, the resulting picture of early Christianity, like the paintings of the Impressionists, had become a blurred image. Efforts to bring it into focus would be encouraged by new discoveries and new methods of NT research.

Part II

NEW TESTAMENT RESEARCH IN THE ERA OF GLOBAL CONFLICT

5

New Discoveries: Linguistic, Geographical, and Historical Research

In the latter part of the nineteenth century, European imperial expansion in Asia and Africa stirred interest in distant lands. New and better modes of transportation facilitated exploration. Pious believers, troubled by the modern world, looked for refuge in the Holy Land. Egypt, which had enshrined the mysteries of the Great Pyramid and the gold of Tutankhamen, proffered even more valuable treasures. In the 1890s, huge quantities of papyri were found in unsuspected places: in mummy cases, in mummified crocodiles, and most of all, in rubbish heaps outside the cities. Leaders in discovery were scholars such as archeologist Sir Flinders Petrie and the Oxford papyrologists B. P. Grenfell and A. S. Hunt. The latter two started digging at Oxyrhynchus in 1896, and in 1898, began a series of publications that finally swelled to more than forty volumes.

Among the discoverers were two Scottish twin sisters, Agnes Smith Lewis (1843–1926) and Margaret Dunlop Gibson (1843–1920), who found, photographed, transcribed, and published important NT manuscripts. Lewis, an expert in Semitic languages, paleography, and text criticism, published a score of scholarly books and several periodical articles. Gibson, who shared her sister's linguistic talents, published Arabic translations of the NT and a critical edition of the Syriac lectionary. The two Victorian ladies, riding camels from Suez to Sinai, made their first visit to St. Catherine's Monastery in 1892. During repeated visits, they continued to find and investigate important manuscripts; the account of their travels reads like a novel.[1] Their most important discovery was a palimpsest of the Old Syriac

---

1. Agnes Smith Lewis, *In the Shadow of Sinai: A Story of Travel and Research from 1895 to 1897* (Cambridge: Macmillan & Bowes, 1898). This book, bound together with a monograph by Gibson (*How the Codex Was Found: A Narrative of Two Visits to Sinai from Mrs. Lewis's Journals, 1892–1893*) has been reprinted (Brighton, UK: Alpha, 1999).

version of the Gospels, dated probably in the fourth century.[2] Lewis wrote the introduction to the critical edition of the manuscript.[3] These sisters provide a single example of extensive geographical exploration, archeological research, and discovery of monuments and inscriptions. In regard to biblical sites, for instance, excavation began at Ephesus in 1863 by J. T. Wood under the auspices of the British Museum. The Austrian Archeological Institute carried on their Ephesian excavations from 1898 to 1913, and resumed them again from 1926 to 1935.

This story of exploration and discovery was interrupted by the tragedy of World War I. The assassin's shot fired in Sarajevo in 1914 echoed around the world. Ignited by this event, the proud nationalism and the jealous imperialism of the preceding decades, fueled by the race for military superiority, exploded into global chaos. The senseless outcome of intrigue and rival alliances, the war was soon transfigured into an ideological crusade: Germany perceived itself as defending western civilization against the pan-Slavism of the Russian east; Britain supposed it was opposing the crimes and barbarism of the "Huns"; America, with illusory idealism, entered the war in order to preserve democracy, to fight a war to end all wars.

NT scholars were not untouched by these tragic events. Institutes were shut down, projects postponed, energies debilitated, careers diverted, and lives lost. The old animosities toward German criticism, lurking in the shadows for generations, emerged into the light of day.[4] Exegetes searched the Scriptures to justify their hostility to the enemy. Jesus, after all, attacked the money changers, and his ethic of nonretaliation, according to the militant apologists, applied to individuals, not to nations. Others struggled to maintain communication across enemy lines, and to support movements for peace and reconciliation. Distracted and crippled in spirit, NT research continued to hobble along, and, in spite of obstacles, was able to accomplish significant results.

WORDS AND THEIR SOCIAL AND RELIGIOUS IMPLICATIONS: ADOLF DEISSMANN (1866–1937)

Adolf Deissmann was born in Langenscheid, the son of a Lutheran pastor and pious mother. "For my whole understanding of religion and religious research," Deissmann wrote, "I am thankful most of all for my parental

---

2. Agnes Smith Lewis, *Light on the Four Gospels from the Sinai Palimpsest* (London: Williams & Norgate, 1913).
3. Robert L. Bensly, J. Rendel Harris, and F. Crawford Burkitt, *The Four Gospels in Syriac: Transcribed from the Sinaitic Palimpsest, with an Introduction by Agnes Smith Lewis* (Cambridge: Cambridge University Press, 1894).
4. See Charles E. Bailey, "The British Protestant Theologians in the First World War: Germanophobia Unleashed," *HTR* 77 (1984): 195–221.

home."⁵ He studied at Tübingen (with Carl Weizsäcker) and in Berlin (with Otto Pfleiderer and Bernhard Weiss). In 1891, he was drawn to Marburg by Georg Heinrici's research on the historical setting of the NT and worked there as an instructor. In 1897, Deissmann was appointed professor at Heidelberg. He made extensive study tours of the Mediterranean world in 1906 and 1909. In 1908, he was called to Berlin as successor of the venerable Bernhard Weiss. Deissmann did extensive archeological research in Ephesus in 1926, 1927, and 1928.

Deissmann was not a theologian—and proud of it! He was, however, deeply religious. For Deissmann, the center of Christianity was not a mechanically inspired book but a nonliterary person—"the living Christ."⁶

> Far away in the East there rises up before us, higher and higher above the thronging crowd of poor and lowly, a Sacred Form. To His own He is already the Saviour and giver of light; to the great world He is invisible as yet in the morning twilight, but it too shall one day bow before Him. In His profound intimacy with God and in manly strength of consciousness of His Messianic mission Jesus of Nazareth is the sheer incarnation of religious inwardness fixed solely on the Kingdom of God, and therefore He is strong to fight and worthy of the highest grace in store for Him—that of being allowed to lay down His life for the salvation of many.⁷

Deissmann believed the Christian ethic should be applied to social and political problems. During the war, he tried to promote understanding among Protestants across national borders, publishing the *Protestant Weekly Letter*.

Deissmann's inaugural dissertation (*Habilitationsschrift*) at Marburg is an analytical investigation of a single phrase: ἐν χριστῷ Ἰησοῦ. In the investigation, Deissmann analyzes the use of the preposition ἐν with a personal singular noun or pronoun in nonbiblical (profane) Greek, and also in Greek that reflects Semitic influence. Comparing the results with Pauline usage, Deissmann concludes that Paul's use is closer to profane Greek than to "biblical" Greek. Paul, he thinks, has employed the common language of the Hellenistic world to create a new religious terminology. "The formula

---

5. "Adolf Deissmann," in *RGS* 1:43. For a survey of Deissmann's life and work, see Hans Lietzmann, "Adolf Deissmann zum Gedächtnis," in *Kleine Schriften, III. Studien zur Liturgie- und Symbolgeschichte zur Wissenschaftsgeschichte*, ed. Der Kommission für Spätantike Religionsgeschichte (Berlin: Akademie-Verlag, 1962), 316–24; Gertrud Frischmuth, "Adolf Deissmann: Ein Leben in Christo für die Una Sancta," in *Ökumenische Profile: Brückenbauer der einen Kirche*, ed. Günter Gloede (Stuttgart: Evangelische Missionsverlag, 1961), 280–90; Wilbert Francis Howard, *The Romance of New Testament Scholarship*, Drew Lectureship in Biography (London: Epworth, 1949), 117–28.
6. Adolf Deissmann, *The New Testament in the Light of Modern Research* (Garden City, N.Y.: Doubleday, Doran, 1929), 174.
7. Adolf Deissmann, *Light from the Ancient East*, trans. Lionel R. M. Strachan (New York: George H. Doran, 1927), 383.

ἐν χριστῷ 'Ιησοῦ created by Paul by the use of an available expression of profane Greek characterizes the relation of the Christian to Jesus Christ as understanding one's self in a local relation to the spiritual Christ."[8]

Deissmann's continuing research of this sort is found in two collections of essays.[9] These essays investigate material from the recently discovered papyri and inscriptions in order to understand the language and literature of Hellenistic Judaism and early Christianity. In one of the essays, Deissmann presents his famous distinction between letters and epistles. According to the distinction, letters are real written communications between particular people; epistles are literary compositions for the larger public. Deissmann believes all the epistles of Paul are letters, whereas he classifies Hebrews and the Catholic Epistles as epistles. In essays on the history of the language of the Greek Bible, Deissmann attacks the earlier notion that biblical Greek was a special, sacred language. Instead, he argues that it was the vernacular of the Hellenistic world—the language found in receipts, student exercises, marriage contracts, and other scraps of writing unearthed in the rubbish heaps of Egypt. In other publications, Deissmann repeats and expands his understanding of biblical Greek.[10] He argues that the antiquated notion of a special "biblical Greek" errs in two ways: it supposes that the Greek of the NT is peculiar; it imagines that the Greek of the NT is uniform. Deissmann believes that only about fifty of the five thousand words of the NT are unique. The Septuagint, although a translation of a Semitic original, also uses the common Greek of its time.[11] The study of NT language, in Deissmann's opinion, illuminates early Christian history: Christianity moved from the restricted Semitic neighborhood into the larger Hellenistic world, adopting the common language and becoming a universal religion.

Deissmann's monumental *Light from the Ancient East* first appeared in 1908 and went through several editions.[12] His thesis is that Christianity must be understood in its historical setting and seen as a movement of the lower classes. However, in his opinion, Christianity was not a proletarian or political movement; it was a religious movement with a future hope, grounded

---

8. *Die neutestamentliche Formel "in Christo Jesu"* (Marburg: N. G. Elwert, 1892), 97.

9. *Bibelstudien* (Marburg: N. G. Elwert, 1895); idem, *Neue Bibelstudien* (Marburg: N. G. Elwert, 1897). In a different arrangement, the essays of these volumes are presented in an English translation: *Bible Studies: Contributions Chiefly from Papyri and Inscriptions to the History of the Language, the Literature, and the Religion of Hellenistic Judaism and Primitive Christianity*, trans. Alexander Grieve (Edinburgh: T. & T. Clark, 1901; repr., Peabody, Mass.: Hendrickson, 1988).

10. *Die sprachliche Erforschung der griechischen Bibel* (Giessen: J. Ricker, 1898); *The Philology of the Greek Bible* (London: Hodder and Stoughton, 1908); idem, *Die Urgeschichte des Christentums im Lichte der Sprachforschung* (Tübingen: J. C. B. Mohr [Paul Siebeck], 1910).

11. See Adolf Deissmann, *Die Hellenisierung des semitischen Monotheismus* (Leipzig: B. G. Teubner, 1903).

12. *Licht vom Osten*, 4th ed. (Tübingen: J. C. B. Mohr [Paul Siebeck], 1923); Eng. trans.: *Light from the Ancient East*.

in God. Deissmann believes the Gospels reflect the culture of the Palestinian villages, and the epistles of Paul, the culture of the Hellenistic cities; Jesus was a carpenter, Paul a tentmaker.

> The result of our observation until now is this: early Christianity in its leading personalities and in the preponderance of its members is a movement of the lower classes. The water of life did not trickle down from the upper class to the many and the small, but bubbled up from the depth of a simple divine spirit; it was drunk first by the lost and the powerless from the great caravan of the unknown and forgotten; again, it was something unpretentious that had flowed from the inexhaustible source into the world, so that the simple were able to drink.[13]

This understanding of Christianity is fostered by the newly discovered sources, and when these sources are followed, the NT can be returned to its original home.

> The New Testament is an exile here in the West, and we do well to restore it to its home in Anatolia. It is right to set it once more in the company of the unlearned, after it has made so long a stay amid the surroundings of modern culture. We have had hundreds of University chairs for the exact, scientific interpretation of the little Book—let us now listen while the homeland of the New Testament yields up its own authentic witness to the inquiring scholar.[14]

Throughout his book, Deissmann shows how the newly discovered material throws light on early Christian social and religious history: the papyri offer information about village life; the excavation of cities such as Pompeii provides data about the Pauline cities. NT terms and concepts find parallels in the remnants of the ancient world. Paul's idea of redemption, for example, reflects the practice of sacral manumission of slaves, witnessed by inscriptions found at Delphi. Illuminated by this new material, the NT shines with its original radiance.

> A book from the ancient East, and lit up by the light of the dawn,—a book breathing the fragrance of the Galilean spring, and anon swept by the shipwrecking north-east tempest from the Mediterranean,—a book of peasants, fishermen, artisans, travelers by land and sea, fighters and martyrs,—a book in cosmopolitan Greek with marks of Semitic origin,—a book of the Imperial age, written at Antioch, Ephesus, Corinth, Rome,—a book of pictures, miracles, and visions,—book of the village and the town, book of the people and the peoples,—the New Testament, if regard be had to the inward side of things, is the great book, chief and singular, of human souls.[15]

---

13. Adolf Deissmann, *Das Urchristentum und die unteren Schichten*, 2d ed. (Göttingen: Vandenhoeck & Ruprecht, 1908), 36.
14. *Light from the Ancient East*, 61.
15. Ibid., 392. Shorter versions of this same material were presented in lectures given at Frankfurt am Main in 1905 (*New Light on the New Testament*, trans. Lionel R. M. Strachan [Edinburgh: T. & T. Clark, 1908]) and at Oberlin College in 1929 (*NT in the Light of Modern Research*).

Also important is Deissmann's book on Paul.[16] The English title is descriptive: *Paul: A Study in Social and Religious History*.[17] Again exploiting the new discoveries, Deissmann's intent is to understand Paul in his historical and geographical setting. Deissmann does not engage in sophisticated sociological analysis, but displays a concern with people and their daily lives, their religious and psychological experience. He studies Paul as a social being, not as a theologian:

> I mean Paul the Jew, who in the days of the Caesars breathed the air of the Mediterranean and ate the bread which he had earned by the labour of his own hands; the missionary whose dark shadow fell on the glittering marble pavement of the great city in the blinding glare of noon; the mystic devotee of Christ who, so far as he can be comprehended historically at all, will be understood not as the incarnation of a system but as a living complex of inner polarities.[18]

As to sources, Deissmann accepts all the canonical Epistles attributed to Paul except Hebrews and the Pastorals as Pauline, and even the latter he considers borderline. For study of the Epistles, Deissmann believes Philemon should be the point of departure, since it is the most letter-like of all the Epistles. Deissmann thinks the imprisonment letters were written from Ephesus, that Ephesians is really "Laodiceans," and that Romans 16 was originally a separate letter sent to Ephesus.

Describing Paul the man, Deissmann views the apostle as a person of violent contrasts. Paul, above all, is a particular kind of mystic. "His mysticism is not acting mysticism, but reacting mysticism, not a mysticism which strives after absorption in the Deity but a mysticism which receives communion with God as a gift of grace." Paul was a Jew, but a Jew of the Greek-speaking dispersion. He became a Christian, according to Deissmann, by his conversion—a mystical experience. "What happened at Damascus ought not to be isolated, but it should be regarded as the basal mystical experience of the religious genius to whom also in later life extraordinary and even ecstatic experiences were vouchsafed."[19]

Deissmann characterizes Paul's religion as a "Christ-mysticism"—a religion of personal communion. "Christ is for Paul not a person of the past, with whom he can only come into contact by meditating on the words that have been handed from him, not a 'historical' personage, but a reality and

---

In the latter work, Deissmann presents critical views on the NT: support of the two-document hypothesis; Luke and Acts written by Luke, travel companion of Paul; the Fourth Gospel by a personal disciple of Jesus who was not the author of the Apocalypse.

16. *Paulus: Eine kultur- und religionsgeschichtliche Skizze*, 2d ed. (Tübingen: J. C. B. Mohr [Paul Siebeck], 1925).

17. Trans. William E. Wilson (1927; repr., New York: HT, 1957).

18. Ibid., x.

19. Ibid., 79, 130.

power of the present, an 'energy,' whose life-giving powers are daily expressing themselves in him, and to whom, since that day at Damascus, he has felt a personal-cult dependence."[20] Paul, according to Deissmann, presents his doctrine of salvation by means of contemporary metaphors such as redemption and adoption; he stresses the crucifixion, but understands sacrificial language as metaphorical.

A summary of Deissmann's understanding of NT religion is presented in lectures he delivered in England in 1923, *The Religion of Jesus and the Faith of Paul*.[21] In regard to Jesus, Deissmann notes that the tradition is fragmentary. Deissmann recommends a method of "indirect observation" whereby one looks behind the fragmentary data to the religious experience of Jesus. From this perspective, the importance of the prayer life of Jesus becomes apparent. Jesus, according to Deissmann, related to God as Father, the loving and forgiving one; and as Lord, the one to whom he was obedient. Deissmann believes Jesus' idea of the kingdom of God is both spiritual and social: it "is both an inner attitude of the individual soul and a programme of revolution for the world."

> And so I would say that the originality of Jesus lies in his whole personality, in the peculiar energy of His experience of the living God. It is not His concepts that are original, but His power; not His formulae, but His confessions; not His dogmas, but His faith; not His system, but His personality. The originality of Jesus lies in the comprehensive uniqueness of His inner life; the new, the epoch-making thing, is Himself.[22]

Adolf Deissmann is a strange mixture of liberal, pietist, and critic. In the liberal tradition he eschews theology and embraces religion. The religion he embraces is a religion of inner mystical piety—a religion that displays a continuity from Jesus to Paul to Deissmann himself. As critic, Deissmann is loyal to the historical method, but for him, new resources provide new perspectives, and new perspectives indicate that the subject of history is real people, social movements, psychological experience. Of continuing importance is Deissmann's research in the papyri, confirming the language of the NT as the common Greek of the Hellenistic age.

---

20. Ibid., 136.
21. Trans. William E. Wilson (New York: George H. Doran, 1923). See also Adolf Deissmann, *Evangelium und Urchristentum* (Munich: J. F. Lehmann, n.d.).
22. *Religion of Jesus*, 114, 149.

GRAMMATICAL AND LEXICOGRAPHICAL RESEARCH: ALEXANDER BUTTMANN AND FRIEDRICH BLASS; HERMANN CREMER AND C. L. W. GRIMM

NT scholars during the Enlightenment made use of the research of classical philologists. In the nineteenth century, some scholars focused their attention on the study of the language of the NT.

Grammar of the NT: Buttmann and Blass

Alexander Buttmann, a teacher in a classical secondary school in Potsdam, had edited a series of grammars by his father, Philipp Buttmann. In the course of preparing an appendix for a new edition, he produced in 1859 a grammar that was virtually a new work. Buttmann's intent was to demonstrate the difference between NT and classical Greek. After a translation was made by J. H. Thayer, Buttmann's *Grammar* was widely used in English-speaking countries.[23] This *Grammar* understands NT Greek as a language influenced by the LXX and the vernacular of the Hellenistic world: the "Macedo-Alexandrian" or common dialect that had evolved from Attic Greek. According to Buttmann (and Thayer), the Greek of the Gospels represents the language of the ordinary people; the Epistles come closer to literary Greek. The *Grammar*, which totals 403 pages, is ordered according to the typical pattern: a first section on forms, a second on syntax.

Friedrich Blass (1843–1907), a professor of classical philology at Halle, had demonstrated his command of classical linguistics with his multivolume work on Attic rhetoric.[24] The first edition of his NT *Grammar* appeared in 1896; the second (1902) became the basis for a popular English edition.[25] After his death, Blass's *Grammar* went through various revisions and editions; in 1913, the editing was carried on by A. Debrunner, and the *Grammar* became a standard text.[26] In Blass's opinion, the Greek of the NT represents the common language of the Hellenistic world—the language illuminated by recent discoveries in Egypt. "Accordingly the language employed in the N.T. is, on the whole, such as was spoken in the lower circles of society, not such as was written in the works of literature." The body of the *Grammar*, a total of 372 pages, follows the conventional outline: a section on phonetics and accidence, and a section on syntax. In analyzing the style of the NT writers, Blass remarks, "The Epistle to the Hebrews is the only piece of writing in the N.T., which in structure of sentences and style

---

23. Alexander Buttmann, *A Grammar of the New Testament Greek*, trans. J. H. Thayer (Andover, Mass.: Warren F. Draper, 1873).

24. *Die Attische Beredsamkeit*, 3d ed., 4 vols. (1887–98; repr., Hildesheim: Georg Olms, 1962).

25. *Grammar of New Testament Greek*, trans. Henry St. John Thackeray, 2d ed. (London: Macmillan, 1905).

26. See Stanley E. Porter and Jeffrey T. Reed, "Greek Grammar since BDF: A Retrospective and Prospective Analysis," *Filología Neotestamentaria* 4 (1991): 143–64.

shows the care and dexterity of an artistic writer."[27] Besides his *Grammar*, Blass published other works on the NT.[28] He wrote commentaries in Latin on Matthew, Luke, John, and Acts, and a commentary on Hebrews in German. Blass had a special interest in Luke and Acts, and developed a unique theory regarding their composition.[29] Largely on the basis of text-critical evidence, Blass believes each appeared in two editions, both written by Luke. The Gospel of Luke, according to Blass, was originally written in the east, and later was revised when Luke came to Rome. Acts, he thinks, was first written in Rome, and then, after Luke's return to the east, was rewritten in an edition addressed to Theophilus.

NT Lexicography: Cremer and Grimm

Hermann Cremer (1834–1903), Professor of Systematic Theology at Greifswald, had a special interest in the NT.[30] His *Lexicon* of NT Greek first appeared in 1866, and went through a series of editions and reprints.[31] The first English translation was published in 1878, based on Cremer's second edition. Material from Cremer's third and fourth editions was added as a supplement to the English edition of 1886. Cremer, in contrast to Deissmann, Buttmann, and Blass, reverts to the traditional view of biblical Greek as "the organ of the Spirit of Christ ... adequate to the new views which the Spirit of Christ reveals."[32] Cremer does not include the whole vocabulary of the NT, but only those words that carry significant theological weight. In overview, Cremer's *Lexicon* comprises more than nine hundred pages, plus indexes of Greek words, synonyms, NT texts, Hebrew words, and biblical-theological subjects. Cremer finds the primary background of NT terms in the HB. He argues at length, for example, that the Johannine λόγος is not to be understood in the context of Philo's usage, but in the setting of the HB, where the word of God is the medium of divine self-disclosure.

C. L. W. Grimm (1807–91), a professor at Jena, was urged by a Leipzig publisher to prepare a new edition of the *Clavis Novi Testamenti philologicae* of C. G. Wilke.[33] As Grimm undertook the project, he discovered that a total

---

27. *Grammar of NT Greek*, 1, 296.
28. See, for example, his *Philology of the Gospels* (London, 1898; repr., Amsterdam: B. R. Gründer, 1969).
29. *Euangelium secundum Lucam sive Lucae ad Theophilum liber prior. Secundum formam quae videtur Romanam* (Leipzig: B. G. Teubner, 1897); idem, *Acta apostolorum sive Lucae ad Theophilum liber alter* (Göttingen: Vandenhoeck & Ruprecht, 1895).
30. See, for example, his *Die eschatologische Rede Jesu Christi Matthäi 24. 25* (Stuttgart: J. F. Steinkopf, 1860). Cremer is also noted for his caustic *A Reply to Harnack on The Essence of Christianity*, trans. Bernhard Pick (New York: Funk & Wagnalls, 1903).
31. *Biblisch-theologisches Wörterbuch der Neutestamentlichen Gräcität*, 7th ed. (Gotha: Friedrich Andreas Perthes, 1893).
32. *Biblico-Theological Lexicon of New Testament Greek*, trans. William Urwick, 4th English ed. (Edinburgh: T. & T. Clark, 1895), iv.
33. See *HNTR* 1:301–5.

rewrite was necessary. The result appeared in 1867 with a new title: *Lexicon graeco-latinum in libros Novi Testamenti*.[34] Although he attends to theological terms, Grimm's main focus is philological. "I have," he wrote, "devoted not a little work and study for explicating those words in which theological ideas are expressed . . . never so that I would exceed the limits of a philological lexicon. Since, on the contrary, the theological province is not appropriate for the author of a philological lexicon."[35] In 1885, the industrious J. H. Thayer translated and expanded Grimm's *Lexicon*.[36] Printing his own contributions in brackets, Thayer added archeological, historical, and bibliographical information. He also attached a valuable appendix that includes lists of Greek words in various categories, for example, words that he thinks are peculiar to the NT. In regard to the use of λόγος in the prologue of the Fourth Gospel, Grimm appears to venture beyond philology into theology. The term describes "the personal (hypostatic) wisdom and power in union with God, his minister in the creation and government of the universe, the cause of all the world's life both physical and ethical, which for the procurement of man's salvation put on human nature in the person of Jesus the Messiah and shone forth conspicuously from his words and deeds."[37]

LINGUISTIC RESEARCH IN ENGLAND: J. H. MOULTON

Philology seems to run in families. Just as Alexander Buttmann carried on the work of his father, Philipp, so James Hope Moulton succeeded his father, William F. Moulton (1835–98). The elder Moulton had served on the NT Company of the biblical Revision Committee.[38] His main contribution to NT linguistics was his translation of the NT *Grammar* by G. B. Winer (1789–1858). Winer, a professor at Erlangen, first published his *Grammik des neutestamentlichen Sprachidioms* in 1822. He continued the project through the sixth edition (1855) when blindness prevented further work. Several English translations of Winer's *Grammar* were published: an American edition by Moses Stuart in 1825[39] and another by J. H. Agnew and O. G. Ebbeke (1840), and a British edition by E. Masson (1859). In 1866, a seventh German edition was produced by Gottlieb Lünemann. An English

---

34. Second ed. (Leipzig: Arnold, 1878).
35. Ibid., ix.
36. Joseph Henry Thayer, *A Greek-English Lexicon of the New Testament* (New York: American Book Co., 1889).
37. Ibid., 382.
38. See p. 82, above.
39. See pp. 23–24, above.

translation of this edition was undertaken by J. H. Thayer.[40] W. F. Moulton's translation, based on Winer's sixth edition, first appeared in 1870 and went through three editions.[41] As the subtitle indicates, Winer's purpose was to provide a grammar as a *Sure Basis for New Testament Exegesis*. In Winer's opinion the Greek of the NT was the language of the age of Alexander and his successors. This language developed in two ways: as a literary form, based on the Attic dialect; as a spoken language of mixed dialects, predominantly the Macedonian. Winer also believes NT Greek displays Semitic influence. W. F. Moulton's edition of Winer comprises some eight hundred pages, and orders the material in three parts: General Character and Diction, Accidence, Syntax. Before his death, Moulton had planned to produce a new edition with the collaboration of his son.[42]

James Hope Moulton (1863–1917) was a descendant of a long line of Methodist ministers.[43] He won a scholarship to King's College, Cambridge, and was elected a fellow in 1888. In 1908, he was named Professor of Hellenistic Greek and Indo-European Philology at the University of Manchester. Moulton developed a friendship with Deissmann and the two engaged in extensive correspondence.[44] On questions of biblical criticism, Moulton was conservative. His interpretation of the Epistle of James for the Peake *Commentary* concluded that James was one of the earliest books of the NT, written by James, the brother of Jesus.[45] Moulton acknowledged non-Pauline features in Ephesians (which he called "Laodiceans"), but believed the epistle expressed Paul's thoughts, written by one of his companions, perhaps Timothy. On a return voyage from India, Moulton's ship was torpedoed, and after three days in a lifeboat, he died at sea. Deissmann wrote to Moulton's brother, "I received the sad news of the sudden tragic death of your brother, my most intimate friend in England and my deserving colleague."[46]

---

40. George Benedict Winer, *A Grammar of the Idiom of the New Testament,* 7th ed. by Gottlieb Lünemann, trans. J. Henry Thayer (Andover, Mass.: Warren F. Draper, 1883).

41. George Benedict Winer, *A Treatise on the Grammar of New Testament Greek: Regarded as a Sure Basis for New Testament Exegesis,* trans. W. F. Moulton, 3d ed. (Edinburgh: T. & T. Clark, 1882).

42. The elder Moulton also collaborated with A. S. Geden on *A Concordance to the Greek Testament,* 3d ed. (Edinburgh: T. & T. Clark, 1926), but the bulk of the work was done by Geden.

43. See W. Fiddian Moulton, *James Hope Moulton* (London: Epworth Press, 1919); Marcus Ward, "James Hope Moulton (born 11th October, 1863)," *London Quarterly and Holborn Review* 188 (1963): 306–14; W. Fiddian Moulton, "James Hope Moulton. 1863–1917: 1. A Biographical Sketch, with Some Account of His Literary Legacies; 2. A Record of Professor J. H. Moulton's Work, with Some Explanation of Its Significance, by A. S. Peake," *BJRL* 4 (1917): 10–23.

44. See G. H. R. Horsley, "The Origin and Scope of Moulton and Milligan's *Vocabulary of the Greek Testament,* and Deissmann's Planned New Testament Lexicon. Some Unpublished Letters of G. A. Deissmann to J. H. Moulton," *BJRL* (1994): 187–216.

45. Arthur S. Peake, ed., *A Commentary on the Bible* (New York: Thomas Nelson & Sons, n.d.), 903–7.

46. Quoted in Horsley, "Origin and Scope," 211.

In 1905, the first edition of J. H. Moulton's *Grammar of New Testament Greek* appeared, and a second edition was published within a few months. This second edition rightly abandoned the subtitle, "based on W. F. Moulton's edition of G. B. Winer's Grammar"; J. H. Moulton's *Grammar* was a totally new work. Actually, only a first volume, consisting of *Prolegomena*, was published. In 1908, a third revised edition appeared, and most of a second volume was ready for the press at the time of Moulton's death.⁴⁷ The work was continued by W. F. Howard, a professor at Handsworth College, Birmingham, and former student of Moulton, who published the second volume on *Accidence and Word-Formation* in three sections (1919, 1921, 1929).

In the preface, Moulton writes, "The main purpose of these *Prolegomena* has been to provide a sketch of the language of the New Testament as it appears to those who have followed Deissmann into a new field of research."⁴⁸ Moulton's central thesis is "that the New Testament was written in the normal Κοινή of the Empire."⁴⁹ As to the general characteristics of the language, Moulton believes Deissmann has demolished the antiquated notion that biblical Greek is a special Hebraic Greek, the language of the Holy Spirit. Instead, Moulton understands NT Greek as the vernacular of the Hellenistic world in which Semitisms are rare. Sources for this common Greek include prose literature of the postclassical age, but especially the inscriptions and nonliterary papyri of Egypt, as well as modern Greek. Although Moulton planned a more complete analysis of accidence and syntax in future volumes, the last six chapters of this volume deal with syntax. For example, in discussing the "Syntax of the Noun," Moulton traces the reduction of cases in NT Greek. He notes that the Greek of the NT represents a transition between the seven cases of primitive Greek and the three cases of modern. As a whole, Moulton's *Grammar* comprises 232 pages plus additional notes, written in a readable style.

J. H. Moulton also contributed to the lexicography of NT Greek.⁵⁰ On the basis of a series of articles he had written for the *Expositor*, Moulton, with the collaboration of George Milligan (professor at Glasgow), published a lexicon. Apparently Moulton had earlier invited E. L. Hicks (who declined) and then Deissmann to participate in the project. Deissmann declined because of his intention to write a lexicon of his own—a project he never

---

47. *A Grammar of New Testament Greek*, vol. 1, *Prolegomena*, 3d ed. (Edinburgh: T. & T. Clark, 1908). See C. Kingsley Barrett, "Biblical Classics: IV. J. H. Moulton: A Grammar of New Testament Greek: Prolegomena," *ExpTim* 90 (1978): 68–71.

48. *Grammar of NT Greek*, x. Moulton's dependence on Deissmann is expressed in his *From Egyptian Rubbish-Heaps* (London: Charles H. Kelly, 1916) and "Treasures of Egypt," in *A Neglected Sacrament and Other Studies and Addresses* (London: Epworth, 1919), 62–71.

49. *Grammar of NT Greek*, xvi.

50. See C. J. Hemer, "Towards a New Moulton and Milligan," *NovT* 24 (1982): 97–123; J. L. North, "'I Sought a Colleague': James Hope Moulton, Papyrologist, and Edward Lee Hicks, Epigraphist, 1903–1906," *BJRL* 79 (1997): 195–206; Horsley, "Origin and Scope."

completed. Words from the first part of the Greek alphabet appeared in fascicles in 1914 and 1915. After Moulton's death, Milligan carried on the work, using notes and references left by Moulton. The whole project was completed in 1929, and a one-volume edition was published the next year.[51] The Moulton/Milligan lexicon makes use of the recently discovered material, especially the Egyptian papyri. The lexicon, consisting of 705 pages, does not include all the words of the NT, but those that are found in the nonliterary sources. With most entries, quotations from the papyri or inscriptions are presented. For example, the use of λόγος in Rom. 14:12, with the meaning "give an account," is illustrated by a papyrus text that reads: "as you are about to give an account to your most illustrious leader." Moulton and Milligan's *Vocabulary* has been used until today with appreciation.

NEW TESTAMENT GEOGRAPHY, HISTORY, AND APOLOGETICS: WILLIAM M. RAMSAY (1851–1939)

Sir William Mitchell Ramsay was born in Glasgow and educated at the University of Aberdeen.[52] In 1873, Ramsay won a scholarship to St. John's College, Oxford, where he distinguished himself in classics. He also studied Sanskrit at Göttingen. In 1880, he was awarded a scholarship for study in Greece, and after a sojourn in Athens, crossed the Aegean to Anatolia, which became his second home. Throughout the remainder of his life, Ramsay made repeated treks across Asia Minor, looking under almost every stone. In 1885, he was appointed professor of classical art and archeology at Oxford, and a year later was named Professor of Humanity (Latin) at Aberdeen. In 1906, he was knighted by Edward VII.

Sir William was a person of strong opinions, and, like the bagpipes of his native Scotland, he was blatant in expressing them. Ramsay did not like theology or theologians—especially German theologians. "I do not follow the prevailing tendency of German criticism of the New Testament," he wrote. "It is wrong because it is narrow, and because it judges from erroneous premises and unjustifiable prejudices."[53] Ramsay's own viewpoint is evident in a section of his book on the cities of Paul, titled "Paulinism in the Graeco-

---

51. James Hope Moulton and George Milligan, *The Vocabulary of the Greek Testament* (London: Hodder and Stoughton, 1949).
52. See Wilbert Francis Howard, "William Mitchell Ramsay: Archaeologist and Historian," *Religion in Life* 8 (1939): 580–90; repr. in Howard's *Romance of NT Scholarship*, 138–55; W. Ward Gasque, *Sir William M. Ramsay: Archaeologist and New Testament Scholar: A Survey of His Contribution to the Study of the New Testament*, Baker Studies in Biblical Archaeology (Grand Rapids, Mich.: Baker, 1966). An autobiographical summary is presented in Ramsay's *The Bearing of Recent Discovery on the Trustworthiness of the New Testament*, 4th ed. (London: Hodder and Stoughton, 1920), 7–31.
53. *The Bearing of Recent Discovery*, ix.

Roman World."⁵⁴ According to Ramsay, Paul viewed pagan civilization as doomed. Paul addresses this predicament with a philosophy of history (which Ramsay affirms) consisting of three principles: (1) "The Divine alone is real: all else is error"; (2) "A Society or a Nation, is progressive in so far as it hears the Divine voice: all else is degeneration"; (3) "All men and every human society can hear the Divine voice; but they must cooperate ere the communication can take place." Thus, in contrast to the process of pagan degeneration and decay, Ramsay believes Paul promotes a religion of progress. "His whole philosophy rests on this idea of growth and development." According to Ramsay, Paul's idea of progress (and his own) combines the Hellenistic principle of freedom of the individual with the Hebrew idea of divine action in history.⁵⁵

Ramsay's Geographical and Historical Research

Ramsay's major contribution is in the area of historical geography. In a succession of monumental works, he demonstrates his mastery of the field. *The Historical Geography of Asia Minor* affirms the importance of geography and topography for understanding history.⁵⁶ Ramsay traces the Roman roads and presents in detail the history of the cities of the various provinces, making use of written sources, inscriptions, and his firsthand observations. A work of major importance, published after his death, is Ramsay's *The Social Basis of Roman Power in Asia Minor*.⁵⁷ Making extensive use of inscriptions, he presents data about such matters as citizenship, marriage, adoption, and family life.

Of importance for NT research is Ramsay's *The Church in the Roman Empire: Before A.D. 170*.⁵⁸ Originally presented at Oxford, these lectures "exemplify to younger students the method of applying archeological, topographical, and numismatic evidence to the investigation of early Christian history."⁵⁹ Ramsay's major concern is the development of Roman policy toward the church. He believes that at the time of Nero, Christians were persecuted for crimes, but by the time of Trajan, they were persecuted for simply bearing the name "Christian." During the Flavian period, according to Ramsay, opposition to Christians became a policy. Ramsay believes 1 Peter was written during this period, around 80. He thinks that Peter wrote the epistle and was executed at Rome, but later than the Neronian perse-

---

54. *The Cities of St. Paul: Their Influence on His Life and Thought* (London: Hodder and Stoughton, 1907; repr., Grand Rapids, Mich.: Baker, 1963), 3–81.
55. Ibid., 12, 14, 33.
56. (London: John Murray, 1890; repr., Amsterdam: Adolf M. Hakkert, 1962).
57. Ed. J. G. C. Anderson (Aberdeen: Aberdeen University Press, 1941). See also William M. Ramsay, *Asiatic Elements in Greek Civilization*, 2d ed. (New Haven: Yale University Press, 1929).
58. (New York: G. P. Putnam's Sons, 1893).
59. Ibid., vii.

cution. Christians were persecuted, according to Ramsay, because they constituted a strong organization that would not assimilate to imperial power. "Christianity was proscribed, not as a religion, but as interfering with that organisation of society which the Empire inculcated and protected."[60]

Also important for early church history is Ramsay's massive *The Cities and Bishoprics of Phrygia*.[61] Many of the sites explored are important for the history of the church, for example, Laodicea, Hierapolis, and Colossae. In regard to these places, Ramsay presents history, religion, social, and political life. References to Christianity appear throughout the work, but major attention is given in Part II (where chapters on Christian inscriptions are presented). Concentrating on a smaller area of south central Asia Minor, Ramsay published, with Gertrude L. Bell, a huge volume titled *The Thousand and One Churches*.[62] Bell, Oxford-educated and later High Commissioner of Iraq, explored with Ramsay the site of the "thousand and one churches" (Bin bir Kilisse) in 1907. Besides these major works, Ramsay wrote some one hundred articles on geography and archeology for the ninth edition of the *Encyclopaedia Britannica*, and more than sixty articles for Hastings's *Dictionary of the Bible*. His captivating essay "Roads and Travel (in NT)" shows Ramsay at his best.[63]

Ramsay's NT Research

In 1900, Ramsay published a commentary on Galatians.[64] He was primarily interested in historical questions, and the commentary is in effect a detailed defense of the south Galatian hypothesis. The first half of the commentary (more than 230 pages) presents "Society and Religion in Central Asia Minor in the Time of Saint Paul." Ramsay's intent is to answer the question: Do the data of the epistle correspond to the social and political situation of north or south Galatia? In 25 B.C.E., both north and south were incorporated into the Roman province of Galatia. According to Ramsay, the cities of the south, such as Antioch of Pisidia and Lystra, were increasingly Romanized, and their citizens called "Galatians." In the north, according to Ramsay's research, the old customs prevailed: the Celtic language was used into the second century, Greek literature and Christian inscriptions did not appear until late, and Jews were scarce. In the south, Greek became the language of cultural life; the cities were on the thoroughfares of Roman communication; Christian inscriptions appear early, and Jews were present in

---

60. Ibid., 372.
61. Two vols. (Oxford: Clarendon Press, 1895, 1897).
62. (London: Hodder and Stoughton, 1909).
63. James Hastings, ed., *A Dictionary of the Bible* (New York: Charles Scribner's Sons, 1908–9), extra vol., 375–402.
64. *A Historical Commentary on St. Paul's Epistle to the Galatians* (New York: G. P. Putnam's Sons, 1900; repr., Grand Rapids, Mich.: Baker, 1979).

large numbers. In short, Ramsay believes the cities of southern Galatia represent the sort of cities addressed by Paul's missionary strategy; the cities of the north do not.

Examples from the body of the commentary display Ramsay's historical concern. In regard to the salutations of the Epistles, Ramsay believes that when Paul includes others besides himself, those mentioned are persons who have a special relation to the recipients. Thus, "all the members of God's family who are with me" (Gal. 1:2) must belong to a church important to the Galatians. In Ramsay's opinion, that church must be Antioch—the place from which Ramsay believes Paul wrote this epistle. Chronological matters are crucial to Ramsay's historical reconstruction. Paul's second visit to Jerusalem (Gal. 2:1-10), in Ramsay's opinion, involved a private meeting between Paul and the Jerusalem leaders (not the Jerusalem Council); this visit corresponds to the visit recorded in Acts 11:29. Ramsay finds the solution to the mystery of Paul's "thorn in the flesh" (2 Cor. 12:7) in Gal. 4:13: the apostle preached to the Galatians first because of a bodily ailment. This indicates to Ramsay that Paul's thorn was malarial fever, contracted in the unhealthy lowlands of Pamphylia, prompting Paul to move to the higher elevation and recuperative climate of Galatia.

Ramsay wrote two important, highly readable books on Paul. In *St. Paul the Traveler and the Roman Citizen*, Ramsay says, "My aim has been to state the facts of Paul's life simply, avoiding argument and controversy so far as was possible in a subject where every point is controverted." Ramsay takes Acts as the primary source. "I shall argue that the book was composed by a personal friend and disciple of Paul, and if this be once established there will be no hesitation in accepting the primitive tradition that Luke was the author."[65] Following and expanding the data from Acts, Ramsay claims that Paul was a citizen of Tarsus, reared in a family of wealth, but disowned because of his conversion to Christianity. Ramsay believes that after the conversion, Paul spent eight years in Tarsus in virtual silence, unsure of his vocation. While working in Antioch, Paul made a second trip to Jerusalem, where he had a vision in the temple (Acts 22:17), inspiring him to Gentile mission.

After his first missionary journey to the cities of south Galatia, Paul, with Barnabas, went to Jerusalem for the Council described in Acts 15. According to Ramsay, the conflict between Paul and Peter (Gal. 2:11-21) occurred prior to the Council. Ramsay thinks the outcome of the Council was a compromise, as the apostolic decree (Acts 15:23-29) indicates: Gentile converts were not required to be circumcised, but were required to observe Jewish customs. On his second missionary journey, Paul visited the south Galatian

---

65. *St. Paul the Traveler and the Roman Citizen*, 3d ed. (London: Hodder and Stoughton, 1897; repr., Grand Rapids, Mich.: Baker, 1962), xxii, 14.

churches for a second time, and, after his departure, Judaizers invaded. Paul learned of this later from Timothy, who, according to Ramsay's reconstruction, returned to his native Galatia after the mission to Corinth, and met Paul in Antioch after Paul's fourth visit to Jerusalem (Acts 18:22); on the basis of that information, Paul wrote Galatians.

Ramsay thinks Paul met Luke for the first time at Troas. Indeed, the Macedonian Paul saw in his vision was, according to Ramsay, none other than Luke. The use of "we" in Acts 16:10 indicates Luke's presence, but disappears in 16:17. Ramsay says, "the author was not arrested, and therefore could not speak in the first person of what happened in the prison." Ramsay, however, seems to be clairvoyant, knowing all sorts of details about the imprisonment. "We must understand that the inner prison was a small cell, which had no window and no opening, except into the outer and larger prison, and that the outer prison, also had one larger door in the opposite wall; then, if there were any faint starlight in the sky, still more if the moon were up, a person in the outer doorway would be distinguishable to one whose eyes were accustomed to the darkness, but the jailor would see only black darkness in the prison."[66]

The rest of Ramsay's account follows Acts closely, describing the missions to Athens, Corinth, Ephesus, the final trip to Jerusalem, the imprisonment, voyage, shipwreck, and arrival in Rome. Along the way, Ramsay, with untypical skepticism, finds the "extraordinary miracles" (Acts 19:11) of Ephesus excessively fanciful. Paul's first trial, according to Ramsay, ended in acquittal; Paul was released and traveled during the years 62–65. The narrative in Acts ends abruptly, Ramsay thinks, because Luke had planned a third volume. Besides his diary and notes, the "Travel Document," Luke got information from people such as Philip and John Mark. "Luke added to these authorities an obvious acquaintance with Paul's own letters."[67]

After the discussion of "Paulinism" (noted earlier), Ramsay's *The Cities of St. Paul* investigates Tarsus and the cities of south Galatia. For each city, Ramsay presents the geographical and topographical setting, the history of the city from earliest times, and the religion of the city. Ramsay views Tarsus as a likely place for Paul to originate and develop his philosophy of history—a city combining eastern and western ideas. According to Ramsay, Paul's mission turned to Gentiles first in Pisidian Antioch (Acts 13:46), because Paul, with his special interest in Gentiles, had superseded Barnabas as leader, and because the mission had entered a new territory.[68]

---

66. Ibid., 219, 221–22.
67. Ibid., 385.
68. Ramsay also published *Pauline and Other Studies in Early Christian History* (London: Hodder and Stoughton, 1906).

Besides the books on Paul, Ramsay produced an intriguing work titled *The Letters to the Seven Churches of Asia*.[69] He sees the Apocalypse as another expression of one of his favorite themes: Christianity as the religion uniting east and west. The author combines the writing of epistles, a typical Hellenistic activity, with the writing of Jewish apocalyptic. Ramsay thinks this combination represents a transition from a Jewish to a Greek perspective, eventuating in the same author's composition of the Fourth Gospel. In discussing the practice of letter writing in the first century, Ramsay notes the close connection between travel and letters. In regard to the Apocalypse, the letters were inserted because "the form of letters had already established itself as the most characteristic expression of the Christian mind, and as almost obligatory on a Christian writer."[70] According to Ramsay, the author of Revelation was the apostle John, banished to Patmos during the persecution under Domitian. The message of the book adresses not the distant future, but the situation of John's own time. Ramsay thinks the seven churches were located on a postal circuit that began in Ephesus, traveled north to Smyrna and Pergamum, and then around to the east and south through the rest of the churches, and back to Ephesus. After these introductory matters, the balance of Ramsay's book presents the seven churches individually in their urban settings, and analyzes the content of each letter. For example, Ramsay vividly describes Ephesus as a modern visitor sees it, and presents its geographical setting and history. Ramsay's account includes a map, a photograph, and drawings of coins illustrating the political and religious life of the city.

Ramsay published several apologetic works. Most extensive is his *Was Christ Born at Bethlehem?*—a defense of the historicity of the census described in Luke 2:1-5.[71] According to the skeptics, no universal census was decreed or enacted by Augustus; a census would not have been promulgated in Herod's kingdom; Mary would not have been required to travel to Bethlehem; and Quirinius was not the governor of Syria at the time of Jesus' birth. Ramsay attempts to answer the objections: since Herod's kingdom was part of the empire, it would have been subject to the enrollment. On the basis of a recently discovered papyrus, Ramsay argues that enrollments by families were enacted in Egypt in fourteen-year cycles. In regard to Quirinius, Ramsay, using an obscure inscription, argues that Quirinius held a position of military leadership in Syria in 6 B.C.E., the time of the first enrollment; later, in 6–9 C.E., he was governor of Syria at the time of the second (Acts 5:37). As to the birth stories as a whole, Luke is reliable, because, in Ramsay's opinion, his source was Mary, the mother of Jesus. In *Luke the*

---

69. (London: Hodder and Stoughton, 1904; repr., Grand Rapids, Mich.: Baker, 1963).
70. Ibid., 35–36.
71. Third ed. (London: Hodder and Stoughton, 1905).

Physician and Other Studies in the History of Religion, Ramsay supports the argument for Lucan authorship on the basis of medical language.[72] Writing about "The Oldest Written Gospel," Ramsay agrees with Harnack that Q is earlier than Mark, but insists that Harnack has not dated it early enough.[73] "There is only one possibility," he concludes, "The lost Common Source of Luke and Matthew . . . was written while Christ was still living."[74]

William Ramsay's research in historical geography, sometimes ignored because of his strident apologetic, made a major contribution to the understanding of NT backgrounds. To be sure, some of his results have proved to be mistaken.[75] Although many critics are not convinced by his defense of the south Galatian hypothesis, Ramsay moved the argument to new ground: the issue was to be decided not solely on grounds of literary data from Acts and the Epistles, but also on the basis of social, cultural, and political data derived from archeology and new areas of historical research such as numismatics and the study of inscriptions. Moreover, Ramsay's critical work on the NT is imaginative and provocative. Yet, the sympathetic W. F. Howard is probably correct: Ramsay "allowed himself to assume a magisterial authority when discussing critical questions that lay outside his own realm of archeology."[76]

LINGUISTIC AND CULTURAL SETTING OF JESUS: GUSTAF DALMAN (1855–1941)

Gustaf Dalman was born and died among the Moravian Brethren.[77] As he wrote, "The Brethren Community of Niesky is my homeland. With it was given to my life and my scholarly endeavor the directions which have continued to determine them."[78] Dalman's father's surname was Marx, but Dalman took the family name of his mother, a pious woman of Swedish descent. In 1874, Dalman began study at the pietist seminary at Gnadenfeld, where, in 1881, he was appointed an instructor. In 1887, Dalman accepted an invitation of Franz Delitzsch to teach at the Institutum Judaicum in Leipzig. After an extensive tour in the Near East (1889–90),

---

72. (London: Hodder and Stoughton, 1908; repr., Grand Rapids, Mich.: Baker, 1956).
73. See pp. 130–31, above.
74. *Luke the Physician,* 89.
75. See Edwin Yamauchi, "Ramsay's Views of Archaeology in Asia Minor Reviewed," in *The New Testament Student and His Field,* vol. 5, *The New Testament Student,* ed. John H. Skilton and Curtis A. Ladley (Phillipsburg, N.J.: Presbyterian and Reformed Publishing Co., 1982), 27–40.
76. "William Mitchell Ramsay," 588.
77. See Julia Männchen, *Gustaf Dalmans Leben und Wirken in der Brüdergemeinde, für die Judenmission und an der Universität Leipzig, 1855–1902* (Wiesbaden: Otto Harrassowitz, 1987); idem, *Gustaf Dalman als Palästinawissenschaftler in Jerusalem und Greifswald, 1902–1941* (Wiesbaden: Harrassowitz, 1993); "Gustaf Dalman," in *RGS* 4:1–29; J. Day, "Dalman, Gustaf Hermann (1855–1941)," in *DBI* 1:241–42.
78. "Gustaf Dalman," *RGS* 4:1.

Dalman was named instructor at the University of Leipzig where he was promoted to associate professor in 1895. In 1902, he was named director of the newly founded Deutsche evangelische Institut für Altertumswissenschaft des heiligen Landes in Jerusalem. When the work of the Institute was suspended by the outbreak of World War I, Dalman was appointed to the faculty at Greifswald, where he established an institute for Palestinian studies.

Linguistic Research

Dalman's main concern in this area was the language of Jesus.[79] An early work presented the history of the use of the name Adonai for God. According to Dalman, the use of the proper name Yahweh declined in the third century B.C.E. By the time of Jesus, אדני (my Lord) was substituted for יהוה. The earliest Christians did not name Jesus אדני but "rabbi" and only later, מרי (my Lord). With Paul, Dalman believes the title κύριος carries meaning expressed by Adonai.

> The naming and presenting of Christ as Lord are unthinkable without the move from Yahweh to Adonai, in which the history of the most important of the OT divine names comes to an end. The dignity of the Lord, in which God at the end of the Old Covenant appears before the people as comprehensible to humans, is transferred to the one in whom the fullness of the deity takes bodily form. The divine name Adonai contained therefore the germ of the final goal of all history, the uniting of all humanity under one head, Christ.[80]

Dalman also produced linguistic tools that facilitated the study of the language of Jesus. His Aramaic *Grammar* was designed to analyze the language spoken by Jews of Palestine in Jesus' time.[81] After completing the *Grammar*, Dalman published a collection of texts designed to be read in connection with his *Grammar*. The second edition was expanded to include texts from Palestinian Aramaic that are parallel to expressions of Jesus.[82] Dalman also produced a lexicon for use in the study of the Targums, Talmud, and Midrash.[83]

Dalman wrote two books that applied the results of his linguistic research to the study of Jesus. Originally published in 1898, Dalman's *The Words of Jesus* was translated into English in 1902. Dalman is convinced that

---

79. See H. Ott, "Um die Muttersprache Jesu: Forschungen seit Gustaf Dalman, *NovT* 9 (1967): 1–25.
80. Gustaf H. Dalman, *Der Gottesname Adonaj und Seine Geschichte* (Berlin: H. Reuther, 1889), 84. Another early work of Dalman presents an anthology of Jewish sources that refer to Jesus: *Jesus Christ in the Talmud, Midrash, Zohar and the Liturgy of the Synagogue*, trans. A. W. Streane (Cambridge: Deighton, Bell, 1893; repr., New York: Arno, 1973).
81. *Grammatik des jüdisch-palästinischen Aramäisch* (Leipzig: J. C. Hinrichs, 1894).
82. *Aramäische Dialektproben unter dem Gesichtspunkt neutestamentlicher Studien*, 2d ed. (Leipzig: J. C. Hinrichs, 1927).
83. *Aramäisch-neuhebräisches Handwörterbuch zu Targum, Talmud und Midrasch*, 3d ed. (Göttingen: Eduard Pfeiffer, 1938).

"Jesus grew up speaking the Aramaic tongue, and that He would be obliged to speak Aramaic to His disciples and to the people in order to be understood." Although Dalman acknowledges that Hebrew was still used as a literary language, he rejects the theory of an original Hebrew Gospel. The Logia, or sayings source, could have been written in Aramaic, but Dalman believes Matthew and Luke used it in a Greek version. The earliest church, he thinks, was bilingual.

> From the very beginning it thus used two languages, and in gatherings of the community the deeds and words of Jesus must have been recounted in Greek and in Aramaic. . . . A gospel source in Greek need not, by reason of its language, have been any later in origin than one written in a Semitic dialect. It is thus possible that the oldest Christian writing may have been composed in Greek.

Since Aramaic documents cannot be assumed, Dalman attempts to investigate the Aramaic words of Jesus that stand behind the Greek of the Gospels. "The more one is convinced that the Gospels contain historically trustworthy communication in regard to the teaching of Jesus, the more important must it appear to get even one step nearer the original by a fresh apprehension of His message in the light of the primary language and the contemporary modes of thought."[84]

After this introductory discussion, the balance of the book presents Dalman's exposition of major ideas of Jesus. For example, some 150 pages discuss Jesus' idea of the sovereignty of God. Dalman believes Jesus originally used the phrase "kingdom of heaven"—a phrase that primarily expresses a religious ideal, realized in the present. "For Him the sovereignty of God meant the divine power which, from the present onwards with continuous progress effectuates the renovation of the world, but also the renovated world into whose domain mankind will one day enter, which is even now being offered, and therefore can be appropriated and received as a blessing." Dalman believes that Jesus used the Aramaic terms for "father" in a distinctive way. "The usage of family life is transferred to God: it is the language of the child to its father." In regard to the phrase "son of man," Dalman notes that it can have the general meaning "human being," and in the time of Jesus, he insists that it was not used as a messianic title. "Jesus called Himself בר אנשא not indeed as the 'lowly one,' but as that member of the human race *(Menschenkind),* in his own nature impotent, whom God will make Lord of the world."[85]

---

84. *The Words of Jesus: Considered in the Light of Post-Biblical Jewish Writings and the Aramaic Language,* trans. D. M. Kay (Edinburgh: T. & T. Clark, 1909), 11, 71, 72.

85. Ibid., 137, 192, 265.

The same sort of material is presented in Dalman's later, *Jesus—Jeshua: Studies in the Gospels*.[86] Of special interest is the lengthy discussion (about a hundred pages) of the Passover. Dalman answers arguments that events described in the Synoptic accounts could not have happened at the time of the festival, and concludes that the Last Supper was a Passover meal. Making use of Jewish sources, Dalman claims that the Supper followed Jewish custom. The cup that Jesus blessed would have been the third of the four Passover cups. "The red wine in the cup turned the mind of Jesus to the past, when the blood on the door-posts of Egypt once wrought redemption, as well as to the near future, when His blood, i.e. His own life, would be poured out."[87]

Geographical-Cultural Research

During his extensive residence in Palestine, Dalman investigated the sites related to Jesus' life. In 1924, he published a popular survey of the *Places and Ways* of Jesus.[88] After a general survey of Palestine, Dalman turns to individual sites. He assumes the birth of Jesus in Bethlehem, and attempts to trace the route of Mary and Joseph. In regard to Jerusalem, Dalman gives careful attention to the location of Golgotha, and concludes that the Church of the Holy Sepulcher is located on the authentic spot. For Dalman, the study of historical geography is theologically important. "What the Christians proclaimed was not a new philosophy or theosophy which can traverse the earth, spaceless and timeless, but the history of Jesus of Nazareth, which would be a myth if it had no connection with actual places."[89]

Dalman's major work is his mammoth seven-volume presentation of the industry and customs of Palestine.[90] Volume 1 deals with the course of the year and the course of the day, that is, seasons and times. Dalman presents data about temperature, rainfall, foliage, and festivals. The second volume is devoted to agriculture, and notes the importance of agricultural practices for understanding the Bible. Dalman deals with such matters as arable land, irrigation, and agricultural tools. Volume 3 reviews the process of the production of flour from harvest to milling. He mentions the NT references to the ox that treads the grain (1 Cor. 9:9; 1 Tim. 5:18), reviews the practice in ancient times, and cites rabbinic parallels. The fourth volume is dedicated to bread, oil, and wine. Dalman notes the use of a mixture of oil and wine as medicine (Luke 10:34). Volume 5 considers fabrics, spinning, weaving,

---

86. Trans. Paul P. Levertoff (London: SPCK, 1929; repr., New York: KTAV, 1971).
87. Ibid., 168.
88. *Orte und Wege Jesu* (Gütersloh: C. Bertelsmann, 1924); Eng. trans.: *Sacred Sites and Ways: Studies in the Topography of the Gospels,* trans. Paul P. Levertoff (New York: Macmillan, 1935).
89. *Sacred Sites*, 380.
90. *Arbeit und Sitte in Palästina,* 7 vols. (1927–41; repr., Hildesheim: Georg Olms, 1964).

and clothing. Dalman thinks the seamless tunic of Jesus (John 19:23) was a one-piece garment that had no lengthwise seam. The sixth volume deals with cattle and milk production, hunting, and fishing. An informative account of the fishing practices in the Sea of Tiberias describes nets, boats, and hooks. The final volume describes houses, poultry, dove production, and beekeeping. Dalman notes various types of roofs, some sod, like the one mentioned in Mark 2:4. The act of preaching from the housetop (Matt. 10:27; Luke 12:3), according to Dalman, would assume a type of Palestinian dwelling with outside stairway. In 1930, Dalman published an extensive one-volume work on the topography, roads, water supply, local traditions, and archeological findings in Jerusalem.[91]

Gustaf Dalman loved every rock and rill of Palestine! However, he was not simply a pious pilgrim who wandered across the Holy Land, eager to retread each footstep of Jesus. For Dalman, love of the land meant exhaustive exploration and critical investigation. His results have continued to enrich the understanding of the historical background and sociocultural setting of the life of Jesus. To be sure, Dalman's linguistic studies are dated, yet he advanced the knowledge of the language of Jesus, and provided basic tools for the investigation of the Jesus' teachings.

THE STUDY OF HISTORICAL BACKGROUNDS

Their coffers filled with new discoveries and armed with new tools, scholars began to assess the value of their treasures for the study of the NT. Some, according to their interest and linguistic specialization, focused on Jewish backgrounds. Others, more at home in Athens than Jerusalem, directed their attention to Hellenism.

RESEARCH IN JEWISH BACKGROUNDS:
EMIL SCHÜRER AND ROBERT HENRY CHARLES

Emil Schürer (1844–1910)

Now and then, a scholar establishes a reputation on the basis of a single work; such was Emil Schürer. Born in Augsburg, he was educated at Erlangen, Berlin, Heidelberg, and Leipzig. He served as an instructor at Leipzig (1869–78) where he was promoted to associate professor in 1873. In 1878, he joined the youthful theological faculty at Giessen, among them his lifelong friend Adolf Harnack.[92] Schürer moved to Kiel in 1890, and to Göttingen in 1895, for the remainder of his career. In point of view, Schürer was

---

91. *Jerusalem und sein Gelände* (Gütersloh: C. Bertelsmann, 1930).
92. See pp. 122–35, above.

sympathetic to Ritschlian liberalism.[93] According to Schürer, Jesus preached God's grace in opposition to the legalistic Judaism of his time.[94] In contrast to the Jewish political understanding, Schürer believes Jesus interpreted the kingdom of God as spiritual and ethical. Jesus, in Schürer's opinion, understood himself as Messiah, but gave to messiahship a new meaning—a messiahship involving suffering and death.[95] For Schürer, Judaism is the dark backdrop before which the vital religion of Jesus is portrayed.

Schürer's monumental *History of the Jewish People* first appeared in 1874 under the title *Lehrbuch der neutestamentlichen Zeitgeschichte*. Two years later, Schürer began the publication of an enlarged two-volume edition with the enduring title *Geschichte des jüdischen Volkes im Zeitalter Jesu Christi*. A third edition of 1898 expanded the second volume into two volumes, and a revised first volume was published in 1901.[96] An English translation, *A History of the Jewish People in the Time of Jesus Christ*, consisting of five weighty tomes and a slim index volume, appeared over the years 1885–96.[97] The enduring value of the work is attested by the publication of an abridged edition of the First Division (the first two volumes of the English version) in 1961 in paperback.[98] More recently, a revision of the entire work, updating the bibliography, making use of sources discovered since Schürer's time (e.g., the Dead Sea Scrolls) and mollifying Schürer's anti-Jewish polemic has been published.[99] In the final German edition, Schürer's work is organized in three parts: I. Political History of Palestine from 175 B.C.E. to 135 C.E.; II. The Internal Conditions (i.e., the organization and religious life of Judaism); III. Judaism in the Dispersion and Jewish Literature. The English edition, based on the second German edition, is presented in two Divisions: I. Political History from 175 B.C.E. to 135 C.E. (bound as two volumes); II.

---

93. See pp. 86–92, above. Schürer dedicated the second part of his *History of the Jewish People* to Ritschl.

94. *Die Predigt Jesu Christi in ihrem Verhältnis zum Alten Testament und zum Judenthum* (Darmstadt: Fr. Würtz, 1882).

95. *Das messianische Selbstbewusstsein Jesu Christi* (Göttingen: Dietrich [W. Fr. Kästner], 1903). See Hans Weder, "Theologie und Religionswissenschaft: Eine Erinnerung an Emil Schürer und Adolf von Harnack," *TLZ* 125 (2000): 1233–44.

96. *Geschichte des jüdischen Volkes im Zeitalter Jesu Christi*, 3 vols., 3d and 4th ed. (Leipzig: J. C. Hinrichs, 1898–1901).

97. Trans. John Macpherson, Sophia Taylor, and Peter Christie (Edinburgh: T. & T. Clark, 1885–96).

98. Emil Schürer, *A History of the Jewish People in the Time of Jesus*, ed. Nahum N. Glatzer (New York: Schocken Books, 1961).

99. Emil Schürer, *The History of the Jewish People in the Age of Jesus Christ (175 B.C.–A.D. 135): A New English Version Revised and Edited by Géza Vermes and Fergus Millar* (Edinburgh: T. & T. Clark, 1973). See Sidney B. Hoenig, "The New Schürer," *JQR* 67 (1976): 47–54; Manahem Stern, "A New English Schürer," *JJS* 25 (1974): 419–24; Géza Vermes and Martin Goodman, "La Littérature juive intertestamentaire à la lumière d'un siècle de recherches et de découvertes," in *Études sur le judaïsme hellénistique: Congrès de Strasbourg (1983)*, ed. R. Kuntzmann and J. Schlosser (Paris: Cerf, 1984), 19–39; Martin Hengel, "Der alte und der neue 'Schürer,'" *JSS* 35 (1990): 19–72.

The Internal Conditions of Palestine, and the Jewish People, in the Time of Jesus Christ (bound as three volumes). For a summary of the content, the English translation, with occasional glances at the more recent editions, provides an adequate representation of Schürer's work.

In the introduction, Schürer affirms the importance of the study of Judaism for the understanding of Christianity. "No incident in the gospel story, no word in the preaching of Jesus Christ, is intelligible apart from its setting in Jewish history."[100] Since Schürer supposes that a major development of the whole era is the ascendance of the Pharisees, he begins his history with the time of their origin, the Maccabean period, and ends it with the time of their triumph, the beginning of the era of the Talmud during the reign of Hadrian. In investigating this history, Schürer divides the history of Palestine (Division I) into two periods. The first includes the time from Antiochus Epiphanes (175 B.C.E.) to the conquest of Pompey (63 B.C.E.). In presenting this period, Schürer depicts the revolt of Mattathias and the military success of Judas Maccabaeus. He describes the reigns of Judas's brothers, Jonathan and Simon. With clarity Schürer unravels the complicated story of the life and work of the later Hasmoneans. He vividly describes the invasion of Pompey, his desecration of the temple, and the end of Jewish independence.

The second period covers the era from 63 B.C.E. to the war of Hadrian (135 C.E.). Regarding this period, Schürer presents a detailed history of the Roman province of Syria. This is followed by an account of the rise and rule of Herod the Great (37–4 B.C.E.). Schürer then recounts the reigns of Herod's sons (Philip, Antipas, and Archelaus) and the rule of the Roman procurators, particularly Quirinius and Pilate. In connection with Quirinius, Schürer presents a lengthy excursus on "The Valuation Census of Quirinius"[101]—an investigation of the historicity of the census reported in Luke 2:1-5. He concludes that the Lucan account contradicts history at two points: the notion of an empire-wide census ordered by Augustus; the belief that a census was conducted in Palestine under Quirinius at the time of the birth of Jesus.[102] Schürer proceeds to depict events in Palestine prior to the war with Rome: the life and reign of Herod Agrippa I, the rule of the Roman procurators Felix and Festus, and the activity of Herod Agrippa II. Schürer describes the Jewish War in detail: the outbreak of revolution, the battles in Galilee, the siege and fall of Jerusalem in 70 C.E. A final section presents events from the destruction of Jerusalem to the revolution and defeat of Bar Kokhba by the forces of Hadrian. According to Schürer, the

---

100. *History of the Jewish People* I, 1:1.
101. Ibid. I, 2:105–43.
102. In the third German edition, Schürer expands his argument, including a refutation of Ramsay's use of recent papyri discoveries to confirm a fourteen-year cycle of enrollments in Egypt in defense of the reliability of Luke.

result was the Romanization of Jerusalem and the triumph of the Pharisees. "Jewish Hellenism, which proclaimed the common brotherhood of man, disappeared, and Pharisaic Judaism, which sharply repudiated all communion with the Gentile world, won universal acceptance."[103]

The second Division of Schürer's *History* describes the internal condition of Palestine and the life of the Jewish people. Schürer believes Jewish life was ruled by the Sanhedrin in Jerusalem. Although its members included the priestly aristocracy, Schürer thinks the Sanhedrin came increasingly under the control of the Pharisaic rabbis. The priests represent a hereditary order whose power was maintained by their sole right to offer sacrifices. Like a naive tourist from a distant land, Schürer observes the temple service with abhorrent dismay:

> But copious as those public sacrifices no doubt were, they still seem but few when compared with the multitudes of private offerings and sacrifices that were offered. It was the vast number of the latter—so vast in fact as to be well-nigh inconceivable—that gave its peculiar stamp to the worship of Jerusalem. Here day after day whole crowds of victims were slaughtered and whole masses of flesh burnt; and when any of the high festivals came round, there was such a host of sacrifices to dispose of that it was scarcely possible to attend to them all notwithstanding the fact that there were thousands of priests officiating on the occasion. But the people of Israel saw in the punctilious observance of this worship the principal means of securing for themselves the favour of their God.[104]

Schürer reserves his major disdain for what he calls "Scribism" (*Schriftgelehrsamkeit*). According to Schürer, this nefarious ideology was based on belief in the divine origin of the Torah. Study of the law became an honored profession, but Schürer complains of the "capricious puerilities" and "extravagances of Jewish exegesis."[105] Indeed, Schürer's antipathy to the religion of Judaism reaches its nadir in a section titled "Life under the Law." He believes the Pharisaic rabbis imposed a rigid system of legalistic obedience.

> All free moral action was now completely crushed under the burden of numberless separate statutory requirements.... In every department of life action no longer proceeds from inward motive, is no longer the free manifestation of a moral disposition, but results from the external constraint of statutory requirement.

A tinge of conscience provokes Schürer to add, "Justice requires us to mention, that many an excellent saying of the learned men of that age, affording proof, that all moral judgment was not stifled under the rubbish of Halachic discussions, has been preserved."[106] Turning to other features of

---

103. *History of the Jewish People* I, 2:319.
104. *History of the Jewish People* II, 1:298–99.
105. Ibid. II, 1:349.
106. Ibid. II, 2:95, 124.

Jewish religion, Schürer discusses the history of the messianic hope from Daniel through 4 Ezra. He believes the failure of the hope to be realized in history led to a focus on the future and the supramundane. In discussing the Essenes, he argues that the original members of this sect broke from the Pharisees and adopted a position of extreme Pharisaism.[107] Schürer also discusses the Jewish diaspora, noting the importance of the synagogue for Jewish life abroad. He thinks the Jews engaged in a successful mission whereby converts were made among the Gentiles.

Schürer devotes an extensive discussion to Jewish literature—a volume of more than 380 pages in the English edition. He orders the material according to two, not entirely distinct, classifications: Palestinian Jewish literature, that is, literature in which Schürer detects a Pharisaic viewpoint; and Graeco-Jewish literature, that is, literature that displays a distinct Hellenistic influence. In regard to the Palestinian literature, Schürer discusses historical documents (e.g., 1 Maccabees), books of gnomic wisdom (e.g., Ben Sira), and hortatory narratives (e.g., Judith). Under the category "pseudepigraphic prophecies," Schürer discusses Daniel, Enoch, and 4 Ezra. In regard to Graeco-Jewish literature, he observes that Hellenistic culture had become universal.

> Judaism and Hellenism now really entered upon a process of mutual internal amalgamation. Judaism, which in its unyielding Pharisaic phase appears so rigidly exclusive, proved itself uncommonly pliable and accommodating upon the soil of Hellenism, and allowed a far-reaching influence to the ascendant Greek spirit.[108]

The literature discussed under this category includes translations of the Scriptures (LXX and Aquila), works revising and completing scriptural literature (e.g., the additions to Daniel), historical works (e.g., Josephus), epic poetry and drama (e.g., Philo the Elder), philosophy (e.g., 4 Maccabees), apologetics (e.g., Josephus, *Against Apion*), Jewish propaganda under a heathen mask (e.g., the Epistle of Aristeas). Schürer gives major attention to Philo of Alexandria. In discussing Philo's thought, Schürer carefully analyzes the idea of the Logos.

Critics of Schürer are not hard to find. Actually, most reviewers, including Jewish scholars, have been appreciative of his work, particularly the historical section.[109] George Foot Moore, who is essentially critical, praises Schürer's book as "an indispensable repertory for all sorts of things about the Jews . . . an immeasurably useful handbook." Moore's criticisms, like

---

107. The new edition of 1973 drastically revises this discussion and adds a section, "The Qumran Community according to the Dead Sea Scrolls."
108. *History of the Jewish People* II, 3:157.
109. See Hoenig, "The New Schürer," 47–54; Stern, "A New English Schürer," 419–24.

those of many others, are directed at Schürer's inadequate understanding of the rabbinic sources and his caricature of Jewish religious life. "But after all allowance is made the final word must be that 'Life under the Law' was conceived, not as a chapter of the history of Judaism but as a topic of Christian apologetic; it was written to prove by the highest Jewish authority that the strictures on Judaism in the Gospels and the Pauline Epistles are fully justified."[110] In spite of these weaknesses, Schürer combined a mastery of material with a lively historical imagination so as to produce a history of Judaism that became the unrivaled authority for more than a half-century.

Robert Henry Charles (1855–1931)

Robert Henry Charles was born in Cookstown, County Tyrone, Ireland.[111] He was educated at Queen's College, Belfast; Trinity College, Dublin; and Exeter College, Oxford. He also studied in Germany. From 1898 to 1906, he worked as Professor of Biblical Greek at Trinity, Dublin. He was also Grinfeld lecturer on the Septuagint and Fellow of Merton College, Oxford. In 1913, he was appointed Canon of Westminster Abbey, where, at first, he bored the congregation with scholarly sermons, but eventually became an effective preacher. He was appointed Archdeacon of Westminster in 1919.

Charles belonged to the liberal wing of the Anglican church. He believed in progressive revelation. "As in nature, so in religion, God reveals Himself in the course of slow evolution."[112] According to Charles, the religion of Israel reached a higher expression in the faith of Jesus and Paul.[113] While a student at Dublin, Charles was troubled by the orthodox picture of hell. This provoked him to a career in the study of Jewish and Christian eschatology. Although pouring over Syriac and Ethiopic texts might seem tedious to some, Charles exclaims that "the toil has been frequently lightened by the joys of discovery, and the task of research has been often one of sheer delight. The pleasures of fox-hunting are not to be compared with

---

110. George Foot Moore, "Christian Writers on Judaism," *HTR* 14 (1921): 237, 240. See Shaye J. D. Cohen, "The Political and Social History of the Jews in Greco-Roman Antiquity: The State of the Question," in *Early Judaism and Its Modern Interpreters*, ed. Robert A. Kraft and George W. E. Nickelsburg, SBLMI (Atlanta: Scholars Press, 1986), 33–56.

111. On the life and work of Charles, see C. F. D'Arcy, "A Brief Memoir," in R. H. Charles, *Courage, Truth, Purity* (Oxford: Basil Blackwell, 1931), xiii–xxxv; H. D. A. Major, "Robert Henry Charles," *Modern Churchman* 46 (1956): 221–26; A. Haire Forster, "Reminiscences of R. H. Charles," *AThR* 39 (1957): 359–60; Howard, *Romance of NT Scholarship*, 105–10.

112. R. H. Charles, *A Critical History of the Doctrine of the Future Life: In Israel, in Judaism, and in Christianity, or Hebrew, Jewish, and Christian Eschatology from Pre-Prophetic Times till the Close of the New Testament Canon* (London: Adam and Charles Black, 1899), vii.

113. An example of Charles's progressive thought can be seen in his exegetical monograph *The Teaching of the New Testament on Divorce* (London: Williams & Norgate, 1921), in which he argues that the "guiltless" party of a divorce is free to remarry.

those of the student in full quest of some truth, some new fact showing itself for the first time within his intellectual horizon."[114]

Texts and Translations: History of Religion

In 1893, Charles published a critical edition of the Book of Enoch—the first in a series of publications of texts of the Jewish pseudepigrapha.[115] Although everyone acknowledges that Jude quotes Enoch, Charles exaggerates when he says, "All the writers of the New Testament were familiar with it, and were more or less influenced by it in thought and diction."[116] Charles believes the document has five main parts, composed in different periods. For example, he thinks the Dream Visions (chs. 83–90) were written between 166 and 161 B.C.E., while the Similitudes (chs. 37–70) were written between 94 and 64 B.C.E. The bulk of Charles's work comprises his translation, accompanied by notes of two types: critical notes on the text; historical and exegetical notes on the translation. Following the same format, Charles published critical editions of other Jewish documents: the Book of the Secrets of Enoch, the Apocalypse of Baruch, the Assumption of Moses, the Ascension of Isaiah, the Book of Jubilees, and the Testaments of the Twelve Patriarchs.[117]

Charles's work on the Jewish texts is consummated in a monumental two-volume collection of the *Apocrypha and Pseudepigrapha*—a work in which Charles enlisted the assistance of other competent scholars.[118] For each book, a critical introduction, an English translation, and critical-exegetical commentary are presented. The introductions treat such matters as text, authorship, date, and theology of the documents. Volume 1 (684 pages) contains the OT Apocrypha. In the introduction, Charles contends that such works as the Wisdom of Solomon display a higher level of "inspiration" than the canonical book of Esther. Although Charles claims that his second volume contains virtually all the noncanonical sources written between 200 B.C.E. and 100 C.E., it actually includes only seventeen

---

114. Quoted by Major, "Charles," 223.
115. *The Book of Enoch* (Oxford: Clarendon Press, 1893).
116. Ibid., 1.
117. *The Book of the Secrets of Enoch* (Oxford: Clarendon Press, 1896); idem, *The Apocalypse of Baruch* (London: Adam and Charles Black, 1896); *The Assumption of Moses* (London: Adam and Charles Black, 1897); *The Ascension of Isaiah* (London: Adam and Charles Black, 1900); *The Book of Jubilees or the Little Genesis* (London: Adam and Charles Black, 1902); *The Greek Versions of the Testaments of the Twelve Patriarchs* (Oxford: Clarendon Press, 1908). Charles's translations of these works were issued in a series of small volumes designed for the general reader, published by the Society for Promoting Christian Knowledge (London) under the title "Translations of Early Documents, Series I, Palestinian Jewish Texts" (1917–29).
118. R. H. Charles, ed., *The Apocrypha and Pseudepigrapha of the Old Testament with Introductions and Critical and Explanatory Notes to the Several Books*, 2 vols. (Oxford: Clarendon Press, 1913). Among those assisting in the project were Agnes Smith Lewis and J. Rendel Harris (see pp. 401–6 below).

documents.[119] A 1983 edition of OT Pseudepigrapha contains fifty-two documents.[120] According to Charles, pseudepigraphic literature developed in reaction to the triumph of Jewish legalism. The establishment of the supremacy of the law left no room for prophecy, so that religious writers had to assume the identity of some ancient seer in order to claim revelation. According to Charles, "Apocalyptic was essentially ethical." The critical work on nine of the documents was undertaken by Charles himself: Jubilees, Martyrdom of Isaiah, 1 Enoch, Testaments of the Twelve Patriarchs, Assumption of Moses, 2 Enoch, 2 Baruch, and Fragments of a Zadokite work. In discussing these documents, Charles makes some interesting comments. For example, "The Book of Enoch is for the history of theological development the most important pseudepigraph of the first two centuries B.C."[121]

In this work on the Jewish texts, Charles shows himself to be a brilliant linguist, a meticulous text critic, and master of a huge amount of bibliographical and historical data. From a modern perspective, Charles's work is not without weaknesses.[122] New material has been discovered, the caricature of legalistic Judaism has been corrected, and the sharp distinction between Hellenistic and Palestinian Judaism has been erased. Nevertheless, Charles's two-volume collection prevailed as the standard source for more than a half-century.

On the basis of his careful research in the sources, Charles produced important works on the history of religion. His *Critical History of the Doctrine of the Future Life* is essentially a historical investigation of Jewish and early Christian eschatology. In Charles's opinion, the failure of the prophetic hope led in the second century B.C.E. to the rise of apocalyptic literature. Whereas the prophets were concerned with this world, apocalyptic focused on the supramundane future. Charles thinks this trend continued in the next century when hope in an earthly kingdom of God was abandoned, and the Messiah was viewed as a supernatural Son of Man. Charles thinks the early Christians transformed Jewish eschatology. Christians believed, "The true Messianic kingdom begins on earth, and will be consummated in heaven; it is not temporary, but eternal; it is not limited to one people, but embraces the righteous of all nations and all times."[123] Charles acknowledges that Jesus used the vivid language of Jewish apocalyptic, but he thinks

---

119. See James H. Charlesworth, "The Significance of the New Edition of the Old Testament Pseudepigrapha," in *La Littérature intertestamentaire: Colloque de Strasbourg (1983)*, ed. André Caquot, Bibliothèque des Centres d'Études Supérieures spécialisées (Paris: Presses Universitaires de France, 1985), 11–28.
120. James H. Charlesworth, *The Old Testament Pseudepigrapha*, 2 vols. (Garden City, N.Y.: Doubleday, 1983).
121. *Apocrypha and Pseudepigrapha* 2:ix, 163.
122. See Charlesworth, "The Significance of the New Edition," 11–28.
123. *Doctrine of the Future Life*, 308–9.

the kingdom of God was essentially ethical, concerned with "the common good of man"—"the community in which the divine will was to be realized."[124] According to Charles, Paul presents an evolving eschatology that moves away from the Jewish apocalyptic of 1 and 2 Thessalonians into the spiritual and the universal eschatology of the imprisonment epistles.

The longer Charles studied apocalyptic, the more he liked it! In *Religious Development between the Old and the New Testaments,* he argues (against most scholars) that the move from prophecy to apocalyptic was not a decline, but an advance.[125] "Apocalyptic and not prophecy was the first to grasp the great idea that all history, alike human, cosmological, and spiritual, is a unity—a unity following naturally as a corollary of the unity of God preached by the prophets. . . . Whereas the scope of prophecy was limited, as regards time and space, that of apocalyptic was as wide as the universe and as unlimited as time."[126] In Charles's view, Christianity further refined apocalyptic: the messianic king became the suffering Son of Man; the hope of a bodily resurrection was transformed into belief in immortality.

Commentary on Revelation

Making use of his text-critical, linguistic, and exegetical skills, together with his knowledge of apocalyptic texts, Charles produced a two-volume *Commentary* on the Apocalypse. Prior to the Commentary, Charles had published *Studies in the Apocalypse,* in which he draws a fundamental distinction between Christian and Jewish apocalyptic: Christian apocalyptic was not pseudonymous, because it did not accede to the Jewish view that revelation had ceased.[127] Charles's *Commentary on Revelation* was published in the series "The International Critical Commentary on the Holy Scriptures of the Old and New Testaments."[128] Begun under the editorship of C. A. Briggs, S. R. Driver, and Alfred Plummer, this series was jointly published by T. & T. Clark (Edinburgh) and Charles Scribner's Sons (New York). The writers were British and American. The first volume appeared in 1895, Driver's *Deuteronomy.* The approach was philological and historical, attempting to avoid theological bias. The series was designed to equal the best of German scholarship, and it continues until today as a major resource for English-speaking students of the Scriptures.

In his preface, Charles asserts that publication at the end of the world war is appropriate, since this is the time "that has witnessed the overthrow

124. Ibid., 314.
125. (London: Williams & Norgate, 1914).
126. Ibid., 24, 32.
127. (Edinburgh: T. &. T. Clark, 1913). After the Commentary, Charles also published *Lectures on the Apocalypse* (London: British Academy, 1922), in which he affirms the continuing relevance of the book of Revelation.
128. *A Critical and Exegetical Commentary on the Revelation of St. John,* 2 vols., ICC (Edinburgh: T. & T. Clark, 1920).

of the greatest conspiracy of might against right that has occurred in the history of the world, and at the same time the greatest fulfillment of the prophecy of the Apocalypse."[129] In a lengthy introduction (more than 150 pages), Charles argues that the author was a Palestinian prophet named John who is not to be identified with either the apostle John or John the Elder. After the death of the author, Charles believes an editor completed the work, rearranged the material, and added interpolations. According to Charles, the author used both Greek and Hebrew sources, including the HB, the Pseudepigrapha, and several books of the NT. Charles believes the final edition could not have been composed prior to the time of Domitian.

According to Charles, the distinctive content of Revelation comes from the author's own psychic experiences—dreams and visions that convey transcendent truth.

> Moreover, if we believe, as the present writer does, that behind these visions there is an actual substratum of reality belonging to the higher spiritual world, then the seer could grasp the things seen and heard in such visions, only in so far as he was equipped for the task by his psychical powers and the spiritual development behind him. . . . In this higher experience the divine insight is won in a state of intense spiritual exaltation, in which the self loses immediate self-consciousness without becoming unconscious, and the best faculties of the mind are quickened to their highest power.

In discussing the theology of the Apocalypse, Charles notes the emphasis on the revelation of God in Christ: "The Son is a revelation of the Father on the stage of the world's history. Hence, as the Father is supreme in power, He is supreme in love going forth in sacrifice. The principle of self-sacrificing love belongs to the essence of the Godhead."[130] Charles's introduction includes a forty-page grammar of the unique Greek of the Apocalypse. In exegesis, Charles adopts an eclectic method: historical and eschatological, philological, literary-critical, tradition-historical, religious-historical, philosophical, and psychical. After the introduction, volume 1 includes the comments on Revelation 1–13; volume 2 presents the comments on chapters 14–22, Charles's critical edition of the Greek text, and his English translation.

As to the format of the commentary, Charles proceeds chapter by chapter, noting the structure of the document. At the beginning of each chapter or section, he presents an introductory analysis of the text. Comments on the Greek phrases of the text are presented verse by verse. For example, in discussing chapters 1 and 2, Charles presents an introduction to the letters to the seven churches. He believes these were actual letters, written earlier and revised for incorporation into the larger book. Commenting on "The

129. Ibid. 1:xv.
130. Ibid. 1:cvi, cxiv.

Message to the Church in Ephesus" (2:1-7), Charles describes the city of Ephesus. He believes "those who claim to be apostles" (v. 2) are the same as the Nocolaitans of 2:6, who are the same as those who "hold to the teaching of Balaam" (2:14); their error, according to Charles, is a failure to observe the apostolic decree (Acts 15:23-29). In regard to "the tree of life that is in the paradise of God" (v. 7), Charles cites parallels from the Testament of Levi and 1 Enoch, and notes that John has transplanted the tree from the Jerusalem temple to the heavenly Jerusalem (22:2); he believes the tree symbolizes immortality.

On Revelation 13, Charles observes that the dragon summons two beasts: the first represents the Roman Empire; the second, the priesthood of the imperial cult. The message of the chapter is that the faithful must keep the commandments of God even though it means martyrdom. In regard to 13:1-10, Charles believes the author used a Jewish apocalyptic source, written shortly after 70. As to details, Charles argues that the beast coming from the sea is a composite of the four beasts of Dan. 7:1-7: the seven heads represent the total number of heads of the four beasts of Daniel; the ten horns come from Daniel's fourth beast; John's beast combines features of a leopard, a bear, and a lion. Commenting on 13:4, Charles says, "In this verse our author takes up the theme which led really to the composition of the book as a whole, the worship of the Beast, the imperial cultus. Since this meant a subordination of the interests of religion to those of the State, it became the chief source of strife between Christendom and the Roman Empire."[131]

In sum, Charles has produced a monumental commentary on the Apocalypse. His research is comprehensive; his skill in source criticism, textual criticism, tradition criticism, linguistic and literary analysis is remarkable; his historical sense and theological sensitivity are impressive. To be sure, many of his critical and exegetical judgments seem overconfident. Moreover, Charles's belief that much of the author's material has come through his own religious experience seems to be in tension with Charles's emphasis on sources and the apocalyptic tradition. The mass of Charles's work, both here and in his research on the Jewish documents, would appear to designate apocalyptic writings primarily as literary compositions, not reports of visionary experiences.

RESEARCH IN HELLENISTIC BACKGROUNDS: PAUL WENDLAND, EDWIN HATCH, AND OTTO PFLEIDERER

Whereas the study of the Jewish backgrounds could affirm a continuity between the revelation of the Hebrew Scriptures and the NT, the study of the Greek backgrounds appeared less congenial. Could early Christianity

---

131. Ibid. 1:351.

have been tainted with paganism? Was not the world's wisdom foolishness with God? One of the first to venture into Alexandria was C. F. Georg Heinrici (1844–1915). Educated at Halle and Berlin, Heinrici taught at Marburg and Leipzig. In his commentaries on the Corinthian correspondence, he frequently cites parallels from Hellenistic literature. Reflecting on this procedure, Heinrici writes, "When the ideas are investigated from the sources and vocabulary of the area out of which they arise, it is possible to gain a solid ground for understanding the elements of Pauline thought." For example, Heinrici finds the background of Paul's idea of "conscience" in Socratic thought, Stoic philosophy, and Philo. Similarly, Heinrici argues that the early church conformed to patterns found in the religious associations and social clubs of Hellenistic society. "Therefore, I have compared the characteristics of Corinthian congregational life with information from the Greek and Roman associations."[132] In a book on Paul, Heinrici contends that the apostle imitated the style of the Cynic-Stoic diatribe, and used images borrowed from the mystery cults.[133]

Paul Wendland (1864–1915)

A more extensive treatment of Hellenism in relation to Judaism and Christianity was published by Paul Wendland.[134] Born in Hohenstein (East Prussia), Wendland held professorships in classics at Kiel, Breslau, and Göttingen, and was noted for his work on Philo. The opening chapter of his *Die hellenistisch-römische Kultur* affirms the importance of Hellenistic language and thought for the development of world history in general and Christianity in particular. Wendland traces the history of Hellenism from the decline of Athens through the rise of Macedonia and the conquests of Alexander to the rule of his successors and the triumph of Rome. The result was the pan-Hellenization of culture, marked by the contrasting features of cosmopolitanism and individualism. In the intellectual realm, Wendland believes the popular philosophers of the time—the Cynics and the Stoics—were driven by a sense of mission. They addressed the ethical issues of the day, and proclaimed their message in the vivid style of the diatribe. Wendland thinks their attack on polytheism and pagan morality paved the way for the Christian proclamation.

---

132. *Das zweite Sendschreiben des Apostel Paulus an die Korinther* (Berlin: Wilhelm Hertz, 1887), 557, 556.
133. *Paulinische Probleme* (Leipzig: Dürr, 1914). Heinrici also published *Hellenismus und Christentum* (Lichterfelde-Berlin: Edwin Runge, 1909)—a work noting parallels between the NT and the Hermetic literature.
134. *Die hellenistisch-römische Kultur in ihren Beziehungen zu Judentum und Christentum* (Tübingen: J. C. B. Mohr [Paul Siebeck], 1912). For a short survey of Wendland's life and work, see Hans Lietzmann, "Paul Wendland," in *Kleine Schriften, III. Studien zur Liturgie- und Symbolgeschichte zur Wissenschaftsgeschichte*, ed. Der Kommission für Spätantike Religionsgeschichte (Berlin: Akademie-Verlag, 1962), 285–88.

Wendland sketches the complex history of religion in the Hellenistic period. He notes the rise of ecstatic religion, the philosophical opposition to the old beliefs, the popularity of foreign faiths and the mystery cults, and the development of the imperial cult. He believes Gnosticism was typical of the syncretism of the time. "Gnosis," says Wendland, "did not actually emerge out of the soil of the Christian church; it is a pre-Christian product whose historical understanding cannot be gained within the boundaries of the history of the church, but only in the wider contexts of the general history of religion." Wendland believes the gnostic ideas of the heavenly redeemer and the cosmic understandings of redemption were influential in the development of Christianity.

> We learn to understand Christianity rightly as a religion of redemption primarily out of this background. . . . The Hellenizing of the doctrine of Jesus was in a certain sense an orientalizing; since it indicated a discussion with the thought-world of the syncretistic religions whose foundation was mostly oriental, whose motifs and ideas were Hellenistic or were indeed Hellenized.[135]

Wendland traces the development of Christianity as a Hellenistic religion. "The preaching of Christ," he writes, "had no relation to Hellenism." However, with the move out of Palestine into the larger world, Hellenistic ideas developed. Wendland detects this development in the stories of the supernatural birth of Jesus and the idea of the preexistent redeemer. Paul, in Wendland's opinion, was important for the Hellenization of Christianity. Although his religious background was in Judaism, Paul's conversion "meant for him a complete break with his Jewish past; . . . it transformed the Pharisaic persecutor of Christians into an apostle of Christ, and the earliest execution of this call must have confirmed him in the knowledge of the new faith as the universal religion of humanity beyond all national and particularistic limitations."[136] Like the philosophers of the day, Paul assumed a natural knowledge of the divine, and his ethics offered parallels to the teachings of the Stoics. According to Wendland, Christianity eventually succeeded the imperial cult to become the universal religion of the Hellenistic age. Going beyond Heinrici, who affirmed the distinctiveness of the Christian religion, Wendland identifies Christianity as a Hellenistic religion.[137]

---

135. *Hellenistisch-römische Kultur*, 165, 185.
136. Ibid., 212, 242–43.
137. Wendland also published an insightful work on the forms of early Christian literature: *Die urchristlichen Literaturformen* (Tübingen: J. C. B. Mohr [Paul Siebeck], 1912). See also Wendland, "Die christliche Literatur," ed. Hans Lietzmann, in *Einleitung in die Altertumswissenschaft*, ed. Alfred Gercke and Eduard Norden, 1/5 (Leipzig: B. G. Teubner, 1923), 1–6.

Edwin Hatch (1835–89)

In England, where resistance was even greater, the pioneer in the study of Hellenistic backgrounds was Edwin Hatch.[138] Born in Derby, Hatch was educated at Pembroke College, Oxford. After nine years as professor of classics at Trinity College, Toronto, he returned to Oxford as vice-principal of St. Mary's Hall. NT scholars remember Hatch for his meticulous work on the *Concordance to the Septuagint*.[139] With the collaboration of a group of scholars, Hatch had finished half of the project by the time of his death. The three-volume work was completed by Henry A. Redpath (1848–1908). Hatch's linguistic research can also be seen in his *Essays in Biblical Greek*.[140] One of the essays presents brief analyses of more than twenty important biblical terms such as δικαιοσύνη. An essay titled "On Psychological Terms in Biblical Greek" investigates the use of καρδία, πνεῦμα, ψυχή and διανοία in the LXX and Hexapla and in Philo.

In his Bampton Lectures (1880) on *The Organization of the Early Christian Churches,* Hatch, reminiscent of Heinrici, argues that the congregations of Christianity were shaped according to patterns already present in the *collegia,* the voluntary associations or social groups found in Graeco-Roman society.[141] Within these associations, administrative officers emerged whose role was primarily financial; they were given the title ἐπίσκοποι. Hatch believes the same type of organizational leadership developed in the early church. In time, a single bishop became the supreme leader, and eventually the notion developed that the bishops succeeded the apostles who had been appointed by Christ. Thus, for Hatch, the historic episcopate, rather than being divinely ordained, was a late development, with its source in pagan society.

The importance of Hellenistic backgrounds is addressed in Hatch's Hibbert Lectures (1888) on *The Influence of Greek Ideas and Usage upon the Christian Church*. Hailed as a classic, this work was reprinted in a paperback edition more than a half-century later.[142] At the outset, Hatch observes that

---

138. For a survey of Hatch's life and work, see Frederick C. Grant's foreword to Hatch's *The Influence of Greek Ideas on Christianity,* HTCL (New York: Harper & Row, 1957); Ieuan Ellis, "Edwin Hatch and the Relative Finality of Christ," *Theology* 78 (1975): 451–59; "Biographical Notices," in *Memorials of Edwin Hatch,* ed. Samuel C. Hatch (London: Hodder and Stoughton, 1890), xv–xliii; W. Sanday, "In Memoriam Dr. Edwin Hatch," *Expositor* 1 (1890): 93–111.

139. Edwin Hatch and Henry A. Redpath, *A Concordance to the Septuagint and Other Greek Versions of the Old Testament (Including the Apocryphal Books),* 3 vols. (Oxford: Clarendon, 1897; repr., Grand Rapids, Mich.: Baker, 1983; 2d ed., Grand Rapids, Mich.: Baker, 1998).

140. (Oxford: Clarendon Press, 1889).

141. Third ed. (London: Rivingtons, 1880). See John S. Kloppenborg, "Edwin Hatch, Churches and *Collegia,*" in *Origins and Method: Towards a New Understanding of Judaism and Christianity* (Sheffield: Sheffield Academic Press, 1993), 212–38. Hatch's book was translated into German by Harnack.

142. Ed. A. M. Fairbairn (London: Williams & Norgate, 1890; repr., HTCL, New York: Harper & Row, 1957).

a comparison between the Sermon on the Mount and the Nicene Creed demonstrates how Christianity was transformed from an ethical religion into a metaphysical system. He believes that Christians were at first hostile to philosophy. "The earliest forms of Christianity were not only outside the sphere of Greek philosophy, but they also appealed, on the one hand, mainly to the classes which philosophy did not reach, and, on the other hand, to a standard which philosophy did not recognize." In time, Christian teachers made use of Greek philosophy, even claiming that Plato purloined his wisdom from Moses. As to ethics, Hatch maintains that the Hellenistic age was a time of moral reformation. Philosophers such as Epictetus advocated control of the passions by reason in harmony with the divine will. Christians, Hatch thinks, increasingly developed an ethic similar to that of the Stoics, stressing virtue and natural law. In the development of theology, Christian thinkers were influenced by Greek philosophy.

> It was in the Gentile rather than in the Jewish world that the theology of Christianity was shaped. . . . Christianity won its way among the educated classes by virtue of its satisfying not only their moral ideals, but also their higher intellectual conceptions. On its ethical side it had . . . large elements in common with reformed Stoicism; on its theological side it moved in harmony with the new movements of Platonism. And those movements reacted upon it. They gave a philosophical form to the simpler Jewish faith, and especially to those elements of it in which the teaching of St. Paul had already given a foothold for speculation. The earlier conceptions remained; but blending readily with the philosophical conceptions that were akin to them, they were expanded into large theories in which metaphysics and dialectics had an ample field.[143]

In conclusion, Hatch acknowledges the process of historical development within Christianity, but contends that the Greek element is not essential to Christianity. He advocates a religion that is both old and new—a religion that affirms the original moral impetus of the teaching of Jesus, but applies it to contemporary life and thought.

Otto Pfleiderer (1839–1908)

Life and Thought

With Pfleiderer, the study of Hellenistic backgrounds was incorporated into a comprehensive view of the history of early Christianity.[144] Pfleiderer was born in Stetten, Württemberg. He studied at Tübingen (1857–61), the last

---

143. Ibid., 124, 238–39.
144. See William V. Kelley, "Pfleiderer at Edinburgh," *Methodist Review* 76 (1894): 794–801; Samuel Plantz, "Dr. Otto Pfleiderer," *Methodist Review* 90 (1908): 883–97; Emanuel Hirsch, *Geschichte der neuern evangelischen Theologie im Zusammenhang mit den allgemeinen Bewegungen des europäischen Denkens* (Gütersloh: C. Bertelsmann, 1954) 5:562–71; Reinhard Leuze, *Theologie und Religionsgeschichte: Der Weg Otto Pfleiderers*, Münchener Universitäts-Schriften, Münchener Monographien zur historischen und systematischen Theologie 6 (Munich: Chr. Kaiser, 1890).

of the important students of F. C. Baur. After serving as a pastor in Heilbronn, Pfleiderer was appointed professor at Jena (1870). In 1875, he moved to the faculty at Berlin, where he remained for the balance of his career.

Although he did not agree with the details of Baur's reconstruction of early Christian history, Pfleiderer approved of his teacher's method and basic theology.[145] Like Baur, Pfleiderer embraced philosophical idealism: truth or the divine spirit is revealed in history; history is the process of the realization of divine purpose; Christianity is the historical expression of universal truth. Pfleiderer published books in various theological areas: philosophy of religion, ethics, history of religion, and history of theology. His basic point of view is evident in his work *Christian Origins*.[146] In this book, Pfleiderer affirms Baur's understanding of Christianity as a historical process that must be investigated by a scientific-historical method—a method that recognizes "the law-abiding order of the universe which ever conditions all human experience."[147]

"In order to understand the origin of Christianity as a historical development," writes Pfleiderer, "the preparation in the ante-Christian world demands first consideration." For Pfleiderer, the Hellenistic backgrounds are of primary importance. Socrates was "a forerunner and a prophet of Christianity," and Philo's idea of the Logos and his stress on universal ethics were significant for Christianity. According to Pfleiderer, Jesus presented his message in the form of Jewish apocalyptic, but this husk contained a true kernel: the idea of unconditional surrender to the will of God. "This kernel of his faith remains the model for all time; it preserves a truth for us, even though history itself has led us to differentiate between the permanent kernel and the temporary form, to recognize the realization of the divine will, no longer in miraculous catastrophes, but in the continuous education of humanity through the natural evolution of social life." "Thus God became for him omnipotence of love,—a father in whom benevolence is not only a quality alongside of others, but is his innermost nature."[148]

Anticipating the work of the history of religion school, Pfleiderer published works on the religious environment of early Christianity.[149] For example, his popular book on Greek philosophy as preparation for Christianity discusses pre-Socratic natural philosophy and the importance of Orphism as a religion of redemption.[150] Turning to Socrates and Plato, Pfleiderer

---

145. See *HNTR* 1:258–69.
146. *Die Entstehung des Christentums* (Munich: J. F. Lehmann, 1905); Eng. trans.: *Christian Origins*, trans. Daniel A. Huebsch (New York: B. W. Huebsch, 1906).
147. *Christian Origins*, 4, 25.
148. Ibid., 31, 33, 94, 99.
149. See pp. 222, 238–53, below.
150. *Die Vorbereitung des Christentums in der griechischen Philosophie*, 2 ed., Religionsgeschichtliche Volksbücher, 3. Reihe, 1. Heft (Tübingen: J. C. M. Mohr [Paul Siebeck], 1912).

notes the significance of Socrates for ethics and Plato's idea of the good for speculative theology. Next to Platonism, Pfleiderer believes Stoicism provided the most important background for Christianity. The Stoics advocated a high ethic and the freedom of the individual. In conclusion, Pfleiderer detects limitations in all Hellenistic philosophies and finds their expectations more fully realized in Christian thought.

Also important for Pfleiderer's emphasis on Hellenistic backgrounds is his *The Early Christian Conception of Christ: Its Significance and Value in the History of Religion*.[151] Here Pfleiderer demonstrates the value of the history of religion method for the study of the development of Christology. "The sphere of comparative religion, I am convinced, offers to the theology of the twentieth century a rich field of labour, whose culture will result in the clearing up of many problems to which Biblical exegesis and criticism have so far found no satisfactory solution."[152] In describing Jesus as the "Son of God," early Christians, in Pfleiderer's opinion, viewed Christ in three ways: (1) as the adopted Son of God (like the king in Israel); (2) as the preexistent divine being (like Philo's Logos); (3) as the virgin-born child (like Buddha and the Greek heroes). In regard to portrayal of Jesus as wonder-worker, Pfleiderer finds parallels in the stories about Heracles, Asclepius, and especially Apollonius of Tyanna.

In assessing this material, Pfleiderer sounds a warning: parallels do not prove historical dependence; parallel expressions do not mean identical ideas. Parallels, he says, are often formal, and Christianity transcends the forms in which it is expressed:

> No one will deny that an ideal is above the limitations of time and coincides with no one of its historical manifestations; but may not the love which conquers the demon of selfishness, which raises the individual soul above the narrow world of self-interest, and in society transforms the natural struggles for existence into the endeavour to realise the moral solidarity of all men—may not this love be rightly conceived as a supernatural power revealing itself as a divine all-attracting force in the souls of men, like the force of gravitation in the material world?"[153]

But why, asks Pfleiderer, did Christian thinkers use this pagan material? Why not simply present the Jesus of history rather than the Christ of faith? Pfleiderer gives two reasons: (1) contemporary expressions were needed to make the message understandable; (2) the historical Jesus had intrinsic limitations. No historical manifestation, according to Pfleiderer, could fully express the transcendent ideal; Jesus was a child of his time and subject to

---

151. (London: Williams & Norgate, 1905); originally published as *Das Christusbild des urchristlichen Glaubens in religionsgeschichtlicher Beleuchtung* (Berlin: Georg Reimer, 1903).
152. *Early Christian Conception of Christ*, 14.
153. Ibid., 164.

its limitations. "It was therefore absolutely necessary that the universal, eternal, and ideal import of His personality should be delivered from the individual and social limitations of its temporal manifestation, and as the real principle of redemption should find concrete expression in a form above the limitations of time."

> Accordingly myth and rite were certainly the most suitable forms of expression for primitive Christian belief. . . . They show us how we ought to let history point the way above history to the eternal and omnipresent God, who is a God of the living and not of the dead; they warn us to free ourselves from the fatal ban of historicism, which seeks God's revelation only in the records of a dead past, and thus loses the power of finding it in the living present.[154]

History of Early Christianity

Pfleiderer's major work is his massive *Primitive Christianity*.[155] Based on his Hibbert Lectures, this greatly expanded work demonstrates development in Pfleiderer's thought since his earlier book on Paul.[156] In particular, Pfleiderer had become increasingly confirmed in his support of Baur's understanding of early Christianity as a progressive historical development, and, consequently, in his rejection of the view of Ritschl and his school (notably Harnack)[157] that early Christianity suffered a fall—its dissolution through Hellenization. According to Pfleiderer, Hellenistic influence was already evident in Paul. "Since the Gentile Christian universal church had been planted by the Pauline preaching in a soil prepared by a long-standing pre-Christian Hellenism, so this Hellenism and that Christian preaching were the two factors from whose relationship the distinction of Gentile Christianity from its beginning is naturally to be explained."[158]

The first volume of *Primitive Christianity* is dedicated to the study of Paul. According to Pfleiderer, Paul clearly perceived the abiding truth of the religion of Jesus. Pfleiderer believes that "Paul, who never saw Jesus in the flesh or listened to His word, nevertheless grasped the innermost spirit of Jesus more purely and more deeply than the first disciples." Paul was reared in Tarsus, a center of the Stoics, whose ethical teachings find parallels in his

---

154. Ibid., 167–68, 169–70.
155. *Das Urchristenthum, seine Schriften und Lehren, in geschichtlichem Zusammenhang* (Berlin: Georg Reimer, 1887); Eng. trans.: *Primitive Christianity: Its Writings and Teachings in Their Historical Connections*, trans. W. Montgomery, ed. W. D. Morrison, 4 vols., TTL (London: Williams & Norgate, 1906–11).
156. *The Influence of the Apostle Paul on the Development of Christianity*, trans. J. Frederick Smith (New York: Charles Scribner's Sons, 1885); idem, *Paulinismus: Ein Beitrag zur Geschichte der urchristlichen Theologie*, 2d ed. (Leipzig: O. R. Reisland, 1890); Eng. trans. of 1st ed.: *Paulinism: A Contribution to the History of Primitive Christian Theology*, trans. Edward Peters, 2 vols. (London: Williams & Norgate, 1877).
157. See pp. 86–92, 122–35 above.
158. *Urchristentum*, v.

epistles. "For the historical student, the special importance of these sayings consists precisely in the fact that they are not dependent on the Christian Gospel, and are therefore of the more significance as witnesses of a widespread ethico-religious mode of thought and feeling in the Graeco-Roman world of that period, which, from its close affinity with the Christian view had, among the heathen, prepared the soil for the Gospel."[159] In his *Christian Origins*, Pfleiderer argues, "Paul transformed the early-Christian enthusiasm, whose ecstatic expressions were so closely related to the orgiastic features of the heathen mysteries, into the principle of a new ethics, which employed the pathos and the power of that enthusiasm in the service of the moral ideals of the life of the congregation."[160]

Discussing Paul's theology, Pfleiderer believes the apostle's view of humanity reflects both Jewish and Hellenistic backgrounds.

> Paul, therefore, teaches, in agreement with the Pharisees, deliverance of the body, but not deliverance of the flesh; in agreement with the Greeks, he teaches liberation from the flesh, from earthly sensuality, not, however, in a disembodied, purely spiritual state, but in a new body appropriate to the circumstances of the heavenly life; therefore not a one-sided deliverance of the spiritual part of man with the permanent abandonment of the bodily, but a deliverance of the whole man, body, soul, and spirit (1 Thess. v. 23), effected, however, by the slaying of the flesh as the present seat of the powers which oppose God.

Pfleiderer thinks that Paul's understanding of redemption also presupposes Hellenistic and Jewish concepts. Paul's idea of the heavenly redeemer reflects the Alexandrian notion of divine mediators, but his idea of redemption also presupposed "the Pharisaic legal religion, according to which God does not forgive unless payment of the debt is made." Nevertheless, Pfleiderer believes the ethical prevails over the legal. Thus, beneath the harsh dogmatic form of a vicarious expiation, there shows itself as the true kernel, the profound thought of a *rebirth of mankind through the inspiring and renewing power of a divine–human deed of love.*[161] In short, Pfleiderer believes Paul escapes the shackles of his historical setting to promote a universal, ethical religion.

The second volume of Pfleiderer's *Primitive Christianity* is devoted to the historical books, that is, the Synoptic Gospels and Acts. Pfleiderer believes Mark to be the earliest and most reliable Gospel. In Pfleiderer's opinion, the phrase "son of man" is an Aramaic term meaning "man" in general. "Accordingly, I hold it to be highly probable that 'the Son of Man' was never a Messianic self-designation of Jesus in any sense whatever, and that,

---

159. *Primitive Christianity* 1:33, 58.
160. *Christian Origins*, 178–79.
161. *Primitive Christianity* 1:291–92, 336, 341.

therefore, all the passages of the Gospels where this sense is unmistakably present do not belong to the oldest tradition." Pfleiderer does not believe, as Baur did, that Acts reflects a Jewish Christian–Gentile Christian conflict of the second century. Nevertheless, Pfleiderer thinks Acts does have a conciliatory purpose. "Everywhere there is manifest the same effort to remove from the hard realities of history that which is unedifying, to tone down the oppositions within Christianity, to reduce conflicts of principle to insignificant differences of opinion—in short, to draw an ideal picture of peace and innocence."[162] On critical matters, Pfleiderer thinks that the author of Luke used Mark and a primitive Aramaic gospel as his primary sources. This Aramaic gospel (Pfleiderer's version of Q) he also believes was used by Mark and Matthew.

In discussing the teaching of Jesus, Pfleiderer decries the modern attempt to eradicate the apocalyptic features of the kingdom. If "what was eschatological, apocalyptic, catastrophic, in Jesus' expectation of the Kingdom is subordinated to our modern ethical, evolutionary, philosophic conception of the Kingdom of God, the inevitable consequence is that . . . what is most characteristic in His mighty appearance on the field of history is painted over with an ideal picture of universal humanity until it becomes unrecognizable." For Pfleiderer, the distinctive thing about Jesus is his person—his opposition to the legalism of the Pharisees, his revival of the spirit of the prophets.

> The union in the mind of Jesus of this glow of apocalyptic hope with the unfailing warmth and practical energy of pitying love to the poor, the distressed, the sinful, was the secret of the magical charm of His personality, of the enthusiasm and heroism of His public life, of His irresistible influence over the masses, and of His power to attract and rivet the devotion of individuals.[163]

Volume 3 deals with Hellenistic backgrounds, apocalyptic writings, Gnosticism, apocryphal books, and early Christian doctrinal and hortatory writings. In regard to backgrounds, Pfleiderer finds the source of the idea of the heavenly redeemer in Hellenistic syncretism. "This conception of the descent of Christ from heaven and return to heaven has its unmistakable counterpart in the descent and ascent of the gods in the myths relating to the descent to hell and to the ascent of souls in the mystery-cults."[164] In regard to the NT apocrypha, Pfleiderer discusses the Acts of John, Acts of Thomas, Acts of Peter, Gospel of Peter, Gospel According to the Egyptians, Gospel According to the Hebrews, and the Acts of Paul. Pfleiderer's review of doctrinal and hortatory works includes Hebrews, Ephesians, Colossians, the Epistles of Ignatius, the Epistle of Polycarp, the Pastoral Epistles, and

---

162. Ibid. 2:36, 289–90.
163. Ibid. 2:401–2, 425.
164. *Primitive Christianity* 3:130.

the Apocalypse. Pfleiderer believes these documents reflect the battle with Gnosticism whereby Christianity borrowed the best from its competitors, survived, and finally triumphed. "In the course of these struggles, and mutual adjustments, of the most diverse elements, Christianity developed into a world-religion which was able to overcome all other religions, for the very reason that it had adopted what was best in them all, and so assimilated its borrowings to its own distinctive principle that, without losing its unity and distinctiveness, it yet presented the most various aspects, and succeeded in satisfying the most manifold needs of human nature."[165]

The final volume gives major attention to the Johannine writings. In regard to the Fourth Gospel, Pfleiderer observes, "This is a doctrinal work in the form of a Gospel." Acording to Pfleiderer, the author has used Mark, Luke, and an apocryphal source similar to the Gospel of the Hebrews. John's theology, in Pfleiderer's opinion, has its background in the Hellenistic thought of the Pauline school and in the Gnosticism the author purports to refute. According to the author, the Logos that has its source in Philo was become flesh—thus, refuting Gnosticism.

> Thus John has not only transformed Philo's abstract metaphysical conception of the Logos into a concrete ethico-religious ideal figure . . . but has also overcome the phantasmal docetism and the fantastic Christological speculations of Gnosticism. He has so united the historical Christ pictured in the Gospel tradition with the Saviour-deity of the Gnostic mysticism that the latter receives from the former historical and ethical concreteness, while the former receives from the latter universality and theological depth.[166]

Like F. C. Baur, Pfleiderer has assumed a comprehensive view that enlists philosophical idealism and scientific criticism in the service of a normative historical Christianity. History is the realm of revelation, and the truth that history unfolds finds its expression in the development of Christianity. Thus, in conflict with the liberal theology of his day, Pfleiderer denied that Christian history had suffered a fall. Instead, Christianity, assimilating elements from its historical environment, continued to progress. However, Pfleiderer played his own version of the liberal shell game. The husk was Jewish legalism and Hellenistic enthusiasm; the kernel was the ethical ideal of Jesus (in spite of its apocalyptic form) as universalized by Paul (in spite of his Jewish limitations and his religious enthusiasm) and continued by John

---

165. Ibid. 3:257.
166. *Primitive Christianity* 4:1, 204. After completing his *Primitive Christianity*, Pfleiderer expanded his work to include the whole of church history: *Entwicklung des Christentums* (Munich: J. F. Lehmann, 1907); Eng. trans.: *The Development of Christianity,* trans. Daniel A. Huebsch (London: T. Fisher Unwin, 1910). In the early part of this book, Pfleiderer confirms his opposition to liberalism's notion that Hellenistic influence denigrated Christianity.

(in spite of his gnostic tendencies) and carried on by subsequent theologians who recognize that truth unfolds in the intellectual evolution of humanity. The norm in all of this is the ethical idealism of Otto Pfleiderer.

SUMMARY

In contrast to the armies of World War I, bogged down in the trenches, NT scholarship made important advances. New discoveries of papyri led to an identification of NT Greek as the common language of the Hellenistic age (Deissmann, Moulton)—an identification that encouraged a perception of the early Christians as a social and religious movement of the common people (Deissmann). Studies in Semitic linguistics opened new insight into the language and words of Jesus (Dalman). Firsthand geographical, archeological, and cultural exploration in Asia Minor (Ramsay) and Palestine (Dalman) provided new data—artifacts, inscriptions, coins—for the reconstruction of early Christian life and history. Exploiting this new material, scholars produced tools what would be effective in the ongoing research on the NT: lexicons (Moulton and Milligan), concordances (Hatch), grammars (Blass, Moulton). Primary texts were collected and published in critical editions to provide abundant sources for the study of historical backgrounds, for example, Charles's classic *Apocrypha and Pseudepigrapha*. Schürer, despite his anti-Jewish bias, produced his *History of the Jewish People*—a comprehensive work that became a standard resource for future generations.

All the scholars of this chapter affirmed the necessity of investigating the NT in its historical-religious setting—an affirmation that would continue to dominate scholarship throughout the new century. Debate would rage, of course, as to which setting—Jewish or Hellenistic—should be considered more important. With Wendland and Pfleiderer, attention was focused on Hellenistic backgrounds—backgrounds that reflected the taint of paganism. This led to the question, How is the relation of Christianity to its setting to be assessed? Do parallels with other religions imply sources or similarities, or differences and distinctions? Is it proper to view Christianity as a Hellenistic cult or an example of the religious syncretism of late antiquity? How does Jesus—whose person and teachings were honored by these scholars—relate to the apocalyptic thought of Judaism? How does Paul—whose ethic and universalism were appealing—relate to the myth and mysteries of the Hellenistic cults? Can new methods be devised that can cope with these issues? Such questions would continue to tantalize NT scholars for generations to come.

6

Methodological Developments

Equipped with new materials, NT scholars shaped new methods. Like their predecessors, they followed the lead of colleagues in other areas of research. Scholars striving to comprehend human life employed the social and psychological sciences. Sociologists investigated the nature and behavior of groups and communities. Observers of humanity, such as Max Weber and Émile Durkheim, developed the sociology of religion. Sigmund Freud peered into the depths of the human psyche, and William James probed the mysteries of religious experience. In order to understand society, these scientists explored the lives of common people: their cults, their rituals, their feelings, their hopes and aspirations.

If these young methods were fruitful in the understanding of modern culture, surely they would benefit the study of the past. Beneath the traditional concern with intellectual history, historians began to investigate the myths and folk literature of the ancient peoples. Richard Strauss was inspired by the antique fables of Till Eulenspiegel. The staid Europeans, bored with the monotony of industrial civilization, developed a fascination for the Orient. The strange novels of Hermann Hesse reveal the enchantment of eastern mysticism, and Max Müller published fifty-one volumes of *The Sacred Books of the East.* The NT, of course, was also a sacred book of the east. Scholars increasingly perceived that it was not produced in the isolation of some theological Patmos, but was adrift in the vast sea of Mediterranean religions.

HISTORY OF RELIGION AND RELATED METHODS

A new approach to the study of the NT was advanced by the "history of religions" school (*religionsgeschichtliche Schule*). Actually, it was a school without a teacher and without pupils, and identification of its members is disputed.[1] From one perspective, the school consisted of scholars who studied, took examinations, and served as instructors at the University of Göttingen in the 1880s and 1890s.[2] The members, important for NT research, included William Wrede, Johannes Weiss, Hermann Gunkel, Albert Eichhorn, Wilhelm Heitmüller, and Wilhelm Bousset—sometimes called the "little faculty" (*kleine Fakultät*) of Göttingen. From a more substantive analysis, the members of the school were scholars who share methods and results: a focus on religion rather than theology, a concern to view the history of Christianity within the course of the larger history of religion, an emphasis on the history of tradition rather than literary criticism, and a conviction that Christianity was decisively shaped by the impact of foreign religions. According to this view, the main representatives are Gunkel, Eichhorn, Heitmüller, and Bousset; Weiss, Paul Wernle, and Heinrich Weinel shared some of the concerns of the school, while Wrede was on the fringes. Orientalists and classical philologists, such as Franz Cumont and Richard Reitzenstein, were adjuncts. To name this group the "history of religion*s*" school represents a mistranslation: the "s" in *religionsgeschichte* does not indicate a plural, but a genitive singular. The members are not concerned with the history of religions, but with the history of one religion, Christianity, within the larger frame of religious history.[3]

THOROUGHGOING ESCHATOLOGY: JOHANNES WEISS, ALBERT SCHWEITZER

In harmony with the concern to view Christianity in its historical setting, two scholars tried to illuminate the beginnings of Christianity with the bright light of Jewish eschatology: Johannes Weiss and Albert Schweitzer.[4]

---

1. See Gerhard Wolfgang Ittel, "Die Hauptgedanken der religionsgeschichtliche Schule," *ZRGG* 10 (1958): 61–78; Karlheinz Müller, "Die religionsgeschichtliche Methode: Erwägungen zu ihrem Verständnis und zur Praxis ihrer Vollzüge an neutestamentlichen Texten," *BZ* 29 (1985): 161–92; Robert Morgan with John Barton, *Biblical Interpretation*, Oxford Bible Series (Oxford: Oxford University Press, 1988), 93–132; H. Boers, "Religionsgeschichtliche Schule," in *DBI* 2:383–87; Ugo Bianchi, *The History of Religions* (Leiden: E. J. Brill, 1975), 150–54.
2. See Gerd Lüdemann, "Die Religionsgeschichtliche Schule," in *Theologie in Göttingen: Eine Vorlesungsreihe*, ed. Bernd Moeller, Göttinger Universitätsschriften A, 1 (Göttingen: Vandenhoeck & Ruprecht, 1987), 325–61; Gerd Lüdemann and Martin Schröder, *Die Religionsgeschichtliche Schule in Göttingen: Eine Dokumentation* (Göttingen: Vandenhoeck & Ruprecht, 1987).
3. See Hermann Gunkel, "The 'Historical Movement' in the Study of Religion," *ExpTim* 38 (1926–27): 532–36.
4. For an insightful analysis of Weiss and Schweitzer within the context of the history of life of Jesus research, see Robert Morgan, "From Reimarus to Sanders: the Kingdom of God, Jesus,

Johannes Weiss (1863–1914)

Toward the end of his career, Johannes Weiss raised the question, "Am I indeed a member of the much-maligned 'history of religion school'?"[5] He notes that though he formerly lectured on the biblical theology of the NT, he now presents the religious history of early Christianity. In an earlier work, Weiss writes, "The history of religion, as developed in modern times, teaches us that the various soteriological, Christological, sacramental, and eschatological ideas and concepts, which we find side by side in the New Testament were pre-existent in Jewish or Hellenic thought or in the syncretism of Oriental religions."[6] However, Weiss is opposed to the notion, advanced by some members of the school, that Christianity is a syncretism of Babylonian, Persian, Egyptian, and Hellenistic religions. "Christianity was from the beginning above all a new way to come to terms with the problem of life.... [T]he outer presentation of this new life in cult and doctrine was simply an insufficient means of expression—like a garment that very imperfectly fits the body."[7]

Johannes Weiss was born in Kiel with a silver briefcase under his arm—destined for an academic career.[8] His father was the venerable Bernhard Weiss, called to Berlin in 1877, esteemed by church and academy.[9] The younger Weiss was educated at Marburg, Berlin, Göttingen, and Breslau. In 1888, he was named instructor at Göttingen and promoted to associate professor two years later. From 1895 to 1908 he served as professor in Marburg, and from 1908 until his untimely death in 1914, at Heidelberg. He was married to the daughter of Albrecht Ritschl. A gifted person, Weiss was an accomplished pianist. He was revered by his students who enjoyed social occasions in his home, among them, Rudolf Bultmann. Weiss was influenced by the religious conservatism of his father and the liberal theology of his teacher and father-in-law, Albrecht Ritschl. However, Weiss's research led him to the conclusion that Ritschl's effort to ground his theology in the NT was hopelessly mistaken. At the same time, Weiss embraced the liberalism of Ritschl as the theology valid for himself and his time. The result was a chasm between historical research and constructive theology.

---

and the Judaisms of His Day," in *The Kingdom of God and Human Society: Essays by Members of the Scripture, Theology and Society Group*, ed. Robin Barbour (Edinburgh: T. & T. Clark, 1993), 80–139.

5. Johannes Weiss, *Die Aufgaben der Neutestamentlichen Wissenschaft in der Gegenwart* (Göttingen: Vandenhoeck & Ruprecht, 1908), 48.

6. *Paul and Jesus*, trans. H. J. Chaytor (London and New York: Harper & Brothers, 1909), 14.

7. *Jesus von Nazareth: Mythus oder Geschichte?* (Tübingen: J. C. B. Mohr [Paul Siebeck], 1910), 25.

8. For an overview of Weiss's life and work, see Berthold Lannert, *Die Wiederentdeckung der neutestamentlichen Eschatologie durch Johannes Weiss*, Texte und Arbeiten zum neutestamentlichen Zeitalter 3 (Tübingen: A. Francke, 1989); F. Crawford Burkitt, "Johannes Weiss: In Memoriam," *HTR* 8 (1915): 291–97; C. Brown, "Weiss, Johannes (1863–1914)," in *HHMBI*, 531–35.

9. See pp. 101–11, above.

Eschatology, Criticism, and Exegesis

Weiss's most influential work is his *Die Predigt Jesu vom Reiche Gottes*—respectfully withheld from publication until after Ritschl's death.[10] Originally published as a short monograph (sixty-seven pages), the second edition expanded the work into a book of more than 250 pages. According to this book, Jesus proclaimed an apocalyptic message: the future, cataclysmic coming of the kingdom of God. Weiss believes that the exorcisms reveal that the power of God is now at work. "Satan's kingdom is already broken," says Weiss, "the rule of God is already gaining ground; but it has not yet become a historical event. The Kingdom of God, in the form that Jesus expected it, is not yet established on earth."[11] In Weiss's opinion, Jesus did not see himself as the founder of the kingdom, but as its herald, demanding repentance. "Precisely from Jesus' own standpoint, his entire activity is not of messianic, but of preparatory character." In time, Jesus came to anticipate his death as a ransom for the sin of the people, and to identify himself with the future Son of Man. Weiss concludes that

> as Jesus conceived of it, the Kingdom of God is a radically superworldly entity which stands in diametric opposition to this world. This is to say that there *can* be no talk of an *innerworldly* development of the Kingdom of God in the mind of Jesus! On the basis of this finding, it seems to follow that the dogmatic religious-ethical application of this idea in more recent theology, an application which has completely stripped away the original eschatological-apocalyptical meaning of the idea, is unjustified.[12]

This hand grenade, tossed into the theological community by a young scion of the academic and religious establishment, created chaos. Weiss had demonstrated that the message of Jesus—the heart of orthodoxy and the hope of liberalism—was mistaken and irrelevant. Critics, of course, did not surrender without firing a shot: Was Weiss's exegesis correct?[13] What of the parables of growth? Had Weiss's critical eye missed the tiny mustard seed? In the wake of the destruction, Weiss himself engaged in a salvation operation.[14] Already amid the apocalyptic rubble of the first edition, Weiss found features of the teaching of Jesus of enduring value: his idea of God and his

---

10. (Göttingen: Vandenhoeck & Ruprecht, 1892); 2d ed., 1900; Eng. trans.: *Jesus' Proclamation of the Kingdom of God*, trans. and ed. R. H. Hiers and D. L. Holland, LJS (Philadelphia: Fortress, 1971). For an analysis of Weiss's work in relation to Ritschl, see Rolf Schäfer, "Das Reich Gottes bei Albrecht Ritschl und Johannes Weiss," *ZTK* 61 (1964): 68–88. After the appearance of his second edition, Weiss published a history of the idea of the kingdom of God from Jesus through Ritschl: *Die Idee des Reiches Gottes in der Theologie* (Giessen: J. Ricker [Alfred Töpelmann], 1901).

11. *Jesus' Proclamation*, 79.

12. Ibid., 82, 114.

13. See Friedemann Regner, "Johannes Weiss: 'Die Predigt Jesu vom Reiche Gottes': Gegen eine theologiegeschichtliche fable convenue," *ZKG* 84 (1973): 82–92.

14. See David Larrimore Holland, "History, Theology and the Kingdom of God: A Contribution of Johannes Weiss to 20th Century Theology," *BR* 13 (1968): 54–66.

ethic of love. In a series of short works, Weiss affirmed the importance of faith in Christ. "We ask: in what form should Christ be preached today as the Lord of the church and of the individual Christian?" Weiss answers, "Our leader here cannot be the historic Christ, but only the Exalted One, about whom we believe that he, if he were among us today, would lead us, so as to transform the world according to the ideas that God reveals to us through history."[15] Nevertheless, Weiss argues that the resurrection faith of the earliest Christians had been grounded in their relation to the person of Jesus. Weiss says that "without the experiences that they had with Jesus, without the impact of his personality, the experiences of the resurrected one would not have stood the test when it was reckoned to confirm the messiahship of Jesus."[16] Thus, Weiss has rehabilitated Jesus—a powerful person of unique relation to God, who taught a universal ethic, who was alive in the memory of the church. Ritschl is dead, but not forgotten.

Besides these works on Jesus, Weiss published a variety of important critical and exegetical studies. In a book on the *Purpose and Literary Character of Acts*, Weiss analyzes the sources and editorial work of the author. He concludes, "I can only understand it as an apology of the Christian religion before the Gentiles in face of the charges of the Jews that shows how it has come about that Judaism has been displaced through Christianity in its world mission."[17] In a literary-critical study of the *Revelation of John*, Weiss detects two levels of composition.[18] He discovers the key in chapter 17, where v. 10 indicates that a sixth king is ruling, while v. 11 refers to an eighth king. The earlier verse, according to Weiss, must belong to an earlier tradition. Weiss believes the identification of the sixth and eighth king is possible because of the Nero redivivus myth whereby Nero (one of the seven) can be identified with Domitian (the eighth). On the basis of this sort of analysis, Weiss concludes that the author, who lived in the time of Domitian, incorporated into his composition an earlier apocalypse, written in the late 60s by John of Asia Minor, the apostle and son of Zebedee.

Weiss's contribution to the study of the Synoptic Gospels includes an extensive (more than four hundred pages) analysis of *Mark*. "The assumption that our second gospel is the oldest is no longer a hypothesis," he writes, "but a scientific conclusion." In Weiss's opinion, Mark is not an

---

15. *Die Nachfolge Christi und die Predigt der Gegenwart* (Göttingen: Vandenhoeck & Ruprecht, 1895), 104, 164.

16. *Jesus im Glauben des Urchristentums* (Tübingen: J. C. B. Mohr [Paul Siebeck], 1910), 11. See Weiss's *Christus: Die Anfänge des Dogmas*, Religionsgeschichtliche Volksbücher, 1. Reihe, 18/19. Heft (Tübingen: J. C. B. Mohr [Paul Siebeck], 1909); Eng. trans.: *Christ: The Beginning of Dogma*, trans. V. D. Davis (London: Philip Green, 1911), 14.

17. *Ueber die Absicht und den literarischen Charakter der Apostelgeschichte* (Göttingen: Vandenhoeck & Ruprecht, 1897), 56.

18. *Die Offenbarung des Johannes: Ein Beitrag zur Literatur- und Religionsgeschichte* (Göttingen: Vandenhoeck & Ruprecht, 1904).

author, but a transmitter of tradition. "It is the church tradition that he reports and transmits to the coming generation; he is only a mediator, not an independent author."[19] Proceeding through Mark, carefully analyzing the details of tradition, Weiss concludes that the author used various types of traditional material: instruction and conflict sayings (*Schul- und Streitgespräche*); logia-type sayings (*Logienartige Gespräche*); words of Jesus, with or without narrative settings; popular traditions of legendary character. In this sort of research, Weiss anticipates form criticism.[20]

A major example of Weiss's exegetical work is his commentary on *1 Corinthians*.[21] First published in 1910 and reprinted in 1925, this commentary continued as the representative volume of the important Meyer series until 1969. In the introduction, Weiss notes that the organization of the Corinthian church reflects features of the synagogue and the Hellenistic guilds and cults. He believes the congregation was troubled by three factions. The Paul party consisted of members loyal to Paul. The party of Apollos included people attracted by his preaching of wisdom; Weiss thinks they are refuted in 1 Cor. 1:18—3:4. The members of the Cephas party are followers of Peter who, according to Weiss, become the major opponents addressed in later parts of the Corinthian correspondence. Weiss believes a Christ-party never existed; the phrase ἐγὼ δὲ Χριστοῦ is an interpolation. According to Weiss, 1 Corinthians is a composite of three letters or letter fragments.

The commentary (more than 380 pages) presents the exegesis according to Weiss's view of the structure of 1 Corinthians. The exegesis proceeds through the Greek text verse by verse. Weiss presents thirty excursuses throughout the commentary on such topics as "the Anthropological Terms of Paul" and "Speaking in Tongues." An example of Weiss's exegetical work can be seen in his analysis of 1 Cor. 1:18-25, "The Foolishness of the Word of the Cross." Since in context Paul is responding to the factions, the prominence given to the term σοφία suggests that it was a slogan of one of the parties, in Weiss's opinion, the loyalists of Apollos. The term as used here represents a syncretistic Hellenistic concept. Weiss says that Paul uses the OT text (v. 19) without concern for its original meaning in Isaiah; Paul simply wants to affirm that God destroyed the wisdom of the wise. In v. 21, Weiss

---

19. *Das älteste Evangelium: Ein Beitrag zum Verständnis des Markus-Evangelium und der ältesten evangelischen Überlieferung* (Göttingen: Vandenhoeck & Ruprecht, 1903), 1, 119.

20. See Walter Schmithals, "Johannes Weiss als Wegbereiter der Formgeschichte," *ZTK* 80 (1983): 389–410. Weiss contributed to a four-volume commentary on the NT, written for the general reader: "Die drei älteren Evangelien," in *Die Schriften des Neuen Testaments: neu übersetzt und für die Gegenwart erklärt*, ed. W. Bousset and W. Heitmüller (Göttingen: Vandenhoeck & Ruprecht, 1916) 1:31–511. In the introduction, Weiss observes that the teachings of Jesus were transmitted by oral tradition, but the tradition was modified and expanded in order to meet the needs of the developing Christian community. See 269–86, below.

21. *Der erste Korintherbrief*, KEK 9 (Göttingen: Vandenhoeck & Ruprecht, 1910).

notes that Paul uses the term κόσμος as a thinking subject, so that the meaning must be "humanity." In stating that humans do not know God, Paul does not conceive of objective knowledge, but refers to the failure of humans to experience a religious relation to God. Later in the commentary, Weiss, making use of contextual and text-critical arguments, contends that 1 Cor. 14:33b-36 ("women should be silent") is a non-Pauline interpolation. In general, Weiss's exegetical work is marked by careful attention to sources and literary structure. He attends meticulously to details: text-critical, linguistic, grammatical. He interprets the material in relation to its historical setting, and displays mastery of Hellenistic material. Weiss's main concern is the historical meaning of the text in relation to the development of early Christian tradition. He is sensitive to theological issues.

History of Early Christianity

Weiss's NT research is summarized in his massive history of *Earliest Christianity*, completed except for the last three chapters at the time of his death.[22] In the first section, Weiss presents the history of the primitive community. He believes the first resurrection appearance (to Peter) took place in Jerusalem. The next section deals with Paul and the Gentile mission. In viewing the Epistles, Weiss believes more attention ought to be given to the process whereby they were collected and edited. Weiss, accepting the south Galatia hypothesis, believes the letter to the Galatians was of crucial importance.

> The Galatian letter . . . has far more significance than merely a literary event. It is the result of a tremendous crisis in the Apostle's life; but over and above that, it is an incident of world history, for in it, for the first time, the freedom of Christianity from Judaism has been argued out so thoroughly that there could never again be a backward step.[23]

Weiss believes Paul probably was imprisoned in Ephesus, but he thinks Philippians, Colossians, and Philemon were written from Rome.

A long section discusses "Paul the Christian Theologian." In this exposition, Weiss frequently notes history of religion parallels.[24] As a writer, Paul makes artful use of a variety of styles.

> Truly, this writer has at his disposal many different means and modes of expression; thus an astonishingly rich and many-sided, spiritually elastic personality unfolds itself to us. . . . The study of Paul's literary art is not only necessary in order to do justice to him, but it is also highly suggestive, and the

---

22. *Das Urchristentum* (Göttingen: Vandenhoeck & Ruprecht, 1914); Eng. trans.: *Earliest Christianity: A History of the Period A.D. 30–150*, ed. Frederick C. Grant, 2 vols. (New York: Harper, 1959).

23. *Earliest Christianity* 1:301.

24. Karl Prümm, "Johannes Weiss als Darsteller und religionsgeschichtlicher Erklärer der Paulinischen Botschaft," *Bib* 40 (1959): 815–36.

deeper one penetrates into it and the more one reads, not only with the eye but also with the ear, so much the stronger becomes the impression of an original and significant personality.[25]

According to Weiss, Paul combines religious experience and theological thought. "He is the outstanding theologian of the Christian Church; since Paul, religion and theology have been so closely coupled together in Christianity that it has not been possible to break their alliance, even to the present day."[26]

In his earlier *Paul and Jesus*, Weiss had affirmed—primarily against Wrede—a continuity between Paul and Jesus.[27] Most important, Weiss believes Paul's faith in Christ was based on his knowledge of the person of Jesus. "Paul's vision and conversion are psychologically inconceivable except upon the supposition that he had been actually and vividly impressed by the human personality of Jesus." On the basis of 2 Cor. 5:16, Weiss argues that Paul had known the historical Jesus. "If we now attempt to conceive the manner in which Paul gained this personal knowledge of Jesus, the simplest and most natural assumption is that he had seen Jesus during His last visit to Jerusalem and perhaps had heard Him speak; he may have been a witness of Jesus' Passion and Crucifixion."[28] In *Earliest Christianity*, Weiss says, "the life and work of the earthly Jesus was of the highest importance to Paul: that Christ became flesh, that he endured all the suffering of a weak and painful human life, and that, as a man, he had yielded himself, in obedience to the will of God, to suffer a bitter death—all this, indeed, constitutes the great fact to which he attributes salvation."[29] Unfortunately (in Weiss's opinion), Paul engaged in christological speculation. He identified Christ with the preexistent being, endangering the humanity of Jesus. Inhaling the rarefied atmosphere of Hellenism, Paul interprets the death and resurrection of Christ as cosmic events whereby the demonic powers were overthrown. By this sort of thought, Weiss thinks, "The historical Jesus is fitted into a system of ideas which did not have him in view." Paul's idea of the unity of the believer with Christ constitutes a mysticism, but in Weiss's opinion, eschatology is more important. Texts such as 2 Thess. 2:2-12 show that Paul was "dependent upon the apocalyptic tradition, but he himself is not an apocalyptist."[30]

Weiss turns to Paul's ethic and his idea of the church. On the basis of the Christian tradition, his own experience, and Jewish and Hellenistic influ-

---

25. *Earliest Christianity* 2:421. In *Die Aufgaben der Neutestamentlichen Wissenschaft in der Gegenwart* (Göttingen: Vandenhoeck & Ruprecht, 1908), Weiss promoted the study of the rhetoric of Paul, noting that the apostle used the style of the Cynic-Stoic diatribe.
26. *Earliest Christianity* 2:423.
27. See pp. 149–50, above.
28. *Paul and Jesus*, 31, 54.
29. *Earliest Christianity* 2:454.
30. Ibid. 2:495, 545.

ences, Paul develops an ethic. His idea of the struggle between flesh and spirit, Weiss thinks, borders on Hellenistic dualism. Paul presents two sacraments, both, according to Weiss, with a double meaning. Baptism is a mystical experience whereby the believer is united with Christ; it also involves a decision of the will with ethical significance. The Lord's Supper is a mystical meal wherein the believer participates in the death of Christ; it is also a remembrance of the fellowship with the person of Jesus.

Looking back over the work of Johannes Weiss, one is impressed by the breadth and depth of his research. He anticipates issues that would continue to occupy scholars in the future: the rhetoric of the Epistles, the development of tradition, form criticism. Weiss's major contribution, of course, is his recognition of the apocalyptic character of Jesus' message of the kingdom of God. This understanding would prevail throughout most of the twentieth century, a stumbling block for scholars and theologians. In making this discovery, Weiss followed historical criticism with both rigor and reluctance: he did not like what he found! Torn between his liberal heritage and his commitment to criticism, however, Weiss insisted on the freedom and integrity of criticism. He affirmed the fundamental principle of Enlightenment research: historical criticism cannot be enlisted in the service of doctrine; it must be rigorously objective. As a result, the central message of Jesus, with its expectation of imminent divine intervention, was shown to be mistaken and hopelessly irrelevant. To be sure, Weiss found features of the early tradition that could provide the ground for authentic Christianity: the person of Jesus with his unique religious experience and profound ethic. This historical person could become the Christ of Paul's faith—a faith that transcended the limits of Jewish apocalyptic and Hellenistic mysticism, a faith of universal ethical religion. It remained for Albert Schweitzer to declare the full impact of Weiss's thesis.

Albert Schweitzer (1875–1965)

Albert Schweitzer's eschatology was much more "thoroughgoing" than Weiss's.[31] Whereas Weiss viewed the teachings of Jesus as eschatological, Schweitzer viewed everything about Jesus—his life, his mission, his messianic consciousness, his teaching, his ethic—as apocalyptic. At the same time, Schweitzer had nothing but contempt for the history of religion school, especially its attempt to find influences on Christianity in oriental and Hellenistic religion. Yet, he borrowed their method, finding in Judaism the background of Jesus, the earliest Christians, and Paul.

---

31. For a comparison of Weiss and Schweitzer, see Wendell Willis, "The Discovery of the Eschatological Kingdom: Johannes Weiss and Albert Schweitzer, in *The Kingdom of God in 20th-Century Interpretation*, ed. Wendell Willis (Peabody, Mass.: Hendrickson, 1987), 1–14.

Schweitzer was born in Upper Alsace, the son of a Lutheran pastor.[32] In 1893, he entered the University of Strasbourg, where he studied philosophy with Wilhlem Windelband and NT with H. J. Holtzmann. He also studied in Paris, where he heard lectures by Auguste Sabatier and took organ lessons from Charles Widor. After completing a dissertation on Kant, Schweitzer earned a degree in theology with a dissertation on the Lord's Supper. From 1902 to 1912, he taught at Strasbourg, served as principal of the theological college, worked as the pastor of a church, and pursued the study of Bach and organ building. As a student, Schweitzer had decided that he would devote his mature life to the service of others. Consequently, he undertook medical studies, and moved to equatorial Africa in 1913. He built and worked in a hospital in Lambaréné for the remainder of his career, giving lectures and organ recitals to support his mission.

Influenced by Kant, Schopenhauer, and Nietzsche, Schweitzer has been called an irrational rationalist. More likely, he should be named a mystic. Schweitzer's basic principle, reverence for life, came to him as he floated up an African river, viewing the sunset over the jungle. According to Schweitzer, all living beings possess a will to live; truth is the affirmation of life:

> Affirmation of life is the spiritual act by which man ceases to live thoughtlessly and begins to devote himself to his life with reverence in order to give it true value. To affirm life is to deepen, to make more inward, and to exalt the will to live. At the same time the man who has become a thinking being feels a compulsion to give to every will to live the same reverence for life that he gives to his own.[33]

Reverence for life means that the creative spirit of God is in all life. The essence of human life is the will, and the ground of human existence is an *Urwill*—the will of God. "The ethic of Reverence for Life is the ethic of Jesus brought to philosophical expression, extended into cosmical form, and conceived of as intellectually necessary."[34] According to Schweitzer, "The concept of Reverence for Life is ethical mysticism."[35]

---

32. Among the many books on the life and thought of Schweitzer, see Albert Schweitzer, *Out of My Life and Thought: An Autobiography*, trans. A. B. Lemke (New York: Henry Holt, 1990); George Seaver, *Albert Schweitzer: The Man and His Mind*, rev. ed. (New York: Harper & Brothers, 1955); Werner Picht, *The Life and Thought of Albert Schweitzer*, trans. Edward Fitzgerald (New York: Harper & Row, 1964); Erich Grässer, *Albert Schweitzer als Theologe*, BHT 60 (Tübingen: J. C. B. Mohr [Paul Siebeck], 1979); John Reumann, "Introduction," in Albert Schweitzer, *The Problem of the Lord's Supper according to the Scholarly Research of the Nineteenth Century and the Historical Accounts*, vol. 1, *The Lord's Supper in Relation to the Life of Jesus and the History of the Early Church*, trans. A. J. Mattill Jr., ed. John Reumann (Macon, Ga.: Mercer University Press, 1982), 1–42; Jackson Lee Ice, *Schweitzer: Prophet of Radical Theology* (Philadelphia: Westminster, 1971).
33. *Life and Thought*, 157.
34. Quoted in Seaver, *Schweitzer*, 309.
35. *Life and Thought*, 237.

Schweitzer's Jesus

Struck by Schleiermacher's observation that Jesus did not command the continuation of the Lord's Supper, Schweitzer probed the connection between the original Supper and the ongoing celebration of the Eucharist.[36] The result was his book *The Problem of the Lord's Supper*.[37] In pursuing the problem, Schweitzer employs a device that he was to use later in his studies of Jesus and Paul: a survey of the history of research. On the basis of the survey—which includes interpretations of the Supper from the Reformation to Schweitzer's own time—Schweitzer concludes that previous research has not solved the problem. In search of a solution, he turns to an analysis of the texts. He notes peculiarities in Mark, the earliest account: Mark does not include the command to eat, and the words "this is the blood of the covenant" (14:24) are spoken *after* the disciples have participated. Schweitzer takes this to mean that Jesus did not present the bread and wine as his body and blood and invite the disciples to partake—features of the story presupposed by the continuing celebration. Accepting Mark as historically reliable, Schweitzer detects two important features of the original event: the saying about the body and blood refers to the secret of Jesus' passion; the words, "I will never again drink of the fruit of the vine until that day when I drink it new in the kingdom of God" (14:25) express the apocalyptic understanding of the kingdom. Later accounts of the Supper, according to Schweitzer, stifle the eschatological note, and seek a rationale for the continuing celebration. "A new interpretation of the Lord's Supper can be built only upon a new interpretation of the life of Jesus, an interpretation which so contains the secrets of the messiahship and of the passion that his solemn action at the final meal becomes comprehensible and understandable."[38]

Schweitzer accepted his own challenge, and published a second volume of his work on the Lord's Supper, a *Sketch* of the life of Jesus.[39] According to Schweitzer, Jesus' apocalyptic conviction "must from the beginning, even in the first Galilean period, have lain at the base of his preaching!"[40] Schweitzer believes Jesus' eschatological message demanded radical ethical obedience

---

36. For an overview of Schweitzer's NT research, see C. K. Barrett, "Albert Schweitzer and the New Testament," *ExpTim* 87 (1975): 4–10; Werner Georg Kümmel, "Albert Schweitzer als Jesus- Paulusforscher," in *Heilsgeschehen und Geschichte*, vol. 2, *Gesammelte Aufsätze 1965–1977*, ed. Erich Grässer and Otto Merk, MTS 16 (Marburg: N. G. Elwert, 1978), 1–11.

37. *Das Abendmahlsproblem auf Grund der wissenschaftlichen Forschung des 19. Jahrhunderts und der historischen Berichte. Heft 1: Das Abendmahl im Zusammenhang mit dem Leben Jesu und der Geschichte des Urchristentums* (Tübingen: J. C. B. Mohr [Paul Siebeck], 1901); Eng. trans.: *Problem of the Lord's Supper*; see John Reumann, "'The Problem of the Lord's Supper' as Matrix for Albert Schweitzer's 'Quest of the Historical Jesus,'" *NTS* 27 (1981): 475–85.

38. *Lord's Supper*, 137.

39. *Das Messianitäts- und Leidensgeheimnis: Eine Skizze des Lebens Jesu* (Tübingen: J. C. B. Mohr [Paul Siebeck], 1956); Eng. trans.: *The Mystery of the Kingdom of God: The Secret of Jesus' Messiahship and Passion*, trans. Walter Lowrie (New York: Macmillan, 1960).

40. *Mystery of the Kingdom*, 48.

in the brief time before the end—an interim ethic. At his baptism, Jesus, according to Schweitzer, recognized himself to be the Messiah, but kept his messiahship secret. Schweitzer thinks Jesus used the title Son of Man to affirm his solidarity with the future apocalyptic figure. At Caesarea Philippi, Peter confessed Jesus as Messiah. Schweitzer thinks Peter had learned the secret at the transfiguration (Mark 9:2-8), which Schweitzer, by clever rearrangement of the text, believes to have occurred prior to the confession (Mark 8:27-33). And how did the high priest learn the secret (Mark 14:61-64)? It had been betrayed, according to Schweitzer, by Judas Iscariot.

Related to the secret of the Messiah is the secret of the passion. According to Schweitzer, Jesus expected the messianic woes: the tribulation of the end time that would befall the faithful. But, when the Twelve returned from their mission, and the Son of Man had not appeared as Jesus had predicted (Matt. 10:23), Jesus, in Schweitzer's reconstruction, drastically revised his view. Not all the faithful, but only Jesus himself—fulfilling the prophecy of Second Isaiah—would suffer and give his life as a ransom for many. At the Last Supper, Schweitzer believes Jesus reveals the mystery of the passion: he will sacrifice himself to inaugurate the messianic feast. After the death of Jesus, Schweitzer believes this dynamic apocalyptic was domesticated. "Therefore with the death of Jesus, and precisely by reason of it, eschatology—notwithstanding that the primitive Christian community still completely lived in it—was virtually done away with." Although Schweitzer admits that Jesus was hopelessly mistaken, he believes Jesus breaks his historical bonds and becomes a model for all time:

> With his death he destroyed the form of his *Weltanschauung*, rendering his own eschatology impossible. Thereby he gives to all people and to all times the right to apprehend him in terms of their thoughts and conceptions, in order that his spirit may pervade their "Weltanschauung" as it quickened and transfigured the Jewish eschatology.[41]

Schweitzer's readers were not appeased; not since Strauss had such a shocking portrait of Jesus been unveiled.[42]

After sketching his outline of Jesus, Schweitzer proceeded to provide a rationale: a history of research, demonstrating that previous attempts to reconstruct the historical Jesus had miserably failed. In the process, Schweitzer produced a classic, *The Quest of the Historical Jesus*.[43] Although it is

---

41. Ibid., 155–56, 158.
42. For contemporary criticisms of Schweitzer, see Werner Georg Kümmel, "Die 'Konsequente Eschatologie' Albert Schweitzers im Urteil der Zeitgenossen," in *Heilsgeschehen und Geschichte: Gesammelte Aufsätze 1933–1964*, ed. Erich Grässer, Otto Merk, and Adolf Fritz (Marburg: N. G. Elwert, 1965), 328–39.
43. *Von Reimarus zu Wrede: Eine Geschichte der Leben-Jesu-Forschung* (Tübingen: J. C. B. Mohr [Paul Siebeck], 1906); Eng. trans.: *The Quest of the Historical Jesus: A Critical Study of Its Progress from Reimarus to Wrede*, trans. W. Montgomery (New York: Macmillan, 1957). The English trans-

marked by careful analysis and brilliant insights, Schweitzer's history is overshadowed by his own apocalyptic picture of Jesus. The survey begins with Reimarus,[44] whose work is praised as "one of the greatest events in the history of criticism," because Reimarus interpreted Jesus in the setting of Jewish apocalyptic thought. Indeed, for Schweitzer, everything between Reimarus and Johannes Weiss "appears retrograde."[45] In the course of the survey, Schweitzer ridicules the rationalists and damns Schleiermacher for his reliance on the Fourth Gospel.[46] Schweitzer, on the other hand, admires the notorious D. F. Strauss[47] because Strauss's Jesus "is a Jewish claimant to the Messiahship, whose world of thought is purely eschatological."[48] However, Schweitzer reserves his sharpest criticism for the authors of the liberal lives of Jesus—scholars such as Theodor Keim, Bernhard Weiss, and Schweitzer's revered teacher, H. J. Holtzmann.[49] In his own time, Schweitzer praises those who recognize the importance of eschatology. The reader of Johannes Weiss "feels like an explorer who after weary wanderings through the billowy seas of reed-grass at length reaches a wooded tract, and instead of swamp feels firm ground beneath his feet."[50] According to Schweitzer, Weiss presents the third great either/or of Jesus research: with Strauss, it is either the historical or the supernatural Jesus; with the Tübingen school, either the Synoptics or John; and with Weiss, either the eschatological or the noneschatological Jesus.

Of importance is Schweitzer's appraisal of Wrede.[51] Schweitzer believes that Wrede's thoroughgoing skepticism and his own thoroughgoing eschatology have totally demolished the liberal picture of Jesus. However, in Schweitzer's opinion, the two views stand in radical opposition: the fourth either/or of Jesus research. "There is, on the one hand, the eschatological solution, which at one stroke raises the Marcan account as it stands, with all its disconnectedness and inconsistencies, into genuine history; and there is, on the other hand, the literary solution, which regards the incongruous dogmatic element as interpolated by the earliest Evangelist into the tradition

---

lation was based on Schweitzer's lst ed. (1906). In 2001, the "First Complete Edition," ed. and trans. John Bowden, was published, FCBS (Minneapolis: Fortress Press). This edition is based on Schweitzer's 2d ed. (1913); it improves Montgomery's translation, adds three chapters (that largely update the discussion), and revises two of the earlier chapters.

44. See *HNTR* 1:170–72.
45. *Quest of the Historical Jesus*, 15, 23 (Complete ed., 15–16, 23). Schweitzer sees in the history of life of Jesus research four main heroes: Reimarus, Strauss, J. Weiss, and himself; see S. J. Gathercole, "The Critical and Dogmatic Agenda of Albert Schweitzer's *The Quest of the Historical Jesus*," *Tyndale Bulletin* 51 (2000): 261–83.
46. See *HNTR* 1:201–20.
47. See *HNTR* 1:246–58.
48. *Quest of the Historical Jesus*, 95 (complete ed., 90).
49. See *HNTR* 1:384–90; pp. 101–22, above.
50. *Quest of the Historical Jesus*, 238 (complete ed., 198).
51. See pp. 144-51, above.

and therefore strikes out the Messianic claim altogether from the historical Life of Jesus."⁵² In response to the latter, Wrede's view, Schweitzer argues that the eschatological element is found in the pre-Marcan tradition, and that Wrede's nonmessianic Jesus cannot explain Jesus' passion and death. Schweitzer counters with the reconstruction of the history he had presented in his earlier sketch, here dramatically summarized.

> The Baptist appears, and cries: "Repent, for the Kingdom of Heaven is at hand." Soon after that comes Jesus, and in the knowledge that He is the coming Son of Man lays hold of the wheel of the world to set it moving on that last revolution which is to bring all ordinary history to a close. It refuses to turn, and He throws Himself upon it. Then it does turn; and crushes Him. Instead of bringing in the eschatological conditions, He has destroyed them. The wheel rolls onward, and the mangled body of the one immeasurable great Man, who was strong enough to think of Himself as the spiritual ruler of mankind and to bend history to His purpose, is hanging upon it still. That is His victory and His reign.⁵³

In the final analysis, Schweitzer had found that the quest for the historical Jesus ended in a blind alley. The Jesus of scholarly reconstruction "is a figure designed by rationalism, endowed with life by liberalism, and clothed by modern theology in an historical garb." In short, scholars dedicated to historical research had constructed a nonhistorical Jesus—a Jesus who mirrored their own presuppositions. Moreover, according to Schweitzer, faith does not rest on the result of historical research. "Not the historical Jesus, but the spirit which goes forth from Him and in the spirits of men strives for new influence and rule, is that which overcomes the world."⁵⁴ Thus, as Schweitzer says in his second edition, "In the last analysis, our relation to Jesus is mystical."⁵⁵

> He comes to us as One unknown, without a name, as of old, by the lake-side, He came to those men who knew Him not. He speaks to us the same word: "Follow thou me!" and sets us to the tasks which He has to fulfil for our time. He commands. And to those who obey Him, whether they be wise or simple, He will reveal Himself in the toils, the conflicts, the sufferings which they shall pass through in His fellowship, and, as an ineffable mystery, they shall learn in their own experience Who He is.⁵⁶

Nevertheless, Schweitzer has himself reconstructed a historical Jesus who, ironically, turned out to be relevant. Schweitzer began with the assumption that pure historical research could reconstruct the historical

---

52. *Quest of the Historical Jesus*, 337 (complete ed., 302).
53. Ibid., 370–71 (this statement is not included in complete ed.).
54. Ibid., 398 (complete ed., 478), 401.
55. *Geschichte der Leben-Jesu-Forschung*, 2d ed. (Tübingen: J. C. B. Mohr [Paul Siebeck], 1913), 641 (complete ed., 486: "Our relationship to Jesus is ultimately of a mystical kind").
56. *Quest of the Historical Jesus*, 403 (complete ed., 487).

Jesus, but he discovered that historical research discovered an apocalyptic, irrelevant Jesus. But for Schweitzer, the very irrelevance of Jesus constitutes his "relevance"—his opposition to decaying civilization, his heroic will to obey the *Urwill*, the will of God.[57] Thus, Schweitzer developed a new hermeneutic of the will—a perception of the will of Jesus that can impact our will so that we are able to become followers of Jesus.[58] The Jesus of the liberals was garbed in the costume of nineteenth-century culture; the Jesus of Schweitzer wore the robe of a heroic, counterculture prophet—the mantel that Schweitzer had taken upon himself.[59]

Schweitzer's Paul

Schweitzer's research on Paul is not as well known.[60] In his book on the *History of Pauline Research*, Schweitzer observes that scholars have tended to psychologize and modernize Paul, missing the conflicts and paradoxes.[61] "They never call attention to the fact that the Apostle always becomes unintelligible just at the moment when he begins to explain something; never give a hint that while we hear the sound of his words the tune of his logic escapes us."[62] Schweitzer also bemoans the tendency of scholars such as Georg Heinrici and Otto Pfleiderer to emphasize Paul's Hellenistic background.[63] On the other hand, Schweitzer hails the work of Richard Kabisch (1868–1914) who recognized that Paul's thought was anchored in Jewish eschatology. Schweitzer berates the history of religion school, especially its

---

57. See David Dungan, "Albert Schweitzer's Disillusionment with the Historical Reconstruction of the Life of Jesus," *PSTJ* 29 (1976): 27–48; Daryl D. Schmidt, "Sane Eschatology: Albert Schweitzer's Profile of Jesus," *Forum*, n.s. 1/2 (1998): 241–60.

58. See Henning Pleitner, *Das Ende der liberalen Hermeneutik am Beispiel Albert Schweitzers* (Tübingen: A. Francke, 1992); Iain G. Nicol, "Schweitzer's Jesus: A Psychology of the Heroic Will," *ExpTim* 86 (1974): 52–55.

59. At his death, Schweitzer left manuscripts that more fully explicate his apocalyptic understanding of the kingdom of God; see Albert Schweitzer, *Reich Gottes und Christentum*, ed. Ulrich Neuenschwander (Tübingen: J. C. B. Mohr [Paul Siebeck], 1967); Eng. trans.: *The Kingdom of God and Primitive Christianity*, trans. L. A. Garrard (New York: Seabury, 1968); Albert Schweitzer, *Reich Gottes und Christentum*, ed. Ulrich Luz, Ulrich Neuenschwander, and Johann Zürcher, Albert Schweitzer: Werke aus dem Nachlass (Munich: C. H. Beck, 1995). In an epilogue written expressly for a book by E. N. Mozley, *The Theology of Albert Schweitzer for Christian Inquirers* (New York: Macmillan, 1951), Schweitzer offers the modern reader a de-eschatologized kingdom: "Only as it comes to be understood as something ethical and spiritual, rather than supernatural, as something to be realised rather than expected, can the Kingdom of God regain, in our faith, the force that it had for Jesus and the early Church" (110).

60. See Werner Georg Kümmel, "Albert Schweitzer als Paulusforscher," in *Rechtfertigung: Festschrift für Ernst Käsemann zum 70. Geburtstag*, ed. Johannes Friedrich, Wolfgang Pöhlmann, and Peter Stuhlmacher (Tübingen: J. C. B. Mohr [Paul Siebeck], 1976), 269–89; Anthony C. Thiselton, "Biblical Classics: VI. Schweitzer's Interpretation of Paul," *ExpTim* 90 (1979): 132–37.

61. *Geschichte der paulinischen Forschung von der Reformation bis auf die Gegenwart* (Tübingen: J. C. B. Mohr [Paul Siebeck], 1911); Eng. trans.: *Paul and His Interpreters: A Critical History*, trans. W. Montgomery (New York: Schocken Books, 1964).

62. *Paul and His Interpreters*, 37.

63. See p. 210, 213–20, above.

use of late sources and the assumption that parallels indicate dependence. As to the notion of a universal myth of a redeemer, Schweitzer writes, "No figure deserving this designation occurs in any myth or in any Mystery-religion; its is created by a process of generalisation, abstraction, and reconstruction."[64]

Schweitzer's book *The Mysticism of Paul the Apostle* begins with an analysis of the apostle's distinctive "Christ mysticism."[65] "The fundamental thought of Pauline mysticism runs thus: I am in Christ; in Him I know myself as a being who is raised above this sensuous, sinful, and transient world and already belongs to the transcendent; in Him I am assured of resurrection; in Him I am a Child of God." According to Schweitzer, Paul's mysticism is historic-cosmic: it relates to a historical and cosmic event, the death of Christ, and it expects his triumphant return. Schweitzer contends that this mysticism did not originate in Hellenism, but in Jewish eschatology. According to Schweitzer, Paul adopts the two-act eschatological drama—seen in the apocalypses of Baruch and Ezra—wherein the Messiah first establishes the messianic kingdom, and, after a period of time, the final consummation will occur. Since the messianic kingdom has already begun, the believer can now participate in the kingdom through Christ-mysticism, through unity with the dying and rising of Christ. Schweitzer finds the background to this thought in the Jewish idea that the elect will be united with the messiah in the messianic kingdom. "The original and central idea of the Pauline Mysticism is therefore that the Elect share with one another and with Christ a corporeity which is . . . capable of acquiring the resurrection state of existence before the general resurrection takes place." This corporeity is expressed in Paul's idea of the body of Christ. "The possession of the Spirit proves to believers that they are already removed out of the natural state of existence and transferred into the supernatural."[66]

According to Schweitzer, Paul's idea of justification is secondary to his eschatology and Christ-mysticism. "The doctrine of righteousness by faith is therefore a subsidiary crater, which has formed within the rim of the main crater—the mystical doctrine of redemption through the being-in-Christ." Similarly, Schweitzer believes the sacraments have their meaning in relation to Jewish eschatology, not Hellenistic religion. Baptism effects unity with the death and resurrection of Christ, and the Lord's Supper effects oneness with the body and blood of Christ. Paul's ethic, according to Schweitzer, is also based on eschatology: through unity with Christ believers are dead to

---

64. *Paul and His Interpreters*, 193.
65. *Die Mystik des Apostels Paulus* (Tübingen: J. C. B. Mohr [Paul Siebeck], 1930); Eng. trans.: *The Mysticism of Paul the Apostle*, trans. W. Montgomery (New York: Henry Holt, 1931; repr., New York: Seabury, 1968; repr. with Foreword by Jaroslav Pelikan; Albert Schweitzer Library (Baltimore: Johns Hopkins University Press, 1998).
66. *Mysticism of Paul*, 3, 115–16, 167.

sin. The highest ethical principle is love—an ethic shared with Jesus. "Out of the zealot Paul, the love of Christ has made a gentle-minded man who only fights with reluctance, always preserves his magnanimity, and has no petty readiness to take offence or desire for self-vindication." According to Schweitzer, Paul is "the patron-saint of thought in Christianity," "the first and greatest of all Christian thinkers."[67] "By raising the eschatological belief in Jesus and the Kingdom of God to the mysticism of fellowship with Christ, Paul has endowed it with a force that enables it to outlast the decline of the eschatological expectation and to be recognized by and integrated into various systems of thought as an ethical Christ-mysticism."[68] Thus, Schweitzer saw reflected in Paul his own image: Paul the freethinker, opposed to the ecclesiastical and academic establishment.

In sum, Schweitzer is an independent and creative mind whose NT research pursues a persistent line of development: from the Lord's Supper, to Jesus, to Paul. With an arrogance excusable only in a genius, he imagines that all preceding work has been mistaken. His passionate arguments, punctuated by either/ors, tend to oversimplify and exaggerate. His emphasis on eschatology, although excessive, offers the intriguing idea of the relation of apocalyptic and mysticism.[69] Also, Schweitzer demonstrates the danger of presuppositions in historical research—paradoxically, both in his critique of others and in his own results. By clever reinterpretation, Schweitzer is able to free both Jesus and Paul for modern faith. Again paradoxically, Schweitzer stresses their relevant irrelevance by isolating them both in Jewish culture. In his effort to protect early Christianity from Hellenistic infection, Schweitzer seems to imagine Paul growing up in Tarsus in quarantine. In any event, Schweitzer sharpened issues that would continue to occupy NT research: the historical Jesus and the Christ of faith, the relation of Paul to Jesus, and the question of the center of Paul's thought. It is ironic that one who spent his whole career battling philosophers and theologians and musicologists and all of civilization would be awarded the Nobel prize for peace—perhaps no candidate deserved it more!

---

67. Ibid., 225, 326, 377, 378.
68. *Life and Thought*, 220.
69. T. Francis Glasson, "Schweitzer's Influence—Blessing or Bane," *JTS* 28 (1977): 289–302, argues that Schweitzer's understanding of Judaism rests on a limited and questionable reading of the sources.

THE HISTORY OF RELIGION SCHOOL

Hermann Gunkel (1862–1932)

The bell that assembled the history of religion school was Hermann Gunkel's dramatic work, *Schöpfung und Chaos* (1895).[70] Gunkel studied in Giessen, Leipzig, and Göttingen. After serving as an instructor in Göttingen, he engaged in OT study and teaching at Halle. He was appointed associate professor at Berlin (1894), and in 1907 was called to a professorship in Giessen. In 1920 he was appointed professor in Halle, where he worked until his retirement in 1927.

Gunkel's mature work was mainly concerned with the HB, but he pioneered procedures that were adopted by NT scholars, notably, the methods of history of religion and form criticism.[71] Gunkel's *Creation and Chaos* has two parts: an investigation of the creation account in Genesis 1, and an analysis of Revelation 12.[72] In the first part, Gunkel argues that Genesis 1 has its background in Babylonian cosmology and mythology. "So thus is our result: the Babylonian Tiâmat-Marduk-Myth has been taken over by Israel and has become a Yahweh-Myth." In the second part, Gunkel contends that in Revelation 12, the Babylonian creation myth has been applied to the eschaton. Following a history of traditions analysis whereby earlier material is seen to have been taken up and shaped by the ongoing tradition, Gunkel claims that the tradition beneath Revelation 12 is a primitive myth. The final text includes details that are unexplained or inconsistent with the text, indicating to Gunkel that the original meaning of the myth has been lost. By analyzing these details, Gunkel is able to draw a distinction between the work of the author and the tradition the author used. Gunkel believes the primitive myth beneath Revelation 12 is Babylonian: the dragon is Tiâmat, the child is the young god Marduk, and the woman is Damkima, the mother of Marduk. "In the ancient era, the myth was a myth of the *Urzeit*,

---

70. See Reinhard Wonneberger, "Gunkel, Hermann (1862–1932)," *TRE* 14:297–300; Hans-Peter Müller, "Hermann Gunkel (1862–1932) in *TPNZJ* 2:241–55; Werner Klatt, *Hermann Gunkel: Zu seiner Theologie der Religionsgeschichte und zur Entstehung der formgeschichtlichen Methode*, FRLANT 100 (Göttingen: Vandenhoeck & Ruprecht, 1969); Walter Baumgartner, "Zum 100. Geburtstag von Hermann Gunkel," VTSup 9, Congress Volume (Leiden: E. J. Brill, 1963) 1–18; François Bovon, "Hermann Gunkel, historien de la religion et exégète des genres littéraires," in *Exegesis: Problèmes de méthode et exercices de lecture (Genèse 22 et Luc 15)*, ed. François Bovon and Grégoire Rouiller, Bibliothèque théologique, Neuchatel: Delachaux & Niestlé, 1975), 86–97.

71. See Leonard J. Coppes, "An Introduction to the Hermeneutic of Hermann Gunkel," *WTJ* 32 (1970): 148–78; Hans Rollmann, "Zwei Briefe Hermann Gunkels an Adolf Jülicher zur religionsgeschichtlichen und formgeschichtlichen Methode," *ZTK* 78 (1981): 276–88.

72. *Schöpfung und Chaos in Urzeit und Endzeit: Eine religionsgeschichtliche Untersuchung über Gen 1 und Ap Joh 12* (Göttingen: Vandenhoeck & Ruprecht, 1895).

which migrated from Babylon to Israel; in the new era, a prophecy of the *Endzeit*."[73]

In 1903, Gunkel published a popular work on the *History of Religion Understanding of the NT*. At the outset, he presents his thesis: "New Testament religion in its origin and development has stood under the influence of foreign religions in its important, indeed, in some of its essential points." To support this assertion, Gunkel first identifies material that clearly comes from the HB and Judaism. He then analyzes the remaining material, and discovers that some of it is un-Jewish and mythical. This material, he believes, has its origin in oriental religion. For example, in the Gospels, Gunkel finds evidence of pagan mythology in the birth stories and the temptation narrative. Following his history of tradition method, Gunkel argues that Paul's idea of a preexistent redeemer of cosmic dimensions cannot have arisen from Judaism or Jesus; such ideas have come to Paul from Persian and Babylonian religion by way of Hellenism. Gunkel concludes, "Christianity is a syncretistic religion."[74] Nevertheless, Gunkel maintains that Christianity is the absolute religion, the highest expression of religious evolution.

Auxiliary Disciplines: Franz Cumont and Richard Reitzenstein

The research of the history of religion school was fostered by scholars who worked in disciplines other than theology. Franz Cumont (1868–1947) served as professor of classical philology at Ghent (1892–1910) and as curator of the royal museum in Brussels (1898–1912). He published an influential, popular book, *The Oriental Religions in Roman Paganism*.[75] In the early chapters, he describes the migration of oriental religions into Rome. These foreign religions were embraced, he believes, because they transcended the old national religions and met the needs of people. In the balance of the book, Cumont turns to the east in order to describe the oriental religions in their original setting. In Asia Minor he finds religions of ecstatic expression; in Egypt, cults of the dying and rising gods; in Syria, the idea of the ascent of the soul; in Persia, the prevalence of dualism. As repository of this current from the east, Rome was inundated by syncretistic religions. "The religious and mystical spirit of the Orient had slowly overcome the whole social organism and had prepared all nations to unite in the bosom of a universal church."[76]

---

73. Ibid., 114, 398.
74. *Zum religionsgeschichtlichen Verständnis des Neuen Testaments,* 3d ed., FRLANT 1 (Göttingen: Vandenhoeck & Ruprecht, 1930), 1, 95.
75. *With an Introductory Essay by Grant Showerman* (Chicago: Open Court, 1911).
76. Ibid., 211.

Born in Breslau, Richard Reitzenstein (1861–1931) held professorships at Giessen, Strasbourg, Freiburg, and Göttingen. His evolving understanding of oriental religion as background to early Christianity came to expression in three major works. In the first of these, Reitzenstein investigates an Egyptian document called *Poimandres*—the first tractate of the Hermetic Literature or *Corpus Hermeticum*.[77] As to the date of the document, Reitzenstein acknowledges that the Hermetic texts were collected in the second century C.E., but he contends that they incorporate older tradition. He thinks the sect that produced Poimandres had its origin in Egypt at about the time of the birth of Christ. In regard to the ideas of the document, Reitzenstein discovers a pre-Christian Gnosticism that expresses the myth of a primal man, the redeemer of all humanity. The myth, in Reitzenstein's opinion, had its ultimate origin in Mesopotamia (Babylonia or Persia). Reitzenstein believes both Paul and John were influenced by these oriental-Hellenistic ideas.

Reitzenstein further develops his theories in *Hellenistic Mystery-Religions*.[78] The first part of this book presents lectures originally delivered at Strasbourg. Reitzenstein, always dazzled by parallels, discovers common features in the various religions of the Orient: a tendency toward universalism, stress on tradition and continuing revelation, the idea of unity with the deity, the hope of salvation. To the original lectures, Reitzenstein has appended twenty additional notes, some of them important for NT research. A sixty-page note on "Paul as a Pneumatic" asserts that the apostle used terms and concepts borrowed from Hellenistic mysticism and Gnosticism. In a note "on the developmental history of Paul," Reitzenstein contends that though Paul used the myth of the divine Anthropos to express his Christology, Paul's Christ does what the mythical redeemer could not do: he dies for the sins of humans. "In spite of the borrowing, his [Paul's] religion remains new and his very own."[79]

Reitzenstein's hypothesis of an ancient, fully developed myth of the Redeemed Redeemer, widely used throughout the Hellenistic world, comes to complete expression in his book on the *Iranian Mystery of Redemption*. In this book, Reitzenstein employs new discoveries and recent research to trace the tradition of the redeemer myth. A collection of manuscripts, the Turfan texts, had recently been discovered in Chinese Turkestan—texts that turned out to be Manichaean, dated in the eighth or ninth century C.E. Mark Lidzbarski, who joined the Göttingen faculty in 1917, had published

---

77. *Poimandres: Studien zur griechisch-ägyptischen und frühchristlichen Literatur* (Leipzig: B. G. Teubner, 1904).

78. *Die hellenistischen Mysterienreligionen: Nach ihren Grundgedanken und Wirkungen*, 3d ed. (1927; repr., Stuttgart: B. G. Teubner, 1956); Eng. trans.: *Hellenistic Mystery-Religions: Their Basic Ideas and Significance*, trans. John E. Steely (Pittsburgh: Pickwick, 1987).

79. *Hellenistic Mystery-Religions*, 423.

research on the Mandaeans. Although they venerated John the Baptist, their literary sources cannot be dated earlier than the seventh century C.E. Nevertheless, in the Manichaean and the Mandaean texts, Reitzenstein detects fragments of what he considered primitive Iranian tradition. Gathering up these fragments, Reitzenstein constructs the redeemer myth: the original Anthropos (a spiritual being from the realm of light) had been imprisoned in the world of darkness, but was released by the personified Gnosis to become the redeemed redeemer of all humanity. The redeemer, who was called Zarathustra in the primitive Iranian myth, Reitzenstein identifies as the Son of Man in Jewish apocalyptic literature. Reitzenstein reaches the conclusion that "the history of religions research provides new knowledge of the gradual transformation of oriental into western religious expression, and gives theology a new means for explaining the terms and the historical meaning of late Jewish and early Christian literature."[80]

Although Reitzenstein can be admired for his broad research and lively imagination, weaknesses in his work are apparent.[81] In fabricating the redeemer myth, he gathered colorful fragments from various times and places, and arranged them into a wondrous mosaic. He assumes that parallels imply dependence. He uses late sources to reconstruct earlier concepts. Yet, critics should not forget that oral tradition precedes writing—that myths that reflect fundamental human fears and aspirations are older than their literary expressions.

History of Religion and the Sacraments: Albert Eichhorn and Wilhelm Heitmüller

Since the history of religion scholars were concerned with cult and worship, they devoted special attention to the sacraments. The work of Albert Eichhorn and Richard Heitmüller is typical. Eichhorn (1856–1926) studied at Leipzig, Erlangen, and Göttingen, and taught at Halle and Kiel, but was never promoted to full professor.[82] His monograph on the *Lord's Supper in*

---

80. *Das iranische Erlösungsmysterium: Religionsgeschichtliche Untersuchungen* (Bonn: A. Marcus & W. Weber, 1921), 150.

81. See Edwin M. Yamauchi, *Pre-Christian Gnosticism: A Survey of the Proposed Evidences* (Grand Rapids, Mich.: Eerdmans, 1973), 171–86; Carsten Colpe, *Die religionsgeschichtliche Schule: Darstellung und Kritik ihres Bildes vom gnostischen Erlösermythus*, FRLANT 78 (Göttingen: Vandenhoeck & Ruprecht, 1961), 171–208; Ugo Bianchi, *The History of Religions* (Leiden: E. J. Brill, 1975), 150–53; Dieter Sänger, "Phänomenologie oder Geschichte? Methodische Anmerkungen zur religionsgeschichtliche Schule," *ZRGG* 32 (1980): 13–27; Richard Nelson Frye, "Reitzenstein and Qumran Revisited by an Iranian," *HTR* 55 (1962): 261–68.

82. See Hans Rollmann, "William Wrede, Albert Eichhorn, and the 'Old Quest' of the Historical Jesus," in *Self-Definition and Self-Discovery in Early Christianity: A Study in Changing Horizons, Essays in Appreciation of Ben F. Meyer*, ed. David J. Hawkin and Tom Robinson (Lewiston: Edwin Mellen, 1990), 79–99; Hugo Gressmann, *Albert Eichhorn und die religionsgeschichtliche Schule* (Göttingen: Vandenhoeck & Ruprecht, 1914); William V. Kelley, "Albert Eichhorn and the History-of-Religion School," *Methodist Review* 99 (1917): 470–73.

the NT contends that the NT accounts of the Supper do not present actual history, but reflect the tradition of the celebration of the Supper in the church. Eichhorn, like other members of the history of religion school, is concerned not simply to reconstruct the historical event, but to analyze its meaning within the developing tradition:

> It is very important for us to recognize the oldest stratum of tradition about Jesus, which is offered to us only in fragments. For the most part, it is covered over with more recent strata, and only by critical procedure can the older strata be uncovered. In this endeavor one will find oneself in harmony with the historical-critical method. On the other hand, it is just as important, indeed, one must say in certain respects even more important, to recognize the transformation of the older traditions and to appreciate the result of the whole process.

In analyzing the NT texts, Eichhorn argues that the words of institution are not historical, since they presuppose the event of the death of Jesus. "The words of the Lord's Supper present the meaning of the death of Christ as a sacrifice as it has developed in the Christian community." Eichhorn believes the early Christians understood themselves in some supernatural way to be eating and drinking the body and blood of Christ. According to Eichhorn, this understanding did not have its origin in the HB or in Judaism, but in oriental syncretistic Gnosticism.[83]

Heitmüller (1869–1926) studied at Greifswald, Marburg, Leipzig, and Göttingen. In 1908, he succeeded Johannes Weiss as professor at Marburg. Later, he served on the faculties at Bonn and Tübingen. According to Heitmüller's *Baptism and the Lord's Supper in Paul,* Paul understood baptism as a mystical rite that incorporated the devotees into Christ, freed them from supernatural powers, and conveyed the divine Spirit. Heitmüller, like Schweitzer, believes justification to be a secondary idea in Paul; he is "the representative of a thoroughly inner, spiritual religiosity." Heitmüller detects a tension in Paul's thought between his sacramental view of baptism and his understanding of faith. In 1 Corinthians 10, the Supper is described as participation in the body and blood of Christ (10:16). In 11:23-26, however, symbolic ideas and Paul's theological interpretation prevail. Thus, Heitmüller believes that the account in chapter 10 represents the older, cultic-sacramental understanding of the Supper. "Christians do not eat the body and blood of a sacrificed animal in order to come to communion with Christ, but, since Christ himself is the sacrifice, they eat the body and blood of Christ, and . . . come into the closest imaginable, completely secret communion with him." Heitmüller thinks this understanding, already present

---

83. *Das Abendmahl im Neuen Testament,* Hefte zur "Christlichen Welt" 36 (Leipzig: J. C. B. Mohr [Paul Siebeck], 1898), 15, 17.

in the church before Paul, had its origin in the syncretistic oriental religion of the Hellenistic world.[84]

Wilhelm Bousset (1865–1920)

Wilhelm Bousset is generally recognized as the brightest star in the galaxy of the history of religion school.[85] A descendant of Huguenots, Bousset was born in Lübeck, the son of a Lutheran pastor. He studied at Erlangen (where orthodoxy dominated), Leipzig (with Harnack), and, against his father's wishes, Göttingen. Bousset became an instructor at Göttingen in 1890, and was named associate professor in 1896. In 1916, he was named professor at Giessen, in spite of the opposition of the Hessian church. The scarcity of food, during and immediately after the war, contributed to the weakening of Bousset's fragile health. He died of a heart attack in 1920.

Bousset's theology was shaped by a variety of influences.[86] Throughout his life, he continued to reflect the warm glow of the religious atmosphere of his parental home. The liberalism he learned from Ritschl and Harnack affirmed the importance of the religion and person of Jesus.[87] This concern with Jesus' person was enhanced by Bousset's admiration of the popular lectures of Thomas Carlyle on heroes and hero worship. Philosophical idealism, with its idea of God's unfolding revelation in history, encouraged Bousset's understanding of the evolution of religion, reaching its apex in Christianity. He was influenced, too, by a revival of the philosophy of J. F. Fries—a philosophy that honored feeling and religious experience.

Bousset expresses his basic beliefs in his book on the *Essence of Religion*, written for the general reader.[88] In this book, Bousset asserts that Christianity is the highest religion, but that it must be seen in the context of religious evolution. According to Bousset, the evolutionary process that produced Christianity began with primitive religion, progressed through national religions, and attained a high level with prophetic religion of the OT—a religion that advocated monotheism and the worth of the individual. With the religions of law—Judaism, Zoroastrianism, and Islam—Bousset believes the upward movement is reversed: religion becomes a brittle legalism, concerned with external ritual. Christianity, according to Bousset, revives the upward advance. Bousset believes Jesus freed religion from nationalism,

---

84. *Taufe und Abendmahl bei Paulus: Darstellung und religionsgeschichtliche Beleuchtung* (Göttingen: Vandenhoeck & Ruprecht, 1903), 16, 32.
85. See Johann Michael Schmidt, "Bousset, Wilhelm (1865–1920)," *TRE* 7:97–101; Anthonie F. Verheule, *Wilhelm Bousset: Leben und Werk: Ein theologiegeschichtlicher Versuch* (Amsterdam: H. A. van Bottenburg, 1973).
86. See Verheule, *Bousset*, 367–92.
87. See pp. 86–92, 122–35, above.
88. *Das Wesen der Religion: Dargestellt an ihrer Geschichte*, 4th ed., Lebensfragen 28 (Tübingen: J. C. B. Mohr [Paul Siebeck], 1920); Eng. trans.: *What Is Religion?* trans. F. B. Low (London: T. Fisher Unwin, 1907).

and Paul freed it from the law. Bousset finds the center of Christianity in the person of Jesus. Paul, who replaced Jesus' gospel about God with faith in Christ, led Christianity into the wider world. However, after the end of the second century, Bousset notes another retrogression: dogmatic Christology and sacramentalism came to dominate. To address modern culture, Bousset believes Christianity must return to Jesus' affirmation of God as forgiving Father. Bousset does not believe that religion can evolve beyond Christianity.[89]

Jesus and Judaism

Given Bousset's religious commitment, it is not surprising that he devoted considerable energy to the study of Jesus. In 1892, he published a book on the *Preaching of Jesus in Contrast to Judaism*. According to Bousset, Judaism in the time of Jesus was a legalistic, national religion; Jesus, by way of contrast, revived the religion of the prophets, and proposed a universal ethic of love. "For Jesus, God was no longer the remote unknown God of Judaism, but the heavenly Father, the essence of personal ethical perfection." In agreement with Judaism, Jesus expected the kingdom of God to come as a supernatural act, but, in Bousset's opinion, Jesus was merely using apocalyptic language to express his certainty of God's triumph. In the final analysis, "the character of Jesus can never be understood on the basis of Judaism and its worldview; here there are total contradictions."[90]

In 1904, Bousset published the immensely popular *Jesus*—a book that went through repeated editions, and was soon translated into Dutch and English.[91] Here Bousset admits that knowledge of the outward course of the life and ministry of Jesus is limited, but contends that we can have considerable insight into his character—"his restrained strength, his pent-up wealth, his calmness in the midst of storm." Bousset believes Jesus was concerned with both the spiritual and the physical, and was able, by psychological influence, to perform healings and exorcisms. In contrast to the externalism of the Pharisees, Bousset believes Jesus' ethic was inward, given urgency by its apocalyptic tenor.

> Heroism, enthusiasm—here was the keynote of Jesus' morality. It meant a boundless devotion to the sacred Will of God, which knew neither condition nor exception, and was continually urging man on from task to task and leav-

---

89. Bousset expresses the same sort of liberal sentiments in another popular book: *Unser Gottesglaube*, Religionsgeschichtliche Volksbücher, 5. Reihe, 6. Heft (Tübingen: J. C. B. Mohr [Paul Siebeck], 1908); Eng. trans.: *The Faith of a Modern Protestant*, trans. F. B. Low (New York: Charles Scribner's Sons, 1909).

90. *Jesu Predigt in ihrem Gegensatz zum Judentum* (Göttingen: Vandenhoeck & Ruprecht, 1892), 51, 130.

91. Fourth ed.; Religionsgeschichtliche Volksbücher; 1. Reihe, 2/3. Heft (Tübingen: J. C. B. Mohr [Paul Siebeck], 1922); Eng. trans.: *Jesus*, trans. Janet Penrose Trevelyan; ed. W. D. Morrison (London: Williams & Norgate, 1906).

ing him no rest; it meant the forcible liberation of the moral element from all the ignobler things which had twined themselves almost indissolubly around it, and the final extrication of the moral law in all its sternness and majesty.[92]

According to Bousset, Jesus became conscious of his messiahship at his baptism, disclosed it to the disciples at Caesarea Philippi, and kept it secret from the crowds to avoid confusion with the popular expectation of a nationalistic messiah. Bousset believes Jesus used the title "Son of Man" to designate his suffering messiahship and his future glory. In Bousset's view, the death of Jesus was the high point in his career, demonstrating his loyalty to his mission and the value of martyrdom. Bousset believes the person of Jesus inspired faith in his resurrection. "And in spite of the separation of time and the frequently exasperating uncertainty of the tradition, we who occupy our place in the history of Jesus through the centuries can still feel his presence near us, with his trust in God and his nearness to God, his relentless moral earnestness, his conquest of pain, his certainty of the forgiveness of sins, and his eternal hope."[93]

In 1903, Bousset published his major work on the *Religion of Judaism in the New Testament Era*.[94] In this book, Bousset presents the history and religion of Judaism from the time of the Maccabean revolt until the defeat of the Jews by Hadrian. The presentation is tendentious: Bousset depicts "late" Judaism according to a dialectic of opposing forces that are resolved in the negative. Thus, in his first section, he describes tendencies toward universalism (seen in the expansion into the diaspora), which are restrained by a persistent nationalism (seen in Maccabean political religion), so that universalism, dear to Bousset's heart, is never really attained. In the next section, Bousset notes a tension between the vital religion of the cult (seen in the joyous participation in the worship of the temple) and the religion of law (seen in the ceremonial and ethical legalism of the scribes); Bousset thinks the latter prevailed.

Turning to religion, Bousset discusses the ideas, practices, and institutions of Judaism. The Jewish faith, according to Bousset, is built on Scripture that has been canonized and interpreted according to a mechanical doctrine of inspiration. He believes the leadership, once in the hands of the noble prophets and pious priests, has been usurped by the scribes who suppose that only those steeped in legalism can be truly pious. With eschatology, Bousset thinks the picture brightens a bit. "In its religion of hope,

---

92. *Jesus* (Eng. trans.), 29, 147.
93. Ibid., 211. See Bousset's later book: *Die Bedeutung der Person Jesu für den Glauben: Historische und rationale Grundlage des Glaubens* (Berlin-Schönberg: Protestantischer Schriftenvertrieb, 1910).
94. *Die Religion des Judentums im späthellenistischen Zeitalter*, 3d ed. Hugo Gressmann, 4th repr. ed. with foreword by Eduard Lohse, HNT 21 (Tübingen: J. C. B. Mohr [Paul Siebeck], 1966).

Judaism shows its finer and inward side."[95] But alas, Bousset believes the hope is restricted by Jewish particularism: the Jews look forward to a future in which Israel's enemies will be destroyed. With apocalyptic literature, Bousset believes eschatology becomes more transcendent. The expected Messiah is a preexistent figure, a Son of Man, who, according to Bousset, combines Jewish messianism and the primitive myth of the Primal Man. In regard to the Jewish doctrine of God, Bousset discovers another tension: the glorious tradition of monotheism is continued, but compromised. "Already," says Bousset, "the way of speaking puts a veil over the essence of God and erects a barrier between God and the believer. The intercourse with God becomes subsumed in the ceremonial."[96] God's action is largely relegated to the past and the future; there are, according to Bousset, no prophets in the present. The relation to God is characterized by fear and a lack of freedom; righteousness is attained by obedience to the law, motivated by a hope of reward. In spite of this prevailing legalism, Bousset detects evidence of genuine religious piety among the ordinary people.

In a final section, Bousset raises a question from the perspective of history of religion: Are the changes that have emerged in Judaism to be explained by direct development from the religion of the OT prophets and the Psalms, or are they the result of foreign influences? Bousset offers reasons to prove the latter: the character of late Judaism is not original, but derived; the religion of late Judaism is not unified, but diverse; the Hellenistic era is a time of syncretizing. The forces that have influenced Judaism, according to Bousset, include Assyrian-Babylonian cosmology, Iranian dualism, Hellenistic syncretism, and the religions of Egypt.

> Finally, not just one religion contributed to the genesis of Christianity, but contact with the religions of the western cultural world, with the period of Hellenistic culture. Alexander the Great had to come and build the Hellenistic kingdom, the confluence of the national cultures from the Euphrates and the Tigris to Alexandria and Rome had to begin, so that the necessary conditions for the genesis of the gospel were created. Judaism was the vessel in which different elements were gathered. Then, through a creative miracle, the new formation of the gospel emerged.[97]

In spite of the popularity of Bousset's book, it deserves sharp criticism.[98] Critics have pointed out that Bousset depended primarily on the Apoc-

---

95. Ibid., 2d ed., 242.
96. Ibid., 364.
97. Ibid., 594.
98. See Felix Perles, *Bousset's Religion des Judentums im neutestamentlichen Zeitalter: kritisch untersucht* (Berlin: Wolf Peiser, 1903); George Foot Moore, "Christian Writers on Judaism," *HTR* 14 (1921): 241–48. Moore writes, "What Bousset lacked in knowledge, he made up, however, in the positiveness and confidence of his opinions, and for the failure to present evidence, by the use of what psychologists call suggestion—unsupported assertion coming by

rypha and Pseudepigrapha, neglecting the rabbinic sources. In his negative evaluation of Judaism, Bousset exploited the anti-Jewish polemic of the NT, and fell into the trap of trying to show the superiority of Christianity by contrasting it with Judaism. The reprinting of the book in 1966 betrays a lack of sensitivity to lessons learned from the Holocaust.

History of Religion and the NT

In his concern to understand early Christianity, Bousset also investigated oriental and Hellenistic religions, with special attention to Gnosticism. His major work on *Gnosis* (1907) was preceded in 1901 by a monograph on a specific feature of gnostic thought: the *Heavenly Journey of the Soul*.[99] Bousset finds references to the journey in Jewish and early Christian texts, for example, in 2 Cor. 12:2, but traces the source to Iranian religion. In the larger work, Bousset observes that Gnosticism has been viewed in two ways: a philosophical way that sees Gnosticism as the Hellenizing of Christianity (e.g., by Harnack); and a way (Bousset's) that sees Gnosticism as a syncretistic religious movement with its origin in the east, incorporating Babylonian and Iranian ideas. An important feature of this Gnosticism, according to Bousset, was the myth of the *Urmensch* or Primal Anthropos. According to the Greek version of the myth, the Proto-Anthropos sinks into the mire of the material world, and human beings share his fate. In Judaism, according to Bousset, the primitive Anthropos is transferred to eschatology; he becomes the messianic Son of Man. Although the Gnostics of the second century identified Christ with the Redeemer, Bousset is convinced that the mythical formulation is pre-Christian. "If one looks more carefully, it will be seen with great clarity that the form of the Redeemer as such was not first introduced from Christianity into gnostic religion, but that it was already existing in some way and under different forms, and that the form of the Redeemer (or the forms of the Redeemer) was later and artificially connected to the figure of the historical Jesus Christ."[100] In short, Bousset affirms Reitzenstein's hypothesis of a widespread, oriental-Hellenistic Redeemer myth.[101]

---

force of sheer reiteration to appear to the reader self-evident or something he had always known" (242).

99. *Hauptprobleme der Gnosis,* FRLANT 10 (Göttingen: Vandenhoeck & Ruprecht, 1907); idem, *Die Himmelreise der Seele, AR* 4 (1901): 229–73; repr., Darmstadt: Wissenschaftliche Buchgesellschaft, 1960.

100. *Hauptprobleme der Gnosis,* 238.

101. In 1912, Bousset summarized his view of Gnosticism in an article published in PW 7:1503–47; repr., Wilhelm Bousset, *Religionsgeschichtliche Studien: Aufsätze zur Religionsgeschichte des Hellenistischen Zeitalters,* ed. Anthonie F. Verheule, NovTSup 50 (Leiden: E. J. Brill, 1979), 44–96. Bousset's work on Gnosticism suffers the same weaknesses as Reitzenstein's (see pp. 240–41, above); for a contemporary criticism, see Adolf von Harnack, "Rezension über: Wilhelm Bousset, Hauptprobleme der Gnosis," in *Gnosis und Gnostizismus,* ed. Kurt Rudolph (Darmstadt: Wissenschaftliche Buchgesellschaft, 1975), 231–37.

More directly related to the NT is Bousset's commentary on *Revelation*. His research on the Apocalypse had been prepared by his book on the *Antichrist*.[102] In this book, Bousset, following Gunkel, finds the ultimate origin of the Antichrist figure in the dragon of Babylonian mythology. The commentary was published in 1896 as the fifth edition in the weighty Meyer commentaries; the 1906 revised edition was reprinted as the representative volume of that series in 1966. In an extensive introduction (179 pages), Bousset investigates the literary character of the Apocalypse. "Concerning the Apocalypse of John as a whole, it surely holds true that it is composed, not viewed, that it is a literary work of art, not the diary of a visionary." Although apocalyptic literature is normally written by a pseudonymous author of the distant past, Bousset believes Revelation was written by an author who presents revelation to his own time. The author, in Bousset's opinion, is John the Elder, a Christian of Asia Minor. Bousset affirms the history of traditions method used by Gunkel, but believes contemporary-historical (*zeitgeschichtliche*) and literary-critical methods should be employed as well. Following these methods, Bousset discovers various levels of tradition, and argues that some of the material comes from a time before the destruction of the temple. Bousset believes that the author has woven previous tradition into a unified composition. "We accept no basic text with gradual expansions, no sources and no mechanically working editor, but an apocalyptic author, who in many points does not create with a free hand, but who assimilates older apocalyptic fragments and traditions, including tradition that now remains obscure." The writer refers to previous persecution, and sees the church of his own time in a mortal struggle with the Roman Empire, the beast, Satan incarnate. Bousset believes all this fits the situation of Domitian, Nero redivivus, the Antichrist.[103]

Bousset's exegesis of Rev. 12:1-17 can serve as an example. This subsection, "The Dragon, the Woman, and the Child," is part of the larger section, "The High Point of the Apocalyptic Prophecy" (Revelation 12–14). Bousset attends to the details of the text, noting evidence of Babylonian cosmology, Iranian mythology, and Jewish messianism. In an excursus on the chapter, Bousset presents his overview of the text. The final composition of the author presents the eschatological battle in which Satan and his servant, the Roman Empire, force the faithful into conflict. In mythical colors, the author depicts the birth and ascension of the Christ, and the fall of Satan,

---

102. *Der Antichrist in der Überlieferung des Judentums, des neuen Testaments und der alten Kirche: Ein Beitrag zur Auslegung der Apocalypse* (Göttingen: Vandenhoeck & Ruprecht, 1895; repr., Hildesheim: Georg Olms, 1983); Eng. trans.: *The Antichrist Legend: A Chapter in Christian and Jewish Folklore*, trans. A. H. Keane (London: Hutchinson, 1896); repr. with Introduction by David Frankfurter, AAR Texts and Translations Series 24 (Atlanta: Scholars Press, 1999).

103. *Die Offenbarung Johannis*, KEK, 6th ed. (Göttingen: Vandenhoeck & Ruprecht, 1906), 16, 129.

who works woes on the faithful. Analyzing this account, Bousset detects unexplained incongruities, for example, the ascent of the child without reference to his life. These incongruities indicate to Bousset the evidence of earlier tradition. The story of the battle of the Archangel with Satan, he thinks, comes from Jewish tradition, but references to the dragon reflect the Babylonian creation myth. Bousset believes the author has reworked these older, non-Christian traditions into his understanding of the current situation. In general, Bousset's exegesis treats text-critical, grammatical, linguistic, and historical details with care and imagination.

Bousset's most important publication, the culmination of his history of religion research, is *Kyrios Christos*. This remarkable book first appeared in 1913; a copy of the edition of 1921 was reprinted in 1965, and an English translation was published in 1970.[104] In the original foreword, Bousset announces the theme: "Kyrios Christos is Jesus of Nazareth in essence as the Lord of his community, venerated in the cultus." The book investigates the history of the development of faith in Christ in early Christianity, beginning with the primitive Palestinian community. Bousset believes the earliest Christians used "Son of Man" as the major title—a title that hailed Jesus as the preexistent Messiah, exalted to the right hand of God. The earliest Christians came to this conviction through faith in the resurrection. "The most important and most central thing in all this is and remains, however, that in the souls of the disciples the rocklike conviction arose that in spite of his death and apparent defeat, indeed precisely through all that, Jesus had become the supra-terrestrial Messiah in glory who would return to judge the world, and that this certainty made possible for them the faith in the substance of the gospel which Jesus represented."[105]

Bousset turns to the faith of the early church as expressed in the Synoptic Gospels—faith in Jesus as Messiah or Christ. Bousset believes Mark presents "fragments of occasional oral tradition which only later were loosely strung together, in which that messianic interest can come to light here and there only in a more incidental fashion." Bousset agrees with Wrede's theory of the messianic secret. "With regard to the facts which he has disclosed I acknowledge his correctness in almost every respect." Although it shaped the tradition to fit its needs, the early church preserved important information about the historical Jesus, especially his parables and his ethical teachings. For Bousset, a decisive shift occurs with the emergence of the

---

104. *Kyrios Christos: Geschichte des Christusglaubens von den Anfängen des Christentums bis Irenaeus*, 5th ed. (Göttingen: Vandenhoeck & Ruprecht, 1965); Eng. trans.: *Kyrios Christos: A History of the Belief in Christ from the Beginnings of Christianity to Irenaeus*, trans. John E. Steely (Nashville: Abingdon, 1970). See Norman Perrin, "Reflections on the Publication in English of Bousset's Kyrios Christos," *ExpTim* 83 (1971): 340–42.

105. *Kyrios Christos* (Eng. trans.), 11, 50.

Gentile community. Most important, the earlier titles "Son of Man" and "Christ" are superseded by *Kyrios* or "Lord." Bousset argues that this use of ὁ κύριος in the absolute and religious sense is *not* found in the Palestinian community, but had its origin in the Hellenistic churches. This title has its significance in the cultic life of the community.

> It is the Lord who holds sway over the Christian life of fellowship, in particular as it is unfolded in the community's worship, thus in the cultus. Around the κύριος the community is gathered in believing reverence, it confesses his name, under the invocation of his name it baptizes, it assembles around the table of the Lord Jesus; it sighs in the fervent cry "Maranatha, come Lord Jesus". . . Thus the community is gathered as a σῶμα around the κύριος as its head, to whom it pays veneration in the cultus.[106]

This title was used in the east to acclaim the king as divine, and in Egypt and Syria to venerate the gods.

In Bousset's opinion, Paul's piety is built upon the *Kyrios* faith he found already formulated in the Gentile churches. Paul develops a Christ-mysticism in which the *Kyrios* is identified with the Spirit. According to Bousset's understanding of Paul's mysticism, the believer is not identified with the Lord, but the community is—the body of Christ. Bousset hears echoes of oriental religion in Paul: the myth of the dying and rising deity in his understanding of baptism; the myth of the Primal Anthropos in his Christology. Although Paul uses these concepts, Bousset affirms "the incomparable greater moral-religious power and the spiritual originality of the apostle."[107]

Bousset believes the Johannine writings present "a singular, relatively original formation, rooted in its own soil, which on the other hand stands in the line of Pauline Christianity." In this literature, the major title is "Son of God"—a title that functions as *Kyrios* does for Paul. Bousset believes the author of the Fourth Gospel reads myth into history. In place of the Pauline idea of the Spirit, Bousset thinks John has substituted the idea of the deification of the believer through ecstatic vision, expressed in the idea of eternal life. According to Bousset, John has abandoned futuristic eschatology. "The few expressions which still preserve the eschatology no longer stand in organic connection with the basic conviction of the Gospel; they were perhaps first added by a redactor who 'ecclesiasticized' the Gospel."[108] According to Bousset, John has transformed Christ mysticism into God mysticism.

Bousset believes the *Kyrios* cult continues to develop in the post apostolic age. The believer is baptized in the name of Jesus, and the Lord is present in the cultic meal. The divine nature of Christ is increasingly affirmed.

---

106. Ibid., 77, 77 n. 97, 134.
107. Ibid., 194.
108. Ibid., 211, 237.

"Thus the deification of Jesus develops gradually and with an inner necessity out of the veneration of the *Kyrios* in earliest Christianity."[109] Functions that belong to God are attributed to the *Kyrios* so that the title "God" can be applied to Christ. Bousset proceeds to present the understanding of Christ as Lord in other literature: later documents of the NT, writings of the Apostolic Fathers, the apologists, and finally, Irenaeus.

Virtually every point in Bousset's *Kyrios Christos* has been contested: his interpretation of the Son of Man, his thesis that the *Kyrios* title arose on pagan soil, his understanding of the religious background that minimizes the HB and exaggerates the oriental cults and myths.[110] From a perspective that stresses religious syncretism, Bousset's attempt to draw a sharp line between Palestinian and Gentile Christianity is surely problematic. What is most surprising is that Bousset fails to follow his history of religion method to its logical conclusion. Although he works arduously to reconstruct Jewish apocalyptic and the oriental redeemer myth, he finds the essence of Christianity untouched by these foreign influences. Bousset's heroes, Jesus and Paul, escape unscathed from the clutches of ecclesiasticizing Judaism and sacramentalizing Hellenism. Although he thinks religions evolve from lower to higher forms, Bousset believes the evolution of Christianity stopped dead in its tracks, nineteen hundred years ago. And the essence of that ultimate religion is the faith and person of Jesus, who, in all his humanness, transcends the limitations of form and time. All of this is reminiscent of Ritschlian liberalism, yet this is a liberalism with a difference: not the intellectual liberalism of nineteenth-century culture, but a liberalism of the cult—of common religious experience and worship.

Peripheral Members: Paul Wernle and Heinrich Weinel

Brief mention may be made of two scholars who sit in the back row of the history of religion school. Paul Wernle (1872–1939) was educated at Bonn and Göttingen, and served on the faculty at Basel. Wernle published a significant work on the Synoptic Problem, but his major contribution to NT research is his massive *The Beginnings of Our Religion*.[111] Originally published

---

109. Ibid., 317.
110. Bousset responded to his contemporary critics in *Jesus der Herr: Nachträge und Auseinandersetzungen zu Kyrios Christos*, FRLANT 25 (Göttingen: Vandenhoeck & Ruprecht, 1916). For more recent criticism, see Larry W. Hurtado, "New Testament Christology: A Critique of Bousset's Influence," *TS* 40 (1979): 306–17.
111. *Die Anfänge unserer Religion*, 2d ed (Tübingen : J. C. B. Mohr [Paul Siebeck], 1904); Eng. trans.: *The Beginnings of Christianity*, trans. G. A Bienemann, ed. W. D. Morrison, 2 vols. (New York: G. P. Putnam's Sons, 1903–4). See also Wernle, *Die synoptische Frage* (Freiburg i. Br.: J. C. B. Mohr [Paul Siebeck], 1899); taking the prologue of Luke as his point of departure, Wernle analyzes the data and reaches a conclusion supporting the two-document hypothesis. For a critique of Wernle, see Hans-Herbert Stoldt, *History and Criticism of the Marcan Hypothesis*, trans. and ed. Donald L. Niewyk (Macon, Ga.: Mercer University Press, 1980), 95–120.

in 1900, the book was dedicated to Bousset and it expresses many of the ideas he espoused. In general, the book is a history of early Christianity from the beginning through the postapostolic age. About Jesus, Wernle writes, "There was in Him something entirely new. . . . But this that was new in Jesus appeared clothed in a contemporary and at bottom unsuitable form, His consciousness as Messiah." As to Paul, his "christology appeared therefore to the Greeks simply as the revelation of a new myth, like those with which they were already familiar, only surpassing them all in grandeur and power." Commenting on Revelation 12, Wernle says, "All this material is of mythological origin. . . . It can be traced back right through Hebrew literature to Babylonian myths, but it has been transmitted by Jewish writers."[112] Later in his career, Wernle became increasingly disenchanted with the history of religion approach. He wrote a critical response to Bousset's *Kyrios Christos* in which he said, "Now I confess my present skepticism concerning the new procedure of the history of religion school, in short, to speak of a myth about the dying and rising savior as a common view, widely disseminated throughout the entire Orient."[113]

Heinrich Weinel (1874–1936) studied at Giessen and Berlin, and served as instructor in Berlin and Bonn; in 1904, he was called to the faculty at Jena.[114] For NT research, Weinel's most significant work is his *Biblical Theology of the NT*. Actually, Weinel is not concerned with the theology of the NT, but with the history of early Christian religion. In the foreword, he writes, "The history of religion method has never been . . . a simple search for parallels, dependencies and origins, but a consideration of the whole of the religious development of humanity that clearly emphasizes the distinctiveness of Christianity, a presentation above all of religion, not of 'doctrines,' not of 'biblical dogmatics', not of 'theology.'"[115] An introductory section, the "history of religion foundation," presents a discussion of religions of redemption, including the mystery religions and apocalyptic Judaism. In comparing Jesus with these religions, Weinel argues that Jesus' religion is essentially different from Jewish apocalypticism and Hellenistic mysticism.[116] In presenting the religion of early Christianity, Weinel includes an extensive discussion of the development of Christology, noting the influence of Gnosticism. Weinel traces the development of Christian mysticism, with particular attention to the Christ-mysticism of Paul and the mysticism of the Johannine literature. In his popular book on Paul, Weinel recognizes

---

112. *The Beginnings of Christianity* 1:55, 188, 372.
113. *Antithesen zu Boussets Kyrios Christos* (Tübingen: J. C. B. Mohr, 1915), 87.
114. See Friedrich Wilhelm Graf, "Der Nachlass Heinrich Weinels," *ZKG* 107 (1996): 201–31.
115. *Biblische Theologie des Neuen Testaments: Die Religion Jesu und des Urchristentums*, 4th ed. (Tübingen: J. C. B. Mohr [Paul Siebeck], 1928), vii–viii.
116. In a monograph, *Ist das "liberale" Jesusbild widerlegt? Eine Antwort an seine "positiven" und seine radikalen Gegner mit besonderer Rücksicht auf A. Drews, Die Christusmythe* (Tübingen: J. C. B. Mohr [Paul Siebeck], 1910), Wernle notes that skeptics such as Drews have distorted the method of history of religion in order to support their own skepticism.

the apostle as a syncretizer.[117] "In Paul two currents meet: that flowing from all religions of antiquity in so far as they have been re-cast in mysteries and Hellenistic philosophy of religion, and that proceeding from the unique religious life of Israel."[118] Basically, Weinel uses the history of religion method in support of liberal theology—a theology that affirms the uniqueness of Jesus, his religion, and his ethics.

In summary, the history of religion school had an enormous influence on NT research. Its scholars illuminated a vast amount of material, previously unknown or ignored. It probed the depths of human experience, and focused attention on the religious and cultic life of the early Christian community. It looked beneath the literary surface to find layers of tradition below, and explored ways to analyze the tradition and assess its importance for early Christian history. To be sure, the history of religion scholars were inclined to exaggerate their method and results, casting a wide net that encompassed all sorts of sources and hypotheses. Yet, no subsequent scholar could ignore their concerns: the relation of early Christianity to its environment (syncretistic or distinctive), the use of Jewish and Hellenistic material in the formulation of the Christian message (material or formal). Two things seemed certain: Christianity did not appear in a vacuum; it was not delivered in a hermetically sealed container.

JEWISH RESEARCH AND THE NEW TESTAMENT: CLAUDE G. MONTEFIORE AND JOSEPH KLAUSNER

Attention has been given above to Christian research on Judaism.[119] On the other hand, important research on the NT by Jewish scholars should also be reviewed.[120] For example, Abraham Geiger (1810–74), a scholarly rabbi who founded an institute for the scientific study of Judaism in Berlin (Hochschule für die Wissenschaft des Judentums), published a three-volume work titled *Das Judentum und seine Geschichte*.[121] This erudite work,

---

117. *Paulus: Der Mensch und sein Werk: Die Anfänge des Christentums, der Kirche und des Dogmas*, 2d ed. (Tübingen: J. C. B. Mohr [Paul Siebeck], 1915); Eng. trans.: *St. Paul: The Man and His Work*, trans. G. A. Bienemann, ed. W. D. Morrison (New York: G. P. Putnam's Sons, 1906 [1st ed. 1904]).

118. *St. Paul*, 10.

119. See pp. 199–209, above.

120. See Joseph Klausner, *Jesus of Nazareth: His Life, Times and Teaching*, trans. Herbert Danby (New York: Macmillan, 1925; repr., Boston: Beacon Press, 1964), 106–24; Uriel Tal, *Christians and Jews in Germany: Religion, Politics and Ideology in the Second Reich, 1870–1914*, trans. Noah Jonathan Jacobs (Ithaca, N.Y.: Cornell University Press, 1975), 160–222.

121. Eng. trans.: *Judaism and Its History*, trans. Charles Newburgh (New York: Bloch, 1911). See Max Wiener, *Abraham Geiger and Liberal Judaism: The Challenge of the Nineteenth Century* (Philadelphia: Jewish Publication Society of America, 1962); Susannah Heschel, *Abraham Geiger and the Jewish Jesus*, Chicago Studies in the History of Judaism (Chicago: University of Chicago Press, 1998); Walter Jacob, *Christianity through Jewish Eyes: The Quest for Common Ground* (Cincinnati: Hebrew Union College Press, 1974), 40–50.

which included a survey of the origin and evolution of Christianity, presented Jesus as a Pharisee. Heinrich Graetz (1817–91), a professor at the University of Breslau, produced a massive eleven-volume *History of the Jews from the Earliest Times to the Present*.[122] In a chapter titled "Messianic Expectations and the Origin of Christianity," Graetz presented Jesus as a religious leader marked by the influence of the Essenes. Heirs of this rich legacy of Jewish scholarship, but with more impact on NT research, were Claude Montefiore and Joseph Klausner.

Claude G. Montefiore (1858–1938)

Born in London, the urbane Claude Montefiore studied at Oxford, where he fell under the spell of Benjamin Jowett.[123] He also attended the Hochschule in Berlin, where he was influenced by Solomon Schechter. Blessed with an abundant bank account, Montefiore devoted himself to research and the support of liberal Jewish causes. From 1915 to 1934, he served as president of University College of Southampton. An articulate spokesman for liberal Judaism, Montefiore viewed God as creator who acts in the laws of nature, not in miracles. Sin, in Montefiore's view, is not the result of a fall, but of failure to do good. The Torah, he thinks, is not infallible, and the prophets are more important than the Pentateuch. "Pure Monotheism, the direct communion of man with God, the direct relation of God to man, the close connection of religion with morality and of morality with religion, the proper place of forms and ceremonies, the absence of priests and intermediaries,—all these things are in liberal Judaism united together."[124] In his tolerant attitude toward Christians, Montefiore looked like a twentieth-century Gamaliel.[125] However, he could be critical. "To increase the lonely greatness of the hero," says Montefiore, "the disciples must be made stupid, the people ungrateful, hard-hearted, wicked. To estimate the Jewish religion (as Christian theologians do) from the New Testament is to produce a caricature."[126]

---

122. English abridged edition: *History of the Jews*, 6 vols. (Philadelphia: Jewish Publication Society of America, 1891–93); see Heinrich Graetz, *The Structure of Jewish History and Other Essays*, trans. and ed. Ismar Schorsch (New York: Jewish Theological Seminary of America, 1975).

123. See *HNTR* 1:353–60. For an overview of Montefiore's life and work, see Lucy Cohen, *Some Recollections of Claude Goldsmid Montefiore 1858–1938* (London: Faber and Faber, 1940); F. C. Burkitt, "Claude Montefiore: An Appreciation," in *Speculum Religionis: Being Essays and Studies in Religion and Literature from Plato to von Hügel: Presented to Claude G. Montefiore* (Oxford: Clarendon, 1929), 1–14; Edward Kessler, ed., *An English Jew: The Life and Writings of Claude Montefiore* (London: Vallentine, Mitchell, 1989).

124. *Liberal Judaism: An Essay* (London: Macmillan, 1903), 193. See also Montefiore's essay "The Spirit of Judaism," in *The Beginnings of Christianity: Part I: The Acts of the Apostles*, ed. F. J. Foakes Jackson and Kirsopp Lake (London: Macmillan, 1939) 1:35–81.

125. See Maurice Gerald Bowler, *Claude Montefiore and Christianity*, BJS 157 (Atlanta: Scholars Press, 1988); Daniel R. Langton, "Claude Montefiore and Christianity: Did the Founder of Anglo-Liberal Judaism Lean to Far?" *JJS* 50 (1999): 98–119.

126. *Liberal Judaism*, 180.

METHODOLOGICAL DEVELOPMENTS 255

Montefiore's major contribution to NT research is his two-volume commentary on the *Synoptic Gospels*. The first volume includes a critical introduction (more than 120 pages) and more than four hundred pages of exegesis on Mark. The second devotes more than 350 pages to Matthew and a little less than three hundred to Luke. Montefiore's introduction presents a judicious analysis of the major issues of Synoptic research. Conversant with a multitude of historical critics, Montefiore accepts the two-document hypothesis. He dates Mark at around 70, and thinks Mark probably used a version of Q. Montefiore believes the gospel records are largely reliable. "Yet, when all has been said, and when criticism has done its worst, it will probably remain true that it is, in large measure, the words ascribed to Jesus in the Synoptic Gospels which argue for the historical character of the man and his life."[127]

Turning to historical matters, Montefiore describes the condition of the Jews in the time of Jesus. He insists that the people loved the law, and were largely sympathetic with the Pharisees. The latter, nevertheless, were not above criticism:

> The tendency of the Pharisees and Rabbis was to interpret the Law more and more strictly, and to increase the wall of legal severance which separated the Jew from the Gentile. It would be unfair to say that the Rabbis deliberately extended the ceremonial at the expense of the moral Law, but it is true to say that their devotion to the non-moral side of the Law did occasionally produce evil results on the moral and spiritual side both in themselves and in their followers.[128]

Nevertheless, Montefiore believes the attacks on the Pharisees attributed to Jesus represent an exaggeration—the prejudice of early Christian anti-Judaism. To be sure, Montefiore acknowledges that Jesus did dispute with the rabbis concerning the law, echoing the proclamation of the preexilic prophets. However, Montefiore observes that the prophets preached in an era before the law was canonized, whereas Jesus spoke in direct conflict with established legal authority. Montefiore believes the conflict primarily concerned cultic matters, so that the priests, together with the Romans, were mainly responsible for the execution of Jesus.

Although Montefiore attends to Greek terms and exegetical details, his commentary is highly readable. In commenting on Mark 2:1-12 (the healing of the paralytic), Montefiore rejects the Christian interpretation that Jesus' act of forgiving sins is a judgment on Judaism's lack of a doctrine of grace:

---

127. *The Synoptic Gospels: An Introduction and a Commentary*, 2d ed., 2 vols. (London: Macmillan, 1927) 1:xcix.
128. Ibid. 1:cxi.

> It is a calumny to say that what Jesus said and did was in accordance with the religion of the prophets and the Psalms, but in contradiction to the 'legal' religion of the Pharisees. Nothing can be proved by more abundant and overwhelming evidence than that the conception of God as forgiving from free grace was a fundamental and familiar feature of the Pharisaic and Rabbinic religion, just as it still remains so.[129]

In regard to Mark 7:1-23, Montefiore says that "from the point of view of Liberal Judaism it might be said that this section is the most important section in Mark, and that its salient and outstanding feature is verse 15" ("there is nothing outside a person that . . . can defile").

> In fact, it destroys the whole conception of *material* or ritual uncleanness in religion . . . which fills up such long, intricate chapters of the Pentateuchal and Rabbinic law. Ritual washings, ablutions, taboos, are all abolished by it, for there is no such thing as ritual impurity. It is one of the greatest sayings in the history of religion. Jesus . . . lays down the principle that there is no such thing as *religious* impurity in a material sense. Religious impurity can only exist within the moral and spiritual sphere.[130]

In his commentary on Matthew, Montefiore notes that the Sermon on the Mount represents a collection of sayings, drawn primarily from Q. In regard to what he takes to be the most important section, Matt. 5:43-48, Montefiore insists that the rabbis did not teach that one should hate one's enemy. He also believes that Jesus, in his conflict with the Pharisees, did not keep his own command "to love your enemies." "If Jesus meant that Christians were to love non-Christians . . . it is singular how completely and persistently his command has been disobeyed." Commenting on the parable of the Good Samaritan in Luke, Montefiore argues that the hero of the parable was originally an Israelite, not a Samaritan—a layperson in contrast to the cultic officials.

> For the parable is one of the simplest and noblest among the noble gallery of parables in the Synoptic Gospels. Love, it tells us, must know no limits of race and ask no enquiry. Who needs me is my neighbour. Whom at the given time and place I can help with my active love, he is my neighbour and I am his.[131]

Montefiore's general estimate of Jesus can be seen in his Jowett Lectures of 1910. He views Jesus as a prophet who proclaimed the eschatological kingdom of God and saw himself as Messiah. Montefiore believes Jesus' concern for outcasts and sinners was unique. The rabbis also "welcomed the sinner in his repentance. But to seek out the sinner, and, instead of

---

129. Ibid. 1:48.
130. Ibid. 1:130, 153.
131. Ibid. 2:79, 468. Montefiore also published *Rabbinic Literature and Gospel Teachings* (London: Macmillan, 1930), in which he prints selections for the Gospels with parallels from the rabbinic literature, and offers comments.

avoiding the bad companion, to choose him as your friend in order to work his moral redemption, this was, I fancy, something new in the religious history of Israel."[132] Montefiore also lectured on Paul. According to Montefiore, the crucial question is, To what extent was the apostle, prior to his conversion, a rabbinic Jew? Montefiore contends that Paul's view of the law, his pessimism, his Christology, his soteriology, and his mysticism are foreign to rabbinic thought and betray the influence of Hellenism. "He was no Rabbinic Jew, and of the Law he knew little more than the fetters, however great and binding he deemed them: to him they had not been transformed into the robe of glory, or transfigured into the crown of joy."[133] Nevertheless, Montefiore recognized Paul as a religious genius, and displays toward him the same spirit of tolerance that characterized his perceptive understanding of early Christian history.

Joseph Klausner (1874–1958)

A dedicated Zionist, Joseph Klausner was less tolerant.[134] He was born in Lithuania, moved to Odessa in 1888, and earned a doctorate from Heidelberg (1902). In 1919, he emigrated to Jerusalem, where he served as professor in the Hebrew University. Klausner's book on the *Messianic Idea* makes a significant contribution to the understanding of NT backgrounds, but his works on Jesus and Paul address crucial issues in NT research.[135]

Klausner's *Jesus of Nazareth*, originally written in Hebrew, first appeared in English translation in 1925. After surveying the history of the life of Jesus research, Klausner concludes that "nearly all the many Christian scholars, and even the best of them, who have studied the subject deeply, have tried their hardest to find in the historic Jesus something which is not Judaism." In reaction, Klausner writes, "Notwithstanding all the efforts of the authors of the Gospels to stress the great opposition between Jesus and Pharisaic Judaism, every step he took, everything he did, every word he spoke, all recall to us . . . the Palestine of his time and contemporary Jewish life and Pharisaic teaching." Klausner continues, "it is sufficient to say that without

---

132. *Some Elements of the Religious Teaching of Jesus: According to the Synoptic Gospels*, Jowett Lectures (London: Macmillan, 1910), 57.
133. *Judaism and St. Paul: Two Essays* (London: Max Goschen, 1914), 115.
134. For a survey of Klausner's life and work, see Jacob, *Christianity through Jewish Eyes*, 71; Moses Brind, "Klausner, Joseph," *UJEnc* 6:411–12.
135. *The Messianic Idea in Israel: From Its Beginning to the Completion of the Mishnah*, trans. W. F. Stinespring (New York: Macmillan, 1955). Here Klausner investigates the history of the idea of the Messiah according to literature from three periods: the prophets, the apocrypha and pseudepigrapha, and the Tannaim. He argues, against the history of religion school, that the messianic idea arose in Israel, not in Babylon or Persia. In an appendix, he draws a distinction between the Christian and the Jewish idea: the messianic idea is essential for Christianity, resulting in a compromising of monotheism; it is not essential for Judaism, but involves a political, this-worldly element. Klausner thinks that after the political failure of Jesus' messianic mission, Christians developed a spiritual understanding of the Messiah.

Pharisaism the career of Jesus is incomprehensible and even impossible, and that despite all the Christian antagonism to the Pharisees, the teaching of the Pharisees remained the basis of early Christian teaching until such time as it gathered within itself elements from non-Jewish sources."[136]

In tracing the career of Jesus, Klausner follows the outline of Mark. Klausner believes Jesus became conscious of his messianic vocation at his baptism.

> But if the kingdom of the Messiah was "at hand," then the Messiah must be in the world: and was there any reason why he, great and imaginative dreamer that he was, he who felt himself so near to God, he who was so filled with the spirit of the prophets, he who felt with every instinct that what above all things was wanted was repentance and good works—was there any reason why he should not be the imminent Messiah?

Klausner observes that Jesus taught in parables and performed what his contemporaries took to be miracles. Klausner thinks the confession at Caesarea Philippi represents a turning point in Jesus' ministry. At that point, Jesus determines to take his cause to Jerusalem—action that betrays a political element in his messianic mission.

> In Jerusalem, the greatest and most holy city of his people, and at the feast of the Passover . . . when Jewish Pilgrims from all the corners of the earth flocked to Jerusalem—there and then Jesus would proclaim his call to repentance and good works, announcing that the Messiah was come . . . and that he was the Messiah. . . . His words were to produce the requisite effect: all people would repent. Then would come difficult times, the days of "the pangs of the Messiah," which would befall Messiah and people alike. But God would bring to pass signs and wonders: Rome would be overthrown . . . by help from on High; and Jesus should be the "Son of man," "the Son of man coming with the clouds of heaven," who was to sit on the right hand of God, and with his twelve disciples, judge the twelve tribes of Israel.[137]

Klausner believes Jesus' action in cleansing the temple enraged the priests, who were instrumental in enlisting the Romans against Jesus. Judas, in Klausner's imagination, was more perceptive than the disciples.

> Judas was an educated Judaean with a keen intellect but a cold and calculating heart, accustomed to criticise and scrutinise; his knowledge of the frailties blinded him to the many virtues of Jesus, virtues which at first had so impressed him and aroused his enthusiasm. It was otherwise with the other disciples, all alike uneducated Galilaeans, dull of intellect but warm-hearted; for them the virtues covered up all the defects, and till the hour of danger they remained faithful to their master, and when the short interval of doubt

---

136. *Jesus of Nazareth: His Life, Times and Teaching,* trans. Herbert Danby (New York: Macmillan, 1925; repr., Boston: Beacon, 1964), 105, 126–27, 216.
137. Ibid., 252, 313.

was past they returned to his holy memory and so cherished the knowledge of his words and deeds that they survive to this day.

In any case, Klausner believes the execution of Jesus was unjust, since he was not really a revolutionary as Pilate had supposed. The result, however, was devastating.

> The Messiah crucified! the "Son of Man" hanged (and so become "a curse of God") by uncircumcised heathen—and yet no help from on high! The great and gracious God, Father of all men, his own heavenly Father, especially near to him, his beloved Son and Messiah—his heavenly Father came not to his help nor released him from his agony nor saved him by a miracle! The dream of his life had vanished: his life's work had perished!

In regard to the resurrection faith, Klausner says, "the nineteen hundred years' faith of millions is not founded on deception. There can be no question but that some of the ardent Galilaeans saw their lord and Messiah in a vision."[138]

Klausner devotes a final section to the teachings of Jesus. He believes Jesus' ethic offers nothing original. "Throughout the Gospels there is not one item of ethical teaching which can not be paralleled either in the Old Testament, the Apocrypha, or in the Talmudic and Midrashic literature of the period near to the time of Jesus." Nevertheless, Klausner believes that Jesus, exaggerating prophetic religion, affirmed a negative ethic; his notion that God bestowed benefits on both the good and the evil, according to Klausner, undermined belief in divine justice.

> This teaching Jesus had imbibed from the breast of Prophetic and, to a certain extent, Pharisaic Judaism; yet it became, on the one hand, the negation of everything that had vitalized Judaism; and on the other hand, it brought Judaism to such an extreme that it became, in a sense non-Judaism. Hence the strange sight:—Judaism brought forth Christianity in its first form (the teaching of Jesus), but it thrust aside its daughter when it saw that she would slay the mother with a deadly kiss.[139]

Klausner's book on Paul was published in Hebrew in 1939. In the first part of the book, Klausner presents an extensive discussion of historical backgrounds with an incisive investigation of diaspora Judaism. Klausner stresses the significance of Paul. "This Saul was the real founder of Christianity as a new religion and a new church after it had been in existence for some years as a Jewish sect and Israelite congregation alone." Klausner believes Paul studied under Gamaliel and probably saw Jesus. "The root and stem of this faith are Jewish, but its branches incline toward the paganism of the period." According to Klausner, Paul turned to the Gentiles out of

---

138. Ibid., 325–26, 353, 359.
139. Ibid., 384, 376.

expediency. "For it was easier to persuade them to adopt a mystical and irrational faith in a dying and rising 'savior' than to persuade Jews." In presenting the missionary activity of Paul, Klausner largely follows Acts, which he thinks was written by the writer of the "we-sections"—a travel companion of Paul. Klausner's portrait of Paul's personality is not flattering. "Saul-Paul was lacking in humility, exceedingly confident of himself, and boastfully condescending."[140]

Turning to Paul's thought, Klausner detects the source of Paul's religion in Hellenistic Judaism. For instance, Paul's idea of flesh and spirit assumes a non-Jewish dualism—a dualism that, according to Klausner, contributes to Paul's confused Christology. "One delusion is founded upon another delusion. The crucified Jesus rose from the dead and lives in his glorious heavenly body, and Paul and the believing 'brethren' live within this dead-alive heavenly Jesus, who is so near to God and has been so exalted as the Son of God that one cannot tell which is more important, God or Jesus!" Although he abandoned the law, Paul, Klausner thinks, advocated a Jewish ethic. "Strange as it may seem, the ethical teaching of Paul is less different from that of Pharisaic Judaism than is the teaching of Jesus." Jesus was a Palestinian Jew; Paul was a Jew of the diaspora.[141]

Montefiore and Klausner offer a different perspective. They provide a corrective to the caricature whereby NT scholars have painted Judaism as the dark background for the brighter portrayal of truth in Jesus and Christianity. At the same time, they, especially Klausner, are not without prejudices of their own.[142] Montefiore, reflecting his liberal Judaism, praises Jesus' disdain for ritual and his passion for morality. Klausner, as a Zionist, notes the importance of political elements within messianism. Both stress the crucial role of the priestly hierarchy in the execution of Jesus. Both note the potent influence of Hellenism on Paul's Jewish heritage. Although Montefiore and Klausner embrace the method and major results of historical criticism, they display more confidence in the reliability of the sources than do many of their Christian counterparts.

---

140. *From Jesus to Paul*, trans. William F. Stinespring (New York: Macmillan, 1943), 303–4, 344, 358, 414.
141. Ibid., 495, 551.
142. See Werner Georg Kümmel, "Jesus und Paulus: Zu Joseph Klausners Darstellung des Urchristentums," in *Heilsgeschehen und Geschichte: Gesammelte Aufsätze 1933–1964*, ed. Erich Grässer, Otto Merk, and Adolf Fritz (Marburg: N G. Elwert, 1965), 81–106. Kümmel contends that Klausner's arguments are sometimes inconsistent, and often represent a misreading of the NT texts.

GOSPEL RESEARCH IN ENGLAND:
WILLIAM SANDAY, B. H. STREETER, F. C. BURKITT

During the nineteenth century, British NT research had tended to be conservative, especially in regard to Jesus. In England, scholarship was wedded to the church, and Anglican theology was devoted to the doctrine of the incarnation.[143] Early in the new century, British scholars focused on the study of the Gospels. A seminar at Oxford, begun in 1894 and continuing for more than a decade, wrestled with the Synoptic Problem. The seminar was chaired by William Sanday, and permanent members included J. C. Hawkins, W. C. Allen, and B. H. Streeter. Along with the widely used Huck *Synopsis*, British scholars made use of the *Synopticon* by Rushbrooke—a monument to the publisher's art.[144] Printed in a large folio volume, this work presents the text in parallel columns, using colored type and symbols to indicate the various interrelationships between Matthew, Mark, and Luke.

One of the first fruits of the Oxford seminar was *Horae Synopticae* by Sir John C. Hawkins.[145] First published in 1899, Hawkins's book is primarily a collection of linguistic data relevant to the Synoptic Problem. The first part deals with words and phrases that are characteristic of each of the Synoptic Gospels. After analyzing the data, Hawkins concludes that the evangelists used sources freely, presenting the material in their own characteristic vocabularies. The second part investigates data that indicate the use of sources. Hawkins argues that the kinds of agreement—identical words, phrases, and sentence constructions—attest to the use of written sources. Assuming the hypothesis that Matthew and Luke used the Logia or Q source, Hawkins detects seventy-two passages that belong to the hypothetical source, and notes that forty-nine of these are placed in different contexts by Matthew and Luke, respectively. Part III presents further statistics and observations related to the origin and composition of each Gospel. Assuming the hypothesis that Matthew and Luke used Mark as a source, Hawkins offers reasons for the omissions or changes of Marcan material by Matthew and Luke. In regard to Matthew, Hawkins notes that the author added OT quotes and grouped sayings into blocks. In regard to Luke, Hawkins presents linguistic data to support his thesis that the author of the "we-sections" of Acts, the rest of Acts, and the Gospel of Luke is one and the same. Hawkins believes the evidence he has collected shows that Matthew

---

143. See R. Morgan, "Historical Criticism and Christology: England and Germany," in *England and Germany: Studies in Theological Diplomacy,* ed. S. W. Sykes (Frankfurt am Main: Peter D. Lang, 1982), 80–112.

144. Originally published in 1892, Albert Huck's text went through various editions, including *A Synopsis of the First Three Gospels,* 9th ed. Hans Lietzmann; Eng. ed. Frank Leslie Cross (Tübingen: J. C. B. Mohr [Paul Siebeck], 1936); W. G. Rushbrooke, *Synopticon: An Exposition of the Common Matter of The Synoptic Gospels* (London: Macmillan, 1880).

145. *Horae Synopticae: Contributions to the Study of the Synoptic Problem,* 2d ed. (1909; repr., Oxford: Clarendon Press, 1968).

and Luke used two sources, and that these sources were probably the recollections of Peter (preserved by Mark) and the Logia of Matthew (identified as Q).[146]

A collection of essays by members of the Oxford seminar was published by Sanday.[147] Sanday contributed the introductory essay, "The Conditions under Which the Gospels Were Written, in Their Bearing upon Some Difficulties of the Synoptic Problem." He notes, for example, that ancient writers did not spread out their sources on a large desk, but consulted scrolls from time to time, with elapsed time between reading and writing. Hawkins contributed two essays. In "Three Limitations of St. Luke's Use of St. Mark's Gospel," he advances the theory that Luke had begun his work prior to discovering Mark, but later incorporated his own earlier composition into the framework of Mark. Hawkins's essay, "Probabilities as to the So-Called Double Tradition of St. Matthew and St. Luke," deals with Q. On the analogy of how he understands Matthew and Luke to have used Mark, Hawkins contends that Q contained material besides that which is common to Matthew and Luke; thus he thinks that some of the peculiar material of Matthew and Luke actually belonged to Q.[148]

B. H. Streeter and W. C. Allen contributed to the Oxford *Studies*. In "On the Original Order of Q," Streeter concludes that "Matthew has entirely disregarded the original context of Q, and used it simply as a quarry from which to hew stones for the building of his great discourses and the enlargement and embellishment of the main structure which he takes over from Saint Mark." Discussing "Saint Mark's Knowledge and Use of Q," Streeter concludes that Mark knew Q. In "The Literary Evolution of the Gospels," Streeter relates the development of the gospel tradition to the history of the early church. Streeter also wrote "Synoptic Criticism and the Eschatological Problem," in which he contends that Q is the least, Mark more, and Matthew the most apocalyptic of the Gospels. W. C. Allen contributed "The Book of Sayings Used by the Editor of the First Gospel," in which he argues that the common material of Matthew and Luke cannot be reduced to a single source. In "The Aramaic Background of the Gospels," Allen argues that this discourse source was probably written in Aramaic.[149]

---

146. For a recent discussion of Hawkins's work, see the debate between W. R. Farmer and Michael Gouldner in *Synoptic Studies: The Ampleforth Conferences of 1982 and 1983*, ed. C. M. Tuckett, JSNTSup 7 (Sheffield: JSOT Press, 1984), 75–104; see also Patrick L. Dickerson, "The New Character Narrative in Luke-Acts and the Synoptic Problem," *JBL* 116 (1997): 291–312.

147. W. Sanday, ed., *Studies in the Synoptic Problem: By Members of the University of Oxford* (Oxford: Clarendon Press, 1911).

148. Ibid., 1–26, 27–29, 95–138.

149. Ibid., 141–64, 157–58, 166–83, 209–27, 425–36, 235–85, 288–312. Allen is also remembered for his *A Critical and Exegetical Commentary on the Gospel According to St. Matthew*, 2d ed., ICC (Edinburgh: T. & T. Clark, 1907). In this work, the representative volume on Matthew in the ICC series for more than a half-century, Allen argues that Matthew used three main sources: Mark, the discourse source, and sources used in common with Luke.

William Sanday (1843–1920)

Sanday, the leader of the Oxford seminar, was a potent force in British scholarship at the turn of the last century.[150] He was born in Nottinghamshire and educated at Oxford. Sanday served for a time as Dean Ireland's Professor of Exegesis, and, in 1895, was appointed Lady Margaret Professor of Divinity at Oxford. His basic point of view is disclosed in his Bampton lectures on *Inspiration*. Actually, the lectures present a discussion of the history of canon, biblical authority, and the doctrine of inspiration in the early church. Sanday believes that the canon was set by the year 200, and that the only inauthentic book in the NT is 2 Peter. He rejects the traditional view of inspiration and adopts an "inductive view," that is, a view that assesses inspiration according to the understanding of the biblical writers themselves. From that perspective, Sanday concludes that the prophets and apostles claim to speak by the Spirit, while some NT writers assume inspiration only in a secondary sense. Luke, for example, writes as a historian, and requires no special divine guidance. Sanday concludes that as the incarnate word "assumed limitations," so also the written Word "had its limitations, corresponding to the progressive stages of moral development in man through which it was to pass and of which it was to be the informing principle."[151] In a lecture responding to Harnack's *What Is Christianity?* Sanday complains that the German theologian had reduced the gospel to a paltry minimum.[152] Against Harnack, Sanday contends that the gospel is not merely the gospel of the Father, but also of the Son. Christology, including theological propositions about Christ, belongs to the essence of Christianity.

At twenty-eight years of age, Sanday launched his scholarly career with a book on the *Fourth Gospel*. He insists that the question of authorship must be decided inductively—by an analysis of the content of the text. In regard to the Gospel's presentation of multiple trips to Jerusalem, Sanday finds evidence in the Synoptics for a Judean ministry prior to the Passion week. He believes the author of John demonstrates accurate knowledge of Jewish customs and the topography of Jerusalem. The story of the raising of Lazarus—"the one great . . . crucial question of the Gospel"—appears to Sanday as a report of an eyewitness. "The Gospel is like the sacred coat 'without seam woven from the top throughout'; it is either all real and true or all fictitious and illusory; and the latter alternative is, I cannot but think, more difficult to accept than the miracle." Sanday thinks that chapter 21

---

150. For an overview of Sanday's life and work, see Walter Lock, "William Sanday," *JTS* 22 (1921): 98–104; B. Chilton, "Sanday, William (1843–1920)," in *DBI* 2:436–37.
151. *Eight Lectures on the Early History and Origin of the Doctrine of Biblical Inspiration* (London: Longmans, Green, 1893), 425–26.
152. *An Examination of Harnack's 'What Is Christianity? A Paper Read before the Tutors' Association on October 24, 1901* (London: Longmans, Green, 1901).

was added by the author who identifies himself as the beloved disciple, who can be none other than the apostle John.[153]

More than thirty years later, Sanday presented lectures on the *Fourth Gospel* at Union Seminary in New York. Although time had elapsed and Sanday had sailed to the New World, his mind had not moved an inch. In reviewing recent skeptical research, Sanday says, "Professor Bacon has been to Germany, and learnt his lesson there too well."[154] In contrast, Sanday argues that John wrote with the Synoptics before him, making deliberate changes. Sanday understands the Fourth Gospel as a "blending of fact and interpretation"—a Gospel that presents "the mind of Christ, seen through the medium of one of the first and closest of His companions."[155] Late in life, however, after decades of mounting the ramparts in defense of John's authenticity, Sanday, looking back over his career, surrendered without offering argument or explanation. "I'm afraid there is one important point on which I was probably wrong—the Fourth Gospel."[156]

Related to his research on the Synoptics are Sanday's lectures on *The Life of Christ in Recent Research*. He confesses at the outset, "while I agree more often with my own countrymen, I learn more from the Germans."[157] Among those from whom he has learned is Johannes Weiss and his view of the eschatological character of Jesus' message. Sanday is less sanguine about Wrede and the theory of the messianic secret. "I consider it to be not only very wrong but also distinctly wrong-headed."[158] Sanday appreciates the work of Schweitzer, but thinks he exaggerates. According to Sanday, Jesus was a teacher as well as a prophet; the Son of Man was an apocalyptic figure, but also a representative of humanity. Sanday approves Holtzmann's affirmation of the messianic consciousness of Jesus.[159] In regard to the history of religion school, Sanday is alarmed: scholars such as Bousset run the risk of dissolving Christianity into the vast sea of general religion. The results of Sanday's gospel criticism are displayed in his popular book on the *Life of Christ*—a book in which he harmonizes information from the Synoptics and John.[160]

---

153. *The Authorship and Historical Character of the Fourth Gospel: Considered in Reference to the Contents of the Gospel Itself: A Critical Essay* (London: Macmillan, 1872), 180, 188.

154. *The Criticism of the Fourth Gospel: Eight Lectures on the Morse Foundation, Delivered in the Union Seminary, New York in October and November, 1904* (New York: Charles Scribner's Sons, 1923), 14. On B. W. Bacon of Yale, see pp. 299–305, below.

155. *Criticism of the Fourth Gospel*, 169.

156. *Divine Overruling* (Edinburgh: T. & T. Clark, 1920), 61. In the latter part of his career, Sanday increasingly identified with theological liberalism; see Mark D. Chapman, "The Socratic Subversion of Tradition: William Sanday and Theology, 1900–1922," *JTS* 45 (1994): 94–116.

157. *The Life of Christ in Recent Research* (Oxford: Clarendon Press, 1907), 38.

158. Ibid., 70. On Wrede, see pp. 147–49, above.

159. See p. 117, above.

160. *Outlines of the Life of Christ*, 2d ed., Fifty-Cent Religious Series (New York: Charles Scribner's Sons, 1912). Sanday also published a useful work on the geographical setting of the life of Jesus: *Sacred Sites of the Gospels: With Illustrations, Maps and Plans* (Oxford: Clarendon Press,

B. H. Streeter (1874–1937)

Seed sown in the Oxford seminar burst into full bloom with Burnett Hillman Streeter.[161] Born in Croydon and educated at Oxford, he was ordained in the Church of England, noted for his personal piety. He held various academic positions at Oxford, including Dean Ireland's Professor of Exegesis. Streeter was killed in an airplane crash in Switzerland.

Streeter's major contribution to NT research is his weighty *The Four Gospels*.[162] Originally published in 1924, this work was slightly revised in 1930 and frequently reprinted. In the first part, dedicated to text criticism, Streeter displays a special interest in the hypothetical Caesarean text. He believes that the early writings of Origen reflect use of the Alexandrian text, but when he moved to Caesarea, Origen adopted the Caesarean text.[163] In general, the texts of the Gospels show a tendency to assimilate (i.e., to harmonize readings of parallel texts), but Mark, according to Streeter, is relatively free from assimilation.

In Part II, Streeter discusses the Synoptic Problem. He adopts the two-document hypothesis. In regard to the priority of Mark, he writes, "A century of discussion has resulted in a consensus of scholars . . . that the authors of the First and Third Gospels made use either of our Mark, or of a document all but identical with Mark." In support of this hypothesis, Streeter presents the familiar arguments from content, order, and the "primitive" character of Mark.[164] Streeter believes the evidence for the independent use of Q by Matthew and Luke is convincing. "But it does not follow, because we accept the view that Q existed, that we can discover exactly which passages in Matthew and Luke were, and which were not derived from it." Although he thinks Mark and Q represent independent traditions, Streeter says, "it is clear that certain items were known to Matthew and Luke both in Mark's version and also in another decidedly different. In fact, to put it paradoxically, the overlapping of Mark and Q is more certain than is the existence of Q."[165]

1903). Along with his gospel research, Sanday made an important contribution to Pauline studies. In collaboration with Arthur C. Headlam, he published *A Critical and Exegetical Commentary on the Epistle to the Romans*, 5th ed., ICC (Edinburgh: T. & T. Clark, 1902)—a monument to nineteenth-century historical research, displaying mastery of the critical disciplines and analytical attention to detail. The commentary remained the representative volume on Romans for the ICC series until 1975.

161. See B. Chilton, "Streeter, Burnett Hillman (1874–1937)," in *DBI* 2:509; Alan Thornhill, *One Fight More* (London: Frederick Muller, 1943).

162. *The Four Gospels: A Study of Origins: Treating of the Manuscript Tradition, Sources, Authorship, and Dates*, rev. ed. (London: Macmillan, 1930).

163. See pp. 397, 408–10, below.

164. For a review and criticism, see D. L. Dungan, "Critique of the Main Arguments for Mark's Priority as Formulated by B. H. Streeter," in *The Two-Source Hypothesis: A Critical Appraisal*, ed. Arthur J. Bellinzoni Jr. (Macon, Ga.: Mercer University Press, 1985), 143–61.

165. *Four Gospels*, 157, 184, 186.

Streeter's distinctive contribution to the discussion of the Synoptic Problem is his hypothesis of a "Proto-Luke." Investigating the sections where Luke does not seem to follow Mark, Streeter detects evidence for the use of a source besides Q, which he calls L. Streeter concludes that Luke, the travel companion and author of Acts, combined Q and L into a single document, Proto-Luke, and later incorporated this material into the framework of Mark to produce his Gospel. Streeter's final position offers a four-document hypothesis. Just as Luke had a special source (L), so also did Matthew (M). According to Streeter, the collecting of tradition took place in major Christian centers: Mark in Rome, Q in Antioch, M in Jerusalem, L in Caesarea. This hypothesis of four documents, Streeter believes, enhances the reliability of the tradition. "Thus the final result of the critical analysis which has led to our formulating the Four Document Hypothesis is very materially to broaden the basis of evidence for the authentic teaching of Christ."[166] Christian centers were decisive, too, for the composition of the Gospels: Matthew, writing around 85 in Antioch, used Q (c. 50), M (c. 60), and Mark (66); Luke, writing around 80, perhaps in Corinth, used L (c. 60) and Proto-Luke.[167]

In Part III, Streeter turns to the Fourth Gospel. He believes its author was a Christocentric mystic who combined Jewish and Greek ideas, and struck a middle course between the Judaizers and the Gnostics. Streeter thinks the author used Mark and Luke as sources, and possibly Matthew. Streeter acknowledges that "John may have been mistaken about his facts, but to him it is as important to emphasise the historical as to see in the historical a symbol of the Eternal." This author, in Streeter's opinion, is John the Elder (not the Apostle) who as a youth had seen Jesus and lived to an old age in Ephesus. He "gave the Church an expression of its belief intellectually acceptable to the Greek mind, yet true to the Jewish thought of God as personal and as one."[168] Besides his work on the Gospels, Streeter is recognized for his research on church order in early Christianity.[169]

---

166. Ibid., 270.

167. Streeter concludes his discussion of the Synoptic Problem with three chapters dealing with secondary issues: In "The Reconstruction of Q," Streeter argues that Q consists of 272 verses, mostly of discourse material. Concerning "The Minor Agreements of Matthew and Luke," he explains these as owing to independent editing of Mark by Matthew and Luke, overlapping of Mark and Q, and textual assimilation. A chapter titled "The Lost Ending of Mark" suggests that the original ending of Mark may have served as a source for John's account of the appearance to Mary Magdalene (20:11-18) and the appearance to the disciples at the Sea of Galilee (21:1-22).

168. *Four Gospels*, 389, 467.

169. *The Primitive Church: Studied with Special Reference to the Origins of the Christian Ministry* (New York: Macmillan, 1929). Here Streeter argues that the NT does not present a single church order, but offers prototypes for episcopalian, presbyterian, and independent systems of church government. "The history of Catholic Christianity during the first five centuries is the history of a progressive standardisation of a diversity which had its origin in the Apostolic age" (50).

F. C. Burkitt (1864–1935)

While Oxford scholars were investigating gospel origins, similar research was carried on at Cambridge. Francis Crawford Burkitt was born in London and educated at Trinity College, Cambridge.[170] In 1905, he was named Norrisian Professor of Divinity at Cambridge. Burkitt shared the typical Anglican concern with the incarnation.

> Christianity stands or falls, lives or dies, with the personality of Jesus Christ; and the Gospel is our introduction to Jesus Christ.... It is the great charm of Christianity that its innermost doctrine is incarnate in the person of its Founder, rather than crystallized into a set of propositions or ordinances.[171]

Burkitt published several works on the Gospels. In 1900, he lectured at Cambridge on the textual criticism and origin of the Gospels.[172] In 1902, he contributed to a symposium on NT criticism with a lecture titled "The Ancient Versions of the New Testament."[173] Somewhat more ambitious is his book *The Earliest Sources for the Life of Jesus*. In this book, Burkitt accepts the two-document hypothesis, but insists that Q cannot be precisely reconstructed. Mark is historically reliable, since, according to Burkitt, it was written by the youth who escaped naked from the arrest of Jesus (Mark 14:52) and later recorded the reminiscences of Peter. Burkitt concludes, "The Gospel according to Matthew is a fresh edition of Mark, revised, rearranged, and enriched with new material; the Gospel according to Luke is a new historical work, made by combining parts of Mark with parts of other documents."[174]

In *The Gospel History and Its Transmission*, Burkitt asserts that "we do not possess enough information to enable us to write a biography of our Lord after the modern pattern," but "we have quite enough in mere bulk to obtain an intelligible picture of the Gospel History." Burkitt writes, "I have attempted to shew you that the Gospel according to Mark presents a reasonably consistent account of the public life of our Lord; and I have tried to indicate to you some general grounds for thinking that its treatment of the

---

170. See Kirsopp Lake, "F. C. Burkitt," *JBL* 55 (1936): 17–19; J. F. Bethune-Baker et al., "Francis Crawford Burkitt," *JTS* 36 (1935): 225–54. As the latter essay indicates, Burkitt contributed to many areas of theological research, including text criticism, Syriac studies, Judaism, and liturgics, as well as the Gospels and early Christianity.
171. *The Gospel History and Its Transmission*, 3d ed. (Edinburgh: T. & T. Clark, 1911), 284.
172. *Two Lectures on the Gospels* (London: Macmillan, 1901).
173. W. Sanday, F. G. Kenyon, F. C. Burkitt, F. H. Chase, A. C. Headlam, and J. H. Bernard, *Criticism of the New Testament: St. Margaret's Lectures* (London: John Murray, 1902), 68–95. Burkitt's competence in text criticism and Syriac is confirmed by his work on the transcription of the Sinaitic Syriac MS that had been discovered in 1892: Robert L. Bensly, J. Rendel Harris, and F. Crawford Burkitt, *The Four Gospels in Syriac: Transcribed from the Sinaitic Palimpsest* (Cambridge: Cambridge University Press, 1894).
174. *The Earliest Sources for the Life of Jesus*, Modern Religious Problems (London: Constable, 1910), 97.

miraculous is what might be expected in an historical, as distinct from a mythical, document coming from Christian sources in the first century."[175] Burkitt believes Luke and Acts were written by a travel companion of Paul who used Josephus as a source. The author of the first Gospel, according to Burkitt, used a collection of Hebrew *testimonia* (a collection of OT prooftexts) that had probably been collected by the apostle Matthew (perhaps to be identified as the Logia mentioned by Papias).[176] In regard to the Gospel of John, perhaps written by a Sadducean Jew, Burkitt says, "The Christ of the Fourth Gospel is not the Christ of history, but the Christ of Christian experience."[177]

The results of Burkitt's gospel criticism can be seen in his *Jesus Christ: An Historical Outline*. In the preface, Burkitt asserts, "I do claim that our documents, properly used, reveal at least the outline of the features of a real Personality and a real Career." Jesus, according to Burkitt, must be understood within his Jewish context. At his baptism, Jesus became convinced of his calling as Messiah, and at Caesarea Philippi, he resolved to take his messianic mission to Jerusalem. "He accepted," says Burkitt, "the contemporary Jewish apocalyptic outlook on the future, the Messianic Feast, the Coming on the clouds of Heaven, the triumph of justice and right as conceived by Jewish thought. This was the reign of 'the Son of Man', and He knew Himself to have been chosen for that exalted office." On the basis of the impact of appearances upon the disciples, Burkitt concludes, "the Resurrection of Jesus is a well-attested fact." In an epilogue, Burkitt speculates that Luke, while he was with Paul in Caesarea, could have received information from one of Philip's daughters. "It may be conjectured with a good deal of probability that these tales in which women figure so markedly may have been handed down to us by Luke from the long memories of a woman disciple."[178]

Besides his work on the Gospels, Burkitt also investigates other areas of NT research. In *Christian Beginnings*, he offers an extended critique of the first two volumes of *The Beginnings of Christianity*, edited by Foakes Jackson and Kirsopp Lake.[179] Burkitt praises the historical work of the authors, but assumes a more conservative stance. For example, he argues that the apostolic decree of Acts 15 is historical; it was not mentioned in Galatians 2, because the meeting reported in that chapter took place earlier, on the occasion of the visit to Jerusalem noted in Acts 11:30. In *Church and Gnosis*, originally presented as lectures at Union Theological Seminary in New

---

175. *The Gospel History and Its Transmission*, 3d ed. (Edinburgh: T. & T. Clark, 1911), 20, 21, 75.
176. See pp. 405–6, below.
177. *Gospel History*, 230.
178. *Jesus Christ: An Historical Outline* (London: Blackie & Son, 1932), vi, 41, 57, 74–75.
179. *Christian Beginnings: Three Lectures* (London: University of London Press, 1924). See pp. 293, 409–10, below.

York, Burkitt assails the history of religion school.[180] Reminiscent of Harnack, he contends that Gnosticism is not a pre-Christian oriental syncretism, but a second-century Christian heresy—a philosophy that attempts to adapt the gospel to the advanced cosmological ideas of the Hellenistic intelligentsia.[181]

In sum, the British scholars made significant contributions to the study of the Gospels. Making use of linguistic analysis, and isolated from the political and academic squabbles beyond the Channel, they added weight to the growing consensus in support of the two-document hypothesis. At the same time, British acceptance of the hypothesis did not signify surrender to the sort of radical criticism advanced in the history of religion school and form criticism in Germany. For the British, the two-document hypothesis, and even more, the four-document hypothesis, were construed to provide evidence for the reliability of the gospel record. Even the Gospel of John, whose authenticity was not universally acclaimed, was thought to provide a significant historical witness, above all, a witness to the history in which revelation had occurred.

FORM CRITICISM:
KARL LUDWIG SCHMIDT, MARTIN DIBELIUS, RUDOLF BULTMANN

Accepting the two-document hypothesis as the solution to the literary relationships of the Synoptic Gospels, form criticism purports to investigate the oral tradition beneath Mark and Q.[182] The term "form criticism" was articu-

---

180. *Church and Gnosis: A Study of Christian Thought and Speculation in the Second Century* (Cambridge: Cambridge University Press, 1932). Burkitt's competence as a historian of early Christianity is confirmed by his contributions to *The Cambridge Ancient History: Volume XII: The Imperial Crisis and Recovery*, ed. S. A. Cook, F. E. Adcock, M. P. Charles, and N. H. Baynes (Cambridge: Cambridge University Press, 1939): "Pagan Philosophy and the Christian Church" (450–75); "The Christian Church in the East" (476–514).

181. On Harnack, see pp. 127–28, above.

182. For general surveys of method and results of form criticism, see Erich Fascher, *Die formgeschichtliche Methode: Eine Darstellung und Kritik*, BZNW (Giessen: Alfred Töpelmann, 1924); Edgar V. McKnight, *What Is Form Criticism?*, Guides to Biblical Scholarship: New Testament Series (Philadelphia: Fortress, 1969); Ludwig Koehler, *Das formgeschichtliche Problem des Neuen Testaments*, Sammlung gemeinverständlicher Vorträge und Schriften aus dem Gebiet der Theologie und Religionsgeschichte 127 (Tübingen: J. C. B. Mohr [Paul Siebeck], 1927); Kendrick Grobel, *Formgeschichte und synoptische Quellenanalyse*, FRLANT 53 (Göttingen: Vandenhoeck & Ruprecht, 1937); Friedrich Büchsel, *Die Hauptfragen der Synoptikerkritik: Eine Auseinandersetzung mit R. Bultmann, M. Dibelius und ihren Vorgängern*, BFCT, Bd. 40, Heft 6 (Gütersloh: C. Bertelsmann, 1939); Eduard Schick, *Formgeschichte und Synoptikerexegese: Eine kritische Untersuchung über die Möglichkeit und die Grenzen der formgeschichtlichen Methode*, NTAbh., Bd. 18, Heft 2–3 (Münster: Aschendorffsche Verlagsbuchhandlung, 1940). For a comprehensive and perceptive investigation of the history and significance of form criticism within the larger history of the analysis of literary forms in relation to philosophical presuppositions and social influences, see Martin J. Buss, *Biblical Form Criticism in Its Context*, JSOTSup 274 (Sheffield: Sheffield Academic Press, 1999).

lated by Eduard Norden in the subtitle of his *Agnostos Theos*: "Investigations of the *Formengeschichte* of Religious Speech."[183] Of course, the idea that tradition about Jesus circulated in oral form prior to the writing of the sources was not new. However, the work of the history of religion scholars provided material and method for the investigation of the oral tradition: the analysis of folk tradition, the study of comparative religion, the focus on cultic life and practice. Moreover, Gunkel had investigated the tradition beneath the sources of the HB and discovered that oral reports took particular forms or *Gattungen*. NT scholars were driven to a similar approach by the impasse created by recent theories about the Gospels. If, as Wrede had argued, the narrative of Mark was a theological and not a historical composition, then study of the history of Jesus was forced to probe the tradition prior to Mark.[184]

A few basic principles are shared by the form critics. They believe that the Gospels are folk literature, not literary compositions, not biography. They believe that the Gospels are collections of small, isolated units of tradition. They believe that these units of tradition were shaped by the faith and life of the Christian community, and that they have their origin and development within a social setting, a *Sitz im Leben*. They believe that these forms follow principles or laws of development, and that they have parallels in other folk and religious traditions. The pioneering work in form criticism was carried out by three major scholars, largely working independently: K. L. Schmidt, Martin Dibelius, and Rudolf Bultmann.

Karl Ludwig Schmidt (1891–1956)

Schmidt was born in Frankfurt am Main, and educated at Marburg and Berlin.[185] During World War I, he suffered a serious head injury. In 1921, Schmidt was called to Giessen as successor of Bultmann. After five years he moved to Jena, and later (1929) to Bonn. In 1933, Schmidt was banned from his teaching position because of his outspoken opposition to the National Socialists. He fled to Switzerland, where he was named professor of NT at Basel in 1935. Recurrence of the ill effects of his war injury forced his retirement in 1953.

---

183. Eduard Norden, *Agnostos Theos: Untersuchungen zur Formengeschichte religiöser Rede* (Stuttgart: B. G. Teubner, 1956). Originally published in 1913, Norden's book investigates Paul's speech in Athens, reported in Acts 17. Norden observes that "the analysis of the Areopagus speech led me to the investigation of the history of forms of religious speech in general" (vii). Actually, Norden's subtitle used the term in the plural: *Formengeschichte* rather than *Formgeschichte*. According to Buss (*Biblical Form Criticism*, 287), the term *Formgeschichte* was coined by M. Dibelius.

184. See pp. 147–49, above.

185. See Andreas Mühling, *Karl Ludwig Schmidt: "Und Wissenschaft ist Leben,"* Arbeiten zur Kirchengeschichte (Berlin: Walter de Gruyter, 1997); Philipp Vielhauer, "Karl Ludwig Schmidt," in *Neues Testament, Judentum, Kirche: kleine Schriften*, ed. Gerhard Sauter (Munich: Chr. Kaiser, 1981), 13–36; Oscar Cullmann, "Karl Ludwig Schmidt, 1891–1956: Ansprache, gehalten beim Begräbnis in Basel am 13. Januar 1956," *TZ* 12 (1956): 1–9; David P. Moessner, "In Memoriam: Karl Ludwig Schmidt (1891–1956)," *TZ* 47 (1991): 3–6.

METHODOLOGICAL DEVELOPMENTS

Schmidt's major contribution to Gospel research is his book on the *Framework of the History of Jesus*.[186] As a point of departure, Schmidt raises the question about the duration of the ministry of Jesus. He notes that conservative scholars tend to follow John, whereas critical scholars prefer Mark's chronology. Schmidt rejects both. He argues that Mark's chronological framework "is just as much an [arbitrary] arrangement as that of the Gospel of John."[187] Schmidt proceeds through the Marcan account, analyzing data that refer to time and place. He discovers that some of Mark's chronological and topological information belongs to the tradition, but much of it comes from his own imagination. Only the passion narrative is different. In regard to that account, the evangelists largely agree, and the narrative represents a primitive tradition that comprehends the story as a whole.[188] Schmidt concludes:

> The earliest outline of the history of Jesus is that of the Gospel of Mark. The instability of the traditions shows how the earliest tradition about Jesus looked: there is no continuous report, but an abundance of individual stories that are ordered generally according to content. These stories, on their own, are not distinctive, since they are linked to the history of early Christianity with its various religious, apologetic, and missionary concerns. . . . But, as a whole, there is no life of Jesus in the sense of a developing biography, no chronological outline of the history of Jesus, but only individual stories, pericopes, which are put into a framework.[189]

Also important for form criticism is Schmidt's essay on the Gospels in relation to the history of literature. According to Schmidt, the attempt to find literary models for the Gospels in Greek biography or Jewish stories is doomed to failure. "The Gospel is fundamentally not cultured literature [*Hochliteratur*] but lowly literature [*Kleinliteratur*], not the accomplishment of an individual author but a book of the people, not biography but cult legend." Schmidt concludes that the Gospels are unique, belonging to no

---

186. *Der Rahmen der Geschichte Jesu: literarkritische Untersuchungen zur ältesten Jesusüberlieferung* (Berlin: Trowitzsch & Sohn, 1919). Schmidt also published a brief summary of form criticism: "Formgeschichte," *RGG* (2d ed.) 2:638–40.

187. *Rahmen der Geschichte*, 17.

188. On the passion narrative, see also Schmidt, "Die literarische Eigenart der Leidensgeschichte Jesu," in *Redaktion und Theologie des Passionsberichtes nach den Synoptikern*, ed. Meinrad Limbeck, Wege der Forschung 481 (Darmstadt: Wissenschaftliche Buchgesellschaft, 1981), 17–20. Schmidt writes: "Before the tradition of Jesus had time to be given the finishing touches as was done with the material outside of the passion narrative, the report of the suffering and death of Jesus was already fixed and could not be changed without damaging the established view of the community" (19).

189. *Rahmen der Geschichte*, 317. For a critique of Schmidt, see C. H. Dodd, "The Framework of the Gospel Narrative," in *New Testament Studies* (Manchester: Manchester University Press, 1953), 1–11. Dodd contends that the outline in Mark is based on the early Christian kerygma, and thus represents a primitive tradition with historical value. A highly critical analysis of Schmidt's argumentation is presented by David R. Hall, *The Gospel Framework: Fiction or Fact? A Critical Evaluation of Der Rahmen der Geschichte Jesu by Karl Ludwig Schmidt* (Carlisle, Cumbria: Paternoster, 1998).

genre of literature; early Christianity is distinctive, not a product of human culture. Form-critical analysis, in Schmidt's view, facilitates the understanding of the nature of early Christianity and its relation to the world.

> Thus the form-critical way of investigation is a theological enterprise. The general philosophical question about content and form is transformed into the theological question about God and world, about Christianity and culture. The radical and positive investigation of the Gospels is an exponent of the fundamental theological question.[190]

The result of Schmidt's form-critical research is presented in his article "Jesus Christ."[191] According to Schmidt, the Gospels present the kerygma of the church:

> [T]he Johannine proclamation of the Logos, who became flesh and dwelt among us . . . is also the hidden theme of the Synoptic Gospels. They do not contain stories of an individual who was the founder and originator of Christianity, but consist of numerous individual reflections on the theme of the incarnation of the Logos.[192]

Although he does not believe the Gospels provide biography, Schmidt thinks they faithfully present the teaching of Jesus: the proclamation of the coming rule God—a cosmic, apocalyptic event. Schmidt also believes Jesus thought himself to be the Messiah. But, as Schmidt thinks his use of the title Son of Man indicates, "Jesus places himself on the same level as his brethren, and at the same time as unique and over them."[193] For Schmidt, the message of the Gospels is the essence of Christianity: the unique historical event in which God is revealed.[194] "What is at issue is not a speculation concerning a Christ myth or an ideal represented by Christ, nor the search for the dominant attributes of a religious genius; we are concerned with

---

190. "Die Stellung der Evangelien in der allegemeinen Literaturgeschichte," in ΕΥΧΑΡΙΣΤΗΡΙΟΝ: *Studien zur Religion und Literatur des Alten und Neuen Testaments: Hermann Gunkel zum 60. Geburtstage, dem 23. Mai 1933,* ed. Hans Schmidt, FRLANT 19 (Göttingen: Vandenhoeck & Ruprecht, 1923) 2:50–134; repr. in *Neues Testament, Judentum, Kirche,* 37–130. The citations above are from the English translation: *The Place of the Gospels in the General History of Literature,* trans. Byron R. McCane (Columbia, S.C.: University of South Carolina Press, 2002), 27, 86. Schmidt's view of primitive Christian writing as distinct from literature is reminiscent of Overbeck, see pp. 141–42, above.
191. "Jesus Christus," *RGG* (2d ed.) 3:110–51; Eng. trans: "Jesus Christ," in *Twentieth Century Theology in the Making: I Themes of Biblical Theology,* ed. Jaroslav Pelikan, trans. R. A. Wilson (London: William Collins Sons, 1969), 93–168.
192. "Jesus Christ," 102. Schmidt's position has affinity with that of Martin Kähler, *Der sogenannte historische Jesus und der geschichtliche, biblische Christus* (Leipzig: A. Deichert, 1896; repr., Munich: Chr. Kaiser, 1956); Eng. trans.: *The So-Called Historical Jesus and the Historic, Biblical Christ,* trans. Carl E. Braaten, Seminar Editions (Philadelphia: Fortress, 1964).
193. "Jesus Christ," 167.
194. See John C. Meagher, "The Implications for Theology of a Shift from the K. L. Schmidt Hypothesis of the Literary Uniqueness of the Gospels," in *Colloquy on New Testament Studies: A Time for Reappraisal and Fresh Approaches,* ed. Bruce Corley (Macon, Ga.: Mercer University Press, 1983), 203–33.

something unique which forms more than simply a part of world history, but which is derived from the context of the scriptures; the task and calling of Jesus as seen in his words and deeds."[195]

Martin Dibelius (1883–1947)

Born in Dresden, the son of a conservative pastor, Martin Dibelius was educated at Neuchâtel, Leipzig, Tübingen, and Berlin.[196] In 1915, he was appointed professor of NT at Heidelberg, where he remained for the balance of his career. Dibelius disliked National Socialism, but though he was under surveillance from time to time, he was never removed from his teaching post. Weakened by the privations of the war, he died of ill health at the age of sixty-four. Dibelius confessed a Christocentric theology that found in the faith of the early Christians the solution to the crises of his time.[197] That faith, as Dibelius observes in his *Jesus*, is a response to the sovereignty of God attested in the signs of the kingdom.[198] "The actuality of God, in its full radical seriousness, manifests itself within time only in the form of 'signs,' and its true sign is the appearance of Jesus."[199] Faith in response to the sovereignty of God also requires obedience to the will of God revealed in Jesus' teaching. "The standard of the Sermon on the Mount and of the Christian," says Dibelius, "is the will of God. The basis of the Christian attitude is the conviction that God's will revealed in Christ's Gospel is the only hope for mankind."[200]

---

195. "Jesus Christ," 168. Besides his work on the Gospels, Schmidt is also remembered for his linguistic and exegetical studies. His perceptive article on ἐκκλησία in *TDNT* has been reprinted and often cited. Also of special interest is Schmidt's monograph, *Die Judenfrage im Lichte der Kapitel 9–11 des Römerbriefes*, ThSt 13 (Zollikon-Zurich: Evangelischer Verlag, 1942), in which he opposes anti-Semitism and the persecution of Jews on the basis of his exegesis of Romans 9–11.

196. See Werner Georg Kümmel, "Dibelius, Martin (1883–1947)," *TRE* 8:726–29; idem, "Martin Dibelius als Theologe," *TLZ* 74 (1949):129–40; repr., in *Heilsgeschehen und Geschichte: Gesammelte Aufsätze 1933–1964*, ed. Erich Grässer, Otto Merk, and Adolf Fritz (Marburg: N. G. Elwert, 1965), 192–206; "Martin Dibelius: Zeit und Arbeit," in *RGS* 5:1–37; Matthias Wolfes, "Schuld und Verantwortung. Die Auseinandersetzung des Heidelberger Theologen Martin Dibelius mit dem Dritten Reich. Mit einer aus dem Nachlass herausgegebenen 'Lebensbeschreibung' aus dem Jahre 1946," *ZKG* 111 (2000): 185–205.

197. See Martin Dibelius, *Geschichtliche und übergeschichtliche Religion im Christentum* (Göttingen: Vandenhoeck & Ruprecht, 1925); repr. as *Evangelium und Welt* (Göttingen: Vandenhoeck & Ruprecht, 1929); idem, *Gospel Criticism and Christology* (London: Ivor Nicholson & Watson, 1935); Germ. trans.: "Evangelienkritik und Christologie," in *Botschaft und Geschichte: Gesammelte Aufsätze*, ed. Günther Bornkamm (Tübingen: J. C. B. Mohr [Paul Siebeck], 1952) 1:293–358.

198. Third ed. with Nachtrag by Werner Georg Kümmel, Sammlung Göschen 1130 (Berlin: Walter de Gruyter, 1960); Eng. trans.: *Jesus*, trans. Charles B. Hedrick and Frederick C. Grant (Philadelphia: Westminster, 1949).

199. *Jesus* (Eng. trans.), 144.

200. *The Sermon on the Mount* (New York: Charles Scribner's Sons, 1940); Germ. trans.: "Die Bergpredigt," in *Botschaft und Geschichte* 1:136–37.

History of Religion, Form and Literary Criticism

As a prelude to his work in form criticism, Dibelius's first major publication was an exercise in the *religionsgeschichtliche* method—an investigation of the *Spiritual World in the Faith of Paul*.[201] Dibelius begins with an analysis of the texts in which Paul speaks of angels, Satan, demons, and the ruler of this age. Dibelius argues that the notion of intermediaries between God and world had its source in Babylonian and Egyptian cosmology. Although he acknowledges that Paul has been influenced by oriental cosmology and Iranian dualism, Dibelius insists that these influences are peripheral, not essential to Paul's thought. For example, Paul employs the myth of the descending and ascending redeemer merely as a metaphor for expressing his Christology. In 1917, Dibelius published a fascinating monograph on the initiatory rites of the mystery cults and their relation to early Christian life.[202] Here he argues that the opponents of Paul at Colossae were converts of a mystery cult similar to the cult of Isis. At the time of his death, Dibelius left an unfinished book on *Paul* in which he argues that the apostle was not a mystic. "The union with Christ is achieved, not in celebrating a mystery nor in the secret hour of an inward vision, but in the troubled and dangerous existence of the missionary—the apostolic life is itself his consecration."[203]

Dibelius's major work on *Form Criticism* first appeared in 1919.[204] In a preface to the English translation of the second edition (1933), Dibelius summarizes:

> The method of Formgeschichte seeks to help in answering the historical questions as to the nature and trustworthiness of our knowledge of Jesus, and also in solving a theological problem properly so-called. It shows in what way the earliest testimony about Jesus was interwoven with the earliest testimony about the salvation which had appeared in Jesus Christ. Thereby it attempts to emphasize and illuminate the chief elements of the message upon which Christianity was founded.

---

201. *Die Geisterwelt im Glauben des Paulus* (Göttingen: Vandenhoeck & Ruprecht, 1909).

202. "Die Isisweihe bei Apuleius und verwandte Initiations-Riten," in *Botschaft und Geschichte: Gesammelte Aufsätze: 2. Zum Urchristentum und zur hellenistischen Religionsgeschichte*, ed. Günther Bornkamm with Heinz Kraft (Tübingen: J. C. B. Mohr [Paul Siebeck], 1956), 30–79; Eng. trans.: "The Isis Initiation in Apuleius and Related Initiatory Rites," in *Conflict at Colossae: A Problem in the Interpretation of Early Christianity Illustrated by Selected Modern Studies*, ed. and trans. Fred O. Francis and Wayne A. Meeks, Sources for Biblical Study 4 (Missoula, Mont.: SBL, 1973), 61–121.

203. *Paul*, ed. Werner Georg Kümmel, trans. Frank Clarke (Philadelphia: Westminster, 1957), 106.

204. *Die Formgeschichte des Evangeliums: Dritte, durchgesehene Auflage mit einem Nachtrag von Gerhard Iber*, ed. Günther Bornkamm (Tübingen: J. C. B. Mohr [Paul Siebeck], 1959); Eng. trans.: *From Tradition to Gospel*, trans. Bertram Lee Woolf, Scribner Library (New York: Charles Scribner's Sons, n.d.).

Dibelius agrees with Schmidt that the Gospels are *Kleinliteratur*, not literary compositions. He also believes they incorporate units of tradition that have their setting in the life of the church. According to Dibelius, the crucial factor in the origin and development of the tradition is the preaching of the early Christians. He writes, "the manner in which the doings of Jesus was [*sic*] narrated was determined by the requirements of the sermon."[205]

Dibelius proceeds to classify the material according to his identification of the forms. He believes the oldest form is the *Paradigm*—a short story that preserves a word or act of Jesus, for example, the healing of the paralytic (Mark 2:1-12). In contrast to the Paradigms are the *Tales* (*Novelle*)—longer stories, embellished with detail and told for the sheer delight in storytelling. These include healings, like the story of the blind man of Bethsaida (Mark 8:22-26), that display conventional features: the seriousness of the disease, the technique of the healer, the proof of the cure. According to Dibelius, the *Legends* are "religious stories in which Jesus brings to light His purity, wisdom, and virtue, or in which the Divine protection and care of Jesus are revealed." The birth stories of Matthew and Luke are examples. Dibelius believes analogies for these forms can be found in rabbinic and Hellenistic literature. In Dibelius's opinion, Mark has compiled the units of tradition in order to present the hidden meaning of Jesus' acts. "In this way the gospel of Mark was written as *a book of secret epiphanies*." As to historicity, Dibelius believes the Paradigms are more reliable, the Tales less, and the Legends still less. "The first understanding afforded by the standpoint of Formgeschichte is that there never was a 'purely' historical witness to Jesus."[206]

The results of Dibelius's classification of the forms are presented in his book *The Message of Jesus Christ*.[207] In the first part, Dibelius presents the reconstructed texts, translated and arranged more or less according to his identification of the forms. The *Old Stories* (*die alten Geschichten*) include all the pericopes Dibelius had classified as Paradigms and a few more. He also includes his reconstruction of the earliest account of the passion narrative. Dibelius identifies thirty-four *Parables*. The vividness of his translation is apparent in his account of the parable of the wicked judge (Luke 18:2-7):

> Once there lived in a city a judge. . . . There also lived in that city a widow, who came to him again and again and pleaded, 'Give me my rights against my enemy!' And for a long time he would not do so. Finally, he got to thinking

---

205. *Tradition to Gospel*, 26.
206. Ibid., 120, 320, 295.
207. *Die Botschaft von Jesus Christus: Die alte Überlieferung der Gemeinde in Geschichten, Sprüchen und Reden* (Tübingen: J. C. B. Mohr [Paul Siebeck], 1935); Eng. trans.: *The Message of Jesus Christ: The Tradition of the Early Christian Communities*, trans. Frederick C. Grant, International Library of Christian Knowledge (New York: Charles Scribner's Sons, 1939).

about it, and said to himself: I don't fear God—that's certain; and I care nothing about what men think; but this widow—I will see that she has her rights, before she becomes a nuisance, and finally comes and scratches my eyes out.[208]

Dibelius also presents *Sayings*, *Great Miracle Tales* (*die grossen Wundergeschichten*), and *Legends*.

In the second part, Dibelius explains his classifications, that is, he presents his form-critical theory and method. In regard to the *Old Stories* (Paradigms), he writes:

> These stories are as a rule briefer, more artless, more vigorous; they paint no picture, they say nothing that is unessential. For this kind of story only one thing was necessary: to provide the setting for Jesus' word and saving deed. The circumstances of his activities were described only in so far as these were required for an understanding of his mission. . . . As a rule . . . they were anecdotes—and it was this kind of story that the preacher of the gospel could use as an illustration in his sermon.

In regard to the *Sayings* of Jesus, Dibelius notes their short, rhythmic character. "For all his admonitions, warnings, and promises were subordinate to the Message: the old world is at an end, God's Kingdom is coming, God Himself draws near to men in judgment and in mercy." The *Miracle Tales*, designed to depict Jesus as a wonder-worker, have a basis in history. "No one would have told such stories about Jesus if he had not actually held the rôle of miracle worker." Although the Gospels include *Legends*, Dibelius believes the tradition was conservative, avoiding fantasies that would have obscured the essential message: "that this earthly Life, lived at a definite historical time in the land of Palestine, was the bearer of God's final and decisive Message to mankind."[209]

Dibelius applied the methods of literary analysis he had used in form criticism to the whole development of early Christian literature in a book on the *History of Early Christian Literature*.[210] In the book, he classifies the Christian writings according to literary categories. Regarding the *Gospels*, he asserts that Mark invented the gospel genre. He believes Matthew wove the teachings of Jesus into the fabric of Mark's account. He thinks Luke intended to write a biography. All three Gospels were written, according to Dibelius, after 70. Dibelius believes the author of the Fourth Gospel, probably a disciple of John the Elder, intended to compose literature. In regard

---

208. *Message of Jesus Christ*, 44.
209. Ibid., 136, 164, 168, 187.
210. *Geschichte der urchristlichen Literatur: I Evangelien und Apokalypsen; II Apostolisches und Nachapostolisches*, SG (Berlin: Walter de Gruyter, 1926); Eng. trans.: *A Fresh Approach to the New Testament and Early Christian Literature*, International Library of Christian Knowledge (New York: Charles Scribner's Sons, 1936).

to *Apocalypses,* Dibelius believes Mark Christianized and incorporated a Jewish apocalypse into his thirteenth chapter. The Revelation of John combines apocalyptic with prophecy, and, Dibelius believes, was written by John the Elder. The *Letter* form was exploited by Paul, but since Paul dictated his epistles, Dibelius thinks they represent Pauline preaching and display the rhetorical features of the speeches of the Cynics. Dibelius also notes other literary expressions that adopted the letter form, for example, Ephesians and 1 Peter, both of which he believes to be pseudonymous. Within the documents of the NT, Dibelius detects other literary forms: exhortation, paraenesis, and liturgical expressions.

Dibelius published extensively on the Acts, using his familiar literary analysis. For example, in an essay on *Acts within the Framework of the History of Early Christian Literature,* he asserts that Acts is unique within the NT.[211] Dibelius believes Acts 13:4—21:18 rests on an itinerary source. In a work on the "Style Criticism" of Acts, Dibelius argues that Acts incorporates independent units of tradition, especially legends such as the story about Eutychus (20:9-12).[212] Concerning questions of historicity, Dibelius writes:

> All these questions can be resolved only after the style-criticism has been carried out; any premature solution of the problems will do more than endanger the integrity of the style-critical method; it will obscure our understanding of the stories themselves. Intrinsically these stories are far removed from the problems of historiography, and it is only when we begin to look away from the questions which have been raised in connection with them that we learn to listen to what the story-tellers have to say to us.[213]

Looking back over the history of early Christian writing, Dibelius acknowledges that the development of literature was inevitable, but he insists that the earlier, preliterary expressions are most important. He says, "it is the works of smaller literary value that are our classical witnesses of primitive Christian faith and life."[214]

The results of form-critical and literary analysis are visible in Dibelius's *Jesus.* At the outset, Dibelius surveys the result of form criticism and concludes that "a 'biography' of Jesus . . . cannot be written." "A movement of an eschatological and Messianic kind in Galilee, distinguished above others by special gifts of its Leader and by the absoluteness of the motives and hope aroused by it—this, but nothing more than this, is what Jesus' ministry

---

211. "Die Apostelgeschichte im Rahmen der urchristlichen Literaturgeschichte," in *Aufsätze zur Apostelgeschichte,* ed. Heinrich Greeven, FRLANT 60 (Göttingen: Vandenhoeck & Ruprecht, 1953), 163–74; Eng. trans.: "The Acts of the Apostles in the Setting of the History of Early Christian Literature," in *Studies in the Acts of the Apostles,* ed. Heinrich Greeven, trans. Mary Ling (New York: Charles Scribner's Sons, 1956), 192–206.
212. "Stilkritisches zur Apostelgeschichte (1923)," in *Aufsätze zur Apostelgeschichte,* 9–28; Eng. trans.: "Style Criticism of the Book of Acts," in *Studies in the Acts,* 1–25.
213. *Studies in the Acts,* 25.
214. *Geschichte der urchristlichen Literatur,* 272.

in Galilee appears to have been." Dibelius believes the message of the kingdom was eschatological and the imminence of God's intervention was signified by miracles incomprehensible to the modern mind. Dibelius thinks Jesus understood Himself to be the Messiah and used the title Son of Man. "The term 'Son of Man,'" says Dibelius, "includes the thought that the Man from heaven who will appear at the end of the world is first to be hidden for a time. Such concealment—in spite of all the signs that he performed—was Jesus' earthly life and suffering." In proclaiming the rule of God, Jesus demanded ethical action—"radical obedience." When the apocalyptic wrappings are stripped away, the permanent treasure of the gospel becomes visible, for the person "who recognizes in the tradition about Jesus the Christ contained in the New Testament the true 'sign' of God will also recognize that this actuality has already begun to come to pass, precisely in the event whose record is the New Testament."[215]

Commentaries

Dibelius contributed to major commentary series. *Handbuch zum Neuen Testament* was founded and edited by Hans Lietzmann.[216] At Lietzmann's death in 1942, Dibelius succeeded him as editor. The first contributions appeared in 1906, consisting of concise commentaries, packed with historical and linguistic data. The third volume of the series was written by Dibelius, and included short commentaries on 1 and 2 Thessalonians, Philippians, Colossians, Ephesians, Philemon, 1 and 2 Timothy, and Titus.[217] In later editions, the commentaries were expanded and published as separate volumes: *An die Kolosser. An die Epheser. An Philemon* (1927); *Die Pastoralbriefe* (1931); *An die Thessalonicher I, II. An die Philipper* (1937). The commentary on the Pastorals was revised in 1955, translated into English in 1972, and included in the important Hermeneia series.[218]

The high point of Dibelius's exegetical research is his masterful commentary on *James* in the venerable Meyer series (*KEK*), founded by H. A. W. Meyer (1800–1873).[219] Originally published in 1921, the editions after 1955 included notes by Heinrich Greeven. A later edition was translated into

---

215. *Jesus* (Eng. trans.), 29, 61, 102, 111, 145.
216. See pp. 434–42, below.
217. *Die Briefe des Apostels Paulus: II Die neun kleinen Briefe,* HNT (Tübingen: J. C. B. Mohr [Paul Siebeck], 1913.
218. *Die Pastoralbriefe,* 3d ed. Hans Conzelmann, HNT 13 (Tübingen: J. C. B. Mohr [Paul Siebeck], 1955); Eng. trans.: *The Pastoral Epistles,* trans. Philip Buttolph and Adela Yarbro, Hermeneia (Philadelphia: Fortress, 1972).
219. See *HNTR* 1:365–70.

English in 1976 as a volume of the Hermeneia series.[220] In discussing the literary genre, Dibelius argues that James is not an epistle; it is paraenesis: a string of ethical exhortations. The "James" to which it is attributed must be James the brother of Jesus, but since evidence against his authorship is overwhelming, Dibelius concludes that the document is pseudonymous. In regard to the history of religion context, Dibelius argues that James is not a Christianized Jewish document, but a Christian document that presents the ethical tradition of the Jewish diaspora in Hellenistic metaphors.

In format, Dibelius orders the material into eight main sections. The exegesis of each section is introduced by an analysis of the text, followed by verse-by-verse interpretation. Throughout the commentary, excursuses on literary, linguistic, and theological topics are interspersed. Dibelius's interpretation of James 2:14-26, "A Treatise on Faith and Works," provides an example. In the analysis, Dibelius notes that the author uses diatribe style. Dibelius believes the phrase "but someone will say" (v. 18) introduces the objection of an opponent, while the words "you senseless person" (v. 20) constitute the answer of the author to the opponent. The major exegetical problem of the text is to determine where the objection ends and the answer begins. In interpreting v. 18, Dibelius attempts to solve the problem. The word of the opponent, "You have faith and I have works" (v. 18), is problematic, since it seems to support the position of the author. Dibelius, however, argues that the contrast of the text is not between "I" and "you," but between "faith" and "works." The translation of the opponent's words should be "one has faith, another has works." Against this, the author, in Dibelius's view, argues that faith and works cannot be separated. As v. 19 makes clear, faith without works is not true faith. Excursuses attached to this section on "Abraham as Example" and "Faith and Works in Paul and James" argue that James affirms the Jewish exegesis of Gen. 15:6, while Paul's idea of faith rests on his own religious experience, and has its background in Hellenistic thought.

In sum, Dibelius made a lasting contribution to NT research. He was master of all the critical disciplines, and he especially made effective use of literary analysis. He also shows that literary analysis is essential to form criticism, and that form criticism is concerned with history of tradition in relation to the development of the church's life and faith. Dibelius's marriage of historical and theological interests bore fruit in his commentaries—works that continue to inform the serious student of the NT.

---

220. *Der Brief des Jakobus,* 10th ed. Heinrich Greeven, KEK (Göttingen: Vandenhoeck & Ruprecht, 1959); Eng. trans.: *A Commentary on the Epistle of James,* trans. Michael A. Williams, Hermeneia (Philadelphia: Fortress, 1976).

Rudolf Bultmann (1884–1976)

Born in Wiefelstede, near Oldenburg, Rudolf Bultmann was the son of a Lutheran pastor.[221] He studied at Tübingen, Berlin, and Marburg. At Berlin he was influenced by Gunkel, and at Marburg by Jülicher and Johannes Weiss. He was appointed instructor at Marburg in 1912, where he was associated with Martin Rade and the liberal theological group, the Friends of the Christian World. In 1916, Bultmann was named associate professor at Breslau. In 1920, he was called to the faculty at Giessen, the successor of Bousset, and a year later was appointed professor of NT at Marburg, where he remained for the rest of his life. Bultmann's door was always open to students, who revered his genial spirit, his lively sense of humor, and his profound religious faith.

History of Religion

Bultmann's early NT research, like that of Dibelius, was closely related to the theory and practice of the history of religion school.[222] In 1910, he submitted his dissertation on the *Style of the Pauline Preaching and the Cynic-Stoic Diatribe*. Bultmann begins by analyzing the style of the diatribe as exemplified by Hellenistic authors such as Seneca and Epictetus. Bultmann shows that the diatribe is dialogical in character, taking the form of saying and countersaying. The speech of the diatribe uses various rhetorical figures, such as paradox, exclamation, rhetorical questions. According to Bultmann, the diatribe argues from conviction and personal experience; the mood of the diatribe is vivid, energetic, and polemical. Turning to Paul, Bultmann finds evidence of the use of diatribe style in the Epistles. However, he believes Paul is different, unconcerned with the rhetorical artifice. "We conclude: *the preaching of Paul made use in part of forms of expression* used in the preaching of *Cynic-Stoic popular philosophers in the diatribe*. We do not

---

221. The discussion of Bultmann here is limited to his contributions to history of religion and form criticism. Bultmann's major hermeneutical and theological work is to be investigated in volume 3 of *HNTR*. It is appropriate to speak of the "early Bultmann," since around 1922 his thought moved from liberalism to dialectical theology. Also, Bultmann's association with Martin Heidegger began at about this time. For a survey of Bultmann's early life and work, see Rudolf Bultmann, "Autobiographical Reflections," in *Existence and Faith: Shorter Writings of Rudolf Bultmann*, ed. Schubert Ogden, Living Age Books (New York: Meridian Books, 1960), 283–88; René Marlé, *Bultmann et l'interprétation du Nouveau Testament,* Théolgie: Études publiées sous la direction de la faculté S. J. de Lyon-Fourvière (Aubier: Éditions Montaigne, 1956); Martin Evang, *Rudolf Bultmann in seiner Frühzeit*, BHT 74 (Tübingen: J. C. B. Mohr [Paul Siebeck], 1988); Karolina De Valerio, *Altes Testament und Judentum im Frühwerk Rudolf Bultmanns*, BZNW 71 (Berlin: Walter de Gruyter, 1994).

222. See Dieter Lührmann, "Rudolf Bultmann and the History of Religion School," in *Text and Logos: The Humanistic Interpretation of the New Testament*, ed. Theodore W. Jennings Jr., SBL Homage Series (Atlanta, Ga.: Scholars Press, 1990), 3–14; Helmut Koester, "Early Christianity from the Perspective of the History of Religions: Rudolf Bultmann's Contribution," in *Bultmann, Retrospect and Prospect: The Centenary Symposium at Wellesley*, ed. Edward C. Hobbs, HTS 35 (Philadelphia: Fortress, 1985), 59–74.

want in conclusion to conceal the fact that the impression of difference is greater than that of similarity."[223]

Bultmann also investigated the *religionsgeschichtliche* setting of the Gospel of John. In an essay on "The History of Religion Background of the Prologue of the Johannine Gospel," originally published in 1923, Bultmann argues that the prologue of the Fourth Gospel rests on a gnostic source that praised the preexistent Sophia.[224] Under Alexandrian influence, Sophia was changed to Logos, and the Logos was incorporated into the myth of the divine bearer of revelation—a myth that had its source in Egyptian, Babylonian, or Persian religion. Bultmann, in an essay titled "The Significance of the Recently Discovered Mandaean and Manichaean Sources for the Understanding of the Gospel of John" (1925), contends that the Johannine Christ can be explicated by the Mandaean literature and Reitzenstein's myth of the redeemed redeemer. Bultmann attempts to support this thesis by presenting quotations from the Mandaean sources in parallel with quotations from the Greek text of John. Although the Mandaean and Manichaean documents are much later, the Mandaean sect, in Bultmann's opinion, originated before 70 and adopted an oriental myth that was still older. Bultmann thinks the author of the Fourth Gospel used the myth to present a nonmythical revelation: a historical event that called humanity into question. "The author is interested only in the *that (Dass)* of revelation, not in the *what (Was)*."[225]

Bultmann's continuing interest in the history of religion is apparent in a later work on *Early Christianity in the Setting of Ancient Religions*.[226] Like members of the *religionsgechichtliche* school, Bultmann believes Christianity's "uniqueness is thrown into sharper relief by setting it against the background of its environment." In discussing the OT heritage, Bultmann asserts that God can only be known in the hearing of the word of God. "God confronts man with his blessing and demand," says Bultmann, "judging him in each successive moment. Every such moment however points towards the future. God is always a God who comes."[227] Turning to Judaism, Bultmann shares the prejudiced anti-Judaism of his predecessors. "God was no longer

---

223. *Der Stil der paulinischen Predigt und die kynisch-stoische Diatribe* (Göttingen: Vandenhoeck & Ruprecht, 1910), 107. For a summary and critique of Bultmann, see Stanley Kent Stowers, *The Diatribe and Paul's Letter to the Romans*, SBLDS 57 (Chico, Calif.: Scholars Press, 1981).
224. "Der religionsgeschichtliche Hintergrund des Prologs zum Johannes-Evangelium," in *Exegetica: Aufsätze zur Erforschung des Neuen Testaments*, ed. Erich Dinkler (Tübingen: J. C. B. Mohr [Paul Siebeck], 1967), 10–35.
225. "Die Bedeutung der neuerschlossenen mandäischen und manichäischen Quellen für das Verständnis des Johannesevangeliums," *Exegetica*, 103.
226. *Das Urchristentum im Rahmen der Antiken Religionen*, Erasmus-Bibliothek, 2d ed. (Zurich: Artemis, 1954); Eng. trans.: *Primitive Christianity in Its Contemporary Setting*, trans. R. H. Fuller, Living Age Books (New York: Meridian Books, 1957).
227. *Primitive Christianity*, 11, 34.

really the God of history, and therefore always the God who was about to come. He was no longer a vital factor in the present: his revelation lay in the past." To be sure, Bultmann insists that Jesus must be understood within Judaism. "Jesus was not a 'Christian,' but a Jew," yet his preaching is "a tremendous protest against contemporary Jewish legalism."[228]

In describing the Greek heritage, Bultmann notes the growth of syncretism in the Hellenistic age and the importance of Gnosticism for understanding Christianity. Both Gnosticism and Christianity see humans as enslaved to a cosmic power.

> Man's redemption—and at this point Primitive Christianity and Gnosticism are in agreement—can only come from the divine world as an event. It is something that must happen to man from outside. Now Christian faith claims that this is precisely what has happened in Jesus of Nazareth.

Bultmann continues:

> The most important development, however, was the interpretation of the person of Jesus in terms of the Gnostic redemption myth. He is a divine figure sent down from the celestial world of light, the Son of the Most High coming forth from the Father, veiled in earthly form and inaugurating the redemption through his work.[229]

However, released from the evil cosmic power, the Christian is free and responsible, called to ethical decision in the world.

Form Criticism

Bultmann's major contribution to form criticism is his monumental *History of the Synoptic Tradition*.[230] Originally published in 1921, a second, unrevised edition appeared in 1931; the third edition (1931) included supplementary notes. Bultmann also published two shorter summaries of his form-critical research: "The Study of the Synoptic Gospels" (1925),[231] and "The New Approach to the Synoptic Problem" (1926).[232] Bultmann had been at work

---

228. Ibid., 60, 71, 72. See De Valerio, *Altes Testament und Judentum*. E. P. Sanders (*Paul and Palestinian Judaism: A Comparison of Patterns of Religion* [Philadelphia: Fortress, 1977]) observes that Bultmann's view of Judaism perpetuates the caricature of Judaism as "the foil over against which the superiority of Jesus is presented" (44).

229. *Primitive Christianity*, 196.

230. *Die Geschichte der synoptischen Tradition*, 3d ed.; FRLANT 29 (Göttingen: Vandenhoeck & Ruprecht, 1957); Eng. trans.: *The History of the Synoptic Tradition*, trans. John Marsh (New York: Harper & Row, 1963).

231. *Die Erforschung der synoptischen Evangelien*, 3d ed., Aus der Welt der Religion 1 (Berlin: Alfred Töpelmann, 1960); repr. in *Glauben und Verstehen: Gesammelte Aufsätze* (Tübingen: J. C. B. Mohr [Paul Siebeck], 1965) 4.1–41; Eng. trans.: "The Study of the Synoptic Gospels," in *Form Criticism: Two Essays on New Testament Research*, trans. Frederick C. Grant, HT (New York: Harper & Brothers, 1962).

232. *JR* 6 (1926): 337–62; repr. in Ogden, *Existence and Faith*, 35–54.

on his *History* for some time, but publication had been delayed owing to the privations of the last years of World War I. In one of the shorter works, Bultmann says, "The purpose of Form Criticism is to study the history of the oral tradition behind the gospels."[233] In the other, he writes of "the goal toward which all this critical work was believed to lead, viz., the attainment of the most accurate possible picture of the life and the teaching of Jesus."[234] Bultmann affirms the basic principles of form criticism, but especially stresses the significance of the move of Christianity from its Palestinian to its Hellenistic setting. Bultmann also recognizes the circular argument of the form-critical method: the study of the elements of the tradition is used to reconstruct the history of the community; but the history of the community is used in the analysis of the tradition.

In the two later works, Bultmann orders the identification of forms somewhat differently, but the definitive understanding is presented in the *History of the Synoptic Tradition*. He begins with the tradition of the sayings of Jesus. For Bultmann, the most important form is the *Apophthegm*: a short, pithy saying or aphorism set in a brief narrative. This form, similar to Dibelius's Paradigm, includes two main types: conflict and didactic sayings (such as the healing of the paralytic of Mark 2:1-5), and biographical apophthegms (such as the story of Jesus in his hometown [Mark 6:1-6]). Bultmann believes the conflict sayings have their origin in the Palestinian church. Another form is seen in the *Dominical Sayings*, which Bultmann divides into three main types. First are the logia or sayings of Jesus as a wisdom teacher (e.g., Matt 6:34b: "Today's trouble is enough for today"). In "Study of the Synoptic Gospels," Bultmann says that "these Wisdom-sayings . . . are least guaranteed to be authentic words of Jesus; and they are likewise the least characteristic and significant for historical interpretation." Second are the prophetic and apocalyptic sayings. Since many of these are distinct from Judaism and free from early Christian tendency, Bultmann believes they represent the earliest and most reliable tradition about Jesus.

> The sayings are distinguished by their brevity and vigor and have their parallels in ancient prophecy, not in contemporary apocalyptic. They are obviously not typical products of apocalyptic fancy, but original utterances of a prophetic personality. One may with perfect right recognize among them authentic words of Jesus.[235]

Third are the legal sayings and church rules—sayings of Jesus that have been transformed into regulations for the life of the church.

---

233. "Study of the Synoptic Gospels," 1.
234. "New Approach," 338.
235. "Study of the Synoptic Gospels," 55, 56.

Besides these three major types, Bultmann analyzes other forms of sayings. The *I-sayings* often represent Jesus posturing as the risen Lord, but some of them, for instance, Luke 11:20 ("if it is by the finger of God that I caste out demons"), Bultmann accepts as authentic. This saying "can, in my view, claim the highest degree of authenticity which we can make for any saying of Jesus: it is full of that feeling of eschatological power which must have characterized the activity of Jesus."[236] In regard to similitudes and parables, Bultmann finds parallels in Jewish literature and notes the tendency of the tradition to allegorize. Bultmann believes the parables follow form-critical laws, for example, they never present more than three characters (law of conciseness) and they put the important point at the end (law of end stress). "We can only count on possessing a genuine similitude of Jesus where, on the one hand, expression is given to the contrast between Jewish morality and piety and the distinctive eschatological temper which characterized the preaching of Jesus; and where on the other hand we find no specifically Christian features."[237]

Bultmann turns to the narrative forms. He classifies the *Miracle Stories* into two categories: healings and nature miracles. These stories are designed to stress the power of Jesus. Bultmann thinks most of them have their origin in the Hellenistic community where abundant parallels can be found in the environment. The *Historical Stories and Legends*—for instance, the account of the baptism of Jesus—are developed in order to depict Jesus as the Messiah. Concerning the *Passion Narrative*, Bultmann writes:

> So I assume that there was a primitive narrative which told very briefly of the arrest, the condemnation by the Sanhedrin and Pilate, the journey to the cross, the crucifixion and death. This was developed at various stages, in part by earlier stories that were available and in part by forms that had newly appeared.[238]

According to Bultmann, the *Easter Narratives* are of two types: empty tomb stories that are secondary and apologetic, and appearances that involve a commission to mission.

Bultmann investigates the editing of the traditional material by the evangelists—a procedure later called "redaction criticism." In regard to the teachings of Jesus, Bultmann believes short, independent sayings were grouped and arranged into discourses. In regard to narrative, Bultmann, like Schmidt, thinks Mark fabricated a framework. "The gospel as a literary type was created, as far as we can see, by Mark, or at any rate was made use

---

236. *History of Synoptic Tradition*, 162.
237. Ibid., 205. This quotation shows that Bultmann, in determining authentic words of Jesus, uses what later became known as the criterion of "dissimilarity."
238. Ibid., 279.

of by him."[239] "So it is a misconception to infer from Mark's ordering of his material any conclusions about the chronology and development of the life of Jesus." Bultmann believes Matthew incorporates Q into Mark's framework in order to provide catechetical instruction for the church. "For our purposes it is essential to recognize that the Gospel of Luke is the climax of the history of the Synoptic tradition in so far as the development which the tradition had undergone from the beginning has gained its greatest success in Luke: the editing and connection of isolated sections into a coherent continuity." Bultmann summarizes the whole process:

> The collection of the material of the tradition began in the primitive Palestinian Church. Apologetic and polemic led to the collection and production of apophthegmatic sections. The demands of edification and the vitality of the prophetic spirit in the Church resulted in the handing on, the production and the collection of prophetic and apocalyptic sayings of the Lord. Further collections of dominical sayings grew out of the need for parenesis and Church discipline. It is only natural that stories of Jesus should be told and handed down in the Church—biographical apophthegms, miracles stories and others.

Bultmann believes the gospel form originates with Mark in the Hellenistic church; it proclaims the kerygma of the Christ myth. "Thus the kerygma of Christ is cultic legend and the *Gospels are expanded cult legends*."[240] The results for life of Jesus research are negative. "We must frankly confess," says Bultmann, "that the character of Jesus as a human personality cannot be recovered by us. We can neither write a 'life of Jesus' nor present an accurate picture of his personality."[241]

Critical reactions to the method and results of form criticism soon appeared.[242] Although the critics acknowledged the value of literary and form-critical analysis, many of them believed Dibelius and Bultmann had overstepped the boundaries of their method. For example, the form critics were accused of making decisions about historicity on the basis of their identification of forms, whereas the form of a tradition tells little or nothing about its truth.[243] And what of the assumption that there must have been a sharp discontinuity between Jesus and the early church? Is it not possible

---

239. "Study of the Synoptic Gospels," 69.
240. *History of Synoptic Tradition*, 349, 367, 368, 370–71.
241. "New Approach," 359.
242. See especially the works of Fascher, Koehler, Büchsel, and Schick listed in note 182 above. For more recent criticism of the work of Dibelius and Bultmann, see Laurence J. McGinley, *Form-Criticism of the Synoptic Healing Narratives: A Study in the Theories of Martin Dibelius and Rudolf Bultmann* (Woodstock, Md.: Woodstock College Press, 1944); Reiner Blank, *Analyse und Kritik der formgeschichtlichen Arbeiten von Martin Dibelius und Rudolf Bultmann*, Theologischen Dissertationen 16 (Basel: Friedrich Reinhardt Kommissionsverlag, 1981).
243. This criticism, valid in part, is not entirely convincing. For example, when a story begins, "Once upon a time," the hearer does not expect a scientific treatise.

that the *Sitz im Leben* might have been a *Sitz im Leben Jesu*? The critics noted, too, that the form critics did not agree among themselves about the identification of the forms or the motives that shaped the forms, that the period of oral tradition was too short for the sort of development Gunkel had detected in the tradition behind the OT, that parallels in rabbinic and Hellenistic literature represent analogy, not genealogy. However, in spite of the opposition, form criticism endured.[244] It highlighted the importance of the oral tradition, and provided a method, however imprecise, for its investigation. Major actors in the ongoing drama of NT research would continue to respond to it—to use, misuse, or dismiss it. Form criticism, of course, did not reach its goal of establishing reliable tradition for the reconstruction of the historical Jesus. However, it did confound the easy answer: that the life of Jesus and the gospel record were one and the same. To turn attention from the objectivity of texts to the vital tradition they expressed may have moved research closer to the meaning of the NT.

SUMMARY

While scholars reviewed in this chapter contribute to the developing methodology of NT research, they offer a variety that defies easy summation. They do agree, however, on the use of the basic historical-critical method and the necessity of understanding the NT documents in their historical setting. They disagree on the relative importance of the various backgrounds. Some (e.g., the British) tend to emphasize Jewish backgrounds. However, in an effort to elevate Christianity above its setting, some (notably Bousset) paint a pejorative picture of the Judaism of the NT period—a distortion corrected by Montefiore and Klausner. The preference for Jewish backgrounds is confounded by Weiss and Schweitzer, who contend that Jesus embraced Jewish apocalyptic—an antiquated Judaism that seemed to render Jesus irrelevant. The history of religion school complicated the issue by finding the background not only in pagan Hellenism, but in the still more remote cults and myths of Babylon and Persia. Although the members of the school claimed the superiority of Christianity, their conclusion that Christianity was a syncretistic religion, shaped by primitive myths, appeared to compromise Christianity's uniqueness.

Closely related to the history of religion school was the method of form criticism. This method, too, exploited the parallels in folk culture and religion. Form criticism, of course, assumed the widely accepted solution of the Synoptic Problem—a solution supported by the calm deliberation

---

244. For more recent developments in form criticism, see Klaus Berger, *Formgeschichte des Neuen Testaments* (Heidelberg: Quelle & Meyer, 1984).

and statistics of the British. However, for the British, the two-document hypothesis—and, even more, Streeter's four documents—served to confirm the reliability of the gospel tradition. The form critics, on the other hand, influenced by Wrede, viewed the earliest written sources, Mark and Q, as tendency documents. At the same time, they believed the oral tradition was shaped by the theological and ecclesiastical demands of the post-resurrection community. The result for Bultmann was complete skepticism about the historical Jesus. In the meantime, the massing of data and the multiplying of methods would contribute to the increasing complexity of NT research.

7

The Advance of American New Testament Research

By the turn of the nineteenth century, the fledgling nation of the United States had begun to soar like an eagle. America emerged as one of the great powers of the world. As in Europe, so in the New World, technology and industry advanced. The vast land was linked from sea to sea by shining rails. The Wright brothers got off the ground and Lucky Lindy flew the Atlantic all alone. From across the ocean came invading hordes of immigrants, and from the babble of the cities, towers were built to heaven. After two years of traditional isolation, the United States entered World War I, reluctant to be entangled in European power struggles. And when the firing ceased, Americans climbed out of the muddy trenches, shunned the League of Nations, and retreated to the distant homeland. Back home, the exhilarating progress was celebrated, but not without tears; the scars of war and reconstruction remained; the armistice between the industrial North and the agrarian South was tenuous. Minorities were repressed, and women gained the right to vote only after a long and relentless struggle.

The religious scene in America mirrored this image of conflict. The separation of church and state had fostered freedom and individualism, and spawned a pluralism of sects and denominations, most claiming loyalty to the Bible. Hailing the virtues of capitalism, many believed competition was healthy, but sometimes open warfare erupted. The bitter conflict between science and religion was dramatized in the infamous Scopes trial in Tennesee, splitting churches and congregations. Heresy trials and quasi heresy trials were frequent, but fortunately, American heretics were not burned at the stake; they simply changed jobs or joined another church. The crucial question was clear: Could religious faith survive in the modern world? And more specifically, what was the relation of reason and revelation, science and Scripture? In this climate, NT research advanced in America in the early years of the twentieth century.

NEW TESTAMENT RESEARCH AT UNION THEOLOGICAL SEMINARY: CHARLES AUGUSTUS BRIGGS AND JAMES MOFFATT

In America, NT research was accomplished primarily in the theological schools. Union Seminary in New York continued the laudable tradition of biblical scholarship established by Edward Robinson and Philip Schaff.[1]

Charles Augustus Briggs (1841–1913)

The life and trials of Charles Augustus Briggs are paradigmatic for American scholarship.[2] Briggs was born in New York; his father was a successful manufacturer of barrels. He was educated at the University of Virginia (1857–60), where he received academic honors and was converted in a religious revival. After serving three months in the Union army, Briggs entered Union Seminary and studied with Edward Robinson.[3] He continued his education in Berlin (1866–69) where he was influenced by Isaac Dorner. In 1874, he joined the faculty at Union, and two years later was named Davenport Professor of Hebrew and Cognate Languages. A contemporary described Briggs as "a dangerous antagonist, always going into the fight in full panoply of knowledge and never fighting as one that beats the air."[4] In 1880, he was named coeditor with Princeton's A. A. Hodge (the son of Charles Hodge)[5] of the *Presbyterian Review*—a journal sponsored by Union and Princeton Theological Seminary to promote unity within the denomination. In reporting the heresy trial of W. Robertson Smith in Scotland, Briggs seemed sympathetic with Smith's OT criticism. Hodge and Benjamin Warfield (who became coeditor in 1888) attacked Briggs and advocated biblical inerrancy.

---

1. See pp. 28–31, 43–52, above; Henry Sloane Coffin, *A Half Century of Union Theological Seminary, 1896–1945: An Informal History* (New York: Charles Scribner's Sons, [c. 1954]); Robert T. Handy, *A History of Union Theological Seminary in New York* (New York: Columbia University Press, 1987).

2. See Mark S. Massa, *Charles Augustus Briggs and the Crisis of Historical Criticism*, HDR 25 (Minneapolis: Fortress, 1990); Max Gray Rogers, "Charles Augustus Briggs: Heresy at Union," in *American Religious Heretics: Formal and Informal Trials*, ed. George H. Shriver (Nashville: Abingdon, 1966), 89–147; Richard L. Christensen, *The Ecumenical Orthodoxy of Charles Augustus Briggs (1841–1913)* (Lewiston: Mellen University Press, 1995); Lefferts A. Loetscher, "C. A. Briggs in the Retrospect of Half a Century," *ThTo* 12 (1955): 27–42; Doug Hill, "Charles Augustus Briggs, Modernism, and the Rise of Biblical Scholarship in Nineteenth-Century America," in *The Bible and the American Myth: A Symposium of the Bible and Constructions of Meaning*, ed. Vincent L. Wimbush, StABH 16 (Macon, Ga.: Mercer University Press, 1999), 71–104.

3. See pp. 28–31, above.

4. Quoted by Loetscher, "C. A. Briggs," 27.

5. See 31–37, above.

In 1883, Briggs published *Biblical Study: Its Principles, Methods, and History.* "Biblical study is the most *important* of all studies," wrote Briggs, "for it is a study of the Word of God, which contains a divine revelation of redemption to the world." Yet Briggs insisted that the Bible must be studied by the same methods used for other ancient books—what he called "evangelical criticism." He acknowledged that the Bible contained errors in chronology and geography, and argued that inspiration was not a matter of words but of meaning. Briggs affirmed plenary inspiration and the infallibility of the Bible; he rejected verbal inspiration and inerrancy. "The form is credible, the substance alone is infallible," said Briggs, "but inerrancy is neither a scriptural nor a symbolical nor a historical term in connection with the subject of Inspiration." According to Briggs, interpretation had to be historical—but also Christocentric: "The Scriptures cannot be understood from the outside by grammar, logic, rhetoric, and history alone. The Bible cannot be understood when involved in the labyrinth of its doctrines. The Bible is to be understood from its centre—its heart—its Christ."[6]

In 1891, Briggs was installed in the newly established Edward Robinson Professorship of Biblical Theology. His inaugural speech addressed the problem of biblical authority.[7] According to Briggs, there are three sources of divine authority: church, reason, and Scripture. The true authority of Scripture, he complained, had to contend with superstition and do battle with bibliolatry. Briggs expanded his polemic in a book entitled *The Bible, the Church and the Reason: The Three Great Foundations of Divine Authority.*[8] In the appendix he listed heroes of the faith who, he believed, shared his opposition to inerrancy, including Augustine, Luther, and Calvin.

In response, editorials and articles in both the religious and the secular press attacked Briggs. His case was tried at the presbyterial and national level. After five days of tedious testimony, the New York presbytery acquitted him, but in 1893, the General Assembly of the Presbyterian Church found Briggs guilty of teaching doctrine contrary to Scripture, and suspended him from the ministry. In the course of the controversy, Union severed its connection with the General Assembly and proceeded as an ecumenical seminary. Briggs abandoned the Presbyterian Church and was ordained an Episcopal priest in 1899. Briggs was active in ecumenical affairs and promoted unity between Catholic modernists and liberal Protestants on the basis of historical criticism.

---

6. Charles Augustus Briggs, *Biblical Study: Its Principles, Methods, and History, together with a Catalogue of Books of Reference* (New York: Charles Scribner's Sons, 1883), 1, 241, 364. On Briggs's Christology, see M. James Sawyer, *Charles Augustus Briggs and Tensions in Late Nineteenth-Century Theology* (Lewiston: Mellen University Press, 1994).

7. *The Authority of Holy Scripture: An Inaugural Address,* 2d ed. (New York: Charles Scribner's Sons, 1891); repr., *Inaugural Address and Defense, 1891/1893,* Religion in America (New York: Arno, 1972).

8. (New York: Charles Scribner's Sons, 1892).

Biblical scholars remember Briggs for his work on the venerable Brown-Driver-Briggs Hebrew Lexicon.[9] However, when he moved to the Robinson chair, Briggs turned increasingly to the study of the NT. This is evident in the revision and expansion of his earlier *Biblical Study* under the title *General Introduction to the Study of Holy Scripture*. For example, in a chapter on the practice of higher criticism, Briggs presents his understanding of NT sources:

> The Gospel of Matthew is a compilation, using the Gospel of Mark and the Logia of Matthew as the chief sources. The Gospel of Luke is a compilation, using the same Gospel of Mark and the Logia of Matthew, and also other Hebraic sources for its gospel of the infancy, and possibly also, another source for the Perean ministry. The book of Acts is a compilation, using a Hebraic narrative of the early Jerusalem Church, and the "We" narrative of a co-traveler with Paul, and probably other sources.

Briggs also reaffirms his commitment to evangelical criticism:

> The valleys of biblical truth have been filled up with the débris of human dogmas, ecclesiastical institutions, liturgical formulas, priestly ceremonies, and casuistic practices. Historical criticism is digging through this mass of rubbish. Historical criticism is searching for the rock-bed of divine truth and for the massive foundations of the Divine Word, in order to recover the real Bible.[10]

Briggs's major contribution to NT research is his investigation of the idea of the Messiah. While still in the Davenport chair, he published a book on the understanding of the Messiah in the HB.[11] In this book, Briggs traces the development of the messianic idea from primitive forms to its highest expression in Isaiah 40–66, prophecy fulfilled in Jesus. "All its phases find their realization in His unique personality, in His unique work, and in His unique kingdom. The Messiah of prophecy," says Briggs, "appears in the

---

9. Francis Brown, S. R. Driver, Charles A. Briggs, *A Hebrew and English Lexicon of the Old Testament, with an Appendix Containing the Biblical Aramaic: Based on the Lexicon of William Gesenius as Translated by Edward Robinson* (Oxford: Clarendon Press, 1980). Originally published in 1907, this lexicon was a reworking of Robinson's 1836 translation of Gesenius. S. R. Driver (professor of Hebrew at Oxford) wrote the articles on pronouns, prepositions, adverbs, conjunctions, and particles. Briggs wrote several articles important for religion, theology, and psychology. Brown (who succeeded Briggs in the Davenport chair) wrote the remaining articles and was responsible for general editing. Many of Brigg's notes for the *Lexicon*, clearly written in his own hand on five by seven-inch pages, are preserved in the Special Collections of the Union Theological Seminary Library. Briggs was also one of the founding editors (with S. R. Driver and Alfred Plummer) of the *International Critical Commentary* series that began to appear in 1895; see p. 207, above.

10. *General Introduction to the Study of Holy Scripture: Principles, Methods, History, and Results of Its Several Departments and of the Whole* (New York: Charles Scribner's Sons, 1899), 327, 531.

11. *Messianic Prophecy: The Prediction of the Fulfilment of Redemption through the Messiah: A Critical Study of the Messianic Passages of the Old Testament in the Order of Their Development*, 7th ed. (New York: Charles Scribner's Sons, 1898); first edition was published in 1886.

Messiah of history."[12] Turning to the NT, Briggs published *The Messiah of the Gospels*. In investigating Mark, Briggs acknowledges, but qualifies, Jesus' idea that the end was near. "It was near in the prophetic sense—that is, the event was certain, but the time uncertain." Matthew, according to Briggs, rightly presents miracles as proof of Jesus' messiahship. However, Briggs believes the miracles of Jesus were not primarily "marvels of miracle-working, displaying power; but miracles of mercy—the healing of the sick, the lame, the blind, the lepers, the deaf and the raising of the dead." Following Luke, Briggs believes Jesus was conscious of his messianic calling at the time of his visit to the temple at twelve years of age.[13]

Briggs goes on to consider *The Messiah of the Apostles*. In investigating the Messiah of the Jewish Christians, he uses the early chapters of Acts, James, and 1 and 2 Peter (both accepted as authentic). In 1 Peter, Briggs detects a novel concept. "The pre-existence of the Messiah as the lamb of sacrifice in the foreknowledge of God is new to the Messianic idea." Briggs accepts all of the Epistles attributed to Paul as authentic. In a meticulous analysis, Briggs argues that Revelation is a composite document, made up of several early apocalyptic sources, each with its distinctive understanding of the Messiah. Regarding the Fourth Gospel, he writes, "The Prologue of the Gospel of John, and the comments of the writer upon his report of the words of Jesus, give us the crown of the structure of the Christology of the New Testament."[14]

Briggs published two books on the life and teaching of Jesus. In *New Light on the Life of Jesus*, Briggs is primarily concerned with chronology.[15] Anticipating K. L. Schmidt, he believes that neither Mark nor John can be followed.[16] Briggs attempts to answer two questions: When did Jesus begin his ministry? What did Jesus do while his disciples were engaged in mission? Regarding the first, he contends that Jesus had a ministry in Galilee prior to the arrest of John the Baptist. Regarding the second, he concludes that Jesus conducted a mission in Judea and Perea while the disciples were carrying out their mission. Briggs speculates that during this time Jesus was accompanied by pairs of disciples: in Judea, with James and John (so that John was able to report the ministry in Jerusalem), in Perea with Matthew and Thomas (so that Matthew's Logia could report Jesus' teachings in Perea). In regard to the Fourth Gospel, Briggs detects layers of tradition: some go back to the apostle John; some are later. For example, sections of the Gospel that refer to the "Jews" and sections that describe the miracles as

---

12. Ibid., 498.
13. *The Messiah of the Gospels* (New York: Charles Scribner's Sons, 1894), 156, 177–78.
14. *The Messiah of the Apostles* (New York: Charles Scribner's Sons, 1895), 48, 462–63.
15. *New Light on the Life of Jesus* (New York: Charles Scribner's Sons, 1904).
16. On Schmidt, see pp. 270–73, above.

"signs" are late. Briggs thinks an original gospel written by the apostle John was edited by a pupil (who prefixed the prologue); chapter 21 was added by a third hand.

In *The Ethical Teaching of Jesus*, Briggs bemoans the lack of attention given to biblical ethics. He thinks Jesus understood the kingdom in three ways: as the kingdom that has been planted and continues to grow, as the kingdom that was coming soon (a prophecy fulfilled at Pentecost), and as the kingdom that would be consummated at the second advent. According to Briggs, Jesus proclaimed a righteousness in sharp contrast to the Pharisees, who "were content if they kept safely within the bounds of external obedience, and felt free to do any amount of wickedness in secret, and even in public, beyond the range of its prohibitions." "The superior righteousness that Jesus had in mind, was . . . a righteousness inspired by a personal relationship to the Father and the Son, and animated by the principle of Christ-like love."[17]

James Moffatt (1870–1944)

Briggs was followed at Union by a succession of brilliant scholars. Mention should be made of Ernest Findlay Scott, British in origin and education, who taught in Canada, and served on the Union faculty from 1919 to 1938. He succeeded M. R. Vincent, who contributed the volume on Philippians and Philemon to the ICC. Scott was noted for his work on the Fourth Gospel and a widely used introduction to the NT.[18] An older contemporary of Scott was J. E. Frame, whose commentary on the Thessalonian letters was also in the ICC. Another immigrant, F. J. Foakes Jackson, who was a dean at Cambridge, was a member of the Union faculty from 1916 to 1933, and was recognized for his work with Kirsopp Lake on the five-volume *The Beginnings of Christianity* (1920–33).[19] But the greatest of these was James Moffatt.

Moffatt was born in Glasgow and educated at the University of Glasgow.[20] After serving parishes in Scotland, he was appointed professor of NT at Mansfield College, Oxford (1911). From 1915 to 1927, Moffatt was Professor of Church History at the Theological College in Glasgow. In 1927, he moved to New York and assumed the Washburn Chair of Church History at Union, where he remained until his retirement in 1938. After retirement, Moffatt lectured from time to time at Drew University, and devoted himself to the work of the translation committee of the Revised Standard Version.

---

17. *The Ethical Teaching of Jesus* (New York: Charles Scribner's Sons, 1904), 167–68, 162.
18. *The Fourth Gospel: Its Purpose and Theology*, 2d ed. (Edinburgh: T. & T. Clark, 1908); idem, *The Literature of the New Testament* (New York: Columbia University Press, 1932).
19. See pp. 409–10, below.
20. See Ernest Findlay Scott, "James Moffatt, 1870–1944," *Religion in Life* 14 (1944–1945): 24–31; E. Best, "Moffatt, James (1880–1944)," in *DBI* 2:159–60; A. J. Gossip, "James Moffatt," *ExpTim* 56 (1944–45): 14–17.

When one of the members of the committee pointed out that a rendering that Moffatt had opposed in the deliberations had actually been taken from Moffatt's own *New Testament,* he replied, "Well, that phrase was right for my translation, but it will not do for this."[21]

Moffatt was a historian, not a theologian, but he was a person of authentic piety who revered the witness of the NT to God's revelation in Christ. His Hibbert Lectures of 1921 are essentially an apology for the historical method. According to Moffatt, this method "shows us the New Testament exactly as it is, neither less nor more. And by putting it back into its original setting the historical method allows it to make its timeless appeal to the conscience and the imagination."[22] In Moffatt's opinion, the historical method cannot engender a religious experience, but it can explicate the vital religious experience of the early Christians so as to stimulate faith for today. In his Shaffer Lectures at Yale (1940), Moffatt declares that the Bible has sacramental power: God speaks through it. Through the Bible, according to Moffatt, "God's self-revelation enters into history and experience, to carry out his purpose and to realize his will, pre-eminently through the life of Jesus Christ on earth."[23]

Moffatt's most important work is his *Introduction* to the NT.[24] He prepared for this work by his earlier *The Historical New Testament.* The earlier book is a presentation of the documents of the NT in chronological order, translated by Moffatt, with historical introductions. In the preface of the first edition, Moffatt bewails the sad state of the science of introduction "hampered by the resurrection of the obsolete, the survival of the unfit, and the prominence of the irrelevant."[25] Moffatt's massive (more than 650 pages) *Introduction* first appeared in 1911; it was slightly revised in 1918 and was frequently reprinted. In the first chapter, Moffatt takes up the Pauline Epistles. He accepts 2 Thessalonians as authentic. He supports the north Galatian hypothesis. He arranges the Corinthian correspondence in four letters: the letter mentioned in 1 Cor. 5:9 (of which a fragment may be found in 2 Cor. 6:14—7:1); 1 Corinthians (which he takes as a unity); the intermediate letter (part of which Moffatt finds in 2 Corinthians 10—13); 2 Corinthians 1–9 (written from Macedonia). Moffatt believes Romans 16

---

21. Quoted by Luther Weigle, *British Weekly,* August 10, 1944, 227.
22. *The Approach to the New Testament,* Hibbert Lectures, 1921, 4th ed. (London: Hodder and Stoughton, 1922), 9.
23. *Jesus Christ the Same: The Shaffer Lectures for 1940 in the Divinity School of Yale University* (New York: Abingdon-Cokesbury, 1940), 208.
24. *An Introduction to the Literature of the New Testament,* 3d ed., ITL (Edinburgh: T. & T. Clark, 1918).
25. *The Historical New Testament: Being the Literature of the New Testament Arranged in the Order of Its Literary Growth and according to the Dates of the Documents; A New Translation: Edited with Prolegomena, Historical Tables, Critical Notes, and an Appendix,* 2d ed. (Edinburgh: T. & T. Clark, 1901), xvii.

was originally a separate letter sent to Ephesus. In regard to Colossians, Moffatt argues for authenticity, and rejects complicated composition theories (like Holtzmann's).[26] He notes that the address to Philemon also includes Apphia, so that this letter is the only epistle in the NT addressed to a woman.

In analyzing the historical literature of the NT, Moffatt devotes forty pages to the Synoptic Problem, and adopts a version of the two-document hypothesis. He asserts, "the priority of Mark to Matthew and Luke no longer requires to be proved." In regard to the tradition, Moffatt contends that what Papias ascribes to Mark is actually an *Urmarcus*, and that the Logia of Matthew (Q) is not a real gospel. "It is thus an apostolic Aramaic treatise which has every likelihood of having been composed prior not only to Mark, but to the Ur-Marcus; it reflects the faith, mission, and sufferings of the primitive Jewish Christian church of Palestine, long before the crisis of 70 A.D. began to loom on the horizon."[27] Moffatt believes that the Gospel of Mark, using the *Urmarcus*, was composed shortly after 70, possibly in Rome. The author of Matthew, writing between 70 and 110, follows Mark, but arranges the material topically. According to Moffatt, the author of Luke uses Aramaic sources in his first two chapters; his special section (9:51—18:34) is a topical arrangement, not an actual travel narrative. Acts makes use of sources, notably the diary of a travel companion of Paul whom Moffatt identifies as Luke the Physician, author of Luke and Acts.

A chapter on "Homilies and Pastorals" treats the rest of the NT Epistles. Moffatt accepts 1 Peter as authentic, though he believes Sylvanus to have been the amanuensis. In Moffatt's judgment, 2 Peter is not authentic nor is Ephesians—a homily that "may be fairly regarded as a set of variations played by a master hand upon one or two themes suggested by Colossians."[28] The Pastorals, according to Moffatt, are treatises written by an unknown Paulinist, probably incorporating some authentic Pauline fragments. A separate chapter on Revelation argues that it is a composite document, written in the time of Domitian (using earlier sources) and edited in the period of Trajan. An extensive chapter on the Fourth Gospel argues that chapter 21 was added by an editor who mistakenly identified the author as an eyewitness. All in all, Moffatt's *Introduction* is a judicious work of enormous erudition that leaves no critical problem untouched.

Moffatt is also remembered for his translation of the NT. His *The New Testament: A New Translation* first appeared in 1913 and later was revised.[29] Moffatt's command of the ancient languages fully qualified him as a translator,

---

26. See p. 114, above.
27. *Introduction*, 180, 203.
28. Ibid., 375.
29. *The New Testament: A New Translation* (New York: Harper & Brothers, 1935).

but he was also skilled in English literature; he wrote a book on the novelist George Meredith and a study of the use of the Bible in Scottish literature. Although the English Revised Version of 1881 offered an accurate translation, it retained the antiquated language of the KJV. In response, new translations, like Moffatt's, appeared.[30] Moffatt, in his preface, writes, "I have endeavoured to make the New Testament, especially St. Paul's epistles, as intelligible to a modern English reader as any version that is not a paraphrase can hope to make them."[31] For example, Moffatt's rendering of Gal. 5:11-12:

> I am 'still preaching circumcision myself,' am I? Then, brothers, why am I still being persecuted? And so the stumbling-block of the cross has lost its force, forsooth! O that those who are upsetting you would get themselves castrated!

Later, exercising his command of Hebrew, Moffatt published a translation of the whole Bible.[32]

Moffatt wrote NT commentaries, the most important of which is a volume for the ICC on *Hebrews*. In an extensive introduction (more than sixty pages), Moffatt argues that the title, "to the Hebrews," was added because of the mistaken notion that the letter was addressed to Jewish Christians. He believes internal evidence proves that the recipients were Gentile Christians who revered the LXX. Moffatt thinks the author was an unidentified Alexandrian who used symbolism, emphasized worship, and acclaimed the finality of God's revelation in Christ.

> The symbolism of the high priesthood and sacrifice of Jesus in the heavenly sanctuary is therefore designed to convey the truth that the relations of men with God are based finally upon Jesus Christ. In the unseen world which is conceived in this naive idealistic way, Jesus is central; through him God is known and accessible to man, and through him man enjoys forgiveness and fellowship with God.[33]

In format, the commentary arranges the material in sections, which are introduced by analyses and general comments, and the text in Moffatt's translation. The comments that follow investigate Greek terms and phrases; secondary and more detailed exegesis is presented in smaller type, and footnotes consider text-critical matters and provide references to ancient and modern sources.

---

30. Among others, an anonymous group of twenty scholars produced *The Twentieth Century New Testament* (1898–1901), and Richard Francis Weymouth published *The Modern Speech New Testament* in 1903.

31. *New Testament*, viii.

32. *A New Translation of the Bible: Containing the Old and New Testaments* (New York: Harper & Brothers, 1926).

33. *A Critical and Exegetical Commentary on the Epistle to the Hebrews,* ICC (Edinburgh: T. & T. Clark, 1924), liii.

Moffatt's comments on Hebrews 1:1-4 may serve as an example. He notes that these verses represent a single sentence that has two subjects: God (vv. 1-2) and the Son (vv. 3-4). The cosmic significance of the Son is mentioned (v. 2) and the author affirms the connection between redemption and creation. Moffatt proceeds through the verses, commenting on Greek phrases, noting parallels in classical sources, and explicating the meaning. For example, the phrase ἐλάλησεν ἡμῖν ("he has spoken to us") includes not only those who heard Jesus, but the revelation to all God's people, including the readers; it does not describe simply the teaching of Jesus, but the whole and final revelation of God in Christ. According to Moffatt, the phrase ἐν ὑψηλοῖς ("on high") is not used by any other NT writer; Moffatt believes that it goes grammatically with ἐκάθισεν ("he sat down") and describes the enthronement and superiority of the Son to the angels. In general, the commentary presents linguistic and grammatical analysis in the service of historical interpretation; it remained the representative volume on Hebrews in the ICC throughout the twentieth century.

Moffatt also contributed two volumes to a series "The Moffatt New Testament Commentary," which uses Moffatt's translation as the text. Written at an intermediate level, the series has been widely used by seminarians and clergy. Moffatt's volume on 1 Corinthians is one of the best. In the introduction, he presents the historical setting, and depicts life in ancient Corinth: "Love and licentiousness formed an alloy, which, like the equally famous Corinthian bronze, was exported as well as enjoyed locally." Interpreting 1:10-17, Moffatt notes that Paul describes the factions of the church in terms used in political discussion by authors such as Aristotle, Herodotus, and Thucydides. In regard to the Christ-party, Moffatt speculates that they may be a group of "ultra-spiritual devotees or high-flying Gnostics who made a mystical Christ, no human leader, the center of religion."[34] To the same series, Moffatt had earlier contributed a commentary on the Catholic Epistles.[35] He also wrote the comments on the Thessalonian correspondence and Revelation for the five-volume "Expositor's Greek Testament," edited by W. Robertson Nicoll.[36]

On the basis of his critical and exegetical research, Moffatt reflected on the theology of the NT. *The Theology of the Gospels* presents Moffatt's understanding of the Christology of the gospel writers. However, he is primarily concerned with the theology of Jesus, which is to be discovered by an

---

34. *The First Epistle of Paul to the Corinthians,* MNTC (New York: Harper & Brothers, 1938), xviii, 10.

35. *The General Epistles: James, Peter, and Judas,* MNTC (New York: Harper & Brothers, 1928).

36. "The First and Second Epistles of Paul the Apostle to the Thessalonians"; "The Revelation of St. John the Divine," in *The Expositor's Greek Testament,* ed. W. Robertson Nicoll (Grand Rapids, Mich.: Eerdmans, 1910) 4:1–54; 5:279–494.

investigation of the theological expressions of the evangelists. In discussing eschatology, Moffatt contends that Jesus viewed the kingdom as both present and future. Jesus' idea of God stressed God as Father and affirmed "the essential affinity of man to God, the sacredness and worth of the present life, and the nearness of God to man in moral and spiritual experience."[37] Moffatt believes the evangelists' understanding of Jesus can be detected by an investigation of christological titles. The title "Son of Man" indicates both the faith of the gospel writers and the self-understanding of Jesus. Moffatt thinks Jesus used "Son of Man" as a title for himself as Messiah, but he modified this by his understanding of himself as the "Suffering Servant."

Moffatt also explicated the theology of the NT by investigating the theological terms "love" and "grace."[38] In these linguistic-theological studies, Moffatt gives attention to the background in classical and Hellenistic authors, and in the HB and Jewish sources. He carefully investigates the use of the Greek terms and their meaning in the various sections of the NT. For example, he contends, exploding a popular misconception, that φιλέω and ἀγαπάω are virtually synonymous in Hellenistic Greek and in the NT. He also asserts, to no one's surprise, that the idea of grace is fundamental to Paul's theology. Elsewhere, Moffatt argues that the center of Paul's thought is not justification, but his idea of the Spirit.[39]

In sum, the Union scholars highlight features of American research. For one, Americans continued to look to the east—sending their professors to Germany to study (Briggs) or importing scholars from Europe to teach (Moffatt). The life and trials of Briggs dramatize another aspect of the American scene: the divisive battle over inspiration. Although essentially conservative on theological and critical issues, Briggs was branded a heretic because he could not subscribe to inerrancy—and also, no doubt, because of his combative behavior. The irenic Moffatt moved much farther to the left on critical matters, harbinger of American liberal criticism. Both Briggs and Moffatt were totally committed to the historical-critical method, embraced as essential to historical and theological understanding.

---

37. *Theology of the Gospels,* Studies in Theology (New York: Charles Scribner's Sons, 1920), 97.
38. *Love in the New Testament* (London: Hodder and Stoughton, 1929); idem, *Grace in the New Testament* (New York: Ray Long & Richard R. Smith, 1932).
39. *Paul and Paulinism,* Modern Religious Problems (Boston: Pilgrim, 1910).

NEW TESTAMENT RESEARCH AT YALE: BENJAMIN WISNER BACON

In the past, Yale had produced scholars such as Jonathan Edwards and Moses Stuart; the tradition was continued at the end of the nineteenth and the beginning of the twentieth century.[40] A notable example is George Barker Stevens (1854–1906). Stevens studied at Yale and in Germany, and in 1886 was appointed professor of NT criticism and interpretation at Yale. In 1895, he moved to the chair of systematic theology, but retained his interest in biblical research. Stevens published a book on the theology of Paul in which he argued that the apostle did not affirm original sin or total depravity.[41] Paul, according to Stevens, advocated an ethical rather than a juridical idea of atonement, and saw love as the essence of God.[42] In a book on the theology of John, Stevens contends that the Fourth Gospel and the Johannine Epistles were written by John the Apostle. According to Stevens, John offers a special theology, mystical and spiritual, and expresses a "moral dualism." Stevens thinks that John "sees the future as already implicit in the present; eternal life as already begun here."[43]

Stevens's best-known book is his *Theology of the New Testament*. In the first part, he presents the teaching of Jesus as recorded in the Synoptic Gospels. In contrast to the Jews who understood the kingdom of God in a nationalistic sense, Jesus, according to Stevens, saw it as spiritual and ethical, present and future. Jesus did not, in Stevens's view, predict his triumphal return within his own generation; that was a mistaken notion of the disciples, who confused Jesus' prediction of the destruction of Jerusalem with his vision of the future consummation. Stevens discusses the theology of the primitive apostles using the discourses of Acts, the Epistle of James, 1 Peter, and Jude as sources.[44] Stevens finds no conflict between James and Paul, but he

---

40. See Roland H. Bainton, *Yale and the Ministry: A History of Education for the Christian Ministry at Yale from the Founding in 1701* (New York: Harper & Brothers, 1957).

41. *The Pauline Theology: A Study of the Origin and Correlation of the Doctrinal Teachings of the Apostle Paul*, rev. ed. (New York: Charles Scribner's Sons, 1897). Stevens had demonstrated his exegetical skill in his *A Short Exposition of the Epistle to the Galatians: Designed as a Text-Book for Class-Room Use and for Private Study* (Hartford: Student Publishing, 1890). Stevens also contributed a book on Paul to the series "The Messages of the Bible," a collection of twelve small volumes covering the whole Bible, edited by Frank K. Sanders and Charles F. Kent: *XI The Messages of Paul: Arranged in Historical Order, Analyzed, and Freely Rendered in Paraphrase, with Introductions* (New York: Charles Scribner's Sons, 1900).

42. Late in life, Stevens wrote *The Christian Doctrine of Salvation*, ITL (New York: Charles Scribner's Sons, 1911), in which he argues that the ethical understanding of atonement is affirmed by Jesus as well as Paul.

43. *The Johannine Theology: A Study of the Doctrinal Contents of the Gospel and Epistles of the Apostle John*, rev. ed. (New York: Charles Scribner's Sons, 1904), 12, 354.

44. Stevens also authored the twelfth volume of "The Messages of the Bible": *XII The Messages of the Apostles: The Apostolic Discourses in the Book of Acts and the General and Pastoral Epistles of the New Testament Arranged in Chronological Order, Analyzed, and Freely Rendered in Paraphrase* (New York: Charles Scribner's Sons, 1900).

detects development in the thought of Peter: at his confession Peter could not accept the suffering of Christ; in the discourses of Acts, he sees the suffering of Christ as according to the saving purpose of God; in 1 Peter, he presents the death of Christ as means of redemption. A section on the Epistle to the Hebrews argues that the author employed the Alexandrian model of two worlds—the external and the invisible—to contrast the old religious system of Judaism to the new religion revealed in Christ. In discussing the theology of Revelation, Stevens is critical of apocalyptic thought because it fails to see that the purposes of God work gradually. Nevertheless, he concludes, "Our Apocalypse, despite its obscurities, stands as a splendid testimony to the undaunted confidence of a persecuted Church that goodness is mightier than evil and that the Kingdom of God will at length prevail."[45]

Benjamin Wisner Bacon (1860–1932)

An important younger colleague of Stevens was Frank Chamberlin Porter, a Yale Ph.D. who taught at the Divinity School from 1889 to 1927. Porter made an impact on his students (including Reinhold and H. Richard Niebuhr) and was especially remembered for his *The Mind of Christ in Paul* (1932). However, his work was eclipsed by the brilliant research of Benjamin Bacon.

Bacon was born in Litchfield, Connecticut, son of a Congregational pastor.[46] As a youth, Bacon studied in preparatory schools in Germany and Switzerland. He continued his education at Yale, where his prowess on the gridiron earned him the title "Freight Train Bacon." Nevertheless, academic awards in classics encouraged him to switch from medicine to ministry. In 1881, he entered the Divinity School and supported himself by playing the violin and leading an orchestra. When Stevens switched to systematic theology, Bacon was given a temporary appointment to teach NT at Yale. In 1897, he was named Buckingham Professor of New Testament Criticism, a position he retained until his retirement in 1928. One of his students, Robert L. Calhoun (who has later to grace the Yale faculty), wrote:

> I seem to remember from the first day onward a marvelous intricacy of internal and external evidence, patristic parallels, Aramaic originals, single, double, and triple traditions, *logia* and redactions, unrolling imperturbably as the Amazon, for us to sink or swim in as we might. Most of us sank . . . yet we did not wholly drown. . . . The inexhaustible patience and gracious restlessness of

---

45. *The Theology of the New Testament*, 2d ed. (1906; repr., ITL; New York: Charles Scribner's Sons, 1946), 562.
46. See Roy A. Harrisville, *Benjamin Wisner Bacon: Pioneer in American Biblical Criticism*, SBL Studies in American Biblical Scholarship 2, Schools and Scholars 2 (Missoula, Mont.: Scholars Press, 1976); Bainton, *Yale and the Ministry*, 213–19; Benjamin Wisner Bacon, "Enter the Higher Criticism," in *Contemporary American Theology: Theological Autobiographies*, 2 vols., ed. Vergilius Ferm (New York: Round Table, 1932) 1:1–50.

a teacher whose full mind engulfed ours and carried them along by massed learning and fluent thought gave us confidence.[47]

Although he had studied in Europe and lectured at Oxford, Bacon never earned a Ph.D. Late in his career he wrote, "I could not even today pass a Yale Ph.D. examination in the required subjects"[48]—an unjustified expression of modesty. Breslau, Oxford, and Harvard awarded him honorary doctorates.

Above all, Benjamin Bacon was a biblical critic. "So far as my life-work has contributed to the development of theology in America," he wrote, "it has been through securing to the methods and results of the higher criticism their rightful place in the progressive work of Reformers, Puritans, and New England divines."[49] His criticism, however, was based on a theology of history, reminiscent of German idealism and the thought of F. C. Baur.[50] Bacon saw history as an evolving process in which God was at work. Like Baur, he interpreted primitive Christian documents in relation to the developing history—to the tensions, conflicts, and syntheses of early Christianity. Reminiscent of the practitioners of history of religion, he adopted an etiological method to discern the origin of religious practices and beliefs.[51] Bacon distinguished two gospels in the NT: the gospel *of* Jesus (Jesus' consciousness of God); and the gospel *about* Jesus (the christological confessions of the early Christians). Bacon believed the modern Christian needed both the religion of Jesus and faith in Christ as modeled in the synthesis of John. Bacon's own faith was Christocentric. He wrote, "An impartial historical estimate will admit that Jesus' life and teachings constitute the highest revelation of man to himself, and since 'the invisible things of the creation are perceived through the things that are made,' this revelation is also the highest of God to man."[52]

An overview of Bacon's NT criticism can be seen in his *Introduction*, written a decade before Moffatt's.[53] Bacon uncharacteristically avoids technical language, but packs the book with critical data. Beginning with the Pauline Letters, Bacon supports the south Galatian hypothesis and the authenticity of 2 Thessalonians. He divides the Corinthian correspondence into the same four letters later identified by Moffatt. He accepts Colossians and

---

47. Quoted by Bainton, *Yale and the Ministry*, 218.
48. "Enter Higher Criticism," 34.
49. Ibid., 1.
50. See *HNTR* 1:258–69.
51. See pp. 222, 238–53, above.
52. Benjamin W. Bacon, *The Sermon on the Mount: Its Literary Structure and Didactic Purpose* (New York: Macmillan, 1902), 1–2.
53. *An Introduction to the New Testament*, New Testament Handbooks (New York: Macmillan, 1902). Later, Bacon published another introduction to the NT, shorter and written for the nonspecialist: *The Making of the New Testament*, Home University Library (New York: Henry Holt, 1912).

Ephesians (locating both in Rome) as authentic, and believes the Pastorals may contain genuine Pauline fragments. Regarding the Synoptic Problem Bacon writes, "The current 'two document" theory—our Mark and the *Logia* as the principal sources of Matthew and Luke—may, therefore, be considered permanently established as giving in outline the ultimate solution."[54] In regard to Luke, he questions the traditional authorship and argues that the author of Acts used a diary written by a travel companion of Paul.

Much of Bacon's scholarly effort was concentrated on the Gospels. In his *Beginnings of the Gospel Story*, Bacon, anticipating form criticism, presents his basic approach:

> The motive of the biblical writers in reporting the tradition current around them is never strictly historical, but always etiological, and frequently apologetic. In other words, their report is not framed to satisfy the curiosity of the critical historian, but, as they frankly acknowledge, to confirm the faith of believers "in the things wherein they have been instructed," to convince the unconverted, or to refute the unbeliever. The evangelic tradition consists of so and so many anecdotes, told and retold *for the purpose of explaining or defending beliefs and practices of the contemporary Church*.[55]

The book is basically a commentary on Mark with a critical introduction. In the introduction, Bacon investigates the tradition and sources used in the composition. He believes the final redactor (R), writing after the destruction of Jerusalem, made use of two major sources: a Petrine narrative (P), and Q. Bacon thinks the earliest tradition about Jesus did not identify him as the apocalyptic Son of Man—an identification the redactor derives from Q. "The apocalyptic conception of Jesus as the Son of man destined to return upon the clouds of heaven seems to be editorially superimposed upon the old Petrine tradition, leaving as the historical significance attached by Jesus himself to his mission the purely religio-ethical and humanitarian."[56] In the commentary, the text, in English translation (RV), is printed at the top of the page, with marginal indications (P, Q, R) of the sources.

Bacon carries on his investigation of the second Gospel in *Is Mark a Roman Gospel?*[57] In regard to the tradition that Mark preserves the reminiscences of Peter, Bacon believes Papias imagined the idea on the basis of his reading of 1 Peter 5:13. Although Bacon has come to the conclusion that

---

54. *Introduction*, 188.
55. *The Beginnings of the Gospel Story: A Historico-Critical Inquiry into the Sources and Structure of the Gospel according to Mark, with Expository Notes upon the Text, for English Readers*, The Modern Commentary (New Haven: Yale University Press, 1909), ix.
56. Ibid., xxxviii.
57. Benjamin W. Bacon, *Is Mark a Roman Gospel?* HTS 7 (Cambridge: Harvard University Press, 1919).

1 Peter is not authentic (reversing the view he had expressed in his *Introduction*), he believes it preserves authentic tradition. Bacon thinks the Gospel of Mark would not have survived unless it had been supported by an important church; that church, he believes, must have been Rome. Bacon supports this conclusion with other evidence: the use of Latinisms, mistakes in Palestinian geography, and Mark's identification of the Last Supper as a Passover meal in support of the Roman position in the Quartodeciman controversy. The final redaction, Bacon thinks, represents a postapostolic harmonizing of the Petrine and Pauline traditions.

The plot thickens with the publication of Bacon's *The Gospel of Mark: Its Composition and Date*. According to Bacon, Papias's observation that Mark did not write the account in order implies that Mark was written after the death of Peter, that is, at a time when Peter would not have been able to correct Mark's arrangement. Also, by means of a complex analysis of Mark 13, Bacon detects an early apocalyptic tradition (originating in the time of Caligula) which was taken up and used by Paul in 2 Thessalonians. In regard to the parables of Mark 4, Bacon discovers a pre-Marcan collection that includes material from Q, influenced by Paul. Bacon also contends that the Christology of Mark is essentially Pauline. Taking all the evidence into consideration, Bacon dates the composition of Mark at around 80.

> In a sense far from that contemplated by the critics of Tübingen Mark is the Gospel of Peter and Paul. Not in an effort at compromise between opposing parties in the Church does it seek the welfare of the whole, but conscious of the great message each Apostle had to convey, and in the spirit of their heroic martyrdom, it opens to the universal brotherhood of Christ the treasure of its apostolic teaching. . . . Not Matthew, as Renan said, mistaking a mere transcript for the original, is the most influential book ever written, but Mark, earliest of our extant Gospels, the first attempt to give to the world a joint message from the martyred Peter and Paul.[58]

In 1910, Bacon published *The Fourth Gospel in Research and Debate*—a book primarily concerned with authorship.[59] Bacon begins with a meticulous investigation of the external evidence. He argues that the tradition for the early martyrdom of the apostle John is strong, and that prior to Irenaeus, a tradition in support of apostolic authorship for the Fourth Gospel is meager. Turning to internal evidence, Bacon argues that the author of the Fourth Gospel used Mark. The details that the author adds to the Marcan framework are, in Bacon's opinion, not the observations of an eyewitness, but apologetic and doctrinal additions. All of this leads Bacon to the

---

58. *The Gospel of Mark: Its Composition and Date* (New Haven: Yale University Press, 1925), 334.
59. *The Fourth Gospel in Research and Debate* (New York: Moffatt, Yard, 1910). For an analysis of Bacon's work on the Fourth Gospel, see D. Moody Smith, "B. W. Bacon on John and Mark," *Perspectives in Religious Studies* 8 (1981): 201–18.

conclusion that the traditional belief in apostolic authorship is untenable.

Bacon's final word on the Gospel of John is expressed in *The Gospel of the Hellenists*, published posthumously. In this book, Bacon comes to the conclusion that the author of the Fourth Gospel is the Elder of Ephesus. The mistaken notion that this Elder's name was John is the result of confusion with the "John" of Revelation—a pseudonym there for the apostle John. Bacon believes a form of Christianity emerged in Ephesus prior to Paul that had its source in Samaria, where Gnosticism and the sect of John the Baptist had flourished—a Hellenistic syncretism that influenced the Elder. According to Bacon, the composition of the Gospel took place in three stages: a composition of discourses, each introduced by a sign (written by the Elder); the expansion of the discourses into a narrative and the addition of the prologue (also by the Elder); editing by a second-century redactor who adapted the material to the Synoptic pattern and added the appendix (chapter 21). Bacon argues that the Gospel plays an important role in transforming the Petrine message of the Synoptics into the universal message of Christianity:

> The Jesus of history remains a glorified martyr of Jewish Messianism unless we see in him also the universal, eternal Christ of Paul—an incarnation of the revealing and redemptive Wisdom of God never to be transcended in human form. Upon this doctrine of the Greek-speaking Church Johannine Christology is built, and upon it the religion of the future must stand, as has the living religion of the past.[60]

Bacon's penchant for meticulous analysis and complex reconstruction is also seen in his *Studies in Matthew*. Bacon believes this Gospel had its origin in Syria, and was composed by a converted rabbi who presents a neo-legalistic understanding of the Christian message. Besides the Gospel of Mark and Q, this redactor, according to Bacon, used S (a primitive source underlying Q), M (a special Matthean source), L (Luke's special source), and N (early Jewish Christian tradition). In discussing the themes of Matthew, Bacon acknowledges that Jesus may have used the title Son of Man—a title that increasingly took on apocalyptic meaning after the crucifixion. Bacon concludes that Matthew represents "a late and degenerate type of Synoptic tradition." Nevertheless, when the debris is cleared away, the authentic religion of Jesus shines through. For example, beneath the Sermon on the Mount is an original discourse of Jesus. "All parts of the discourse alike, exordium, theme and application, are visibly dominated by the characteris-

---

60. *The Gospel of the Hellenists*, ed. Carl H. Kraeling (New York: Henry Holt, 1933), 309–10. Attention to early Christology is also given in Bacon's *The Apostolic Message: A Historical Inquiry* (New York: Century, 1925), and in his *Jesus the Son of God or Primitive Christology: Three Essays and a Discussion* (New Haven: Yale University Press, 1911).

tic feature of Jesus' religious thought, his unswerving faith in the all-wise, all-loving, all-controlling Father in heaven."[61]

With Benjamin Bacon, American scholarship reached parity with the Europeans. He demonstrates mastery of the sources, analytical skill, and originality—all grounded in a theological understanding of history. Bacon was alert to the complex interrelation of early Christian literature and developing Christian tradition. His risky reconstructions, like the crenellated turrets of an intricate sand castle, would be washed away by later scholarship. Yet his dedication to biblical research, the passion with which he worked, his refusal to surrender to easy answers—all this would inspire and confound students for years to come.

THE CHICAGO SCHOOL:
ERNEST DEWITT BURTON, SHAILER MATHEWS, SHIRLEY JACKSON CASE, EDGAR JOHNSON GOODSPEED

Whereas Bacon's intricate NT criticism was intelligible only to the intellectual elite, the Chicago School took its message to the masses.[62] "We had a Cause," wrote Shailer Mathews, "the extension of correct, and as we believed, inspiring views of the Bible. We could not be cloistered scholars; we were to serve a religious movement."[63] This cause had been present since the founding of the new University of Chicago in 1892. The first president was William Rainey Harper (1856–1906), a Yale Ph.D. who had taught at the Baptist Union Theological Seminary in Morgan Park, Illinois. In 1886, Harper moved to Yale, where his lectures on the HB packed the largest

---

61. *Studies in Matthew* (New York: Henry Holt, 1930), 260, 345. Earlier, Bacon had presented a book-length investigation of the Sermon: *The Sermon on the Mount: Its Literary Structure and Didactic Purpose* (New York: Macmillan, 1902). Bacon never realized his intention to write a life of Jesus, but a sketch of his project is presented in his *The Story of Jesus and the Beginnings of the Church: A Valuation of the Synoptic Record for History and for Religion* (New York: Century, 1927). According to Bacon, the decisive event in Jesus' career was his decision to take his message to Jerusalem—an action that led to his execution as an insurrectionist. Bacon believes Jesus understood himself as Messiah, interpreted according to the idea of the Suffering Servant. The teachings of Jesus, according to Bacon, were essentially ethical and religious; later tradition misconstrued them as apocalyptic.

62. Charles Harvey Arnold, *Near the Edge of Battle: A Short History of the Divinity School and the "Chicago School of Theology"* (Chicago: Divinity School Association, University of Chicago, 1966); Creighton Peden, *The Chicago School: Voices in Liberal Religious Thought* (Bristol, Ind.: Wyndham Hall, 1987); W. Creighton Peden and Jerome A. Stone, eds., *The Chicago School of Theology: Pioneers in Religious Inquiry*, vol. 1, *The Early Chicago School, 1906–1959*, Studies in American Religion 66a (Lewiston: Edwin Mellen, 1996); J. Coert Rylaarsdam, "Introduction: The Chicago School—and After," in *Transitions in Biblical Scholarship*, ed. J. Coert Rylaarsdam (Chicago: University of Chicago Press, 1968), 1–16; Robert W. Funk, "The Watershed of the American Biblical Tradition: The Chicago School, First Phase, 1892–1920," *JBL* 95 (1976): 4–22; Thomas H. Olbricht, "New Testament Studies at the University of Chicago: The First Decade 1892–1902," *ResQ* 22 (1979): 84–99.

63. Shailer Mathews, *New Faith for Old: An Autobiography* (New York: Macmillan, 1936), 72.

classroom on the campus. When the new university was founded in Chicago, with the generous support of John D. Rockefeller, Harper agreed to become president—provided he could continue to teach Hebrew. From the beginning, Chicago was dedicated to research and graduate education. The Baptist Union Seminary became the Divinity School of the University, located in the heart of the campus.

The "Chicago School" is variously identified. Arnold, for example, considers the development of the Divinity School from 1906 to 1966 to constitute the history of the Chicago School. However, he characterizes the first phase (1906–26) as "The Era of Socio-Historical Method." Rylaarsdam, who is mainly concerned with biblical research, focuses on the sociohistorical method. He sees Mathews as the pioneer and Case as the main practitioner. The method is distinctly American, with little influence from European and confessional traditions.[64] For NT research, then, it is proper to view the Chicago School as characterized by a distinctive methodology. Burton is the founder; Mathews and Case are the major representatives; Goodspeed is a colleague.

Ernest DeWitt Burton (1856–1925)

Harper had an uncanny knack for attracting talented scholars to Chicago. His choice to head the NT department was E. D. Burton.[65] Born in Granville, Ohio, Burton was the son of a Baptist minister. He studied at Griswold College in Davenport, Iowa, and Dennison University in Ohio. In 1882, he graduated from Rochester Theological Seminary, and the next year joined the faculty at Newton Theological Institution in Massachusetts. In 1887, he studied at Leipzig and traveled in Europe. At first, Burton declined Harper's offer; the students at Newton had petitioned him not to leave. But Harper's persistence and the vision of the new university, rising on the prairie south of the burgeoning city, proved irresistible. Burton served as head of the NT department from 1902 to 1923, when he was appointed president of the university, a post he held until his death from cancer in 1925. During his years at Chicago, Burton served as editor of *Biblical World* (a journal designed to communicate modern biblical study to a popular audience) and the more scholarly *American Journal of Theology*.

Burton, a person of genuine piety, was frequently attacked for his devotion to historical criticism. "To all criticisms of myself," he said, "I have only the answer that I stand where I do in my convictions because I am forced to

---

64. William J. Hynes, *Shirley Jackson Case and the Chicago School: The Socio-Historical Method*, SBLBSNA 5 (Chico, Calif.: Scholars Press, 1981), 1–14.

65. See Thomas Wakefield Goodspeed, *Ernest DeWitt Burton: A Biographical Sketch* (Chicago: University of Chicago Press, 1926); Olbricht, "New Testament Studies at the University of Chicago," 91–94; Funk, "Watershed of the American Biblical Tradition," 8–17.

stand there as an honest student of the evidence."⁶⁶ Burton's understanding of the biblical scholar's task is set forth in his essay "The Function of Interpretation in Relation to Theology."⁶⁷ According to Burton, the goal of theology "is to discover the truths concerning God, and the relation between God and the universe, and to coordinate these truths, as far as practicable, into a self-consistent system." "Theology," he continues, "sets no limits to its possible sources save the limits of the universe, and no limits to its available sources save the limits of human knowledge concerning the universe." This cosmic outlook sets the course for the concern with natural theology that characterizes the Chicago School.⁶⁸

In regard to interpretation, Burton identifies two types: the interpretation of expression, which is found in art, music, and literature; the interpretation of facts, which is the prerogative of history. The study of history, however, requires an assessment of the meaning of the facts. Biblical history, which Burton believes to present progressive revelation, has an interpretative center. "The great figure of Jesus Christ will stand forth in bold and clear relief, as the central figure of this whole history, himself the one great fact which alone gives us the clue to the meaning of the rest—the supreme and crowning revelation of all that long history of the revelation of God to man, and of man to himself." The preliminary work of the biblical historian, however, is to be completed by the theologian. "To the latter will belong, without dispute, the important task of coordination and systematization, the statement in organized form of the great truths concerning God and his relation to the world which biblical history reveals." The foundational task of interpretation must be done again and again. "But no sooner will it be once accomplished than it will require to be repeated, this time with the additional thoroughness which the results first reached enable us to attain, and so on, time after time, till we attain such perfection as is possible to human minds."⁶⁹

Early in his career, Burton gave attention to Greek grammar and linguistics. His *Syntax of Moods and Tenses in New Testament Greek* first appeared as a pamphlet in 1888 and was expanded into a book in 1893.⁷⁰ In the first part, on tenses, Burton notes that the main function of tense in NT Greek is not to denote time, but to indicate progress. In the second part, on moods, Burton

---

66. Quoted by Goodspeed, *Burton*, 44; see also "Why I Am Content to Be a Christian," in Ernest DeWitt Burton, *Christianity and the Modern World: Papers and Addresses*, ed. Harold R. Willoughby (Chicago: University of Chicago Press, 1927), 3–10.
67. "The Function of Interpretation in Relation to Theology," *AJT* 2 (1898): 52–79. For Burton's view of the scope and task of NT research, see his essay, "The Present Problems of New Testament Study," *AJT* 9 (1905): 201–37.
68. "Functions of Interpretation," 53, 55.
69. Ibid., 71, 72, 72–73.
70. Ernest DeWitt Burton, *Syntax of the Moods and Tenses in New Testament Greek*, 3d ed. (Chicago: University of Chicago Press, 1898).

analyzes the use of the moods in main and subordinate clauses. In general, his work is careful, analytical, and detailed, displaying command of classical Greek and the major NT grammars. In 1891, Burton published a monograph, *The Study of New Testament Words*, and in 1898 he expressed his intention to produce a dictionary of NT terms—a project never completed.[71] However, in the course of work on his Galatians commentary, Burton engaged in extensive linguistic research, and some of the results were published in *Spirit, Soul, and Flesh*.[72] After completion of the commentary, he took up the dictionary project again, only to be interrupted by his appointment to the university presidency. At the time of his death, he left a manuscript that was published posthumously under the title *New Testament Word Studies*.[73]

Burton's philological work came to fruition in his major work, an extensive (more than five hundred pages) commentary on *Galatians*. In the introduction, Burton presents a lengthy discussion of the history of Galatia, and concludes that the churches addressed in the epistle are the churches of the southern part of the province. As to the time and place of writing, Burton believes Galatians was written after the Jerusalem conference and after Paul's second visit to south Galatia (Acts 16:1-6). The place of writing, he thinks, was probably Ephesus, the date, c. 52. According to Burton, the letter responded to the turmoil caused by Judaizers who had invaded the Galatian churches. "But the central purpose of the letter is to arrest the progress of the judaising propaganda with its perverted gospel of salvation through works of the law, which the Galatians were on the very point of accepting, and to win them back to faith in Jesus Christ apart from works of the law, the gospel which Paul himself had taught them." Burton believes the early church was divided by three factions: the Jerusalem leaders, who accepted Paul's mission, but honored the law; the Judaizers, who insisted on keeping the law and circumcision; Paul, who affirmed the validity of the law, but rejected its authority. Religion, according to Paul, "is not conformity to statues, or non-conformity, but a spiritual relation to God expressed in the word 'faith,' and an ethical attitude toward man, summed up in the word 'love.' . . . Thus he makes religion personal rather than ecclesiastical, and morality a social relation grounded in religion." Burton believes this doctrine has its background in the prophets and is in harmony with the teachings of Jesus.[74]

---

71. *The Study of New Testament Words* (Hartford: Student Publishing, 1891).
72. *Spirit, Soul, and Flesh* (Chicago: University of Chicago Press, 1918). An appendix in Burton's commentary on Galatians presents lexicographical studies on twenty-one major Greek terms.
73. *New Testament Word Studies*, ed. Harold R. Willoughby (Chicago: University of Chicago Press, 1927).
74. *A Critical and Exegetical Commentary on the Epistle to the Galatians*, ICC (Edinburgh: T. & T. Clark, 1921), lv, lxiv.

One or two examples can illustrate Burton's exegesis. He sees Gal. 1:11-12 as part of the personal portion of the letter where Paul is defending his authority. These verses present the claim that Paul did not receive his gospel from humans, but directly from God. Burton attends to detail. For example, in regard to v. 11, he discusses the textual variant δέ in place of γάρ, and concludes that γάρ is preferable. In discussing the phrase τὸ εὐαγγέλιον τὸ εὐαγγελισθὲν ὑπ' ἐμοῦ Burton says the use of the aorist tense indicates that Paul is referring to the gospel he had preached in Galatia. The word ἀποκαλύπτω (v. 12) means "a divine disclosure of a person or truth, involving also perception of that which is revealed by the person to whom the disclosure is made . . . a personal experience, divine in its origin . . . personal to himself and effectual."[75] In regard to Gal. 3:13, Burton presents several possible interpretations to explain how Christ became a curse "for us." He rejects interpretations that see Christ as a substitutionary victim of the wrath of God. According to Burton, the verse means that Christ fell under the curse of the law, not under the curse of God.[76]

In general, Burton engages in linguistic and grammatical analysis in order to determine the historical meaning of the text: what Paul intended to write to the Galatians at that particular time. Burton is a master of detail and analytical skill; he is in command of a huge amount of secondary sources; he addresses virtually all the critical and exegetical issues. In scope and depth, Burton's commentary matches anything that the Europeans had produced. It remained the representative volume of the ICC on Galatians for the rest of the century.[77]

Burton also devoted himself to the study of the Gospels. In 1904, he published *Some Principles of Literary Criticism and Their Application to the Synoptic Problem*. Burton begins by articulating principles that he believes are implicit in the literary relation of documents in general. For example, when there is a literary relationship between two documents, it can be assumed

---

75. Ibid., 41.
76. Burton's concern with the doctrine of atonement is seen in chapters on noncanonical Jewish literature and the NT in Ernest DeWitt Burton, John Merlin Powis Smith, and Gerald Birney Smith, *Biblical Ideas of Atonement: Their History and Significance* (Chicago: University of Chicago Press, 1909). Burton concludes, "The common doctrine of the New Testament is that as sin creates alienation between God and man, making man the object of divine displeasure, so repentance, faith in Jesus, adoption of that principle of life which Jesus exemplified preeminently in his death, is the basis of forgiveness and acceptance with God" (265).
77. Besides his commentary on Galatians, Burton also published popular study books on Paul and the apostolic age: *A Handbook of the Life of the Apostle Paul: An Outline for Classroom and Private Study* (Chicago: University of Chicago Press, 1906); *The Records and Letters of the Apostolic Age: The New Testament Acts, Epistles, and Revelation in the Version of 1881 Arranged for Historical Study* (New York: International Committee of Young Men's Christian Associations, 1895). Burton also coauthored a short, nontechnical introduction: Ernest DeWitt Burton and Fred Merrifield, *The Origin and Teaching of the New Testament Books, Outline Bible-Study Courses of the American Institute of Sacred Literature* (Chicago: University of Chicago Press, 1914).

that one is derived from the other. When three documents are involved, the relationship is more complex, and Burton prints four diagrams presenting the variety of possibilities. If the relationship involves nonextant sources as well as the three documents, even more possibilities are evident. Next, Burton applies these principles to the study of the Synoptics. He argues that differences indicate that each Gospel is an independent composition, while agreements indicate literary dependence. Burton investigates the agreements in detail and presents fourteen diagrams to depict the various possibilities. Then he proceeds to eliminate the possibilities that provide the least satisfactory solutions. He concludes: "We must remain content apparently with that which the evidence seems clearly to establish, namely, that the common source of the threefold narrative of Matt., Mark, and Luke must have contained substantially the material which we now have in our present gospel of Mark."[78]

This result, Burton observes, does not fully solve the problem, since it does not explain the common, non-Marcan material found in Matthew and Luke. Burton presents ten diagrams—some assuming use of Matthew by Luke or Luke by Matthew, and some assuming the use of another nonextant source, showing possible relationships. After analyzing the possibilities and eliminating the least satisfactory solutions, Burton concludes that Matthew and Luke used, as well as Mark, a hypothetical source he calls "X." However, Burton does not believe this conclusion explains why Matthew and Luke present this non-Marcan material in different arrangements. This leads him to the conclusion that X consisted of two or more documents. Further investigating the data, Burton detects evidence for still other sources. His final solution to the Synoptic Problem: there are four major sources: Mark (substantially as we have it), M (a special Matthean source, probably the Logia mentioned by Papias), P (a Perean document used by Luke and Matthew), G (a Galilean document used by Luke and Matthew); there are several minor sources: the infancy story of Matthew, the infancy story of Luke, and narrative peculiar to Matthew, and narrative peculiar to Luke.

The strength of Burton's argument is his attempt to work inductively, deriving principles from the literary relation of documents in general. He does not refer to the solutions of other scholars, and is largely free from the theological and academic struggles that have plagued the Europeans. To be sure, many of the decisions that Burton makes in constructing his hypothesis are open to question, despite his analytical skill. His work, in any case, illustrates the complexity of the problem.

---

78. *Some Principles of Literary Criticism and Their Application to the Synoptic Problem,* University of Chicago Decennial Publications 5 (Chicago: University of Chicago Press, 1904), 24.

In 1904, Burton published an *Introduction to the Gospels*, designed for college students and beginning seminarians. After his death, this book was revised in accord with Burton's later views.[79] Here Burton takes up each Gospel in canonical order. He thinks Matthew was written by a Palestinian Christian to prove that Jesus was the Jewish Messiah. In regard to Mark, Burton detects internal evidence that he believes supports authorship by John Mark. Luke, in Burton's opinion, was written by a Jew of broad perspective or a Gentile proselyte of Judaism. In his original edition, Burton argued that John was written by an eyewitness. The revised edition incorporates his later view: the Fourth Gospel was written by a Jew who moved from Palestine to a Hellenistic region after 70, and did not write until around 110, making it unlikely that the author could have been an eyewitness. As to sources, Burton thinks the author used the Synoptics, a narrative source, and a discourse source—the whole composition reworked by a later editor. To facilitate the study of the Gospels, Burton published, in conjunction with other scholars, a series of synopses or harmonies of the Gospels.[80]

Shailer Mathews (1863–1941)

Born in Portland, Maine, Mathews was educated at Colby College, where he was influenced by Albion W. Small, later of the University of Chicago, the father of American sociology.[81] Mathews received his theological education at Newton Theological Institution, where he studied under Burton. In 1890–91, Mathews went to the University of Berlin, concentrating on the study of history and economics. Small had planned to invite Mathews to the sociology department at Chicago, but Burton acted first (1894), persuading Mathews to teach NT, and later, historical theology. In 1908, Mathews was named Dean of the Divinity School, a post he held until 1933. In order to promote the modern understanding of the NT and early Christianity,

---

79. *A Short Introduction to the Gospels*, rev. ed. Harold R. Willoughby (Chicago: University of Chicago Press, 1926).

80. William Arnold Stevens and Ernest DeWitt Burton, *A Harmony of the Gospels for Historical Study: An Analytical Synopsis of the Four Gospels*, 3d ed. (New York: Charles Scribner's Sons, 1904); a guide to the use of earlier editions of the *Harmony* was also published: Ernest DeWitt Burton and Shailer Mathews, *Constructive Studies in the Life of Christ: An Aid to Historical Study and a Condensed Commentary on the Gospels: For Use in Advanced Bible Classes*, rev. ed. (Chicago: University of Chicago Press, 1901). Later, a synopsis was published that did not include the Fourth Gospel: Ernest DeWitt Burton and Edgar Johnson Goodspeed, *A Harmony of the Synoptic Gospels for Historical and Critical Study* (New York: Charles Scribner's Sons, 1917); this was followed by a synopsis based on the Westcott–Hort text: Ernest DeWitt Burton and Edgar Johnson Goodspeed, *A Harmony of the Synoptic Gospels in Greek* (Chicago: University of Chicago Press, 1920).

81. See Shailer Mathews, *New Faith for Old: An Autobiography* (New York: Macmillan, 1936); William D. Lindsey, *Shailer Mathews's Lives of Jesus: The Search for a Theological Foundation for the Social Gospel* (Albany: State University of New York Press, 1997), 34–69; Shailer Mathews, *Jesus on Social Institutions*, ed. Kenneth Cauthen, LJS (Philadelphia: Fortress, 1971), xiii–lxxi; Arnold, *Edge of Battle*, 35–42.

Mathews traveled as much as fifty thousand miles a year, delivering an average of 150 addresses annually. Mathews was involved in a host of causes: he edited a series of books encouraging the political activity of women; he served as President of the Federal Council of Churches and President of the Northern Baptist Convention.

In point of view, Mathews opposed speculative metaphysics and every kind of orthodoxy—at first fundamentalism, later neoorthodoxy. He believed the criterion of truth was pragmatic and functional: truth was that which most effectively met the needs of human beings in society.[82] Mathews's theological method was grounded in naturalism and humanism, and dedicated to empirical and sociological analysis. "I came to see," he wrote, "that theological doctrines had a social origin, that they were the product of group action in the interests of group solidarity and that they were really analogies which were the outcome of what I called creative social minds."[83] Mathews affirmed evolution and developed a theology of social process.[84] His study of the French Revolution fostered his view of early Christianity as a revolutionary movement, but the excesses of the Revolution led him to reject radical action in favor of gradual progress.[85] According to Mathews:

> [T]he gospel is a message of the redemptive love of the God of Law; . . . of a spiritual and therefore more individual life beyond death made possible by the transformation of the repentant human personality by dynamic personal union with the God of Love . . . ; and of a regenerate society that shall bring blessing to the individual because of the socialization of the regenerate spiritual life of individuals,—all revealed as realizable and morally just by the supreme teaching, the spiritual experiences, the sinless life, the death and the resurrection of the historical Jesus.[86]

This understanding of the gospel Mathews calls "modernism"—"the use of scientific, historical, social method in understanding and applying evangelical Christianity to the needs of living persons." The God who is revealed in Jesus is the "cosmic Personality—or Spirit" who is at work in the evolutionary processes of nature and history.

> Though we take the wings of the telescope and fly to the utmost reach of space, God must be there. Though we descend to the depth of atoms, there, too, He must sustain us. Though we trace the course of human evolution and social transformation, there, too, must God be found.

---

82. See William Lindsey, "'Somebody, Somehow, Somewhere, and Somewhen': Shailer Mathews and the Socio-Historical Interpretation of Doctrine," *American Journal of Theology and Philosophy* 20 (1999): 191–215.
83. *New Faith*, 283.
84. Mathews was invited to be a witness for the defense at the Scopes trial. He was unable to attend, but his five hundred-word statement was read into the record.
85. Shailer Mathews, *The French Revolution: A Sketch*, rev. ed. (New York: Longmans, Green, 1901).
86. *The Gospel and the Modern Man* (New York: Macmillan, 1910), 76.

Sin, according to Mathews, is failure to follow the immanent divine will. "To be saved is to be transformed by new relations with spiritual forces both human and divine.... Salvation is more than rescue.... It is newness of life, a likeness to Christ which finds its expression in good will." Salvation, in Mathews's opinion, is both individual and social. In short, Mathews is an evangelical modernist.[87]

Early in his career, Mathews published *The Social Teaching of Jesus: An Essay in Christian Sociology*. Originally written as an article for the *American Journal of Sociology*, this work, rewritten in book form, was widely read and frequently reprinted. By Christian sociology, Mathews means "the social philosophy and teachings of the historical person Jesus the Christ." Mathews acknowledges that Jesus was not a student of sociology, but insists that he was a keen observer of human nature, concerned with social relationships. Mathews believes that Jesus' social teaching is expressed in his idea of the kingdom of God. "By the kingdom of God Jesus meant an ideal (though progressively approximated) social order in which the relation of men to God is that of sons and (therefore) to each other, that of brothers." In the balance of the book, Mathews proceeds to explicate the meaning of the teachings of Jesus for social institutions. For example, discussing Jesus' idea of the family, Mathews, totally ignoring the critical problems, notes Jesus' lofty view of women:

> It was a virgin who bore the Saviour; a woman to whom he, as a child, was subject, and by whom, in all probability, he was trained and educated; to a woman, so far as we have any record, he gave the first clear proclamation of his Messiahship. His first miracle was wrought because of the faith and at the solicitation of his mother. A woman, who because of her grateful faith poured over him the costly ointment, is the only person to whom he promised an immortality of remembrance. Women ministered to his needs and supplied him the means of support. Among the last words Jesus spoke upon the cross were those with which he commended Mary to the care of his beloved disciple. A woman was the first at the tomb, the first to see the risen Christ, the first to believe on him, and the first to bear testimony to the resurrection.

In regard to eschatology, Mathews at this time was confident that Jesus' social vision will be realized. "The world will," he writes, "by virtue of man's endeavor and God's regenerating power, have been transformed into the kingdom. And the triumph of this new and perfected humanity, this eternal

---

87. Shailer Mathews, *The Faith of Modernism* (New York: Macmillan, 1925), 35, 115–16, 108, 91. Mathews distinguished modernism from liberalism. He believed liberalism was guilty of doctrinal reductionism, whereas modernism advocated a theology of social process. See William D. Lindsey, "Shailer Mathews on Doctrinal Development: Parallels between American Protestant Modernism and European Roman Catholic Modernism," *American Journal of Theology and Philosophy* 11 (1990): 115–32.

fraternity which he described and instituted and for which centuries have travailed—this is the coming of the Lord."[88]

The optimism of this early book was chastened in Mathews's later writings. Under the impact of historical events, particularly the War, and on the basis of his ongoing historical research, Mathews developed a more realistic assessment of early Christian eschatology.[89] A decisive step was taken in his *The Messianic Hope in the New Testament*. In this book, Mathews defines messianism as "that fixed social belief of the Jewish people that Jehovah would deliver Israel and erect it into a glorious empire to which a conquered world would be subject."[90] Messianism, Mathews believes, takes two forms: a revolutionary messianism (seen in the radicalism of the Zealots) and an eschatological messianism (expressed in the writings of the Pharisees). Among the main features of eschatological messianism, Mathews lists the idea of the two ages, the expectation of future judgment, the kingdom of the Jews, God's final triumph, the resurrection of the dead, and, in some sources, the coming of a personal Messiah.[91]

Turning to the messianism of Jesus, Mathews asks, How much of the messianism of the early Christians has been read back into the teachings of Jesus? He answers with his version of what was later called the criterion of dissimilarity: "that saying is more probably genuine which treats of messianic matters in any other way than that which characterized apostolic belief." Yet, if a saying found in Mark is also found in Matthew and Luke, Mathews believes that saying can be accepted with considerable confidence—the criterion of multiple attestation. Using these criteria, Mathews concludes that Jesus presented two views of the kingdom: the kingdom is present and gradually growing; the kingdom is eschatological and future.

> Any strict definition of the kingdom of God as used by Jesus must be eschatological. With Jesus as with his contemporaries the kingdom was yet to come. Its appearance would be the result of no social evolution, but sudden, as the gift of God; men could not hasten its coming; they could only prepare for membership in it.

Mathews believes Jesus understood himself to be the Messiah and used the title "Son of Man" to designate his messianic role. Mathews thinks Jesus

---

88. *The Social Teaching of Jesus: An Essay in Christian Sociology* (New York: Macmillan, 1897), 3, 54, 98–99, 228–29.

89. See Lindsey, *Shailer Mathews's Lives of Jesus*, 125–73.

90. *The Messianic Hope in the New Testament,* Decennial Publications of the University of Chicago (Chicago: University of Chicago Press, 1905), 3.

91. Mathews's concern with Jewish backgrounds is also seen in his *A History of New Testament Times in Palestine: 175 B.C.–70 A.D.*, rev. ed., New Testament Handbooks (New York: Macmillan, 1910). Of special interest is Mathews's discussion of the social life of the Palestinian Jews (157–78). In his *The Social Gospel* (Philadelphia: Griffith & Rowland, 1910), Mathews praises the concern with social teaching in the Talmud (118).

broke with the Pharisaic messianism on the basis of his idea of God as Father—the idea that led Jesus to abandon nationalism and affirm a universal kingdom. In an effort to rescue Jesus from apocalypticism, Mathews contends that the form of Jesus' teaching is eschatological while its essence is religious and spiritual:

> The center of his teaching is not the kingdom of God, with its mingled ethnic and political connotation; it is *eternal life*—the life which, because it is like God's persists across death in the joy of the divine life. . . . The conception was not given by Judaism, it was given by the conscious experience of Jesus. . . . Life in the enjoyment of eternity!—that is the supreme good.

And why did Jesus adopt the offensive apocalyptic language? "It was because he saw himself so supreme that he was forced to use the extremist valuations of his day and people to express his own self-consciousness."[92]

Mathews turns to the messianism of the apostles, giving major attention to Paul. He believes that the apostle adopted the main features of Pharisaic messianism, but modified it according to his experience of Christ. "Both by his experience and his antecedents Paul could hardly have made anything but eschatological messianism the co-ordinating schema of a system that centered about a belief that Jesus was the Christ." Consequently, Paul describes salvation in apocalyptic terms, as "deliverance from death" and "the entrance of the 'redeemed,' through the resurrection of the body, into that glorious life which was to come to those who believed in the Anointed King." Can such a messianic view make sense to modern people who hold a scientific view of the universe? asks Mathews. In answer, he reverts to the liberal distinction between kernel and husk. "Eschatological messianism is not the material but the form of Paulinism." The essence of Paul's thought, according to Mathews, is found in his religious experience—his sense of reconciliation with God and consciousness of divine sonship. Mathews discovers the same distinction in the eschatology of the early church. "Formally, therefore, the church was a group of messianists awaiting a kingdom that never came and indifferent to all customs of society except those that were evil; essentially the church was a group of men and women endeavoring to let the new religious and ethical life that had come to them from God through accepting Jesus as Christ express itself in social relations." Finally, Mathews discloses the hermeneutic by which he distills this sort of meaning from the texts:

> There must be, first, a precise interpretation of the Gospel as it stands in the New Testament, in its own terms and from its own point of view. Second, there must be a discrimination between the messianic and kindred interpretative formulas and concepts, on the one hand, and on the other, the facts in the

92. *Messianic Hope in the New Testament.*, 58, 82, 123, 129.

records of the life of Christ and of Christian experience which fair-minded criticism, psychology, and sociology will regard as assured. Then, third, there will be the presentation of these facts, through the use of such interpretative and pedagogical concepts as will do for today what the various concepts of the New Testament did for their day.[93]

Mathews's final assessment of the eschatological element of the NT is seen in his *Jesus on Social Institutions*. Originally published in 1928, this book interprets the eschatology of Jesus in terms of the revolutionary spirit of the times. "For, without leading revolt, he was to live and teach in the atmosphere of revolution, use the language of revolution, make the revolutionary spirit the instrument of his message, and organize a movement composed of men who awaited a divinely given new age."[94] According to Mathews, Jesus believed the eschatological kingdom of God was immanent, but saw love as the main feature of God's rule. Thus, Mathews believes the idea of love, grounded in Jesus' view of God as Father, was a cosmic principle. Moved by this principle, Jesus, according to Mathews, presented teachings important for social institutions. Although he acknowledges that Jesus did not offer a social program, Mathews insists that Jesus proclaimed a social gospel—a gospel that can transform modern society.

Mathews's distinctive understanding of the relation between theology and sociology is set forth in his book on the *Atonement*. At the outset, he argues that doctrines have a social origin:

> In order to understand a doctrine one must know not only the time and place of its formulation, but also the social and religious tension which gave rise to it. Strictly speaking, there is no history of doctrine; there is only the history of the people who made doctrines. A theology is a function of the religious life of a given period and this in turn is the expression of a social order conditioned not only by elements of culture, like philosophy, literature, and science, but also by the creative economic and political forces which engage in the production of the social order itself.

In regard to atonement, Mathews believes that Christians affirm the importance of the death of Christ, but interpret it according to various patterns that reflect their historical and social context. The early Christians, according to Mathews, understood the death of Christ according to the messianic pattern; Augustine, according to the imperial pattern; Anselm, according to the pattern of feudalism; the Reformers, according the pattern of monarchy. Mathews believes modern Christians ought to understand the atonement according to a pattern of process—according to an understanding of God informed by scientific knowledge. From this perspective, Mathews sees

---

93. Ibid., 174, 185, 206, 315–16, 320.
94. *Jesus on Social Institutions*, 12.

God as the personality-creating force in the universe. This truth Mathews finds at the heart of the life and teaching of Jesus. "For to him love was in the cosmic process. The God of nature was a Father."[95]

Shirley Jackson Case (1872–1947)

Case was born on a farm in New Brunswick, Canada.[96] After graduation from Acadia University (1893), he was ordained and served as a part-time Baptist minister. Case received the B.D. from Yale Divinity School in 1904. While working on his Ph.D. (under Porter and Bacon), he taught Greek at Yale.[97] After completing his degree, Case accepted Burton's invitation to join the NT faculty at Chicago (1908). In 1923, he became chair of the Church History department, and in 1933 he was named Dean of the Divinity School. After retirement, Case taught for a time at Bexley Hall in Ohio. In 1940 he moved to Florida, where he was appointed Professor of Religion at Florida Southern College and Dean of the Florida School of Religion. Case continued to teach until the day he died of a cerebral hemorrhage.

Case thought he had been born a liberal. However, he considered Harnack's (and Mathews's) attempt to salvage Christianity by drawing the distinction between form and essence to be mistaken.[98] Case believed the quest for an abstract essence involved "violently lopping off from the gospel tree a great wealth of luxuriant foliage." Case's own approach was to evaluate religion according to its social function. "Religious worth was not to be measured by the source from which ideas or practices had been originally derived, but to know their origin and history enabled the student to appraise their functional significance in the life of the people by whom they had been espoused." The subject of research, therefore, was persons in society. "Henceforth," says Case, "I determined to know nothing among theologies save the beliefs and quests of real people." Instead of an essence, Case affirmed a relativity.

> The truth of dogma is never absolute; it will always be relative and functional. Every item in Christian belief at any period in history is a product of the experience and conviction of Christian people, and can be regarded as valid only

---

95. *The Atonement and the Social Process* (New York: Macmillan, 1930), 11, 202. In statements of this sort, Mathews anticipates ideas of Whiteheadian process theology that were to develop in the later Chicago School.

96. See Hynes, *Shirley Jackson Case*, 15–140; Shirley Jackson Case, "Education in Liberalism," in *Contemporary American Theology: Theological Autobiographies,* ed. Vergilius Ferm (New York: Round Table, 1932) 1:107–25; Paul Schubert, "Shirley Jackson Case, Historian of Early Christianity: An Appraisal," *JR* 29 (1949): 30–46: C. C. McCown, "Shirley Jackson Case's Contribution to the Theory of Sociohistorical Interpretation," *JR* 29 (1949): 15–29; Arnold, *Edge of Battle,* 47-52.

97. Case honored his teachers by editing a *Festschrift* for Porter and Bacon: *Studies in Early Christianity* (New York: Century, 1928).

98. See pp. 122–25, above.

so long as it serves adequately to express the sincerest convictions and deepest experiences of each new generation of Christian persons.[99]

Case, who was essentially a historian, offers a summary of his thought in *The Christian Philosophy of History*. In this book, Case asserts that there are three ways of viewing history. According to the providential view (represented by Judaism and early Christianity), God is the ruler of history and the role of humans is relatively insignificant. According to the human view (an understanding developed in the nineteenth century), humans participate in and are responsible for history. According to the dualistic or dialectical view (a more recent spasm of the providential view, seen in Karl Barth), history is the arena of conflicting forces; God is remote and humans are helpless. The balance of Case's book explicates and advocates the second, the human view.

> Human history draws its deductions from the observable facts of the recoverable temporal sequence without primary reference to what may have been in the mind of God before the beginning of time or what may be his intentions regarding the outcome of cosmic events when measurable time has issued in eternity. . . . It shuns metaphysical speculation and worships at the shrine of empiricism.

Case believes that God works in history and that history is a process in which humans are responsible participants. "The Kingdom of God cometh not with observation but by dint of strenuous endeavor on the part of men who serve him from generation to generation throughout the evolving centuries."[100]

Typical of Case's approach is his first important book, *The Evolution of Early Christianity*. In this book, Case argues that Christianity must be understood in its historical setting and according to its progressive development. "Christianity can be ultimately and comprehensively conceived only in the developmental sense, as the product of actual persons working out their religious problems in immediate contact with their several worlds of reality, the process being renewed in the religious experience of each new generation."[101] Like the members of the history of religion school,[102] Case believes early Christianity must be understood in its setting within the syncretistic culture of the Mediterranean world. According to Case, early Christianity was indelibly tainted by the Hellenistic religions of redemption—the mystery cults and Gnosticism.

---

99. "Education in Liberalism," 112, 113, 114, 115. See Shirley Jackson Case, "The Problem of Christianity's Essence," *AJT* 17 (1913): 541–62. Paul Schubert ("Shirley Jackson Case") points out that Case's own commitment to science tended to be absolutist.

100. *The Christian Philosophy of History* (Chicago: University of Chicago Press, 1943), 56–57, 218.

101. *The Evolution of Early Christianity: A Genetic Study of First-Century Christianity in Relation to Its Religious Environment* (Chicago: University of Chicago Press, 1914), 25.

102. See pp. 222, 238–53, above.

In details they exhibit varying characteristics, but they all alike seek to meet the widespread demand for an individual salvation to be procured primarily by the aid of the deity.... The human spirit, conscious of its frailty and helpless at the loss of older sanctions, eagerly turned toward those cults which offered a personal salvation based upon a divine redemptive transaction. Among the oriental religions of redemption which attempted to meet this situation, Christianity was the last to arise, but it ultimately triumphed over all its rivals.

Christianity triumphed, Case believes, because it answered the deepest needs of people in their time—a model of what Christians ought to do today.

> But in the last analysis it owed its triumph to the activity of loyal individuals who not only answered the call of God as they heard it in their own lives or discerned it on the pages of history, but who learned, consciously or unconsciously, to read the divine will as revealed in the "signs of the times." They were sensitive to the religious forces within their environment, and so drew inspiration from its life and responded to its needs by conserving, heightening, and supplementing current religious values.... If Christians today would be true successors of those ancient worthies they too must make religion an affair of life and growth commensurate with the needs of the present generation.[103]

Case, in later publications, continued and refined his method of investigating early Christianity. In *The Social Origins of Christianity*, he advocates the study of early Christian literature according to the sociohistorical approach—an approach that has parallels to form criticism.[104] "Social emphasis ... calls for the revitalizing of the literature, not by reading into it the life of a subsequent age, but by visualizing in realistic fashion the very life of the place and time in which the various New Testament books were produced."[105] From this perspective, Case sees Jesus instigating social change, a threat to the religious and political establishment. After the crucifixion, the followers of Jesus formed a new society, and with Paul, the new society moved into an urban environment. According to Case, the dynamic of the Pauline communities was dissipated by the increasing concern with ecclesiastical institution. Finally, in the fourth century, Christianity was embraced as the stabilizing force of the Roman empire.[106]

Case was adamant in his belief that Christians should not retreat from society. This conviction led him, like Mathews, to attack the millennialism

---

103. *Evolution of Early Christianity*, 329, 369.
104. See pp. 269–86, above. In a brief review of Fascher's *Die formgeschichtliche Methode* ("Reopening the Synoptic Problem," *JR* 5 [1925]: 428–30), Case mentions the major works on the subject by Dibelius, Schmidt, and Bultmann, and calls for "more and better *Formgeschichte*" (431).
105. *The Social Origins of Christianity* (Chicago: University of Chicago Press, 1923), 31.
106. Case relates the story of the establishment of Christianity in detail in *The Social Triumph of the Ancient Church* (New York: Harper & Brothers, 1933).

that flourished in the era of World War I. In *The Millennial Hope*, Case addresses the question, "Are the ills of society to be righted by an early and sudden destruction of the present world, or is permanent relief to be secured only by a gradual process of strenuous endeavor covering a long period of years?" Case attempts to answer the question by a historical investigation. According to his reading of the sources, ancient religions—both Gentile and Jewish—hoped for salvation from supernatural forces. In this setting, Jesus uttered his teachings in apocalyptic form, and his followers, spellbound by belief in his resurrection, awaited his immanent triumphal return.

> But at no time in this period did Christians generally come to realize that it was their mission to win the world by a gradual process of spiritual transformation. Only in the Fourth Gospel does the consciousness of this task seem to be awakening, but even here it does not come to clear and full expression.

Case concludes that apocalyptic teachings of the Bible cannot be applied today. The study of history proves that apocalyptic predictions have been wrong, and the world, according to Case's unshakable optimism, is getting better, not worse.[107]

Case's interest in eschatology encouraged him to publish a commentary on *Revelation*. He interprets the book historically as addressed to Christians of Asia Minor in the era of Domitian—a time when resistance to emperor worship threatened their existence.

> Finding themselves hopelessly in the minority, it is not surprising that Christians regarded the existing order of things as a state of irredeemable wretchedness from which ultimate deliverance could be secured only through some desperate act of divine intervention. Their situation made possible a ready acceptance of belief in the early end of the world and in a speedy return of Christ to establish a new régime of perfection upon the earth.

Classifying Revelation as an example of apocalyptic literature, Case sees it as the product of both literary composition and visionary experience. Case interprets the beast from the sea (13:1) as representing imperial power, and the beast from the earth (13:11) as representing the priesthood of the imperial cult. In the final chapter, Case presents a brief history of the interpretation of the Apocalypse in which he advocates a strictly historical method. "With this method in hand the long-misunderstood mysteries of Revelation are easily solved."[108]

For Case, apocalypticism was a mere symptom of a more dangerous disease: supernaturalism. In 1946, Case published *The Origins of Christian*

---

107. *The Millennial Hope* (Chicago: University of Chicago Press, 1918), v, 154.
108. *The Revelation of John: A Historical Interpretation* (Chicago: University of Chicago Press, 1919), 14–15, 406.

Supernaturalism, which, except for a chapter titled "The Survival of Supernaturalism," was a reissue of his earlier *Experience with the Supernatural in Early Christian Times*.[109] The thesis of the book is that the supernatural features of Christianity are not essential, but were imported from the environment. "The original genius of Christianity as a moral and spiritual way of life is seen to have been gradually overlaid with a veneer of otherworldly imagery that obscured the fundamental nature of the new religion." Supernaturalism, according to Case, was rampant in the ancient world; only the Epicureans—heroes in Case's eyes—opposed it. Surrounded by clouds of visions and apparitions, the early Christians supposed they had seen the risen Jesus. "Had not the disciples of Jesus been 'unlearned and ignorant men' (Acts 4:13)—Galilean peasants and fisherfolk—they might have had more scruples against believing that Jesus had actually appeared to Peter." Things got progressively worse, according to Case, when Christians proceeded to institutionalize the supernatural, developing elaborate liturgy and vested hierarchy. "Thus Christianity triumphed not by abolishing the yearning of the heathen for access to the supernatural but by intensifying and heightening the customary techniques for attaining this goal." Case believes the remedy is to be found in religious naturalism—a recognition that God's "presence is most clearly manifest in the operations of natural law, in the emergence of social ideals, in the upsurgence of human morality, and in the spiritual outreach of religious living."[110]

Beneath the rubble of early Christian apocalyptic and supernaturalism, Case searched for the historical Jesus. In the introduction to his *Jesus: A New Biography*, Case affirms the two-document hypothesis and the importance of Mark as a historical source. "Although the evangelist had only a secondary interest in the personal religious living of his incomparable hero, the colors appropriate to the Christ of faith were not spread so thickly upon the canvas as to obscure completely the earlier outlines of an earthly Jesus."[111] In examining the oral tradition, Case echoes the form critics.

> At the start, activities and teachings of Jesus were recalled only in isolated fashion.... These first accounts owed their origin, not to the literary impulses of outstanding authors, but to the activity of various inconspicuous disciples who rehearsed individual sayings or incidents from the lifetime of Jesus for practical use in the Christian cause. First orally, and then in written form,

---

109. *The Origins of Christian Supernaturalism* (Chicago: University of Chicago Press, 1946); idem, *Experience with the Supernatural in Early Christian Times* (New York: Century, 1929).
110. *Origins*, v, 27, 120, 233.
111. *Jesus: A New Biography* (Chicago: University of Chicago Press, 1927), 22. Earlier, Case had defended the historicity of Jesus in response to writers such as Arthur Drews who imagined that Jesus never existed: *The Historicity of Jesus: A Criticism of the Contention That Jesus Never Lived, a Statement of the Evidence for His Existence, an Estimate of His Relation to Christianity* (Chicago: University of Chicago Press, 1912).

these fluid memories gradually crystallized into more formal units of tradition that ultimately were embalmed in our present gospels.

Case also believes that the units of tradition can be classified according to content and purpose in relation to the developing tradition, and that the relation of elements of the tradition to the social environment (what the form critics called *Sitz im Leben*) can serve as a criterion for authenticity.

> Every statement in the records is to be judged by the degree of its suitableness to the distinctive environment of Jesus, on the one hand, and to that of the framers of gospel tradition at one or another stage in the history of Christianity, on the other. When consistently applied, this test will prove our safest guide in recovering from the present gospel records dependable information regarding the life and teaching of the earthly Jesus.[112]

Although Case has subtitled his work a "biography," he acknowledges, "it is quite impossible to reconstruct a full itinerary of Jesus' career." What can be known of Jesus must be seen in his setting within Judaism. Case emphasizes the social; he gives attention to agricultural and commercial life, and to the religious institutions. He notes that Jesus belonged to the artisan class, and that he may have labored in the rebuilding of Sepphoris. At his baptism, according to Case, Jesus became conscious of his prophetic calling. Case believes the conflict between Jesus and the Pharisees was exaggerated by the later tradition. "In his sympathies and aims Jesus had more in common with them than with any other Jewish party of his day."[113]

Case's primary concern is the religion of Jesus. He begins with an investigation of the religion Jesus lived. According to Case, the investigation is complicated by the developing tradition. "From a very early date the Christian movement had included within itself both the religion of Jesus and the religion about Jesus, both the Jesus of history and the Christ of dogma." As to the religion of Jesus, Case thinks Jesus saw himself primarily as prophet and teacher. Case believes it would have been psychologically impossible for Jesus to identify himself with the apocalyptic Son of Man. Jesus did, according to Case, understand himself as Son of God, that is, he felt a close personal relation with God. "The outstanding feature of Jesus' religion was the prophet's characteristic awareness of the presence of God." Most important for Case is the religion that Jesus taught. These teachings are depicted in colors that reflect the rural life of Galilee—a sign to Case of their authenticity. Case admits that Jesus shared the apocalyptic expectations of his contemporaries, but argues that Jesus' main concern was to change people, to prepare them for the coming kingdom—the good life, the higher social order.

---

112. *Jesus*, 97–98, 115.
113. Ibid., 276, 305.

Jesus proclaimed that the good life was the perfect life. . . . No limit was to be set either to the ideal or to the effort necessary for worthy religious living. . . . Poverty, hunger, affliction, and persecution, when incurred in the pursuit of this high goal, were to be accounted blessings. . . . He who would do the will of God acceptably must stand ready to sacrifice all else, even life itself, in his pursuit of the heavenly treasure. And what Jesus demanded of others he himself was ready to perform. His own loyalty to the ideals that he preached carried the prophet from his carpenter's home in Nazareth to Christendom's cross on the Golgotha hill.

In the final analysis, Case's lucid book, unencumbered by footnotes, presents a stirring portrait of the liberal Jesus.[114]

Edgar Johnson Goodspeed (1871–1962)

Goodspeed was not fully committed to the sociohistorical method, and his relations with Case were not always cordial.[115] Nevertheless, he belonged to the inner circle of the University of Chicago. Goodspeed was born in Quincy, Illinois, the son of a Baptist minister. In 1876, the family moved to Chicago and then to Morgan Park, where his father became financial officer at the Baptist Union Theological Seminary. The older Goodspeed was instrumental in securing J. D. Rockefeller's support for the seminary, and later, for the university. Edgar graduated from Dennison University (1890), where he studied classics and played on the baseball team. After a year of study at Yale, he followed Harper back to Chicago, where he received the Ph.D. in 1898. After two years of study in Berlin and travel in the Near East, Goodspeed was appointed instructor at the University of Chicago (1902). He was promoted to full professor in 1915, and was named head of the NT department (succeeding Case) in 1923. After retirement in 1938, he moved to California, where he continued to write and lecture at UCLA. Throughout his life, he was closely associated with the American Baptist Church.

Goodspeed devoted himself to higher criticism and developed a distinctive theory in regard to the publication of the Pauline Letters. This theory evolved in a series of publications, beginning with Goodspeed's *The*

---

114. Ibid., 339, 378, 441. Case also published *Jesus through the Centuries* (Chicago: University of Chicago Press, 1932), a book that traces the developing understanding of Jesus from the beginning until modern times. Case's belief that persons were important for shaping history is seen in his *Makers of Christianity: From Jesus to Charlemagne* (New York: Henry Holt, 1934).

115. See Edgar J. Goodspeed, *As I Remember* (New York: Harper & Brothers, 1953); James I. Cook, *Edgar Johnson Goodspeed: Articulate Scholar*, SBLBSNA 4 (Chico, Calif.: Scholars Press, 1981), 1–7; James Harrel Cobb and Louis B. Jennings, *A Biography and Bibliography of Edgar Johnson Goodspeed* (Chicago: University of Chicago Press, 1948). Goodspeed was not untouched by the concerns of the Chicago School; in his *The Formation of the New Testament* (Chicago: University of Chicago Press, 1926), he wrote, "As a collection the New Testament is a social product. It grew out of the needs and moods of the early churches" (vii).

Formation of the New Testament.[116] According to Goodspeed's reading of the data, the author of Acts did not know the Pauline Letters. However, after the publication of Acts, Goodspeed finds evidence for the influence of the Pauline Letters in virtually all the NT documents. "The existence of a Pauline collection is therefore the key to the new letter-writing movement of the end of the first and the beginning of the second centuries."[117] At this point in his thinking, Goodspeed believed the original order of the Pauline Letters could be detected in the Muratorian canon, which listed the Corinthian letters first, followed by Ephesians. Goodspeed speculates that this arrangement had been devised in Corinth, where Ephesians—which he believes had originally been in first place—had been replaced by Corinth's favorite letters. The original collection of the letters, Goodspeed thinks, was made at Ephesus, where Ephesians was written as an introduction.

As well as his view of the Epistles, this book advances Goodspeed's theory in relation to the collection of the four Gospels and the emergence of the NT canon. As to the Gospels, Goodspeed claims that Mark was the earliest, written in Rome. Matthew, according to Goodspeed, made use of Mark. Goodspeed thinks Luke was probably composed in Ephesus. The Fourth Gospel, he believes, was also written in Ephesus, where he thinks the fourfold gospel collection was made around 125. Goodspeed proceeds to trace the history of the canon. He thinks Justin's mention of the "Memoirs of the Apostles" refers to the collection of the canonical Gospels. By 180, Goodspeed believes the canon had taken definite shape, consisting of a collection of Gospels and a collection of Pauline Epistles, with Acts as the connecting link.

Goodspeed further develops his theory in *New Solutions of New Testament Problems*.[118] In this book, he expands his argument that Ephesians was written as an introduction to the Pauline collection. First, he argues that Ephesians was not written by Paul. Goodspeed also notes that the phrase "in Ephesus" (1:1) is lacking from some of the early manuscripts. Although Ephesians is included in all the early collections of the Pauline Epistles, Goodspeed discovers no occasion in Paul's career that could have provoked such a letter. Ephesians, according to Goodspeed, includes ideas from all of the Pauline Letters, indicating that it was written as a general letter, introducing the collection. Goodspeed proceeds to expand his argument concerning the impact of the Pauline collection on subsequent NT literature. For example, the letters of Revelation are presented as a corpus with an

---

116. In 1916, Goodspeed had published a short introduction to the NT that does not mention the theory. However, it is incorporated in the later revision: *The Story of the New Testament*, 2d ed. (Chicago: University of Chicago Press, 1929).

117. *Formation*, 25.

118. (Chicago: University of Chicago Press, 1927).

introductory letter.[119] The introductory letter uses the Pauline epistolary formula "grace and peace" (Rev. 1:4), and Revelation (21:14), like Ephesians (2:20), refers to the foundation of the apostles. Goodspeed notes that at first glance, the Pauline collection appears to contain eight letters written to six churches, but actually Philemon was addressed to a church. Goodspeed thinks it is actually the letter to Laodicea mentioned in Col. 4:16. Thus, the Pauline collection, like the letter corpus in Revelation, includes a general introductory letter followed by letters to seven churches, ending in both cases with a letter to Laodicea.[120]

In *The Meaning of Ephesians*, Goodspeed concentrates on the question of authorship. He surmises that the collector of the Pauline Letters would have known one or two letters of Paul. When this author read Acts, he was prompted, according to Goodspeed, to conjecture that Paul had written other letters; this encouraged him to visit the churches, collect the letters, and write an introduction. In examining Ephesians, Goodspeed discovers that although it reflects knowledge of all the Pauline Letters, it reproduces three-fifths of the content of Colossians. This leads Goodspeed to suppose that the author's favorite epistle was Colossians, that he also knew Philemon (Laodiceans), and that he was, therefore, probably a resident of Asia. "The writer of Ephesians," says Goodspeed, "was thus the earliest student of the letters of Paul—indeed, we may truly say, the first interpreter of them. His own letter, which may fairly be called an epistle, is in a sense a commentary upon them."[121] Goodspeed proceeds to present a short commentary on Ephesians in which he attempts to demonstrate that his theory of composition provides the proper perspective for interpreting the epistle. The balance of the book (pp. 82–165) presents a chart of parallels designed to prove that Ephesians is dependent on the nine authentic letters of Paul, and especially on Colossians.

In *New Chapters in New Testament Study*, Goodspeed focuses on Ephesus as a center for the production of Christian literature. According to Good-

---

119. John Knox (*Never Far from Home: The Story of My Life* [Waco, Tex.: Word Books, 1975], 101–2), a distinguished NT scholar in his own right, recounts an incident that Goodspeed reported to his students. After he had deposited the manuscript of *The Formation of the New Testament* at the University of Chicago Press, Goodspeed and his wife set out by car for California. As he drove, it suddenly occurred to him that the seven letters in Revelation were introduced by a general letter, but he could not remember for certain. At the end of the day's drive, he checked into his room at the hotel and rushed to the Gideon Bible in order to confirm his expectation.

120. Goodspeed also develops his theory by showing the impact of the Pauline collection on 1 Peter (also an encyclical), the Pastorals, and the Johannine letters. *New Solutions* also contains three chapters on Luke and Acts wherein Goodspeed argues vehemently against C. C. Torrey's claim that Acts 1–15 is based on an Aramaic source, written c. 50. This book also includes a chapter on Hebrews and a chapter that argues that the original ending of Mark can be reconstructed by the use of Matthew.

121. *The Meaning of Ephesians* (Chicago: University of Chicago Press, 1933), 10.

speed, it was the place where more than half of the documents of the NT were composed and collected. "So for one momentous generation, Ephesus was the literary focus of early Christianity, and by its compositions—three letters to Corinth, Luke-Acts, Ephesians, Revelation, the Gospel of John, the letters of John; and by its compilations—the Pauline, Ignatian and Johannine letters and the four gospels—influenced Christianity more than Jerusalem, Antioch or Rome."[122] Also in this book, Goodspeed contends that introductions to the NT should be written with his hypothesis as the organizing principle: the publication of the Pauline corpus constitutes the watershed; the writings of Paul and Luke-Acts precede, and all the rest of the literature follows. In this book, Goodspeed also argues that all of the documents of the NT were originally written in Greek; the theory of Aramaic originals is confounded, Goodspeed argues, by the dearth of Aramaic literature in the NT era—an argument that was later undermined by the discovery of the Dead Sea Scrolls. An insightful chapter on pseudepigraphy notes the prevalence of the practice in Judaism and early Christianity. Goodspeed thinks the author of Ephesians could hardly have claimed authorship for himself, since virtually everything he wrote he borrowed from Paul. First Peter, according to Goodspeed, was a pseudonym, enlisting the authority of Peter to mollify the anti-Romanism of Revelation. A final chapter on modern apocrypha surveys hoaxes and fraudulent documents such as the "Letter from Heaven" and the "Gospel of Josephus."[123]

Goodspeed put his proposal to practice in *An Introduction to the New Testament*—a highly readable exercise in higher criticism.[124] Goodspeed begins with an analysis of the Pauline Letters. He accepts 2 Thessalonians as authentic. He believes Galatians was addressed to churches of the southern part of the province. He believes, like Moffatt, that Paul wrote a total of four letters of Corinth. He thinks Romans 16 was originally a letter of recommendation of Phoebe to Ephesus. Philippians (a composite of two letters) and Colossians, according to Goodspeed, were written from the Roman imprisonment. In regard to Ephesians, Goodspeed is attracted by the conjecture of his student John Knox that the author was Onesimus, the slave who later became bishop of Ephesus. Also written prior to the publication of the Pauline collection were the Synoptic Gospels. Goodspeed accepts the tradition that Mark preserves the reminiscences of Peter. The Logia of Papias Goodspeed believes to have been an oral gospel, not a written source

---

122. *New Chapters in New Testament Study* (Chicago: University of Chicago Press, 1937), 49.
123. Goodspeed had treated this subject in greater detail in *Strange New Gospels* (Chicago: University of Chicago Press, 1931); among the more interesting documents surveyed: "The Crucifixion of Jesus, by an Eye Witness," "The Confessions of Pontius Pilate," "The Twenty-Ninth Chapter of Acts."
124. (Chicago: University of Chicago Press, 1937).

used by Matthew and Luke. Goodspeed thinks the use of first person plural in Acts indicates that the author, Luke, was a participant in the events.

Goodspeed presents a separate chapter reiterating his theory about the collection of the Pauline epistles. He presents a chart designed to show that Revelation, Hebrews, 1 Clement, 1 Peter, John, Ignatius, Polycarp, James, Marcion, the Pastoral Epistles, and 2 Peter—all know all or most of the letters of Paul. Goodspeed's chapter on Ephesians expands his earlier arguments. In regard to the original order of the Pauline collection, Goodspeed offers a new hypothesis based on Knox's observations about Marcion's order. This order (Galatians, Corinthians, Romans, Thessalonians, Laodiceans [Ephesians], Colossians, Philippians, Philemon) follows the principle of decreasing length, except for Galatians and Ephesians (which Marcion called "Laodiceans"); on the basis of length, Ephesians should have preceded Thessalonians. Goodspeed concludes that Marcion, because of his preference for Galatians, switched Ephesians with Galatians. Goodspeed concludes that Ephesians was originally first—the proper place for the general letter that introduces the whole collection.

The rest of the *Introduction* deals with NT documents written after Ephesians and the publication of the Pauline collection. In regard to the Gospel of John, Goodspeed thinks it was written by a Greek Christian to communicate the gospel to the Greeks. "In fact, the gospel may be said to be intensely Greek from Prologue to Epilogue in every fiber of both thought and language." Goodspeed continues, "In John, Resurrection, Second Coming, and the gift of the Spirit are made one."[125] Goodspeed believes the appendix, John 21, was written by one of the editors of the four-gospel collection who attempts to identify the author as the "beloved disciple." The actual author, according to Goodspeed, was John the Elder of Ephesus who also wrote the Johannine Epistles. Goodspeed thinks the Pastoral Epistles were written c. 150 to counter Marcion's rejection of the OT.

Goodspeed's final statement on his Ephesian hypothesis is expressed in his book *The Key to Ephesians*. In this book, Goodspeed waxes sentimental about the theory that Onesimus is the collector of the Pauline Letters and the author of Ephesians. "I don't know how this mere conjecture may strike the reader," he writes, "but it fills my eyes with tears. The emancipated slave lives to build his protector a monument more enduring than bronze!"[126] Seventy-four pages of this book are devoted to the English translation of the chart that had appeared in Greek in the *Meaning of Ephesians*. Viewed as a whole, Goodspeed's hypothesis displays creative imagination. It rests, of course, on two basic premises: that the author of Acts did not know the Pauline letters, and that Ephesians was not written by Paul. Although the

---

125. *Introduction*, 308, 299.
126. *The Key to Ephesians* (Chicago: University of Chicago Press, 1956), xv.

latter is widely accepted, the relation of Acts to the Epistles is a matter of debate. Beyond these basic premises, the details of Goodspeed's theory pile conjecture upon conjecture—that Philemon is Laodiceans, that Acts was written in Ephesus, that the collector of the letters was the author of Ephesians, and so on.[127]

Goodspeed devoted much energy to translating the NT. At a meeting of the New Testament Club of Chicago, he read a paper on modern translations. In response, Case quipped that since Goodspeed found so many flaws in these versions, he ought to do one himself. Although this remark evoked laughter at Goodspeed's expense, a representative of the University Press who was present took the suggestion seriously, and persuaded Goodspeed to undertake the project. In 1923, he published *The New Testament: An American Translation*.[128] "The aim of the present translation," he wrote, "has been to present the meaning of the different books as faithfully as possible, without bias or prejudice, in English of the same kind as the Greek of the original, so that they may be continuously and understandingly read."[129] This accurate, lucid translation presents the text in paragraphs, with chapter and verse indications in the margin. Goodspeed was especially concerned to follow American, rather than British usage; thus, "corn fields" and "ears of corn" (Mark 2:23, KJV) become "wheat fields" and "heads of wheat." Difficult theological terms are translated into simple language; thus, "the righteousness of God" becomes "God's way of uprightness." Goodspeed's translation of Luke 24:38b-39 is typical: "Why are you so disturbed, and why do doubts arise in your minds? Look at my hands and feet, for it is I myself! Feel me and see, for a ghost has not flesh and bones, as you see I have." Occasionally, colloquialism prevails: "Goodbye, and the Lord be with you always. Again I say, goodbye" (Phil. 4:4).

The publication of the translation provoked an immediate outcry, even in the secular press. When Goodspeed's translation of the Lucan version of the Lord's Prayer was cited, he was accused of impiously shortening the prayer of Jesus. On the other hand, some newspapers printed the whole translation serially, and a Chicago radio station broadcast extensive readings from Goodspeed's version. Later, in joint editorship with J. M. Powis Smith and

---

127. Goodspeed's interest in early Christian literature extended beyond the canon. He published a concordance of the Apostolic Fathers (*Index patristicus sive clavis patrum apostolicorum operum* [1907; repr., Naperville, Ill.: Alec R. Allenson, 1960]) and a concordance of the second-century apologists (*Index apologeticus sive clavis Iustini Martyris operum aliorumque apologetarum pristinorum* [Leipzig: J. C. Hinrichs, 1912]) and *Die ältesten Apologeten: Texte mit kurzen Einleitungen* (Göttingen: Vandenhoeck & Ruprecht, 1914). Goodspeed also authored the popular *A History of Early Christian Literature* (Chicago: University of Chicago Press, 1942).
128. (Chicago: University of Chicago Press, 1923).
129. Ibid., v.

with the cooperation of a group of OT scholars, Goodspeed published a translation of the whole Bible.[130] Also with Smith, Goodspeed published *The Short Bible: An American Translation*—a selection of the most important sections of the Bible, arranged in chronological order.[131] At the suggestion of a former student, S. Vernon McCasland, Goodspeed translated the Apocrypha, and since earlier English translations had followed Miles Coverdale (who had translated from Latin), Goodspeed was apparently the first to publish an English translation from the original language.[132]

In response to criticism, Goodspeed trekked across the country, delivering some 125 popular lectures opposing the KJV, and defending modern translations in general and his own in particular. One of his favorite observations was that the KJV, which was supposed to have been kept in pristine purity since its inception in 1611, had actually been changed frequently, notably in a thorough revision in 1769 by Benjamin Blayney. By 1948, Goodspeed's translation in its various forms had sold more than a million copies. Goodspeed also published books about translations. His *The Making of the English New Testament* presents a lively history of English translations from William Tyndale (1525) to 1925. In this book, Goodspeed notes the captivity of later translators to the language of the earlier. "It is not too much to say that William Tyndale wrote nine-tenths of the King James New Testament."[133] Goodspeed further demonstrates this tendency in *Problems of New Testament Translation*.[134] He considers 115 problem texts from Matthew to Revelation, showing how traditional renderings have continued to dominate later translations.

Publications from Goodspeed's later years are disappointing. His book on *Paul*, for example, largely represents, in vivid prose, the account of Acts.[135] Originally published in 1950, Goodspeed's *Life of Jesus* acknowledges that a biography cannot be written, but attempts to present a chronological account of the ministry of Jesus. Goodspeed believes the baptism of Jesus was decisive.

> It was doubtless the climax of much religious reflection and experience, but it was none the less the great moment, the decisive hour, not only in Jesus' life but in human experience. One man had at last been caught up as no one before into the vision of God, to be his spokesman, his Chosen, his Beloved, his Son.

---

130. *The Bible: An American Translation* (Chicago: University of Chicago Press, 1931).
131. (Chicago: University of Chicago Press, 1933).
132. *The Apocrypha: An American Translation* (Chicago: University of Chicago Press, 1938).
133. *The Making of the English New Testament* (Chicago: University of Chicago Press, 1925), 51.
134. (Chicago: University of Chicago Press, 1945).
135. *Paul* (Philadelphia: John C. Winston, 1947). Goodspeed also published *The Twelve: The Story of Christ's Apostles* (Philadelphia: John C. Winston, 1957).

Goodspeed tends to rationalize the miracles. For example, in regard to the Gerasene demoniac, Goodspeed writes, "Jesus humored him, and the man's cries and movements so frightened the animals that they rushed in panic over the edge of the cliff into the lake." Goodspeed softens Jesus' blow to the Syrophoenician woman; "she was too much in earnest to be hurt by his language, or perhaps something in his manner told her this was not really his own attitude." Goodspeed thinks Jesus used apocalyptic language to express a spiritual and ethical message. "Jesus was well aware that God's violent triumph through an apocalyptic judgment would not be the noblest triumph for God's cause; its noblest triumph would be won only through winning the hearts of men to the will of God."[136]

The Chicago School made a distinctive contribution to NT research. Much of its work, of course, perpetuated the tradition of European scholarship. All of the Chicago scholars had studied in Germany, and their work in linguistics and exegesis (Burton) and higher criticism (Goodspeed) followed earlier patterns, though with fresh imagination and fewer footnotes. Case and Mathews share with the history of religion school the concern for historical backgrounds, and Case is similar to the form critics in his analysis of tradition. The Chicago scholars, like their colleagues at Union and Yale, embrace liberalism's concern with Jesus and his ethical teaching, even though their historical research could not deny his apocalypticism. Much of this liberalism, of course, represents a lingering pietism; all of the Chicago scholars were devoted Baptists. The distinctive feature of the Chicago School—seen especially in Mathews and Case—is the development of the sociohistorical method. The method, grounded in naturalism and humanism, is rigorously empirical, functional, pragmatic, and democratic. The subject is persons in society; truth is historical process; the goal is Christian social order.

AMERICAN WOMEN IN NEW TESTAMENT RESEARCH

In the first volume of this *History*, the only woman mentioned was Mary Anne Evans (novelist George Eliot), the brilliant translator of D. F. Strauss's revolutionary *Life of Jesus*.[137] Earlier in this volume, the role of Agnes Smith Lewis and her sister Margaret Dunlop Gibson in the discovery and publication of

---

136. *A Life of Jesus,* HT (New York: Harper & Brothers, 1956), 43, 92, 119, 127. Goodspeed's final contribution to NT research, *Matthew: Apostle and Evangelist* (Philadelphia: John C. Winston, 1959), supposes that Jesus appointed Matthew, the tax collector, to keep records of Jesus' teaching; years later, Matthew, living in Antioch, received a copy of Mark, which he combined with his own records to produce the Gospel of Matthew.

137. *HNTR* 1:250–51.

important manuscripts was noted.[138] These exceptions prove the rule: women were not members of the exclusive club of male scholarship. They were not admitted to the academic institutions where scholars were trained, and they had no access to the positions from which scholarship was dispensed. Recently, however, careful research has demonstrated that the feminine contribution to theological literature was much larger than had been recognized.[139] In the nineteenth century, women, who have been largely ignored, made important contributions to NT research.

The Grimké sisters, Sarah and Angelina, Quaker converts from the Episcopalian aristocracy of South Carolina, were activists in the antislavery movement and advocates of women's rights.[140] Angelina published *Appeal to Christian Women of the South* (1836), in which she argues that the Scriptures, properly interpreted, oppose slavery. "Read the Bible then," she writes, "it contains the words of Jesus, and they are spirit and life. Judge for yourselves whether he sanctioned such a system of oppression and crime."[141] The sisters left the South to lecture in New England, where their opposition to slavery found a receptive audience, but their audacity to speak in churches was denounced.[142] In response to the dictum that women should not voice their opinions in the public forum, Sarah wrote "Letters on the Equality of the Sexes and the Condition of Women" (1837). "In examining this important subject," she says, "I shall depend solely on the Bible to designate the sphere of woman, because I believe that almost every thing that has been written on this subject, has been the result of a misconception of the simple truths revealed in the Scriptures, in consequence of the false translation of many passages of Holy Writ."[143] For others, the view of the Bible was less sanguine. Lucretia Coffin Mott, a Quaker minister, preached a sermon in 1849 in Philadelphia that claimed that "the great error in Christendom is, in regarding these scriptures taken as a whole as the plenary inspiration of God, and their authority as supreme."[144]

---

138. See pp. 177–78, above.
139. See Patricia Demers, *Women as Interpreters of the Bible* (New York: Paulist, 1992); Marla J. Selvidge, *Notorious Voices: Feminist Biblical Interpretation, 1500–1920* (New York: Continuum, 1996); Carolyn De Swarte Gifford, "American Women and the Bible: The Nature of Woman as a Hermeneutical Issue," in *Feminist Perspectives on Biblical Scholarship*, ed. Adela Yarbro Collins, SBLBSNA (Chico, Calif.: Scholars Press, 1985), 11–33; Amy Oden, ed., *In Her Words: Women's Writings in the History of Christian Thought* (Nashville: Abingdon, 1994).
140. See Gerda Lerner, *The Grimké Sisters from South Carolina: Pioneers for Woman's Rights and Abolition* (New York: Oxford University Press, 1998). Later the sisters were disowned by the Quakers, and were attracted toward utopian religious ideas and spiritualism.
141. Quoted by Gifford, "American Women and the Bible," 17.
142. Among leading clergy who opposed the Grimkés were Lyman Beecher and Leonard Bacon, grandfather of Yale NT scholar B. W. Bacon. Angelina Grimké married the noted abolitionist Theodore Weld; among their friends was Henry B. Stanton, who married Elizabeth Cady.
143. Quoted by Gifford, "American Women and the Bible," 18–19.
144. Quoted by Oden, *In Her Words*, 296.

Since biblical texts had been used in the suppression of women, feminine scholars were provoked to pursue critical exegesis. Antoinette Brown, a native of New York State, believed she had been called to ministry.[145] In 1846, she entered Oberlin Collegiate Institute in Ohio. Upon finishing the literary course, she stayed on to study theology. Although she completed the program, she was not granted a degree or approved for ordination. Perhaps as compensation, her student paper on 1 Cor. 14:34-35 and 1 Tim. 2:11-12 was published in the *Oberlin Quarterly*. Making use of lexicons such as Liddell and Scott and citing classical sources and NT scholars, Brown presents a careful linguistic study in which she argues that these texts do not deny the *right* of women to teach, but oppose *inappropriate* speaking or teaching. She concludes, "Where have any of the inspired writers said, I suffer not a woman to teach in public, and to stand up in the name of her Redeemer, administering the cup of salvation to the lips of dying immortals, even though her spirit is yearning to break unto them the bread of eternal life?"[146] Later in life (1853), Antoinette Brown Blackwell was ordained (probably the first ordained woman in America), and served a Congregational parish in New York State. She remained active in feminist causes, and published works in science, philosophy, and poetry.

Translations

American women were active in biblical translation. Julia Evelina Smith was born in Glastonbury, Connecticut, in 1792, her father a Yale-educated lawyer, her mother a talented linguist.[147] When William Miller's prediction that the end of the world would come in the early 1840s failed, Julia Smith concluded that his translation of the Bible must have been faulty. To correct this and other mistakes, Smith spent seven years producing five translations of the Bible: two from Greek (LXX and NT), two from Hebrew, and one from Latin (the Vulgate)—the three languages, she observed, that hung over the head of the crucified Savior (John 19:20). Originally, Smith had no intention of publishing her translation, but in 1872, Julia and her sister Abby became embroiled in an extended tax dispute with the Glastonbury officials. "We thought it might help our cause," wrote Julia in 1875, "to have it known that a woman could do more than any man has ever done, while

---

145. See Elizabeth Cazden, *Antoinette Brown Blackwell: A Biography* (Old Westbury, N.Y.: Feminist Press, 1983); Selvidge, *Notorious Voices*, 105–20.
146. "Exegesis of I Corinthians XIV, 34,35 and I Timothy II, 11,12," *Oberlin Quarterly* 4 (1849): 373.
147. See Susan J. Shaw, *A Religious History of Julia Evelina Smith's 1876 Translation of the Holy Bible: Doing More Than Any Man Has Ever Done* (San Francisco: Mellen Research University Press, 1993); Emily Walter Sampson, "'More Than Any Man Has Ever Done': Julia Smith's Search for the Meaning of God's Word," *BRev* 14 (1998): 41–45, 54–55; Madeleine B. Stern, "The First Feminist Bible: The 'Alderney' Edition, 1876," *Quarterly Journal of the Library of Congress* 34 (1977): 23–31; Selvidge, *Notorious Voices*, 214–26.

we are denied protection from any quarter, made to pay more money than any of the inhabitants of the place, without voice in the matter."[148] Doing "more than any man has ever done" was to translate the whole Bible. As Smith knew, translators such as Wycliffe and Tyndale had been assisted by others, while the hallowed King James Version was the work of more than forty underachievers.

Smith's translation was published in 1876, the centennial of the nation, by the American Publishing Company of Hartford—a company that published Mark Twain's *Tom Sawyer* the same year.[149] Smith responded to the charge that her efforts were presumptuous:

> I cannot be afraid of criticism, for let any one get a thorough knowledge of any language, especially one of such perfect grammatical construction, and let it be rendered literally word for word without the consideration of the writer . . . but let the book testify for itself without addition or subtraction. . . . Never have I considered myself above others for having translated the Bible.[150]

Above all, Smith strove for a literal translation: historical present is translated as present tense; articles are translated only if they appear; the same English word is used for every occurrence of a Greek term (a principle Smith does not always follow).[151] Romans 3:21-26 provides an example:

> But now without law the justice of God has been made apparent, being testified by the law and by the prophets; And the justice of God by faith of Jesus Christ to all and upon all believing: for there is no distinction: For all have sinned, and failed of the glory of God; Being justified as a gift by his grace by the redemption which is in Christ Jesus: Whom God had set before a propitiatory by faith in his blood, for a manifestation of his justice by passing over of sins before existing, in the sufferance of God; For the manifestation of his justice now in time: for him to be just, and justifying him of the faith of Jesus.

In regard to texts about women, Smith does not shrink from the literal, as in the case of 1 Tim. 2:11-15:

---

148. Julia E. Smith, *Abby Smith and Her Cows, with a Report of the Law Case Decided Contrary to Law* (1877; repr., New York: Arno, 1972), 57.
149. *The Holy Bible: Containing the Old and New Testaments, Translated Literally from the Original Tongues* (Hartford: American Publishing Company, 1876). See Harold P. Scanlin, "Bible Translation by American Individuals," in *The Bible and Bibles in America*, ed. Ernest S. Frerichs, SBLBAC (Atlanta, Ga.: Scholars Press, 1988), 58; P. Marion Simms, *The Bible in America: Versions That Have Played Their Part in the Making of the Republic* (New York: Wilson-Ericson, 1936), 149–50; Harry M. Orlinsky and Robert Bratcher, *A History of Bible Translation and the North American Contribution*, SBLBSNA (Atlanta: Scholars Press, 1991), 79–81.
150. *Abby Smith*, 62.
151. In translating the HB, Smith is oblivious to the principle of the "waw-consecutive" whereby the imperfect tense after the letter *waw* is construed as perfect tense. Smith usually renders the imperfect as the future. For example, Gen. 8:6-7: "Noah shall open the window of the ark which he made. And he shall send forth the raven, and it shall go forth."

> Let the woman, in freedom from care, learn in all subjection. And I trust not the woman to teach, neither to exercise authority over the man, but to be in freedom from care. For Adam was first formed, then Eve. And Adam was not deceived, but the woman, having been deceived, was in the transgression. And she shall be saved through bringing forth children, if they remain in faith and love and consecration with discretion.

To be sure, in v. 11, Smith translates ἡσυχίᾳ "in freedom from care" rather than "in silence" (KJV), but the primary meaning of the term is "quietness" or "rest." In 1 Cor. 14:34, Smith translates, "Let your women be silent in the churches," where the term is σιγάτωσαν from σιγάω—a term Smith consistently translates "be silent" in its other nine occurrences in the NT.

Another contribution to the history of translation was made by Helen Barrett Montgomery.[152] Montgomery, who had studied Greek at Wellesley, was the first woman to become president of the Northern Baptist Convention. To celebrate the one-hundredth anniversary of the American Baptist Publication Society, she published the *Centenary Translation: The New Testament in Modern English* (1924).[153] Her purpose is "To offer a translation in the language of everyday life, that does not depart too much from the translations already familiar and beloved."[154] Montgomery's translation is based on the Greek text used for the Revised Version of 1881. Each NT book is provided with a brief introduction that deals with such matters as date, author, and characteristics. Montgomery is aware of critical problems, but reaches conservative conclusions. She believes the Pastoral Letters to be authentic and the Fourth Gospel to have been authored by John the apostle. However, she notes Harnack's theory that Hebrews was written by Priscilla.[155] On textual matters, Montgomery is more innovative: she prints John 10:19-30 before John 10:1-18, and relegates the account of Judas's death in Acts 1:18-19 to the footnotes.

In contrast to Smith's literalism, Montgomery's translation of Rom. 3:21-26 displays a concerted effort to make a difficult text understandable.

> But now, quite apart from the law, a righteousness coming from God has been fully brought to light, continually witnessed by the Law and the Prophets. I mean a righteousness coming from God through faith in Jesus Christ for all who believe. For there is no distinction between Jew and Gentile, since all have sinned and lack the glory which comes from God; but they are now being justified by his free grace through the deliverance that is in Christ Jesus. For God openly set him forth for himself as an offering of atonement through

---

152. See Sharyn Dowd, "Helen Barrett Montgomery's Centenary Translation of the New Testament: Characteristics and Influences," *Perspectives in Religious Studies* 19 (1992): 133–50.
153. (Philadelphia: Judson, 1924). See Orlinsky and Bratcher, *History of Bible Translation*, 93–94; Simms, *Bible in America*, 150–52.
154. Montgomery, *Centenary Translation*, Introduction.
155. See p. 134, above.

faith, by means of his blood, in order to show forth his righteousness—since in his forbearance he had passed over the sins previously committed—to show forth his righteousness, I say, at this present time; that he himself might be just and yet the justifier of him who has faith in Jesus.

Montgomery's translation also reflects feminist concerns. She identifies Phoebe as "a minister of the church at Cenchreae," noting in the footnote, "The word used is διάκονος, a masculine noun, meaning 'minister' or 'servant.'" Most striking is Montgomery's translation of 1 Cor. 14:34-35 where she puts in quotation marks the entire command that woman should not speak. In the footnote, she writes, "Paul is probably quoting a sentence from the Judaizers."[156] All in all, Montgomery presents a reliable, readable translation.

Commentary: *The Woman's Bible*

The Woman's Bible was the brainchild of Elizabeth Cady Stanton (1815–1902), a lifelong combatant in the battle for women's rights.[157] As a girl, Stanton learned Greek from the minister who lived next door. She was reared a strict Presbyterian, but became increasingly convinced that the Bible had been misused in the suppression of women. At the 1885 meeting of the National Woman Suffrage Association, Stanton supported the following resolution:

> Resolved, That we call on the Christian ministry . . . to teach and enforce the fundamental idea of creation, that man was made in the image of God, male and female, and given equal rights over the earth, but none over each other. And, furthermore, we ask their recognition of the scriptural declaration that, in the Christian religion, there is neither male nor female, bond nor free, but all are one in Christ Jesus.[158]

Late in life, Stanton decided that a commentary should be produced to present a feminist understanding of the Bible. Stanton believed historical-

---

156. Dowd ("Montgomery's Centenary Translation," 142–50) believes Montgomery is dependent on the work of Katharine C. Bushnell who published as a series of Bible studies, "God's Word to Women" (1921).
157. See Selvidge, *Notorious Voices*, 95–105; Oden, *In Her Words*, 314–20; Lois W. Banner, *Elizabeth Cady Stanton: A Radical for Woman's Rights*, ed. Oscar Handlin, Library of American Biography (Boston: Little, Brown, 1980); Elisabeth Griffith, *In Her Own Right: The Life of Elizabeth Cady Stanton* (New York: Oxford University Press, 1984); Jeanne Stevenson-Moessner, "Elizabeth Cady Stanton, Reformer to Revolutionary: A Theological Trajectory," *JAAR* 62 (1994): 673–89; Dorothy C. Bass, "Women's Studies and Biblical Studies: An Historical Perspective," *JSOT* 22 (1982): 10–12; Anne Todd, "The Woman's Bible: 100 Years Ahead of Its Time?" *Daughters of Sarah* 21 (1995): 47–51; Suzan E. Hill, "The Woman's Bible: Reformulating Tradition," *Radical Religion* 3 (1977): 23–30; James H. Smylie, "*The Woman's Bible* and the Spiritual Crisis," *Soundings* 59 (1976): 305–28; Ruth Page, "Elizabeth Cady Stanton's *The Woman's Bible*," in *Feminist Theology: A Reader*, ed. Ann Loades (London: SPCK, 1990), 16–23.
158. Elizabeth Cady Stanton, *Eighty Years and More (1915–1897): Reminiscences* (London: T. Fisher Unwin, 1898), 381.

critical scholarship would be useful in subverting the male-dominating orthodox doctrine of biblical authority and inspiration. Consequently, she invited female Hebrew and Greek scholars to participate, but most of them declined, anxious to avoid guilt by association. More than twenty women agreed to contribute, including eight published authors, three Universalist ministers, and various freethinkers, including Mrs. Robert Ingersoll. Among the most militant was Matilda Joslyn Gage, whose major book *Woman, Church and State: A Historical Account of the Status of Woman through the Christian Ages* was essentially a chronicle of the repression of women by religion, especially Christianity. The major villain in the plot was Paul, whom Gage characterized as "intolerant," "unscrupulous," "the first Jesuit in the Christian church," "the Protestant Pope." Nevertheless, Gage believed the Holy Spirit represented the feminine aspect of the Deity, and wrote, "When woman interprets the Bible for herself, it will be in the interest of a higher morality, a purer home."[159]

The work on Stanton's *Woman's Bible* took more than six years. The procedure was for the participants to cut out all the texts in the Authorized Version that refer to women, paste them in a notebook, and write comments. Early in the project, Helen Gardener wrote, "I have begun already with Paul's Epistles, and am fascinated with the work. The untenable and unscientific positions he takes in regard to women are very amusing."[160] The final product appeared in 1898 when Stanton was more than eighty years of age.[161] Part I includes comments on the Pentateuch, Part II on Joshua through Revelation. Stanton presents her point of view in the Introduction:

> The only points in which I differ from all ecclesiastical teaching is that I do not believe that any man ever saw or talked with God, I do not believe that God inspired the Mosaic code, or told historians what they say he did about woman, for all the religions of the world degrade her, and so long as woman accepts the position that they assign her, her emancipation is impossible.[162]

The comments in *The Woman's Bible* do not deal extensively with critical issues. Stanton, who wrote most of the material, is moderate. She accepts the Fourth Gospel as written by the apostle John, "the bosom friend of Jesus,"[163] but observes that the style of Revelation is so different that the same author could not have written both. More radical criticism is offered by Ellen Battelle Dietrick. "As for passages now found in the New Testament

---

159. *Woman, Church and State: A Historical Account of the Status of Woman through the Christian Ages: With Reminiscences of the Matriarchate*, 2d ed. (New York: Truth Seeker, 1900; repr. in the series American Women: Images and Realities; New York: Arno, 1972), 54, 424.

160. Quoted by Stanton, *Eighty Years and More*, 392.

161. Elizabeth Cady Stanton, *The Woman's Bible: Parts I and II* (1895, 1898; repr. in the series American Women: Images and Realities (New York: Arno, 1972).

162. Ibid., Part I, 12.

163. Ibid., Part II, 138.

epistles of Paul, concerning women's non-equality with men and duty of subjection, there is no room to doubt that they are bare-faced forgeries, interpolated by unscrupulous bishops, during the early period in which a combined and determined effort was made to reduce women to silent submission, not only in the Church but also in the home and in the State."[164]

In the Preface to Part II, Stanton responds to a clergyman who had declared Part I (1895) to be the work of the devil:

> This is a grave mistake. His Satanic Majesty was not invited to join the Revising Committee. . . . Moreover, he has been so busy of late years attending Synods, General Assemblies and Conferences, to prevent the recognition of women delegates, that he has had no time to study the languages and "higher criticism."

Stanton was convinced that the NT was worse than the HB in oppressing women. However, most of the contributors found an exception in Jesus. "Jesus taught us, as no one else has ever done it, the humanness of God and the divineness of man, so that, standing there eighteen hundred years ago, he has naturally and infallibly attracted the eyes, the thought, the love, the reverence of the world." An anonymous commentator writes, "I think that the doctrine of the Virgin birth as something higher, sweeter, nobler than ordinary motherhood, is a slur on all the natural motherhood of the world."[165]

The Appendix contains letters written in response to *The Woman's Bible*, mostly sympathetic. However, Frances E. Willard, author of *Woman in the Pulpit* (1888) and president of the National Woman's Christian Temperance Union, expressed her belief that Christianity and the Bible had mainly advanced the cause of women. The National American Suffrage Association, meeting in Washington, D.C., in 1896, voted—over the strong protest of Susan B. Anthony—to declare that the Association had no official connection with *The Woman's Bible*. In any event, Stanton's work confirms what the history of NT research has repeatedly demonstrated: interpretation is shaped by the perspective of the interpreter. With Stanton, however, an important new perspective was provided.

NT Research

In the 1890s, women began to join the Society of Biblical Literature (founded, 1880).[166] Among the first was Mary E. Woolley, who taught at

---

164. Ibid., 150.
165. Ibid., 8, 115, 114.
166. See Ernest W. Saunders, *Searching the Scriptures: A History of the Society of Biblical Literature, 1880–1980*, SBLBSNA 8 (Chico, Calif.: Scholars Press, 1982), 8–9, 33, 83–84; Bass, "Women's Studies and Biblical Studies," 6–12.

Wellesley and later became president of Mount Holyoke College. Louise Pettibone Smith published a paper in the *Journal of Biblical Literature* in 1917, and served as secretary of the Society, 1950–51.[167] A highly regarded faculty member at Wellesley (1915–53), Smith held a doctorate from Bryn Mawr and had studied with Karl Barth at Bonn. She played a significant role in introducing Bultmann to America by her translation (with Erminie Huntress Lantero) of his monumental *Jesus*—appropriately retitled *Jesus and the Word*. Three other examples can provide samples of NT research by women in the period prior to World War II.

Silva Lake (formerly Mrs. Robert New) made important contributions to text criticism. She engaged in text-critical research with the support of a Guggenheim Fellowship from 1929 to 1931, and in 1936 was awarded a Ph.D. from Brown University. An example of her work is seen in *Family Π and the Codex Alexandrinus: The Text according to Mark*. In this careful, detailed analysis, Lake presents a history of the research about this group of manuscripts and their relation to the important uncial, Alexandrinus. She describes the manuscripts that belong to this family (a total of twenty-one) and presents her reconstruction of their generic relationship. She concludes, "The reconstructed text of Family Π, therefore, represents a manuscript older than the Codex Alexandrinus and affords another witness to a text which must have existed in the early part of the fifth century, if not before."[168] Later, Lake collaborated with her second husband, Kirsopp Lake, on a similar work on Family 13.[169] Silva and Kirsopp Lake also published a concise, well-informed *Introduction* to the NT.[170] They accept the two-document hypothesis in regard to the Synoptic Problem, and believe the Fourth Gospel may have been written by John the Elder. The Lakes doubt the authenticity of the Pastoral and Catholic Epistles. In general, their *Introduction* presents the data and alternative hypotheses, and leaves the decisions to the reader.

Mary Edith Andrews, a graduate of the Chicago School, made a significant contribution to Pauline research. Educated at Oberlin College, she received a B.D. from Chicago Theological Seminary and the Ph.D. from the University of Chicago (1931) where she studied with Case and Goodspeed. She served as Professor and head of the Department of Religion at Goucher College in Baltimore. Andrews was elected President of the National Asso-

---

167. See Edward C. Hobbs, ed., *Bultmann, Retrospect and Prospect: The Centenary Symposium at Wellesley*, HTS 35 (Philadelphia: Fortress, 1985), xi–xii, 88–113.

168. *Family Π and the Codex Alexandrinus: The Text according to Mark*, SD 5 (London: Christophers, 1937), ix.

169. *Family 13 (The Ferrar Group): The Text according to Mark, with a Collation of Codex 28 of the Gospels*, SD 11 (London: Christophers, 1941). On Kirsopp Lake, see pp. 406-10, below.

170. Kirsopp Lake and Silva Lake, *An Introduction to the New Testament* (London: Christophers, 1938).

ciation of Biblical Instructors, and served for a time as editor of the *Journal of Bible and Religion.*

Andrews's major work is *The Ethical Teaching of Paul.* In the introduction, she observes that Paul's theology has been exploited at the expense of his ethics. What is needed, she thinks, is a careful investigation of the latter by means of the sociological method. "The theologians have dwelt upon his ideas; the present study would analyze his behavior in the effort to find his practical bases for the achievement of the good life in the varied human relationships of his experience." Andrews believes the key to understanding Paul is to be found in his religious experience: "Paul's originality lies in his conception of the individual Christian as under the guidance of the Spirit, and in his conception of the community as formed of Spirit-guided individuals." Andrews believes Paul was a person of exaggerated self-assurance and unstable emotions. "He is an intensely emotional person," she writes, "on the heights or in the depths most of the time." In dealing with the Corinthians—mostly members of the working class who were plagued with problems of pagan morality—Paul, Andrews thinks, gave mixed ethical signals. His eschatology leads him to support the status quo; his preference for celibacy yields to the acceptance of marriage to avoid immorality. Paul's strictures on women's participation in worship, Andrews believes, contradict his theory of equality in Christ. "Theoretically, being *en Christo* was the point of fundamental importance; practically, it was of slight importance against Paul's inherited prejudices and the exigencies of the immediate situation."[171]

Andrews raises the question, Was Paul an intellectual? Noting the work of Bultmann, Andrews says that the predominant intellectuals of the day were the Stoics. However, referring to the research of Paul Wendland and Richard Reitzenstein, she contends that Paul was more in harmony with Hellenistic mysticism and Gnosticism than with Stoicism. Turning to Jewish influences, Andrews says, "The intellectual content of resurrection, Parousia, appeal to Scripture, confidence in God the Father, is quite overbalanced by Paul's thoroughly un-Jewish conduct." She concludes, "The predominance of practical problems . . . shows that Paul has been greatly over-estimated as an intellectual, particularly as the important early Christian theologian."[172]

Another product of the Chicago School was Mary Redington Ely Lyman. Born in Vermont, Ely graduated from Mount Holyoke College and earned at B.D. at Union Theological Seminary, New York. After additional study at Cambridge, she received her Ph.D. at the University of Chicago in 1924.

---

171. *The Ethical Teaching of Paul: A Study in Origin* (Chapel Hill: University of North Carolina Press, 1934), 8, 35, 52, 98.
172. Ibid., 144, 169.

She taught at Vassar, Barnard, Sweet Bryar Colleges, and in 1950, was named Jesup Professor of English Bible at Union Seminary.

Mary Redington Ely's major work is *Knowledge of God in Johannine Thought.* Like Andrews, she embraces the sociohistorical method and exploits the results of history of religion research.

> The increasing understanding of the evolutionary nature of Christianity has carried with it a truer appreciation of the purpose and character of its early writings. The documents are now seen to be susceptible of interpretation only in the light of the conditions of life which lay behind them. The older view, which . . . used theological interpretation as the method of research, has given place to a consideration of the New Testament writings as means through which to view the community life of which they were an expression.

The major concern of this book is "the discovery of the causes at work which produced in the mind of the writer an emphasis upon knowledge of God as essential to religion." Ely believes this can be accomplished only by studying the Fourth Gospel in its setting within the religious syncretism that flourished in Ephesus.[173]

Ely begins with an analysis of the terms for knowing—οἶδα, γινώσκω, γνωρίζω. These terms, according to Ely, indicate a rational and intellectual concern, yet they are shaped by the author's religious experience, influenced by his historical context. In regard to Judaism, Ely notes the prophetic legacy of ethics and the current expressions of legalism and apocalyptic. She finds the background to the Johannine idea of the Logos in Philo, and notes the stress on emotion and ritual in the Hellenistic mysteries. Ely believes Gnosticism represents a pre-Christian synthesis of oriental ideas and redemptive religion—a synthesis that sees esoteric knowledge as the way to salvation. Ely investigates the Hermetic literature, acknowledging the late date of the sources, but detecting the sort of syncretism that she thinks would have been found at Ephesus at the end of the first century.

Ely concludes that the author makes use of Hellenistic materials, but affirms a religion that is intellectual and ethical. His ethical concern is seen in his understanding of the relation of knowledge to love, and his rational concern is apparent in his presentation of theology as biography—a revelation in history, confirmed by evidence, witnesses, and signs.

> And here appears the discriminating, creative gift of the author of the Fourth Gospel, that accepting from Hellenistic religion its redemption motif, he thrust into it a new concept of "knowledge" which was partly a fusion of Hellenic philosophical notions and Old Testament ethical evaluations. . . . [H]e has brought to the Hellenistic notion of "knowledge" that is illumination and comes to man by the avenue of ecstasy or vision, a correction which, on the content side, is a progressive, personal fellowship with Jesus, the Son of God,

---

173. *Knowledge of God in Johannine Thought* (New York: Macmillan, 1925), 9, 11.

and on its process side, recognizes the need of man's reflective powers, and challenges not only his emotional, but his intellectual nature as well.[174]

All in all, this is a very perceptive book, fully informed by the German and French sources, and employing the sociohistorical method with religious sensitivity.[175]

Mary Ely Lyman's contribution to the historical quest is seen in her *Jesus* (1937)—a volume in the series Hazen Books on Religion. These small books, aimed at the popular audience, were written by esteemed authors such as Walter Horton and Henry P. Van Dusen. The fact that Lyman was chosen to write the volume on Jesus shows the high regard in which she was held by the scholarly community. Lyman thinks a general outline of the career of Jesus is presented in the Synoptic Gospels. She believes he was moved by a sense of urgency, and had "faith in the possibilities of human nature." Lyman believes the central feature of the teaching of Jesus was the kingdom—"the righteous rule of God." Although she acknowledges that Jesus accepted the apocalyptic idea of the imminence of the kingdom, Lyman believes he modified it. "He gave new meaning to the thought of the Kingdom by making it completely a moral and spiritual concept." Jesus, she thinks, saw himself primarily as prophet. "His own view then seems to be in harmony with that of the poet-prophet of the exile who portrayed a Suffering Servant of the Lord." The impact of Jesus is seen in the NT and in the ongoing history of Christianity:

> Jesus is now, as he has been all through the Christian centuries, more than a teacher of ethics, more than the spokesman of a great system of teaching. Behind the teaching is the life, the concrete embodiment of the ideal in living, that carries over these centuries an enthusiasm, a winsomeness, a power that no system of ethics could ever give. Here is incentive to our achievement: that we see the ideal actually at work.[176]

In short, Lyman presents a concise, lucid account of the liberal Jesus.

CONSERVATIVE REACTION:
BENJAMIN B. WARFIELD AND J. GRESHAM MACHEN

The sort of criticism that triumphed at Union, Yale, and Chicago—illustrated by the work of such scholars as Andrews and Lyman—provoked a potent reaction from conservatives, spearheaded by the theologians of

---

174. Ibid., 150–51.
175. Later Ely published a book on the Gospel of John for the general reader: Mary Redington Ely Lyman, *The Fourth Gospel and the Life of To-Day* (New York: Macmillan, 1931). In this book, she argues that historical study demonstrates the relevance of the Fourth Gospel for modern thought, especially the importance of grounding theological thought in historical fact. She locates the Gospel in Ephesus early in the second century.
176. *Jesus*, Hazen Books on Religion (New York: Association, 1937), 8, 15, 21, 32, 53.

Princeton Seminary. In the early stages, this counterattack was led by Benjamin B. Warfield, erudite heir of the intellectual tradition of Charles Hodge.[177] Warfield remained within the mainstream of American Christianity, contributing articles to the leading journals and encyclopedias. Early in the twentieth century, however, the battle became increasingly bitter, and the fundamentalist-modernist controversy exploded. Liberalism, embracing evolution and advances in science, became increasingly popular. American culture, traditionally religious, became increasing pluralistic and secular. Scholars such as Mathews made converts to modernism, and liberalism captured theological seminaries across the country.[178]

In reaction, conservatism hardened into fundamentalism.[179] A movement that flourished in the 1920s, fundamentalism was a combination of various conservative religious trends—dispensationalism, millennialism, revivalism—with the supernaturalism and biblicism of the Princeton theologians. In 1910, the General Assembly of the Presbyterian Church affirmed five essential doctrines that came to be known as the "fundamentals": inerrancy of Scripture, the virgin birth of Christ, substitutionary atonement, the physical resurrection, and the miraculous power of Christ. From 1910 to 1915, a series of twelve little volumes titled *The Fundamentals* was published, advocating a variety of conservative ideas, but agreeing on one thing: the danger of biblical criticism. During World War I, the anti-Teutonic sentiment that swept the country inspired the fundamentalists to see in German NT research a threat as dreadful as the Kaiser's stealthy U-boats.

In 1922, Harry Emerson Fosdick, destined to become America's most popular preacher with a weekly radio broadcast heard across the nation, delivered a sermon entitled, "Shall the Fundamentalists Win?"[180] Fosdick, a Professor at Union Seminary, had been called as continuing guest preacher at New York's First Presbyterian Church. In the sermon, Fosdick declared

---

177. See pp. 31–37, above.
178. See William R. Hutchison, *The Modern Impulse in American Protestantism* (Cambridge: Harvard University Press, 1976).
179. See Ernest R. Sandeen, *The Origins of Fundamentalism: Toward a Historical Interpretation*, Facet Books: Historical Series 10 (Philadelphia: Fortress, 1968); idem, *The Roots of Fundamentalism: British and American Millenarianism* (Chicago: University of Chicago Press, 1970); George M. Marsden, *Fundamentalism and American Culture: The Shaping of Twentieth-Century Evangelicalism: 1870–1925* (New York: Oxford University Press, 1980); Ferenc Morton Szasz, *The Divided Mind of Protestant America, 1880–1930* (Tuscaloosa: University of Alabama Press, 1982); Mark A. Noll, *Between Faith and Criticism: Evangelicals, Scholarship, and the Bible in America*, SBL Confessional Perspectives Series (San Francisco: Harper & Row, 1986); Timothy P. Weber, "The Two-Edged Sword: The Fundamentalist Use of the Bible," in *The Bible in America: Essays in Cultural History*, ed. Nathan O. Hatch and Mark A. Noll (New York: Oxford University Press, 1982), 101–20.
180. William R. Hutchison, ed., *American Protestant Thought: The Liberal Era*, HT (New York and Evanston: Harper & Row, 1968), 170–82. Fosdick's sermon was published in the *Christian Century*, June 8, 1922; *The Christian Work*, June 10, 1922; and as a pamphlet, "The New Knowledge and the Christian Faith" (1922).

that three of the fundamentalists' basic doctrines were unessential: the virgin birth, the verbal inspiration and infallibility of Scripture, and the literal second coming of Christ. Although Fosdick intended his sermon to be a plea for tolerance, the fundamentalists heard it as a call to arms. Intellectual conservatives like J. Gresham Machen, who shared the fundamentalist view of Scripture, were further infuriated when Fosdick published *The Modern Use of the Bible*. Fosdick, who was no match for Machen as a biblical scholar, championed historical criticism and the scientific worldview, arguing that the antique thought forms of the Bible had to be updated. "It is impossible that a Book written two to three thousand years ago should be used in the twentieth century A.D. without having some of its forms of thought and speech translated into modern categories."[181] For Machen, updating meant betrayal—a betrayal he was later to detect and decry in Princeton Seminary and in the Presbyterian Church.

Benjamin B. Warfield (1851–1921)

Warfield was born near Lexington, Kentucky, the son of a prosperous farmer.[182] He was educated at the College of New Jersey (later Princeton University), where he graduated at the head of his class (1871). After study in Europe, Warfield decided on a career in the ministry and entered Princeton Theological Seminary. After graduation in 1876, he spent at year in Europe, where he studied at Leipzig. From 1878 to 1887, Warfield taught NT at Western Theological Seminary, Allegheny, Pennsylvania. In 1887, he was named Professor of Didactic and Polemical theology at Princeton Seminary, where he taught for thirty-three years. F. L. Patton, formerly president of the Seminary, described Warfield: "Tall, erect, with finely moulded features and singular grace and courtesy of demeanor, he bore the marks of a gentleman to his finger tips."[183] Warfield's writings, primarily periodical essays and encyclopedia articles, have been collected into ten volumes.[184]

---

181. *The Modern Use of the Bible*, Lyman Beecher Lectureship in Preaching (New York: Macmillan, 1924), 129.
182. See Samuel G. Craig, "Benjamin B. Warfield," in Benjamin Breckinridge Warfield, *Biblical and Theological Studies*, ed. Samuel C. Craig, The Benjamin B. Warfield Collection (Philadelphia: Presbyterian and Reformed Publishing, 1968), xi–xlviii. W. Andrew Hoffecker, *Piety and the Princeton Theologians: Archibald Alexander, Charles Hodge, Benjamin Warfield* (Phillipsburg, N.J.: Presbyterian and Reformed Publishing, 1981), 95–155; idem, "Benjamin B. Warfield," in *Reformed Theology in America: A History of Its Modern Development*, ed. David F. Wells (Grand Rapids, Mich.: Eerdmans, 1985), 60–86; Jack B. Rogers and Donald K. McKim, *The Authority and Interpretation of the Bible: An Historical Approach* (New York: Harper & Row, 1979), 323–48.
183. Quoted by Craig, "Warfield," xvi.
184. *The Works of Benjamin B. Warfield*, 10 vols. (1927–32; repr., Grand Rapids, Mich.: Baker, 1981). Selections from Warfield's writings are printed in the multivolume series "The Benjamin B. Warfield Collection" (Phillipsburg, N.J.: Presbyterian and Reformed Publishing); for a shorter representative selection, see Mark A. Noll, *The Princeton Theology, 1812–1921* (Grand Rapids, Mich.: Baker, 1983), 241–316; John E. Meeter, ed., *Selected Shorter Writings: Benjamin B. Warfield*, 2 vols. (Nutley, N.J.: Presbyterian and Reformed Publishing, 1970–73).

Warfield's inaugural address at Princeton was expanded into an essay, "The Idea of Systematic Theology."[185] Like Hodge, Warfield believed theology to be a science. Like science, theology presupposes the reality of a subject matter (God), the capacity of the human mind to comprehend (common sense), and a medium of communication (Scripture). "Theology is therefore that science which treats of God and of the relations between God and the universe."[186] According to Warfield, God can be known only by God's revelatory action—in nature, in history, and in religious experience, but most of all, in Scripture. In relating systematic theology to the other disciplines, Warfield delineates important distinctions: apologetic theology establishes presuppositions; exegetical theology provides the material for biblical theology; biblical theology orders the material provided by exegetical theology; and systematic theology, the crowning discipline, presents revealed truth in its rational arrangement.

Warfield revered the Calvinist tradition with its stress on divine sovereignty and grace, on human depravity and salvation by divine intervention. Like Hodge, he qualified his Calvinism by adopting Scottish commonsense philosophy. From this perspective, Warfield viewed theology as primarily concerned with facts. The facts, he believed, were not limited to phenomena of nature (creation), but to the supernatural acts of the transcendent God (Creator). In his essay "The Essence of Christianity," Warfield opposed the naturalism and anthropocentrism of liberalism.[187] "Christianity, clearly, is not a natural evolution of the religious spirit of man, with a more or less accidental connection with the man Jesus; it is a particular religion instituted by Christ and given once for all its specific content by His authority."[188] In opposition to natural religion, Warfield affirms the supernatural. In his essay "Christian Supernaturalism," he argues that Christianity is through and through a supernatural religion.[189] "The confession of a supernatural God, who may and does act in a supernatural mode, and who acting in a supernatural mode has wrought out for us a supernatural redemption, interpreted in a supernatural revelation, and applied by the supernatural operations of His Spirit—this confession constitutes the core of the Christian profession."[190]

---

185. Noll, *Princeton Theology*, 241–61; *Works* 9:49–87.
186. Noll, *Princeton Theology*, 246.
187. In Benjamin Breckinridge Warfield, *The Person and Work of Christ*, ed. Samuel G. Craig, The Benjamin B. Warfield Collection (Philadelphia: Presbyterian and Reformed Publishing, 1950), 479–530; repr. in Benjamin Breckinridge Warfield, *Christology and Criticism* (New York: Oxford University Press, 1929), 393–444.
188. *Person and Work*, 513.
189. In Benjamin Breckinridge Warfield, *Biblical and Theological Studies*, ed. Samuel C. Craig, The Benjamin B. Warfield Collection (Philadelphia: Presbyterian and Reformed Publishing, 1968), 1–21; *Works* 9:25–46.
190. "Christian Supernaturalism," *Biblical and Theological Studies*, 21.

View of Scripture

Warfield's research presupposes his basic view of Scripture, and his view of Scripture is grounded in his doctrine of special revelation.[191] According to Warfield, revelation is given by God in three stages: in the patriarchal age by theophany, in the prophetic era by inward inspiration, and in the age of the Spirit by the written word. The supreme revelation is the fact of God's self-disclosure in the flesh, and, in the NT, the meaning of that fact is revealed.

> The entirety of the New Testament is but the explanatory word accompanying and giving its effect to the fact of Christ. And when this fact was in all its meaning made the possession of men, revelation was completed and in that sense ceased. Jesus Christ is no less the end of revelation than He is the end of the law.[192]

The revelation in the NT is confirmed by Warfield's doctrine of inspiration.[193] According to Warfield, inspiration is a distinctive, unique action of the Spirit.

> That it is such an influence as makes the words written under its guidance, the words of God; by which is meant to be affirmed an absolute infallibility (as alone fitted to divine words), admitting no degrees whatever—extending to the very word, and to all the words. So that every part of Holy Writ is thus held alike infallibly true in all its statements, of whatever kind.[194]

Warfield opposes the mechanical idea of inspiration, that is, the idea that the writers were the penmen of God, taking down dictation by rote. Instead, "the whole Bible is recognized as human, the free product of human effort in every part and word. And at the same time, the whole Bible is recognized as divine, the Word of God, his utterances, of which he is in the truest sense the Author."[195] Thus, according to Warfield, there is a concurrence of the divine and the human in the words of Scripture.

Warfield finds his view of inspiration confirmed by the biblical writers.[196] For Warfield, this is not a circular argument, but simply a demonstration that this doctrine, like all of his doctrines, is biblical. He argues that the

---

191. See Cornelius Van Til, "Introduction," in Benjamin Breckinridge Warfield, *The Inspiration and Authority of the Bible*, ed. Samuel G. Craig, The Benjamin B. Warfield Collection (Phillipsburg, Pa.: Presbyterian and Reformed Publishing, 1948), 3–68; John H. Gerstner, "Warfield's Case for Biblical Inerrancy," in *God's Inerrant Word: An International Symposium on the Trustworthiness of Scripture*, ed. John Warwick Montgomery (Minneapolis: Bethany Fellowship, 1973), 115–42; Mike Parsons, "Warfield and Scripture," *Chm* 91 (1977): 198–220.
192. The Biblical Idea of Revelation," in *Inspiration and Authority*, 96.
193. "Inspiration and Criticism," in *Inspiration and Authority*, 419–42; *Works* 1:395–425.
194. "Inspiration and Criticism," *Inspiration and Authority*, 420.
195. "The Divine and Human in the Bible,"in Noll, *Princeton Theology*, 279.
196. "The Biblical Idea of Inspiration," in *Inspiration and Authority*, 131–66; *Works* 1:77–112.

word θεόπνευστος does not mean "inspired of God," but "God breathed," that is, it describes the product of the "creative breath of God." Warfield discusses three major texts that he believes affirm his doctrine of inspiration. Second Timothy 3:16 he translates, "Every Scripture, seeing that it is God-breathed, is as well profitable."[197] Second Peter 1:19-21 Warfield understands to say that all Scripture is prophecy and that prophecy is "moved by the Holy Spirit." John 10:34-35 presents a word from the Psalms as Scripture and asserts that "the scripture cannot be annulled." Warfield believes the inspiration and authority of Scripture are also affirmed when Jesus and the NT writers says "it is written," or "God said," or "the scriptures say."[198] Although these texts do not explicitly affirm inerrancy, Warfield believes they present the Bible as the word of God, and if God speaks through the Bible, the words of the Bible, regardless of human freedom and the limitations of language, must be true.

Warfield acknowledges that errors have crept into the NT during the copying and printing of the text; inerrancy is restricted to the original autographs.[199] However, Warfield does not adopt this view as an escape into an illusive hypothetical text, protected from critical scrutiny. He believes that the extant texts closely approximate the originals, and, except for some minor textual details, are without error or contradiction. Warfield also contests the claims of many higher critics when he asserts that "modern biblical criticism has not disproved the authenticity of a single book of our New Testament."[200] This raises the question of Warfield's understanding of canon. In his inaugural at Western Theological Seminary, Warfield had acknowledged that 2 Peter did not appear in canonical lists until late, yet he argued that its eventual appearance must have meant earlier acceptance. In his essay "The Formation of the Canon of the New Testament," Warfield argues that canonicity precedes the *recognition* of books as canonical.[201] "The Canon of the New Testament was completed when the last authoritative book was given to any church by the apostles, and that was when John wrote

---

197. "The Biblical Idea of Inspiration," *Inspiration and Authority*, 132–33, 134.

198. See "'It Says': 'Scripture Says': 'God Says,'" in *Inspiration and Authority*, 299–348; idem, "The Terms 'Scripture and 'Scriptures' as Employed in the New Testament," in *Inspiration and Authority*, 229–41.

199. "The Inerrancy of the Original Autographs," in Noll, *Princeton Theology*, 268–74. Warfield's attention to the autographs results from his understanding of text criticism. In 1886, he published *An Introduction to the Textual Criticism of the New Testament*, 3d ed. (London; Hodder and Stoughton, 1890). Although this was a student handbook, it argued that the same methods should be used for the study of the text of the NT as for other ancient documents. Warfield supported the genealogical method that groups manuscripts according to errors; he largely agreed with the method and results of Westcott and Hort. See Theodore P. Letis, "B. B. Warfield, Common-Sense Philosophy and Biblical Criticism," *American Presbyterians: Journal of Presbyterian History* 69 (1991): 175–90.

200. "Inspiration and Criticism," *Inspiration and Authority*, 429.

201. *Inspiration and Authority*, 411–16; *Works* 1:415–56.

the Apocalypse, about A.D. 98." "The early churches, in short, received, as we receive, into their New Testament all the books historically evinced to them as given by the apostles to the churches as their code of law; and we must not mistake the historical evidences of the slow circulation and authentication of these books over the widely-extended church, for evidence of slowness of 'canonization' of books by the authority or the taste of the church."[202]

An example of Warfield's belief in biblical inerrancy is presented in his essay "The Prophecies of Paul."[203] In essence, this is an exegetical study, designed to demonstrate that Paul was not mistaken about the end of the world. Warfield believes the Thessalonians, misunderstanding Paul's first letter, expected the end to come soon. Paul corrected them with 2 Thessalonians, presenting predictions that Warfield believes were largely fulfilled with the destruction of Jerusalem. According to Warfield, 1 Corinthians presents the resurrection of the spiritual body as a body of "flesh and bones" (Luke 24:39) in which the Spirit fully dominated. Paul's reference to "flesh and blood" that cannot inherit the kingdom (1 Cor. 15:50) Warfield interprets as moral, not physical. In all the Pauline texts, Warfield detects evidence that Paul remained uncertain about the time of the end.[204]

Warfield's higher criticism is illustrated by his contribution to the "Temple Bible"—a series that presents nontechnical introductions and exegetical notes on the biblical (KJV) texts. Warfield's contribution is *Acts and Pastoral Epistles*. In his introduction to Acts, Warfield speculates that the author of Luke and Acts planned a third volume. That author, in Warfield's opinion, is Luke, the travel companion of Paul. "It is scarcely likely that anyone but a physician would have written just as this book is written." In his introduction to the Pastorals, Warfield adopts the hypothesis that Paul was released from prison in Rome, made a trip to Crete and Ephesus, and was imprisoned for a second time in Rome. Since 1 and 2 Timothy and Titus were written at a later time, Warfield believes their style and vocabulary reflect a situation different from the earlier letters. "We cannot feel surprise to find the 'Pastoral Epistles' therefore very much alike, and in the very points in which they resemble one another very much unlike the rest of Paul's epistles." Warfield's notes basically explain details of the text: identification of persons, explanation of terms, textual variants.[205]

---

202. "The Formation of the Canon of the NT," *Inspiration and Authority*, 415, 416. Gary Steven Shogren ("Christian Prophecy and Canon in the Second Century: A Response to B. B. Warfield, *JETS* 40 [1997]: 609–26) argues that Warfield's claim that prophecy ended with the closing of the canon (at the end of the first century) is not supported by second-century church fathers.

203. In *Biblical and Theological Studies*, 463–502; *Works* 2:601–40.

204. According to Warfield, inspiration does not convey omniscience, and inerrancy applies only to statements that the author intended. See Moisés Silva, "Old Princeton, Westminster, and Inerrancy," *WTJ* 50 (1988): 65–80.

205. *Acts and Pastoral Epistles: Timothy, Titus, and Philemon*, The Temple Bible (London: J. M. Dent, 1902), xxiv, xxxvi, 127.

Biblical Theology

Warfield's major contribution to NT research is in biblical theology. In accord with his understanding of revelation, he gives attention to Jesus and Christology. His essay "The Historical Christ" originally appeared as "Jesus Christ" in the prestigious *The New Schaff-Herzog Encyclopedia of Religious Knowledge*.[206] In regard to sources for the study of Jesus, Warfield adopts a version of the two-document hypothesis: a primitive narrative source (virtually the sole source of Mark) was used by Matthew and Luke, and they also used another source for the sayings of Jesus. According to Warfield, the Fourth Gospel was written by an eyewitness who supplemented the Synoptics. Jesus, in Warfield's reading of the Gospels, saw his whole life as fulfillment of his supernatural messianic mission. Although Warfield affirms the humanity of Jesus, he writes, "The Jesus of the New Testament is not fundamentally man, however divinely gifted: he is God tabernacling for a while among men, with heaven lying about Him not merely in his infancy, but throughout all the days of His flesh." Jesus, according to Warfield, presented himself as the founder of the kingdom of God, and his miracles prove that the kingdom was present. "For a time," speculates Warfield, "disease and death must have been almost banished from the land."[207]

Warfield's understanding of Jesus is expanded in his essay "The Supernatural Birth of Jesus," originally written at the request of the editors of the highly regarded *American Journal of Theology*.[208] Warfield begins with a definition: "I shall take 'the supernatural birth of Jesus' in its highest sense—that of the truly miraculous birth of Jesus from a virgin mother, without intervention of man." On the basis of this definition, Warfield proceeds to argue that belief in the supernatural birth of Jesus is essential to Christianity because of three basic elements. First, the whole life of Jesus must be seen as supernatural. Second, the supernatural birth is crucial to a proper understanding of the incarnation:

> The Christianity of the New Testament, remembering the two natures . . . offers us in our Lord's person, not a mere man (perhaps in some sense made God), nor a mere God (perhaps in some sense made man), but a true God-man, who, being all that God is and at the same time all that man is, has come into the world in a fashion suitable to his dual nature, conceived indeed in a virgin's womb, and born of woman and under the law, but not by the will of the flesh, nor by the will of man, but solely by the will of God who he is.

---

206. "The Historical Christ," in *Person and Work of Christ*, 5–33; *NSHERK* 6:50–60; *Christology and Criticism*, 149–77; *Works* 3:149–77.
207. "The Historical Christ," *Person and Work*, 19, 31.
208. *AJT* 10 (1906): 21–30; *Biblical and Theological Studies*, 157–68; *Christology and Criticism*, 447–58; *Works* 3:447–58.

Finally, the supernatural birth is essential to the doctrine of redemption, because redemption requires a redeemer without sin, and this is possible, in Warfield's opinion, only on the basis of a supernatural birth.[209]

Warfield's essay "The Person of Christ According to the New Testament" is an exercise in NT Christology.[210] Warfield begins with Paul, giving attention to major texts. In regard to Phil. 2:5-9, Warfield believes the phrase "form of God" means that Christ possessed those characteristics that belong to God as God. Although the text says that Christ "emptied himself," Warfield does not believe it means that Christ abandoned his divine nature in assuming his human nature; "emptying," says Warfield, should be understood metaphorically, not literally. In interpreting Rom. 8:3, Warfield observes that God sent Christ "not in sinful flesh, but only 'in the likeness of sinful flesh.'"[211] Warfield's understanding of Pauline Christology is expanded in his essay, "The Christ That Paul Preached"—an essay that gives careful attention to Rom. 1:1-7.[212] According to Warfield's exegesis, the two designations, Son of David and Son of God, do not imply temporal sequence or change (as if Jesus were first Son of David, and only later Son of God). Paul "is distinguishing elements in the constitution of our Lord's person, by virtue of which He is at one and the same time both the Messiah and the Son of God. He became of the seed of David with respect to the flesh, and by the resurrection of the dead was mightily proven to be also the Son of God with respect to the Spirit of holiness."[213]

In the essay on the "Person of Christ," Warfield also attends to the Christology of the Gospels. The prologue of John affirms the deity and preexistence of Christ. "In some sense distinguishable from God, He was in an equally true sense identical with God." In regard to John 14:28 where Jesus is reported to say "the Father is greater than I," Warfield writes, "Obviously this means that there was a sense in which He had ceased to be equal with the Father, because of the humiliation of His present condition, and in so far as this humiliation involved entrance into a status lower than that which belonged to Him by nature." Similarly, in response to Mark 13:32 where Jesus says that the Son does not know the day or the hour of the parousia,

---

209. "The Supernatural Birth of Jesus," *Biblical and Theological Studies*, 160, 164–65. Warfield's stress on the humanity of Jesus is seen in his essay "On the Emotional Life of Our Lord" (*Person and Work of Christ*, 93–145), in which he analyzes the three main emotions of Jesus presented in the gospel narratives: compassion, anger, and joy. Warfield believes Jesus' anger was fully justified. "Jesus' anger is not merely the seamy side of his pity; it is the righteous reaction of his moral sense in the presence of evil. But Jesus burned with anger against the wrongs he met with in his journey through human life as truly as he melted with pity at the sight of the world's misery: and it was out of these two emotions that his actual mercy proceeded" (122).
210. *Person and Work of Christ*, 37–70; *Works* 2:175–209.
211. "The Person of Christ according to the NT," *Person and Work of Christ*, 45.
212. *Person and Work of Christ*, 73–90.
213. "The Christ that Paul Preached," *Person and Work of Christ*, 84.

Warfield comments, "When He speaks of 'the Son' (who is God) as ignorant, we must understand that He is designating Himself as 'the Son' because of His higher nature, and yet has in mind the ignorance of His lower nature; what He means is that the person properly designated 'the Son' is ignorant, that is to say with respect to the human nature which is as intimate an element of His personality as is His Deity."[214]

Closely related to his Christology and crucial to his theology is Warfield's understanding of the atonement. In his article "The Chief Theories of the Atonement," Warfield identifies various theories of atonement in regard to their effective termination, for example, theories that see the work of Christ terminating in Satan (bringing release), in humans (inducing ethical action), or in God (satisfying divine justice).[215] According to Warfield, the proper theory sees the work of Christ terminating in both God and humans, but primarily in God (wherein Christ is satisfaction for sin and affirmation of divine justice). Warfield's view of atonement is expanded in other essays. In "The New Testament Terminology of Redemption," he presents a sophisticated linguistic analysis of λύτρον and related terms.[216] Warfield investigates the usage of these terms in classical and Hellenistic sources and in the LXX. In regard to the OT, he concludes that the understanding of redemption at cost or by payment of ransom is always explicit or implicit. In the NT, the term ἀπολύτρωσις refers to the redemption accomplished in Christ. "It is quite clear in sum that ἀπολύτρωσις in the New Testament is conceived, in accordance with its native connotation, and its usage elsewhere, distinctly as a ransoming; and that implication must be read in it on every occasion of its occurrence."[217] In "Christ Our Sacrifice," Warfield engages in history of religion research.[218] He detects two main ideas of sacrifice in ancient religion: sacrifice understood apart from the idea of sin (for example, sacrifice as a gift); sacrifice understood as related to the idea of sin (that is, piacular sacrifice). "Any unbiased study of the Levitical system must issue, it seems to us, in the conviction that this system is through and through, in its intention and effect, piacular." In accord with the OT, the NT uses sacrificial language to depict the crucifixion. Warfield concludes, "the New Testament writers, in employing this language to describe the death of Christ, intended to represent that death as performing the functions of an expiatory sacrifice."[219]

In sum, the work of Warfield reflects a vigorous and incisive theological mind, skilled in historical and exegetical research, fully comprehensive of

---

214. "Person of Christ," *Person and Work of Christ*, 53, 61, 63.
215. *NSHERK* 1:349–56; *Person and Work of Christ*, 351–69; *Works* 9:261–80.
216. *Person and Work of Christ*, 429–75; *Works* 2:327–72.
217. "The NT Terminology of Redemption," *Person and Work of Christ*, 467.
218. *Person and Work of Christ*, 391–426; *Works* 2:401–35.
219. "Christ Our Sacrifice," *Person and Work of Christ*, 413, 424.

the scholarship of his opponents (including the Germans)—all dedicated to an apologetic and polemic biblical theology that is characterized by emphasis on supernaturalism and biblical inerrancy. In the last analysis, assessment of Warfield's work will depend on the presuppositions and theological perspectives of his critics.[220] Supporters of his work are justified in their protest against a theological perspective that rules out the supernatural a priori or denigrates the biblical idea of inspiration. On the other hand, critics may wonder whether a criticism that posits the inerrancy and harmony of the primary sources can allow a genuine historical investigation. For example, it is difficult to believe that original readers of Luke 24:39 would have understood the text to describe a spiritual body, or that the original readers of 1 Cor. 15:42-57 would have understood the spiritual body to have had flesh and bones. Also, for critics in the tradition of Herder and Coleridge,[221] Warfield would appear to offer a one-dimensional Bible—a Bible reduced to objective facts and doctrines, a Bible deprived of the depth and variety of literary expression. In any event, this debate would continue to disturb the ongoing history of NT research.

J. Gresham Machen (1881–1937)

Life and Theological Perspective

The mantel of Warfield fell on J. Gresham Machen, and with it, a double portion of the polemic spirit. Machen was in born Baltimore, the son of a prominent lawyer.[222] He was educated at Johns Hopkins University, where he graduated at the head of his class (1901). In 1902, he reluctantly entered Princeton Seminary with no intention of ordination to the ministry. Machen spent a year of study in Germany (1905–6), first at Marburg and then at Göttingen. At Marburg he was captivated by the liberal Wilhelm Herrmann because of "the contagious earnestness, the deep religious feeling of the man."[223] About his experience at Göttingen, Machen was later to

---

220. See the debate between Dunn and Nicole: James D. G. Dunn, "The Authority of Scripture according to Scripture," *Chm* 96 (1982): 104–22; Roger Nicole, "The Inspiration and Authority of Scripture: J. D. G. Dunn versus B. B. Warfield," *Chm* 97 (1983): 198–215.

221. *HNTR* 1:177–83, 339–43.

222. For biography, see Ned B. Stonehouse, *J. Gresham Machen: A Biographical Memoir* (Grand Rapids, Mich.: Eerdmans, 1954); D. G. Hart, *Defending the Faith: J. Gresham Machen and the Crisis of Conservative Protestantism in Modern America* (Baltimore: Johns Hopkins University Press, 1994); J. Gresham Machen, "Christianity in Conflict," in *Contemporary American Theology: Theological Autobiographies*, ed. Vergilius Ferm (New York: Round Table, 1932), 245–74; C. Allyn Russell, *Voices of American Fundamentalism: Seven Biographical Studies* (Philadelphia: Westminster Press, 1976), 135–61; Bradley J. Longfield, *The Presbyterian Controversy: Fundamentalists, Modernists, and Moderates*, Religion in America Series (New York: Oxford University Press, 1991), 28–53.

223. Machen, "Christianity in Conflict," 255.

write, "My admiration for Bousset's learning and brilliancy were later increased by his book, *Kyrios Christos,* which appeared in 1913. Not since the time of F. C. Baur, it seems to me, has there appeared such an original, comprehensive and grandly conceived re-writing of early Christian history." Indeed, throughout his stormy career, Machen continued to respect the scholars with whom he sharply disagreed. "I have never been able to give myself the comfort which some devout believers seem to derive from a contemptuous attitude toward men on the other side of the great debate; I have never been able to dismiss the 'higher critics' en masse with a few words of summary condemnation."[224]

While continuing to struggle with his faith and vocational decision, Machen accepted—without creedal or ministerial commitments—an invitation to teach Greek at Princeton Seminary. During his early years at Princeton, Machen's doubts gradually dissolved and his faith deepened. In 1914, Machen was named assistant professor of NT and ordained to the Presbyterian ministry. From that time forth, Machen assumed a theological position as immovable as the Rock of Gibraltar. He returned from service with the YMCA in France during the last year of the Great War to see orthodox Calvinism and the old Princeton theology under siege in church and seminary. In 1926, Machen's election as Professor of Apologetics and Ethics was reviewed by the General Assembly of the Presbyterian Church (PCUSA), and an examination committee was sent to Princeton. In an effort to resolve the internal tensions, the seminary was reorganized, and in 1929, Machen, for whom compromise was betrayal, resigned. Within the year, and a month before the crash of the stock market, Machen led in the founding of Westminster Theological Seminary in Philadelphia. In 1933, he founded an independent mission board in reaction to the liberalism he detected in the Presbyterian missionary program. In reaction, Machen was tried and suspended from the Presbyterian church as a schismatic (1935). In 1936, he was instrumental in founding the Orthodox Presbyterian church. During a demanding speaking tour, exposed to the winter winds of North Dakota, Machen contracted pneumonia and died on January 1, 1937.

Was Machen a fundamentalist?[225] Although he loathed the label, Machen sympathized with many of the doctrines. He was devoted to the fundamen-

---

224. Ibid., 255, 260, 257–58.
225. For Machen's theological perspective, see W. Stanford Reid, "J. Gresham Machen," in *Reformed Theology in America: A History of Its Modern Development,* ed. David F. Wells (Grand Rapids, Mich: Eerdmans, 1985), 102–18; D. G. Hart, "When Is a Fundamentalist a Modernist? J. Gresham Machen, Cultural Modernism, and Conservative Protestantism," *JAAR* 65 (1997): 605-33; George M. Marsden, *Understanding Fundamentalism and Evangelicalism* (Grand Rapids, Mich.: Eerdmans, 1991), 182–202; idem, "J. Gresham Machen, History, and Truth," *WTJ* 42 (1979): 157–75; Roy A. Harrisville and Walter Sundberg, *The Bible in Modern Culture: Theology and Historical-Critical Method from Spinoza to Käsemann* (Grand Rapids, Mich.: Eerdmans, 1995) 180–202; Terry A. Chrisope, "J. Gresham Machen and the Modern Intellectual Crisis," *Presbyterion* 24 (1998): 92–109.

tals, especially to supernaturalism and the inerrancy of Scripture. Machen was a Southerner in attitude, a supporter of states' rights and racial segregation. On the other hand, he was an upper-middle-class person, urban and urbane. He rejected dispensationalism and millenarianism. In contrast to fundamentalist piety, Machen opposed Prohibition and approved smoking. Since the church was a voluntary organization, Machen believed it had every right to enforce its rules without tolerance. However, in regard to society (an involuntary association), Machen was a libertarian. He opposed the idea of imposing Christian principles and practices on society, for example, prayer in the public schools. Thus, he became an unwitting ally of many intellectuals who advocated the secularizing of American culture.[226]

Actually, Machen was not a theologian but a historian. He shared the Princeton theology of Warfield—a strict Calvinism combined with Scottish commonsense philosophy. Machen's apologetic theology is set forth in his popular book *Christianity and Liberalism*, first published in 1923. In face of the liberal threat, Machen calls for militant action. He declares, "the really important things are the things about which men will fight." Machen's thesis is that liberalism is not Christianity: liberalism is naturalism; Christianity is a supernatural religion. Machen says, "the believer in the supernatural regards everything that is done as being the work of God. Only, he believes that in the events called natural, God uses means, whereas in the events called supernatural He uses no means, but puts forth His creative power." Machen also attacked the popular liberal notion that Christianity teaches the universal fatherhood of God and the "brotherhood of man." According to Machen, only members of the household of faith could rightly call God "Father," and only members of the community of faith were really "brothers." The religion of Jesus, so dear to the liberals, was, in Machen's opinion, not Christianity. For Paul and the early Christians, Christ was the object of faith, not as moral example, but as God's action for redemption. "The fundamental thing is that God Himself, and not another, makes the sacrifice for sin—God Himself in the person of the Son who assumed our nature and died for us, God Himself in the Person of the Father who spared not His own Son but offered Him up for us all." Machen concludes, "Christianity is being attacked from within by a movement which is anti-Christian to the core."[227]

Machen's theological position is confirmed and expanded in his later works. In *What Is Faith?*, he attacks the anti-intellectualism of his day, and

---

226. The caustic columnist H. L. Mencken, who ordinarily ridiculed the fundamentalists, praised Machen: "Dr. Machen was to [William Jennings] Bryan as the Matterhorn is to a wart. His Biblical Studies had been wide and deep, and he was familiar with the almost interminable literature of the subject. Moreover, he was an adept theologian, and had a wealth of professional knowledge to support his ideas. Bryan could only bawl" (quoted by Hart, *Defending the Faith*, 59).

227. *Christianity and Liberalism* (Grand Rapids, Mich.: Eerdmans, 1946), 2, 99, 132, 173.

advocates the grammatico-historical method of biblical interpretation. He says, "religion is here made to depend absolutely upon doctrine; the one who comes to God must not only believe in a person, but he must also believe that something is true; faith is here declared to involve acceptance of a proposition." According to Machen, faith is a gift of the Spirit of God, but it also requires knowledge. Machen declares, "Christianity is founded squarely, not merely upon ideals, but upon facts. But if Christianity is founded upon facts, then it is not entirely independent of science; for all facts must be brought into some sort of relation."[228]

In *The Christian Faith in the Modern World*, originally a series of radio addresses delivered in 1935, Machen emphasizes the primacy of Scripture. Like Warfield, Machen affirms the inspiration and inerrancy of the original writings. "Only the autographs of the Biblical books . . . were produced with that supernatural impulsion and guidance of the Holy Spirit which we call inspiration." Machen declares, "What a dreadfully erroneous thing it is to say merely that the Bible contains the Word of God. No, it is the Word of God. It is the Word of God when it records the facts." According to Machen, the NT clearly "teaches that the Father is God and the Son is God and the Holy Spirit is God, and that these three are not aspects of the same person but three persons standing in a truly personal relationship to one another." Similarly, "when the Christian says that Jesus Christ is God, or when he says that he believes in the deity of Christ, he means that same person who is known to history as Jesus of Nazareth existed before he became man, from all eternity as infinite, eternal and unchangeable God, the second person of the holy Trinity." According to Machen, the resurrection was an objective event, not a hallucination. If the latter were true, "It means that if there had been a good neurologist for Peter and the others to consult there never would have been a Christian Church."[229]

NT Research

Although generations of students used Machen's *New Testament Greek for Beginners*,[230] his main contribution to NT research is found in two major books: his book on Paul and his book on the virgin birth.[231] *The Origin of Paul's Religion* was originally presented as the Sprunt Lectures at Union Theological Seminary, Richmond, Virginia.[232] Machen's purpose is to

---

228. *What Is Faith?* (New York: Macmillan, 1925), 47, 242.
229. *The Christian Faith in the Modern World* (New York: Macmillan, 1936), 39, 58, 130, 134, 205.
230. (New York: Macmillan, 1923).
231. On Machen's NT research, see D. G. Hart, "Fundamentalism, Inerrancy, and the Biblical Scholarship of J. Gresham Machen," *JPH* 75 (1997): 13–28; Cullen I. K. Story, "J. Gresham Machen: Apologist and Exegete," *Princeton Seminary Bulletin* 2 (1979): 91–103.
232. (Originally published by Macmillan in 1921; repr., Grand Rapids, Mich.: Eerdmans, 1946).

demonstrate the importance of Paul for the origin of Christianity. Machen is also concerned to refute false interpretations of the apostle: the liberal view (that Paul merely explicates the religion of Jesus), the thesis of Wrede (that Paul's religion is not based on Jesus), and the belief of Bousset (that Paul's background is to be found in Hellenism).[233] Paul's conversion, according to Machen, was not a subjective experience, but an objective, one might even say, a "physical" event.

> Only, it must have been a real person whom Paul met on the road to Damascus—not a vision, not a mere sign. . . . But if it was really Jesus, the sight of His face and the words of love which He uttered may have been amply sufficient, provided the heart of Paul was renewed by the power of God's Spirit, to transform hatred into love.[234]

In discussing Paul's career, Machen gives extensive attention to Acts 15 and Galatians 2, and concludes that the two texts probably refer to the same event, the Jerusalem Council. Following the Western text, he argues that the apostolic decree (Acts 15:23-29) was concerned only with morals, and thus did not constitute an additional requirement placed on Paul. Machen also contends that no major schism existed between Paul and Peter; the conflict at Antioch, according to Machen, had to do with Peter's behavior, not his principles.

Turning to Paul's theology, Machen contends that the apostle's faith was based on Jesus, and was in essential harmony with the faith of the earliest disciples. "There is only one possible conclusion—the heavenly Christ of Paul was also the Christ of those who had lived with Jesus of Nazareth." Machen believes that Paul's presentation of Jesus as the supernatural redeemer mirrors the message of the Gospels. As to the background of Paul's thought, Machen insists that Paul was a Pharisee, virtually untouched by the Hellenistic Judaism of the diaspora. Machen, like many other NT scholars, enriches Paul at the expense of the Jews. He says, "it seems clear that the religion of the Pharisees at the time of Paul was burdened with all the defects of a religion of merit as distinguished from a religion of grace." Above all, Machen insists that Paul's message of redemption in Christ is totally distinct from the syncretistic religions of Hellenism. Paul, according to Machen, advocated a forensic view of justification whereby God pronounces the guilty to be not guilty, since the guilt has been borne by Christ, the substitutionary, atoning sacrifice. This view, Machen thinks, was shared by the disciples of the Jerusalem church, who, like Paul, confessed the supernatural Messiah as Lord. Machen concludes:

---

233. See pp. 149–50, 249–52.
234. *The Origin of Paul's Religion*, 68.

> The religion of Paul was not founded upon a complex of ideas derived from Judaism or from paganism. It was founded upon the historical Jesus. But the historical Jesus upon whom it was founded was not the Jesus of modern reconstruction, but the Jesus of the whole New Testament and of Christian faith; not a teacher who survived only in the memory of His disciples, but the Saviour who after His redeeming work was done still lived and could still be loved.[235]

Machen's book received positive reviews on both sides of the Atlantic—even from those who disagreed with him—and rightly so. It is the work of a keen mind, a scholar of great erudition. Machen addresses all the important issues and presents impressive arguments. He has mastered the secondary sources and presents his opponents' views fairly and without rancor. Nevertheless, some of Machen's readers find it difficult to conceive of Paul as totally immune to Hellenism, or to believe that the crisis of the death and resurrection involved no shred of discontinuity between the Jesus of history and the Christ of faith.

The Virgin Birth of Christ is Machen's magnum opus—a classic statement of the doctrine. Originally presented as lectures at Columbia Theological Seminary (1927), the book was first published in 1930. How Machen accomplished the immense amount of research displayed in this work while he was center of the storm that raged in church and seminary is testimony to his enduring fortitude. Machen begins by showing that belief in the virgin birth was widespread in the church of the second century. Turning to the NT evidence, Machen presents a detailed analysis of the data from Luke. He argues that Luke 1:5—2:52—the whole birth narrative—belongs to the original Gospel, written by Luke, who had contact with the earliest witnesses. Machen also contends that the hymns of Luke 1 are not Greek compositions of Luke or Jewish hymns that have been inserted. Machen claims, for example, that "the Magnificat in its Greek form is actually derived from a Semitic song of Mary herself."

> Our conclusion, then, is that the entire narrative in Lk. i-ii finds both its climax and its centre in the virgin birth of Christ. A superficial reading may lead to a contrary conclusion; but when one enters sympathetically into the inner spirit of the narrative one sees that the virgin birth is everywhere presupposed.[236]

Machen's treatment of Matthew is much briefer. He argues that the first two chapters are not a later addition, and that the whole section assumes the virgin birth. Machen devotes considerable attention to the Sinaitic Syriac text of Matt. 1:16, which reads: "Joseph, to whom was betrothed Mary

---

235. Ibid., 136, 179, 317.
236. *The Virgin Birth of Christ,* 2d ed. (New York: Harper & Brothers, 1932), 95, 164.

the Virgin, begat Jesus called the messiah." Although he finds the text secondary, Machen contends that even if the original had read "Joseph begat Jesus," it would not contradict the virgin birth because "begat" in the genealogy only means "had a legal heir." Machen proceeds to compare the Lucan and Matthean accounts. The evidence that the two accounts arose independently supports Machen's argument for the antiquity and authenticity of the virgin birth tradition. In response to some of the details of the accounts, for example, the mysterious movements of Matthew's star, Machen tends to shift from his usual concern with facts toward figurative interpretation. The accounts, he says, "are portraits rather than photographs." Nevertheless, the point at which the two agree, the virgin birth of Jesus, Machen takes as a fact, confirmed by historical research. The God who created the heavens and the earth did not abandon the freedom to create.

> So, at His own good time, there did enter, we think, into the course of this world a creative work for the redemption of sinful man, a creative work which was begun by the stupendous miracle of the virgin birth. It is only as such a stupendous miracle, only as a part of such a work of redemption, that the virgin birth of Christ can ever be accepted as a fact by reasonable men.[237]

Machen turns to his most difficult challenge—the silence of the rest of the NT about the virgin birth. He argues that the contemporaries of Jesus assumed he was the child of human parents because Joseph and Mary had not told anybody about the miracle. Mark did not report the virgin birth because, in Machen's opinion, it did not fit his purpose, and besides, Machen thinks Mark only related data that Peter knew as an eyewitness. The omission by John does not, in Machen's view, imply a tension between birth and preexistence, but simply indicates that the miraculous birth does not serve his purpose. Machen believes that Paul's description of God's Son as "born of woman" (Gal. 4:4) neither affirms nor denies the virgin birth; it indicates that Jesus was born like other humans. According to Machen, the conception was the miracle; the birth was normal. Only after Pentecost, says Machen, does Mary disclose her secret so that it eventually makes its way into Luke and Matthew.

> So, within the little circle of believing and sympathetic women or near friends, she may have been led to breathe things too sacred and mysterious to be spoken of to mortal ears before. These things, of course, were not repeated at once to the official governors of the Church. . . . Still less were they included in missionary sermons, where the great effort was to adduce facts which could be attested directly by all, and where the humble woman's mystery would have brought nothing but slander and scorn. But when the story was finally told, there is no evidence that it aroused any opposition at all from

---

237. Ibid., 186, 199, 265.

those who were already disciples of Christ. And so, possibly supplemented by a record that Joseph had left, the marvellous tale of the mother of the Lord found its way into the Gospel tradition and creeds of the Church, and into the inmost hearts of Christians of all centuries.[238]

Machen turns to the question: Where did the idea of the virgin birth originate? First, he argues that it could not have arisen in Judaism on the basis of stories about special births in the HB. Machen believes that Isa. 7:14 predicted the supernatural conception of Jesus, but he observes that the Jews did not understand the text as prophesying the virgin birth of the Messiah. Next, Machen argues that the idea of the virgin birth did not arise on pagan soil. He presents two main reasons: the fundamental hostility of early Christianity to paganism, and the Jewish-Palestinian character of the birth narratives. In particular, Machen argues against the theory that as Christianity moved into the Gentile world the idea of the Son of God increasingly took on physical character. The Christian idea of the virgin birth, he contends, is radically different from the pagan stories of gods cavorting with humans. "The conclusion to which we are obliged to come after examination of the whole subject of 'alternative theories' is that if the doctrine of the virgin birth of Christ did not originate in fact, modern critical investigation has at any rate not yet succeeded in showing how it did originate."[239]

Machen concludes his book with a discussion of the importance of the doctrine of the virgin birth. Above all, Machen believes the virgin birth to be crucial to Christology. According to Machen, the virgin birth fixes the time of the incarnation.

> To that doctrine it is essential that the Son of God should live a complete human life upon this earth. But the human life would not be complete unless it began in the mother's womb. At no later time, therefore, should the incarnation be put, but at that moment when the babe was conceived. There, then, should be found the stupendous event when the eternal Son of God assumed our nature, so that from then on He was both God and man.

Also Machen believes the virgin birth explains how Jesus escaped the sin and guilt of humans, and thus was able to function as redeemer.

> How, except by the virgin birth, could our Saviour have lived a complete human life from the mother's womb, and yet have been from the very beginning no product of what had gone before, but a supernatural Person come into the world from outside to redeem the sinful race? . . . Deny or give up the story of the virgin birth, and inevitably you are led to evade either the high Biblical doctrine of sin or else the full Biblical presentation of the supernatural Person of our Lord.[240]

---

238. Ibid., 265.
239. Ibid., 379.
240. Ibid., 394, 395.

In sum, Machen's *Virgin Birth*, like all of his works, is a monument to profound faith, rigorous research, and reasoned argument. At the very least, Machen has demonstrated that the virgin birth is not some irrational hangover of the pre-scientific mind. He has also demonstrated that competent historical criticism can be dedicated to conservative doctrines. Machen's argument is strongest where he deals with the origin of the doctrine. It is weakest where he deals with the silence of the bulk of the NT; the fact that twenty-five books of the NT never mention the virgin birth hardly supports Machen's view that it is essential to Christianity. Moreover, Machen's understanding of supernatural concept as a fact raises questions. Do Luke and Machen share the same biological understanding of conception? How does the "fact" of the virgin birth affect the humanity of Jesus? Since Jesus was born of a human mother, how does he elude the original sin of humanity? Is it possible—scandalous to Warfield and Machen—to see the virgin birth primarily as doctrine rather than essentially as fact?

SUMMARY

The research reviewed in this chapter documents the advance of NT scholarship in America. Works like Moffatt's *Introduction* and Burton's *Galatians* represent the tradition of grammatical-historical criticism at a high level of achievement. This is also true of Bacon's work on the Gospels and Goodspeed's on the Epistles. Although American research displays great variety, it is unanimous in its acceptance of the historical-critical method. Indeed, those who appear farthest apart—the Chicago School on the left and the Princeton theologians on the right—are the most dedicated to empiricism, rationalism, and the scientific method. This simply shows that acceptance of the same method does not (in contrast with the natural sciences) assure the same results. Use of the scientific method in biblical research involves other factors, for example, the presupposition of varying worldviews, differences regarding the selection and perception of the data. The Chicagoans saw history as social process; the Princetonians focused on the facts. However, for Warfield and Machen the facts were believed to include supernatural events and intellectual doctrines—presupposing a worldview radically different from the natural theology and humanism of Mathews and Case.

This ontological chasm illustrates another prominent feature of American research—the persistence of conflict. The Chicago School published popular literature, and its members, especially Mathews, were outspoken missionaries of modernism; they vociferously attacked orthodoxy, supernaturalism, millenarianism, and fundamentalism. The Princeton theologians, for example, Machen, addressed the larger public by radio broadcasts; he did not hesitate to castigate the liberals as non-Christians. The striking feature is that both the liberals and the conservatives produced "heretics"; both Briggs and Machen were defrocked by their denomination, indeed, by the same denomination, the northern Presbyterians. The divisive issue that would continue to plague American Christianity was the question of the inspiration and authority of Scripture, brought into focus by the dogma of inerrancy.

The character of the issues that arise in this chapter is distinctively American. The sociohistorical method, on the one hand, and fundamentalism, on the other, are particularly American phenomena. They reflect the basic American preoccupation with pragmatism—the concern with the solid facts and how they function. This is also revealed in the way criticism is employed—essentially in the service of some pragmatic goal. The contributors to *The Woman's Bible*, for example, believed criticism would be helpful in opposing slavery, advocating temperance, and gaining the vote. Thus, criticism could oppose orthodoxy and support modernism, or support fundamentalism and oppose liberalism—all in the service of human enlightenment. Beneath this prevailing pragmatism was a fundamental religious commitment—this, too, was typical of American ideology. Virtually all the scholars reviewed were persons of faith, mostly ordained clergy, mainly Presbyterians and Baptists. Research primarily took place in divinity schools, training persons for ministry in the church. For all the concern with textual, linguistic, and historical detail, NT research in American struggled to remain democratic, relevant to the life and faith of the people.

8

Conservative Alternatives on the Continent

American fundamentalism has no perfect parallel in Europe. European biblical research, however, produced scholars who were alarmed by the advance of theological liberalism, rationalistic criticism, and cultural secularism. In a time of the shaking of the foundations, conservatives sought stability. The old order was gone, with its delicate balance of powers, its inbred clan of monarchies, its era of peace and prosperity. World War I, which amassed the destructive power of the whole globe, annihilated millions of people, rewarded the merciless victors, and left Europe in ashes that would later ignite into an even greater holocaust. A bloody revolution, inspired by radical social and economic theories, triumphed in Russia. Totalitarian regimes, supported by military might and repressive politics, triumphed in Italy, Spain, and Germany.

As the towers of European culture tumbled, conservative theologians called for a rebuilding of the old foundations. Christian civilization, they declared, was based on unshakable truths: the Bible as the Word of God, Jesus as the Prince of Peace, and the God of Scripture as the supernatural ruler of the universe. From this perspective, many recent biblical scholars were blamed as abettors of the current chaos. The practitioners of the history of religion method, for example, had concluded that Christianity was neither supernatural nor unique. The writers of the NT, they claimed, had imported ideas and practices from the pagan cults, creating a tainted syncretism, at home in the Hellenistic world, but irrelevant for the crises of the modern world. In reaction, a theologian such as Paul Feine, writing in 1919, could affirm the sustaining power of a more traditional faith.

> The Great War has given Christian theology a new task. There are among our German people many Christians who would not have been able to bear the burden of the war years, if they had not had and learned the solid

foundation of faith to see the temporal in the light of the eternal. Thus they were powerfully reminded to remember Jesus Christ, the same yesterday, today, and forever.[1]

CRITICS OF THE HISTORY OF RELIGION: ERNST VON DOBSCHÜTZ AND PAUL FEINE

Ernst von Dobschütz (1870–1934)

Born in Halle, Ernst von Dobschütz was educated at universities in Leipzig, Halle, and Berlin. He began his teaching career at Jena (1898), where he was promoted to associate professor in 1899. He moved on to professorships at Strasbourg (1904), Breslau (1910), and Halle (1913).[2]

Von Dobschütz was primarily devoted to philological and historical research. In a book on the *Apostolic Age*, he reviews recent publications, noting problems in early church history that have not been fully solved. As to the origin of the church, von Dobschütz believes modern criticism correctly affirms the importance of the resurrection. However, he believes it sometimes errs in construing the resurrection as a psychological experience rather than a real historical happening. In assessing the relation of the earliest church to Judaism, von Dobschütz contends that ethics is more important than eschatology. He says that "all sources indicate that for Jewish Christianity the eschatological thought given in the special messianic confession had less significance than practical, ethical behavior." Von Dobschütz believes Gentile Christianity should be investigated in its historical setting, but not according to the procedures of the history of religion school. He says, "we must make every effort to put ourselves back into that ancient time so that we gradually come to the position that we are no longer struck by what the Christianity of that day had in common with the religiosity of the time, but that which distinguished it, that which attracted the people of that time to Christianity."[3]

The leader of Johannine Christianity in Asia Minor, according to von Dobschütz, was not John the apostle, but John the Elder—a noble advocate of historical and ethical religion in the face of docetism. "Thus in the person of John of Asia Minor, Jewish Christianity has given to pagan Christianity the most valuable thing that it has: the proper counterbalance against Hellenistic intellectualism, spiritualism, and mysticism." Indeed, von Dobschütz believes the major error of the history of religion scholars is their

---

1. *Theologie des Neuen Testaments,* 8th ed. (Berlin: Evangelische Verlagsanstalt, 1953), iv.
2. For a survey of von Dobschütz's life and work, see "Ernst von Dobschütz," in *RGS* 4:31–62.
3. *Probleme des apostolischen Zeitalters* (Leipzig: J. C. Hinrichs, 1904), 52, 78.

exaggeration of Hellenistic influences, and their distortion of Christianity as a syncretistic religion.

> This "pan-oriental" or "Near Eastern" religion of syncretism is based essentially on an abstraction drawn from the comparison between the ancient Babylonian-Persian on the one hand, and the Gnostic-Mandaean on the other. . . . The enthusiasm of history of religion instinctively accepts its postulates as proved reality.

According to von Dobschütz, the distinctiveness of Christianity is grounded in the person of Jesus and expressed in ethical behavior. When this is recognized, "we can truly claim for Christianity, but never for any particular form of it, an absoluteness."[4]

Von Dobschütz's own concern with ethical Christianity is more fully expressed in his book *Christian Life in the Primitive Church*.[5] In this work, what he "endeavours to investigate is not the ethical teaching of primitive Christianity, but its real morals." Von Dobschütz begins with an investigation of the Pauline churches. He notes that the converts at Corinth, permeated with paganism, were called to a new morality. "It is astonishing what Christianity in a relatively short time made out of these motley and confused heathen groups, earnest men working out their salvation with fear and trembling, saints fully aware of the moral tasks of their consecration." Turning to the Jerusalem church, von Dobschütz contrasts Christian morality with Judaism, which he caricatures as concerned with externals and "trifling pedantries." In Gentile Christianity after Paul, von Dobschütz finds a laudable concern with morality that continues into the second century, "due to the power which issued from Jesus Christ and actually transformed men. The certainty and confidence of faith based on Him with reliance on God's grace in Jesus Christ, begot in Christians a matchless delight in doing good."[6] Influenced by liberalism and lingering piety, von Dobschütz finds the center of Christianity in morality. He stands like a sentry on the wall, ready to protect the distinctive character of the Christian religion from invasion by foreign influence.

---

4. Ibid., 94, 137, 136.
5. *Die urchristlichen Gemeinden: Sittengeschichtliche Bilder* (Leipzig: J. C. Hinrichs, 1902); Eng. trans.: *Christian Life in the Primitive Church*, trans. George Bremner, ed. W. D. Morrison (London: Williams & Norgate, 1904).
6. *Christian Life*, xv, 137, 379. Von Dobschütz also published a history of early Christianity for the non-specialist: *Das apostolische Zeitalter*, Religionsgeschichtliche Volksbücher, 1. Reihe, 9. Heft (Halle: Gebauer-Schwetschke, 1904); Eng. trans.: *The Apostolic Age*, trans. F. L. Pogson (Boston: American Unitarian Association, 1910). An example of von Dobschütz's exegetical work can be seen in his commentary on the Thessalonian epistles in the Meyer series.

Paul Feine (1859–1933)

Paul Feine was born at Golmsdorf, near Jena. He studied at Jena and Berlin. In 1893, he was appointed instructor at Göttingen, and in 1894, named professor of NT on the Protestant faculty at Vienna. He was called to Breslau in 1907 (to succeed and counter Wrede) and he moved to Halle in 1910.[7]

Feine is remembered for his *Introduction to the NT*.[8] First published in 1912, this work was reprinted in 1918, and revised in 1923. Feine's work is a model of brevity (267 pages) and clarity, yet, like a computer chip, it packs much information into a small space. Feine's arrangement generally follows the order of the NT: the Gospels (in canonical order), the Pauline Letters (in chronological order), the Catholic Epistles, and the Apocalypse. Feine's critical judgments are conservative. Regarding the Synoptic Problem, he adopts a version of the two-document hypothesis: Mark (used by Matthew and Luke) was based on a *Grundschrift* (an *Urmarcus*) written in the 40s. The author of Matthew and Luke also used the Logia source, written, Feine believes, by the apostle Matthew. According to Feine, both the Fourth Gospel and Revelation were written by John the son of Zebedee. Feine believes the Pastoral Epistles contain authentic material, though he thinks they were edited after Paul's death. In Feine's opinion, the only pseudonymous document in the NT is 2 Peter.

Much of Feine's scholarly attention was directed to Paul. In 1906, he published a popular work *Paul as a Theologian*.[9] According to Feine, Paul was not a systematic theologian, but, nevertheless, "the greatest thinker and the greatest theologian of primitive Christianity. The lucidity and keenness of his mind made him the first to perceive Christianity as a new religion, a world religion."[10] Basic to Paul's thought, in Feine's judgment, is his conversion—an experience in which Christ became the center of his religion. Feine is convinced that Paul's Christology is based on the historical Jesus, untainted by Hellenistic mythology. Justification, according to Feine, is not the exclusive center of Pauline thought.

---

7. For an overview of Feine's life and work, see "Paul Feine," in *RGS* 5:39–84.

8. *Einleitung in das Neue Testament*, 3d ed., Evangelisch-Theologische Bibliothek (Leipzig: Quelle & Meyer, 1923). In 1936, Feine's *Einleitung* was thoroughly revised by Johannes Behm. In 1963, it was revised (largely rewritten) by W. G. Kümmel, and popularly described as the Feine-Behm-Kümmel *Introduction*. The fourteenth edition (1965) was translated into English by A. J. Mattill and published a year later. In 1973, Kümmel produced a major revision (17th edition) which was translated by Howard Clark Kee and published in 1975 by Abingdon.

9. *Paulus als Theologe*, Biblische Zeit- und Streitfragen (Lichterfelde-Berlin: Edwin Runge, 1906); Eng. trans.: *St. Paul as a Theologian*, 2 vols., Foreign Religious Series (New York: Eaton & Mains, 1908).

10. *Paul as Theologian* 1:10.

And yet the idea of justification is only one of the different forms in which the Christian faith of the apostle clothed itself. In so far as justification concerns an act of God, the doctrine is parallel to reconciliation, redemption, salvation. As far as the religious experience of man is considered, the same content is found in forgiveness of sin, reception of life, regeneration, divine adoption.[11]

A weightier book on the apostle Paul (more than six hundred pages) appeared in 1927. The first part of the book reviews the history of Pauline studies. Feine begins with the "intellectual-doctrinal view" (represented by scholars such as Baur and Holtzmann), which, he thinks, misconstrues Paul as a *Systematiker*. Even more mistaken is the viewpoint of devotees of the history of religion school. Feine scores their misuse of parallels and their failure to assess the date of their sources. In particular, he finds Reitzenstein's redeemer myth to be a scholarly fabrication, and Gunkel's view of Christianity as a syncretism to be historically wrong. Against Heitmüller, Feine contends that Christian baptism was not borrowed from the mystery religions, and contra Bousset, he argues that the confession of Jesus as Lord (which had been pronounced already in Palestine) conveys no notion of a Hellenistic cult deity. The eschatological interpreters fare no better. For example, Schweitzer's portrait of Paul as a preacher of apocalyptic-cosmic-mystical salvation is, according to Feine, without support in the sources. Feine is especially critical of scholars (such as Wrede) who fail to recognize the continuity between Paul and Jesus. Feine's own view is "that Paul in all the essential elements of his Christian faith—in Christology, doctrine of redemption, ethics, position regarding the law, understanding of baptism and the Lord's Supper, eschatology—is dependent on Jesus, but that the shape of this faith reflects individual and contemporary conditions."[12]

The balance of the book presents Feine's own understanding of the historical Paul. He argues that the apostle is in essential agreement with the earliest Christians. "Thus, Paul stands not as an innovator, creator of new ideas, founder of the Christian faith or of a special gospel, but he stands in a line with the primitive church and with their preaching—a line which is the direct continuation of what had been begun in the earthly activity of Jesus."[13] Indeed, Feine, like Johannes Weiss,[14] is convinced that Paul had known the historical Jesus—a knowledge implied by 2 Cor. 5:16. Acts 22:3 and 26:4 suggest to Feine that Paul had grown up in Jerusalem, and Gal. 3:1 suggests that Paul had witnessed the crucifixion. After investigating various

---

11. Ibid. 2:55–56.
12. *Der Apostel Paulus: Das Ringen um das geschichtliche Verständnis des Paulus*, BFCT 2/12 (Gütersloh: C. Bertelsmann, 1927), 164. On the history of religion school and the eschatological interpreters, see pp. 222–53, above.
13. *Apostel Paulus*, 403.
14. See pp. 223–29, above.

possible parallels in Egypt, Babylon, and Persia, Feine concludes that Christianity is distinctive. "The fundamental difference is that we believe in a living, history-moving God who . . . in the person of Christ has intervened in history."[15]

Feine broadens his investigation of early Christian thought in his *Theology of the New Testament*, first published in 1910. At the outset, Feine defines the subject:

> The theology of the NT is the presentation of the content of the preaching of Jesus, and the faith of the apostles and earliest Christians based on this preaching, according to the documents of the NT. Its task therefore is historical. Thus it intends to establish the factual situation of a tradition of the past by means and methods of historical science. But we engage in this research as Christian theologians with the conviction that the content of the NT is unique and normative for us today.

In discussing Jesus, Feine contends that the alleged history of religion parallels tend to relativize him. Instead, Feine thinks Jesus should be hailed as the revelation of an absolute religion. The teachings of Jesus, Feine maintains, have their background in the HB and Judaism. Jesus' message of the kingdom of God refers to the eschatological future, but also, in Feine's opinion, to a relationship with God, planted in the present and flourishing in the church. According to Feine, John's theological expressions differ from Paul's, but they agree on essential points. Feine acknowledges that John borrows terminology from the Hellenistic environment, but contends that his meaning is different. The Logos, in Feine's exegesis, has its background in the HB, not in Philo. "The sound of the words, the atmosphere that hangs over the Gospel, appears to be Greek, but the content can only be understood on the basis of the revelation-theology of John."[16]

After surveying the theological views of the remaining parts of the NT, Feine presents the main ideas of NT theology: the death of Christ as atonement for sin; the Holy Spirit as the gift that unites believers with Christ; salvation given by Christ and received by repentance and faith; baptism and the Lord's Supper as religious practices founded by Christ; ethics as obedience to Christ, expressed in community. In sum, Feine, like von Dobschütz, opposes the results of the history of religion school. Although Christianity should be viewed in its historical setting, it must be seen over against its environment as a distinctive religion.

---

15. *Apostel Paulus*, 509–10.
16. *Theologie des Neuen Testaments*, 8th ed. (Berlin: Evangelische Verlagsanstalt, 1953), 1, 338. Feine also published *Die Religion des Neuen Testaments*, Evangelisch-Theologische Bibliothek (Leipzig: Quelle & Meyer, 1921)—a work that shows his concern with religion (in contrast to systematic theology), but largely confirms what he had written in the *Theologie*.

CONSERVATIVE CRITICISM:
THEODOR ZAHN AND ADOLF SCHLATTER

Theodor Zahn (1838–1933)

Born in Mörs (near Essen), Zahn studied at Basel, at Erlangen (where he came under the sway of J. C. K. von Hofmann), and at Berlin.[17] In 1865, he moved to Göttingen, where he was an instructor and university preacher. He was told by an official that, "As preacher, you are indeed indispensable; as an instructor, quite superfluous." With no hope for a chair at Göttingen, he accepted appointment as professor at Kiel (1877). In teaching, Zahn's goal was to promote "a historical understanding of the beginning of Christianity based on an independent investigation of the sources." In 1878, Zahn was named successor of Hofmann at Erlangen, but, unlike his mentor, did not prescribe a system of thought. "I have never had my own system," he wrote, "nor attempted to build one." At Erlangen, Zahn engaged in extensive research, dedicated to "securing the history of the New Testament canon and the demand of historical understanding of the New Testament." In 1888, he moved to Leipzig, but after four years returned to Erlangen, and remained there for the rest of his career.[18]

A summary of Zahn's theology can be seen in his book *The Apostles' Creed*. He believes the creed was used as a baptismal confession in Rome prior to 120. Taking up the articles one by one, Zahn argues that they are all biblical and true. For example, in regard to the third article, he defends the doctrine of the virgin birth of Jesus. The fifth article (missing from some versions of the creed) concerning Christ's descent into hell, according to Zahn, is historically valid: after Jesus' death, his soul entered into fellowship with the departed spirits so that he could be the redeemer of prior generations. In regard to the affirmation of the resurrection of the flesh (the tenth article), Zahn claims that it does not contradict 1 Cor. 15:50 ("flesh and blood cannot inherit the kingdom of God"). Paul, according to Zahn, was contending that humans in their natural state could not be raised; they had to be transformed. Zahn concludes:

> [The Creed] does not contain one sentence which cannot be well derived from the history and teaching of Jesus, and the explanatory and illustrative teaching and preaching of the Apostles. . . . For it does not contain a single

---

17. See Theodor Zahn, "Mein Werdegang und meine Lebensarbeit," in *RGS* 1:221–48; A. J. Bandstra, "Zahn, Theodor (1838–1933)," in *HHMBI*, 398–402; Erich H. Kiehl, "Theodor Zahn," in *BITC*, 50–58; Uwe Swarat, *Alte Kirche und Neues Testament: Theodor Zahn als Patristiker*, Theologische Verlagsgemeinschaft (Wuppertal: R. Brockhaus, 1991).
18. Zahn, "Mein Werdegang," 15, 13, 18, 19.

sentence which does not correspond with an event in the historical revelation of God essential for sanctifying faith.[19]

Canon and Introduction

Zahn was vitally concerned with early Christian tradition, and he gave concentrated attention to the history of the NT canon.[20] His major contribution, a massive two-volume work, is a monument of scholarly erudition, leaving no detail untouched.[21] Zahn also edited a nine-volume series of studies on the canon.[22] A summary of his research is presented in his *Outline of the History of the New Testament Canon*.[23] Here Zahn begins in the third century and traces the history of the canon backwards. In the period from 170 to 220, the church was moved to limit the apostolic writings in face of the Montanist claim to new inspiration. Widely accepted, according to Zahn, were four Gospels, thirteen Epistles of Paul, Acts, and the Apocalypse. Hebrews was accepted in the east, and among the Catholic Epistles, 1 John and 1 Peter were widely recognized. Less secure were the rest of the Catholic Epistles, and in some locations, books like the Shepherd of Hermas and the Didache were accepted. In the period from 140 to 170, Zahn believes the canon was crucial in the church's struggle with heretics. In Zahn's view, the orthodox canon was not created in reaction to Marcion's canon; instead, Marcion was reacting to the church's tradition of authoritative documents. Other heretics, for instance the Valentinians, used the canonical books, confirming the authenticity of the tradition. In Zahn's opinion, Justin's notice of the "memoirs of the apostles" is a sure reference to the four canonical Gospels. Pushing canonicity further back, Zahn concludes that canonical collections of four Gospels and the letters of Paul (including the Pastorals) were made between 80 and 110.[24] However, in a

---

19. *The Apostles' Creed: A Sketch of Its History and an Examination of Its Contents*, trans. C. S. Burn and A. E. Burn (London: Hodder and Stoughton, 1899), 213.

20. See Bruce M. Metzger, *The Canon of the New Testament: Its Origin, Development, and Significance* (Oxford: Clarendon, 1987), 23–24.

21. *Geschichte des Neutestamentlichen Kanons*, 2 vols. (Erlangen: A. Deichert [Georg Böhme], 1889, 1890).

22. *Forschungen zur Geschichte des neutestamentlichen Kanons und der altkirchlichen Literatur*, 9 vols. (Leipzig: A. Deichert [Werner Scholl], 1881–1916).

23. *Grundriss der Geschichte des Neutestamentlichen Kanons: Eine Ergänzung zu der Einleitung in das Neue Testament*, 2d ed. (Leipzig: A. Deichert [Georg Böhme], 1904; repr., Wuppertal: R. Brockhaus, 1985).

24. Against this hypothesis, see Adolf Harnack, *Das Neue Testament um das Jahr 200: Theodor Zahn's Geschichte des neutestametlichen Kanons* (Freiburg, i. Br.: J. C. B. Mohr [Paul Siebeck], 1889), 110: "This presentation is no history, since the criticism is Tendenz-Criticism. On the basis of the results that are provided here, the announced presentation of the prehistory of the NT in the second century can only be unfounded." Despite sharp disagreements, Harnack and Zahn maintained a friendship and carried on correspondence from 1873 to 1929; see Friedr. Wilh. Kantzenbach, "Adolf Harnack und Theodor Zahn: Geschichte und Bedeutung einer gelehrten Freundschaft," *ZKG* 83 (1972): 226–44.

lecture on the enduring significance of the canon, Zahn admits that the tradition was not sacrosanct, yet he concludes that it was eminently reliable.

> We do not believe in the infallibility of the ancient church that collected, sifted, and preserved the twenty-seven books of the NT as canon. We do not underestimate the human factor that worked in the process, and we do not renounce the duty, by continual research and investigation of the written word of God, to become ever more certain. But the history of the New Testament until today gives us good ground for the confidence in which we apply to this book of books the old evangelical confession: *the Word of God endures forever.*[25]

Zahn's contribution to higher criticism is presented in his mammoth *Introduction to the NT*.[26] A work of more than 1,100 pages, Zahn's two volumes provide critical introductions to the books of the NT according to his understanding of their chronological order. Copious notes, printed in smaller type, are presented at the end of each section—notes that include references to countless ancient and modern sources. Zahn begins with the Epistle of James. He thinks it was written around 50 from Jerusalem by James the brother of Jesus. In Zahn's opinion, this epistle was known by Paul. In regard to the Pauline Letters, Zahn believes Galatians to be the earliest, written from Corinth, and addressed to the churches of south Galatia. First Thessalonians was written shortly after Timothy's arrival in Corinth, and 2 Thessalonians, whose authenticity Zahn staunchly defends, a few months later. According to Zahn, 1 Corinthians was written in 57 after Paul had written an earlier letter and visited Corinth for a second time. Zahn accepts 2 Corinthians as a unity. He believes Romans (including chapter 16) was written to enlist support for Paul's proposed mission to the west. According to Zahn, Philemon and Colossians were written from a first imprisonment at Rome. Ephesians, which Zahn argues at length to be authentic, was a circular letter, originally sent to Laodicea and other churches of the area. Philippians, accepted by Zahn as a unity, was written later from the same imprisonment. Zahn is convinced that the Pastoral Epistles cannot be fit into Paul's career prior to his imprisonment, and he vigorously contends that Paul was released from prison, traveled to Spain and to the east, and was back in prison in Rome so as to be executed in 66, or at the latest in 68. Thus, Zahn concludes that 1 Timothy and Titus were

---

25. *Die bleibende Bedeutung des neutestamentlichen Kanons* (Leipzig: A. Deichert [Georg Böhme], 1898), 61.
26. *Einleitung in das Neue Testament,* 2 vols. (Leipzig: A. Deichert [Georg Böhme], 1897, 1899; repr. Wuppertal: R. Brockhaus, 1994); Eng. trans.: *Introduction to the New Testament,* trans. Fellows and Scholars of Hartford Theological Seminary, ed. Melancthon Williams Jacobus, 2d ed., 3 vols. in 1 (New York: Charles Scribner's Sons, 1917; repr., Edinburgh: T. & T. Clark, 1971). For a short summary of his work on introduction, see Theodor Zahn, *Grundriss der Einleitung in das Neue Testament* (Leipzig: A. Deichert [Werner Scholl], 1928).

written during the interval, and 2 Timothy during the second imprisonment. In supporting the authenticity of these epistles, Zahn denies that they reflect a later church order, oppose a later heresy, or express un-Pauline style or theology.

In regard to the Catholic Epistles, Zahn believes 1 Peter to be authentic, although he supposes that Silvanus was responsible for the composition. Zahn makes an extensive case for the authenticity of 2 Peter, which he dates prior to 1 Peter. Zahn believes 2 Peter was used by Jude (which is also authentic), thus confirming its Petrine authorship. Hebrews, in Zahn's opinion, was a real letter, written to a particular group at a particular time: a Jewish Christian congregation of Rome, around 80. Zahn does not believe it was written by Paul, and probably not by Barnabas, though Apollos is possibly the author. Therefore, Zahn is willing to accept as canonical a document of dubious authorship.

Turning to the Gospels and Acts, Zahn observes that the Synoptic Problem has not been solved, and calls for more attention to tradition. Beginning with Mark, Zahn accepts Papias's assertion that Mark preserved the witness of Peter. Zahn thinks internal evidence indicates a Palestinian author, and Latinisms support the tradition of Mark's association with Peter in Rome. Zahn accepts the tradition that Matthew was the earliest Gospel, written by Matthew (or Levi) the tax collector. However, he believes parallels between Matthew and Mark indicate a literary relationship. He concludes that Mark used the original Aramaic Matthew as a source, and the translator of the Greek Matthew used Mark. In regard to the third Gospel, Zahn believes it and the Acts of the Apostles were written by Luke, the travel companion of Paul. Zahn also accepts Friedrich Blass's theory that Luke wrote an earlier version of Acts and later revised it himself.[27] In Zahn's opinion, Luke planned to write a third volume. As to sources, Zahn believes Luke used Mark, but not the Aramaic Gospel of Matthew. The non-Marcan material that Luke has in common with Matthew Zahn attributes to other sources (oral and written). He thinks the source for Luke's infancy narratives is Mary.

Zahn believes John the apostle moved to Ephesus and wrote the Fourth Gospel, three epistles, and the Apocalypse. In regard to the Gospel, Zahn detects internal evidence that supports this tradition. Chapter 21, which Zahn believes was written by disciples of John while he was still alive, confirms Johannine authorship. According to Zahn, John, writing around 80 to 90, used Mark, probably Luke, and possibly Matthew as sources. Zahn acknowledges that the discourses of the Fourth Gospel are not verbatim reports, but believes they faithfully represent the meaning of the teachings

---

27. See p. 185, above.

of Jesus. In supporting Johannine authorship of the Apocalypse, Zahn investigates the tradition about John the Elder, and concludes that John the Elder and John the apostle are one and the same. The apparent differences in style between the Gospel and Revelation represent, in Zahn's opinion, different subject matter.

All in all, Zahn's *Introduction* is a work of enormous erudition, displaying relentless commitment to the historical-critical method. His conclusions, while not always convincing, are supported by abundant sources and cogent reasoning. His arguments from patristic sources are substantial, even though he does not agree with some elements of the tradition. Zahn's analysis of style is less satisfactory, and his assessment of theological relationships is often unconvincing. For example, the attempt to harmonize the eschatology of the Fourth Gospel and the apocalyptic of Revelation betrays a lack of theological precision.[28]

Commentaries

Beginning in 1903, Zahn edited a series of major commentaries, *Kommentar zum Neuen Testament*, to which he contributed seven volumes: Matthew, Luke, John, Acts, Romans, Galatians, and Revelation. In the introduction to the first volume, Zahn's own *Gospel of Matthew*, he notes the need of a new series. The Meyer commentaries, for example, Zahn believes to be overloaded with details and plagued with unreliable interpretations. Zahn summarizes the task of the exegete:

> The interpreter as such has only to draw out from what the writer says, what he meant and wanted to say; and he does not have to answer the question whether what is written is true, and where it is concerned with the narration of facts. The latter is rather the task of the historian. The interpreter of the Gospels . . . has always to illuminate as a written product particular texts which serve the historical writer as sources, and thereby to prepare for the historian.[29]

In regard to critical matters, Zahn confirms what he says in his *Introduction*: Papias's reference to the Logia is actually a reference to Matthew's original

---

28. On the basis of his conservative assessment of the documents, Zahn published nontechnical works on Jesus and the early church. His *Grundriss der Geschichte des Lebens Jesu* (Leipzig: A. Deichert [Werner Scholl], 1928) orders the career of Jesus according to the chronology of the Fourth Gospel, harmonizes the accounts of all four Gospels, and affirms the historicity of the miracles. His *Grundriss der Geschichte des Apostolischen Zeitalters* (Leipzig: A. Deichert [Werner Scholl], 1929) uses Acts as primary source and harmonizes data from the Epistles. Zahn also published *Skizzen aus dem Leben der Alten Kirche*, 2d ed. (Erlangen: A. Deichert [Georg Böhme], 1898), dealing with such topics as "Missionary Methods in the Age of the Apostles," "Slavery and Christianity in the Ancient Word," and "The History of Sunday in the Early Church."

29. *Das Evangelium des Matthäus*, KNT (Leipzig: A. Deichert [Georg Böhme], 1903; repr. Wuppertal: R. Brockhaus,1984), 1.

Aramaic Gospel, written around 65; the Greek translation was made around 90. The commentary proper, consisting of almost seven hundred pages, is arranged according to Zahn's understanding of the structure of the Gospel. The comments, presented in running paragraphs, deal with historical, linguistic, and theological matters, always with attention to the tradition. Extensive footnotes add exegetical details, cross-references, and references to secondary sources.

Zahn's exegesis of 16:13-28 can serve as an example. Under the subsection "The Confession of Peter and the Announcement of the Passion," Zahn devotes twenty pages, written in two long paragraphs, to this text. He notes that in listing the names of those with whom Jesus is identified, only Matthew mentions Jeremiah. This suggests to Zahn that Matthew perceived a special similarity between Jesus and Jeremiah, the prophet of mercy and misfortune. Zahn points out that Matthew's version of Peter's word goes beyond the confession of Messiah to include "Son of God."

> Jesus himself, as the Son, Jesus in his unique relation to God as his Father is this secret. Only the knowledge of the secret, conferred by the Father of Jesus and mediated through the personal experience in company with Jesus . . . guarantees therefore the correct content and unshakable certainty of the confession, that he and no other is the Christ.[30]

According to Zahn, Jesus' word that Simon was Peter, the rock on which the church would be built, refers to the work that Peter would do in founding the church. Zahn notes that this is the first time the term ἐκκλησία is used in the Gospel, but believes the idea of church goes back to Jesus. Zahn thinks Jesus continues the metaphor of building, and thus depicts the opposition to the church as the gates of Hades, and Peter, as the superintendent of the building, the keeper of the keys. Peter, in Zahn's opinion, is simply representative of the authority of the apostles—an authority not to be transferred to others.

Zahn's other commentaries further explicate his critical and exegetical concerns. The commentary on *Luke* (more than seven hundred pages in length) illustrates Zahn preoccupation with factual history.[31] For example, he devotes serious attention to the census described in 2:1-5. Zahn notes that Luke and Josephus agree that a census took place; they only disagree about the date. Zahn, using an inscription and other historical data, argues that a census was carried out in Judea prior to the death of Herod at a time when Quirinius held authority in Syria. In short, Zahn believes Luke to be a more reliable historian than Josephus. Zahn's commentary on John illus-

---

30. Ibid., 536.
31. *Das Evangelium des Lucas,* 3rd and 4th ed., KNT (Leipzig: A. Deichert [Werner Scholl], 1913; repr., Wuppertal: R. Brockhaus, 1988).

trates his attention to exegetical detail.[32] On the basis of grammar, text criticism, and context, he argues that a full stop should be placed at the end of v. 3. Thus, the translation should read: "everything came into being through him, and apart from him not a single thing came into being that came into being."[33] Zahn's commentary on *Romans* demonstrates his use of exegetical detail in the service of theology.[34] In regard to 3:24-25, he discusses the interpretation of "through the *redemption* that is in Christ Jesus." He notes that the basic meaning of ἀπολύτρωσις is release from custody by the payment of a ransom, but sometimes the term is used simply to mean "release" without reference to payment. In this text, Zahn believes Paul is affirming God's action of redemption through Christ, not the paying of a ransom. Zahn's *Galatians* commentary illustrates his penchant for harmonizing.[35] In commenting on 1:15, Zahn supposes the three days of blindness depicted in Acts 9:8-9 to be the outward expression of the inner experience Paul describes in Gal 1:16.

In all these commentaries Zahn demonstrates mastery of the materials and skills of exegesis—text criticism, linguistics, grammar. This exegetical work, though dedicated to historical reconstruction, has theological significance, for Zahn believes the historical message of the NT to be truth for today. In his dedication to tradition, Zahn has enormous confidence in the scholars of the ancient church and very little in those of his own time. Like the wine tasters of Jesus' parable, Zahn says, "The old is good" (Luke 5:39).

Adolf Schlatter (1852–1938)

In the genealogy of NT scholarship, Schlatter, like Melchizedek, is without father or mother; he stands alone.[36] Biologically, he was born in Sankt Gallen, Switzerland, to a father who had sought baptism in a free church, and a mother who remained loyal to the Swiss reformed establishment. Schlatter's decision to pursue theology was transforming. "To those who ask me about the day of my conversion," Schlatter wrote, "I am inclined to

---

32. *Das Evangelium des Johannes*, KNT (Leipzig: A. Deichert [Werner Scholl], 1921; repr., Wuppertal: R. Brockhaus, 1983).
33. Other exegetes put the full stop within v. 3, prior to ὃ γέγονεν, and translate, for example, with the NRSV: "All things came into being through him, and without him not one thing came into being. What has come to being . . ."
34. *Der Brief des Paulus an die Römer*, 1st and 2d ed., KNT (Leipzig: A. Deichert [Georg Böhme], 1910).
35. *Der Brief des Paulus an die Galater*, 3d ed. Friedrich Hauck, KNT (Leipzig: A. Deichert [Werner Scholl], 1922; repr., Wuppertal: R. Brockhaus, 1990).
36. See Werner Neuer, *Adolf Schlatter: Ein Leben für Theologie und Kirche* (Stuttgart: Calwer, 1996); idem, *Adolf Schlatter: A Biography of Germany's Premier Biblical Theologian*, trans. Robert W. Yarbrough (Grand Rapids, Mich.: Baker, 1996); Theodor Schlatter, ed., *Adolf Schlatters Rückblick auf seine Lebensarbeit: Zu seinem hundertsten Geburtstag* (Gütersloh: C. Bertelsmann, 1952); "Adolf Schlatter," in *RGS* 1:145–71; Robert W. Yarbrough, "Adolf Schlatter," in *BITC*, 59–72; Robert Stupperich, "Adolf Schlatters Berufungen," *ZTK* 76 (1979): 100–17.

answer that my decision to study theology was my conversion."[37] In 1871, he entered the University of Basel, where he studied history with Jakob Burckhardt. Schlatter moved to Tübingen in 1873, and was captivated by Johann Tobias Beck. In 1875, Schlatter returned to Basel to take his examinations and receive ordination. After a few years of pastoral work, Schlatter in 1881 studied and taught for a time in Bern. In 1888, he was called to the faculty at Greifswald. Five years later, Schlatter was invited to a professorship at Berlin to counter the advance of liberalism. In 1898, he joined the faculty at Tübingen. Schlatter officially retired in 1922 (at age seventy), but continued to lecture until 1930. After this second retirement, he continued his research, and in the years from 1929 to 1937, produced nine major commentaries and some eighty other scholarly works. As well as his research in the NT and early Christianity, Schlatter made important contributions to systematic theology and ethics.

Theology and Method

Schlatter's theology is difficult to comprehend, written in a convoluted style that defies comprehension even by native German intellectuals.[38] Basic to his thought is his idea of history. On the one hand, Schlatter opposes what he calls the "atheistic" view of history, that is, the view that history can be understood without regard to God.[39] In Schlatter's opinion, this constitutes an a priori decision that precludes the possibility of a true understanding of history. On the other hand, Schlatter opposes Greek rationalism: the separation of the intellectual from the wholeness of life. Schlatter similarly opposes Immanuel Kant's concern with abstract thought and his skepticism about empirical knowledge. In Schlatter's view, history must be seen as a complex of events involving cause and effect. In this history, God acts for revelation. The supreme act of revelation is the life of Christ—what Schlatter calls the life-act *(Lebensakt)* of Christ. Since God has acted in history, Schlatter believes theology is concerned with the study of a particular history: the biblical history of Christ.

---

37. *Rückblick*, 37.
38. Stephen F. Dintaman, *Creative Grace: Faith and History in the Theology of Adolf Schlatter,* American University Studies 7, Theology and Religion 153 (New York: Peter Lang, 1993); Albert Bailer, *Das systematische Prinzip in der Theologie Adolf Schlatters*, AzTh 2/12 (Stuttgart: Calwer, 1968); Gottfried Egg, *Adolf Schlatters kritische Position: gezeigt an seiner Matthäusinterpretation*, AzTh 2/14 (Stuttgart: Calwer, 1968); Eberhard Güting, "Zu den Voraussetzungen des systematischen Denkens Adolf Schlatters," *Neue Zeitschrift für systematische Theologie und Religionsphilosophie* 15 (1973): 132–47; Robert Morgan, ed., *The Nature of New Testament Theology: The Contribution of William Wrede and Adolf Schlatter,* Studies in Biblical Theology 2/25 (Naperville, Ill.: Alec R. Allenson, 1973); Werner Neuer, "Die Bedeutung Adolf Schlatters für Theologie und Kirche heute," *Theologische Beiträge* 20 (1989): 191–203.
39. "Atheistic Methods in Theology," trans. David R. Bauer, in Neuer, *Schlatter: A Biography*, 211–25; original: Adolf Schlatter, "Atheistische Methoden in der Theologie," BFCT 9 (1905) 5:229–250; repr. in Adolf Schlatter, *Zur Theologie des Neuen Testament und zur Dogmatik: Kleine Schriften*, ed. Ulrich Luck (Munich: Chr. Kaiser, 1969), 134–50.

According to Schlatter, the study of history has two aspects: observation *(Beobachtung)* and judgment *(Urteil)*. Observation, the act of seeing *(Sehakt)*, requires, like natural science, the study of the facts. Schlatter never tires of saying, "Science is first seeing and secondly seeing and thirdly seeing and again and again seeing."[40] At the same time, observation must also be open to the action of God in creation and in miracle. Moreover, observation is no mere empiricism: it involves the life experience of the observer. "So in every piece of work done according to the norms of historical science, the writer and the reader should be aware that a historical sketch can only take shape in the mind of a historian, and that in this process the historian himself, with all his intellectual furniture, is involved."[41] Judgment, the second aspect of the study of history, involves decision: the appropriation of the actions of history by the observer. In studying the NT, the believer accepts the claim of the NT and is moved to faith and a transformed life. In Schlatter's view, the NT can be understood only by those who accept its claim.

Schlatter's view of Scripture can be characterized as historic-pneumatic, that is, a synthesis between authoritative tradition recorded by inspired apostles and the present activity of the Spirit in the life of the believer.

> The inspiration of the apostles has as presupposition their being sent by Christ and arises out of this history. Again, the Spirit leads them into history, since it wants no emptying and repression of human life, but creates humans whose thought and will stems from God, so that they think what God thinks, and will what God wills.[42]

For Schlatter, the whole of Scripture witnesses to the grace of God in history. The center of Scripture is Christ. "An account of the history of Jesus, his messengers and his community therefore precedes a New Testament theology and serves as its basis."[43] Schlatter is not concerned with a Jesus of historical reconstruction, but with the Christ presented by the apostles: the inner life of Jesus. Looking into this inner life, Schlatter perceives a Jesus who recognized himself as the unique, preexistent Son of God. This inner life comes to expression in deeds and words of Jesus, and the evangelists and apostles record these words and deeds. Schlatter detects a continuity of facts: from the words and deeds of Jesus to the words and deeds of the apostolic witness. "I saw also no cleft between the call of Israel to repentance and the founding of the Christian church, between the work of Peter in Jerusalem and that of Paul among the Greeks; instead, I possessed a unified NT, not because I had given it unity by my skill and apologetic, but because

---

40. "Atheistic Methods," 218.
41. "The Theology of the New Testament and Dogmatics," in R. Morgan, ed., *Nature of NT Theology* (117–66), 125–26; this essay originally was published as "Die Theologie des Neuen Testaments und die Dogmatik," BFTC 13 (Gütersloh: C. Bertelsmann, 1909) 2:7–82; repr. in Schlatter, *Zur Theologie des NT und zur Dogmatik,* 203–72.
42. Quoted in Bailer, *Das systematische Prinzip,* 80.
43. "Theology of the NT," 156.

a strongly interconnected history, which was created from the same forces, has produced, from the beginning of Jesus, the community, assembled by the disciples, and its documents."[44]

In interpreting Scripture, Schlatter does not follow the conventions of Enlightenment scholarship, and he rarely cites the works of others.[45] Schlatter believes preoccupation with critical minutiae, piling up Babels of footnotes that reach to heaven, diverts from the main concern: to observe the facts, to probe the meaning of the words. In particular, like von Dobschütz and Feine, he decries the method of history of religion. "The necessary task of New Testament theology remains undone so long as it lurches up and down the wide front of the statistics and history of all religions in an attempt to establish how far back anticipations of and analogies to the ideas of the New Testament can be found."[46] Steering a course between the rocks of biblicism on the right and the abyss of rationalism on the left, Schlatter follows a criticism that is concerned with both history and doctrine.

Philology, Criticism, and History

Schlatter's first major work is his prize-winning book *Faith in the New Testament*.[47] In the early chapters, Schlatter presents his understanding of the background of the Christian idea of faith. The Palestinian synagogue, he thinks, stressed faith as obedience to law, leading to a preoccupation with works and concern with the realization of righteousness in the future. As a result, Schlatter supposes that Judaism had pushed God out of the present, and put human religion in place of personal relation to God. Schlatter believes that Jesus was the creator of the doctrine of faith alone. "The originator of the formula "sola fide" is Jesus; he said: 'only believe' (Mk. 5:36); but we do not understand his call to faith rightly, if we mean by it that he expected nothing from humans, and that nothing worked in them other than pure faith."[48] Instead, Schlatter believes that faith for Jesus means a new relation to God that transforms the believer, resulting in a life of response to God's love by concrete acts of love.

According to Schlatter, the early Christian idea of faith involved obedience. "The community turned with undivided interest to its ethical task: to

---

44. Quoted in T. Schlatter, *Rückblick*, 233–34.
45. See Peter Stuhlmacher, "Adolf Schlatter's Interpretation of Scripture," *NTS* 24 (1978): 433–46; Wolfgang J. Bittner, "Methodische Grundentscheide in der exegetischen Arbeit Adolf Schlatters am Beispiel seiner Schriften zum Johannes-Evangelium," in *Die Aktualität der Theologie Adolf Schlatters,* ed. Klaus Bockmühl (Giessen: Brunnen, 1988), 113–17.
46. "Theology of the NT," 144.
47. *Der Glaube im Neuen Testament,* 6th ed. (Stuttgart: Calwer, 1982). In 1883, Schlatter's monograph won a prize offered by a Christian foundation in the Hague. This book served as an inspiration for Kittel's famous *Theological Dictionary of the New Testament*; the first volume of Kittel's *Dictionary* was dedicated to Schlatter, and Kittel's preface of 1933 reads, "*Der Glaube im Neuen Testament* is a model for the investigation of biblical theological terms" (*TDNT* 1:ix).
48. *Glaube im NT,* 99.

obey the word of Jesus and to serve God through work pleasing to him." Schlatter is convinced that faith is central to Paul's thought, grounded in his conversion experience. Faith is response to God's action in Christ, especially seen in Paul's stress on the crucifixion. "From the cross no other result can be drawn than that faith with its denial of work, law, and justice, and with its affirmation of the righteousness of God, which, since it is one with grace, provides for us justification." But, cautions Schlatter, this does not mean that Paul is opposed to good works. "As the work of Christ for humanity remains unfruitful without faith, so faith is unfruitful and useless if it does not become the root of love, lest out of it arises that willing and acting that serves God and others." Turning to the apostles of the church at Jerusalem, Schlatter investigates the understanding of faith in James, Peter, and Matthew. According to Schlatter, Matthew stresses the necessity of works. Turning to the Fourth Gospel, Schlatter finds essential agreement between John and Paul.

> This unity with Paul arises from the fact that John, like Paul, has directed the entire religious thought and will with conscious clarity toward Christ. Both understand faith in Christ as the root and basis of their entire piety, and view that as the transition into a unity with Christ that makes effective and fruitful everything that he is and has.[49]

Schlatter's critical views are presented in his *Introduction to the Bible*—a historical-critical investigation of all the books of the HB and NT. Schlatter believes that "much of our current biblical research is sick. . . . Types of thinking that deny God and Christ gain power over us theologians, and where they become powerful, they exercise a great influence on the historical investigation into the content and origin of the Bible." After more than 250 pages of introduction to the books of the Hebrew Scriptures, Schlatter turns to the time between the Testaments, and caricatures the Pharisees.

> In place of faith, the scribe by his strivings came only into a sick, exaggerated self-consciousness. . . . Therefore, he directed his attention more eagerly and exclusively to the external regulations of the Scripture, to that which one could legalistically formulate and keep under surveillance. With the zeal that one placed on these things, one boasted before God and humans. So humans became great and God small, and the religion of Israel dried up and became, instead of devotion to God, admiration and reverence for that which the Jew was and did.[50]

---

49. Ibid., 291, 344, 372–73, 509. After a final summarizing chapter, Schlatter adds over sixty pages that present his analysis of the Hebrew and Greek terms on which his work is based.
50. *Einleitung in die Bibel*, 4th ed. (Stuttgart: Calwer, 1923), 6, 268. For a critique of Schlatter's anti-Judaism, see Joseph B. Tyson, *Luke, Judaism, and the Scholars: Critical Approaches to Luke-Acts* (Columbia, S.C.: University of South Carolina Press, 1999), 42–65.

Schlatter begins his investigation of the NT with the first three Gospels—documents that he believes present a reliable record. "There can be no doubt that what they narrate to us, they have held for reality, and come before us in a most straightforward sense as writers of history."[51] Schlatter gives little attention to the Synoptic Problem, but his later works indicate that he supports the priority of Matthew (written in the 60s), Mark's use of Matthew, and Luke's use of Mark. According to Schlatter, Mark was written by John Mark, and Luke by the travel companion of Paul who also wrote Acts.

Regarding the Pauline Letters, Schlatter writes, "Paul presented the epistle as a substitute for the spoken word and so the churches received it." Schlatter accepts the thirteen letters attributed to Paul as authentic, and supports the hypothesis of a second Roman imprisonment to provide the occasions for the writing of the Pastoral Epistles. Colossians, written during the first imprisonment, opposes an early form of Gnosticism; Schlatter thinks that "the source of the whole movement is older than Christianity and is to be found in the mystical wisdom and theology of Israel." Schlatter believes Philippians vividly reflects the many sides of Paul. "We find here also the teacher who awakens and clarifies the ethical judgment of the church, the adviser who tries to lead it in the way of God, the polemicist who forcefully defends the boundaries between what is Christian and not Christian, the theologian who knows how to unfold the truth of God in its fullness, the apostle who with highest authority gives instructions in the name of God."[52]

Turning to the Catholic Epistles, Schlatter is convinced that all are authentic except 2 Peter. He believes the different perspectives of James and Paul are mutually complementary. "That both sides of the Christian life have been so clearly recognized and expressed within the circle of the apostles is not a sign of their weakness and disunity, but rather of their spiritual power and greatness, and does not constitute an imperfection but the truth and wholesomeness of the Bible." "The unity which Scripture needs and has consists in this: that all its instructions are linked together into a whole to which I can shift no point without the whole being moved, can throw away no part without my losing the whole, and can agree with no part without my being drawn and led into the whole." Moreover, the Bible is the Word of God, given by divine inspiration. "If the Scripture gives us a clear, distinct picture of God, then it is certain that it has its origin in God. The Word that reveals God to us is God's own word to us." Yet, although Schlatter embraces a high doctrine of biblical authority, he rejects inerrancy. "The Bible does not possess this inerrancy either in its historical writing or in its

---

51. Ibid., 280.
52. Ibid., 356, 401, 407.

instruction." "Since God speaks through humans, so He makes them his messengers as humans with all their weakness."[53]

On the basis of his understanding of the documents, Schlatter published a history of the *Church in the New Testament Period*, originally published in 1910 with the title *Die Lehre der Apostel*.[54] According to Schlatter, the church began on the first Easter, which was followed by the gift of the Spirit on Pentecost. The new community was distinct from Judaism, for Judaism had rejected the Messiah who had founded the church. Schlatter, in presenting the expansion of the church, follows the narrative of Acts, adding details from the Epistles. According to Schlatter, Peter engaged in a mission to Babylon, and did not arrive in Rome until after the death of Paul. The apostle John, in Schlatter's opinion, migrated to Asia shortly after Paul's death, and wrote Revelation from his exile on Patmos, after 70, and the Fourth Gospel from Ephesus, around 80. "For St John the foundation of faith lay solely in Jesus himself—not in a metaphysical Christology or a doctrine of the Trinity, not in speculation about the life of God before the creation or of the eternal glory of the Son, but in a particular history."[55] The final chapters of Schlatter's history trace the fate of the Jewish church and the continuing work of the apostles in the Gentile churches.

NT Theology and Exegesis

Since Schlatter believes Christ to be the center of the NT, his most important book is his *History of Christ*.[56] Originally published in 1909 under the title *Das Wort Jesu*, this book was the first volume in Schlatter's *Theology of the NT*. "Therefore," writes Schlatter, "the knowledge of Jesus is the foremost, indispensable component of New Testament theology." According to Schlatter, the life of Jesus must be investigated by the historical method. "It is the historical objective that should govern our conceptual work exclusively and completely."[57] The sources for Schlatter's reconstruction are the four Gospels. Schlatter believes Jesus was born of a virgin, fulfilling Isaiah's prophecy; he was the preexistent Son of God entering into human life. Jesus, according to Schlatter, was conscious from his boyhood of his messianic vocation; he could speak Greek, but was untouched by Hellenistic ideas. Schlatter believes Jesus' baptism was a decisive point in his career— the sign of his divine Sonship and his call to mission. In contrast to John,

---

53. Ibid., 444, 481, 478, 483, 483.
54. *Die Geschichte der ersten Christenheit.* 2d ed., BFCT (Gütersloh: C. Bertelsmann, 1926. Repr., Stuttgart: Calwer, 1983); Eng. trans.: *The Church in the New Testament Period,* trans. Paul P. Levertoff; London: S.P.C.K., 1955).
55. *Church in the NT Period,* 299.
56. *Die Geschichte des Christus,* 2d ed. (Stuttgart: Calwer, 1922, repr. 1984); Eng. trans.: *The History of the Christ: The Foundation for New Testament Theology,* trans. Andreas J. Köstenberger (Grand Rapids, Mich.: Baker, 1997).
57. *History of Christ,* 19, 18.

Jesus took his message to the masses. Schlatter believes Jesus' earliest contact with his disciples was in Judea.

Jesus' mission, according to Schlatter, was to offer God's grace to Israel. "For Jesus the decisive event lay in man's hearing, in his being sought by divine grace, and in accepting and obeying God's call." According to Schlatter, Jesus understood the kingdom as the eschatological community, both present and future. Schlatter believes Jesus, in referring to himself, used both the titles Son of God and Son of Man:

> By "Son of God" he said that he had his life from and for God. When he simultaneously called himself the Son of Man, he said that he had and wanted to have his life from and for man. While the one name expressed his closeness to God, the other expressed his closeness to man.

Schlatter observes that "the account of miracles is everywhere inextricably interwoven with tradition." According to Schlatter, Jesus was closer to the Zealots than to any of the other Jewish sects.[58]

In the latter part of his mission, Jesus pronounced judgment on Jerusalem. Since the disciples had found it difficult to accept his approaching death, Jesus, according to Schlatter, repeatedly instructed them about his passion and resurrection. Schlatter, who claims to be concerned with facts, sometimes veers into speculation.

> Jesus also revealed the completeness of his divine sonship by appropriating the concept parallel to eternity, omnipresence. If he freed himself through the former concept from time, he distanced himself by the latter from space. He could think of himself as omnipresent, likewise, merely by attributing completeness to his relationship with God. He also did not conceive of his omnipresence in gnostic terms and did not promise that something of him or in him would be everywhere with the disciples, neither a power proceeding from him nor a nature residing in him. He himself would be with them. The concept was established simply by the fact that he was omnipresent as God was omnipresent. His concept of eternity had the same form: he was eternal since God was eternal.

According to Schlatter, Jesus cleansed the temple for a second time and celebrated the Passover meal a day early. As to the responsibility for the crucifixion, Schlatter writes:

> Jesus suffered his crucifixion as the act of the nation. . . . That he was delivered into the hands of the Gentiles and that he met his end at the cross, likewise, was felt to be particularly weighty, because Israel thereby expelled him from the community. Therefore the guilt for his death is not placed on Pilate, and Israel is not left with the excuse that Roman rule was guilty of injustice that led to the Christ's crucifixion.

---

58. Ibid., 117, 134–35, 175.

Schlatter thinks the strange portents—the darkened sun, the severed veil of the temple—reveal God at work. The events of Easter were not, in Schlatter's opinion, visions or legends; they were factual happenings, confirming faith in Jesus as Christ and Son of God.[59]

Schlatter's work on NT theology continues in his book *The Theology of the Apostles*, originally published in 1910 with the title *Die Lehre der Apostel.*[60] The first section investigates the basic ideas of the early disciples: their doctrine of God as Creator of the world, and Christ as revealer of God and redeemer of humanity. Turning to individuals, Schlatter reviews the convictions of the early apostles. He believes that Peter's theology (as 1 Peter indicates) is grounded in the outcome of Jesus' earthly life: "his cross, resurrection, exaltation, and return." The history of Christ, Schlatter believes, was faithfully recorded by the apostle Matthew. "The preeminence given to Matthew's Gospel among the books of the New Testament is a result of his compilation of Jesus' discourses. The man who arranged and connected Jesus' sayings in such a way belongs, together with Paul and John, to the great religious teachers of mankind." According to Schlatter, James, the brother of Jesus and leader of the Jerusalem church, stressed a faith that required obedience, based on the ethical teaching of Jesus. Schlatter sees in John a variety of doctrinal expressions: in Revelation, he prophesies the triumph of Christ over Gnostics and Romans; in 1 John, he affirms the norm of love; in the Fourth Gospel, he emphasizes faith in Jesus as unique Son of God. According to Schlatter, John's presentation of Christ as Logos does not have its source in Greek thought or Philo, but in the HB. Schlatter believes the eschatology of the Gospel of John and the Apocalypse to be in harmony. "Thus both texts describe the eschatological process similarly in its dual aim: Jesus comes for the glorification of his community, and he comes in order to establish God's reign over the world."[61]

Schlatter gives extensive consideration (about two hundred pages) to the theology of Paul. In Schlatter's opinion, Paul is not a speculative thinker. "He talks about God's revelation, not his nature, about the gift of Christ, not about his communion with God; about the reality of sin, not its possibility and origin; about the effect Jesus' death has on us, not his reconciling power by which he moves God." Paul's thought is grounded in the HB, and stresses the action of God in Christ. According to Schlatter, Paul viewed Christ as the preexistent mediator of creation, yet based his faith on the facts of the historical Jesus. Most important is God's saving work accomplished by the death of Christ.

---

59. Ibid., 307, 367.
60. *Die Theologie der Apostel,* 2d ed. (Stuttgart: Calwer, 1922); Eng. trans.: *The Theology of the Apostles: The Development of New Testament Theology,* trans. Andreas J. Köstenberger (Grand Rapids, Mich.: Baker, 1999).
61. *Theology of the Apostles,* 52–53, 69–70, 161.

But by recognizing Christ's death as signifying the death of all, Paul indicates that Jesus' vicarious representation did not merely remain an attempt or wish, but that it accomplished its goal and procured help for mankind by which it becomes God's community. . . . But because he dies not because of his own guilt but because of that of mankind, his cross reveals God's verdict to mankind, and because he was sent into the flesh not for his own sake but for ours, his death is the end of the flesh and the establishment of that communion with God that is brought about through the Spirit.[62]

Schlatter published several commentaries on the NT. In 1900, he began a series for the nonspecialist, *Erläuterungen zum Neuen Testament*; these treat every book in the NT, and have been collected and published in three volumes.[63] Late in life Schlatter produced major critical commentaries on Matthew, John, Luke, James, 1 and 2 Corinthians, Mark, Romans, the Pastoral Epistles, and 1 Peter. Schlatter's commentary on *Romans* can serve as an example.[64] In this commentary, Schlatter presents no detailed critical introduction. He simply notes that Paul is writing in Corinth, about to depart for Jerusalem, and is thus concerned with the relation of the gospel to Judaism. Schlatter says, "Paul paid no attention to the consideration of whether the majority of the community were of Gentile or Jewish origin."[65] In format, the commentary proper (more than 270 pages) orders the material according to Schlatter's understanding of the structure of the letter. The comments are presented in running paragraphs, and attend to Greek terms and phrases (transliterated in the English version). There are almost no footnotes, and few references to secondary, critical literature. The main concern is theological.

Schlatter sees 3:21-31, "Humans Believing in Christ," as an important part of the first main section of the letter: "The Revelation of the Righteousness of God for Believers" (1:18—8:39). In discussing 3:22, Schlatter argues that *dia pisteos* ("through faith") goes with *dikaiosune* ("righteousness"), not with *pephanerotai* ("has been disclosed"); that is, Paul is describing the character of righteousness, not the way in which it is revealed. Schlatter argues against the interpretation that Paul is describing the faith of Jesus; instead, Christ is the object of faith—the one in whom God acts for redemption. In regard to *hilasterion* ("sacrifice of atonement," v. 25), Schlatter detects an allusion to the cover of the ark of the covenant, but believes Paul is presenting a contrast: action on the day of atonement was hidden; the action depicted here is public. According to Schlatter, Paul is stressing

---

62. Ibid., 200, 263.
63. *Erläuterung zum Neuen Testament* (Stuttgart: Calwer, 1922–23, repr., 1987).
64. *Gottes Gerechtigkeit: Ein Kommentar zum Römerbrief* (Stuttgart: Calwer, 1935; repr. 1991); Eng. trans.: *Romans: The Righteousness of God,* trans. Siegfried S. Schatzmann (Peabody, Ma.: Hendrickson, 1995). See Peter Stuhlmacher, "Adolf Schlatter als Paulusausleger—ein Versuch," *Theologische Beiträge* 20 (1989): 176–90.
65. *Romans*, 6.

God's action; God is not acted upon or moved by the sacrifice of atonement. Schlatter also rejects the idea that Paul believes the death of Christ was a foreordained necessity. Paul's "God did not end up in a predicament in which he had to assert himself."[66] According to Schlatter, believers receive the grace of God that fulfills the law so that they can be obedient to Christ, able to serve God. In contrast to many interpreters, Schlatter puts great emphasis on the third main section of the epistle: "Christianity in Action" (12:1—15:13). In this section, Paul declares "what believers are to do, what it is that gives them their common action and unites them as a community."[67]

In this (as in his other commentaries), Schlatter displays skillful exegesis in the service of theology. He affirms the orthodox view of Paul—justification by God's grace received by faith—as the central theme of the apostle's thought. Yet, in the details, Schlatter presents his own distinctive understanding, especially his emphasis on the importance of ethics: sanctification as well as justification. Although he attends to the exegetical details, Schlatter's main method is to grapple rigorously with the meaning of the text. Schlatter is steeped in Paul's thought, and he offers profound insights—though not always with clarity. Whatever else may be said about Schlatter, he is not guilty of oversimplification.

In overview, Schlatter's complex work is difficult to evaluate.[68] He has been criticized for everything from his writing style to his inadequate source criticism. Nevertheless, he can be honored for his bold independence and his rejection of scholarly trivia in favor of concern with crucial issues. Although his neglect of the work of others may seem to smack of arrogance, Schlatter's intent is to focus on the text itself, undistracted by secondary criticism. Nevertheless, his superficial treatment of the problem of the Son of Man, for example, suggests that he could have learned more from others. Schlatter's plea for historical objectivity and rigorous observation of the facts seems qualified by his affirmation of the necessity of faith and the importance of the inner life. Although he scorns intellectualism, his own work is highly theological and speculative. Finally, one can ask if Schlatter's intentional historical objectivity does justice to the depth of faith and meaning that he himself so profoundly perceives in the NT.

---

66. Ibid., 101.
67. Ibid., 225, 227.
68. For a review of criticism of Schlatter's work by his contemporaries, see Andreas J. Köstenberger, "Preface: The Reception of Schlatter's New Testament Theology 1909–23," in Schlatter, *Theology of the Apostles*, 9–22; repr., *Southern Baptist Journal of Theology* 3 (1999): 40–51. For more recent assessment of Schlatter, see Robert W. Yarbrough, "Modern Reception of Schlatter's New Testament Theology," in Schaltter, *Theology of the Apostles*, 417–31; repr., *Southern Baptist Journal of Theology* 3 (1999): 52–65.

ROMAN CATHOLIC BIBLICAL RESEARCH: MARIE-JOSEPH LAGRANGE (1855–1938)

Lagrange was a wise man who built his scholarship upon a rock; for him, the rock was Peter on whom the church was built, and the church, he believed, received the canon of Scripture, and rightly interpreted it according to inspired tradition.[69] Albert Lagrange was born in Bourge-en-Bresse. After receiving his doctorate in law in Paris, Lagrange turned to theology and entered the seminary of Saint-Sulpice at Issy-les-Moulineaux. In 1879, he entered the Dominican order and took the name Marie-Joseph. When the order was expelled from France, Lagrange continued his studies at Salamanca, and was ordained in 1883. In 1884, he returned to France and taught and studied at the Catholic Institute in Toulouse. In 1888, he was sent by his order to the University of Vienna to pursue Near Eastern studies. At the age of thirty-five (1890), Lagrange was dispatched to Jerusalem to found a school of biblical studies. Years later, he remembered his arrival:

> I was moved, seized, gripped by this sacred land, and I abandoned myself to the delightful appreciation of distant and historic times. I had so loved the book, and here I was gazing at its setting! Not a single doubt remained in my mind about the aptness of pursuing biblical study in Palestine.[70]

Near St. Stephen's church, in a building that had been a slaughterhouse, Lagrange started the École Pratique d'Études Bibliques (now called École Biblique et Archéologique Française). In 1892, Lagrange founded the *Revue biblique*—the first major Roman Catholic periodical dedicated to the critical study of Scripture.

Lagrange, quite contrary to his intention, became embroiled in the modernist controversy within the Roman Catholic Church.[71] In response to the movement to modernize the church's doctrine, Leo XIII had reaffirmed biblical authority, but allowed room for historical research. Lagrange was in agreement.

---

69. See F.-M. Braun, *L'œuvre du Père Lagrange: étude et bibliographie* (Fribourg: Éditions de l'Imprimerie St-Paul, 1943); Eng. trans.: *The Work of Père Lagrange*, trans. Richard T. A. Murphy (Milwaukee: Bruce, 1963); Bernard Montagnes, *Le Père Lagrange (1855–1938): L'exégèse catholique dans la crise moderniste* (Paris: Cerf, 1995); L.-H. Vincent, "Le Père Lagrange," *RB* 47 (1938): 321–54; Jerome Murphy-O'Connor, *The École Biblique and the New Testament: A Century of Scholarship (1890–1990)*, NTOA (Göttingen: Vandenhoeck & Ruprecht, 1990); M.-J. Lagrange, *Père Lagrange: Personal Reflections and Memoirs*, trans. Henry Wansbrough (New York: Paulist, 1985); Richard Murphy, ed., *Lagrange and Biblical Renewal*, Aquinas Institute Studies 1 (Chicago: Priory, 1966); C. E. T. Kourie, "Leading Lights in Twentieth-Century Roman Catholic Biblical Scholarship: Marie-Joseph Lagrange (1855–1938)," *Theologia Evangelica* 24/3 (September 1991): 37–43.

70. Lagrange, *Personal Reflections*, 19.

71. See p. 163, above.

I have always remained loyal to the traditional belief, reaffirmed by Leo XIII—although not as revealed dogma—that the Scriptures assert nothing that is erroneous. But the Pope had accepted that, in scientific matters, the inspired writer is speaking according to appearances, so that what he writes must not be taken as a categorical statement of fact.[72]

In 1903, the Pontifical Biblical Commission was established, and the *Revue biblique* designated as its official organ. With the election of Pius X, however, the papacy moved to the right, rejecting the biblical criticism of the modernists. Lagrange, who had embraced the methods of Enlightenment criticism, was mistakenly identified with the modernists, and for a time his work was suspended. Lagrange was submissive. "I am prepared to reject opinions I have expressed if they are rejected or reproved by the Holy See, and I submit to it in the same way anything I write in the future."[73] Lagrange, who had been attacked for his research on the HB, turned to the study of the NT. In this he proved himself to be no modernist, opposing at every turn the work of Alfred Loisy.[74] Lagrange spent the years of World War I in France. After the war, he returned to Jerusalem for a period of fruitful work. In 1935, ill health forced his return to France, where he died three years later.

Point of View and Method

Lagrange was primarily a historian and exegete.[75] He subscribed to Roman Catholic tradition and dogma, and was influenced by the venerable theologian of his order, Thomas Aquinas. Lagrange was committed to historical criticism, and used criticism to challenge the modernists on their own playing field. His commentaries investigate the texts in their original language, not the official Vulgate. He engaged in the study of Paul to demonstrate his theological competence, and his concern to correct what he considered to be Lutheran misinterpretation.

In 1902, Lagrange lectured at the Catholic Institute in Toulouse on the *Historical Method*.[76] In the lectures, he says, "I hold the first duty of biblical criticism to be submission to the authority of the Catholic church as the necessary consequence of the very principle of revelation." As the Council of Trent had declared, all the books of the canon are authoritative and inspired. "Just as miracles confirm revelation, so does inspiration preserve

---

72. Lagrange, *Personal Reflections*, 72.
73. Ibid., 149.
74. See pp. 163–72, above.
75. See Richard T. A. Murphy, trans., *Père Lagrange and the Scriptures* (Milwaukee: Bruce, 1946); François Refoulé, "La méthode historico-critique et le Père Lagrange," *RSPT* 76 (1992): 553–87.
76. *La méthode historique, surtout à propos de l'Ancien Testament*, Ebib (Paris: V. Lecoffre, 1903); Eng. trans.: *Historical Criticism and the Old Testament*, trans. Edward Myers (London: Catholic Truth Society, 1905).

supernatural teaching, and is to us a token of God's paternal designs in the work of our salvation, or, as the men of old were wont pleasantly to say, it is a letter we receive from our Father."[77] Lagrange distinguishes between recording and teaching. In recording, writers conform to the limitations of their culture, so that error is possible. In teaching, writers present the inspired teaching of divine revelation, without error. Lagrange does not specify how the interpreter is to distinguish fallible recording from infallible teaching, but cultural limitations are obviously identified by historical research, and infallible teaching is, for Lagrange, confirmed by the tradition of the church.

Lagrange's view of biblical criticism is presented in lectures he gave at the end of World War I, *The Meaning of Christianity according to Luther and His Followers in Germany*.[78] Lagrange is skeptical of the meticulous scholarship flowing from the east side of the Rhine. In order to avoid being inundated, Lagrange believes orthodox scholarship should try to excel in the use of the critical tools. "We must apply ourselves to philology and history with more earnestness; we must unite our efforts, to secure the advantages derived from association and continuity; we must be ready, too, in the light of better knowledge of language and of the history of doctrine to sacrifice untenable theses." According to Lagrange, scientific criticism can be adopted because God is the author of science. This does not mean, however, that supernatural events should be precluded a prioi. "Living by supernatural influence, believing in the divinity of Jesus Christ, she [the Church] is prepared to accept the statement of the Gospels that the Son of God made man, worked miracles, announced future events, promised to send the Holy Ghost. She accepts at their face value texts written under deep conviction of the reality of the supernatural." Moreover, Lagrange believes that God has entrusted these texts to the care of the Church. "He has, consequently, seen to it that this revelation be preserved intact. It is contained in the Sacred Books; it is necessary then that the Church, the custodian of revelation, be assured of transmitting faithfully the meaning of the Word of God." In support of his position, Lagrange argues that the Church shares the faith of the NT, and therefore is sensitive to its meaning. Lagrange also points out that, according to Catholic teaching, truth is not confined to Scripture, so that the exegete is not compelled to find every point of dogma in the Bible. Lagrange also observes that the church provides a collective opinion, thus avoiding novelties and individualistic or idiosyncratic interpretations.[79]

---

77. *Historical Criticism*, 31, 87.
78. Trans. W. S. Reilly (New York: Longmans, Green, 1920); original: *Le sens du christianisme d'après l'exégèse allemande* (Paris: J. Gabalda, 1918).
79. *Meaning of Christianity*, 21, 366, 35.

The balance of Lagrange's lectures trace the history of NT research from the Reformation to his own time. The trouble began, according to Lagrange, with Luther's individualistic misunderstanding of Paul. It continued with the skepticism of the deists and the rationalism of the nineteenth-century Protestants. Lagrange believes criticism reached its low point with Strauss's substitution of myth for history, and Baur's unhistorical reconstruction of early Christianity. As to more recent trends, Lagrange thinks the apocalyptic approach of Johannes Weiss and Albert Schweitzer represents a misunderstanding of both Jewish eschatology and the teachings of Jesus. Lagrange abhors the notion that Christianity was a syncretistic religion. "The trouble with men who study the history of religions is that they see resemblances everywhere, and consequently—much more grave—dependencies everywhere; and with these they establish a relationship without taking dates and values sufficiently into consideration."[80]

Backgrounds and Commentaries

Lagrange was a prolific author whose bibliography numbers twenty-nine books and 248 articles. In regard to historical backgrounds, Lagrange published two important books on Judaism. His *Judaism before Jesus Christ*, a massive work of more than six hundred pages, is essentially a survey of the history and religion of Judaism in the period from Antiochus IV to the Jewish Revolt.[81] Lagrange gives special attention to the literature of the period and the development of eschatology. According to Lagrange, the major religious ideas of Judaism in this era include: the unity of God (who was addressed as "Father" in prayers) and the idea of retribution in the future life. In an earlier work, Lagrange had investigated *Messianism according to the Jews*. This book begins with a survey of the messianic idea of Hellenistic Jewish scholars, particularly Josephus and Philo. Turning to Jewish apocalyptic literature, Lagrange notes that these writings represent a special genre, characterized by pseudonymity and the disclosure of secrets by visions and symbols. "Between the religious vigor of the inspired Scriptures and the sensible naturalism of the Greeks, the apocalypses appear as a false genre whose overheated passions are not able to move the people from complacency."[82] In regard to the Messiah, Lagrange discovers variety: some texts offer an eschatology without a messiah, while others present a messiah who is a historical figure, and still others, a transcendent, supernatural messiah. The common theme that Lagrange detects in all is the overthrow of the present evil order by divine intervention.

---

80. Quoted by Étienne Magnin in Murphy, *Père Lagrange*, 131.
81. *Le judaïsme avant Jésus-Christ*, 3d ed., Ebib (Paris: J. Gabalda, 1931).
82. *Le messianisme chez les Juifs*, Ebib (Paris: J. Gabalda, 1909), 135.

Lagrange published major critical commentaries on all four Gospels and two of the Pauline Epistles. In 1910, the first edition of his commentary on *Mark* appeared; it was revised in the fourth edition of 1928 and reprinted in 1947.[83] In an extensive introduction (more than 170 pages), Lagrange reviews the tradition concerning John Mark, the son of Mary of Jerusalem, companion of Paul and Barnabas on the first missionary journey. He also notes the tradition that Mark recorded the reminiscences of Peter in Rome—a tradition Lagrange believes confirmed by data from the NT and internal evidence from the Gospel. Lagrange reviews recent criticism, but accepts the tradition of the church that Matthew is the earliest Gospel. Nevertheless, Lagrange believes Mark presents a reliable account. In regard to doctrine, Lagrange acknowledges that Mark's understanding of the kingdom of God is influenced by Jewish apocalyptic, but argues that the parables present the idea of gradual growth. Lagrange thinks the title "Son of Man" depicts both the humanity and the messianic glory of Jesus.

As to the commentary proper (more than 460 pages), Lagrange's fourth edition follows the format that is used throughout the Études bibliques series. The Greek text is printed at the top of the left-hand page, and the French translation on the facing (right-hand) page. The comments are printed below in running paragraphs, ordered according to the chapters of the text, with subsections indicated by titles. The comments deal with terms and phrases, and include extensive references to ancient and modern sources; excursuses are added at the appropriate places. Regarding Mark 8:27-30, titled "The Messianic Confession of Peter," Lagrange begins with a description of the location and history of the region of Caesarea Philippi. On v. 28, he observes that no one is reported to have identified Jesus as Messiah—a detail that serves Mark's intent to emphasize the confession of Peter. Lagrange believes that Mark's omission of Jesus' response to Peter as the rock on which the church was built is the result of the modesty of Peter (Mark's source). Jesus' charge that the disciples should not disclose his messianic identity (v. 30) is due, in Lagrange's opinion, to Jesus' conviction that the crowds would not comprehend his understanding of messiahship.[84]

In 1921, Lagrange published a commentary on *Luke*.[85] In an extensive introduction (more than 165 pages), Lagrange investigates the sources. He believes that Mark was Luke's main written source, and that Luke also used the hypothetical original gospel of Matthew, written in Aramaic. According

---

83. *Évangile selon saint Marc,* 4th ed., Ebib (Paris: J. Gabalda, 1947).
84. For other examples of Lagrange's interpretation of Mark, especially in contrast to the exegesis of Loisy, see Nadia M. Lahutsky, "Paris and Jerusalem: Alfred Loisy and Père Lagrange on the Gospel of Mark," *CBQ* 52 (1990): 444–64; for example, on 3:31-35 (concerning the "brothers" of Jesus), Lagrange, after careful analysis of linguistic and grammatical details, concludes that the text does not contradict the perpetual virginity of Mary.
85. *Évangile selon saint Luc,* 8th ed., Ebib (Paris: J. Gabalda, 1948).

to Lagrange, Luke also used other sources, including Mary's reminiscences of the events of the birth and boyhood of Jesus. Lagrange views the work of Luke within the tradition of the Greek historians, and believes he was concerned to present the facts as foundation for faith. Luke's Christology, in Lagrange's opinion, is not higher than Mark's, although Luke's unique use of the title "Savior" emphasizes the Christ of Christian belief. Lagrange thoroughly investigates the vocabulary, grammar, and style of Luke; he finds expressions that have parallels in the Epistles, but denies that Pauline ideas are read into Luke's Gospel. In regard to the text, Lagrange rejects Blass's theory (adopted by Zahn) that Luke wrote two editions of his Gospel and Acts.[86] The actual commentary, more than six hundred pages, follows the format and character of the other volumes of the series.

Lagrange first published his commentary on *Matthew* in 1923.[87] In the introduction (more than 180 pages), he investigates and confirms the tradition that the first Gospel was written by Matthew, one of the Twelve, the tax collector called "Levi" by Mark and Luke. According to Lagrange, Matthew wrote in Jerusalem in Aramaic for Palestinians prior to 70. In regard to the Synoptic Problem, Lagrange asserts that the widely accepted two-document hypothesis denies reliable tradition, and undermines the authority of Matthew. Lagrange's solution, reminiscent of Zahn, is that Mark used the original Aramaic gospel of Matthew, and that the Greek translator of canonical Matthew used Mark. Like the other commentaries in the series, Lagrange's comments (545 pages) attend to text-critical, linguistic, grammatical, and historical details, displaying mastery of an enormous amount of ancient and modern sources.

In 1925, Lagrange published a commentary on the *Gospel of John*.[88] The lengthy introduction (more than 190 pages) gives much attention to the question of authorship. On the basis of internal evidence, Lagrange concludes that the author was an eyewitness, to be identified with the beloved disciple, who, according to Lagrange, can be no other than John the son of Zebedee. Lagrange finds support for this view in the tradition that early on and universally supports Johannine authorship. According to Lagrange, this author knew the other Gospels, and assumed that his readers knew the gospel tradition. In relating the content of John to that of the Synoptics, Lagrange believes it crucial to distinguish the private from the public ministry of Jesus. In the Synoptics, which record the public ministry, Jesus had said that the secrets of the kingdom would be revealed to the disciples. These secrets, according to Lagrange, are revealed in the private

---

86. See p. 185, above.
87. *Évangile selon saint Matthieu,* 8th ed., Ebib (Paris: J. Gabalda, 1948).
88. *Évangile selon saint Jean,* 7th ed., Ebib (Paris: J. Gabalda, 1948).

instruction given to the disciples, notably in the discourses of the latter part of the Gospel of John. Lagrange concludes, "the Fourth Gospel is a very valuable source that should be used with all conceivable diligence in order to know the *Life of Jesus* about which it specifies, better than the Synoptics, the chronological framework; and that it is a supplement, wholly in accord with its proper purpose, which is to put in full light Jesus as Messiah and Son of God."[89]

Lagrange's lengthy commentary (535 pages) follows the format of the Études bibliques series and displays Lagrange's concern with exegetical details in the service of theological interpretation. For example, he finds three themes in 1:1: the Logos before creation, the Logos in relation to God, and the divine nature of the Logos. Lagrange notes the use of Logos by the Stoics, but argues that John's use has its background in the HB. According to Lagrange, the phrase πρὸς τὸν Θεόν ("with God") expresses both the unique relation of the Logos to God and the Logos as distinct person. Lagrange believes the idea of creation through the Logos (1:3) indicates creation accomplished by the thought or intelligence of God; the phrase δι' αὐτοῦ (here and in Col. 1:16) does not mean subordination. "The thought of John," says Lagrange, "is simply that the Word who was God cooperated in the creation of all things, being the thought which God had conceived and which he expressed outwardly in some way. The Logos collaborated without ceasing to be God."[90]

In 1928, Lagrange published *The Gospel of Jesus Christ*—in effect a commentary on a harmony of the four Gospels.[91] Lagrange presents the material in 321 sections, ordered primarily according to the chronology of John; he prints the texts in parallel columns, from left to right: Luke, Mark, Matthew, and John. In investigating the prologue to Luke, Lagrange summarizes his final position on the Synoptic Problem: Matthew wrote first (in Aramaic); Mark presented the tradition of Peter, but also used Aramaic Matthew; Luke followed Mark's order, and put the discourse material of the Aramaic Matthew into its proper settings; the translator of Greek Matthew used Mark as a source. To this commentary on the Gospels, Lagrange attaches an epilogue, "The Gospel of Jesus Christ, God and Man." In this epilogue, Lagrange presents a survey of the life of Jesus. He believes Jesus' understanding of the kingdom was religious and ethical, in contrast to the

---

89. Ibid., cxcvi.
90. Ibid., 6–7.
91. *L'Évangile de Jésus-Christ*, 2d ed., Ebib (Paris: J. Gabalda 1954); Eng. trans.: *The Gospel of Jesus Christ*, trans. Members of the English Dominican Province, 2 vols. (Westminster, Md.: Newman, 1958). The synopsis on which the comments are based originally appeared in Greek, *Synopsis evangelica graece*, edited by Lagrange in collaboration with C. Lavergne (Barcelona, 1926). In the English translation, the material from the Synopsis is according to: *A Catholic Harmony of the Four Gospels, Being an Adaptation of the "Synopsis Evangelica" of P. Lagrange*, ed. John Barton (London: Burns, Oates & Washbourne, 1930).

nationalistic idea of the Jews. According to Lagrange, Jesus was fully human, but without sin. Lagrange also opposes the liberal Protestant notion that Jesus' message is only a gospel about God—an arid universalism that affirms the fatherhood of God and the brotherhood of humans. Instead, Lagrange sees the message as the gospel about Christ, the Son of God. "It lay in nothing else but Christ's own declarations, which left no room for doubt, compelling the disciples (even as they compel us) to leave Him unless they believed in the words of eternal life—declarations which His miracles prepared the way for and confirmed by endowing them with the authority of God Himself; declarations, finally which were recognized to be in harmony with the Scriptures."[92]

In the interval between his Mark and Luke commentaries, Lagrange produced commentaries on *Romans* and *Galatians*. In the introduction to the *Romans* commentary, Lagrange contends that the majority of the members of the Roman church were Gentiles.[93] He believes Paul wrote to encourage them to welcome Jewish Christians who were returning from the exile earlier imposed by Claudius. Lagrange understands 3:21-30 to develop the main theme of the epistle. Lagrange investigates the meaning of ἀπολύτρωσις (v. 24), and concludes that it includes the idea of ransom, in harmony with other texts that refer to paying a price. Lagrange believes that ἱλαστήριον (v. 25) does not refer to the mercy seat, but presents Jesus as God's instrument of expiation. Lagrange's *Galatians* adopts the north Galatian hypothesis. In relation to Romans, Lagrange believes this epistle represents an earlier stage in Paul's thinking. In discussing the opponents of Paul, Lagrange distances the Judaizers (converts from the Pharisaic Judaism) from James and the Jerusalem leaders. Lagrange argues that Paul's conversion, as recounted in chapter 1, is based on the revelation of Christ as Son of God—an event quite unlike the subjective experience of Luther. Lagrange believes the term καλέσας (v. 15) describes both Paul's call and his conversion. "He became apostle at the same time he was converted."[94]

Canon, Text, and Historical Context

Late in life, Lagrange began the publication of a multivolume series titled *Introduction to the Study of the NT*. The first volume was dedicated to the investigation of the canon.[95] At the outset, Lagrange presents the Catholic position: the church did not create the canon, but received the sacred books, written by the apostles. Lagrange affirms two principles of canonicity:

---

92. *Gospel of Jesus Christ* 2:325.
93. *Saint Paul: Épître aux Romains*, 4th ed., Ebib (Paris: J. Gabalda, 1950).
94. *Saint Paul: Épître aux Galates*, 2d ed., Ebib (Paris: J. Gabalda, 1925), 14.
95. *Introduction à l'étude du Nouveau Testament: Première partie: Histoire ancienne du canon du Nouveau Testament*, 2d ed., Ebib (Paris: J. Gabalda, 1933).

apostolic origin and ecclesiastical use. He gives special attention to seven problematic books—Hebrews, James, the Apocalypse, and the short Catholic Epistles (2 Peter, Jude, 2 and 3 John)—and presents evidence for their early use. Like Zahn, Lagrange rejects the notion that the church delineated the canon in reaction to Marcion; instead, the argument against Marcion (for example, by Irenaeus) presupposes a prior authoritative collection of apostolic writings. Lagrange investigates the usage of NT documents in various regions during the third and fourth centuries, and concludes that the canon was fixed by the beginning of the fifth century. In a final chapter, Lagrange acknowledges that the acceptance of the canon is ultimately a matter of faith. This faith, however, he believes to be confirmed by the inspired tradition. "The church made its decision according to the use it has made of these books, use about which it was not able to be mistaken, being assisted by the Holy Spirit that had inspired them."[96]

The second volume of the *Introduction* deals with Textual Criticism.[97] Lagrange begins with a history of modern editing of the text from Robert Étienne (1550) to A. Merk (1933). Speaking for himself, Lagrange advocates the genealogical method whereby variants are analyzed so as to group manuscripts into families. To evaluate variants, Lagrange uses the recognized criteria, for example, Griesbach's principle that the harder reading is to be preferred.[98] The balance of this massive work (more than 650 pages) is devoted to an investigation of the text according to the sections of the canon. In regard to the Gospels, Lagrange analyzes the Greek texts according to their major recensions. He affirms the importance of the early Egyptian text represented by Codex Vaticanus (B) and Codex Sinaiticus (ℵ), but rejects the idea (of Westcott and Hort) that these represent a neutral text. Lagrange also recognizes the importance of the "Western Text" represented by Codex Bezae (D), and agrees with recent text-critical research in identifying a "Caesarean" text, represented by Codex Koridethi (Θ) and the Chester Beatty Papyrus (P[45]). Lagrange turns to the ancient versions, giving detailed attention to the Syriac, Latin, Coptic, and Gothic texts. This same procedure is repeated for the rest of the canon: Acts of the Apostles (where Lagrange finds evidence for an early Antiochene recension), Epistles of Paul, Catholic Epistles, and the Apocalypse.

Apparently, Lagrange had planned a third volume of the *Introduction* to be dedicated to literary criticism. This, however, was never accomplished. Instead, Lagrange jumped to a fourth volume on *Historical Criticism*. In response to the claim of the history of religion scholars that Christianity was

---

96. Ibid., 178.
97. *Introduction à l'étude du Nouveau Testament: Deuxième partie: Critique textuelle, II La critique rationnelle*, Ebib (Paris: J. Gabalda, 1935).
98. *HNTR* 1:142–43.

a syncretistic religion, borrowing extravagantly from its religious neighbors, Lagrange focuses on a single example of Hellenistic religion, Orphism. This example, he thinks, is particularly appropriate, because Orphism is a syncretistic oriental religion of redemption. Lagrange begins with a survey of recent research on Orphism. In the course of the investigation, Lagrange deals with the sources, the origin of Orphism, initiation into the Orphic cult, and Orphism as a religion of salvation. A final chapter is devoted to the relation of Christianity to Orphism, in which Lagrange investigates features of Orphism that have alleged parallels in Christianity. For example, in regard to the idea of the union of the believer with a suffering and dying god, Lagrange contends that the mysteries do not envisage a god who freely accepts death as expiation for the sins of others. Paul's idea of unity with Christ is, according to Lagrange, not borrowed from paganism, but grounded in his own experience of Christ. In conclusion, Lagrange says that "we believe we have given solid reasons to conclude that Christianity borrowed nothing from the religious sect of the Orphics."[99] Nevertheless, Lagrange believes the Hellenistic religions prepared the way for Christianity by voicing the aspiration of people for redemption—a redemption realized in Christ.

With Lagrange at the helm, Roman Catholic scholarship navigates into the mainstream of NT research. He shows that a scholar can be a devout believer and expert critic at the same time. To be sure, Lagrange's criticism has encouraged him to jettison orthodox beliefs like biblical inerrancy and the primacy of the Vulgate. On the other hand, his commitment to the authority of the church has moved him to adjudicate critical questions (for example, the Synoptic Problem) on the basis of the tradition. Lagrange, however, openly acknowledges his presuppositions, and his view of tradition allows him to escape the strictures of *sola scriptura* and at the same time to affirm a high doctrine of biblical authority. Although much of his work is devoted to apologetics, Lagrange performs the apologetic task with exceptional skill.

SUMMARY

Although the scholars of this chapter have been grouped together, they display differences. Von Dobschütz and Feine reflect the liberal tradition with emphasis on the teachings of Jesus, although the stress on morality (von Dobschütz) is affirmed by Schlatter. Although all the scholars of this chapter are committed to the historical-critical method, the focus on facts by

---

99. *Introduction à l'étude du Nouveau Testament: IV Critique historique. I Les mystères: l'Orphisme*, Ebib (Paris: J. Gabalda, 1937), 222.

Zahn and Schlatter has parallels with the empiricism of the Princeton theologians of the preceding chapter. Also, these scholars (including von Dobschütz and Feine) attack the advancing consensus of liberal criticism, in particular, the work of the history of religion school. The attack is aimed at the notion that parallels imply dependence and that Christianity is a syncretism. As historical critics, these scholars agree that early Christianity must be investigated in its historical setting. But to avoid the shadow of paganism, they locate the background in Judaism, or better, in the HB, since they tend to denigrate the Pharisaic Judaism of the first century. Moreover, these scholars are reluctant to portray Jesus and the early Christians with the pigment of apocalyptic, so that even Schlatter and Lagrange slide toward the religious-ethical understanding of the kingdom of God. In particular, the source of the Johannine Logos and the Pauline christological formulations is not to be found in Hellenism (Feine, Schlatter, Lagrange). Although the argument might be effective in regard to John and Paul, it tends to ignore the question of how these terms were understood by John's readers in Ephesus and Paul's in Corinth.

The scholars of this chapter stress continuity—from the OT prophets to Jesus to the early Christians to Paul to John. This emphasis encourages a harmonizing whereby distinctions are blurred, and the individuality of the authors is sacrificed to the unity of the canon. A high estimate of the canon is thought to be confirmed by a reliable tradition, which Zahn, without sufficient explanation of his rationale, enlists in the defense of his critical conclusions about the NT. Lagrange, on the other hand, follows a theology of tradition that has been carefully crafted over the years by Catholic theologians. Zahn and Lagrange agree (for different reasons) that the church did not create canon, but simply received what was already apostolic, thus, essentially canonical. Because of his theology of tradition, Lagrange is able to leave the closing of the canon to a relatively late date, whereas Zahn—in support of authenticity and reliability—pushes formalizing of the canon as early as possible. Joined with the high doctrine of the canon, these scholars hold a lofty view of inspiration. Yet, although they consider the records highly reliable, they do not advocate inerrancy.

All the scholars of this chapter exemplify a profound religious faith. Schlatter, for example, insists that unless one shares the biblical claim, one cannot understand the Bible. He also effectively attacks criticism—atheistic criticism—that excludes a priori the supernatural, the miraculous, the action of God. Of course, exposing the presuppositions of others does not prove that one's own are valid. Although empathy with the message of the NT—like the empathy required to appreciate music—may be essential to understanding, the question can be raised as to what is the biblical claim; what is the chord to which the listener must resonate? Answering these questions requires criticism and runs the risk of circular argument. As the scholars of this chapter demonstrate, their presuppositions determine their results—contrast, for example, Zahn and Lagrange on Peter's confession.

As to critical details, the scholars of this chapter are notable for their critical judgments, for example, the priority of Matthew (Zahn, Schlatter, and Lagrange). In this decision, Lagrange is influenced by the Catholic tradition, whereas Zahn and Schlatter seem anxious to confirm reliability and apostolic authority (Matthew, an eyewitness and apostle, rather than Mark). The same motivation probably explains the support of the authenticity of the Pastoral and Catholic Epistles (except for 2 Peter, according to Feine and Schlatter). This is probably true, too, for the Johannine literature, although ascribing both the Fourth Gospel and Revelation to the same author appears to compromise critical judgments and theological precision. Critics, however, who easily dismiss these conservative conclusions need to be reminded that they, too, harbor presuppositions and prejudices; they, too, engage in circular arguments and fanciful reconstructions. Of course, one does not have to agree with Zahn, Schlatter, and Lagrange to appreciate their work. They do not, after all, fully agree among themselves. Yet to read them with appreciation is to be challenged by three of the great minds of NT research.

9

The Refining of Historical Criticism

The era of the two world wars was a time of uncertainty. At the end of World War I, Europe was in a shambles. Germany, the center of biblical studies, had been humiliated, burdened with reparations. All was quiet on the western front except for the shouts of the victorious Allies. But they, too, remembered the horrors of the trenches, and hoped for a brighter future through the collective security of the League of Nations. This hope was dashed with the triumph of totalitarianism in Italy and Germany. Yet, while the optimism of the Weimar Republic failed, democracy flourished in Britain and America. The Western world was a picture of contrasts: the Jazz Age and the Prohibition amendment; the amassing of wealth and the crash of the stock market. The phonograph brought the jazz singer into the living room, and Hollywood entertained the masses. But mass entertainment could not feed the folk who lost their jobs and stood in bread lines. Scholars such as Oswald Spengler could herald the "decline of the West," while ordinary people absorbed the anti-intellectual folk wisdom of Will Rogers.

In this period, scientific technology continued to advance and dominate the marketplace. Henry Ford produced inexpensive cars for the common people. In 1930, transcontinental air passenger service took off in the United States. New technologies facilitated the refining of NT research. Better methods of transportation encouraged the search for ancient artifacts. Improved photography developed facsimile copies of forgotten manuscripts, exposing the hidden treasures of remote libraries to the bright light of the scholar's desk. Modern chemistry distilled solutions that could erase the patina of later writing to uncover the primitive script of a fragile palimpsest. Equipped with new techniques, NT scholars carried on their relentless research, warily emerging into the brave new world.

NT research in this period also reflects the variety and uncertainty of the times. The new discoveries of the earlier era are evaluated, refined, and appropriated. Manuscripts that had been overlooked are found in secluded monasteries. Text criticism is advanced with ambitious proposals and cautious refinements. In regard to Jewish backgrounds, attention is turned to rabbinic material and the debate about its relevance. The history of religion method, corrected by the conservatives, is widely accepted and domesticated in commentaries and exegetical monographs. Dramatic reconstructions of early Christian history are proposed, then accommodated to more moderate assessments. In point of view, liberalism, once the harbinger of progress, has become the establishment. New theological movements, shaken by the crisis of the times, are largely ignored, and older philosophical models are revived and perpetuated. Scholars cry "Peace" when there is no peace.

CONTINUING DISCOVERY AND RESEARCH IN TEXT CRITICISM: HERMANN FREIHERR VON SODEN, JAMES RENDEL HARRIS, AND KIRSOPP LAKE

In 1881, text criticism had reached a high point in the publication of *The New Testament in the Original Greek* by B. F. Westcott and F. J. A. Hort.[1] These two scholars had mastered text-critical methodology and produced a text, based on what they believed to be an ancient "neutral" text, very close to the original. Yet, in listing Greek MSS on which their text was built, they included no papyri. Actually, only nine NT papyri were known in 1900, and most of the papyri (more than a hundred) now used by text critics were discovered in the twentieth century. Also, in the interim since 1881, critics had come to question Westcott and Hort's theory of a neutral text and their disdain for the so-called Western text. At the same time, scholars, following the genealogical method employed by their predecessors, found evidence for new families of MSS, and saw signs of another ancient text-type called the Caesarean. Text criticism is sometimes seen as the most objective of the biblical disciplines. However, as the discussion below will demonstrate, text criticism thrives on hypotheses, conjectures, and emendations. According to Kirsopp Lake and his colleagues, "Ultimately all intelligent criticism is subjective."[2]

---

1. See pp. 62–65, above.
2. Kirsopp Lake, Robert P. Blake, and Silva New, "The Caesarean Text of the Gospels of Mark," *HTR* 21 (1928): 336.

Hermann Freiherr von Soden (1852–1914)

Von Soden, one of the most diligent text critics of the early twentieth century, was born in Cincinnati, Ohio, and educated in Tübingen, Germany.[3] After serving parishes in southern and northern Germany, von Soden began teaching at the University of Berlin (1889), and eventually was promoted to professor of NT. His theological perspective is revealed in his popular book on the life of Jesus.[4] According to von Soden, Jesus saw himself as Messiah—one who enjoyed a unique relation to God as Father, whose mission addressed the inner life, the salvation of souls. This same liberal outlook is reflected in his critical conclusions, disclosed in his book *The History of Early Christian Literature.*[5] For example, von Soden denies the authenticity of 2 Thessalonians, Ephesians, and the Pastoral Epistles, and rejects the apostolic authorship of all the Johannine literature.[6]

Von Soden's massive text-critical work, bound in four hefty volumes, is arranged in two parts. In the foreword, von Soden expresses gratitude to Elise Koenigs for her support, which financed visits to libraries in Europe and the Near East by some forty-five scholars who contributed to the project. In Part I (*Untersuchung*), Section 1 (Textual Evidence), von Soden reveals the purpose of text criticism. "The final goal of the concern with the varied traditional forms of the text of the NT documents is the restoration of the text that the authors of these documents once set before their readers."[7] After a survey of the work of the early text critics, von Soden turns to the research of the last half of the nineteenth century. He decries what he calls the "bankruptcy" of criticism from Bengel to Westcott and Hort, particularly the ignoring of a vast amount of important material. In order to investigate this mass of material, von Soden devises a new system for identifying MSS. This system attempts to identify MSS according to their date. For example, for codices of the Gospels written prior to the tenth century, von Soden uses Arabic numbers from 1 to 99; tenth-century MSS are indicated

---

3. For biographical information, see "Soden, Hans Karl Hermann, Freiherr von," in *NSHERK* 10:495; Bruce M. Metzger, *The Text of the New Testament: Its Transmission, Corruption, and Restoration,* 2d ed. (New York: Oxford University Press, 1968), 138–39.

4. *Die wichtigsten Fragen im Leben Jesus* (Berlin: Alexander Duncker, 1907).

5. *Urchristliche Literaturgeschichte (Die Schriften des Neuen Testaments)* (Berlin: Alexander Duncker, 1905); Eng. trans.: *The History of Early Christian Literature: The Writings of the New Testament,* trans. J. R. Wilkinson, ed. W. D. Morrison, CTL 13 (London: Williams & Norgate, 1906).

6. Von Soden also published a short, nontechnical commentary on Philippians (*Der Brief des Apostels Paulus an die Philipper,* 2d ed. [Tübingen: J. C. B. Mohr (Paul Siebeck), 1906]) and contributed a volume (*Hebräerbrief, Briefe des Petrus, Jakobus, Judas* [3d ed.; Tübingen: J. C. B. Mohr (Paul Siebeck), 1899]) to the respected series Hand-Commentar zum Neuen Testament of which he, along with such notables as H. J. Holtzmann, was an editor.

7. *Die Schriften des Neuen Testaments in ihrer ältesten erreichbaren Textgestalt, auf Grund ihrer Textgeschichte,* 2d ed., 4 vols. (Göttingen: Vandenhoeck & Ruprecht, 1911, 1913) 1:1.

by numbers 1000–1099. He has a different system for the Epistles, and for MSS from the eleventh and following centuries. In order to indicate what part of the canon the MSS contain, von Soden uses δ (διαθήκη) for MSS of the whole NT, ε (εὐαγγέλιον) for MSS of the Gospels, and α (ἀπόστολος) for MSS that include the Epistles and Revelation.

Von Soden proceeds to present a list of the extant MSS according to the libraries in which they are located. He also provides a list indicating how the system used by previous editors (a system devised by Wettstein and revised by Gregory) relates to his new system.[8] For example, the MS that the previous system identifies as B (Codex Vaticanus), von Soden identifies as δ1; ℵ (Sinaiticus) is δ2; D (Bezae) is δ5. Von Soden also presents a list of all the extant MSS arranged according to their content (δ, ε, and α codices) in chronological order with a brief description of each MS. This list includes a total of 2,339 codices. Von Soden also offers a list of patristic commentaries, and discusses material that is added to MSS, for example, subscriptions.

In the second section of Part I ("Forms of the Text: A"), von Soden presents his theory of the genealogical relation of the texts of the Gospels. He believes there are three ancient text-types, each the result of an early recension of the text. The K (Koine) text became dominant in the second millennium. An early representative of this text is seen in ε6 (according to Gregory, Ω) which von Soden dates in the seventh century. In a complex analysis, von Soden detects several subtypes of the K text. He believes the earliest form of this text was a recension made by Lucian of Antioch in the fourth century. The H (Hesychian) text has its main representatives in δ1 (B) and δ2 (ℵ). Von Soden believes a common ancestor underlies these two codices—a recension made around the end of the third century by Hesychius, an Alexandrian scholar. The I ('Ιερουσαλήμ, Jerusalem) text has its main representatives in the Italian Latin, Sinaitic Syriac, and δ5 (D). Von Soden also divides this text into subgroups. Beneath these various forms was an original text, the result, von Soden thinks, of a recension made in Palestine, probably late in the third century under the tutelage of Pamphilus. Von Soden studies the relation of these text-types to each other, and concludes that they have a common ancestor—what he calls the I-H-K text. In an effort to reconstruct this original text, von Soden investigates the ancient versions (Old Latin and Old Syriac) and the texts used by patristic authors before Origen. He concludes that the original I-H-K text was used in the second century by Irenaeus, but that it had been corrupted by the influence of Tatian's Diatessaron. "Tatian's Diatessaron is basically the sole source for all the more significant variations of the text of the Gospels."[9]

---

8. *HNTR* 1:104.
9. *Schriften des NT* 2:1633.

When these variations are eliminated, von Soden thinks the text of 140 C.E. can be reconstructed—a text very close to the autographs. In the third section of Part I ("Forms of the Text: B"), von Soden applies the same procedures he has used for the Gospels to the analysis of the text of the Epistles and the Apocalypse, with essentially the same result.

In Part II, von Soden presents his critical text, that is, his attempt to reconstruct the original I-H-K text—the text "in its earliest attainable form." In the foreword, he confidently asserts that careful study of his results will confirm his theory of a Palestinian recension (the I Text) and will obliterate the phantom of the Western text. Von Soden's introduction explains his complicated critical apparatus (that is, the footnotes that present the evidence for textual variants). He includes evidence from all the Greek MSS that support his three main text-types, the evidence from the ancient versions (Coptic, Old Latin, Old Syriac, Vulgate, and Peshitta), and citations from the fathers of the first four centuries—a huge amount of material. Von Soden arranges the apparatus under the text in three parts: a section that contains variants that could belong to the original text, a section that contains variants that are important for understanding the three main recensions, and a section (printed in smaller type) that includes variants of lesser importance. In indicating the textual evidence, von Soden uses his new method of identifying MSS and his special signs for the three text-types: I, H, and K. Since there are many subtexts indicated by symbols, for instance, K^c and I^a (the I Text has more than twenty subtexts), the apparatus is extremely difficult to use.[10]

Von Soden's reconstructed text, almost nine hundred pages, is printed at the top of the page—usually about one-third, or, in the case of the Gospels, one-fourth of the page, with the three-part apparatus below. The NT books are presented in the order: Gospels, Acts, Catholic Epistles, Pauline Epistles, and the Apocalypse. As examples of the text, the secondary endings of Mark (16:9-20) are printed in smaller type, as is the account of the adulteress (John 7:53—8:11). The notorious text of 1 John 5:7 ("in heaven, the Father, the Word, and the Holy Spirit, and these three are one. And there are three that bear witness of earth") is not included in von Soden's text; he relegates it to the third section of his apparatus.

---

10. To aid in the use of von Soden's complicated system of signs, a key had been published: Friedrich Krüger, *Schlüssel zu von Soden's Die Schriften des Neuen Testaments in ihrer ältesten erreichbaren Textgestalt hergestellt [Göttingen] 1902–1913. Gegenüberstellung der in von Soden's Apparat vorkommenden Sigla und der entsprechenden in Gregorys Liste* (Göttingen: Vandenhoeck & Ruprecht, 1927). A guided tour through one example of von Soden's apparatus is provided by Kurt Aland and Barbara Aland, *The Text of the New Testament: An Introduction to the Critical Editions and to the Theory and Practice of Modern Textual Criticism*, trans. Erroll F. Rhodes (Grand Rapids, Mich.: Eerdmans, 1987), 41–43.

To those uninitiated in the vast mysteries of text criticism, von Soden's work is a mountain of research, crammed with data, bristling with details, abounding in complex analysis and imaginative reconstruction. Most experts, however, have been critical.[11] Not since the building of the tower of Babel had so much effort produced so little results. Kirsopp Lake pronounced von Soden's text a "tragic failure."[12] Von Soden's hypotheses concerning the three ancient recensions (and their editors) allege more than the evidence allows. His theory of a primitive I-H-K text puts too much weight on the K text—the late text that is clearly inferior. Besides, for all his attention to detail, von Soden's work is marred by errors in collating and recording; his failure to spell Westcott (sometimes "Weskott") and Hort (sometimes "Horst") consistently does not inspire confidence. Unfortunately, von Soden's complicated system of notation has discouraged scholars from recognizing that von Soden's edition "is a necessary tool for textual critics . . . a vast quarry of information that is unavailable elsewhere."[13]

James Rendel Harris (1852–1941)

Von Soden's ardor for hypotheses is totally eclipsed by the meteoric brilliance of James Rendel Harris's imagination. Born in Plymouth, England, Rendel Harris was educated at Cambridge, where he was influenced by F. J. A. Hort.[14] He began his teaching at Cambridge as a lecturer in mathematics, but in 1881, the year of the publication of the Westcott-Hort edition, he turned to text criticism. The next year he migrated to America, where he taught at Johns Hopkins, and later at Haverford College (1885 to 1892). In 1893, Harris returned to Cambridge as lecturer in paleography. Ten years later he was appointed professor at Leiden, but, after a few months, he resigned in order to become director of studies at Woodbrooke, the Quaker center in Birmingham. In 1918, Harris was appointed curator of oriental MSS at the John Rylands Library in Manchester—a post from which he retired in 1925, suffering from failing eyesight. In 1896, he and his wife spent six months organizing relief for the Armenians who were suffering persecution in Asia Minor. While traveling to the east on the Mediterranean, his ship was torpedoed by the Germans in 1916—a tragedy

---

11. See K. Aland and B. Aland, *The Text of the New Testament*, 22–23, 40–43; Metzger, *Text of the NT*, 142–43; Hans Lietzmann, "H. v. Sodens Ausgabe des Neuen Testaments," in *Kleine Schriften, II Studien zum Neuen Testament,* ed. Kurt Aland, TU 68 (Berlin: Akademie, 1958), 239–48, originally published in *ZNW* 15 (1914): 323–31.
12. *The Text of the New Testament,* 6th rev. ed. Silva New, Oxford Church Text Books (London: Rivingtons, 1928), 78.
13. K. Aland and B. Aland, *Text of the New Testament,* 23.
14. For a survey of Harris's life and work, see C. A. Phillips, "Rendel Harris," *ExpTim* 52: 349–52.

repeated on his return trip the following year when he survived in the lifeboat in which J. H. Moulton perished.[15]

For Harris, text criticism was a hands-on discipline. He discovered MSS, photographed, transcribed, and edited them. According to Harris, "The history of the text of the New Testament is the most perplexing of the unsolved problems of the universe, and has almost as many missing links as the chain of life itself."[16] An overview of Harris's work is seen in his lively lecture series, *Side-Lights on New Testament Research*.[17] In these lectures, Harris approves the work of Westcott and Hort, for example, their designation of the longer ending of Mark (16:9-20) as not original. Using his boundless imagination, Harris, investigating the Armenian version, concludes that this ending of Mark was the work of Ariston, an elder mentioned by Papias. Harris also agrees that the prayer of Jesus recorded in Luke 23:34 ("Father, forgive them") is not original. Harris supposes that it was added by the same scribe who interpolated the story of the adulteress (John 7:53—8:11) after Luke 21:38—a story that had its origin, according to Harris, in the Gospel of the Hebrews. Harris also discusses the practice of textual emendation, and offers one of his own. He believes "Enoch" has been incorrectly omitted from the text of 1 Peter 3:19. According to Harris, a text that originally described Enoch's trip to Hades has been misconstrued to support the superstitious notion that Jesus descended into the underworld.

Harris dedicated considerable effort to the transcribing and editing of MSS. One of the early examples is his work on the Didache, or *The Teaching of the Apostles*.[18] In 1885, Harris had published photographs of three pages of the recently discovered text of the document, and in 1887, the Patriarch of Jerusalem had allowed the entire MS to be photographed and sent to America to be studied. Harris's book includes his transcription of the text, his critical commentary, and ten plates of the photographic copy of the MS. In 1889, Harris spent seventeen days at St. Catherine's at Sinai where he discovered and photographed a Syriac translation of the second-century *Apology of Aristides*—a work he later published with introduction, translation, and notes.[19] During the visit to St. Catherine's, Harris also investigated and later published *Biblical Fragments from Mount Sinai*.[20] This book presents a

---

15. See pp. 186–89, above.
16. *On the Origin of the Ferrar-Group: A Lecture on the Genealogical Relations of New Testament MSS. Delivered at Mansfield College, Oxford on Nov. 6th, 1893* (London: C. J. Clay and Sons, 1893), 5.
17. *Seven Lectures Delivered in 1908, at Regent's Park College, London*, Angus Lectureship (London: Kingsgate, 1908).
18. *The Teaching of the Apostles, Newly Edited, with Facsimile Text and a Commentary: From the MS. of the Holy Sepulchre, Jerusalem* (London: C. J. Clay and Sons, 1887).
19. *The Apology of Aristides on Behalf of the Christians: From a Syriac MS. Preserved on Mount Sinai*, TS 1/1 (Cambridge: University Press, 1891).
20. (London: C. J. Clay and Sons, 1890).

general description of the fragments and brief descriptions of the sixteen fragments. For example, Number 9 is a bilingual (Greek and Arabic) uncial MS of Matthew 13, and Number 16 is a fragment of a previously unknown Syriac version of the Pauline letters.

The year 1893 found Harris back at Sinai. The year before, Agnes Smith Lewis had discovered the famous palimpsest of the Sinaitic Syriac.[21] When a return was planned for additional study of the MS, Lewis requested that Harris join the scholarly team that included her sister, Margaret Dunlop Gibson, R. L. Bensly, and F. C. Burkitt.[22] The team spent forty days at St. Catherine's, transcribing the MS; the results were published the following year.[23] In 1909, Harris discovered among his own collection of documents a Syriac MS of the *Odes of Solomon* and the *Psalms of Solomon*. On the basis of this text and other MSS, Harris (along with his student, Alphonse Mingana) published a critical text of the *Odes*, with introduction and English translation.[24]

Harris's major contribution to text criticism is his persistent work on the Western text. He began his investigation in 1890, with his book on *The Diatessaron of Tatian*.[25] After a survey of what is known of Tatian's career, Harris reviews the MSS on which the reconstruction of the Diatessaron is based—two Arabic texts, now located in Rome. He also reports notices of the *Diatessaron* in ancient authors. Harris sees in the *Diatessaron* an early form of the so-called Western text, and detects evidence for the existence of a harmony of the Gospels prior to Tatian.

Pursuing his interest in the Western text, Harris published a book on its main representative, Codex Bezae (D). He begins by tracing the life of the Codex backwards from the time it was donated to the University of Cambridge by Theodore Beza. Harris locates it in France in the tenth century, and in southern Gaul in the sixth. In quest of the earlier life of the MS, Harris investigates the interrelation of the Greek and Latin texts of this bilingual MS, and concludes, against the majority view that the Latin had been influenced by the Greek, that the opposite is true. "We have now verified completely the hypothesis to which our investigations of the Beza text led us, viz. that the Greek text has been thoroughly and persistently Latinized." In regard to the type of text represented by D, Harris detects evidence that it was in existence prior to Irenaeus, and hazards a bold conclusion: "We have

---

21. See pp. 177–78, above.
22. See pp. 267–69, above.
23. Robert L. Bensly, J. Rendel Harris, and F. Crawford Burkitt, *The Four Gospels in Syriac: Transcribed from the Sinaitic Palimpsest, with an Introduction by Agnes Smith Lewis* (Cambridge: University Press, 1894).
24. Rendel Harris and Alphonse Mingana, eds., *The Odes and Psalms of Solomon*, 2 vols. (Manchester: University Press, 1916, 1920).
25. *The Diatessaron of Tatian: A Preliminary Study* (London: C. J. Clay and Sons, 1890).

shewn reason for believing that the whole body of Western Latin readings go back into a single bilingual copy, the remote ancestor of the Codex Bezae."[26] Harris believes this early text influenced the Egyptian versions, the Alexandrian codices, and Tatian. He thinks this ancestor of Bezae had been influenced by the Syriac text tradition and by Montanism; its origin, according to Harris, was in Rome or Carthage. In another monograph, Harris concludes, "I have sought to recover the Latin of that famous text from the neglect or contempt into which it has fallen, and to shew to the critical students of the New Testament that this text is of all texts the most important for the recovery of the rude and primitive rendering of the Gospels and the Acts which was current in the early part of the second century."[27]

Related to his work on the Western text is Harris's investigation of a collection of MSS called the Ferrar Group. W. H. Ferrar had identified a group of four MSS that seemed to have a genealogical relationship, and after his death in 1871, his work was carried on and published by T. K. Abbott in 1877. The four MSS included in the family or group were the minuscule codices 13, 69, 124, and 346. In 1893, Harris presented a lecture, *On the Origin of the Ferrar-Group*, in which he reviews the research since Abbott.[28] Abbé Martin had demonstrated that three of the Ferrar codices had originated in southern Italy or Sicily, and that Codex 543 should be added to the group. Harris also discovered that some of the MSS of the Ferrar Group contain numerical notations similar to those found in the subscriptions of some Syriac MSS; he concludes that the ancestor of the Ferrar Group had been influenced by the Old Syriac text. In *Further Researches into the History of the Ferrar-Group*, Harris notes that Kirsopp Lake had identified three more MSS as belonging to the group: Codices 788, 826, and 828.[29] Harris also observes that of the total of eight MSS, five have their origin in southern Italy or Sicily. He proceeds to investigate menologies (records of saints arranged in the order of the calendar) found in Codex 13 and Codex 346. The saints listed, Harris discovers, were related to southern Italy or, especially, to Sicily. He also finds tracts attached to three of the Ferrar MSS that include geographical references to north Africa and display Arabic influence. He concludes that the author of the original MS behind these three MSS (69, 346, 543) was a twelfth-century scribe named Nilus Doxapatrius—according to Harris, a Sicilian Christian who had access to Arabic books on geography.

---

26. *Codex Bezae: A Study of the So-Called Western Text of the New Testament,* TS 2/1 (Cambridge: University Press, 1891), 107, 171.

27. *The Codex Sangallensis (Δ): A Study in the Text of the Old Latin Gospels* (London: C. J. Clay and Sons, 1891), 1.

28. *On the Origin of the Ferrar-Group: A Lecture on the Genealogical Relations of New Testament MSS. Delivered at Mansfield College, Oxford on Nov. 6th, 1893* (London: C. J. Clay and Sons, 1893).

29. (London: C. J. Clay and Sons, 1900).

In investigating MSS, Harris made use of stichometry, that is, the analysis of the length and number of lines in a MS. In his monograph *Stichometry*, he observes that ancient MSS were measured by *stichoi* (lines or verses).[30] Copyists were paid by the hundred lines, so that the length of the line became standardized, normally a line of sixteen syllables. Euthalius, a bishop whom Harris dates in the fourth century, produced an edition of Acts and the Epistles that included stichometric notes in the margin. Harris believes Euthalius was following the system of notation that was used in the library of Pamphilus in Caesarea, and that this system discloses the form of the text of the third century. On the basis of his understanding of this form, Harris draws conclusions about the content of the text, for instance, that the account of the adulteress was not included, but the longer ending of Mark was. In *New Testament Autographs*, Harris applies stichometry to the investigation of Codex Vaticanus (B) and Codex Sinaiticus (ℵ).[31] On the basis of the number of lines in the columns of these MSS, Harris believes he is able to reconstruct the lines of the original texts from which they were copied. He concludes that B was copied from a MS of fourteen lines to a page, and ℵ from a MS of twelve lines; the originals from which these two great codices were copied, Harris thinks, were close in form and content to the autographs of the NT.[32]

Using his text-critical skills, Harris developed a theory about early Christian *Testimonies*, that is, collections of OT texts used in controversy with the Jews.[33] Specific reference to *Testimonia* is found in Cyprian, but Harris detects evidence for their earlier existence in such phenomena as the same sequence of quotations used by different writers, and the attributing of quotes to the wrong authors (as in Mark 1:2). Harris also believes there is evidence of the early and widespread use of testimonies in patristic and NT documents. On the basis of a late *Testimonia* found at Mount Athos and other shreds of evidence, Harris reaches an amazing conclusion:

> The foregoing results have brought us to a complete verification of the thesis that the original Testimonia of the Christian Church was collected by Matthew the Apostle, and circulated in the first instance under his name; they are the *Logia* to which Papias refers, and these *Logia* are not the *Sayings of Jesus*, as one was at first inclined to assume.[34]

---

30. (London: C. J. Clay and Sons, 1893).
31. Supplement *AJP* 12 (Baltimore: Isaac Friedenwald, n.d.).
32. Weaknesses of Harris's argument are pointed out by Frederic G. Kenyon (*Handbook to the Textual Criticism of the New Testament*, 2d ed. [London: Macmillan, 1926], 34–35), for instance, that papyri that have been discovered do not fit Harris's pattern.
33. James Rendel Harris, with the assistance of Vacher Burch, *Testimonies*, 2 vols. (Cambridge: University Press, 1916, 1920).
34. Ibid., 124.

Although many scholars accepted the existence of the testimony collections, few could agree to their Matthean origin and Dominical authority.[35] But even Harris could not have dreamed that the pre-Christian origin of the *Testimonia* would be confirmed by the discovery of the Dead Sea Scrolls.[36]

It is difficult to do justice to Harris in a short space.[37] Even his audacious conclusions are supported by evidence and argument, however flimsy and fanciful. Moreover, Harris's tendency to venture beyond the evidence should not be allowed to detract from his accomplishments. He expanded text-critical methodology and he showed that the so-called Western text was more valuable than Westcott and Hort had allowed; he also showed that it was not "western"—that it was strongly influenced by the Syriac textual tradition. As Kirsopp Lake says, "By no means everything which Rendel Harris said has stood the test of further examination, especially his own, but his original work on Codex Bezae set the problems and for thirty years determined the course of controversy."[38]

Kirsopp Lake (1872–1946)

Lake was born in Southampton and educated at Oxford.[39] While in Oxford, he worked as a cataloger of Greek MSS at the Bodleian Library. He succeeded Harris at Leiden, where he taught early Christian literature and NT exegesis. In 1913, he lectured in the United States, and the next year was called to the faculty at Harvard. Lake had been considered for a post at Cambridge, but his book on the *Resurrection* was viewed as dangerously liberal. In 1919, he was appointed professor of ecclesiastical history at Harvard Divinity School. In 1932, Lake resigned from the Divinity faculty, under the scandal of his Reno divorce and marriage to his student Silva, the former Mrs. Robert New. Lake retreated to the Harvard history department, and continued to lecture on the Bible as literature—a course popular with undergraduates.

Lake's point of view is revealed in *The Historical Evidence for the Resurrection of Jesus Christ*. According to Lake, "The first task of the historical

---

35. See Albert C. Sundberg, Jr., "On Testimonies," *NovT* 3 (1959): 268–81.
36. See Joseph A. Fitzmyer, "'4Q Testimonia' and the New Testament," in *Essays on the Semitic Background of the NT* (London: Geoffrey Chapman, 1971), 59–89.
37. Some conservative scholars were pleased with Harris's work *The Origin of the Prologue to St John's Gospel* (Cambridge: University Press, 1917), which located the background of the Logos in the OT wisdom tradition and not in Philo or Hellenism. However, they were scandalized by his monograph *The Twelve Apostles* (Cambridge: W. Heffer & Sons, 1927), which concluded that one of the twelve was "Judas Thomas," the twin brother of Jesus.
38. K. Lake, *The Text of the New Testament*, 6th ed. by Silva New, Oxford Church Text Books (London: Rivingtons, 1949), 74.
39. See H. D. A. Major, "Kirsopp Lake (1872–1946)," *Modern Churchman* 46 (1956): 330–32; Gerard K. Lake, "Biographical Note," in *Quantulacumque: Studies Presented to Kirsopp Lake*, ed. Robert P. Casey, Silva Lake, and Agnes K. Lake (London: Christophers, 1937).

inquirer is to collect the pieces of evidence; the second is to discuss the trustworthiness and meaning of each separate piece; and the third is to reconstruct the events to which the evidence relates." Lake launches his inquiry with a survey of the accounts of the resurrection in chronological order, beginning with Paul. "St Paul believed that the resurrection body of the Lord was from the beginning spiritual, and not material." Turning to the Synoptic Gospels, Lake concludes that the earliest record is found in Mark; the Gospels of Matthew and Luke add material, drawn from other traditions. Lake also analyzes the accounts of the resurrection in the Gospel of John, the Gospel of Peter, and the Gospel of the Hebrews.[40]

On the basis of this collection of the evidence, Lake advocates a reconstruction of the historical tradition by the methods of text criticism. He contends, "the reconstruction of an original tradition from forms of later dates and of divergent contents must be guided by exactly the same principle as is the reconstruction of an original text from a number of extant MSS. In each case the fundamental problem is the retracing of the line of development followed by the various authorities, and the solution depends chiefly on the ability to detect errors of transmission and to explain their existence." Using this method, Lake argues that Paul preserves the earliest tradition: the risen Christ was not flesh and blood. Later tradition, countering the docetists, developed the ideas of the physical resurrection, the empty tomb, and the ascension. As to the appearances, Lake believes the first was to Peter in Galilee, aroused by his sense of the presence of the living personality of Jesus. Lake, reflecting the history of religion perspective, says, "we have to consider the possibility that the phenomenon which we call the Resurrection of Christ cannot be isolated, but must be considered in connexion with others which belong to the same class." Thus, for Lake (in contrast to the early Christians) the resurrection was not a unique event, but an illustration of a larger truth: life triumphs over death.[41]

Lake made significant contributions to NT textual criticism. His earliest book is *The Text of the New Testament*, a pocket-sized manual, first published in 1900. According to Lake, "The object of all textual criticism is to recover so far as possible the actual words written by the writer."[42] This goal is pursued in four steps: (1) the study of each MS by itself, (2) comparisons of MSS and arrangement of them into groups, (3) assessment of archetypes and construction of a provisional text, (4) conjectural emendation of the provisional text. Lake proceeds to describe the materials of text criticism: Greek MSS, early versions, patristic quotations, liturgical evidence, chapter divi-

---

40. *The Historical Evidence for the Resurrection of Jesus Christ*, CTL 21 (London: Williams & Norgate, 1907), 6, 27.
41. Ibid., 167, 275.
42. *Text of the New Testament*, 1.

sions, and stichometry. He reviews the history of modern text criticism and concludes with a chapter on research since Westcott and Hort. Among others, he notes the work of Harris on Codex Bezae and Lewis on the Sinaitic Syriac together with work on the old Latin, proving the importance of the Western text. Lake also reviews studies of families of MSS such as the Ferrar Group, and entertains the possibility of the Caesarean text.

Like Harris, Lake edited MSS, most notably *Codex Sinaiticus.*[43] His splendid facsimile edition, published in a large folio volume, was based on photographs that Lake and his first wife Helen had made in St. Petersburg in the summer of 1908.[44] In the introduction, Lake recounts the discovery of the MS by Tischendorf, and investigates its history.[45] Since the text includes the Eusebian canons (signs in the margins, dividing the text), the Codex cannot be earlier than Eusebius. Lake interprets the paleographical evidence to suggest that Sinaiticus and Codex Vaticanus (B) were produced by the same scriptorium. Lake concludes, "all the arguments from history, criticism, palaeography, and orthography combine to give to the view that the codex is an Egyptian MS. of the fourth century a probability which cannot be approached by any other theory."[46] Lake believes the original copying of the NT part of the MSS was by a single scribe, though the MS was corrected by several hands. The balance of the book presents the photographic plates of the MS.[47]

Concerned with the genealogical relation of MSS, Lake investigated families of MSS. In 1902, he published a monograph titled *Codex 1 of the Gospels and Its Allies.*[48] This group of MSS he calls "Family 1." It includes Codices 1, 118, 131, and 209. To collate these MSS, Lake traveled to libraries in Basel, Rome, and Venice. He concludes that they all depend on a common ancestor, and represent a type of text close to the Old Syriac and similar to the text of Family 13 (the Ferrar Group). The balance of the book prints the text of Codex 1 with critical apparatus. Some years later, Lake, together with Robert P. Blake, published an essay on the Koridethi Codex (Θ).[49] The authors note that scholars since Westcott and Hort have given attention to texts that are intermediate between the Western text and the Alexandrian text. Lake and Blake believe Koridethi (a ninth-century uncial MS) to be a

---

43. *Codex Sinaiticus Petropolitanus: The New Testament, the Epistle of Barnabas and the Shepherd of Hermas* (Oxford: Clarendon Press, 1911).

44. The MS was moved to the British Museum in 1933, and now resides in the British Library in London.

45. *HNTR* 1:323–25.

46. *Codex Sinaiticus,* xv.

47. Lake also edited and published *The Apostolic Fathers with an English Translation by Kirsopp Lake,* 2 vols., LCL (Cambridge: Harvard University Press, 1913). He also translated and edited the Loeb edition of Eusebius's *Ecclesiastical History.*

48. TS 7/3 (Cambridge: University Press, 1902).

49. Kirsopp Lake and Robert P. Blake, "The Text of the Gospels and the Koridethi Codex," *HTR* 16 (1923): 267–86.

hybrid of this type. Studying the variants, they conclude that this MS is closer to B than D, and that it is related to Family 1 and Family 13. This line of investigation is continued in a monograph by Lake, Blake, and Silva New on the Caesarean text.[50] The authors recount research suggesting the existence of such a text-type, including Lake's work on Family 1, Family 13, and Θ, and Streeter's theory that Origen began to use a text of this type when he moved from Alexandria to Caesarea.[51] After studying the common variants of these texts, the authors conclude: "That a common text is shared by these authorities is clear, but any attempt to divide the family into smaller groups of manuscripts results in remarkable and instructive failure."[52] In studying the patristic evidence for this text, they discover that Origen actually used the so-called Caesarean text while he was still in Alexandria, and continued to use an Alexandrian text after his arrival in Caesarea; but in his later writings, he used the "Caesarean" text. After detecting Caesarean readings in the Georgian, Armenian, and Syriac versions, the authors conclude that three types of text were used at the end of the third century: Western, Caesarean, and Neutral (or Alexandrian).

Lake's work in higher criticism is illustrated by his book *The Earlier Epistles of St. Paul: Their Motive and Origin*.[53] However, more important is his work in editing, along with F. J. Foakes Jackson, the five-volume *Beginnings of Christianity*—an exhaustive study of the Acts of the Apostles.[54] The first volume, *Prolegomena I*, appeared in 1920 and contained 480 pages. The preface indicates that the purpose of the volumes is to investigate the historical development of early Christianity as a synthesis of Greco-Oriental and Jewish religions in the Roman Empire. The chapters in this volume are the joint work of Foakes Jackson and Lake. They include chapters on the Jewish world and primitive Christianity, for example, "The Public Teaching of Jesus and His Choice of the Twelve," and "The Disciples in Jerusalem and

---

50. Kirsopp Lake, Robert P. Blake, and Silva New, "The Caesarean Text of the Gospels of Mark," *HTR* 21 (1928): 208–404.

51. See pp. 338, 265. above.

52. "Caesarean Text," 256. Actually, recent scholarship has divided the so-called Caesarean text into a pre-Caesarean and a recensional Caesarean text; see Bruce M. Metzger, *Chapters in the History of New Testament Text Criticism*, NTTS 4 (Grand Rapids, Mich.: Eerdmans, 1963), 42–72.

53. (London: Rivingtons, 1911). Here Lake approves Harnack's theory that 1 Thessalonians was written to Gentile Christians, and 2 Thessalonians to the Jewish converts at Thessalonica. Lake believes the Corinthian correspondence originally consisted of four letters. He thinks a short version of Romans was composed prior to the Jerusalem Council (Acts 15) and sent to churches in the neighborhood of Antioch. Lake also writes, "Christianity has not borrowed from the Mystery Religions, because it was always, at least in Europe, a Mystery Religion itself" (p. 215). See also the notice of Lake's *An Introduction to the New Testament* (London: Christophers, 1938) written in collaboration with his second wife, Silva, see p. 338, above.

54. F. J. Foakes Jackson and Kirsopp Lake, eds., *The Beginnings of Christianity, Part I: The Acts of the Apostles*, 5 vols. (London: Macmillan, 1920–33); vols. 4 and 5 were reprinted by Baker in 1966.

the Rise of Gentile Christianity." Volume 2 *(Prolegomena II)* offers a critical introduction to Acts. No chapter in this 539-page volume is explicitly attributed to Lake, but some of the chapters were jointly written by the editors; for example, in a section on the composition and purpose of Acts, a chapter titled "The Greek and Jewish Traditions of Writing History" was authored by H. J. Cadbury and the editors. Volume 3 is devoted to a study of the text of Acts; it was written by J. H. Ropes.

Volume 4, composed by Lake and Cadbury, presents the English translation and commentary on Acts. The two scholars had different interests: Cadbury's were linguistic and literary, Lake's were historical and doctrinal. The result is a combined effort, with Lake acting as the final editor. "The first object of a commentary," according to these scholars, "is to explain as accurately as possible what the writer meant to say, neither exaggerating nor extenuating his ambiguities, so that in some ways the best commentary is a literal translation."[55] The comments deal with the exegetical details: textual, historical, linguistic, and grammatical; the commentary is punctuated by extensive references to ancient and modern sources. Volume 5 presents additional notes to the commentary. Seventeen of these notes were written by Lake, including "The Ascension," "The Death of Judas," "Proselytes and God-Fearers," "The Apostolic Council of Jerusalem," "Paul's Route in Asia Minor," "The Unknown God," "The Chronology of Acts."

In sum, the *Beginnings of Christianity* is a monumental work—the most extensive investigation of a NT book by English-speaking scholarship. It epitomizes the scholarship of Kirsopp Lake—a historian equipped with text-critical and linguistic skills. He made a lasting contribution to our knowledge of early Christianity and our understanding of the text of the NT. To be sure, text critics since Lake have found the theory of the Caesarean text as a distinct text-type to be questionable.[56] Nevertheless, Lake's work in pursuit of the Caesarean, especially in the Gospels, has added to our knowledge of the history of the NT text.

The text-critical work of Sir Frederic G. Kenyon should be mentioned. Kenyon, director of the British Museum from 1909 to 1930, and father of the distinguished Palestinian archeologist Kathleen Kenyon, wrote important works in paleography and text criticism of nonbiblical Greek papyri. In regard to the NT, he published *Handbook to the Textual Criticism of the New Testament*—an excellent summary of the history, materials, and methods of textual criticism.[57] Of special interest is Kenyon's lectures on *Recent*

---

55. Ibid., 4:viii.
56. See K. Aland and B. Aland, *Text of the New Testament*, 66; Eldon Jay Epp and Gordon D. Fee, *Studies in the Theory and Method of Textual Criticism* (Grand Rapids, Mich.: Eerdmans, 1993), 8, 89–92; Metzger, *Chapters in the History of NT Text Criticism*, 42–72.
57. 2d ed. (London: Macmillan, 1912). A short, updated version appeared in 1937 under the title, *The Text of the Greek Bible: A Students Handbook*, 2d ed. (London: Duckworth, 1949).

THE REFINING OF HISTORICAL CRITICISM 411

Developments in the Textual Criticism of the Greek Bible—a well-informed, readable history of NT text criticism.[58] In his later *Our Bible and the Ancient Manuscripts,* Kenyon concludes that five ancient text-types can be identified: Byzantine, Alexandrian, Caesarean, Western, and Syriac.[59]

In regard to biblical texts, Kenyon edited and published important NT MSS. His edition of one of the treasures of the British Library, *Codex Alexandrinus,* includes a short introduction that presents the history and description of the MS.[60] The balance of the edition contains a photographic facsimile, in reduced size, of the text. Among the most important events in the study of the NT text was the discovery of the Chester Beatty Papyri. Kenyon published introductions, critical texts, and photographic facsimiles of the MSS in a series of fascicles, beginning in 1933 with a *General Introduction.*[61] In this Introduction, Kenyon recounts the acquisition of the MSS by Sir A. Chester Beatty—a wealthy engineer turned collector—from a dealer around 1930. The collection includes three MSS of the NT: 30 leaves of the Gospels and Acts (P^{45}), 10 leaves of the Pauline Epistles (P^{46}), and 10 leaves of Revelation (P^{47}). The leaves consist of papyri that had been bound in a codex, and can be dated early in the third century, thus, one hundred years earlier than the great Codices B and ℵ. These papyri represent a mixed text-type like the "Caesarean," between the Alexandrian and the Western. Subsequent fascicles included the critical texts and photographic facsimiles.[62] In 1936 and 1937, Kenyon published two supplementary fascicles containing the text and facsimile of the Pauline Letters.[63] As well as the 10 leaves of the original collection, these fascicles include 30 leaves of the same codex that had been acquired by the University of Michigan and additional leaves that Chester Beatty in the meantime had obtained. The result is a MS of 86 leaves (of an original 104) that include all of the Pauline Letters (plus Hebrews) except 2 Thessalonians, Philemon, and the Pastoral Epistles. Thus, the Chester Beatty papyrus of the Epistles of Paul (P^{46}) is the earliest extant MS of the NT in substantial size.

---

58. Schweich Lectures 1932 (London: British Academy, 1933).
59. 4th ed. (New York: Harper Brothers, 1938).
60. *The Codex Alexandrinus: New Testament and Clementine Epistles* (London: British Museum, 1909).
61. *The Chester Beatty Biblical Papyri: Descriptions and Texts of Twelve Manuscripts on Papyrus of the Greek Bible, Fasciculus I General Introduction* (London: Emery Walker, 1933).
62. *Fasciculus II Gospels and Acts: Text* (London: Emery Walker, 1933); idem, *Fasciculus II Gospels and Acts: Plates* (London: Emery Walker, 1934); idem, *Fasciculus III Pauline Epistles and Revelation: Text* (London: Emery Walker, 1934); idem, *Fasciculus III Revelation: Plates* (London: Emery Walker, 1936).
63. *The Chester Beatty Biblical Papyri: Descriptions and Texts of Twelve Manuscripts on Papyrus of the Greek Bible, Fasciculus III Supplement: Pauline Epistles: Text* (London: Emery Walker, 1936); idem, *Fasciculus III Supplement: Pauline Epistles: Plates* (London: Emery Walker Limited, 1937).

NEW TESTAMENT GRAMMAR AND LEXICOGRAPHY: ARCHIBALD THOMAS ROBERTSON AND WALTER BAUER

In 1913, the task of editing Friedrich Blass's widely used *Grammatik des neutestamentlichen Griechisch* (fourth edition) was assumed by Albert Debrunner (1884–1958), professor of Indo-European and classical philology at the University of Bern.[64] Debrunner rearranged Blass's Grammar, collecting principles into the main text and relegating details to the footnotes. He also extensively revised the sections on phonology, accidence, and word formation. In 1943, Debrunner made another extensive revision (seventh edition) wherein many of the notes were put into an appendix. A later edition in 1954 (ninth) disassembled the appendix and inserted much of the material back into the text. In 1961, Blass/Debrunner was published in English—a *Grammar* highly regarded on both sides of the Atlantic.[65]

Archibald Thomas Robertson (1863–1934)

A year after Debrunner's edition, and four hundred years after the appearance the Complutensian Polyglot, Archibald Thomas Robertson published his massive *A Grammar of the Greek New Testament in the Light of Historical Research*.[66] Robertson was born near Chatham, Virginia, but grew up on a farm in North Carolina.[67] In 1876, he was baptized, and began his lifelong loyalty to the Southern Baptist Church. After graduating from Wake Forest College, Robertson enrolled in the Southern Baptist Theological Seminary at Louisville, Kentucky, and received the Th.M. in 1888. In 1892, Robertson was appointed professor at Southern Baptist, and remained in that post until a day in 1934 when he dismissed his class early and went home and died of a stroke. According to a former student, "No one who ever sat in his class can forget the consecrated enthusiasm with which he unfolded the meanings of the Greek New Testament."[68] On matters of higher criticism, Robertson is conservative.[69] However, like many conservative critics, Robertson's view of lower criticism is in full accord with the most advanced research.[70]

---

64. See pp. 184–85, above.
65. Friedrich Blass and Albert Debrunner, *A Greek Grammar of the New Testament and Other Early Christian Literature*, trans. Robert W. Funk (Chicago: University of Chicago Press, 1961). The editing of the German editions was assumed by Friedrich Rehkopf in 1975 (14th ed.) (Göttingen: Vandenhoeck & Ruprecht).
66. (New York: George H. Doran, 1914).
67. See Everett Gill, *A. T. Robertson: A Biography* (New York: Macmillan, 1943); Edgar V. McKnight, "A. T. Robertson," in *BITC*, 93–104.
68. Quoted in Gill, *A. T. Robertson*, 114.
69. See his *Luke the Historian in the Light of Research* (Edinburgh: T. & T. Clark, 1920); idem, *A Harmony of the Gospels for Students of the Life of Christ: Based on the Broadus Harmony in the Revised Version* (New York: Harper & Brothers, 1922).
70. See his *An Introduction to the Textual Criticism of the New Testament* (Nashville: Broadman Press, 1925).

Prior to publishing his "Big Grammar," as his family and friends liked to call it, Robertson produced *A Short Grammar of the Greek New Testament*.[71] As the subtitle indicates, this handbook was written *For Students Familiar with the Elements of Greek*; it is an intermediate, systematic grammar. In the preface, Robertson expresses a fundamental principle: "At bottom exegesis is grammatical."[72] This *Short Grammar* went through repeated editions, and was translated into Italian, German, French, Spanish, and Dutch.

Robertson's *A Grammar of the Greek New Testament in the Light of Historical Research* is indeed a "big" grammar, totaling more than 1,200 pages, plus additional notes, and indices of subjects, Greek words, and quotations; the "List of Works Most Often Referred To" is more than twenty pages in length. As Robertson says, "No one who has not done similar work can understand the amount of research, the mass of detail and the reflection required in a book of this nature."[73] In the "Introduction" (Part I), Robertson presents a thoroughly informed and fully articulated account of his grammatical theory. He begins with a survey of the history of NT grammar in the nineteenth century. In discussing the modern period, he praises the work of Adolf Deissmann in obliterating the distinction between biblical and profane Greek, and he affirms J. H. Moulton's appropriation of the new linguistic discoveries for understanding NT grammar.[74] Robertson also hails the work of F. Bopp, K. Brugmann, and B. Delbrück in comparative philology. "The N.T. Greek is now seen to be not an abnormal excrescence, but a natural development in the Greek language."[75] Within the history of the language, Robertson believes NT Greek belongs to the age of the Koine—the common, vernacular Greek of the Hellenistic period. As the recent finds of papyri and inscriptions show, words once considered features of a distinctive biblical Greek are actually words of the Koine.

Robertson turns to "Accidence" (Part II), that is, analysis of the forms of words. A chapter on "Word Formation" treats such matters as etymology, roots, compound words, and personal names. A chapter on "Orthography and Phonetics" deals with the spelling of Greek words and the sound of Greek letters. In a chapter on "The Declensions," Robertson notes the tendency of the language to reduce the number of case endings and to replace the functions of the declensions by the use of prepositions. Nevertheless, he insists, "It is clear therefore that in Greek the usual seven (eight with the vocative) Indo-Germanic cases are present, though in a badly mutilated condition as to form."[76]

---

71. (New York: George H. Doran, 1908).
72. Ibid., vii.
73. *Grammar of Greek NT*, vii.
74. See pp. 179–80, 188–89, above.
75. *Grammar of Greek NT*, 30.
76. Ibid., 249.

The bulk of Robertson's *Grammar* (pages 379–1208) is dedicated to "Syntax," that is, the arrangement of words in order to express meaning. The method that Robertson adopts is historical: analysis of syntax according to the evolution of the language. In discussing the eight cases (nominative, vocative, accusative, genitive, ablative, locative, instrumental, dative), Robertson acknowledges the "blending of the forms while insisting on the integrity of the case-ideas." Other chapters deal in detail with adverbs, prepositions, adjectives, and the pronoun. A chapter on the article (more than forty pages), illustrates Robertson's concern with detail. He observes that the function of the article is to make words definite, and that when a word is indefinite, the article is not used. However, a word without the article may be definite. "The anarthrous noun may *per se* be either definite or indefinite."[77] In regard to the verb, Robertson believes use of the tenses in Greek is widely misunderstood. Tense, according to Robertson, must not be seen primarily as referring to time, but as expressing the kind of action (*Aktionsart*). Greek verbs express three types of action: punctiliar, durative (or linear), and completed (or perfected). Punctiliar action is expressed by the aorist; durative by the present, imperfect, and future; perfected by the present perfect, past perfect, future perfect, and the infinitive. At length, Robertson discusses mode, verbal nouns (the infinitive and the participle), particles, and figures of speech.

Robertson's *Grammar* is a monumental accomplishment. Although verbose, repetitious, and burdened with quotations from secondary sources, the *Grammar* displays great erudition and the mastery of an enormous amount of primary and secondary material. The inclusion of indices of Greek words and NT references makes the *Grammar* eminently useful as an exegetical tool. Within the presentation, the reader may sense a tension: on the one hand, Robertson insists on the simplicity of Koine Greek—the reduction of details and erosion of fine points; on the other, his concern with the rudimentary eight cases and his analysis, for example, of the aorist tense as constative, ingressive, and effective (pages 831–35) seems to betray a preoccupation with grammatical precision and detail. As Robertson admits in his discussion of the aorist, "One is in constant danger of over-refinement here."[78] E. J. Goodspeed, not accustomed to handing out bouquets to conservatives, wrote, "Prof. Robertson has placed all serious students of the N.T. in Greek under lasting obligations by assembling and organizing the results of modern philological study and archeological materials in a N.T. Grammar, which for its comprehensive scope and modern point of view may fairly be called unrivalled."[79]

77. Ibid., 448, 796.
78. Ibid., 835.
79. Quoted by Gill, *A. T. Robertson*, 199. A synthesis of Robertson's scholarship is seen in his six-volume commentary, *Word Pictures in the New Testament* (New York: Harper & Brothers, 1930–33). Written for the general reader, these volumes include comments on all the books of the NT and constitute a treasury of linguistic and grammatical information.

Walter Bauer (1877–1960)

Bauer made significant contributions in two areas of NT research: lexicography and the history of early Christianity. His revolutionary understanding of the latter will be reviewed later in this chapter. Walter Bauer was born in Königsberg, and studied at Marburg, Berlin, and Strasbourg.[80] In 1903, he became an instructor at Marburg, and in 1913, he was named associate professor at Breslau. He moved to Göttingen in 1916, where he was promoted to full professor in 1919. Bauer retired from teaching in 1945, but continued his research.

According to an American expert, "Bauer established himself as the outstanding scholar in the four-hundred-year history of New Testament lexicography."[81] Bauer became involved in lexicographical research when, at the death of Erwin Preuschen in 1920, the publishers invited him to prepare a revision of Preuschen's *Vollständiges Griechisch-Deutsches Handwörterbuch zu den Schriften des NTs und der übrigen urchristlichen Literatur.*[82] Bauer accepted the invitation with misgivings, since he had not been inclined toward lexicography. In any case, Preuschen's work was flawed by serious weakness: it did not relate early Christian writings to the historical development of Greek literature, and it did not make adequate use of the recently discovered papyri and inscriptions. On the other hand, Preuschen's work had obvious strengths: it was apparently the first lexicon to give definitions in German (instead of Latin), and it included other early Christian literature as well as the documents of the NT canon. Bauer corrected the weakness and enhanced the strengths. Looking back on his work, Bauer said:

> The farther I go in lexicographical work, the greater is my amazement at the boldness with which I entered upon this undertaking almost thirty years ago. However, I have also increasingly recognized my obligation to stand on my own feet, and to add the results of my own research to that which the previous form of the book owed to the diligence of others.[83]

Although the first part of Bauer's lexicon was ready for the press in 1924, the completed work did not appear until 1928, published as the second edition, with the title: *Griechisch-Deutsches Wörterbuch zu den Schriften des NTs und der übrigen urchristlichen Literatur, von Walter Bauer.* Thus, the work was no longer identified as a "handbook" (it had been increased in size), and

---

80. On the life of Bauer, see F. W. Gingrich, "Walter Bauer 1877–1960," *NTS* 9 (1962–63): 1–2; Georg Strecker, "Walter Bauer—Exegete, Philologe und Historiker," *NovT* 20 (1978): 75–80.
81. Gingrich, "Walter Bauer," 2. For a review of Bauer's lexicographical research, see F. Wilbur Gingrich, "The Contributions of Professor Walter Bauer to New Testament Lexicography," *NTS* 9 (1962–63): 3–10.
82. Giessen: Alfred Töpelmann, 1910.
83. *Griechisch-Deutsches Wörterbuch zu den Schriften des Neuen Testaments und der übrigen urchristlichen Literatur,* 4th ed. (Berlin: Alfred Töpelmann, 1952), vii.

the lexicon, appropriately, was acknowledged to be the work of Bauer. A third, fully revised edition, appeared in 1937, and a fourth in 1952. In this monumental work, NT Greek is viewed in the context of the history of Greek literature. The lists of abbreviations include 78 publications of papyri and inscriptions, 223 nonbiblical authors of antiquity, and 174 modern authors. The fourth edition contains 1,634 columns (two to a page), and the fifth edition of 1957–58 includes 1,789 columns—much of the work on the latter editions accomplished while Bauer was suffering from poor eyesight.

In 1957, an English edition, based on Bauer's fourth edition, was published as *A Greek-English Lexicon of the New Testament and Other Early Christian Literature*, translated and augmented by William F. Arndt and F. Wilbur Gingrich.[84] A second English edition, revised and augmented by F. Wilbur Gingrich and Frederick W. Danker, based on Bauer's fifth edition of 1958, appeared in 1979 with Bauer's name appropriately printed on the spine.[85] This second English edition includes an essay by Bauer titled "An Introduction to the Lexicon of the Greek New Testament," originally published in 1955.[86] In this essay, Bauer affirms the same understanding of NT Greek as Robertson: the Greek of the NT is the Koine—the common language of communication in the Hellenistic age. Although Bauer acknowledges that the NT Greek has been influenced by the language of the LXX, this does not suggest the existence of a special "biblical" Greek. Words like μαρτυρία and πειράζω, once thought to be peculiar, are found in nonbiblical sources. Bauer notes some of the interesting details of his fourth edition. "There is no longer any doubt in my mind that ἀδελφοί can mean 'brothers and sisters' in any number."[87] In the lexicon itself, he writes, "The plural can also mean siblings of a different sex."[88] Bauer also notes that Memnon of Asia Minor, a younger contemporary of Paul, would not have addressed the Lycaonians (of south Galatia) as Γαλάται (Gal. 3:1).

Bauer's greatness as a lexicographer is seen in two features of his work: his discovery of a large number of new and original parallels, and his careful analysis of difficult words, for example, prepositions. "As a result of Professor Bauer's work," writes F. W. Gingrich, "the lexical treatment of the

---

84. *A Translation and Adaptation of Walter Bauer's Griechisch-Deutsches Wörterbuch zu den Schriften des Neuen Testaments und der übrigen Literatur, Fourth Revised and Augmented Edition*, by William F. Arndt and F. Wilbur Gingrich (Chicago: University of Chicago Press, 1957).

85. (Chicago: University of Chicago Press, 1979). A third English edition by F. W. Danker, based on the 6th German edition (1988) by Kurt and Barbara Aland, was published by the University of Chicago Press in 2000.

86. Originally published as "Zur Einführung in das Wörterbuch zum Neuen Testament," ConBNT 15 (1955).

87. *Greek-English Lexicon*, 2d ed., xxvii.

88. *Griechisch-Deutsches Wörterbuch*, 4th ed., column 28.

N.T. and early Christian literature is more adequate than that of any other section in the whole field of Greek literature."[89] And what is said of Bauer can be said of all the scholars discussed in this section: the text critics have provided us with a text of the NT that is vastly better attested than the text of any other ancient document; the grammarians and the lexicographers have equipped us with tools for exegesis that are unsurpassed in any other historical or literary discipline.

RESEARCH IN JEWISH BACKGROUNDS: HERMANN L. STRACK AND PAUL BILLERBECK, AND GEORGE FOOT MOORE

Strack and Billerbeck

These two scholars are remembered for their massive *Kommentar zum Neuen Testament aus Talmud und Midrasch*. Hermann L. Strack (1848–1922) was born in Berlin, and studied in Berlin and Leipzig.[90] After a period of work in the imperial library in St. Petersburg, he joined the faculty at Berlin (1877). In a lecture delivered to an international conference on the Jewish mission, Strack presents his idea of the essence of Judaism:

> The Jews are a community that is held together not only through blood relationship, but also, and in a higher level, through reminiscences of a significant past, namely, of great acts of God and great mutual suffering, and through hope in regard to the future. On the basis of these memories and hopes, the Jews possess an exalted self-consciousness that makes it difficult for them to feel and acknowledge the depth of human depravity and the necessity of an extraordinary act of God for the redemption of humanity.[91]

Although he believed Jews should be converted to Christianity, Strack opposed anti-Semitism. Against charges made in the popular press, Strack argued that the Jews were not guilty of religious crimes, and he supported his argument with citations from Jewish works that advocated love of neighbor and mercy toward all.[92]

---

89. "Contributions of Professor Walter Bauer," 10.
90. See Ralf Golling and Peter von der Osten-Sacken, eds., *Hermann L. Strack und das Institutum Judaicum in Berlin,* Studien zu Kirche und Israel 17 (Berlin: Institut Kirche und Judentum, 1996).
91. *Das Wesen des Judentums: Vortrag gehalten auf der Internationalen Konferenz für Judenmission zu Amsterdam,* Schriften des Institutum Judaicum 36 (Leipzig: J. C. Hinrichs, 1906), 23.
92. Hermann L. Strack, *Sind die Juden Verbrecher von Religionswegen?* Schriften des Institutum Judaicum in Berlin 28 (Leipzig: J. C. Hinrichs, 1900). See also Strack's *The Jew and Human Sacrifice: Human Blood and Jewish Ritual: An Historical and Sociological Inquiry,* trans. from 8th ed. Henry Blanchamp (London: Cope and Fenwick, 1909). Strack also published a book that presents a collection of texts from patristic sources and the Talmud in regard to Jesus: *Jesus, die Häretiker und die Christen nach den ältesten Jüdischen Angaben: Texte, Übersetzung und Erläuterungen,* Schriften des Institutum Judaicum in Berlin 37 (Leipzig: J. C. Hinrichs, 1910).

Strack published an Aramaic grammar. He had planned this work as early as 1879, but when he learned of E. F. Kautzsch's projected *Grammatik des Biblisch-Aramäisch* he abandoned the project. However, when Kautzsch's work finally appeared in 1884, Strack noted that it was designed for scholars. This led him to publish a manual grammar for students who had a knowledge of Hebrew.[93] In the short space of twenty-eight pages, Strack summarizes the principles of Aramaic grammar; to this he adds a collection of the Aramaic texts from Ezra and Daniel, and concludes with an Aramaic-German lexicon.

Strack's command of the rabbinic literature is attested in his *Introduction to the Talmud*.[94] Originally published in 1887, the book was extensively revised in the fourth edition (1908) and expanded in the fifth (1920). The English translation, based on the fifth edition, was issued by the Jewish Publication Society, which recognized Strack as the leading Protestant authority of his time on rabbinic literature. Strack begins by explaining the meaning of basic terms such as "Mishnah" (the collection of traditional law until the end of the second century C.E.) and "Tannaim" (the teachers of the period of the Mishnah). He sketches the history of traditional teaching, oral and written—both believed to go back to Moses. Strack gives attention to the arrangement of the Mishnah: its six main divisions, each divided into tractates—a total of sixty-three tractates. He presents the history of the two Talmuds, Palestinian and Babylonian. He notes the difference of opinion about the Talmud. "Among the orthodox Jews the 'holy Talmud' is spoken of in terms of highest reverence; in the mind of many Christians it stands for a medley of absurd and coarse statements, as well as of hostile utterances against Christianity." The proper view, according to Strack, is to see the various teachings in their different contexts, and to recognize that they do not constitute a unified, homogeneous statement. "Accordingly it is highly preposterous to cause all the utterances of a single rabbi found in

---

93. The grammar first appeared as *Abriss des biblischen Aramäisch* (Leipzig: J. C. Hinrichs, 1896); in the second and later editions, it was titled *Grammatik des Biblisch-Aramäischen mit den nach Handschriften berichtigten Texten und einem Wörterbuch*, 4th ed. (Leipzig: J. C. Hinrichs, 1905).

94. *Einleitung in Talmud und Midras*, 5th ed. (Munich: C. H. Beck, 1930); Eng. trans.: *Introduction to the Talmud and Midrash*, (Philadelphia: Jewish Publication Society, 1931; repr., New York: Meridian Books, 1959). A completely rewritten edition has been published: H. L. Strack and G. Stemberger, *Einleitung in Talmud und Midrasch* (Munich: C. H. Beck, 1982); Eng. trans.: *Introduction to the Talmud and Midrash*, trans. Markus Bockmuehl (Edinburgh: T. & T. Clark, 1991).

the Talmud to stand without further ado as 'teaching of the Talmud' or to hold Judaism responsible for such utterances." An informative chapter on the hermeneutics of the Talmud deals with rabbinic methods of interpretation. Strack also presents a brief description of the life and work of the most important rabbinic teachers.[95]

As to the famous *Kommentar*, the respective roles of the two scholars, Strack and Billerbeck, is not entirely clear. The foreword to the first volume of the *Kommentar* (1922), jointly written by Strack and Billerbeck, says that Strack had worked for ten years on the material prior to enlisting the collaboration of Billerbeck in 1906. The foreword to the second volume, written by Billerbeck in 1923, notes that Strack had died the previous year, but had left a full manuscript. In the foreword to volume 4 (1928), Billerbeck expresses continuing appreciation for Strack. "As editor Professor Strack rendered the greatest service for the appearance and dissemination of the work."[96] On the other hand, Joachim Jeremias, to whom Billerbeck on his deathbed entrusted his work, attributes the major accomplishment of the commentary to Billerbeck. According to Jeremias, Billerbeck, as a pastor preparing sermons, had discovered that the standard commentaries on the NT did not provide adequate material from the Jewish backgrounds. He began studying rabbinic literature, and published articles that caught the eye of Strack. According to Jeremias, Strack tried to persuade Billerbeck to write a systematic presentation of Talmudic theology, but Billerbeck agreed instead to collect and translate Jewish parallels to the NT—and so began the collaboration on the Commentary. Jeremias concludes, "So as uncontested are the services that Hermann L. Strack rendered through the encouragement and planning, as also through the provision of literature and the securing of financial support . . . and finally through the oversight of the manuscript of the first volume—in the writing of the work he was not at all involved."[97] Probably the lack of clarity results from the modesty of Billerbeck, a parish pastor, and the prestige of Strack, a professor in Berlin.

Paul Billerbeck (1853–1932) was born in Prussia and educated in Greifswald and Leipzig. Ordained in 1879, he spent his entire career serving pastorates in an area now part of Poland. Like the Pharisees who tithed mint and dill, he spent his life sifting through the rabbinic literature, finding the smallest seeds, but missing the plant that had grown into a tree.

At the outset, Strack and Billerbeck present their purpose in writing the commentary:

---

95. *Introduction to the Talmud* (Meridian, 1959), 87, 89.
96. Hermann L. Strack and Paul Billerbeck, *Kommentar zum Neuen Testament aus Talmud und Midrasch*, 4 vols. (Munich: C. H. Beck, 1922–28), 4:v.
97. Joachim Jeremias, "Billerbeck, Paul (1853–1932)," *TRE* 4:641.

We did not intend to present an actual interpretation of the New Testament, but that which is understood on the basis of material from the Talmud and Midrash; we intended to present objectively the beliefs, the ideas, and the life of the Jews in the time of Jesus and earliest Christianity. . . . We protest emphatically against the idea that a conclusion should be drawn about actual or alleged views prevailing in contemporary Judaism on the basis of the material collected here.[98]

The result is a monumental accomplishment: a total of four volumes (bound as five) including volume 1 on Matthew (1,055 pages), volume 2 on Mark, Luke, John, and Acts (853 pages), volume 3 on the Epistles and Revelation (857 pages), and volume 4 (with two parts, bound separately) presenting excursuses on particular texts. The work includes comments, but is primarily a collection of parallels to the NT texts, translated into German. Most of the parallels are from the rabbinic sources, but other sources, including Josephus, the Apocrypha, and the Pseudepigrapha, are also included.

A few examples can illustrate the character of the *Kommentar*. On Matt. 5:43 ("You have heard that it was said, 'You shall love your neighbor and hate your enemy'"), Strack and Billerbeck say, "The first part of the saying stems from Lev. 19:18; the second part cannot be attested in the sources. The whole is a popular maxim by which the average Israelite in Jesus' day ordered his behavior toward friend and enemy." In commenting on the first part of the verse, Strack and Billerbeck note that Deut. 10:19 instructs Israelites to love the stranger, that is, the foreigner who lives among them. This, they say, implies that the "neighbor" refers exclusively to Israelites, and does not imply a love for humanity. In regard to the second part of the verse, they continue, "Hate is in general seen by the synagogue as something reprehensible; but in some circumstances it is allowed or even commanded." A section in smaller print, supporting the idea that hate is commanded, quotes a rabbi who counsels hate toward an evildoer: "It is a duty to hate such a person, since it is said, 'The Fear of Yahweh is hatred of the evil one.'"[99]

In regard to Matt. 23:15 ("you cross land and sea to make a single convert"), Strack and Billerbeck acknowledge that Jewish missionary activity after 70 C.E. was rare, but claim that it was extensive in the time of Jesus:

> The saying of Jesus in 23:15 is the clearest witnesses to the zeal of the Judaism of his time in the making of proselytes. That we do not find similar definite evidence in the rabbinic sources is not surprising: this literature offers historical material from the time of Jesus only sparsely.

---

98. *Kommentar zum NT aus Talmud*, 1:vi.
99. Ibid. 1:353, 364, 366.

On Mark 14:36 ("Abba, Father"), Billerbeck says that the Greek phrase ἀββα ὁ πατήρ is a translation from Aramaic meaning "my father." He finds very little evidence in the rabbinic sources for individuals referring to God in this way, though references to "our father" are more frequent. "The individual feared, with the address 'my father,' to become overly familiar, and thereby to violate respect for God."[100]

The reference to the necessity for the Messiah to suffer (Luke 24:26) provides the occasion for an excursus on "The Suffering and Dying of the Messiah in the Ancient Synagogue." In regard to the Son of David messiah, Billerbeck notes that the time of the Messiah will be a time of suffering, but that the Messiah himself will not suffer; he will triumph. In the second century C.E., the idea of the Son of Joseph emerged—a messiah who would die in battle prior to the coming of the Son of David. Another lengthy excursus deals with the *Memra Yahweh*. Billerbeck contends that the term *memra* (word) is used primarily as a substitute for the name of God, and that it does not represent a hypostasis between God and the world. "The result of the foregoing exposition in regard to the Johannine Logos is that the expression 'Memra of the Lord' is a purely formal substitute for the Tetragrammaton, and thus it is not suitable to serve as the point of departure for the Logos of John."[101]

Among the excursuses of volume 4, the one on "the Passover meal" is typical. Billerbeck presents an account of how the meal was observed by Jews in the time of Jesus, including such matters as the preparation for the meal, and the securing, preparing, and roasting of the lamb. The actual celebration of the meal is presented in detail in the Mishnah, for example, the drinking of four cups. Billerbeck assumes that the Lord's Supper was a Passover meal; he harmonizes the NT texts, and interprets them in the light of Jewish practice. The cup of the new covenant, for example, he takes to be the third cup of the Passover celebration.[102]

In sum, the Strack-Billerbeck commentary offers an enormous collection of rabbinic material, made available to the German reader. Jeremias writes:

> A field of research basically important for the understanding of the Gospels, which was previously a terra incognita, accessible only to a few specialists, the Jewish environment of Jesus and the early church has been opened for

---

100. Ibid. 1:926; 2:50.
101. Ibid. 2:333.
102. Aids to the use of the commentary have been published as separate volumes: *Rabbinischer Index*, ed. Joachim Jeremias, assisted by Kurt Adolph (Munich: D. H. Beck, 1956); this is an index of the material according to references to the Talmud, Pseudepigrapha, Targums, Midrashim, Other Haggadic Works, Medieval works, Prayers, Authors; and *Verzeichnis der Schriftgelehrten, Geographisches Register*, ed. Joachim Jeremias, assisted by Kurt Adolph (Munich: C. H. Beck, 1961); this is an index of the rabbinic teachers who are cited, and the geographical places mentioned in the Commentary.

general use to the theological world since 1922. Through it a new basis for New Testament exegesis, especially of the Gospels, was created.[103]

Similarly, George Foot Moore, always alert to Christian distortions of Judaism, praises Strack-Billerbeck as "An immense collection of parallels and illustrations from all parts of the rabbinical literature, in trustworthy translation, with the necessary introductions and explanations."[104] Post-Holocaust scholarship, however, has been critical.[105] The critics charge that material is taken out of context, that parallels are heaped up in excess without appreciation of the authentic spirit of Judaism. They argue, too, that rabbinic material from a later date is used to illuminate NT texts, even though the *Kommentar* notes the sources and dates of the parallels cited. Many will agree with James Dunn, who acknowledges the validity of the criticisms, but concludes, "they do not destroy the value of Strack-Billerbeck."[106] Of course, for the understanding of Judaism, the weakness of the commentary is built into the design: rabbinic material is presented in parallel to NT texts; the Christian sources are the lens through which Jewish teaching is viewed. This procedure might be analogous to the notion that knowledge of Shakespeare can be derived from parallels found in *Poor Richard's Almanack*.

George Foot Moore (1851–1931)

In contrast to Billerbeck, George Foot Moore tried to understand Judaism in its own right. Moore, whose remains rest in the ancient burial ground at Andover, not far from those of Moses Stuart, was born in Westchester, Pennsylvania.[107] He was educated at Yale and Union Theological Seminary, New York. Ordained to the Congregational ministry in 1878, Moore served for a time as pastor in Ohio. In 1883, he was appointed professor of OT at Andover Theological Seminary. He moved to Harvard in 1902, where he remained until his retirement in 1928. Moore served as editor of scholarly journals, including the *Harvard Theological Review* and the *Journal of Biblical Literature*. During his Andover years, he concentrated on the study of the HB, and his commentary on Judges (1895) remained the representative volume of the *International Critical Commentary* series through the twentieth

---

103. "Billerbeck," 642.
104. *Judaism in the First Centuries of the Christian Era: The Age of the Tannaim*, 2 vols. (Cambridge: Harvard University Press, 1927) 1:215–16.
105. See Samuel Sandmel, "Parallelomania," *JBL* 81 (1962): 8–11; E. P. Sanders, *Paul and Palestinian Judaism: A Comparison of Patterns of Religion* (Philadelphia: Fortress, 1977), 42–44, and references throughout the book.
106. James D. G. Dunn, "They Set Us in New Paths VI. New Testament: The Great Untranslated," *ExpTim* 100 (1989): 204.
107. On Moses Stuart, see pp. 21–27, above. On Moore, see Morton Smith, "The Work of George Foot Moore," *Harvard Library Bulletin*, 15 (1967): 169–79.

century. At Harvard, Moore's main field was the history of religions. He devoted the last twelve years of his life to the study of Judaism.

Moore published important works on the history of religions. In *The Birth and Growth of Religion*, he offers a psychological-sociological account of the evolution of religion.[108] Moore believes polytheistic religions evolved into henotheistic, and eventually into monotheistic religions. The highest religions, he believes, combine a religion of salvation with philosophical reflection; they are both moral and intellectual. Moore's *History of Religions*, originally published in 1913, presents a compact survey of the religions of the world. Volume 1 reviews the religions of China, Japan, Egypt, Babylonia, Syria, and India; attention is also given to Zoroastrianism and the religion of the ancient Greeks and Romans. Volume 2 is devoted to Judaism, Christianity, and, as Moore calls it, "Mohammedanism." About this volume Moore says, "The three religions with which it deals are so intimately related to one another that in a morphological classification they might be regarded as three branches of monotheistic religion in Western Asia and Europe." As to method, Moore declares:

> The historian of religion has to do more than exhibit the facts impartially and in just proportion, trace the origin and development of ideas and institutions, and define the forces internal and external, which were operative in this development. He must endeavour to understand and appreciate ways of thinking and feeling remote from his own, and help his readers to a like apprehension. To do this, he must put himself, as far as imagination can go, into the position and attitude of those who formed and entertained these ideas; he must learn to think other men's thoughts after them, as they thought them, and to enter with sympathetic intelligence into their feelings.

Moore's survey of Judaism includes chapters on the religion of ancient Israel, the age of the prophets, the school and the synagogue (the period investigated in his major work on *Judaism*), and a final chapter on medieval and modern Judaism. In regard to Christianity, Moore understands Jesus primarily as a teacher of morality. Paul, according to Moore, presents a unique religion that was largely misunderstood. "The main current of Christian thought did not, as is often imagined, take its rise in Paul, it did not even pass through him; rather it flowed by him as around a rock in the bed of a stream."[109]

Moore's famous essay "Christian Writers on Judaism" has been noted earlier.[110] The essay contends that Christian treatment of Judaism from the

---

108. Morse Lectures of 1922 at Union Theological Seminary, New York (New York: Charles Scribner's Sons, 1924).
109. *History of Religions*, 2 vols., rev. ed., ITL (New York: Charles Scribner's Sons, 1949) 2:vii, x, 136.
110. *HTR* 14 (1921): 197–254. See pp. 203–4, 246–47, above.

time of Justin Martyr to the present has been improperly apologetic and polemical. The first section deals with Christian scholarship prior to the end of the eighteenth century. The second reviews scholarship from the nineteenth century to the present. In this period, the work of August Friedrich Gfroerer, a student of F. C. Baur, is praised. "It was the first time that the attempt had been made to portray Judaism as it was, from its own literature, without apologetic, polemic, or dogmatic prepossessions or intentions." In sharp contrast is Ferdinand Weber's *System der altsynagogalen palästinischen Theologie* (1880)—a work that presents a distorted Judaism as a backdrop for Christianity. Moore acknowledges that Emil Schürer's *History of the Jewish People in the Time of Jesus* includes much useful material, but contends that the chapter on the law (which largely follows Weber) is Christian apologetic, not history. In regard to W. Bousset's *Die Religion des Judentums im neutestamentlichen Zeitalter*, Moore scores the author's meager knowledge of rabbinics, and concludes, "it was not Judaism as a religion, but Judaism as a background, environment, source, and foil that he had in mind." In general, Moore finds Christian scholarship guilty at two main points: the charge that Judaism perceives God as remote, and the caricature of Jewish legalism. Moore believes that what is needed is "the critical ordering and evaluation of Jewish sources."[111]

Moore attains his intention in his masterpiece *Judaism in the First Centuries of the Christian Era: The Age of the Tannaim*.[112] The purpose of the work is to study the religion of Judaism in the time from Herod to circa 200 C.E. The first part of the introduction presents a historical survey and statement of the significance of this history. "In the light of subsequent history the great achievement of these centuries was the creation of a normative type of Judaism and its establishment in undisputed supremacy throughout the wide Jewish world." According to Moore, normative Judaism—that is, the standard Jewish religion that he depicts in these volumes—was established by the end of the second century C.E. In the survey of this history, beginning with Ezra and Nehemiah, Moore attends to the rise of the Pharisees—the forerunners of normative Judaism. The scribes, who were associated with the Pharisaic party, "mediated to the people the knowledge of the law, impressed upon them by precept its authority, and set them the example of punctilious observance of its minutiae." Moore traces the move of the Pharisaic leadership out of Jerusalem, and the founding of a school at Jamnia (70 C.E.) and later (135 C.E.) at Sepphoris and Tiberias. Around 200 C.E., an authoritative edition of the Mishnah was produced by Patriarch Judah

---

111. Ibid., 225, 245, 253.
112. 3 vols. (Cambridge: Harvard University Press, 1927, 1930).

(called "Judah, the Prince," or simply, "the Rabbi"). The normative Judaism that developed in the schools of Palestine and Babylonia triumphed, and, according to Moore, Hellenized Judaism disappeared. The result, in Moore's opinion, was a revealed religion—a religion in which the will of God is revealed in the law. In this kind of religion, disobedience to the law requires repentance, but ultimately salvation is a gift of God. Moore observes, "the legal conception of sin leads directly to the recognition that the only remedy for sin is God's forgiving grace, having its ground in his mercy, or his love, and its indispensable condition in repentance, a moral renovation of man which is compared to a new creation, with its fruit in works meet for repentance."[113]

The second part of Moore's introduction considers the sources. He contends that the apocalypses should not be accepted as primary sources for investigating normative Judaism, but he accepts the Gospels as sources, and believes the rabbinic sources to be relevant for the understanding of the Gospels:

> It is the relation between the Gospels and the teaching of the rabbis . . . which makes them the important source they are for a knowledge of the Judaism of their time, and on the other hand makes the rabbinical sources the important instrument they are for the understanding of the Gospels. The Gospels with the first part of the Acts of the Apostles are thus witnesses to authentic Jewish tradition, while the apocalypses (and the kindred elements in the Gospels) represent groups, or at least tendencies, outside the main current of thought and life.[114]

Moore observes that there are three main classes of rabbinic sources: the Mishnah, the Tannaite Midrash, and the homiletic commentaries or Midrashim. He also notes the importance of such sources as the Testaments of the Twelve Patriarchs and the Book of Jubilees, along with the historical writings, including 1 and 2 Maccabees and Josephus.

The bulk of Moore's two main volumes presents a systematic account of the major beliefs of "normative Judaism." The first part deals with the essential character of Judaism as a revealed religion. According to this religion, the will of God has been disclosed in the written and unwritten law. "As revelation, explicit or by clear implication, all this law has the same divine origin and authority; the infraction of even the seemingly most trivial prescription may be followed by incommensurable consequences, for it is not the trivial rule that is transgressed or neglected, but the unitary law of God which is broken." According to rabbis, the unwritten law was preserved

---

113. Ibid. 1:3, 67, 117.
114. Ibid. 1:132.

in a tradition that went back to Moses. Ultimately, the twofold law, written and unwritten, was viewed as eternal, existing before creation and revealed at Sinai. This divine revelation was taught in the synagogue and the rabbinic schools. The "endeavor to educate the whole people in its religion created a unique system of universal education, whose very elements comprised not only reading and writing, but an ancient language and its classic literature." According to Moore, "The conviction that Judaism as the one true religion was destined to become the universal religion was a singularity of the Jews. No other religion in their world and time made any such pretension or cherished such aspirations." This universalism, Moore believes, encouraged mission, so that Judaism became "the first great missionary religion of the Mediterranean world."[115]

The second main part takes up the idea of God. According to Moore, normative Judaism embraced a personal understanding of God, and viewed justice and mercy as the main features of the divine character. Moore vigorously refutes the notion that the Jews believed God to be remote and unreachable. He points out that concepts like *shekina* (glory) and *memra* (word) do not represent intermediaries but circumlocutions for the divine name—a name that should not be used trivially or in connection with magic.

> We have seen that the idea of God was eminently personal. He was supramundane but not extramundane; exalted but not remote. He was the sole ruler of the world he had created, and he ordered all things in it in accordance with his character, in which justice and mercy were complementary, not conflicting, attributes.[116]

In the third main part, Moore explicates the Jewish understanding of man, sin, and atonement. He observes that Judaism believed humans were made in the image of God with freedom to choose right or wrong. Sin is understood as disobedience to the revealed will of God. According to Moore, the Jews believed that ritual atonement functioned to expiate ritual sins, but that the expiation of all sins required repentance. "The Mishnah . . . makes repentance the indispensable condition of the remission of every kind of sin, and this, with the other side of it, namely, that God freely and fully remits the sins of the penitent, is a cardinal doctrine of Judaism; it may properly be called the Jewish doctrine of salvation."[117]

The fourth main part of Moore's *Judaism* considers religious observances. He notes that the two fundamental observances are circumcision and the Sabbath. Although the observance of the Sabbath disallowed thirty-

---

115. Ibid. 1:235, 322, 323, 324.
116. Ibid. 1:423.
117. Ibid. 1:500.

nine major types of behavior (divided into 1,521 subcategories), the Sabbath, in Moore's opinion, was not observed as a burden, but as a joyous festival. In regard to the complex rules about food and purity, Moore emphasizes Judaism as a revealed religion in which rules are obeyed because God willed them.

> If this is what is meant by the "legalism" of the Scribes and Pharisees, the name cannot be denied them, though another derivative of *lex*, "loyalty," would express their conscious attitude better. It is pertinent to add that from this point of view observances are not the "externals" of religion, the outgrown vestments of ideas; conformity to the revealed will of God is the essence of religion.

The fifth and sixth parts of Moore's work deal with morals and piety. He acknowledges that Jews affirmed a doctrine of retribution, involving reward and punishment, but insists that, according to the Jews, salvation cannot be earned. "It should be remarked, further, that 'a lot in the World to Come,' which is the nearest approximation in rabbinical Judaism to the Pauline and Christian idea of salvation, or eternal life, is ultimately assured every Israelite on the ground of the original election of the people by the free grace of God, prompted not by its merits, collective or individual, but solely by God's love, a love that began with the Fathers." In regard to the Pharisees, Moore acknowledges "that many sincere Pharisees thought better of themselves in comparison with other men than it is good for any man to think, and that their superior airs were often very disagreeable. . . . But that the Pharisees as a whole were conscious and calculating hypocrites whose ostentatious piety was a cloak for deliberate secret villainy is unimaginable in view of the subsequent history of Judaism."[118]

In a final (seventh) section, Moore discusses Jewish eschatology. He believes the idea of resurrection arose from the doctrine of retribution: reward and punishment would be reckoned after death. Moreover, the triumph of God's purposes required a restoration of Israel and the righteous individuals. According to Moore, many Jews expected the future to involve the restoration of a golden age of the past. Thus, he finds that some hope for a king like David—a messiah who was neither preexistent nor supernatural. Views (or lack of views) about the messiah differed:

> Any attempt to systematize the Jewish notions of the hereafter imposes upon them an order and consistency which does not exist in them. . . . [T]heir religious significance lies in the definitive establishment of the doctrine of retribution after death, not in the variety of ways in which men imagined it.[119]

---

118. Ibid. 2:78, 94–95, 193.
119. Ibid. 2:389.

Moore's third volume is a collection of notes on various topics, such as "Sanhedrin" and "Nazareth." A note on Paul contends that the apostle's argument in regard to the Jewish understanding of sin and salvation rests on two premises repugnant to the spirit of Judaism: (1) that righteousness under the law required perfect conformity to the law, and (2) that God cannot forgive penitent sinners and bestow on them salvation by grace. In regard to the first, Moore quotes rabbis who say that the righteous person is not required to obey every command of the law. In regard to the second, Moore finds it difficult to understand how Paul could have failed to understand the Jewish doctrine of repentance and divine forgiveness. "How a Jew of Paul's antecedents could ignore, and by implication deny, the great prophetic doctrine of repentance, which, individualized and interiorized, was a cardinal doctrine of Judaism, namely, that God, out of love, freely forgives the sincerely penitent sinner and restores him to his favor—that seems from the Jewish point of view inexplicable."[120]

All in all, Moore's *Judaism* is a spectacular achievement. It displays command of a huge amount of complex material, evaluated by a skilled historian of religion. Most important, Moore, in contrast to most of his predecessors, presents Judaism in its own right. He corrects two earlier misconceptions: that the Jews viewed God as distant, and that Judaism was an extreme legalism, devoid of the idea of grace. To be sure, later scholarship would object to Moore's use of the term "normative" Judaism, and insist that Judaism displayed more variety than Moore acknowledged.[121] Although sympathetic to Judaism, Moore is not totally uncritical. Moreover, his apologetic for Judaism rests convincingly on his understanding of Judaism as a revealed religion: what has been misconstrued as legalism is faithful obedience.[122]

RESEARCH IN HELLENISM: ARTHUR DARBY NOCK

As Billerbeck and Moore investigated Judaism, others probed the Hellenistic backgrounds of the NT. Previous research had been dominated by the history of religion school. Newer studies searched the sources, but were

---

120. Ibid. 3:151.
121. See Smith, "Work of G. F. Moore," 179; James Riley Strange, "G. F. Moore and E. E. Urbach Revisited," in *The Annual of Rabbinic Judaism: Ancient, Medieval, and Modern*, ed. Alan J. Avery-Peck, William Scott Green, and Jacob Neusner, vol. 2 (Leiden: Brill, 1999), 141–59. In the preface to the third volume of *Judaism*, Moore anticipates this criticism, and admits that texts like the Damascus Document indicate that Judaism exhibits considerable variety. However, he reaffirms his idea of "normative Judaism," and contends that "continuity and progress" are more important than "diversity and dissent" (vi).
122. When Moore says that rabbis made selections from Scripture and tradition on the basis of "their own higher conceptions," he seems unwittingly to compromise the principles of revealed religion in favor of his own liberalism; see Frank C. Porter, "Judaism in New Testament Times," *JR* 8 (1928): 30–62.

more cautious in assessing their significance. An example worthy of note is the work of the Scottish scholar H. A. A. Kennedy (1866–1934).[123] Educated in Edinburgh, Kennedy taught for a time at Knox College, Toronto, before assuming the NT chair at New College, Edinburgh. His first significant publication, *Sources of New Testament Greek, or the Influence of the Septuagint on the Vocabulary of the New Testament*, is an analysis of the words of the NT, demonstrating that NT Greek was not a distinctive biblical language, but the vernacular of the Hellenistic age.[124] Regarding the background of the NT, Kennedy was convinced that Philo had been neglected in the study of early Christianity. His book *Philo's Contribution to Religion* presents extensive quotes from the Alexandrian philosopher that Kennedy thinks have parallels in the NT.[125] More cautious is Kennedy's earlier *St. Paul and the Mystery-Religions*. In the preface, Kennedy expresses appreciation for the work of the history of religion school, and later in the book, notes the impact of Hellenistic syncretism on the apostle: "Its atmosphere would surround him like the air which he breathed."[126] However, Kennedy traces the true background of Paul's thought to the HB, and concludes that Paul's religion is not a Hellenistic syncretism, nor, more specifically, a mystery religion.[127]

Arthur Darby Nock (1902–63)

Arthur Darby Nock was born in Portsmouth, England, and educated at Cambridge.[128] In 1930, at age twenty-eight, he was appointed Frothingham Professor of History of Religion at Harvard. He served for many years as editor of the *Harvard Theological Review*. Nock delivered the Gifford Lectures in 1939 and 1946, which, except for his study of Posidonius, remained unpublished. Once a practicing Anglican, Nock became an agnostic with religious

---

123. John Baillie, "Kennedy, Harry Angus Alexander (1866–1934)," *Dictionary of National Biography 1931–40,* 504–5.
124. (Edinburgh: T. & T. Clark, 1895). Kennedy was apparently unaware of the discoveries of the large quantity of papyri and the work of Deissmann and Moulton that was going on at about the same time (see pp. 177, 179–83, 186–89, above); his research was restricted to the texts of the NT, the LXX, and older Greek literature.
125. (London: Hodder and Stoughton, 1919).
126. *St. Paul and the Mystery-Religions* (London: Hodder and Stoughton, 1913), 30.
127. Kennedy is also remembered for his work in NT theology. His *St Paul's Conceptions of the Last Things*, Cunningham Lectures, 2d ed. (London: Hodder and Stoughton, 1904), contrasts Paul's doctrine of the resurrection with the Greek idea of immortality, and argues that Paul advocated a spiritual resurrection. Kennedy's highly regarded *The Theology of the Epistles* (New York: Charles Scribner's Sons, 1920) treats the thought of all the NT epistles except the Johannine. Kennedy contends that the center of Paul's thought is communion with Christ, and that Pauline influence on 1 Peter has been exaggerated. Kennedy also wrote the comments on Philippians for the *Expositor's Greek Testament*, ed. W. Robertson Nicoll, 5 vols. (London: Hodder and Stoughton, 1897–1911); repr., Grand Rapids, Mich.: Eerdmans, 1956) 3:397–473.
128. See Krister Stendahl, "Arthur Darby Nock, 21.II.1902–11.I.1963," *Numen* 10 (1963): 236–37; E. R. Dodds and Henry Chadwick, "Obituary: Arthur Darby Nock," *JRS* 53 (1963): 168–69; Crane Brinton, Frank M. Cross Jr., Fred N. Robinson, Krister Stendahl, and Zeph Stewart, "Arthur Darby Nock, 21.II.1902–11.I.1963," *HTR* 57 (1964): 65–68.

sensitivity. He was noted for his warm and boisterous personality, like a character out of Dickens. Those who knew him well mention his "lovable eccentricities, and the effervescent gaiety which effectively hid from all but a few the private griefs and anxieties of a lonely and vulnerable man."[129]

In regard to his own scholarship, Nock was self-critical. "I see only half the literature," he said, but continued, "I realize that others see only a third, but still I should miss things."[130] As a result, much of Nock's work was confined to articles and reviews. Many of these have been collected, edited by Zeph Stewart, and published under the title *Arthur Darby Nock: Essays on Religion and the Ancient World.*[131] The two volumes of this work, containing more than five hundred pages each, include articles and reviews written between 1925 and 1963—a total of fifty-nine items. A few samples are of special interest for NT research.

"Paul and the Magus," commenting on Acts 13:6-12, reviews the encounter of Paul and the magician Elymas in Cyprus.[132] Nock discusses the meaning of the term μάγος and the significance of magic in the Hellenistic world. He thinks Elymas was some sort of religious adviser to the proconsul Sergius Paulus. According to Nock, the blindness that falls on Elymas shows that the magician is outplayed in his own game. It indicates that judgment accompanies the divine mission, and that Christian miracle is superior to pagan magic. An essay on "Gnosticism"[133] affirms, in opposition to the history of religion school, "the traditional view of Gnosticism as a Christian heresy with roots in speculative thought."[134] Nock also offers a short summary of his assessment of NT backgrounds.

> If we are to understand the development of early Christianity, we must always bear in mind its diversified Jewish background. In fact, the contribution of Greek thought to Christianity in its first hundred years came primarily through Hellenistic Judaism. The teaching of Jesus had its roots in a Palestinian culture of mainly Semitic speech, but teaching about the Christ had its roots largely in Greek-speaking Judaism such as we know primarily at Alexandria.[135]

---

129. Dodds and Chadwick, "Arthur Darby Nock," 169.
130. Quoted in Brinton et al., "Arthur Darby Nock," 68.
131. 2 vols. (Cambridge: Harvard University Press, 1972).
132. Ibid. 1:308–30; originally published in *The Beginnings of Christianity*, V *Additional Notes*, ed. F. J. Foakes Jackson and K. Lake (1933; repr., Grand Rapids, Mich: Baker, 1966), 164–88.
133. *Essays on Religion* 2.940–59; originally published in *HTR* 57 (1964): 255–79.
134. Ibid. 2:956.
135. Ibid. 2:945. Nock contributed to the study of the Hellenistic environment of early Christianity with his editorial work, in collaboration with A.-J. Festugière, on the Hermetic literature: A. D. Nock and A.-J. Festugière, eds., *Corpus Hermeticum*, 4 vols., Collection des universités de France (Paris: "Les Belles Lettres," 1945, 1954); this is recognized as the authoritative text of the Hermetic documents.

Nock's mastery of Hellenistic religion is confirmed by his book *Conversion: The Old and the New in Religion from Alexander the Great to Augustine of Hippo*.[136] "By conversion" writes Nock, "we mean the reorientation of the soul of an individual, his deliberate turning from indifference or from an earlier form of piety to another, a turning which implies a consciousness that a great change is involved, that the old was wrong and the new is right." Nock observes that after Alexander, syncretistic cults, combining Greek and oriental ideas, moved from the East to the West. Carried by soldiers and migrants, these cults spread their message by written and oral propaganda, rituals and rumors of miracles. They promised escape from fate and death; they satisfied curiosity about the world and the mysteries of the East. "Yet the surprising thing is the slightness of the change which they effected in the fundamental temper of the people among whom they took root." Within this world of competing religions, Nock notes that Christianity was remarkably successful.

> The success of Christianity is the success of an institution which united the sacramentalism and the philosophy of the time. It satisfied the inquiring turn of mind, the desire to escape from Fate, the desire for security in the hereafter; like Stoicism, it gave a way of life and made man at home in the universe, but unlike Stoicism it did this for the ignorant as well as for the lettered. It satisfied also social needs and it secured men against loneliness.

In an imaginative chapter, Nock takes up the question of how Christianity was viewed by pagans. He believes they were impressed by the Christian stress on morality—a morality empowered by the claim of the possession of the Spirit. Pagans were familiar with the idea of intermediaries between the gods and humans, but, according to Nock, the idea of the incarnation of the deity was unique. "The Christian householder brought forth from his store things old and new: the old was not obsolete and the new was not incomprehensible."[137]

Nock's knowledge of Hellenistic religion is applied to the study of early Christian literature in his *Early Gentile Christianity and Its Hellenistic Background*. This book is actually a collection of three essays that had been published earlier.[138] In the essay "Early Gentile Christianity and Its Hellenistic Background," originally published in 1928, Nock notes that Christians made their first converts among Jews, and then among Gentiles associating with the synagogues of the Diaspora.[139]

---

136. (Oxford: Clarendon, 1933).
137. Ibid., 7, 160, 210–11, 253.
138. HTCL (New York: Harper & Row, 1964).
139. In *Essays on the Trinity and the Incarnation*, ed. A. E. J. Rawlinson (London: Longmans, Green, 1928); repr. in Stewart, *Essays in Religion* 1:49–133.

In this Hellenistic world there was then a great and confusing array of cults, old civic worship, sometimes now recovering after generations of decay, new Caesar-worship, and also the now rising religions of the individual. In a way they were competing for his attachment: at the same time they were ready to blend or be equated, and showed little tendency to that exclusiveness which was a distinctive feature of Judaism and Christianity.[140]

In the essay "The Theology of Christianity as a Mission-Religion," Nock contends that the influence of Hellenism should not be exaggerated. "It must be added," he writes, "that 'saviour-gods' and mysteries probably did not bulk so large in the life of the first century A.D. as in modern study."[141] Nock believes the title "Kyrios" for Jesus was first used by Christians of Jerusalem, but when Paul used it before Gentile audiences, Jesus was seen as Lord in relation to the lords and deities of the Hellenistic cults. Nock acknowledges that elements of the "redeemer myth" had been present earlier, but he believes that the fully developed myth is post-Pauline. Nock also contends that the Christian rites of baptism and the Lord's Supper were little influenced by the Hellenistic cults. In his essay "Hellenistic Mysteries and Christian Sacraments," originally published in 1952, Nock writes, "To argue as I have done is not to suggest that pagan mysteries had no influence on the development and acceptance of Catholic Christianity; the surprise is that on the evidence they had so little."[142]

Nock turns directly to the NT with his book *St. Paul*, originally published in 1938.[143] Nock is not concerned with later interpretations of Paul: "we shall try to forget for the moment all that happened after his execution at Rome, and, instead, seek as far as we can to view Paul as a man of the first century, living and moving and teaching in its peculiar conditions." Nock views Paul as a zealous devotee of orthodox Judaism who had been converted by a vision that led him to identify Jesus as Messiah. Nock acknowledges that Paul was influenced by Hellenistic ideas, but insists that "Jewish eschatological presuppositions were certainly the starting-point of Paul's Christianity." Paul's religion was Christocentric. "Christ and the Spirit were everything."[144]

Nock surveys the Pauline Letters in chronological order. He accepts 2 Thessalonians as authentic, and believes Galatians was addressed to churches in north Galatia. He sees the Corinthian correspondence as a composite of four letters. The opponents attacked in 2 Corinthians 10–13

---

140. *Early Gentile Christianity*, 17.
141. Ibid., 29.
142. Ibid., 144. This essay was originally published in *Mnemosyne*, series 4, vol. 5 (Leiden: E. J. Brill, 1952).
143. Repr., HTCL (New York: Harper & Row, 1963).
144. Ibid., 20, 77, 80.

Nock takes to be Judaizing Christians from Jerusalem. He believes the eschatology of 2 Corinthians 5 represents a "new doctrine."

> The passage of the Christian to the promised life is now seen from the standpoint of the individual; the transformation which had been expected as one of the concomitants of the appearance of Christ starts now and is a gradual continuous process; and death is followed not by sleep in Christ, but by union with him. Further, the bodily existence of the present is conceived as something burdensome and cramping. The result has definite affinities with Hellenistic personal mysticism such as had found its way into Jewish circles.

In discussing Romans, Nock finds little support for the orthodox doctrine of atonement. "Where Paul differs from much later thought is that he does not think of God as needing satisfaction; God himself provides the remedy." In regard to the later epistles, Nock locates Colossians, Philemon, and Philippians in the Roman imprisonment. Ephesians and the Pastoral Epistles, in Nock's opinion, were not written by Paul. Nock concludes that "it is Paul more than any other man who was responsible for the fact that Christianity was not a Jewish sect but an independent body with an independent life."[145]

On the whole, A. D. Nock offers a breath of fresh air. An independent thinker with exceptional knowledge of the religion of the Hellenistic period, he refuses to join any of the warring parties. On the one hand, Nock avoids a "parallelomania" that reduces Christianity to a Hellenistic syncretism. On the other, he refuses to degrade paganism as a foil over against a pure and superior Christianity. Nock praises Christianity's moral and intellectual commitment while avoiding Christian imperialism.

THE HISTORY OF EARLY CHRISTIANITY:
HANS LIETZMANN, MAURICE GOGUEL, AND WALTER BAUER

Since F. C. Baur, most NT scholars have been church historians as well as exegetes. The two approaches are mutually beneficial. On the one hand, careful linguistic and grammatical analysis of the sources undergirds historical reconstruction. On the other hand, the larger historical reconstruction provides the framework in which the details of criticism find their significance. The process is a heremeutical circle: the data are viewed within a comprehensive vision, and in the process, the data revise the comprehensive vision. Practitioners of the dual approach need to be both philologians and philosophers. Three worthy examples appear in the era between the two great wars: Hans Lietzmann, Maurice Goguel, and Walter Bauer.

---

145. Ibid., 203, 212–13, 247.

Hans Lietzmann (1875–1942)

Life and Theological Perspective

Hans Lietzmann was born in Düsseldorf.[146] His mother died at his birth, and he was raised by his stepmother. He was educated at the high school in Wittenberg, where he excelled in classics and dedicated his life to the combined study of philology and theology. His university studies were pursued at Jena and Bonn. In 1905, Lietzmann accepted an invitation to the faculty at Jena. In 1921, he declined a call to Berlin, but two years later accepted a second call and moved to Berlin in 1924, worthy successor of Adolf von Harnack. Lietzmann traveled widely, working in the Vatican library and participating in archeological research in Rome and Constantinople. He was opposed to National Socialism and associated with the Confessing Church. After a lengthy illness, Lietzmann died in 1942. Heinrich Bornkamm recalls one of his last visits with Lietzmann when he found him listening to a broadcast of Beethoven's Ninth, a copy of the score in hand.

Lietzmann has been criticized as a devotee of historicism, that is, preoccupation with the objective reconstruction of factual history. To be sure, Lietzmann was a philologian, committed to the objective study of the data. In a letter to Bultmann, he wrote, "I have set for myself no other goal than that once formulated by von Ranke, namely, to recount 'how it actually was,' and I recognize that this goal can be reached with our means only incompletely."[147] However, despite this commitment to objectivity, Lietzmann's historical work is built on theological foundations. He believes Christianity had its beginning in the history of Jesus, in whom the will and activity of God was disclosed. Lietzmann insists that the study of history must be sensitive to the activity of God. "For the Christian, world history in all times has the same meaning: it is the history of the kingdom of God; it is history of salvation."[148]

In an essay titled "The Theologian and the New Testament," Lietzmann takes up the question: Can the historical-critical method be applied to the

---

146. See "Hans Lietzmann," in Hans Lietzmann, *Kleine Schriften, III Studien zur Liturgie- und Symbolgeschichte zur Wissenschaftsgeschichte,* ed. Komission für Spätantike Religionsgeschichte, TU 74 (Berlin: Akademie-Verlag, 1962), 331–68; Heinrich Bornkamm, "Hans Lietzmann," *ZNW* 41 (1942): 1–12; Kurt Aland, *Glanz und Niedergang der deutschen Universität: 50 Jahre deutscher Wissenschaftsgeschichte in Briefen an und von Hans Lietzmann* (1892–1942) (Berlin: Walter de Gruyter, 1979). Aland's work includes a biographical introduction (more than 150 pages) plus a huge collection (more than eight hundred pages) of Lietzmann's correspondence; see Rudolf Smend, "Glanz und Niedergang der deutschen Universität," *EvT* 40 (1980): 181–88.

147. Quoted in Wilhelm Schneemelcher, "Lietzmann, Hans Karl Alexander (1875–1942)," *TRE* 21 (1991): 195.

148. Quoted in Dietmar Wyrwa, "Hans Lietzmanns theologisches Verständnis der Kirchengeschichte," in *450 Jahre Evangelische Theologie in Berlin,* ed. Gerhard Besier and Christof Gestrich (Göttingen: Vandenhoeck & Ruprecht, 1989), 418.

NT by Christians who accept it as the word of God?[149] In answer, he asserts that the NT is revelation of God, but that it is subject to the contingencies of history. This means that interpretation of the NT requires historical-philological study. "The first duty of the New Testament exegete is to want to hear and accept only the words of the apostles and to strive with complete passivity for nothing other than the right understanding."[150] However, mere objective exegesis is not adequate for the Christian who hears in the words of the Bible the call of God. The word of God can be heard in Scripture, according to Lietzmann, when historical study is informed by faith—a faith that employs a spiritual exegesis that works in harmony with historical-critical research.

NT Research
From early in his career, Lietzmann published studies that have to do with text, canon, and early Christian documents. A number of Lietzmann's text-critical essays have been collected in the second volume of his *Kleine Schriften*. He also published works on the Muratorian Fragment, the early Christian creeds, and the Didache.[151] Always anxious to produce tools for students and scholars, Lietzmann undertook the revision of Albert Huck's widely used gospel *Synopsis*, which had originally appeared in 1892.[152] Lietzmann's prolegomena presents in the original languages the patristic texts that refer to the Gospels, including citations from Papias, Irenaeus, and the Muratorian Fragment. The *Huck–Lietzmann Synopsis* became standard in Europe and America, its wide recognition attested, for example, by the *Gospel Parallels*—a synopsis that presents the text of the RSV in pericopes arranged and numbered according to the Huck–Lietzmann system.[153]

Lietzmann's view of the canon is expressed in his delightful book *How Did the Books of the New Testament Become Holy Scripture?*—originally presented as a vacation course for schoolteachers.[154] According to Lietzmann, the

---

149. "Der Theolog und das Neue Testament," in Hans Lietzmann, *Kleine Schriften, II Studien zum Neuen Testament*, ed. Kurt Aland, TU 68 (Berlin: Akademie-Verlag, 1958), 3–8; originally published in *Einführung in das Neue Testament*, ed. Rudolf Knopf, 4th ed. (Giessen, 1934; 5th ed., Berlin: Alfred Töpelmann, 1949), 1–5.

150. *Kleine Schriften, II*, 5.

151. *Das Muratorische Fragment und die Monarchianischen Prologe zu den Evangelien*, KlT 1 (Bonn: A. Marcus und E. Weber, 1921); idem, *Symbole der Alten Kirche*, 5th ed., KlT 17/18 (Berlin: Walter de Gruyter, 1961); idem, *Die Didache*, 5th ed., KlT 6 (Berlin: Walter de Gruyter, 1948); Eng. trans.: *The Teaching of the Twelve Apostles with Apparatus Criticus*, 2d ed. (Cambridge: Deighton, Bell, 1907).

152. Albert Huck, *Synopse der drei ersten Evangelien*, 9th ed. Hans Lietzmann (Tübingen: J. C. B. Mohr [Paul Siebeck], 1936); Eng. ed.: *A Synopsis of the First Three Gospels*, ed. Frank Leslie Cross (Tübingen: J. C. B. Mohr [Paul Siebeck], 1936).

153. (New York: Thomas Nelson & Sons, 1949).

154. *Wie wurden die Bücher des Neuen Testaments heilige Schrift?: Fünf Vorträge*, Lebensfragen 21 (Tübingen: J. C. B. Mohr [Paul Siebeck], 1907); repr. in *Kleine Schriften, II*, 15–98.

question must be answered historically. He begins by investigating the NT itself. He notes that Paul accepted the authority of the Hebrew Scriptures, but also claimed himself to have received divine revelation. Lietzmann points out that the author of 2 Peter knew a collection of Paul's letters. Thus, two ideas important for the canon are already witnessed in the NT: the authority of the apostles, and the collection of apostolic documents. Turning to the noncanonical writings, Lietzmann notes that 1 Clement affirms the authority of the apostles, but fails to quote 1 Corinthians 15 to support belief in the resurrection. Lietzmann thinks Ignatius knew the Gospel of John and the letters of Paul, but does not cite them as Scripture. Justin's "Memoirs of the Apostles," in Lietzmann's opinion, included other documents beside the four canonical Gospels. Irenaeus argues for four Gospels, no more, no less, and accepts the authority of Paul, thus presenting what Lietzmann recognizes as a canon of Gospels and epistles by the end of the second century. Lietzmann believes the closing of the canon was encouraged by the struggle with the Gnostics and Marcion.

Lietzmann's exegetical work is seen in his contributions to the *Handbuch zum Neuen Testament*—a series of commentaries begun under his editorship in 1906. The purpose of the series was to provide material that facilitated the interpretation of the NT in its historical setting—an answer to the prayer of the history of religion school. Thus the commentaries include abundant parallels from contemporary sources, particularly Hellenistic, made readily available to the exegete. Early editions of the commentary were short, and sometimes the work on more than one NT book was bound into a single volume. For example, commentaries on all three of the Synoptics by Erich Klostermann were bound in one volume. In later editions, commentaries on Mark, Matthew, and Luke—all written by Klostermann—were bound as separate commentaries. Other contributors to the series include Walter Bauer (John), Erwin Preuschen (Acts), Martin Dibelius (the shorter letters of Paul), Hans Windisch (Hebrews and the Pastoral Epistles), and Ernst Lohmeyer (Revelation). Lietzmann wrote the commentaries on the longer Pauline letters, collected into a single volume under the title *Die Briefe des Apostel Paulus*, later issued in three separate volumes. The series also included a grammar of NT Greek (by Ludwig Radermacher), Bousset's book on Judaism,[155] and commentaries on the Apostolic Fathers. In the preface to volume 22 of the *Handbuch*, Lietzmann addresses the complaint that the volumes, with their philological and historical thrust, do not really provide exposition of the texts useful to the preacher.[156]

---

155. See pp. 245–47, above.
156. "Eine Bemerkung zur Exegese des Neuen Testaments," in *Kleine Schriften, II*, 9–11; originally published in *HNT* 22:v–vii.

In response, Lietzmann contends that "scientific exegesis is the precondition of all true biblical preaching."[157]

Lietzmann's commitment to scientific research in the history of religion mode is illustrated in his commentaries. His exegesis of *1 and 2 Corinthians* was completed in 1907, and expanded and published as a separate volume in 1923.[158] There is no critical introduction; historical-critical matters are treated in the commentary and in excursuses. As typical of the series, the text, in German translation, is printed at the top of the left-hand page; comments are below and continued on the right-hand page. The comments are succinct, accompanied by extensive references and citations from ancient and modern sources. In regard to 1 Cor. 1:10-12, for example, Lietzmann observes that "Chloe" means "the blond"—a name frequently used for slave women. In an excursus on "the Parties in Corinth," Lietzmann argues that there were four factions in the Corinthian church. On the basis of context and style, he contends that those who claim to belong to Christ constitute a separate faction, mentioned again in 2 Cor. 10:7. Lietzmann also includes, after his comments on 1 Cor. 10:21, an excursus on cult meals. He presents material from the papyri and inscriptions illustrating how the table used in the meals was identified as the table of the deity. Lietzmann also presents a floor plan of a meat market in Pompeii that includes a chapel of the imperial cult.

Lietzmann's commentary on *Galatians* first appeared in 1910; it was expanded and issued as a separate volume in 1923.[159] An excursus on "Galatia" reviews the history of the Celts in northern Asia Minor, and the incorporation of their area into the Roman Empire in 25 B.C.E.—an account punctuated with references from inscriptions and ancient authors. Lietzmann concludes that the epistle was addressed to churches of the northern area—the original area of the ethnic Celts. Commenting on 2:1-10 (concerning the Jerusalem Council), Lietzmann argues that Paul knew nothing of the apostolic decree described in Acts 15:23-29. Lietzmann notes that in the list of leaders in Gal. 2:9 James is usually listed first, but that in some MSS, Peter is put at the top of the list.

Lietzmann's *Romans* originally appeared in 1906; in 1928, it was revised and expanded to become volume 8 in the series.[160] The fourth edition of 1933 was prefaced by an essay on the introduction to the history of the text of the Pauline Letters.[161] In this essay, Lietzmann asserts that Paul's letters

---

157. "Bemerkung zur Exegese," 11.
158. *An die Korinther I. II,* 4 ed. Werner Georg Kümmel, HNT 9 (Tübingen: J. C. B. Mohr [Paul Siebeck], 1949).
159. *An die Galater,* 4th ed., HNT 10 (Tübingen: J. C. B. Mohr [Paul Siebeck], 1971).
160. *An die Römer,* 5th ed., HNT 8 (Tübingen: J. C. B. Mohr [Paul Siebeck], 1971).
161. "Einfuhrung in die Textgeschichte der Paulusbriefe," in ibid., 1–18.

were collected early in the second century. He identifies three major types of text: Egyptian, Western, and Koine. He argues that the Koine is secondary, and that the Western, though early, is flawed by additions and corrections; the Egyptian is the most reliable text. In the commentary itself, Lietzmann contends that the church of Rome was essentially Gentile in composition. An excursus on 16:24 reviews and rejects the hypothesis that chapter 16 was originally a letter addressed to Ephesus. In commenting on 3:21-31, Lietzmann presents an excursus on ΙΛΑΣΤΗΡΙΟΝ. He notes the use of the term in inscriptions for votive offerings and its use in the LXX for כפרת, the cover of the ark of the covenant. In regard to Paul's use, Lietzmann argues that reference to the cover on the ark would have required a clearer explanation.

Lietzmann's interest in theological exegesis is seen in his book on the *Son of Man*, written when he was only twenty-one years old. He begins by observing that Jesus did not use the Greek phrase ὁ υἱός τοῦ ἀνθρώπου. "Thus, every attempt to understand the speech of Jesus in a deeper sense by analysis of the Greek form is methodologically absolutely inadmissible, and the entire effort that has been applied to this question has become unfruitful." The question is: What is the meaning of the Aramaic phrase בר נשא that the Greek represents? Lietzmann investigates the meaning of the Aramaic phrase in the Targums and the Talmud and finds no use of it as a messianic title. In Daniel, the phrase "son of man" refers to a human figure in contrast to beasts, and in Enoch, according to Lietzmann, the phrase is not a messianic title. Lietzmann acknowledges that "Son of Man" is used as a title in the Gospels, but contends that "Jesus never assumed for himself the title 'Son of Man,' since it never existed in Aramaic, and on linguistic grounds, cannot exist." Lietzmann thinks Jesus used the phrase simply to mean "man" or as a substitute for the personal pronoun. The use of the phrase as a messianic title, according to Lietzmann, arose in early Christianity in connection with the expectation of the triumphant return of Christ when Daniel was misread as referring to the future Messiah as Son of Man.[162]

Research in the History of Early Christianity

In 1915, Lietzmann published a fascinating book on Peter and Paul in Rome. The book is a thorough investigation of the literary and archeological evidence concerning the deaths and burials of Peter and Paul. Lietzmann reviews the evidence in early calendars and papal lists, celebrations of the chair of Peter, and the feasts of Peter and Paul. He also analyzes the archeological data concerning the catacomb of St. Sebastian and the ceme-

---

162. *Der Menschensohn: Ein Beitrag zur neutestamentlichen Theologie* (Freiburg i. Br.: J. C. B. Mohr [Paul Siebeck], 1896), 25, 85.

tery under St. Peter's in Rome. He recounts the history of the building of the churches of St. Peter and St. Paul. He concludes:

> The foregoing investigation has shown that the present location of the graves of Peter and Paul can be confirmed by around the year 200. In the year 258, the bones of the apostles were taken from these two burial places to the catacombs to be protected. Under Constantine, the relics were returned to their original locations, and since that time have remained there undisturbed.

Lietzmann then takes up the question, What of the tradition prior to 200? He argues that literary evidence, notably 1 Clement, supports the deaths of Peter and Paul in Rome. "In all probability, Peter and Paul died the death of martyrs in Rome under Nero."[163]

Better known, but equally controversial, is Lietzmann's *Mass and Lord's Supper*—a work originally published in 1926.[164] In essence, the book is an investigation of the eucharistic rites of the church for the purpose of detecting the origin and meaning of the Lord's Supper. Working backwards through the history of the church, Lietzmann detects two early liturgical forms: the Egyptian and the Roman (or Hippolytan). The Egyptian, as seen in the liturgy of Serapion, stresses the symbolism of the elements of the Eucharist. This liturgy, in Lietzmann's opinion, did not originally include a narrative of the institution of the Supper or the idea of the celebration as remembrance. Lietzmann finds an early expression of this form in the Didache. He believes it represents the practice of the earliest church in Jerusalem. It had its origin, according to Lietzmann, in the common meals of Jesus with the disciples. Lietzmann believes the Last Supper was such a meal; it was not, in his opinion, a Passover meal. On the other hand, the Roman form of the liturgy, represented by Hippolytus, stressed the institution of the Supper and the celebration of the Supper as remembrance of the death of Christ. This form, according to Lietzmann, had its origin in Paul. Lietzmann thinks that Paul received this understanding of the Supper by revelation "from the Lord" (1 Cor. 11:23). Although Lietzmann presents abundant data, careful analysis, and imaginative reconstruction, most

---

163. *Petrus und Paulus in Rom: Liturgische und archäologische Studien* (Bonn: A. Marcus und E. Weber, 1915), 165, 176.

164. *Messe und Herrenmahl: Eine Studie zur Geschichte der Liturgie*, 3d ed., Arbeiten zur Kirchengeschichte 8 (Berlin: Walter de Gruyter, 1955); Eng. trans.: *Mass and Lord's Supper: A Study in the History of the Liturgy*, trans. Dorothea H. G. Reeve, Introduction and Supplementary Essay by Robert Douglas Richardson (Leiden: E. J. Brill, 1953–79). Lietzmann's theory of two early forms of the Lord's Supper is presented in brief form in his *Die Entstehung der christlichen Liturgie nach den ältesten Quellen* (Darmstadt: Wissenschaftliche Buchgesellschaft, 1963), originally published in TU 74, and reprinted in *Kleine Schriften, III*.

scholars are not convinced that two distinct forms of the Eucharist existed in the apostolic age.[165]

Lietzmann's magnum opus is his four-volume *History of the Early Church*—one of the most readable and informative treatments of the subject produced in the twentieth century.[166] For the history of NT research, most important is the first volume, *The Beginnings of the Christian Church*, originally published in 1932. This volume surveys the history of the apostolic and postapostolic ages up to the mid-second century. Opening chapters set the stage with a review of the history of Palestine and the religion of Judaism in this period. In studying Jesus, Lietzmann insists on use of the historical-critical method.

> But in spite of all the transformation effected by tradition, we see in every direction the genuine rock of reliable information upon which the historian can build—if only he will deal with the sources of primitive Christianity by the same methods as all other existing sources. That means, however, that he must approach them as an expert and disinterested judge, not as a critic who is sceptical on principle. There is only one historical method; if we hear of special methods for religion, history, legend, form-criticism, and the history of worship, we must remember that these are not new methods, but new standpoints calculated to supplement each other and to refine the one historical method.

In regard to the Gospels, Lietzmann accepts the two-document hypothesis, and believes Jesus' message of the kingdom was eschatological. He also says, "No person of judgment to-day can any longer doubt that Jesus possessed miraculous power, and worked 'miracles' as understood in the ancient sense; and to the historian, the extant records, just because of their popular character, flash light from very many facets, and are more valuable than dry official reports could be; for from them comes a reflection of His acts and deeds which pierces far into the deeps of human nature." In Lietzmann's opinion, Jesus viewed himself as Messiah, but modified the popular expectation. "He allowed the apocalyptic conceptions to remain, and glow on the horizon; but He took the seeds of the Kingdom, which were replete with divine power, and planted them in the hearts of those hearers who repented and believed."[167]

---

165. See Richardson's "Introduction" in *Mass and Lord's Supper*; A. J. B. Higgins, "Important and Influential Foreign Books: H. Lietzmann's 'Mass and Lord's Supper' (Messe und Herrenmahl)," *ExpTim* 65 (1953–54): 333–36.

166. *Geschichte der alten Kirche*, 3d ed., 4 vols. (Berlin: Walter de Gruyter, 1944); Eng. trans.: *A History of the Early Church*, 2d ed., 4 vols., trans. Bertram Lee Woolf (New York: Charles Scribner's Sons, 1949–52); in the English edition, the volumes are published as separate works: *The Beginnings of the Christian Church*, *The Founding of the Church Universal*, *From Constantine to Julian*, *The Era of the Church Fathers*.

167. *Beginnings* (vol. 1 of *History of the Early Church*), 45–46, 50, 56.

In regard to the first church in Jerusalem, Lietzmann affirms the importance of the resurrection faith and notes the problem of the resurrection fact. "But the verdict on the true nature of the event described as the resurrection of Jesus, an event of immeasurable significance for the history of the world, does not come within the province of historical inquiry into matters of fact; it belongs to the place where the human soul touches the eternal." After a survey of the Jewish Diaspora, Lietzmann recognizes the significance of Paul.

> Paul did not initiate missionary work to the Gentiles; even without him, Christianity would have extended round the Mediterranean; but he gave the religion of Jesus the form in which it was capable of conquering the world, without receiving damage to its own soul. He had never sat at the feet of the Master, but nevertheless was the only one amongst the Apostles who really understood Him.

Paul's theology, according to Lietzmann, stressed the idea of the righteousness of God.

> God's righteousness must indeed demand punishment and expiation from the sinner; this expiation was made to God when the innocent and sinless Jesus voluntarily bore the punishment of sin, and suffered death. He suffered death as a vicarious, expiatory sacrifice on behalf of sinful mankind. Thereby He reconciled God, satisfied His righteousness, which had demanded expiation, and opened in this manner the way of mercy which can bring to the Christian believer the necessary righteousness.

Lietzmann believes a tension existed between the Pauline churches and the Jewish church in Jerusalem. He thinks Peter may have brought the apostolic decree of Acts 15:23-29 to Corinth.[168]

In investigating the postapostolic age, Lietzmann attends to the literature. He interprets the Epistle of James as a polemic against Paul. "But when the author carries the discussion further, and understands by 'works' the exercise of all the Christian virtues; and when faith is for him the rational acceptance of a proposition, it becomes clear that he had not the least understanding of Paul."[169] Hebrews, according to Lietzmann, is a tract that affirms the preexistence of Christ, written in imitation of Paul. First Peter he judges to be pseudonymous, and the Pastoral Epistles, also pseudonymous, are concerned with church order in the face of Jewish gnostic opponents. In regard to the Gospel of John, Lietzmann concludes that it was not written by an eyewitness; he accepts the tradition of the early martyrdom of John the son of Zebedee. According to Lietzmann, the "beloved disciple" is an ideal, not a person.

---

168. Ibid., 62, 112, 116.
169. Ibid., 202.

Lietzmann notes the importance of Marcion. "He was the first really to proclaim, on a theological basis, the existence of a New Testament as a collection of writings, and to put it, not alongside, but in the place, of the Old Testament." Lietzmann also gives considerable attention to Gnosticism, which he takes to be a pre-Christian, syncretistic religion.

> The examples that we have cited so far show that gnosis arose apart from Christian influence. Indeed, it is older than Christianity, and is a phenomenon of pagan syncretism, which mingled Greek and oriental religion in the greatest variety of forms, filled them out with mystical traits, and, at the same time, combined them with philosophical ideas and modes of thought. . . . But in its critical early period, Christianity was practically untouched by gnosticism which, at that time, was itself obviously only just showing signs of beginning.[170]

With Hans Lietzmann, historical understanding of early Christian literature reaches a high point. Lietzmann is equipped with all the tools of historical research—text critical, archeological, linguistic—and, at the same time, he has the historical imagination that inspires credible reconstruction. He preserves, with appropriate moderation, the legacy of the history of religion school. Lietzmann is concerned with the theological significance of the sources, but he understands theology historically: history is the medium of divine revelation. The theology that emerges is a type of liberalism—a faith grounded in the life and teaching of Jesus, a faith that resonates to the worship of the common meals of the disciples, a faith that affirms the early Christian stress on morality. To be sure, Lietzmann has not fully worked out the relation of history and theology; he has produced no sophisticated hermeneutic, nor articulated a theological ontology of history. Yet, one cannot expect everything of a person who has done so much and done it so well.

Maurice Goguel (1880–1955)

Life, Thought, and Early Works

Maurice Goguel was born in Paris, the son of a Lutheran pastor.[171] He studied in Paris and at Marburg, where he was influenced by the liberalism of Wilhelm Herrmann. Most of Goguel's career was spent at the Faculté Libre de Théologie de Paris, where he began teaching at age twenty-five. Goguel

---

170. Ibid., 256–57, 277.
171. See Marcel Simon, "Maurice Goguel (1880–1955)," in Maurice Goguel, *The Primitive Church*, trans. H. C. Snape (New York: Macmillan, 1964), 7–11; Alan H. Jones, *Independence and Exegesis: The Study of Early Christianity in the Work of Alfred Loisy (1857–1940), Charles Guignebert (1857–1939) and Maurice Goguel (1880–1955)*, BGBE 26 (Tübingen: J. C. B. Mohr [Paul Siebeck], 1983); Oscar Cullmann, "Maurice Goguel (1880–1955)," in *Oscar Cullmann: Vorträge und Aufsätze, 1925–1962*, ed. Karlfried Fröhlich (Tübingen: J. C. B. Mohr [Paul Siebeck], 1966), 667–74; Frank Michaéli, "Vies parallèles: Adolph Lods et Maurice Goguel," *ETR* 52 (1977): 385–401.

succeeded Alfred Loisy (1927) and Charles Guignebert (1937) at the Sorbonne. According to Oscar Cullmann, "Maurice Goguel is doubtless one of the greatest to whom our discipline is most indebted."[172]

Goguel belongs to the liberal tradition in France that goes back to Ernst Renan, and more recently, to Alfred Loisy.[173] This tradition was also represented by Charles Guignebert (1867–1939), who was sympathetic to the history of religion school and devoted to rigorous, nontheological exegesis. Goguel had studied with Auguste Sabatier (1839–1901), who promoted the critical method and opposed orthodoxy. Goguel was also influenced by Henri Bergson, the prophet of creative evolution and the inner vital impulse (*élan vital*). The concern with the inner life and evolution led Goguel to an interest in psychology and sociology. He began his theological career with the intent to study systematic theology, but came to the conviction that theology had to be grounded in history, and as a result he became a historian of Jesus and early Christianity.

Early in his career, Goguel published monographs on the *Johannine Idea of the Spirit* and the history of the *Eucharist* in the early church. In the book on the Spirit, written when Goguel was only twenty-two, he argues that the primary background of the idea of the Spirit in the Fourth Gospel is to be found in the Christian tradition. Goguel concludes, "For our author, the sole religious problem is this: How can a person acquire eternal life? And he responds, By the gift of the Spirit which will be given to those who believe in Christ, for the Spirit is that which makes alive."[174] Goguel's book on the Eucharist begins with an investigation of the Last Supper, which he believes not to have been a Passover meal or to have included the command to repeat in remembrance. The breaking of bread in the early church Goguel understands as the common meal of the community—a simple practice that evolved into the sacramental observance of Paul. In the Fourth Gospel, the main presentation of the Eucharist, Goguel thinks, is to be found in the account of the feeding of the multitude. Goguel says, "John thinks only about a spiritual communion with the glorified Christ. The consumption of the flesh and the blood is only allegorical."[175]

Goguel's Introduction

Goguel produced two major works: a massive introduction to the NT and a three-volume survey of the history of early Christianity. A short summary cannot do justice to Goguel's *Introduction*, a four-volume work (bound as

---

172. "Goguel," 674.
173. On Renan, see *HNTR* 1:375–84. On Loisy, see pp. 163–72, above.
174. *La notion johannique de l'Esprit et ses antécédents historiques, Étude de théologie biblique* (Paris: Fischbacher, 1902), 145.
175. *L'Eucharistie: des origines à Justin Martyr* (La Roche-sur-Yon: Imprimerie Centrale de l'Ouest, 1910), 214–15.

five), containing some 2,500 pages, that is not complete, since it does not include Hebrews, the Catholic Epistles, or Revelation.[176] No major critical introduction to the NT had been published in French since F. L. Godet's work of 1893–98[177] and the work of the Catholic scholar E. Jacquier (first edition, 1903–8). Goguel's general ordering of the material is canonical: volume 1 deals with the Synoptic Gospels, volume 2 with the Fourth Gospel, volume 3 with Acts, and volume 4 (bound as two volumes) with the Pauline Epistles.

Volume 1 on the Synoptics presents a history of the Synoptic Problem, terminating in the triumph of the two-document hypothesis. Goguel concludes, "the establishment of the priority of Mark is one of the most certain results of criticism."[178] Goguel devotes considerable attention to the agreements of Matthew and Luke against Mark, but concludes that these do not constitute a serious impediment to Marcan priority. Turning to the Logia (or Q), Goguel argues that this source, a collection of teachings, was used independently (in different editions) by the authors of Matthew and Luke. Goguel believes the Logia was written before 70, probably in Palestine. Taking up the Synoptics individually, Goguel develops ideas he had published in an earlier work on the second Gospel.[179] In regard to the integrity of Mark, Goguel contends that the original ending had been cut off because it recounted resurrection appearances not in harmony with the Jerusalem tradition. Goguel believes Mark was composed in Rome after 70 by a Palestinian who made use of the Logia and the reminiscences of the preaching of Peter; it was modified by an editor some dozen years later. In regard to Matthew, Goguel believes the author used three sources: Mark, the Logia, and a variety of other sources. Goguel rejects the tradition of Matthew as author, and concludes that the Gospel was written between 80 and 90. As to Luke, Goguel believes the author (who was not Luke) used Mark, the Logia, and a variety of distinctive Lucan sources.

Goguel devotes more than five hundred pages (volume 2) to the critical introduction to the Fourth Gospel. He reviews the history of the Johannine problem, and investigates the tradition about John, concluding (in agreement with Lietzmann) that John the apostle suffered an early martyrdom. Goguel thinks the author knew and assumed that his readers knew the Synoptic tradition, and also that the author made use of other traditions, some ancient and reliable. Goguel gives considerable attention to the identifica-

---

176. *Introduction au Nouveau Testament,* 4 vols., Bibliothèque historique des religions (Paris: Ernest Leroux, 1923–26).
177. See *HNTR* 1:372.
178. *Introduction* 1:74.
179. *L'Évangile de Mark et ses rapports avec ceux de Matthieu et de Luc: essai d'une introduction critique à l'étude du second évangile,* BEHE, Sciences Religieuses (Paris: Ernest Leroux, 1909).

tion of the "beloved disciple." In his view, a later editor who wrote and added chapter 21 to the Gospel, also added references to this figure, identifying him with John, in order to claim apostolic authorship for the Gospel. Goguel concludes that John the son of Zebedee is not the author, though John the Elder may have participated in the editing. Goguel proposes a date between 90 and 110, and believes the original composition may have been in Syria, the later editing in Asia Minor.

In regard to Acts (volume 3), Goguel gives extensive attention to the text, and concludes that the Western text is secondary. Goguel argues that the author did not know the letters of Paul, and did not use Josephus as a source. He believes the composition involved a complex process: an original work written by Luke was used by the writer of the "book to Theophilus," which was later edited by an interpolator who mutilated the prologue and added the account of the ascension. The date of the original, according to Goguel, was around 80–90. Although he thinks Acts contains legendary material, Goguel believes the author uses sources of historical value.

Goguel has a special interest in Paul, and devotes two parts of volume 4 (bound as two separate volumes) to the apostle. For investigating Paul, Goguel identifies three main sources: the Pauline Epistles, Acts, and the apocryphal Acts of Paul. In the Epistles, Paul "does not appear as a stained glass saint, but as a person of flesh and bone and of emotions of singular intensity, and it is this personality that they revive for us. Where ancient theology believed to find paragraphs of a doctrinal treatise, there is actually a living human being."[180] In regard to the apocryphal Acts, Goguel acknowledges that they offer little historical information, although their failure to mention a second imprisonment of Paul is, according to Goguel, a significant argument from silence. Goguel believes Paul persecuted Christians because they identified the crucified Jesus as Messiah. Goguel is skeptical of interpreting the conversion of Paul on the analogy of the religious experience of Luther. Goguel accepts 2 Thessalonians as authentic, though he believes it to have been addressed to Berea. According to Goguel, neither 1 nor 2 Corinthians is a unity, and the Corinthian correspondence includes parts of six letters. In regard to the situation at Corinth, Goguel finds only three factions in the church; the phrase "I belong to Christ" he takes as a textual gloss or interpolation. Goguel believes Galatians was written to the churches of north Galatia. In regard to Romans, Goguel concludes that the original letter consisted of 1:1—16:23. As to the death of Paul, Goguel says the details are shrouded in mystery; Paul may have been sentenced to slavery in the mines. Goguel believes Philippians was written from an Ephesian imprisonment, Colossians and Philemon from Caesarea.

180. *Introduction* 4:62.

Taken as a whole, Goguel's *Introduction* represents an enormous accomplishment; the work is exhaustive and exhausting. No issue of critical introduction is ignored. Goguel displays mastery of all the critical skills and a mountain of material. Although some of his judgments are idiosyncratic, he usually resists the temptation to draw conclusions unwarranted by the data. The result is a French introduction, fully cognizant of and totally undaunted by the scholarship on the other side of the Rhine—an introduction that largely supports the growing critical consensus: the two-document hypothesis, the unauthenticity of the Fourth Gospel, the unevenness of evidence in Acts, and the post-Pauline origin of Ephesians and the Pastoral Epistles.

History of Early Christianity

Goguel, who seldom sinned on the side of brevity, presents his history of early Christianity in a trilogy under the general title *Jésus et les origines du Christianisme*. The first volume of *The Life of Jesus* was originally published in 1932.[181] A few years earlier Goguel had written a book in defense of the historicity of Jesus.[182] Goguel, like other historical critics, had been alarmed by the claim of popular writers that Jesus was merely a myth.[183] These skeptics had taken the plowshares of NT criticism and beat them into swords to attack the historical basis of the Christian faith. In France, the attack had been led by P. L. Couchoud, the personal physician of the anticlerical novelist Anatole France.[184] According to Couchoud, Jesus was not a historical but a spiritual reality, the product of collective mystical experience. Goguel reviews the evidence from non-Christian and then from Christian sources, and concludes, "The historical reality of the personality of Jesus alone enables us to understand the birth and development of Christianity, which otherwise would remain an enigma, and in the proper sense of the word, a miracle."[185]

In *Life of Jesus*, Goguel assumes that Mark's account provides a reliable outline of the main features of Jesus' ministry. In investigating the tradition recorded in the Gospels, Goguel considers criteria for determining authenticity. For example, he says, "every time we find, attributed to Jesus or recommended by him, an attitude which is contrary to that which is current in the very earliest form of the Church, there is room to suppose that we are

---

181. *La vie de Jésus* (Paris: Payot, 1932); Eng. trans.: *The Life of Jesus,* trans. Olive Wyon (New York: Macmillan, 1933); repr., *Jesus and the Origins of Christianity,* 2 vols., HTCL (New York: Harper & Brothers, 1960).
182. *Jésus de Nazareth: mythe ou histoire?* (Paris: Payot, 1925); Eng. trans.: *Jesus the Nazarene: Myth or History?* trans. Frederick Stevens (New York: D. Appleton, 1926).
183. See pp. 252 (n. 116), 321 (n. 111), above.
184. Couchoud's book, *Le Mystère de Jésus*, appeared in 1924.
185. *Jesus the Nazarene*, 316.

in the presence of an historical fact."[186] However, Goguel cautions against using this criterion negatively: "we have no right to affirm that every word or saying of Jesus which is in harmony with the conceptions of the Christianity of the Apostolic age is not authentic." Indeed, the "criterion of dissimilarity" is to be qualified by the use of what came to be known as "the criterion of coherence." "The sayings of Jesus whose authenticity can be established can, in their turn, serve as a touchstone for estimating the authenticity of other sayings, which are either in connexion with, or in complete harmony with them."[187]

On the basis of his study of the tradition, Goguel, with astounding confidence, tries to reconstruct a chronology: Jesus is with John the Baptist at the end of 26 C.E. and the beginning of 27; in the spring of 27, he returns to Galilee and begins his ministry; in September of 27, he leaves Galilee and goes to Jerusalem; in December of 27, he leaves Jerusalem and retreats to a solitary place (Perea); at the Passover of 28 he returns to Jerusalem and meets his death. In regard to the early Galilean ministry, Goguel says:

> Returning from the Jordan with the certainty that he had received from God the mission to announce to the Jews that God willed, by a free gift of His love, to open to repentant men the gates of the coming Kingdom, Jesus went forth to proclaim this Kingdom whose members would obey God wholly, and would realize the divine perfection in their own lives. He did not pose either as an enemy or as a reformer of the ancient tradition, but his wholly spiritual conception of the Kingdom, the way in which he conceived the nature of obedience towards God, led him to adopt a free and progressive attitude towards the tradition and the Law, an attitude which roused the Pharisees against him.[188]

In the latter part of the Galilean ministry, Jesus reacts to the crisis created by what Goguel construes as Herod's decision to execute Jesus. Goguel sees in the feeding of the multitude a turning point: Jesus understood his action as anticipating the messianic banquet; the people misunderstand his messiahship as political. At Caesarea Philippi, Jesus, according to Goguel, becomes increasingly concerned to instruct the disciples about his messianic role—a role that requires suffering. "Through the idea that his sufferings were necessary for the coming of the Kingdom of God, Jesus was led beyond the sense of a simple prophetic vocation and to regard himself, no longer simply as the herald of the Kingdom of God, but as the one who was

---

186. *Life of Jesus*, 206. In the reprint edition, this and the following references are found in vol. 1, *Prolegomena to the Life of Jesus*.
187. Ibid., 207–8.
188. Ibid., 358. In the reprint edition, this and the following references are found in vol. 2, *The Life of Jesus*.

to realize it himself, who, after having been humiliated and rejected, would appear as the glorious Son of Man."[189]

As Goguel's chronology indicates, Jesus had a longer ministry in Jerusalem than the Synoptics indicate. Goguel believes the passion narrative rests on early, independent tradition, and that it was the first part of the tradition to be written down. In the extant records, Goguel detects a mixture of fact and fiction: the betrayal of Judas is historical, while the denial of Peter is not; the cry of dereliction is historical, while the penitent thief is not. About Gethsemane, Goguel asserts, "Although this incident cannot be regarded as literally accurate, on a higher plane, it is true. In an admirable allegory it expresses what took place in the soul of Jesus."[190] Thus, Goguel sees Jesus as presenting a new understanding of God, grounded in his own religious experience. Written in a time of skepticism, Goguel's book is, in spite of some significant methodological and critical observations, largely an exercise in historical overconfidence.[191]

The second volume of Goguel's trilogy, *La naissance du christianisme*, reviews the history of the early church after the death of Jesus.[192] At the outset, Goguel affirms a strict historical approach. "When we come to the history of religions or of one particular religion, we must not abandon the rigorous standard of historical criticism in order to square the result of research with the postulate of this or that theology; . . . The business of the historian is only to establish the facts and set them out in order by their mutual connection."[193] Goguel believes the history of the church begins with the rise of the resurrection faith. In discussing the resurrection, Goguel presents the results of his earlier, larger work, on the *Faith in the Resurrection of Jesus*—one of Goguel's most impressive books.[194] In this earlier book, Goguel begins by analyzing the accounts of the resurrection found in the NT texts. In these texts, Goguel traces an evolving tradition that began with belief in the exaltation of Christ as Messiah and ended with the idea of the resurrection as proof of Christianity. In analyzing the tradition, Goguel begins with the idea of the empty tomb. He believes this idea originated from the belief that Jesus had been exalted to heaven—a belief that led to the assumption that the tomb must have been empty. Then, according to Goguel, the "fact" of the empty tomb was confirmed by the appearance of

---

189. Ibid., 392.
190. Ibid., 495.
191. See C. Leslie Mitton, "Important and Influential Foreign Books: Goguel's 'Life of Jesus,'" *ExpTim* 65 (1953–54): 259–63.
192. (Paris: Payot, 1946); Eng. trans.: *The Birth of Christianity*, trans. H. C. Snape (New York: Macmillan, 1954).
193. *Birth of Christianity*, 10–11.
194. *La foi à la résurrection de Jésus dans le christianisme primitif: étude d'histoire et de psychologie religieuses*, BEHE, Sciences religieuses 47 (Paris: Ernest Leroux, 1933).

angels at the tomb, and finally, resurrection appearances of Jesus were linked to the empty tomb. In investigating the tradition of the empty tomb, Goguel asks why the early tradition contained no description of Jesus' actual departure from the tomb. He answers: the original understanding of the resurrection did not involve a material exit from the tomb, but a spiritual exaltation.

> In good time, by an evolution . . . the idea of the transferal to heaven was replaced by that of the reanimation of the body of Jesus; the idea of the celestial life of Christ remaining, however, from the religious and theological point of view, the essential element of the resurrection faith. The discovery of the empty tomb became, then, a kind of preface to the appearances, which were considered veritable proof of the resurrection.[195]

Thus, for Goguel, in contrast to a host of scholars, the tradition of the empty tomb was earlier than the tradition of the resurrection appearances.

Turning to the appearances, Goguel reviews the major texts in Paul and the Gospels. In regard to the location of appearances, Goguel contends that the Galilean tradition is older. He thinks the idea of the ascension developed when belief in the immediate transfer to heaven was replaced by earthly appearances that occurred for a limited interval between the death and exaltation of Jesus. Of special interest is Goguel's psychological analysis of the appearances. He thinks there were two types of Christophany: (1) to a person who had come to believe that Jesus was alive in heaven, but had not yet come to the belief in appearances on earth prior to the parousia, for instance, Peter; (2) to a person who had not been a personal follower of Jesus, but had learned of appearances to persons like Peter, for instance, Paul. According to Goguel, the first resurrection appearances were to those who had known Jesus; their belief in the resurrection was based on their personal relation to him. The appearance to Peter, Goguel thinks, "created an epidemic of Christophanies."[196] For Paul, conversion was the result of faith working subliminally in his conscience; he knew of the appearances to Peter and others—a knowledge that burst into transforming vision whereby Jesus appeared as Messiah.

After the discussion of the resurrection faith, Goguel's *Birth of Christianity* investigates the failure of Christianity to develop within the framework of Judaism. Goguel recounts the history of the church in Jerusalem, noting the change of leadership from Peter to James whereby the church became increasingly anti-Pauline. Turning to the development of Christianity within the framework of Hellenism, Goguel traces the rise of the Hellenists (Greek-speaking Jewish Christians) in Jerusalem and their mission that

---

195. Ibid., 224.
196. Ibid., 430.

founded the church in Antioch. In recounting the Jerusalem conference, Goguel notes the increasing conflict between Jewish and Gentile Christianity, evident in the later confrontation of Peter and Paul at Antioch. After 70, the Gentile church separated from Judaism, and the universalism of Paul triumphed. Goguel describes the development of religious thought seen in the later documents of the NT. For example, he sees in the Fourth Gospel a theology radically different from the thought of the Apocalypse. "The Johannine Apocalypse and the Fourth Gospel are the terminals of two processes of development which are so different from each other that one is tempted to say that they conflict with each other, one of them affirming that salvation will be realised in a realm beyond by the destruction of the sinful world, the other insisting on a new kind of life which is present here and now."[197]

The third and final book of Goguel's trilogy, *L'Église primitive*, surveys the doctrine, organization, worship, and ethics of the early church.[198] In the introduction, Goguel expresses his dissatisfaction with the Catholic view, whereby Christianity was perceived as the continuation of the church founded on Peter, and with the Protestant view whereby a radical break was perceived at the end of the apostolic age, and the subsequent history (prior to the sixteenth century) was seen in decline. In regard to doctrine, Goguel describes the faith of the Jerusalem Christians: "It is a society which is provisionally deprived of its leader and awaits his return."[199] With Paul, the church was viewed as the body of Christ—a community of believers in whom the spirit of Christ was present. In post-Pauline Christianity, Goguel detects an increasing preoccupation with apostolic tradition and sound doctrine.

In regard to the organization of the early church, Goguel traces the evolution from charismatic leadership to the monarchical episcopate. He reviews the development of the idea of Roman primacy, and discusses at length the use of the words "you are Peter" (Matt. 16:18) in support of the authority of the bishop of Rome. Goguel investigates the literary and archeological evidence concerning Peter's ostensible sojourn in Rome, and concludes, "it may be that Peter never came to Rome or, if he came, he only played an obscure part there."[200] In regard to worship, Goguel notes the influence of Jewish practice on the Jerusalem church. For the Jerusalem Christians, baptism was a simple rite of initiation, but with Paul, according to Goguel, it became a sacrament. Turning to ethics, Goguel notes Jesus'

---

197. *Birth of Christianity*, 280.
198. (Paris: Payot, 1947); Eng. trans.: *The Primitive Church*, trans. H. C. Snape (New York: Macmillan, 1964).
199. *Primitive Church*, 50.
200. Ibid., 223.

stress on obedience to God. Paul, according to Goguel, construes ethics in terms of an indicative and imperative, and John advocates an ethic moved by the Spirit. Goguel believes that toward the end of the century a legalism emerged in which morality was seen as the condition of salvation, rather than its result. In conclusion, Goguel writes:

> Jesus did not foresee the Church; he did not found it. But from his actions it took its rise. Its origin lay with his personality, which acted through the intermediary of those convictions and feelings which he created. The Church was created out of the trust and hopes; in other words, the faith with which his words and actions, and still more his being and character, inspired those who were grouped round him.[201]

The reader who has waded through the many pages of Goguel's history cannot help but be impressed by its comprehensive review of the life of the church from its beginning to mid-second century. Compared with Lietzmann, Goguel's work is more detailed, less readable, and even tedious. Like Lietzmann, Goguel affirms the importance of Jesus, the preference to consider worship and ethics rather than dogma and ecclesiasticism. Although the two historians use the same methods and materials, they arrive at different results.

Walter Bauer as Historian and Exegete

That there are various ways of interpreting early Christianity is demonstrated by Walter Bauer. Bauer's life and work as a lexicographer was reviewed earlier.[202] His work as a historian is equally important.[203] Bauer was particularly fascinated by postapostolic Christianity, and worked extensively in noncanonical sources. Research in this area had been facilitated by the efforts of Edgar Hennecke, a student of Harnack who spent forty years as a pastor, but devoted himself to the study of the NT Apocrypha.[204] In 1904, Hennecke published, in collaboration with a few other scholars, *Neutestamentliche Apokryphen in deutscher Übersetzung und mit Einleitungen*—a collection of early Christian apocryphal documents in German translation with critical introductions.[205] Later, again with the collaboration of other scholars, Hennecke published a companion volume, *Handbuch zu neutestamentlichen Apokryphen*—a work that expanded the introductions and notes. In 1959, an English translation of Hennecke's *New Testament Apocrypha*,

---

201. Ibid., 577.
202. See pp. 415–17, above.
203. See Wilhelm Schneemelcher, "Walter Bauer als Kirchenhistoriker," *NTS* 9 (1962–3): 11–22.
204. See W. Schneemelcher, "Edgar Hennecke in memoriam," *TLZ* 76 (1951): 567.
205. (Tübingen: J. C. B. Mohr [Paul Siebeck], 1904).

based on the third edition by Wilhelm Schneemelcher, was published.²⁰⁶ A second English edition, based on the sixth edition of Hennecke-Schneemelcher, appeared in 1991.²⁰⁷ Prior to 1959, the English reader had relied on *The Apocryphal New Testament*, edited by Montague Rhodes James—a work with meager introductions, lacking documents discovered since its publication in 1924.²⁰⁸

Bauer's major book on *Orthodoxy and Heresy* was anticipated by two earlier works. In 1903, he published a study on the *Apostolos*, that is, the canon of the Epistles, used in Syria from the middle of the fourth to the middle of the fifth century.²⁰⁹ In 1909, Bauer published a fascinating book on the life of Jesus in the age of the NT apocrypha.²¹⁰ The book is an investigation of descriptions of Jesus found in documents from the early second century to the time of Origen. In regard to the birth of Jesus, Bauer finds texts that speculate about such matters as the length of the pregnancy and happenings inside Mary's womb. In regard to the ministry of Jesus, Bauer discovers that the apocryphal documents tend to add details, for example, the identification of the mount of transfiguration as Tabor. He notes that some sources increase attendance at the Last Supper so as to include James and some women. Some later sources, Bauer points out, present descriptions of the actual event of the resurrection; some increase the number of witnesses, and extend the period of appearances to as long as twelve years. From his analysis of the data, Bauer deduces the factors that he believes shaped the developing tradition: the concern to preserve the tradition by correcting and harmonizing, the desire to interpret more fully the life of Jesus by adding details and identifying people and places, the effort to meet the ongoing needs of the churches by enhancing Jesus' role as leader and fulfillment of divine prophecy.

Bauer's *Orthodoxy and Heresy* first appeared in 1934.²¹¹ Bauer believes earlier historians viewed the data from the perspective of orthodoxy, assuming a line of continuity from Jesus through the early Christians to the orthodoxy of the ancient church. From this perspective, heresy was seen as an invasion from outside or a falling away from earlier truth. Bauer challenges

---

206. Eng. trans. ed. R. McL. Wilson, 2 vols. (Philadelphia: Westminster, 1963, 1965).

207. Eng. trans. and ed. R. McL. Wilson, 2 vols. (Louisville: Westminster/John Knox, 1991, 1992).

208. Montague Rhodes James, *The Apocryphal New Testament, Being the Apocryphal Gospels, Acts, Epistles and Apocalypses* (Oxford: Clarendon, 1924).

209. *Der Apostolos der Syrer in der Zeit von der Mitte des vierten Jahrhunderts bis zur Spaltung der Syrischen Kirche* (Giessen: J. Ricker [Alfred Töpelmann], 1903).

210. *Das Leben Jesu: Im Zeitalter der neutestamentlichen Apokryphen* (Darmstadt: Wissenschaftliche Buchgesellschaft, 1967).

211. *Rechtgläubigkeit und Ketzerei im ältesten Christentum*, 2 ed. Georg Strecker (Tübingen: J. C. B. Mohr [Paul Siebeck], 1964); Eng. trans.: *Orthodoxy and Heresy in Earliest Christianity*, ed. Robert A. Kraft and Gerhard Krodel (Philadelphia: Fortress, 1971); except for minor corrections, the second German edition preserves Bauer's text; the English translation revises the footnotes.

this established view by an investigation of Christianity in various geographical areas. In Edessa he finds variety, including followers of Bardesanes and Marcion. "And the investigation of these beginnings for the history of Christianity in Edessa," says Bauer, "has made us aware of a foundation that rests on an unmistakably heretical basis. In relation to it, orthodoxy comes to prevail only very gradually." In Egypt, Bauer notes the early presence of gnostic Christians. He identifies Demetrius of Alexandria (189–231) as the first true representative of orthodox Christianity—a bishop who banished Origen, but did not reject Clement, who was actually closer to Gnosticism.

> Thus even into the third century, no separation between orthodoxy and heresy was accomplished in Egypt and the two types of Christianity were not yet at all clearly differentiated from each other. Moreover, until late in the second century, Christianity in this area is decidedly unorthodox.[212]

Turning to Asia Minor, Bauer recalls the conflict within the church at Antioch in the time of Peter and Paul. He also notes the attack on heresy recorded in the letters of the Apocalypse and the Pastoral Epistles. In regard to Rome, Bauer sees in 1 Clement the attempt to assert the authority of Rome over Corinth. He also traces the increasing efforts of Rome to claim apostolic authority.

Bauer follows his geographical survey with an analysis of the factors involved in the conflict between orthodoxy and heresy. For example, in the case of Montanism, Bauer notes how the orthodox argued on the basis of the OT and apostolic authority. The OT, however, was rejected by the Gnostics, who claimed the support of early Christian literature, notably the Gospel of John. According to Bauer, Marcion was successful because the ground had already been prepared by the earlier, wide extent of heresy. Marcion's appropriation of Paul rendered Paul's authority problematic, for some, even heretical. In Bauer's view, the Pastoral Epistles were written in Rome to accommodate Paul to orthodoxy, and to refute Marcion. "The price the Apostle to the Gentiles had to pay to be allowed to remain in the church was the complete surrender of his personality and historical particularity."[213] In brief, Bauer believes heresy preceded orthodoxy; the development of orthodoxy was relatively late.

Reaction to Bauer has been mixed.[214] On the one hand, his work has been praised. Martin Dibelius, for example, recognizes in the book "the two talents

---

212. *Orthodoxy and Heresy*, 43, 59.
213. Ibid., 227.
214. See ibid., Appendix 2, "The Reception of the Book," by Georg Strecker, revised and augmented by Robert A. Kraft, 286–316; H. E. W. Turner, *The Pattern of Christian Truth: A Study in the Relations between Orthodoxy and Heresy in the Early Church* (London: Mowbray, 1954), 39–80; Thomas A. Robinson, *The Bauer Thesis Examined: The Geography of Heresy in the Early Church* (Lewiston: Edwin Mellen, 1988); Michel Desjardins, "Bauer and Beyond: On Recent Scholarly Discussions of Αἵρεσις in the Early Christian Era, *Second Century* 8 (1991): 65–82; Hans Dieter Betz, "Orthodoxy and Heresy in Primitive Christianity," *Int* 19 (1965): 299–311.

that have made German scholarship the pillar of German respectability: the meticulous investigation of the most minute aspects, and boldness of construction in larger matters."[215] On the other hand, Bauer has been sharply criticized. He is accused, for example, of arguing from silence, of overstatement, of forcing the material into the mold of his own hypothesis; some contest the details of his analysis. On one point there is wide agreement: the use of the terms *orthodoxy* and *heresy* is misleading; these terms are meaningful only from a later perspective, and they are ill chosen since they imply value judgments. What Bauer appears to have demonstrated is that there was considerable variety in early Christianity. With later developments of creed, canon, and episcopacy, the limits of variety were restricted.

As well as being a lexicographer and a historian, Bauer was also a commentator, the author of the commentary on *John* in the Lietzmann series.[216] In his preliminary remark, Bauer insists that the Fourth Gospel can only be understood in its setting within the religions of its time. Most important, according to Bauer, is gnostic syncretism—a pre-Christian religion that is illuminated by the study of the Mandaean and Manichaean literature. As typical of the series, the commentary includes no critical introduction, but a section at the end of the commentary deals with matters of higher criticism. In regard to author, place, and date, Bauer rejects the tradition. He thinks John the apostle died an early martyrdom, and that the Gospel was not written by an eyewitness or a Palestinian. The place of writing, he thinks, was probably Syria, the date, 100–125. According to Bauer, the author intended to oppose Gnosticism, even though he had himself been influenced by gnostic ideas. Bauer thinks the author knew the tradition about Jesus, including the Synoptics and some apocryphal gospels. His purpose, according to Bauer, was to replace other gospels with his own—the true Gospel. In spite of various disruptions and displacements, Bauer believes the Fourth Gospel represents a unified literary composition.

Bauer begins the commentary with an excursus on the ΛΟΓΟΣ. He notes that the author introduces the term without explanation, assuming that his readers understand it. The background, according to Bauer, is not be to found in the HB, but in Hellenistic Jewish sources that view Wisdom as an intermediary between God and the world. Bauer believes the term *Logos* is appropriate for identifying this intermediary with a historical man. The immediate background is to be found in Philo, and the author was also influenced, according to Bauer, by the image of the heavenly redeemer of Hellenistic syncretism, reflected in the Hermetic literature, Iranian religion, and the beliefs of the Mandaeans.

---

215. Quoted by Strecker, "Reception of the Book," 290.
216. *Das Johannesevangelium*, 3d ed., HNT 6 (Tübingen: J. C. B. Mohr [Paul Siebeck], 1933). See Erich Fascher, "Walter Bauer als Kommentator," *NTS* 9 (1962–63): 23–38.

In commenting on the wedding at Cana, for example, Bauer notes that three days after the prophecy that the disciples would see heaven opened (1:51), this story discloses the power and glory of Jesus. In regard to v. 2:4, Bauer cites parallels in OT, NT, and Hellenistic sources to indicate that the phrase τί ἐμοὶ καὶ σοί is Hebraic and means "leave me alone," or "don't bother me." According to Bauer, with references to classical and Hellenistic usage, the term γύναι is not an address of disrespect, but when used by a son, adds to the sharpness of the rejection of the mother's request. The cryptic mention of "my hour" refers to the glory that will be revealed through the miracle; the expression is frequent in the Fourth Gospel with reference to Jesus' death, which, according to Bauer, is inseparable from the idea of his glorification. Bauer thinks the excessive amount of wine (between 472.74 and 703.11 liters, by his calculation) is designed to demonstrate the magnitude of the miracle. As to the meaning of the account, Bauer believes the story is a multivalent sign, similar to the wine miracle that accompanied the epiphany of Dionysus—a sign that anticipates, among other things, the abundance of the messianic meal. In sum, Bauer is a skillful exegete who maintains the tradition of the history of religion school.

MASTERY OF HISTORICAL EXEGESIS:
HANS WINDISCH AND ERNST LOHMEYER

In the era prior to World War II, historical-critical study of the NT reached its zenith. New discoveries would be made and methods would be refined, but the basic grammatico-historical method of the Enlightenment, with its empiricism and rationalism, its long tradition of tireless scrutiny of the sources, its increasing consensus of critical results, was practiced with an unsurpassed devotion and competence. Germany, where the movement had most vigorously flourished, presents two very different, notable examples: Hans Windisch and Ernst Lohmeyer.

Hans Windisch (1881–1935)

Hans Windisch was born in Leipzig, where he became an instructor at the university in 1908.[217] From 1914 to 1929, he was professor of NT at Leiden in neutral Netherlands, where he was able to pursue his research, removed

---

217. For summaries of Windisch's life and work, see Erik Beijer, "Hans Windisch und seine Bedeutung für die neutestamentliche Wissenschaft," *ZNW* 48 (1957): 22–49; John Reumann, "Introduction," in Hans Windisch, *The Spirit-Paraclete in the Fourth Gospel*, trans. James W. Cox, Facet Books: Biblical Series 20 (Philadelphia: Fortress, 1968), iii–xiv; Marinus de Jonge, "Hans Windisch als Neutestamentler an der Universität Leiden (1914–1929)," in *Texte und Geschichte: Facetten theologischen Arbeitens aus dem Freundes- und Schülerkreis Dieter Lührman zum 60. Geburtstag*, ed. Stefan Maser and Egbert Schlarb, Marburger Theologische Studien 50 (Marburg: N. G. Elwert, 1999), 47–65.

from the ravages of World War I. In 1929, Windisch was called to the faculty at Kiel. He remained there until 1935, when he moved to Halle as successor of Ernst von Dobschütz. In the midst of a discussion with Erich Klostermann, Windisch died suddenly at age fifty-four.

Early Works

Windisch's commitment to historical-critical exegesis in the service of theology is seen in his book *Baptism and Sin in Primitive Christianity up to Origen*.[218] In this book, Windisch is concerned with a vexatious problem: Christians who have been freed from sin in baptism continue to sin. After an investigation of the idea of freedom from sin in the HB and Judaism, Windisch argues that Jesus revived the prophetic ideal: a call for repentance and life without sin. Although Paul acknowledged that Christians sinned after baptism, he believes, according to Windisch, that sinlessness could be achieved. Windisch discusses the issue in relation to the other literature of the NT, the Apostolic Fathers, the apologists, and patristic authors. For his own part, Windisch believes that Christians, inspired by the forgiving spirit of Jesus, can be transformed and moved toward sinless living.

The importance of Jesus for Christian life and ethics is seen in Windisch's early work *The Messianic War and Early Christianity*. This work reacts to a book by Karl Kautsky on the origin of Christianity that offered a Marxist interpretation and viewed Jesus as the leader of a revolutionary movement. In typical history of religion fashion, Windisch begins with a review of the messianic idea in Jewish history and eschatology. Turning to Jesus, Windisch acknowledges that Jesus claimed to be Messiah, but contends that he did not understand messiahship in a political or military sense. Windisch accepts John's account of the words of Jesus, "My kingdom is not from this world" (18:36). "The whole appearance and the whole history of Jesus," says Windisch, "is therefore a *protest against revolutionary messianism*." For Windisch, the significance of Jesus is seen in his meaning for religion and ethics. "He came in order to make known the ethical-religious claims of God to humans in full purity and clarity."[219]

Windisch's competence in higher criticism is demonstrated by his book *John and the Synoptics*. As the subtitle indicates, Windisch is concerned with the question, "Did the Fourth Evangelist intend to supplement or replace the earlier Gospels?" He opts for the latter, that is, that the author of John intended to write an autonomous, absolute Gospel, replacing all the others. Before developing his argument, Windisch discloses his critical presupposi-

---

218. *Taufe und Sünde im ältesten Christentum bis auf Origenes: Ein Beitrag zur altchristlichen Dogmengeschichte* (Tübingen: J. C. B. Mohr [Paul Siebeck], 1908).
219. *Der messianische Krieg und das Urchristentum* (Tübingen: J. C. B. Mohr [Paul Siebeck], 1909), 42, 95.

tions: the Fourth Gospel was written around 100; it contains Palestinian tradition; the author was not an eyewitness. Windisch argues that the author knew the Gospel of Mark and probably also Matthew and Luke. The bulk of Windisch's book is dedicated to demolishing the age-old theory that the Fourth Gospel was written to supplement the earlier Gospels. Windisch attempts to refute this theory by investigating the composition as a whole and the relevant texts individually. He concludes, "The Fourth Gospel is no collection of supplements; it intends neither to supplement older accounts nor to be supplemented by them, but to give a description of the story of Jesus that is understandable in itself, self-contained, complete, and that replaces all the previous older documents."[220] In a fascinating chapter, Windisch attempts a psychological explanation for the author's self-understanding. Windisch believes the author adopts prophetic speech, that is, he speaks prophetically out of his own religious experience; by possession of the gift of the Spirit, he believes he is in contact with Christ, so that his words become an actual representation of the deeds and words of Jesus.

Major Works

In 1928, Windisch published his important book *The Meaning of the Sermon on the Mount*.[221] He understands this work as a case study in exegetical method—a method that adheres strictly to a historical, as distinguished from a theological, exegesis.

> I acknowledge without reserve the validity of theological exegesis, and, above all, of Biblical theology, as a supplement to the historical study of the religion of primitive Christianity. I protest only against a fusion, or a too intimate association, of the two disciplines. We must learn to distinguish in principle between historical and theological exegesis, and the point at which historical exegesis stops and "interpretation," that is, theological exegesis, begins, must in each case be made plain.

Windisch believes the Sermon on the Mount offers a pertinent example, since theological exegesis has tended to idealize or Paulinize it. At the outset, Windisch acknowledges that the Sermon is conditioned by eschatological expectation, but points out that it also includes teaching from the wisdom tradition. "Actually the Sermon does embody groups of sayings and individual logia that are exclusively oriented to the crisis, but it also

---

220. *Johannes und die Synoptiker: Wollte der vierte Evangelist die älteren Evangelien ergänzen oder ersetzen?* UNT 12 (Leipzig: J. C. Hinrichs, 1926), 87.

221. *Der Sinn der Bergpredigt: Ein Beitrag zum geschichtlichen Verständnis der Evangelien und zum Problem der richtigen Exegese*, 2d ed., UNT 16 (Leipzig: J. C. Hinrichs, 1937); Eng. trans.: *The Meaning of the Sermon on the Mount: A Contribution to the Historical Understanding of the Gospels and to the Problem of Their True Exegesis*, trans. S. MacLean Gilmour (Philadelphia: Westminster, 1950). The second edition by Martin Dibelius incorporates corrections and minor revisions that Windisch had left at his death.

subordinates to this dominant sanction a rich fund of traditional matter in which the eschatological situation either is not involved or is present only as a secondary factor."[222]

Windisch critiques the work of modern interpreters who assume the teachings of Jesus must somehow be made to support theological notions of their day. According to these interpreters, "Jesus cannot have taught something that is no longer understood or accepted in Heidelberg or Marburg." Windisch particularly opposes theological interpreters who suppose the Sermon intentionally presents impossible demands, designed to throw the hearers into despair, so that they must await salvation by grace. In contrast, Windisch insists that Jesus gave commands and expected them to be obeyed. "Since the demands are obvious deductions from the very essence of religious wisdom, every pious man must and can recognize and fulfill them. The idea of impracticability appears absolutely senseless within the framework of a correct understanding of the Sermon on the Mount." Windisch continues, "The Sermon on the Mount is an ethic of obedience that is based on two cardinal propositions, that God now proclaims his will by means of Jesus, and that the devout and pious man must now obey it."[223]

Windisch, with sensitivity all too rare among NT scholars, investigates the attitude toward Judaism expressed in the Sermon. He recognizes that Jesus differed from the rabbis: that he was not concerned with ceremonial laws; that he did not emphasize tradition. However, Windisch insists that the Gospel of Matthew has exaggerated the polemic against Judaism. He bewails Matthew's biased representation of "the teaching of the rabbis and Pharisees as a religion of external legalism, of moral and religious superficiality, of immoral passion for revenge and hypocrisy. . . . The capacity to appreciate what is relatively good in Judaism and what is held in common with Judaism has been destroyed, and the greatness and novelty of Jesus' teaching have been exaggerated until they have become absolute." As Windisch observes, "The reader is in danger of carrying away from the Sermon on the Mount, as well as from the denunciatory discourse in Matt., ch. 23, an utter caricature of rabbinism."[224]

Once historical exegesis has been properly performed, Windisch believes theological exegesis to be appropriate. "The task of theological exegesis is to relate the religious and theological content of the Bible, as it has been determined by historical exegesis, to the individual in his immediate situation, and to do this in such a way that it comes home to him as God's message directed to his particular need." According to Windisch's

---

222. *Meaning of the Sermon*, 18, 39.
223. Ibid., 56, 96, 120.
224. Ibid., 143, 150.

theological exegesis, the Sermon presents ethical commands that the readers should obey, but at the same time it presents the mercy and grace of God, and, in its eschatological references, it implies the cross. "The cross atones for all the sins of the faithful, including their many transgressions of Jesus' teaching in the Sermon on the Mount." Thus, Windisch appears to believe that theological exegesis is justified in detecting and applying implications and "principles that are enunciated in the Sermon." As to how theological exegesis discerns these principles and by what theological norms they are evaluated and applied, Windisch is not clear. Apparently, what he opposes is the effort to read particular teachings and modern applications into the texts, and to claim that these are the true teachings of the texts themselves. In this regard, Windisch believes historical exegesis exercises a critical function. "The task of historical exegesis is to abstract itself from its own time, which is always in change and in flux; to reach back into the past, the static and the fixed; to hold up a mirror to every theology, even (and especially) to one that advances 'pneumatic' claims; . . . and to oppose the original structure and original motivation of that tradition to all dogmatizing and modernizing reinterpretations."[225]

Windisch's book *Paul and Christ* shows his unswerving loyalty to the method of the history of religion school.[226] For that school, the interpretation of Jesus as a "divine man" (θεῖος ἀνήρ) was commonplace. However, with Windisch, not only Jesus, but also Paul is depicted according to this model. Windisch begins by reviewing examples from Graeco-Roman antiquity—figures such as Pythagoras and Apollonius of Tyana—who exemplify the characteristics of the divine man. The balance of the book attempts to demonstrate how Paul and Christ, in parallel, have been depicted according to these characteristics. Windisch begins with their vocational experiences. "The baptism of Jesus and the conversion of Paul viewed from a history of religion perspective are two similarly formed visionary experiences that for both indicate the call to a holy office and the preparation for it."[227] Windisch also believes that Paul and Jesus are presented as pneumatics who perform charismatic functions: they are bearers of revelation, mediators between God and the community. According to Windisch, both Paul and Christ are viewed as exhibiting the characteristics of the mystagogue: Paul is a steward of the mysteries of God; and the Johannine Christ utters mystical teachings about himself.

Although Windisch has collected an abundance of history of religion material, and exercised a lively imagination, his book offers the critics an

---

225. Ibid., 154, 187, 192, 195, 213.
226. *Paulus und Christus: Ein biblisch-religionsgeschichtlicher Vergleich,* UNT 24 (Leipzig: J. C. Hinrichs, 1934).
227. Ibid., 134.

easy target.²²⁸ Parallels are found in excess, and Windisch's indiscriminate application of them leaves the impression that almost any hero from Hermes to Harnack could be classified as a divine man. Also, Windisch's treatment of the sources is unclear: Is the historical Paul of the Epistles a divine man, or is the Paul of Acts and the early tradition a divine man—or both? The intrusion of a foreign figure (the divine man)—to some degree the creation of modern scholarship—confuses rather than clarifies the historical understanding of Jesus and Paul.

Commentaries

Windisch contributed to two leading commentary series. For the Meyer series, he wrote the volume on *2 Corinthians*.²²⁹ The first five editions of the commentary on this Epistle were written by H. A. W. Meyer,²³⁰ and editions six through eight by C. F. G. Heinrici (1844–1915). The ninth edition was to have been prepared by Johannes Weiss who had written the Meyer commentary on 1 Corinthians.²³¹ However, Weiss died in 1914, and the assignment was given to Windisch, who had participated in Weiss's seminar at Marburg in 1901–2. Windisch believes the distinctive feature of 2 Corinthians is its expression of the personal relation of Paul to the church, so that "my ultimate goal was to make understandable from the epistle the personality of the writer (as person and as apostolic witness)."²³² In pursuit of this goal, Windisch views Paul in his historical setting, illuminated by material from his Jewish and Hellenistic background. In the introduction, Windisch gives detailed attention to the problem of integrity. He concludes that 2 Corinthians is a composite of two letters: 2 Corinthians 1–9, and 2 Corinthians 10–13, which he believes to have been written two months later. Windisch thinks the opposition to Paul consists of a coalition of the gnostic pneumatics of 1 Corinthians and Jewish wandering preachers who later invaded the church.

Windisch's comments on 2 Cor. 5:1-10 can serve as an example of his exegetical research. In regard to 5:1, he says that the introductory clause "if our earthly tent is destroyed" means "when our death takes place." He notes that "tent" as a metaphor for body is used in Wisdom 9:15—a metaphor frequent in the Greek philosophers, including Pythagoras and Plato, and in

---

228. See Karl Prümm, "Zur Früh- und Spätform der religionsgeschichtlichen Christus Deutung von H. Windisch," *Bib* 42 (1961): 391–422; 43 (1962): 22–56.
229. *Der zweite Korintherbrief*, 9th ed., KEK (1924; repr., Göttingen: Vandenhoeck & Ruprecht, 1970).
230. See *HNTR* 1:365–70.
231. See pp. 226–27, above.
232. *Zweite Korintherbrief*, v.

the Hermetic literature and Philo.[233] According to Windisch, these sources view death not only as the destruction of the old tent, but as moving to a new dwelling. The new house, "the building from God," stands in contrast to the earthly tent—a contrast that Windisch interprets as an expression of Hellenistic dualism. According to Windisch, the phrase ἐν τοῖς οὐρανοῖς goes with οἰκίαν, indicating that the house already exists in the heavens—a dwelling that the believer will enter immediately upon death. Windisch notes that with the term ἐπενδύσασθαι (v. 2) the metaphor is changed: the new condition is symbolized by a new garment, and the homeless person is now depicted as naked. Referring to Rev. 3:18, Windisch believes that Paul assumes, with his contemporaries, that the condition of nakedness makes unity with the Lord impossible; Windisch presents references from Plutarch and Josephus which indicate that naked bodies should not appear before the deity. In regard to v. 4, Windisch argues that the phrase "so that what is mortal may be swallowed up by life" reflects the same transformation described in 1 Cor. 15:52-54. However, in that text, the transformation would take place at the parousia, whereas here, according to Windisch, the transformation will happen at death. In place of any reference to the parousia, this text concludes with God's gift of the Spirit, confirmation of the hope of transformation. According to Windisch, this text excludes any notion of soul-sleeping or an intermediate state. In an excursus, "The Fate of Dying Christians in this Epistle and the Earlier Epistles," Windisch contends that Paul's eschatology in 2 Corinthians 5 has changed from that expressed in 1 Thessalonians 4 and 1 Corinthians 15. The change—the idea that the believer would be united with Christ at death—is the result, according to Windisch, of Paul's experience in Asia, where he reflected on his own impending demise.

To the series *Handbuch zum Neuen Testament* Windisch contributed commentaries on Hebrews, the Catholic Epistles, and the Epistle to Barnabas. Originally written in 1913, the expanded version of the commentary on Hebrews (1931) welcomes the recently available history of religion material: "the Mandaean texts exercise their function to serve as oriental commentaries to the NT. . . . [T]he foundation of the Mandaean religion is an oriental gnosis, which was very early blended together with Jewish, and then with Christianized gnosis." In a brief introduction, Windisch contends that the title "to the Hebrews" was later added on the basis of a superficial reading of the content. Windisch presents other critical observations at the end of the commentary: Hebrews is a lecture or homily, sent as an epistle; the

---

233. Windisch's recognition of the importance of Philo for NT backgrounds is seen in his early work *Die Frömmigkeit Philos und ihre Bedeutung für das Christentum: Eine religionsgeschichtliche Studie* (Leipzig: J. C. Hinrichs, 1909).

author was not Paul; the date was in the 80s; the place of writing was Rome; the church addressed was essentially Gentile. In regard to the theology of the document, Windisch believes the unknown author was an independent thinker who was much influenced by Hellenism and Hellenistic Judaism. "Thus the religion of Hebrews gives absolutely the impression of a mystery religion."[234] Windisch's commentary on the Catholic Epistles displays the same concern with historical interpretation, informed by Jewish and Hellenistic parallels.[235]

In retrospect, Hans Windisch is an accomplished representative of the liberal historical criticism of the nineteenth century. He strives for objective historical reconstruction, free from theological presuppositions. He exploits the method of the history of religion school. Windisch is disturbed by new ventures in theological interpretation, but seems unaware of his own presuppositions: acceptance of the Enlightenment worldview; commitment to an ethical religion, exemplified in the life and teaching of Jesus. In effect, Windisch is a defender of the liberal, historical-critical establishment, yet he performs this role with commendable clarity and originality.

Ernst Lohmeyer (1890–1946)

Ernst Lohmeyer was born in Dorsten, Westphalia, the son of a village pastor.[236] He studied theology, philosophy, and oriental languages in Tübingen, Leipzig, Berlin, and Erlangen. After serving in the army during World War I, Lohmeyer studied with Dibelius at Heidelberg, where he was named instructor. In 1920, he succeeded Bultmann at Breslau, and, after a year, was promoted to full professor. Lohmeyer was opposed to National Socialism and associated with the Confessing Church. Disciplined for his political views, he was removed to the less conspicuous university at Greifswald, where he was named professor in 1936. In 1939, Lohmeyer was called to military duty, and served as an officer in Poland, the Netherlands, Belgium, and Russia. In 1943, because of his age, he was relieved of military duty, and returned to teaching in Greifswald. After the victory of the Russians, on the eve of his inauguration as rector of the university, Lohmeyer was seized, imprisoned, and eventually shot by the Soviets—an outcome kept secret until 1995. Apparently, he was executed because of his resistance to the authoritarian East German Communist control of the university.

---

234. *Der Hebräerbrief,* 2d ed., HNT 14 (Tübingen: J. C. B. Mohr [Paul Siebeck], 1931), Vorwort, 135.

235. *Die katholischen Briefe,* 3d ed., HNT 15 (Tübingen: J. C. B. Mohr [Paul Siebeck], 1951). This commentary first appeared in 1911; it was revised and expanded in the edition of 1930; the third edition of 1951 is a reprint, with notes added by H. Preisker.

236. See Oscar Cullmann, "Ernst Lohmeyer (1890–1946)," in *Oscar Cullmann,* 663–66; Wolfgang Otto, ed., *Freiheit in der Gebundenheit: Zur Erinnerung an den Theologen Ernst Lohmeyer anlässlich seines 100. Geburtstages* (Göttingen: Vandenhoeck & Ruprecht, 1990); James R. Edwards, "Ernst Lohmeyer—ein Schlusskapitel," *EvT* 56 (1996).

In contrast to Windisch, Lohmeyer recognized that philosophical presuppositions are unavoidable. His own theology was grounded in German idealism, and he was influenced by his friend and Breslau colleague, Richard Hönigswald, a neo-Kantian.[237] Basic to Lohmeyer's understanding of early Christianity is a philosophy of history reminiscent of Hegel: history is the dialectical unfolding of the Absolute. According to this view, there is a dialectic of revelation and its concrete expression in history—a dialectic that is resolved in eschatology. Lohmeyer is dedicated to the study of the historical manifestation, and captivated by a faith that finds meaning beyond history. He believes the theology of Paul, for example, must be investigated in its distinct historical character, but also in relation to its timeless understanding of the transcendent Idea.[238] Thus, Lohmeyer believes the interpreter of early Christianity is confronted with dualisms: the otherworldly and the this-worldly; the divine and the human; faith and knowledge. According to Lohmeyer, the absolute and eternal is realized in the historical Jesus; in him, history is both continued and transcended.

Important Monographs

In the time between the wars, Lohmeyer published his seminal study of Phil. 2:5-11.[239] According to Lohmeyer's analysis, the text is a conscious poetic construction with two main parts. The first part (vv. 6-8), made up of three strophes, presents the movement of Christ to earth; the second part (v. 9-11), also made up of three strophes, presents the exaltation of Christ. "From all of these factors the conclusion is necessary that this poem presents a foreign composition taken over by Paul; it is a type of traditional early Christian hymn." Lohmeyer finds evidence of Semitic influence, but concludes that the hymn was originally composed in Greek. Lohmeyer proceeds to analyze the content of the hymn, making use of an approach that combines history of religion and philosophical idealism. For example, he thinks the description of being equal with God as a robbery (NRSV: "something to be exploited") recalls the Iranian myth of the assault upon the divine in the *Urzeit*. Summarizing the whole hymn, Lohmeyer writes:

---

237. See Erik Esking, *Glaube und Geschichte in der theologischen Exegese Ernst Lohmeyers: Zugleich ein Beitrag zur Geschichte der neutestamentlichen Interpretation*, ASNU 18 (Lund: Gleerups, 1951); Günter Haufe, "Ernst Lohmeyer—Theologische Exegese aus dem Geist des philosophischen Idealismus," in Otto, *Freiheit in der Gebundenheit*, 88–97.

238. See Ernst Lohmeyer, *Grundlagen paulinischer Theologie*, BHT 1 (Tübingen: J. C. B. Mohr [Paul Siebeck], 1929).

239. *Kyrios Jesus: Eine Untersuchung zu Phil. 2:5-11*, SHAW (1927/28) 4 (Heidelberg: Carl Winter, 1928); see Colin Brown, "Ernst Lohmeyer's *Kyrios Jesus*," in *Where Christology Began: Essays on Philippians 2*, ed. Ralph P. Martin and Brian J. Dodd (Louisville: Westminster/John Knox, 1998), 6–42.

One strophe [v. 6] presents the thesis: the initial being of the divine form. Two strophes [vv. 7, 8] establish the antithesis: the historical being in human lowliness. Three strophes [vv. 9, 10, 11] confess the synthesis: the revelation of the Kyrios before whom all bow down.[240]

Analyzing the content of each strophe in detail, Lohmeyer continues to combine philological and theological exegesis. For example, he believes the phrase "form of a slave" (v. 7) alludes to the servant of Second Isaiah, and that being found ὡς ἄνθρωπος (v. 7) refers to the Aramaic "son of man." In regard to the fourth strophe (v. 9) Lohmeyer notes that the verb ὑπερύψωσεν is used only here in Paul. Lohmeyer emphasizes the fact that the text does not mention resurrection, but instead, the exaltation of Christ. He understands this to be a non-Pauline emphasis, indicating a pre-Pauline theological tradition.

In summing up his results, Lohmeyer concludes that the hymn depicts universal and cosmic events. He believes it combines the concepts "Son of Man" and "Kyrios" and presents a primitive Christology similar to the Johannine Logos. "Thus John is the conserver, Paul the innovator."[241] In Lohmeyer's opinion, the hymn resolves the Jewish problem of the dialectic between God and the world: the divine being comes into history, and the historical Jesus is confessed as Lord. This radically new exegesis makes use of the history of religion method, while standing the conclusion of the history of religion school on its head: the designation of Jesus as Kyrios is the confession of pre-Pauline Jewish Christianity; Logos Christology is actually earlier than Paul. However, in spite of Lohmeyer's penetrating analysis and creative imagination, his historical and theological reconstruction has not been widely followed. His literary analysis, on the other hand, has become axiomatic, so that most modern texts and translations print Phil. 2:6-11 in poetic form.

The same combination of critical analysis and imaginative reconstruction is found in Lohmeyer's book *Galilee and Jerusalem*.[242] The burden of the work is to prove that two different Christologies, Galilean and Jerusalem, were confessed in earliest Christianity. Rudimentary evidence is apparent in the accounts of the resurrection appearances in the NT: some of the accounts report appearances is Galilee, others, in Jerusalem. Turning to an analysis of the texts, Lohmeyer notes that Mark 14:28 and Mark 16:7 predict that the disciples would *see* Jesus in Galilee. Lohmeyer distinguishes this "seeing" (active) from "appearing" (passive), and contends that it refers to seeing Christ in the parousia. Lohmeyer thinks the account in Matt. 28:16-

---

240. *Kyrios Jesus*, 8, 30.
241. Ibid., 76.
242. *Galiläa und Jerusalem*, FRLANT 52 (Göttingen: Vandenhoeck & Ruprecht, 1936).

20 confirms this, because this account does not, in his opinion, stress the resurrection, but emphasizes the authority of the *exalted* Christ—the same emphasis Lohmeyer detects in the recognition of Jesus as "Lord" in John 21:7. In all of these accounts, Lohmeyer notes, the place of the Christophanies is Galilee. Turning to Paul's account in 1 Cor. 15:5-8, Lohmeyer notes that no mention is made of the place, but that Paul stresses the occurrence of the resurrection on the third day. Lohmeyer also observes that Luke stresses the third day (9:22; 18:33; 24:7, 21, 46), and believes this provides a connection with Paul, so that Paul is understood as supporting the Jerusalem Christophanies. Lohmeyer concludes that there are two traditions regarding the appearances: Galilean, supported by Mark, Matthew, and John 21; and Jerusalem, supported by Luke and Paul.

Lohmeyer proceeds to investigate these two traditions as they relate to the history of Jesus and the primitive church. He observes that for Mark (and Matthew) most of the ministry of Jesus took place in Galilee. "The outline of the life of Jesus in the Gospel of Mark rests on the clear theological idea that God has chosen the despised Galilee for his eschatological work and gospel."[243] According to John (1–20), on the other hand, the main activity of Jesus takes place in Jerusalem. Lohmeyer points out that Luke has modified the outline of Mark, reducing the Galilean activity and locating important events in Samaria, and seeing Jerusalem as the place where Jesus accomplishes his work as messianic king. Turning to the history of the early church, Lohmeyer notes the importance of Jerusalem in the Acts narrative—the place where the Spirit is poured out. Lohmeyer believes Paul also affirms the beginning of the church in Jerusalem (Rom. 15:19). Only hints of what Lohmeyer takes to be the priority of the Galilean tradition can be detected in Acts: a mission to Galilee is mentioned, but not described (9:31); the leadership of James is apparent, but not explained. Analyzing these and extrabiblical texts, Lohmeyer finds evidence for a Son of Man Christology in Galilee. He believes Galilean Christianity is prior:

> [I]t is clear that this twofold mission has emerged not only from different places, but also from different christological grounds: the Galilean mission is connected with the brothers of the Lord and the historical life of the hidden Son of Man; the Jerusalem with the Twelve and the fact of the pouring out of the Spirit in Jerusalem. To the former correspond the Galilean, to the latter, the Jerusalem Christophanies.[244]

---

243. Ibid., 34.
244. Ibid., 100. Lohmeyer's sympathy with Galilean Christianity is evident in his *Kultus und Evangelium* (Göttingen: Vandenhoeck & Ruprecht, 1942); Eng. trans.: *Lord of the Temple: A Study of the Relation between Cult and Gospel*, trans. Stewart Todd (Richmond, Va.: John Knox, 1962).

Lohmeyer's delineation of two different kinds of early Christianity, though the result of historical research, is influenced by his dialectical understanding of history. According to Lohmeyer, Galilee confesses, Κύριος Ἰησοῦς; Jerusalem confesses, Χριστὸς Ἰησοῦς; the two confessions are combined in the pre-Pauline hymn of Phil. 2:11, Κύριος Ἰησοῦς Χριστός; to this early Christian synthesis Lohmeyer resonates. For him, the essence of early Christology is found in the combination of two concepts: the servant of Second Isaiah and the eschatological Son of Man. "The servant of God is a figure in whose life and work the present power of the Holy Spirit is evident; the Son of Man is that which carries out the powerful and decisive eschatological decision of God concerning the work of fulfillment."[245]

Commentaries

Like Windisch, Lohmeyer contributed to both the Meyer and the Lietzmann series.[246] Written for the former, Lohmeyer's commentary on Mark appeared in 1937.[247] In the foreword, he notes that his commentary will focus on Mark's narrative of the life of Jesus, even though Mark cannot provide the basis for a biography. An introductory section investigates titles of Jesus that are used in the Gospel. Lohmeyer believes "Son of Man" is most important.

> He who bears the name Son of Man is thus a transcendent form, a foreigner in this age and Lord of the coming aeon; with him is the coming eschatological event present. And he is at the same time a human form, a Jew among Jews, child of his land and his history; with him every present aspect of his work is directed to the coming aeon and every event of his life to the highest sign of the eschatological day. This double divine–human designation is not only the secret of his essence, but also of the decree of God through which the coming aeon is brought into the present and the present into the future. It holds these two in hiddenness, which is only the shell of revelation, so that both lead to a revelation in glory.[248]

According to Lohmeyer, this title not only expresses the thought of the author, it also represents Jesus' own understanding of his role.

The importance of the Son of Man title is also apparent in Lohmeyer's exegesis of Mark 8:27—9:1, a pericope Lohmeyer titles "The Secret of the Son of Man." For Lohmeyer, this text is not a biographical, but a theologi-

---

245. Ernst Lohmeyer, *Gottesknecht und Davidsohn*, 2d ed., FRLANT 61 (Göttingen: Vandenhoeck & Ruprecht, 1953), 123.

246. See Dieter Lührmann, "Ernst Lohmeyers exegetisches Erbe," in Otto, *Freiheit in der Gebundenheit*, 53–87.

247. *Das Evangelium des Markus*, 15th ed., KEK (Göttingen: Vandenhoeck & Ruprecht, 1959); Lohmeyer's original was the tenth edition of 1937; minor corrections were made in the eleventh (1951); subsequent editions are reprints of the eleventh.

248. Ibid., 6.

cal turning point. The first part of the text (8:27-29) presents the identity of the Son of Man. In an introductory comment, Lohmeyer observes that the location of the event in Caesarea Philippi may be historically accurate, but in Mark, he believes the intention is to present the Galilee of the Gentiles as the place of revelation. When Jesus asks, "Who do people say that I am?" Lohmeyer sees in the use of ἄνθρωποι a reference to the perspective of humanity. The question to the disciples, he thinks, presumes a different perspective—the perspective of faith, asking about the secret of the Son of Man. In regard to Peter's answer, Lohmeyer believes the use of the article (ὁ χριστός) identifies Jesus as *the* king or priest or prophet of the end time. Peter's answer is corrected by the second part of the text (8:30-33), which presents "The Way of the Son of Man." Lohmeyer believes the background of the idea of the suffering Messiah is to be found in Second Isaiah and that it is joined with the idea of the Son of Man in application to Jesus. Throughout this commentary, Lohmeyer engages in text-critical, linguistic, grammatical, and historical research in the service of theological meaning.

Lohmeyer made other contributions to the Meyer series. He had intended to publish his commentary on *Matthew* soon after the completion of his Mark, but the war intervened. The commentary finally appeared posthumously, edited by Werner Schmauch, who attempted to be as faithful to Lohmeyer as possible.[249] A distinctive feature of the commentary is Lohmeyer's claim that some texts usually thought to be dependent on Mark are actually based on an early, non-Marcan tradition. Lohmeyer also contributed the commentary on *Philippians, Colossians, and Philemon* to the Meyer series.[250] The Philippians commentary, for example, includes an introduction in which Lohmeyer contends that this epistle was written from the Caesarean prison in the late summer of 59. In regard to Colossians, Lohmeyer opts for Pauline authorship, and explains the distinctive features of the vocabulary and thought as reflecting the situation of Paul's address to his opponents—representatives of a Hellenistic-Jewish Gnosticism.

The independent and distinctive character of Lohmeyer's scholarship is attested by his remarkable commentary on the *Revelation of John*, published in the Lietzmann series.[251] A section on general matters, printed at the end

---

249. Ernst Lohmeyer, *Das Evangelium des Matthäus*, ed. Werner Schmauch, 3d ed., KEK, Sonderband (Göttingen: Vandenhoeck & Ruprecht, 1962); Schmauch's first edition appeared in 1955, and slightly revised in 1958; the third edition is a reprint.

250. *Die Briefe an die Philipper, an die Kolosser und an Philemon*, 11th ed. Werner Schmauch, KEK (Göttingen: Vandenhoeck & Ruprecht, 1956); Lohmeyer's commentary (eighth edition) appeared in 1930; the ninth (1956) was a reprint; the tenth by W. Schmauch added notes, and the eleventh is a reprint.

251. *Die Offenbarung des Johannes*, 2d ed., HNT 16 (Tübingen: J. C. B. Mohr [Paul Siebeck], 1953); originally published in 1926, the second edition (by G. Bornkamm) incorporates a few notes that Lohmeyer had left at his death.

of the book, presents Lohmeyer's introduction to the Apocalypse. In regard to the form of the document, Lohmeyer writes, "No book of the NT shows such a seemingly confused and confusing abundance of features and images, but also such a self-contained and systematic unity as the Apocalypse of John."[252] The unity of the book is evidenced in the complex way in which the number seven has been carefully used throughout the composition—a feature Lohmeyer detects in the main structure of the document and in a multitude of lesser arrangements, stylistic patterns, and details.

Lohmeyer believes the message of Revelation is presented through three closely related spheres of understanding: God and Christ, the believers, and the world. God is the ruler of all, and Christ has all the attributes of God, but there is a tension between the eternal Christ and the Christ who died in history. The believers also display a tension: their names are written in the eternal book, but they have been purchased by the blood of the Lamb; they belong to eternity, but they are caught in history. The world participates in a similar tension: it is separated from God and under the power of evil, but it is the creation of God and Christ is its Lord. In all of this exposition, Lohmeyer's typical dialectic is apparent.

> But this apparent dualism is at the same time only a reflection of that double relation that Christ has to eternity and time, and thereby to history and the world, which at the same time characterizes the believers. As the historical essence of Christ has eternal validity, so also the historical existence of the world; but the former confirms the timeless connection of Christ with God and thereby also of the church with God and Christ; the latter, the timeless separation from God. This historical and timeless opposition demands a solution, and again it is eschatology that must provide the resolution of these opposites.

The eschatological drama that resolves the dialectic of history includes, according to Lohmeyer, the actual events of Roman history. However, the meaning of the Apocalypse must not be reduced to a political interpretation, for "no historical experience or observation determines the eschatological drama." Thus, according to Lohmeyer, the meaning transcends the historical; the eternal is revealed in history.[253]

Lohmeyer refuses to classify Revelation as an apocalyptic document, and identifies points of contrast: in apocalyptic, the message is hidden, whereas in Revelation, the meaning is open; in apocalyptic, the past is guarantee for the prediction of the future and the present is meaningless, whereas in Revelation, the meaning of the future is in the present; in apocalyptic, the seer is the revealer, whereas in Revelation, the revealer is Christ. Lohmeyer dis-

---

252. Ibid., 184.
253. Ibid., 191, 194.

cerns a relationship between the thought of the Johannine Apocalypse and the Johannine Gospel: the Christ who is revealed in the beginning and end of the Apocalypse is revealed in the life and death of Jesus in the Fourth Gospel. However, the author of Revelation cannot, in Lohmeyer's opinion, be John the son of Zebedee or an apostle. Nevertheless, Lohmeyer believes that the thought of Revelation is not Hellenistic, but Palestinian—probably the work of John the Elder.

Standing in the light of Lohmeyer's colorful mixture of meticulous criticism and creative vision, the observer is dazzled. Seldom since F. C. Baur had a NT scholar displayed such mastery of critical analysis and theological reconstruction. Criticism, of course, seems easy.[254] Lohmeyer has imposed a nineteenth-century philosophy on the ancient sources; he finds in the documents reflections of his own theological image. In the light of such obvious criticisms, Lohmeyer's enduring contributions are all the more striking. For example, no interpreter of Philippians 2 would ignore his work. Although this is owing to Lohmeyer's critical skills, it may also indicate that a conscious and informed presupposition of a philosophy of history facilitates the analysis and reconstruction of history. In the case of Lohmeyer, there also may have been a latent force—never overt in his publications—the trials of his own tragic history. In the midst of the ravages of war, he was sustained by a vision of the eternal.

SUMMARY

In this chapter an amazing phenomenon is apparent: although Enlightenment criticism has been practiced for two centuries, scholars continue to propose new hypotheses, novel reconstructions. This is exemplified by Harris's theory of the testimonies, Goguel's view of the empty tomb, Bauer's understanding of heresy and orthodoxy, and Lohmeyer's interpretation of Philippians 2. All of this witnesses to the creativity and imagination of a multitude of scholars—a variety of personalities, united in dedication to the understanding of the NT.

The work of these scholars has been facilitated by the refining of the tools of the discipline. As their primary source, the scholars use critical texts based on a vast collection of manuscripts, recently augmented by discovery and publication of papyri (Chester Beatty). Many of these manuscripts have been published in facsimile and critical editions by scholars such as Kenyon and Lake. The critical NT texts result from the work of scholars like von Soden who analyze, arrange, and evaluate the manuscripts in relation to textual tradition and text-critical theory. Although the resulting critical

---

254. See Esking, *Glaube und Geschichte*, 208–9; 240–42.

texts are not autographs, they approximate the originals with a degree of reliability far beyond that of any other ancient document. These scholars are aided, too, by excellent reference works in grammar (Robertson) and lexicography (Bauer).

The scholars agree that the NT has to be interpreted in its historical setting. The understanding of Judaism has been advanced by research in the rabbinic literature (Strack-Billerbeck), and by the effort to understand Judaism in its own right (Moore), and not as a foil over against Christianity (Windisch). The method of the history of religion has been adopted with caution about excessive parallels, careless dating of documents, and fabricated theories. That Paul and John—and their readers—were influenced by Hellenistic beliefs and practices is widely accepted, as demonstrated by the commentaries of Bauer, Windisch, and Lohmeyer—and the whole Lietzmann series. Debates continue about the details, for example, the origin and nature of Gnosticism (Nock versus the Germans).

Scholars in this chapter witness to the continuing problem of presuppositions. Windisch and Lohmeyer represent opposing views. Windisch calls for a nontheological exegesis while Lohmeyer interprets texts in relation to a philosophy of history. Lietzmann advocates scientific objectivity, yet insists that the understanding of history must be open to the activity of God. The claim to objectivity—untainted by presuppositions—is immediately suspect, though a scholar such as Nock—without faith commitments—demonstrates a high degree of objectivity and productivity. In any event, the hermeneutical question—the question of methodology in relation to ontology—needs to be considered. In the meantime, scholars with varying presuppositions—recognized, denied, or unconscious—have been able to make new and significant contributions to NT research.

Epilogue

The period from 1870 to 1940 produced a mountain of NT research. Most basic, the historical-critical method was universally adopted. In the nineteenth century, it was embraced in America, notably in the work of Moses Stuart. Also in America, the method was enlisted in the battle of conflicting causes: by Andrews Norton and Theodore Parker in defense of Unitarianism; by Charles Hodge in support of Calvinist orthodoxy. In England, where criticism had been resisted, the Enlightenment approach was adopted and refined by Hort, Lightfoot, and Westcott.

Progress was made in the area of text criticism. Manuscripts were discovered by Agnes Smith Lewis and Rendell Harris, and a large quantity of papyri, notably the Chester Beatty manuscripts, was found and published (for example, by F. G. Kenyon). The genealogical method of grouping and analyzing manuscripts was advanced by such scholars as Harris and Silva and Kirsopp Lake. The result was the end of the authority of the Received Text and the publication of new critical texts such as those of Westcott and Hort and Bernhard Weiss. Von Soden also contributed to the knowledge of the history and reconstruction of the text, though his idiosyncratic nomenclature buried his results under a bushel of complexity.

This period also produced a better understanding of NT linguistics. With the discovery of a heap of nonliterary papyri in Egypt, the Greek of the NT was found to be not a special tongue, handed down from heaven for the creation of holy writ, but the everyday language of ordinary people. The significance of this discovery was grasped by Adolf Deissmann, and its results blossomed into new grammars by Friedrich Blass, J. H. Moulton, and A. T. Robertson, and vastly improved lexica by Moulton (with Milligan) and Walter Bauer.

New methods were developed. The history of religion school took up the older attention to historical backgrounds and exploited it in new ways.

Members of the school believed ideas and practices originating in Babylonia and Persia had wandered through myth and ritual into Hellenistic Judaism and early Christianity. The myth of a cosmic redeemer, believed by scholars like Reitzenstein to be widespread in the Hellenistic world, was viewed as a model for formulating NT Christology. Cultic rituals and meals were thought to shape the early Christian rites of baptism and the Lord's Supper (A. Eichhorn and W. Heitmüller). According to Bousset, Jesus was worshiped in the Gentile churches as the Lord of a Hellenistic, syncretistic cult. These radical views were countered by the defensive tactics of scholars like von Dobschütz and Feine. The Hellenistic backgrounds, which had been the main concern of the history of religion scholars, were more cautiously studied by scholars such as Wendland, Hatch, and Nock. In any case, the obligation to interpret Jesus and early Christianity in their historical and religious setting was everywhere affirmed.

The data for the investigation of NT backgrounds were enriched by the geographical research in Palestine by Edward Robinson and in Asia Minor by William Ramsay. Palestinian language, culture, economy, and society were investigated in situ by Gustaf Dalman. The preference for Jewish backgrounds was typical of scholars (for example, Feine and Lagrange) who sought to protect early Christianity from pagan pollution. Material for research in Judaism was provided by the publication of primary sources, notably R. H. Charles's editions of the apocrypha and pseudepigrapha. Texts from the rabbinic sources were set in parallel with the NT by the massive commentary of Strack and Billerbeck. The history of Judaism in the NT period was rehearsed in detail by Emil Schürer, but his assessment of Jewish religion (like that of Bousset) caricatured Judaism as a foil for Christianity (a view reflected in several scholars; Windisch is a notable exception. A more authentic interpretation of Judaism—treating Judaism in its own right—was provided by G. F. Moore. From a Jewish perspective, Montefiore displayed sympathy with Jesus and his teachings, and along with Klausner (who stressed the Jewishness of Jesus), showed that Christian anti-Judaism (even within the NT) contradicted the ethical precepts of Jesus.

Related to the work of the history of religion school was the method of form criticism. This method attempted to analyze the developing oral tradition about Jesus. The practitioners of the method assumed the priority of Mark, but were driven behind the written accounts to the earlier tradition because they had been convinced (by Wrede) that Mark (like John) was a tendency document, concerned more with doctrine than with history. Wrede's work had dealt a crippling blow to scholars who supposed that the two-document hypothesis confirmed the reliability of Mark and Q—one preserving the tradition of Peter, the other, the tradition of Matthew. K. L. Schmidt further undermined their position by contending that the framework of Mark's Gospel was largely a fabrication of the author. Other practitioners of the *formgeschichtliche* method, Martin Dibelius and Rudolf Bultmann, investigated the development of the tradition according to principles and formal parallels detected in the oral tradition of other folk religions. Most important, they recognized the role of the later church in shaping the tradition—a factor compounding the difficulty of the quest for the historical Jesus. Related to form criticism was the sociohistorical method developed by the Chicago School, especially Mathews and Case. These scholars, trained in the social sciences, viewed early Christianity as a social movement, originating in an ancient society and culture, and moved by social and economic forces.

New methods spawned new theories and variations on the old: Blass's theory concerning the twofold composition of Luke-Acts; Holtzmann's theory about the composition of Colossians; Harnack's theory that Prisca wrote Hebrews; Streeter's hypothesis of a Proto-Luke; Harris's theory that Q was an early Christian *testimonia*; Goodspeed's theories concerning Ephesians; W. Bauer's theory that heresy preceded orthodoxy; Lohmeyer's theory about early Galilean Christianity; Machen's defense of the virgin birth. But the greatest of these was the apocalyptic hypothesis of Johannes Weiss and Albert Schweitzer. Weiss exploded the liberal image of the kingdom of God as ethical and spiritual, and argued that it was an apocalyptic phenomenon. With Schweitzer, apocalyptic was not limited to Jesus' teaching, but was extended to his whole career. In the wake of Schweitzer, scholars throughout this period were driven to a desperate effort to salvage Jesus—to reclaim his continuing relevance and universal significance.

The debate about the apocalyptic Jesus illustrates a broader problem: the ideological varieties with which the NT was approached. The end of the nineteenth century, especially in Europe, saw the dominance of liberalism in academic circles and in the study of the Bible. Opposition to the triumph of liberalism came from many quarters. In America, where liberalism had captured seminaries and invaded pulpits, the nineteenth-century work of Hodge was revived and refined by Warfield and Machen, who articulated a unique doctrine of verbal inspiration and biblical inerrancy. Although in a different way, some European scholarship advanced the conservative counterattack. Zahn argued that the tradition was reliable, the NT documents early and authentic. Schlatter, who grounded his work in a theology of history, affirmed the Bible as divine revelation. Conservative criticism was aided by Lagrange, who remained loyal to the Catholic doctrine of Scripture and tradition while practicing incisive historical criticism.

Besides these ideologies on the left and the right, other approaches to the NT emerged. Skeptics like Overbeck and Loisy attacked both liberalism and orthodoxy. The beginnings of feminist heremeutic were expressed in translations by J. Smith and H. B. Montgomery, *The Woman's Bible*, the text-critical work of Silva Lake, and the criticism and exegesis of Andrews and Ely. These women, like Parker and the Chicago School, affirmed the relevance of the NT for social issues—the struggle against slavery and the battle for woman's suffrage.

Underlying these ideological differences where profound problems—differences in worldview and clashing philosophies of history. Theological questions arose in regard to basic presuppositions. For example, what sort of worldview is assumed by the historical-critical method? On the one hand, the Enlightenment sees history, like nature, as a unity, functioning according to natural law. Unique or supernatural events, from this perspective, cannot be entertained by historical research. Theologians like Schlatter, on the other hand, declare that this understanding of historical method precludes a priori the action of God in history, denying a theological interpretation of history and an authentic reading of the sources. According to this view, understanding the NT requires participation in the biblical faith. But the question arises: What is the biblical faith (or faiths)? And the answer to that question requires historical research—a research that involves presuppositions and runs the risk of circular argument (or perhaps, offers a sophisticated hermeneutical circle). In any event, the hermeneutical question—the question of the methodology beneath the method—was not solved prior to World War II, and remained a crucial issue for biblical studies in the postwar period.

As to higher criticism, the period produced a large shelf of introductions to the NT, most notably those of Holtzmann, Jülicher, Moffatt, Zahn, and Goguel. Out of these and other higher critical works, a growing consensus of liberal criticism emerged. The two-document hypothesis was promoted by the deliberate work of the British (Sanday, Streeter, and Burkitt) and Burton in Chicago. An important contribution to gospel research was made by Jülicher's study of the parables. In regard to Pauline Epistles, the Pastorals and Ephesians were increasingly considered pseudonymous, despite the vigorous arguments of Zahn. Almost no one (except earlier scholars like Stuart) accepted the Pauline authorship of Hebrews. In regard to the Corinthian correspondence, 2 Corinthians was increasingly seen as a composite. Debate about the destination of Galatians continued, though the north hypothesis, over the protest by Ramsay, claimed the majority. The authenticity of the Catholic Epistles was debated, though virtually everyone (except Zahn) rejected 2 Peter. Debate continued concerning the Johannine literature, though many concluded that the Fourth Gospel and the Apocalypse were not by the same author, and several (against the arguments of scholars like Westcott, B. Weiss, and Feine) abandoned the apostolic authorship of the Gospel of John. No one denied that John was primarily a theological Gospel, but several insisted that it embodied reliable tradition (e.g., Weizsäcker, Sanday, and Goguel). Acts remained a battleground with varying views of its historical value, theological tendency, and authorship. Support for Lucan authorship and an early date came from scholars as far apart as Harnack and Ramsay. Some (notably Overbeck) did not agree, and many acknowledged that the author had an ax to grind (for example, Reuss and Pfleiderer). The analysis of the style of Acts by Dibelius is noteworthy, and the mammoth *Beginnings of Christianity* was an unequaled achievement in historical criticism.

In regard to synthetic work—exegesis and theology—this period produced some remarkable works. Commentaries, which constitute the most boring literary genre devised by humans, offered some exceptions: the readable book on the *Synoptic Gospels* by Montefiore and Lohmeyer's captivating commentary on the *Apocalypse*. Stuart's commentary on *Revelation* was a stunning achievement for its time and place. Perceptive theological commentaries were represented by the *Romans* commentaries of Hodge and Schlatter. As to fulfilling the essential purpose of commentaries—to provide informed critical introduction, meticulous analysis of text-critical and linguistic details, the discriminating collection of history of religion parallels, together with historical imagination and theological sensitivity—this period produced some laudable examples. The three big series—the Meyer, the Lietzmann, and the ICC—consistently followed high standards. Classic examples can be seen in Burton's *Galatians*, Charles's *Revelation*, J. Weiss's *1 Corinthians*, and Dibelius's *Epistle of James*. Accomplishments in NT theology were exemplified by the contrasting works of Holtzmann and Schlatter. Holtzmann articulated liberalism: stress on the ethics of Jesus and the religious experience of Paul, salvation as the reconciling action of divine love. Schlatter emphasized the preexistence of Christ and Paul's doctrine of Jesus as vicarious sacrifice. Several scholars detected development in Paul's thought (R. H. Charles, B. Weiss, Holtzmann)—usually away from apocalyptic to something more theologically respectable. Also, many scholars found the high point of NT theology in the Fourth Gospel, though the background of John's thought—Hellenistic or Hebrew—was debated. Sensitivity to the symbolic and poetic character of NT language was expressed by Bushnell.

In regard to matters of substance, attention was given to the life of Jesus and the history of the early church. Most scholars agreed that a biography of Jesus was impossible, although valiant efforts were made by B. Weiss and Goguel. Also, several smaller "Lives" were published (for example, by Bousset, Goodspeed, Ely), and Case even called his book "A New Biography." Following in the steps of Schweitzer, a host of scholars pursued the quest for the historical Jesus, and many produced studies on the teachings of Jesus.

Of special interest was the enigma of the messianic consciousness of Jesus. Ironically, biographies were thought to be impossible, but psychological analysis was ventured. Typical was Holtzmann's book on the messianic consciousness of Jesus. Holtzmann and many others (Jülicher, Wernle) argued that Jesus recognized himself to be the Messiah, but understood messiahship in some new, unique way. This approach, of course, was flatly rejected by Wrede's messianic secret and Schweitzer's apocalyptic Jesus. The new way, according to most advocates of this view, involved the recognition of the necessity of messianic suffering (Schürer, Bousset). Related to this approach, extensive efforts were launched to comprehend the meaning of the "Son of Man"—all the way from the theory of Wellhausen, Dalman, Pfleiderer, and Lietzmann (that it was only an Aramaic term for "man") to apocalyptic interpretations grounded in Daniel, refined in Enoch, and transformed by modern theological anthropology. An imaginative resolution of the issue was the conviction that Jesus reinterpreted the Son of Man in fusion with the figure of the Suffering Servant of Second Isaiah (Moffatt, Lohmeyer)—a view appealing to twentieth-century theologians, perhaps baffling to first-century Galileans. As on the cliff at Nazareth, the historical Jesus passed through the midst of the scholars and went on his way.

In regard to early church history, the sharp conflicts that F. C. Baur had detected in Antioch and Corinth were reduced to minor skirmishes. To be sure, scholars recognized disagreements, but these were not between Paul and Peter, or even James. These were conflicts between Paul's freedom and universalism, on the one hand, and the legalistic and nationalistic Judaizers, on the other. Similarly, emphasis was placed on the line of continuity between Jesus and Paul, contra Wrede's picture of Paul as the second founder of Christianity. The idea of continuity assumed new vitality when Johannes Weiss (and Klausner and Feine) argued that Paul had personally seen Jesus, heard his teaching, and possibly beheld his crucifixion. This theory illustrates another feature of NT research in this period: building hypotheses on minimal evidence.

As this summary shows, NT research in the period between the Franco-Prussian War and World War II became increasingly complex. The discovery of new materials, the development of new methods, the proposal of new hypotheses—all contributed to the expansion of NT research. This increasing complexity, however, is not the result of some dire plot to steal the Bible from the laity. Scholars of all persuasions have contributed; Schlatter's work is at least as complex as Holtzmann's, and it was a liberal (Harnack) who sought simplification. Nevertheless, it is ironic that the interpretation of a book written in ordinary language for ordinary people had become so complex. Actually, the complexity of the research should not be surprising.

EPILOGUE 477

Although in Koine, the NT is written in a foreign language. Though set in real history, that history is distant. Although expressing folk religion, that religion is not ours. Moreover, the NT, for all is supposed simplicity, deals with profound matters—God and God's revelation, the nature and destiny of humans. Without texts, translations, and commentaries (all products of research) the NT would not have been preserved, let alone understood. The problem, of course, is the great variety and conflicting character of the secondary sources. Yet, rather than viewing this material as a mess of pottage, one can see it as a priceless heritage. There is not a book reviewed in this volume that would not help the reader to a fuller understanding of the NT. To be sure, some are more helpful than others. Although some scholars are dull and difficult, many are stimulating—all witnessing to the ongoing vitality of the biblical message and the unbounded creativity of the human intellect. Those who seek to understand the NT stand in their debt.

Select Bibliography

INTRODUCTION

General Works on the History of New Testament Interpretation

Bray, Gerald. *Biblical Interpretation: Past and Present.* Downers Grove, Ill.: InterVarsity, 1996.

Burkett, Delbert. *The Son of Man Debate: A History and Evaluation.* Society for New Testament Studies Monograph Series 107. Cambridge: Cambridge University Press, 1999.

Dawes, Gregory W., ed. *The Historical Jesus Quest: Landmarks in the Search for the Jesus of History.* Louisville: Westminster John Knox, 1999.

Duling, Dennis C. *Jesus Christ through History.* San Diego: Harcourt Brace Jovanovich, 1979.

Dungan, David Laird. *A History of the Synoptic Problem: The Canon, the Text, the Composition, and the Interpretation of the Gospels.* Anchor Bible Reference Library. New York: Doubleday, 1999.

Gasque, W. Ward. *A History of the Interpretation of the Acts of the Apostles.* Peabody, Mass.: Hendrickson, 1989.

Glover, Willis B. *Evangelical Nonconformists and Higher Criticism in the Nineteenth Century.* London: Independent, 1954.

Grant, Robert, with David Tracy. *A Short History of the Interpretation of the Bible.* 2d rev. ed. Philadelphia: Fortress Press, 1984.

Greschat, Martin, ed. *Theologen des Protestantismus im 19. und 20. Jahrhundert I, II.* Urban-Taschenbücher 284, 285. Stuttgart: W. Kohlhammer, 1978.

Harrisville, Roy A., and Walter Sundberg. *The Bible in Modern Culture: Baruch Spinoza to Brevard Childs.* 2nd ed. Grand Rapids, Mich.: Eerdmans, 2002.

Hirsch, Emanuel. *Geschichte der neuern evangelischen Theologie im Zusammenhang mit den allgemeinen Bewegungen des europäischen Denkens.* Vol. 5. Gütersloh: C. Bertelsmann, 1954.

Howard, Wilbert Francis. *The Romance of New Testament Scholarship.* Drew Lectureship in Biography. London: Epworth, 1949.

Hurth, Elisabeth. *In His Name: Comparative Studies in the Quest for the Historical Jesus.* European University Studies 23: Theology. Frankfurt am Main: Peter Lang, 1989.
Jones, Maurice. *The New Testament in the Twentieth Century: A Survey of Recent Christological and Historical Criticism of the New Testament.* London: Macmillan, 1934.
Kloppenborg Verbin, John S. *Excavating Q: The History and Setting of the Sayings Gospel.* Edinburgh: T. & T. Clark, 2000.
Kümmel, Werner Georg. *The New Testament: The History of the Investigation of Its Problems.* Translated by S. McLean Gilmour and Howard C. Kee. Nashville: Abingdon, 1972.
Latourette, Kenneth Scott. *Christianity in a Revolutionary Age: A History of Christianity in the 19th and 20th Centuries.* 5 vols. New York: Harper & Row, 1958–62. Repr., Grand Rapids, Mich.: Zondervan, 1969.
McKim, Donald K., ed. *Historical Handbook of Major Biblical Interpreters.* Downers Grove, Ill.: InterVarsity, 1998.
Morgan, R. "Historical Criticism and Christology: England and German." Pages 80–108 in *England and Germany: Studies in Theological Diplomacy.* Edited by S. W. Sykes. Studies in the Intercultural History of Christianity 25. Frankfurt am Main: Peter D. Lang, 1982.
Morgan, Robert, with John Barton. *Biblical Interpretation.* Oxford Bible Series. Oxford: Oxford University Press, 1988.
Neill, Stephen, and Tom Wright. *The Interpretation of the New Testament, 1861–1986.* 2d ed. Oxford: Oxford University Press, 1988.
O'Neill, J. C. *The Bible's Authority: A Portrait Gallery of Thinkers from Lessing to Bultmann.* Edinburgh: T. & T. Clark, 1991.
Riches, John K. *A Century of New Testament Study.* Cambridge: Lutterworth, 1993.
Rogers, Jack B., and Donald K. McKim. *The Authority and Interpretation of the Bible: An Historical Approach.* New York: Harper & Row, 1979.
Rogerson, John, Christopher Rowland, and Barnabas Lindars, eds. *The History of Christian Theology. Volume 2: The Study and Use of the Bible.* Grand Rapids, Mich.: Eerdmans, 1988.
Stange, Erich, ed. *Die Religionswissenschaft der Gegenwart in Selbstdarstellungen.* 5. vols. Leipzig: Felix Meiner, 1925–29.
Stoldt, Hans-Herbert. *History and Criticism of the Marcan Hypothesis.* Translated by Donald L. Niewyk. Macon, Ga.: Mercer University Press, 1980.
Weaver, Walter P. *The Historical Jesus in the Twentieth Century.* Harrisburg, Pa.: Trinity Press International, 1999.
Welch, Claude. *Protestant Thought in the Nineteenth Century. Volume 2: 1870–1914.* New Haven: Yale University Press, 1985.

1. NEW TESTAMENT RESEARCH IN AMERICA DURING THE NINETEENTH CENTURY

General Works

Ahlstrom, Sydney. *A Religious History of the American People.* New Haven: Yale University Press, 1972.

———. "Theology in America: A Historical Survey." Pages 232–321 in *The Shaping of American Religion*. Edited by James Ward Smith and A. Leland Jamison. Religion in American Life 1. Princeton Studies in American Civilization 5. Princeton: Princeton University Press, 1969.

———, ed. *Theology in America: The Major Protestant Voices: From Puritanism to Neo-Orthodoxy*. American Heritage Series. Indianapolis: Bobbs-Merrill, 1967.

Bainton, Roland H. *Yale and the Ministry: A History of Education for the Christian Ministry at Yale from the Founding in 1701*. New York: Harper & Brothers, 1957.

Brown, Jerry Wayne. *The Rise of Biblical Criticism in America, 1800–1870: The New England Scholars*. Middletown, Conn.: Wesleyan University Press, 1969.

Campbell, Jerry Dean. "Biblical Criticism in America, 1858–1892: The Emergence of the Historical Critic." Ph.D. diss., University of Denver, 1982.

Chable, Eugene Robert. "A Study of the Interpretation of the New Testament in New England Unitarianism. " Ph.D. diss., Columbia University, 1955.

Cherry, Conrad. *Nature and Religious Imagination: From Edwards to Bushnell*. Philadelphia: Fortress Press, 1980.

Conser, Walter H., Jr. *Church and Confession: Conservative Theologians in Germany, England, and America: 1815–1866*. Macon, Ga.: Mercer University Press, 1984.

Foster, Frank Hugh. *A Genetic History of the New England Theology*. New York: Russell & Russell, 1963.

Frerichs, Ernest S., ed. *The Bible and Bibles in America*. Society of Biblical Literature. The Bible in American Culture. Atlanta, Ga.: Scholars Press, 1988.

Grusin, Richard A. *Transcendentalist Hermeneutics: Institutional Authority and the Higher Criticism of the Bible*. Post-Contemporary Interventions. Durham, N.C.: Duke University Press, 1991.

Handy, Robert T. *A History of Union Theological Seminary in New York*. New York: Columbia University Press, 1987.

Herbst, Jurgen. *The German Historical School in American Scholarship: A Study in the Transfer of Culture*. Ithaca, N.Y.: Cornell University Press, 1965.

Klaiss, Donald Stanley. "The History of the Interpretation and Criticism of the New Testament in America, 1620–1900." Ph.D. diss., University of Chicago, 1934.

Miller, Glenn T. *Piety and Intellect: The Aims and Purposes of Ante-Bellum Theological Education*. Studies in Theological Education. Atlanta: Scholars Press, 1990.

Noll, Mark A., ed. *The Princeton Theology, 1812–1921: Scripture, Science, and Theological Method from Archibald Alexander to Benjamin Breckinridge Warfield*. Grand Rapids, Mich.: Baker, 1983.

Sandeen, Ernest R., ed. *The Bible and Social Reform*. Society of Biblical Literature Centennial Publications. The Bible in American Culture. Philadelphia: Fortress Press, 1982.

Simms, P. Marion. *The Bible in America: Versions That Have Played Their Part in the Making of the Republic*. New York: Wilson-Ericson, 1936.

Toulouse, Mark G., and James O. Duke, eds. *Makers of Christian Theology in America*. Nashville: Abingdon, 1997.

Williams, George Hunston, ed. *The Harvard Divinity School: Its Place in Harvard University and in American Culture*. Boston: Beacon, 1954.

Wright, Conrad. *The Beginnings of Unitarianism in America*. Boston: Starr King, 1955.

Edwards

Primary Sources

Edwards, Jonathan. *Apocalyptic Writings: "Notes on the Apocalypse," An Humble Attempt.* Vol. 5 of *The Works of Jonathan Edwards.* Edited by Stephen J. Stein. New Haven: Yale University Press, 1977.

———. *The "Miscellanies" (Entry Nos. a–z, aa–zz, 1–50).* Vol. 13 of *The Works of Jonathan Edwards.* Edited by Thomas A. Schafer. New Haven: Yale University Press, 1994.

———. *The "Miscellanies" (Entry Nos. 501–832).* Vol. 18 of *The Works of Jonathan Edwards.* Edited by Ava Chamberlain. New Haven: Yale University Press, 2000.

———. *Notes on Scripture.* Vol. 15 of *The Works of Jonathan Edwards.* Edited by Stephen J. Stein. New Haven: Yale University Press, 1998.

———. *Original Sin.* Vol. 3 of *The Works of Jonathan Edwards.* Edited by Clyde A. Holbrook. New Haven: Yale University Press, 1970.

———. *Religious Affections.* Vol. 2 of *The Works of Jonathan Edwards.* Edited by John E. Smith. New Haven: Yale University Press, 1959.

Secondary Sources

Cherry, Conrad. "Symbols of Spiritual Truth: Jonathan Edwards as Biblical Interpreter." *Interpretation* 39 (1985): 263–71.

———. *The Theology of Jonathan Edwards: A Reappraisal.* Gloucester, Mass.: Peter Smith, 1974.

Gerstner, John H. *The Rational Biblical Theology of Jonathan Edwards.* 3 vols. Powhatan, Va.: Berea Publications, 1991.

Laurence, David. "Jonathan Edwards, John Locke, and the Canon of Experience." *Early American Literature* 15 (1980): 107–23.

Logan, Samuel T., Jr. "The Hermeneutics of Jonathan Edwards." *Westminster Theological Journal* 43 (1980): 79–96.

Pfisterer, Karl Dieterich. *The Prism of Scripture: Studies on History and Historicity in the Work of Jonathan Edwards.* Anglo-American Forum 1. Bern: Herbert Lang, 1975.

Stein, Stephen J. "Providence and the Apocalypse in the Early Writings of Jonathan Edwards." *Early American Literature* 13 (1978–79): 250–67.

———. "The Quest for the Spiritual Sense: The Biblical Hermeneutics of Jonathan Edwards." *Harvard Theological Review* 70 (1977): 99–113.

———. "The Spirit and the Word: Jonathan Edwards and Scriptural Exegesis." Pages 118–30 in *Jonathan Edwards and the American Experience.* Edited by Nathan O. Hatch and Harry S. Stout. New York: Oxford University Press, 1988.

Turnbull, Ralph G. "Jonathan Edwards—Bible Interpreter." *Interpretation* 6 (1952): 422–35.

Norton

Primary Sources

Norton, Andrews. "A Defense of Liberal Christianity." *The General Repository and Review* 1 (January 1812): 1–25.

———. *The Evidences of the Genuineness of the Gospels.* Vol. 1. 2d ed. Cambridge, Mass.: John Owen, 1846. Vols. 2 and 3. Cambridge: George Nichols, 1848.

———. *The Evidences of the Genuineness of the Gospels.* Abridged ed. Boston: American Unitarian Association, 1873.

———. *Inaugural Discourse, Delivered before the University in Cambridge, August 10, 1819.* Cambridge, Mass.: Hilliard and Metcalf, 1819.

———. *Internal Evidences of the Genuineness of the Gospels.* Boston: Little, Brown, 1855.

———. *A Statement of Reasons for Not Believing the Doctrines of Trinitarians, concerning the Nature of God and the Person of Christ.* 3d ed. Boston: Walker, Wise, 1859.

———. *A Translation of the Gospels, with Notes.* 2 vols. 5th ed. Cambridge: John Wilson and Son, 1882.

Secondary Sources

Habich, Robert D. "Emerson's Reluctant Foe: Andrews Norton and the Transcendental Controversy." *The New England Quarterly* 65 (1991): 208–37.

Handlin, Lilian. "Babylon est delenda—the Young Andrews Norton." Pages 53–85 in *American Unitarianism: 1805–1865.* Edited by Conrad Edick Wright. Boston: Massachusetts Historical Society, 1989.

Turner, James. "Religion et langage dans l'Amérique du XIXe siècle: Le cas étrange de Andrews Norton." *Revue de l'histoire des religions* 110 (1993): 431–62.

Parker

Primary Sources

Collins, Robert E. *Theodore Parker: American Transcendentalist: A Critical Essay and a Collection of His Writings.* Metuchen, N.J.: Scarecrow, 1973.

Commager, Henry Steele, ed. *Theodore Parker: An Anthology.* Boston: Beacon, 1960.

Parker, Theodore. *A Critical and Historical Introduction to the Canonical Scriptures of the Old Testament.* From the German of Wilhelm Martin Leberecht de Wette. Translated and Enlarged by Theodore Parker. 2d ed. 2 vols. Boston: Charles C. Little and James Brown, 1850.

———. *A Discourse of Matters Pertaining to Religion.* Edited by Thomas Wentworth Higginson. The Works of Theodore Parker. Centenary Edition 1. Boston: American Unitarian Association, 1907.

———. "*Das Leben Jesu, kritisch bearbeitet* von Dr. David Friedrich Strauss." Tübingen: 1837, 2 voll. 8vo. *The Life of Jesus,* critically treated, etc. Second improved edition (1st edition, 1835; 3d, 1839), *The Christian Examiner and General Review* 28 (third series, vol. 10; no. 3, July 1840): 273–316.

———. "Relation of the Bible to the Soul." *The Western Messenger* 8, no. 8 (December 1840, January 1841): 337–40; 388–93.

Secondary Sources

Dirks, John Edward. *The Critical Theology of Theodore Parker.* Columbia Studies in American Culture 19. New York: Columbia University Press, 1948. Repr., Westport, Conn.: Greenwood, 1970.

Miller, Perry. "Theodore Parker: Apostasy within Liberalism." *Harvard Theological Review* 54 (1961): 275–95.

Stuart

Primary Sources

Stuart, Moses. *A Commentary on the Apocalypse.* 2 vols. Andover: Allen, Morrill and Wardwell, 1845.
———. *A Commentary on the Epistle to the Hebrews.* 2 vols. London: John Miller, 1828.
———. *A Commentary on the Epistle to the Romans with a Translation and Various Excursuses.* 2d ed. Andover: Gould and Newman, 1835.
———. *Elements of Interpretation: Translated from the Latin of J. A. Ernesti and Accompanied by Notes with an Appendix Containing Extracts from Morus, Beck and Keil.* 3d ed. Andover: Mark Newman, 1827.
———. *Exegetical Essays on Several Words Relating to Future Punishment.* Andover: Flagg and Gould, 1830. Repr., Rosemead, Calif.: Old Paths Book Club, 1954.
———. *Letters to the Rev. Wm. E. Channing, Containing Remarks on His Sermon Recently Preached and Published at Baltimore.* Andover: Flagg and Gould, 1819.
———. *Miscellanies, Consisting of I. Letters to Dr. Channing on the Trinity. II. Two Sermons on the Atonement. III. Sacramental Sermon on the Lamb of God. IV. Dedication Sermon—Real Christianity. V. Letter to Dr. Channing on Religious Liberty. VI. Supplementary Notes and Postscripts of New Additional Matter.* Andover: Warren F. Draper, 1957.
———. "Review of 'The Evidences of the Genuineness of the Gospels, by Andrews Norton, Vol. I, Boston, 1837.'" *American Biblical Repository* 11, no. 33 (April 1838): 266–343.

Secondary Sources

Giltner, John Herbert. *Moses Stuart: The Father of Biblical Science in America.* Biblical Scholarship in North America. Society of Biblical Literature Centennial Publications. Atlanta: Scholars Press, 1988.
Granquist, Mark. "The Role of 'Common Sense' in the Hermeneutics of Moses Stuart." *Harvard Theological Review* 83 (1990): 305–19.
Stephens, Bruce M. "Breaking the Chains of Literalism: The Christology of Moses Stuart." *The Covenant Quarterly* 50 (1992): 34–47.

Robinson

Primary Sources

Robinson, Edward. *The Bible and Its Literature; An Inaugural Address, Delivered in the Mercer-Street Church in the City of New York, January 20, 1841. With the Charge by the Rev. William Patton.* New York: Office of the American Biblical Repository, and the American Eclectic, 1841.
———. *Biblical Researches in Palestine, and in the Adjacent Regions: A Journal of Travels in the Year 1838, by E. Robinson and E. Smith.* 2 vols. Boston: Crocker and Brewster, 1856.
———. *A Harmony of the Four Gospels in English, according to the Common Version. Newly Arranged, with Explanatory Notes.* 12th ed. Boston: Crocker & Brewster; London: Wiley & Putnam, 1866.
———. *A Harmony of the Four Gospels in Greek, according to the Text of Hahn, Newly Arranged with Explanatory Notes.* Rev. ed. Boston: Crocker and Brewster, 1862.

———. *Later Biblical Researches in Palestine, and in the Adjacent Regions: A Journal of Travels in the Year 1852, by E. Robinson and E. Smith and Others.* 2d ed. Boston: Crocker and Brewster, 1871.

———. "Philology and Lexicography of the New Testament." *The Biblical Repository* 4, no. 13 (January 1834): 154–82.

Secondary Sources

Abel, F.-M. "Edward Robinson and the Identification of Biblical Sites." *Journal of Biblical Literature* 58 (1939): 365–72.

Alt, Albrecht. "Edward Robinson and the Historical Geography of Palestine." *Journal of Biblical Literature* 58 (1939): 373–77.

Bewer, Julius A. "Edward Robinson as a Biblical Scholar." *Journal of Biblical Literature* 58 (1939): 355–63.

Stinespring, W. F. "The Critical Faculty of Edward Robinson." *Journal of Biblical Literature* 58 (1939): 379–87.

Williams, Jay G. *The Times and Life of Edward Robinson: Connecticut Yankee in King Solomon's Court.* Society of Biblical Literature Biblical Scholarship in North America 19. Atlanta: Society of Biblical Literature, 1999.

Hodge

Primary Sources

Hodge, Charles. *A Commentary on the Epistle to the Ephesians.* Grand Rapids, Mich.: Eerdmans, n.d.

———. *Commentary on the Epistle to the Romans.* Rev. ed. Philadelphia: Alfred Martien, 1873.

———. *An Exposition of the First Epistle to the Corinthians.* New York: A. C. Armstrong & Son, 1894.

———. *An Exposition of the Second Epistle to the Corinthians.* New York: George H. Doran, 1859.

———. *Systematic Theology.* 3 vols. Grand Rapids, Mich.: Eerdmans, 1952.

Noll, Mark A., ed. *Charles Hodge: The Way of Life.* Sources in American Spirituality. New York: Paulist Press, 1987.

Secondary Sources

Danhof, Ralph John. *Charles Hodge as a Dogmatician.* Goes, Netherlands: Oosterbaan & Le Cointre, 1929.

Gerstner, John H. "The Contributions of Charles Hodge, B. B. Warfield, and J. Gresham Machen to the Doctrine of Inspiration." Pages 347–59 in *Challenges to Inerrancy: A Theological Response.* Edited by Gordon R. Lewis and Bruce Demarest. Chicago: Moody, 1984.

Hoffecker, W. Andrew. *Piety and the Princeton Theologians: Archibald Alexander, Charles Hodge, and Benjamin Warfield.* Phillipsburg, N.J.: Presbyterian and Reformed Publishing, 1981.

Noll, Mark A., ed. *The Princeton Defense of Plenary Verbal Inspiration, Fundamentalism in American Religion, 1880–1950.* New York: Garland, 1988.

———, ed. *The Princeton Theology, 1812–1921: Scripture, Science and Theological Method from Archibald Alexander to Benjamin Breckinridge Warfield.* Grand Rapids, Mich.: Baker, 1983.
Olbricht, Thomas H. "Charles Hodge as an American New Testament Interpreter." *Journal of Presbyterian History* 57 (1979): 117–33.
Wells, Jonathan. *Charles Hodge's Critique of Darwinism: An Historical-Critical Analysis of Concepts Basic to the 19th Century Debate.* Studies in American Religion 27. Lewiston, N.Y.: Edwin Mellen, 1988.

Bushnell

Primary Sources

Bushnell, Horace. *Christ in Theology.* American Religious Thought of the 18th and 19th Centuries. New York: Garland, 1987.
———. *Christian Nurture.* New York: Charles Scribner, 1864.
———. *God in Christ: Three Discourses Delivered at New Haven, Cambridge and Andover, with a Preliminary Dissertation on Language.* New York: Charles Scribner's Sons, 1910.
———. *Nature and the Supernatural, as Together Constituting the One System of God.* New York: Charles Scribner's Sons, 1889.
———. *The Vicarious Sacrifice, Grounded in Principles Interpreted by Human Analogies.* 2 vols. New York: Charles Scribner's Sons, 1877.
———. *Views of Christian Nurture, and of Subjects Adjacent Thereto.* 2d ed. Hartford: Edwin Hunt, 1848.
Smith, David L., ed. *Horace Bushnell: Selected Writings on Language, Religion, and American Culture.* American Academy of Religion Studies in Religion. Chico, Calif.: Scholars Press, 1984.

Secondary Sources

Crosby, Donald A. *Horace Bushnell's Theory of Language: In the Context of Other Nineteenth-Century Philosophies of Language.* The Hague: Mouton, 1975.
Duke, James O. *Horace Bushnell: On the Vitality of Biblical Language.* Society of Biblical Literature. Biblical Scholarship in North America. Chico, Calif.: Scholars Press, 1984.
Johnson, William Alexander. *Nature and the Supernatural in the Theology of Horace Bushnell.* Studia Theologica Lundensia 25. Lund: CWK Gleerup, 1963.
Smith, David L. *Symbolism and Growth: The Religious Thought of Horace Bushnell.* American Academy of Religion Dissertation Series 36. Chico, Calif.: Scholars Press, 1981.

Schaff

Primary Sources

Lange, John Peter. *The Gospel According to Matthew, together with a General Theological, and Homiletical Introduction to the New Testament.* Translated from 3d ed. by Philip Schaff. A Commentary on the Holy Scriptures: Critical, Doctrinal, and Homiletical, by John Peter Lange, vol. 1 of the New Testament. New York: Charles Scribner, 1865.

Lange, John Peter, and F. R. Fay. *The Epistle of Paul to the Romans.* Translated by J. G. Hurst. Edited by P. Schaff and M. B. Riddle, 2d ed. A Commentary on the Holy Scriptures; Critical, Doctrinal, and Homiletical by John Peter Lange, vol. 5 of the New Testament. New York: Scribner, Armstrong, 1875.

Nichols, James Hastings, ed. *The Mercersburg Theology.* Library of Protestant Thought. New York: Oxford University Press, 1966.

Penzel, Klaus, ed. *Philip Schaff: Historian and Ambassador of the Universal Church: Selected Writings.* Macon, Ga.: Mercer University Press, 1991.

Schaff, Philip. *Christ and Christianity: Studies on Christology, Creeds and Confessions, Protestantism and Romanism, Reformation Principles, Sunday Observance, Religious Freedom, and Christian Union.* New York: Charles Scribner's Sons, 1885.

———. *History of the Apostolic Church; with a General Introduction to Church History.* Translated by Edward E. Yeomans. New York: Scribner, Armstrong, 1874.

———. *The Person of Christ: His Perfect Humanity as Proof of His Divinity, with Impartial Testimonies to His Character.* Rev. ed. New York: Georg H. Doran, 1913.

———. *What Is Church History? A Vindication of the Idea of Historical Development.* Philadelphia: J. B. Lippincott, 1846.

Yrigoyen, Charles, Jr., and George M. Bricker, eds. *Reformed and Catholic: Selected Historical and Theological Writings of Philip Schaff.* Pittsburgh: Pickwick, 1979.

Secondary Sources

Lotz, David W. "Philip Schaff and the Idea of Church History." Pages 1–35 in *A Century of Church History: The Legacy of Philip Schaff.* Edited by Henry W. Bowden. Carbondale: Southern Illinois University Press, 1988.

Penzel, Klaus. "Church History in Context: The Case of Philip Schaff." Pages 217–60 in *Our Common History as Christians: Essays in Honor of Albert C. Outler.* Edited by J. Deschner, L. T. Howe, and K. Penzel. New York: Oxford University Press, 1975.

2. THE ESTABLISHMENT OF HISTORICAL CRITICISM IN GREAT BRITAIN

General Works

Borsch, Frederick Houk, ed. *Anglicanism and the Bible.* Anglican Studies Series. Wilton, Conn.: Morehouse Barlow, 1984.

Edwards, David L. *Christian England (Volume 3): From the Eighteenth Century to the First World War.* Grand Rapids, Mich.: Eerdmans, 1984.

Elliott-Binns, L. E. *The Development of English Theology in the Later Nineteenth Century.* Burroughs Memorial Lectures, 1950. London: Longmans, Green, 1952.

———. *English Thought, 1860–1900: The Theological Aspect.* Greenwich, Conn.: Seabury, 1956.

Gore, Charles, ed. *Lux Mundi: A Series of Studies in the Religion of the Incarnation.* London: John Murray, 1889.

Gregory, Caspar René. *Canon and Text of the New Testament.* International Theological Library. New York: Charles Scribner's Sons, 1924.

Metzger, Bruce M. *The Canon of the New Testament: Its Origin, Development, and Significance.* Oxford: Clarendon Press, 1987.

———. *The Text of the New Testament: Its Transmission, Corruption, and Restoration.* 3d ed. New York: Oxford University Press, 1992.

Morgan, R. "Historical Criticism and Christology: England and Germany." Pages 80–108 in *England and Germany: Studies in Theological Diplomacy.* Edited by S. W. Sykes. Studies in the Intercultural History of Christianity 25. Frankfurt: Peter D. Lang, 1982.

Pals, Daniel L. *The Victorian "Lives" of Jesus.* Trinity University Monograph Series in Religion 7. San Antonio, Tex.: Trinity University Press, 1982.

Pfleiderer, Otto. *The Development of Theology in Germany since Kant: And Its Progress in Great Britain since 1825.* Translated by J. Frederick Smith. 3d ed. London: George Allen & Unwin, 1909.

New Testament Studies before and in the Time of the Cambridge Three

[Cassels, W. R.]. *Supernatural Religion: An Inquiry into the Reality of Divine Revelation.* Popular Edition. London: Watts, 1902.

Davidson, Samuel. *An Introduction to the Study of the New Testament, Critical, Exegetical, and Theological.* 2 vols. London: Longmans, Green, 1868.

Edersheim, Alfred. *The Life and Times of Jesus the Messiah.* 2 vols. New York: E. R. Herrick, n.d.

Farrar, Frederic W. *History of Interpretation.* Bampton Lectures, 1885. Grand Rapids, Mich.: Baker, 1961.

———. *The Life of Christ.* 2 vols. London: Cassell, Petter & Galpin, 1874.

Seeley, J. R. *Ecce Homo: A Survey of the Life and Work of Jesus Christ.* Everyman's Library 305. London: J. M. Dent & Sons, 1908.

Hort

Primary Sources

Hort, Fenton John Anthony. *The Apocalypse of St John I–III: The Greek Text, with Introduction, Commentary, and Additional Notes.* London: Macmillan, 1908.

———. *The Epistle of St James: The Greek Text with Introduction, Commentary as far as Chapter IV, Verse 7, and Additional Notes.* Repr. in F. J. A. Hort, *Expository and Exegetical Studies: A Compendium of Works Formerly Published Separately.* Minneapolis: Klock & Klock, 1980. (This volume also includes: *Prolegomena to St Paul's Epistles to the Romans and the Ephesians*; *The First Epistle of St Peter*; *The Apocalypse of St John.*)

———. *The First Epistle of St Peter, I.1—II.17: The Greek Text with Introductory Lecture, Commentary and Additional Notes.* London: Macmillan, 1898.

———. *Judaistic Christianity: A Course of Lectures.* Cambridge: Macmillan, 1894.

———. *Prolegomena to St Paul's Epistles to the Romans and the Ephesians.* London: Macmillan, 1895.

———. *Two Dissertations: I On ΜΟΝΟΓΕΝΗΣ ΘΕΟΣ in Scripture and Tradition. II On The 'Constantinopolitan' Creed and Other Eastern Creeds of the Fourth Century.* Cambridge: Macmillan, 1876.

Westcott, Brooke Foss, and Fenton John Anthony Hort. *The New Testament in the Original Greek: Introduction and Appendix.* New York: Harper & Brothers, 1882.

Secondary Sources

Burgon, John William. *The Revision Revised. Three Articles Reprinted from the Quarterly Review*. London: John Murray, 1883.

Colwell, Ernest C. "Hort Redivivus: A Plea and a Program." Pages 131–55 in *Transitions in Biblical Scholarship*. Edited by J. Coert Rylaarsdam. Essays in Divinity. Chicago: University of Chicago Press, 1968.

Patrick, Graham A. "1881–1981: The Centenary of the Westcott and Hort Text." *Expository Times* 92 (1980–81): 359–64.

———. "F. J. A. Hort, 1828–1892: A Neglected Theologian." *Expository Times* 90 (1978–79): 77–81.

Rupp, E. G. *Hort and the Cambridge Tradition: An Inaugural Lecture*. Cambridge: Cambridge University Press, 1970.

Lightfoot

Primary Sources

Lightfoot, J. B. *The Apostolic Fathers. Part I. S. Clement of Rome: A Revised Text with Introductions, Notes, Dissertations, and Translations*. 2 vols. London: Macmillan, 1890.

———. *The Apostolic Fathers. Part II. S. Ignatius. S. Polycarp: Revised Texts with Introductions, Notes, Dissertations, and Translations*. 3 vols. 2d ed. London: Macmillan, 1889.

———. *Biblical Essays*. London: Macmillan, 1893.

———. *The Christian Ministry*. London: Macmillan, 1901.

———. *Dissertations on the Apostolic Age: Reprinted from Editions of St Paul's Epistles*. London: Macmillan, 1892.

———. *The Epistle of Paul to the Galatians: With Introductions, Notes and Dissertations*. Grand Rapids, Mich.: Zondervan, n.d.

———. *Essays on the Work Entitled Supernatural Religion: Reprinted from The Contemporary Review*. London: Macmillan, 1889.

———. *Historical Essays*. London: Macmillan, 1896.

———. *Notes on the Epistles of St Paul (I and II Thessalonians, I Corinthians 1–7, Romans 1–7, Ephesians 1:1-14): Based on the Greek Text from Previous Unpublished Commentaries*. Classic Commentary Library. Grand Rapids, Mich.: Zondervan, 1957.

———. "Recent Editions of St Paul's Epistles." *Journal of Classical and Sacred Philology* 3 (1856): 81–121.

———. *Saint Paul's Epistles to the Colossians and to Philemon: A Revised Text with Introductions, Notes, and Dissertations*. 3d ed. London: Macmillan. 1879.

———. *Saint Paul's Epistle to the Philippians: A Revised Text with Introduction, Notes, and Dissertations*. London: Macmillan, 1927.

Secondary Sources

Barnard, L. W. "Bishop Lightfoot and the Apostolic Fathers." *Church Quarterly Review* 161 (1960): 423–35.

Barrett, C. K. "Quomodo historia conscribenda sit." *New Testament Studies* 28 (1982): 303–20.

Kaye, Bruce N. "Lightfoot and Baur on Early Christianity." *Novum Testamentum* 26 (1984): 193–224.

Richards, Paul H. "The Interpreter at Work: XVI. J. B. Lightfoot as a Biblical Interpreter." *Interpretation* 8 (1954): 50–62.

SELECT BIBLIOGRAPHY

Treloar, Geoffrey R. *Lightfoot the Historian: The Nature and Role of History in the Life and Thought of J. B. Lightfoot (1828–1889) as Churchman and Scholar.* Wissenschaftliche Untersuchungen zum Neuen Testament 2/103. Tübingen: Mohr Siebeck, 1998.

Westcott

Primary Sources

Westcott, Brooke Foss. *Christus Consummator: Some Aspects of the Work and Person of Christ in Relation to Modern Thought.* London: Macmillan, 1887.
———. *The Epistle to the Hebrews: The Greek Text with Notes and Essays.* London: Macmillan, 1889.
———. *The Epistles of St John: The Greek Text with Notes and Essays.* 2d ed. Cambridge: Macmillan, 1886.
———. *A General Survey of the History of the Canon of the New Testament.* 7th ed. London: Macmillan, 1896.
———. *A General View of the History of the English Bible.* 3d edition by William Aldis Wright. New York: Macmillan, 1922.
———. *The Gospel According to St John: The Authorized Version with Introduction and Notes.* London: John Murray, 1894.
———. *The Gospel According to St. John: The Greek Text with Introduction and Notes.* Edited by A. Westcott. 2 vols. Grand Rapids, Mich.: Eerdmans, 1954.
———. *The Gospel of Life: Thoughts Introductory to the Study of Christian Doctrine.* London: Macmillan, 1892.
———. *The Gospel of the Resurrection: Thoughts on Its Relation to Reason and History.* London: Macmillan, 1906.
———. *An Introduction to the Study of the Gospels.* 7th ed. London: Macmillan, 1888.
———. "New Testament." Volume 2, pages 506–34 in *A Dictionary of the Bible.* Edited by William Smith. 3 vols. London: John Murray, 1863.
Westcott, Brooke Foss, and Fenton John Anthony Hort. *The New Testament in the Original Greek.* New York: American Book Company, n.d.
———. *The Revelation of the Father: Short Lectures on the Titles of the Lord in the Gospel of St John.* London: Macmillan.
———. *Saint Paul's Epistle to the Ephesians: The Greek Text with Notes and Addenda.* Grand Rapids, Mich.: Eerdmans, 1950.

Secondary Sources

Barrett, C. K. *Westcott as Commentator: The Bishop Westcott Memorial Lecture, 1958.* Cambridge: Cambridge University Press, 1959.
Kuist, Howard Tillman. "The Interpreter at Work: XV. Brooke Foss Westcott (1825–1901)." *Interpretation* 7 (1953): 442–52.
Newsome, David. *Bishop Westcott and the Platonic Tradition: The Bishop Westcott Memorial Lecture, 1968.* Cambridge: Cambridge University Press, 1969.
Olofsson, Folke. *Christus Redemptor et Consummator: A Study in the Theology of B. F. Westcott.* Acta Universitatis Upsaliensis: Studia Doctrinae Christianae Upsaliensia 19. Uppsala: Uppsala University, 1979.

3. THE TRIUMPH OF LIBERALISM ON THE CONTINENT

Ritschl

Primary Sources

Ritschl, Albrecht. *Ausgewählte Werke in Einzelausgaben*. Edited by Klaus Scholder. Vol. 5: *Für und wider die Tübingen Schule*. Stuttgart-Bad Cannstatt: Friedrich Frommann (Günther Holzboog), 1975.

———. *Die christliche Lehre von der Rechtfertigung und Versöhnung: Erster Band: Die Geschichte der Lehre*. Bonn: Adolph Marcus, 1870. English translation: *A Critical History of the Christian Doctrine of Justification and Reconciliation*. Translated by John S. Black. Edinburgh: Edmonston and Douglas, 1872.

———. *Die christliche Lehre von der Rechtfertigung und Versöhnung: Zweiter Band: Der biblische Stoff der Lehre*. Bonn: Adolf Marcus, 1874.

———. *Die christliche Lehre von der Rechtfertigung und Versöhnung: Dritter Band: Die positive Entwickelung der Lehre*. Bonn: Adolph Marcus, 1874. English translation: *The Christian Doctrine of Justification and Reconciliation: The Positive Development of the Doctrine*. Edited by H. R. Mackintosh and A. B. Macaulay. Library of Religious and Philosophical Thought. Clifton, N.J.: Reference Book, 1966.

———. *Die Entstehung der altkatholischen Kirche: Eine kirchen- und dogmengeschichtliche Monographie*. 2d ed. Bonn: Adolph Marcus, 1857.

———. *Gesammelte Aufsätze*. Freiburg i. Br.: J. C. B. Mohr (Paul Siebeck), 1893.

———. *Instruction in the Christian Religion*. Translated by Alice Mead Swing. Pages 171–286 in Albert Temple Swing, *The Theology of Albrecht Ritschl*. New York: Longmans, Green, 1901.

———. *Three Essays: Theology and Metaphysics, "Prolegomena" to The History of Pietism, Instruction in the Christian Religion*. Translated by Philip Hefner. Philadelphia: Fortress Press, 1972.

———. "Über den gegenwärtigen Stand der Kritik der synoptischen Evangelien." Pages 1–51 in *Gesammelte Aufsätze*. Freiburg i. Br.: J. C. B. Mohr (Paul Siebeck), 1893.

———. "Ueber geschichtliche Methode in der Erforschung des Urchristenthums." *Jahrbücher für Deutsche Theologie* 1 (1861): 429–59. Repr., pages 469–99 in Ferdinand Christian Baur, *Ausgewählte Werke in Einzelausgaben*. Edited by Klaus Scholder. Vol. 5: *Für und wider die Tübingen Schule*. Stuttgart-Bad Cannstatt: Friedrich Frommann (Günther Holzboog), 1975.

———. "Zum Verständnis des Prologs des johanneischen Evangeliums. Ein Vorschlag." *Theologische Studien und Kritiken* 48 (1875): 576–82.

Secondary Sources

Hefner, Philip. "Baur Versus Ritschl on Early Christianity." *Church History* 31 (1962): 255–78.

Marsh, Clive. *Albrecht Ritschl and the Problem of the Historical Jesus*. San Francisco: Mellen Research University Press, 1992.

McCulloh, Gerald W. *Christ's Person and Life-Work in the Theology of Albrecht Ritschl with Special Attention to Munus Triplex*. Lanham, Md.: University Press of America, 1990.

Ringleben, Joachim, ed. *Gottes Reich und menschliche Freiheit: Ritschl-Kolloquium (Göttingen 1989)*. Göttinger theologische Arbeiten 46. Göttingen: Vandenhoeck & Ruprecht, 1990.
Schäfer, Rolf. "Das Reich Gottes bei Albrecht Ritschl und Johannes Weiss." *Zeitschrift für Theologie und Kirche* 61 (1964): 68–88.
Weyer-Menkhoff, Stephan. *Aufklärung und Offenbarung: Zur Systematik Theologie Albrecht Ritschls*. Göttinger theologische Arbeiten 37. Göttingen: Vandenhoeck & Ruprecht, 1988.

Reuss

Primary Sources

Reuss, Édouard. *La Bible, traduction nouvelle avec introductions et commentaires*. 12 vols. Paris: Sandoz et Fischbacher, 1874–81.

———. *Bibliotheca Novi Testamenti Graeci cuius editiones ab initio typographiae ad nostram aetatem impressas quotquot reperiri potuerunt collegit digessit illustravit*. Brunsvigae: C. A. Schwetschke et Filium (M. Bruhn), 1872.

———. *Histoire du canon des saintes-écritures dans l'église chrétienne*. 2d ed. Strasbourg: Treuttel et Wurtz, 1863. English translation: *History of the Canon of the Holy Scriptures in the Christian Church*. Translated by David Hunter. Edinburgh: James Gemmell, 1884.

———. *History of Christian Theology in the Apostolic Age*. Translated from the 3d ed. by Annie Harwood, with a preface and notes by R. W. Dale. 2 vols. London: Hodder and Stoughton, 1872–74.

———. *History of the Sacred Scriptures of the New Testament*. Translated from the 5th German ed. by Edward L. Houghton. 2 vols. Boston: Houghton, Mifflin, 1884.

Secondary Sources

Caquot, André. "Reuss et Renan." *Revue d'histoire et de philosophie religieuses* 71 (1991): 437–42.
Causse, A. "La Bible de Reuss et la renaissance des études d'histoire religieuse en France." *Revue d'histoire et de philosophie religieuses* 9 (1929): 1–31.
Jacob, Ed. "Édouard Reuss, un théologien indépendant." *Revue d'histoire et de philosophie religieuses* 71 (1991): 427–35.
Vincent, Jean Marcel. *Leben und Werk des frühen Eduard Reuss: Ein Beitrag zu den geistegeschichtlichen Voraussetzungen der Bibelkritik im zweiten Viertel des 19. Jahrhunderts*. Beiträge zur evangelischen Theologie 106. Munich: Ch. Kaiser, 1990.
———. "Le 'Rationalisme Mystique' d'Édouard Reuss et ses incidences sur *La Bible*." *Revue d'histoire et de philosophie religieuses* 74 (1944): 43–66.
———. "Die Stellung Eduard Reuss' zur Baurschen Tendenzkritik." *Theologische Zeitschrift* 50 (1994): 1–8.

Weizsäcker

Weizsäcker, Carl. *Das apostolische Zeitalter der christlichen Kirche*. 2d ed. Freiburg i. Br.: J. C. B. Mohr (Paul Siebeck), 1892. English translation: *The Apostolic Age of the Christian Church*. Translated by James Millar. 2 vols. Theological Translation Library. London: Williams and Norgate, 1894–95.

———. *Untersuchungen über die evangelische Geschichte: ihre Quellen und den Gang ihrer Entwicklung.* 2d ed. Tübingen: J. C. B. Mohr (Paul Siebeck), 1901.

B. Weiss

Primary Sources

Weiss, Bernhard. *Die Apostelgeschichte: Textkritische Untersuchungen und Textherstellung.* Texte und Untersuchungen 8/3. Leipzig: J. C. Hinrichs, 1893.

———. *Der Codex D in der Apostelgeschichte: Textkritische Untersuchung.* Texte und Untersuchungen 17/1 (Neue Folge 2/1). Leipzig: J. C. Hinrichs, 1897.

———. *Der erste Petrusbrief und die neuere Kritik.* Biblischen Zeit- und Streitfragen 2/9. Lichterfelde-Berlin: Edwin Runge, 1906.

———. *Die Evangelien des Markus und Lukas.* 9th ed. Kritisch-exegetischer Kommentar über das Neue Testament (Meyer-Kommentar). Göttingen: Vandenhoeck & Ruprecht, 1901.

———. *Die Geschichtlichkeit des Markusevangeliums.* Biblische Zeit- und Streitfragen. Lichterfelde-Berlin: Edwin Runge, 1905.

———. *Der Hebräerbrief in zeitgeschichtlicher Beleuchtung.* Texte und Untersuchungen 35/3 (3. Reihe; 5/3). Leipzig: J. C. Hinrichs, 1910.

———. *Der Jakobsbrief und die neuere Kritik.* Leipzig: A. Deichert (Georg Böhme), 1904.

———. *Der Johanneische Lehrbegriff in seinen Grundzügen untersucht.* Berlin: Wilhelm Hertz, 1862.

———. *Das Johannesevangelium als einheitliches Werk geschichtlich erklärt.* Berlin: Trowitzsch & Sohn, 1912.

———. *Die Katholischen Briefe: Textkritische Untersuchungen und Textherstellung.* Leipzig: J. C. Hinrichs, 1892.

———. *Kritisch exegetisches Handbuch über den Brief des Paulus an die Römer.* 7th ed. Kritisch-exegetischer Kommentar über das Neue Testament (Meyer-Kommentar). Göttingen: Vandenhoeck & Ruprecht, 1886.

———. *Das Leben Jesu.* 4th ed. 2 vols. Stuttgart: J. G. Cotta, 1902. English translation: *The Life of Christ.* Translated by J. W. Hope and M. G. Hope. 3 vols. Clark's Foreign Theological Library. Edinburgh: T. & T. Clark, 1883–84.

———. *Lehrbuch der Biblischen Theologie des Neuen Testaments.* 3d ed. Berlin: Wilhelm Hertz, 1880. English translation: *Biblical Theology of the New Testament.* Translated from 3d ed. by David Eaton and James E. Duguid. 2 vols. Clark's Foreign Theological Library. Edinburgh: T. & T. Clark, 1882–83.

———. *Lehrbuch der Einleitung in das Neue Testament.* Berlin: Wilhelm Hertz, 1886. English translation: *A Manual of Introduction to the New Testament.* Translated by A. J. K. Davidson. 2 vols. Foreign Biblical Library. New York: Funk & Wagnalls, 1889.

———. *Das Marcusevangelium und seine synoptischen Parallelen.* Berlin: Wilhelm Hertz, 1872.

———. *Das Matthäus-Evangelium.* 9th ed. Kritisch-exegetischer Kommentar über das Neue Testament (Meyer-Kommentar). Göttingen: Vandenhoeck & Ruprecht, 1898.

———. *Das Matthäusevangelium und seine Lucas-Parallelen.* Halle: Buchhandlung des Waisenhauses, 1876.

———. *Das Neue Testament: Handausgabe der Griechischen Texte.* 3 vols. Leipzig: J. C. Hinrichs, 1896–1905.

———. *Die Paulinischen Briefe im berichtigten Text mit kurzer Erläuterung zum Handgebrauch bei der Schriftlektüre.* Leipzig: J. C. Hinrichs, 1896.
———. *Der Petrinische Lehrbegriff: Beiträge zur biblischen Theologie, sowie zur Kritik und Exegese des ersten Briefes Petri und der petrinischen Reden.* Berlin: Wilhelm Schultze, 1855.
———. *Der Philipper-Brief ausgelegt und die Geschichte seiner Auslegung kritisch dargestellt.* Berlin: Wilhelm Hertz, 1859.
———. *The Present Status of the Inquiry concerning the Genuineness of the Pauline Epistles.* Reprinted from *The American Journal of Theology*, Vol. 1, No. 2, April 1897. Chicago: University of Chicago Press, 1897.
———. *Die Quellen des Lukasevangeliums.* Stuttgart: J. G. Cotta, 1907.
———. *Die Quellen der Synoptischen Überlieferung.* Texte und Untersuchungen 32 (3. Reihe; 2/3). Leipzig: J. C. Hinrichs, 1908.
———. *The Religion of the New Testament.* Translated by George H. Schodde. New York and London: Funk & Wagnalls, 1905.
———. *Textkritik der Paulinischen Briefe.* Texte und Untersuchungen 14/3. Leipzig: J. C. Hinrichs, 1896.
———. *Die Vier Evangelien im berichtigten Text, mit kurzer Erläuterung zum Handgebrauch bei der Schriftlektüre.* Leipzig: J. C. Hinrichs, 1900.

Secondary Sources

Gregory, Caspar René. "Bernhard Weiss and the New Testament." *American Journal of Theology* 1 (1897): 16–37.

Holtzmann

Primary Sources

Holtzmann, Heinrich Julius. *Die Entstehung des Neuen Testaments.* Religionsgeschichtliche Volksbücher I. Reihe; 11. Heft. Tübingen: J. C. B. Mohr (Paul Siebeck), 1906.
———. *Evangelium, Briefe und Offenbarung des Johannes.* Hand-Commentar zum Neuen Testament 4. Freiburg i. Br.: J. C. B. Mohr (Paul Siebeck), 1891.
———. *Judenthum und Christenthum im Zeitalter der apokryphischen und neutestamentlichen Literatur.* Volume 2 of *Geschichte des Volkes Israel und der Entstehung des Christenthums.* By Georg Weber und Heinr. Holtzmann. Leipzig: Wilhelm Engelmann, 1867.
———. *Lehrbuch der historisch-kritischen Einleitung in das Neue Testament.* 2d ed. Sammlung Theologischer Lehrbücher. Freiburg i. Br.: J. C. B. Mohr (Paul Siebeck), 1886.
———. *Lehrbuch der neutestamentlichen Theologie.* 2d ed. 2 vols. Tübingen: J. C. B. Mohr (Paul Siebeck), 1911.
———. *Das messianische Bewusstsein Jesu: Ein Beitrag zur Leben-Jesu-Forschung.* Tübingen: J. C. B. Mohr (Paul Siebeck), 1907.
———. *Die Pastoralbriefe, kritisch und exegetisch behandelt.* Leipzig: Wilhelm Engelmann, 1880.
———. *Praktische Erklärung des I. Thessalonicherbriefes.* Edited by Eduard Simons. Tübingen: J. C. B. Mohr (Paul Siebeck), 1911.
———. *Die Synoptiker. Die Apostelgeschichte.* Hand-Commentar zum Neuen Testament 1. Freiburg i. Br.: J. C. B. Mohr (Paul Siebeck), 1889.

———. *Die synoptischen Evangelien: Ihr Ursprung und geschichtlicher Character.* Leipzig: Wilhelm Engelmann, 1863.

Secondary Sources

Peabody, David B. "Chapters in the History of the Linguistic Argument for Solving the Synoptic Problem: The Nineteenth Century in Context." Pages 47–68 in *Jesus, the Gospels, and the Church: Essays in Honor of William R. Farmer.* Edited by E. P. Sanders. Macon, Ga.: Mercer University Press, 1987.

———. "H. J. Holtzmann and His European Colleagues: Aspects of the Nineteenth-Century European Discussion of Gospel Origins." Pages 50–131 in *Biblical Studies and the Shifting of Paradigms, 1850–1914.* Edited by Henning Graf Reventlow and William Farmer. Journal for the Study of the Old Testament: Supplement Series 192. Sheffield: Sheffield Academic Press, 1995.

Steck, Karl Gerhard. "Heinrich Julius Holtzmanns Beitrag zur Kontroverse über Schrift und Tradition." Pages 371–87 in *Hören und Handeln: Festschrift für Ernst Wolf zum 60. Geburtstag.* Edited by Helmut Gollwitzer and Hellmut Traub. Munich: Chr. Kaiser, 1962.

Harnack

Primary Sources

von Harnack, Adolf. *Die Apostellehre und die jüdischen beiden Wege.* 2d ed. Leipzig: J. C. Hinrichs, 1896.

———. *Beiträge zur Einleitung in das Neue Testament I: Lukas der Artz: Der Verfasser des dritten Evangeliums und der Apostelgeschichte.* Leipzig: J. C. Hinrichs, 1906. English translation: *New Testament Studies I: Luke the Physician: The Author of the Third Gospel and the Acts of the Apostles.* Translated by J. R. Wilkinson. 2d ed. Crown Theological Library 20. London: Williams & Norgate, 1909.

———. *Beiträge zur Einleitung in das Neue Testament II: Sprüche und Reden Jesu: Die zweite Quelle des Matthäus und Lukas.* Leipzig: J. C. Hinrichs, 1907. English translation: *New Testament Studies II: The Sayings of Jesus: The Second Source of St. Matthew and St. Luke.* Translated by. J. R. Wilkinson. Crown Theological Library 23. New York: G. P. Putnam's Sons, 1908.

———. *Beiträge zur Einleitung in das Neue Testament III: Die Apostelgeschichte.* Leipzig: J. C. Hinrichs, 1908. English translation: *New Testament Studies III: The Acts of the Apostles.* Translated by J. R. Wilkinson. Crown Theological Library 27. New York: G. P. Putnam's Sons, 1909.

———. *Beiträge zur Einleitung in das Neue Testament IV: Neue Untersuchungen zur Apostelgeschichte und zur Abfassungszeit der synoptischen Evangelien.* Leipzig: J. C. Hinrichs, 1911. English translation: *New Testament Studies IV: The Date of the Acts and of the Synoptic Gospels.* Translated by J. R. Wilkinson. Crown Theological Library 33. London: Williams & Norgate, 1911.

———. *Beiträge zur Einleitung in das Neue Testament V: Über den privaten Gebrauch der Heiligen Schriften in der alten Kirche.* Leipzig: J. C. Hinrichs, 1912. English translation: *New Testament Studies V: Bible Reading in the Early Church.* Translated by J. R. Wilkinson. Crown Theological Library 36. London: Williams & Norgate, 1912.

———. *Beiträge zur Einleitung in das Neue Testament VI: Die Entstehung des Neuen Testaments und die wichtigsten Folgen der neuen Schöpfung.* Leipzig: J. C. Hinrichs, 1914.

English translation: *New Testament Studies VI: The Origin of the New Testament and the Most Important Consequences of the New Creation.* Translated by J. R. Wilkinson. Crown Theological Library 45. London: Williams & Norgate, 1925.

———. *Die Briefsammlung des Apostels Paulus und die anderen vorkonstantinischen christlichen Briefsammlungen: Sechs Vorlesungen aus der altkirchlichen Literaturgeschichte.* Leipzig: J. C. Hinrichs, 1926.

———. *Das Christentum und die Geschichte: Ein Vortrag.* Leipzig: J. C. Hinrichs, 1895. English translation: *Christianity and History.* Translated by Thos. Bailey Saunders. London: Adam & Charles Black, 1896.

———. *Die Entstehung der christlichen Theologie und des kirchlichen Dogmas: Sechs Vorlesungen.* Bücherei der christlichen Welt. Gotha: Leopold Plotz, 1927.

———. *Entstehung und Entwickelung der Kirchenverfassung und des Kirchenrechts in den zwei ersten Jahrhunderten; nebst einer Kritik der Abhandlung R. Sohms: "Wesen und Ursprung des Katholizismus," und Untersuchungen über "Evangelium," "Wort Gottes" und das trinitarische Bekenntnis.* Leipzig J. C. Hinrichs, 1910. English translation: *The Constitution and Law of the Church in the First Two Centuries.* Translated by F. L. Pogson. Edited by H. D. A. Major. Crown Theological Library 31. London: Williams & Norgate, 1910.

———. *Aus der Friedens- und Kriegsarbeit. Reden und Aufsätze.* Neue Folge 3. Giessen: Alfred Töpelmann, 1916.

———. *Geschichte der altchristlichen Literatur bis Eusebius.* 2d ed. by Kurt Aland. 2 vols. in 4. Leipzig: J. C. Hinrichs, 1958.

———. *Lehrbuch der Dogmengeschichte.* Vol. 1, *Die Entstehung des kirchlichen Dogmas.* Sammlung Theologischer Lehbücher. Freiburg i. Br.: J. C. B. Mohr (Paul Siebeck), 1886. English translation: *History of Dogma.* Vol. 1. Translated from 3d ed. by Neil Buchanan. New York: Russell & Russell, 1958.

———. *Die Lehre der Zwölf Apostel, nebst Untersuchungen zur ältesten Geschichte der Kirchenverfassung und des Kirchenrechts.* Texte und Untersuchengen 2 (1886) 1, 2. Leipzig: J. C. Hinrichs, 1884.

———. *Marcion: Das Evangelium vom fremden Gott: Eine Monographie zur Geschichte der Grundlegung der katholischen Kirche.* 2d ed. Texte und Untersuchungen 45. Leipzig: J. C. Hinrichs, 1924. English translation: *Marcion: The Gospel of the Alien God.* Translated by John E. Steely and Lyle D. Bierma. Durham, N.C.: Labyrinth, 1990.

———. *Die Mission und Ausbreitung des Christentums in den Ersten drei Jahrhunderten.* 2d ed. Vol. 1, *Die Mission in Wort und Tat.* Leipzig: J. C. Hinrichs, 1906. English translation: *The Mission and Expansion of Christianity in the First Three Centuries.* Translated by James Moffatt. Harper Torchbooks/The Cloister Library. New York: Harper & Brothers, 1961.

———. *Outlines of the History of Dogma.* Translated by Edwin Knox Mitchell, with an Introduction by Philip Rieff. Boston: Beacon, 1957.

———. *Studien zur Geschichte des Neuen Testaments und der alten Kirche: I Zur neutestamentlichen Textkritik.* Arbeiten zur Kirchengeschichte. Berlin: Walter de Gruyter, 1931.

———. "Über die Sicherheit und die Grenzen geschichtlicher Erkenntnis: Ein Vortrag." Pages 3–23 in Adolf v. Harnack, *Erforschtes und Erlebtes. Reden und Aufsätze.* Neue Folge 4. Giessen: Alfred Töpelmann, 1923.

———. "Die Verklärungsgeschichte Jesu, der Bericht des Paulus (I. Kor. 15,3ff.) und die beiden Christusvisionen des Petrus." Sitzungsberichte der preussischen Akademie der Wissenschaften 7 (1922): 62–80. Repr., Berlin: Akademie der Wissenschaften (Walter de Gruyter), 1922.

———. *Das Wesen des Christentums: Sechzehn Vorlesungen vor Studierenden aller Fakultäten im Wintersemester 1899/1900 an der Universität Berlin gehalten.* 1900. Repr., Leipzig: J. C. Hinrichs, 1929. English translation: *What Is Christianity?* Translated by Thomas Bailey Saunders. Introduction by Rudolf Bultmann. Harper Torchbooks/The Cloister Library. New York: Harper & Brothers, 1957.

———. *Aus Wissenschaft und Leben. Reden und Aufsätze.* Neue Folge 2. Giessen: Alfred Töpelmann, 1911.

Secondary Sources

Bammel, Ernst. "The Jesus of History in the Theology of Adolf v. Harnack." *Modern Churchman* 19 (1976): 90–112.

Döbertin, Winfried. *Adolf von Harnack: Theologe, Pädagoge, Wissenschaftspolitiker.* European University Studies; Series XXIII: Theology, Vol. 258. Frankfurt am Main: Peter Lang, 1985.

Glick, G. Wayne. "Nineteenth Century Theological and Cultural Influences on Adolf Harnack." *Church History* 29 (1959): 157–82.

———. *The Reality of Christianity: A Study of Adolf von Harnack as Historian and Theologian.* Makers of Modern Theology. New York: Harper & Row, 1967.

Jantsch, Johanna. *Die Entstehung des Christentums bei Adolf von Harnack und Eduard Meyer.* Habelts Dissertationsdrucke: Reihe alte Geschichte. Bonn: Rudolf Habelt, 1990.

Meijering, E. P. *Theologische Urteil über die Dogmengeschichte: Ritschls Einfluss auf von Harnack.* Beihefte zur Zeitschrift für Religions- und Geistesgeschichte 20. Leiden: E. J. Brill, 1978.

Zahn-Harnack, Agnes von. *Adolf von Harnack.* 2d ed. Berlin: Walter de Gruyter, 1951.

4. THE RETURN OF SKEPTICISM

Overbeck

Primary Sources

Overbeck, Franz. *Christentum und Kultur: Gedanken und Anmerkungen zur modernen Theologie.* Edited by Carl Albrecht Bernoulli. 1919. Repr., Darmstadt: Wissenschaftliche Buchgesellschaft, 1963.

———. "Introduction to the Acts of the Apostles." Vol. 1, pages 2–81 in *The Contents and Origin of the Acts of the Apostles, Critically Investigated, by Edward Zeller.* Translated by Joseph Dare. Theological Translation Fund. London: Williams & Norgate, 1875.

———. *Das Johannesevangelium: Studien zur Kritik seiner Erforschung.* Edited by Carl Albrecht Bernoulli. Tübingen: J. C. B. Mohr (Paul Siebeck), 1911.

———. *Kurze Erklärung der Apostelgeschichte von Dr. W. M. L. DeWette, vierte Auflage bearbeitet und stark erweitert von F. O.* Leipzig, 1870.

———. *Werke und Nachlass: 1 Schriften bis 1873.* Edited by Ekkehard W. Stegemann and Niklaus Peter. *2 Schriften bis 1880.* Edited by Ekkehard W. Stegemann and Rudolf Brändle. 4 *Kirchenlexicon Texte Ausgewählte Artikel A–I.* Edited by Barbara von Reibnitz. 5 *Kirchenlexicon Texte Ausgewählte Artikel J–A.* Edited by Barbara von Reibnitz. 6/1 Kirchenlexicon Materialien: Christentum und Kultur. Edited by Barbara von Reibnitz. Stuttgart: J. B. Metzler, 1994–96.

Secondary Sources

Brändle, Rudolf, and Ekkehard W. Stegemann, eds. *Franz Overbecks unerledigte Anfragen an das Christentum*. Munich: Chr. Kaiser, 1988.

Eberlein, Hermann-Peter. *Theologie als Scheitern? Franz Overbecks Geschichte mit der Geschichte*. Theologie in der Blauen Eule 3. Essen: Die Blaue Eule, 1989.

Emmelius, Johann-Christoph. *Tendenzkritik und Formengeschichte: Der Beitrag Franz Overbecks zur Auslegung der Apostelgeschichte im 19. Jahrhundert*. Forschungen zur Kirchen- und Dogmengeschichte 27. Göttingen: Vandenhoeck & Ruprecht, 1975.

Luehrs, Robert B. "Christianity against History: Franz Overbeck's Concept of the *Finis Christianismi*." *Katallagete* 5 (1975): 15–20.

Pfeiffer, Arnold. *Franz Overbecks Kritik des Christentums*. Studien zur Theologie und Geistesgeschichte des Neunzehnten Jahrhunderts 15. Göttingen: Vandenhoeck & Ruprecht, 1975.

Vielhauer, Philipp. "Franz Overbeck und die neutestamentliche Wissenschaft." *Evangelische Theologie* 10 (1950/51): 193–207. Repr., pages 235–52 in *Aufsätze zum Neuen Testament*. Theologische Bücherei 31. Munich: Chr. Kaiser, 1965.

Wrede

Primary Sources

Wrede, William. *Über Aufgabe und Methode der sogenannten Neutestamentlichen Theologie*. Göttingen: Vandenhoeck & Ruprecht, 1897. English translation: "The Task and Methods of 'New Testament Theology.'" Pages 68–116 in *The Nature of New Testament Theology: The Contribution of William Wrede and Adolf Schlatter*. Edited by Robert Morgan. Studies in Biblical Theology, Second Series 25. Naperville, Ill.: Alec R. Allenson, 1973.

———. *Charakter und Tendenz des Johannesevangeliums*. Sammlung gemeinverständlicher Vorträge und Schriften aus dem Gebiet der Theologie und Religionsgeschichte. Tübingen: J. C. B. Mohr (Paul Siebeck), 1933. Reprint of pages 178–231 in William Wrede, *Vorträge und Studien*. Tübingen: J. C. B. Mohr (Paul Siebeck), 1907.

———. *Die Echtheit des zweiten Thessalonicherbriefs*. Texte und Untersuchungen. Neue Folge 9/2. Leipzig: J. C. Hinrichs, 1903.

———. *Die Entstehung der Schriften des Neuen Testaments*. Lebensfragen: Schriften und Leben 18. Tübingen: J. C. B. Mohr (Paul Siebeck), 1907. English translation: *The Origin of the New Testament*. Translated by James S. Hill. Harper's Library of Living Thought. London: Harper & Brothers, 1909.

———. *Das literarische Rätsel des Hebräerbriefs*. Forschungen zur Religion und Literatur des Alten und Neuen Testaments 8. Göttingen: Vandenhoeck & Ruprecht, 1906.

———. *Das Messiasgeheimnis in den Evangelien: Zugleich ein Beitrag zum Verständnis des Markusevangeliums*. Göttingen: Vandenhoeck & Ruprecht, 1901. English translation: *The Messianic Secret*. Translated by J. C. G. Greig. Library of Theological Translations. Cambridge: James Clarke, 1971.

———. *Paulus*. 2d ed. Religionsgeschtliche Volksbücher 1. Reihe, 5/6. Tübingen: J. C. B. Mohr (Paul Siebeck), 1907. English translation: *Paul*. Translated by Edward Lummis. 1908. Repr., Lexington, Ky.: American Theological Library Association, 1962.

———. *Vorträge und Studien*. Tübingen: J. C. B. Mohr (Paul Siebeck), 1907.

Secondary Sources

Morgan, Robert. "Re-Reading Wrede." *Expository Times* 108 (1997): 207–10.

Robinson, William C., Jr. "The Quest for Wrede's Secret Messiah." *Interpretation* 27 (1973).

Rollmann, Hans. "*Paulus alienus:* William Wrede on Comparing Jesus and Paul." Pages 23–45 in *From Jesus to Paul: Studies in Honour of Francis Wright Beare.* Edited by Peter Richardson and John C. Hurd. Waterloo: Wilfrid Laurier University Press, 1984.

———. "William Wrede, Albert Eichhorn, and the 'Old Quest' of the Historical Jesus." Pages 79–99 in *Self-Definition and Self-Discovery in Early Christianity: A Study in Changing Horizons.* Edited by David J. Hawkin and Tom Robinson. Studies in the Bible and Early Christianity 26. Lewiston: Edwin Mellen, 1990.

Schreiber, Johannes. "Wellhausen und Wrede: eine methodische Differenz." *Zeitschrift für die neutestamentliche Wissenschaft und die Kunde der ältesten Kirche* 79 (1988): 24–41.

Taylor, Vincent. "Important and Influential Foreign Books: W. Wrede's The Messianic Secret in the Gospels." *Expository Times* 65 (1953–54): 246–50.

Tuckett, Christopher, ed. *The Messianic Secret.* Issues in Religion and Theology 1. Philadelphia: Fortress Press, 1983.

Wellhausen

Primary Sources

Wellhausen, Julius. *Analyse der Offenbarung Johannis.* Abhandlungen der königlichen Gesellschaft der Wissenschaften zu Göttingen. Philologisch-Historische Klasse. Neue Folge 9/4. Berlin: Weidmann, 1907.

———. *Einleitung in die drei ersten Evangelien.* Berlin: Georg Reimer, 1905. 2d ed. Berlin: Georg Reimer, 1911. Repr., pages 1–176 in *Evangelienkommentare.* Berlin: Walter de Gruyter, 1987.

———. *Erweiterungen und Änderungen im vierten Evangelium.* Berlin: Georg Reimer, 1907.

———. *Das Evangelium Johannis.* Berlin: Georg Reimer, 1908. Repr., pages 601–746 in *Evangelienkommentare.* Berlin: Walter de Gruyter, 1987.

———. *Das Evangelium Lucae übersetzt und erklärt.* Berlin: Georg Reimer, 1904. Repr., pages 459–600 in *Evangelienkommentare.* Berlin: Walter de Gruyter, 1987.

———. *Das Evangelium Marci übersetzt und erklärt.* 2d ed. Berlin: Georg Reimer, 1909. Repr., pages 321–457 in *Evangelienkommentare.* Berlin: Walter de Gruyter, 1987.

———. *Das Evangelium Matthaei übersetzt und erklärt.* 2d ed. Berlin: Georg Reimer, 1914. Repr., pages 177–320 in *Evangelienkommentare.* Berlin: Walter de Gruyter, 1987.

———. *Israelitische und Jüdische Geschichte.* 9th ed. Berlin: Walter de Gruyter, 1958.

———. *Kritische Analyse der Apostelgeschichte.* Abhandlungen der königlichen Gesellschaft der Wissenschaften zu Göttingen. Philologisch-Historische Klasse. Neue Folge 15/2. Berlin: Weidmann, 1914.

———. *Die Pharisäer und die Sadducäer: Eine Untersuchung zur inneren jüdischen Geschichte.* Greifswald: L. Bamberg, 1874.

Secondary Sources

Bovon, François. "Julius Wellhausen's Exegesis of Luke 15:11-32." Pages 118–13 in *Exegesis: Problems of Method and Exercises in Reading (Genesis 22 and Luke 15): Studies Published under the Direction of François Bovon and Grégoire Rouiller*. Translated by Donald G. Miller. Pittsburgh Theological Monograph Series 21, Pittsburgh: Pickwick, 1978.

Dahl, Nils A. "Wellhausen on the New Testament." Pages 89–110 in *Julius Wellhausen and His Prolegomena to the History of Israel*. Edited by Douglas A. Knight. *Semeia* 25 (1983).

Rouiller, Grégoire. "Julius Wellhausen: His Historical and Critical Method." Pages 97–117 in *Exegesis: Problems of Method and Exercises in Reading (Genesis 22 and Luke 15)*.

Timmer, John. *Julius Wellhausen and the Synoptic Gospels: A Study in Tradition Growth*. Academisch Proefschrift. University of Amsterdam. Rotterdam: Bonder-Offset N.V., 1970.

Jülicher

Primary Sources

Jülicher, Adolf. "Adolf Jülicher." Pages 159–200 in *Die Religionswissenschaft der Gegenwart in Selbstdarstellungen* 4. Edited by Erich Stange. Leipzig: Felix Meiner, 1928.

———. *Einleitung in das Neue Testament*. Grundriss der theologischen Wissenschaften 3/1. 3d and 4th ed. Tübingen: J. C. B. Mohr (Paul Siebeck), 1901. English translation: *An Introduction to the New Testament*. Translated by Janet Penrose Ward. New York: G. P. Putnam's Sons, 1904.

———. "Die Geschichte des Neuen Testaments." Pages 1–30 in *Die Schriften des Neuen Testaments: neu übersetzt und für Gegenwart erklärt*. Edited by W. Bousset and W. Heitmüller. 3d ed., 1. Halbband, 1–30. Göttingen: Vandenhoeck & Ruprecht, 1916.

———. *Die Gleichnisreden Jesu. Erster Teil: Die Gleichnisreden Jesu im Allgemeinen. Zweiter Teil: Auslegung der Gleichnisreden der drei ersten Evangelien*. 2d ed. Tübingen: J. C. B. Mohr (Paul Siebeck), 1910.

———. *Neue Linien in der Kritik der evangelischen Überlieferung*. Vorträge des Hessischen und Nassauischen theologischen Ferienkurses 3. Giessen: Alfred Töpelmann, 1906.

———. "Parables." Pages 3563–67 in *Encyclopaedia Biblica: A Critical Dictionary of the Literary, Political and Religious History, the Archaeology Geography and Natural History of the Bible* 3. Edited by T. K. Cheyne and J. Sutherland Black. London: Adam and Charles Black, 1902.

———. *Paulus und Jesus*. Religionsgeschichtliche Volksbücher. 1. Reihe; 14. Heft. Tübingen: J. C. B. Mohr (Paul Siebeck), 1907.

———. "Die Religion Jesu und die Anfänge des Christentums bis zum Nicaenum (325)." Pages 41–128 in J. Wellhausen, A. Jülicher, et al., *Die Christliche Religion. I Hälfte: Geschichte der christlichen Religion*. Die Kultur der Gegenwart 1/4. Berlin: B. G. Teubner, 1906.

Secondary Sources

Harnisch, Wolfgang, ed. *Gleichnisse Jesu: Positionen der Auslegung von Adolf Jülicher bis zur Formgeschichte*. Wege der Forschung 366. Darmstadt: Wissenschaftliche Buchgesellschaft, 1982.

Ulrich, Mell, ed. *Die Gleichnisreden Jesu 1899–1999: Beiträge zum Dialog mit Adolf Jülicher.* Beihefte zur Zeitschrift für die neutestamentliche Wissenschaft 103. Berlin: Walter de Gruyter, 1999.

Loisy

Primary Sources

Loisy, Alfred. *Les Actes des Apôtres.* Paris: Émile Nourry, 1920.
———. *Choses passées.* Paris: Émile Nourry, 1913. English translation: *My Duel with the Vatican: The Autobiography of a Catholic Modernist.* Translated by Richard Wilson Boynton. New York: E. P. Dutton, 1924.
———. *L'Épître aux Galates.* Paris: Émile Nourry, 1916.
———. *Études bibliques.* 3d ed. Paris: Alphonse Picare et Fils, 1903.
———. *Études évangéliques.* Paris: Alphonse Picard et Fils, 1902.
———. *L'Évangile et l'Église.* Paris: Alphonse Picard et Fils, 1902. English translation: *The Gospel and the Church.* Translated by Christopher Home. Introduction by Bernard B. Scott. Lives of Jesus Series. Philadelphia: Fortress Press, 1976.
———. *L'Évangile selon Luc.* Paris: Émile Nourry, 1924.
———. *L'Évangile selon Marc.* Paris: Émile Nourry, 1912.
———. *Les évangiles synoptiques.* 2 vols. Ceffonds: the Author, 1907–8.
———. *Jésus et la tradition évangélique.* Paris, 1910. Repr., Frankfurt: Minerva, 1971.
———. *Les livres du Nouveau Testament, traduits du grec en français avec introduction général et notices.* Paris: Émile Nourry, 1922.
———. *Mémoires: pour servir à l'histoire religieuse de notre temps.* 3 vols. Paris Émile Nourry, 1930–31.
———. *Les mystères païens et le mystère chrétien.* Paris: Émile Nourry, 1914.
———. *La naissance du christianisme.* Paris: Émile Nourry, 1933. English translation: *The Birth of the Christian Religion.* Translated by L. P. Jacks. London: George Allen & Unwin, 1948.
———. *Les origines du Nouveau Testament.* Paris, 1936. Repr., Frankfurt: Minerva, 1971. English translation: *The Origins of the New Testament.* Translated by L. P. Jacks. New York: Macmillan, 1950.
———. *Le quatrième évangile.* 2d ed. *Les épîtres dites de Jean.* Paris: Émile Nourry, 1921.
———. *Remarques sur la littérature épistolaire du Nouveau Testament.* Paris: Émile Nourry, 1935.

Secondary Sources

Burke, Ronald. "Loisy's Faith: Landshift in Catholic Thought." *Journal of Religion* 60 (1980): 138–64.
Dietrich, Wendell S. "Loisy and the Liberal Protestants." *Studies in Religion* 14 (1985): 303–11.
Hill, Harvey. "La Science Catholique: Alfred Loisy's Program of Historical Theology." *Zeitschrift für neuere Theologiegeschichte/Journal for the History of Modern Theology* 3 (1996): 39–59.
Jones, Alan H. *Independence and Exegesis: The Study of Early Christianity in the Work of Alfred Loisy (1857–1940), Charles Guignebert (1857–1939) and Maurice Goguel (1880–1955).* Beiträge zur Geschichte der biblischen Exegese 26. Tübingen: J. C. B. Mohr (Paul Siebeck), 1983.

Moran, Valentine G. "Loisy's Theological Development." *Theological Studies* 40 (1979): 411–52.

———. *(Re)reading, Reception, and Rhetoric: Approaches to Roman Catholic Modernism.* American University Studies 7, Theology and Religion 206. New York: Peter Lang, 1999.

Turvasi, Francesco. *The Condemnation of Alfred Loisy and the Historical Method.* Uomini e Dottrine 24. Rome: Edizioni de Storia e Letteratura, 1979.

5. NEW DISCOVERIES: LINGUISTIC, GEOGRAPHICAL, AND HISTORICAL RESEARCH

Deissmann

Deissmann, Adolf. "Adolf Deissmann." Pages 43–78 in *Die Religionswissenschaft der Gegenwart in Selbstdarstellungen* 1. Edited by Erich Stange. Leipzig: Felix Meiner, 1925.

———. *Evangelium und Urchristentum. (Das Neue Testament im Lichte der historischen Forschung.)* Beiträge zur Weiterentwicklung der christlichen Religion 3. Munich: J. F. Lehmann, n.d.

———. *Licht vom Osten: Das Neue Testament und die neuentdeckten Texte der hellenistisch-römischen Welt.* 4th ed. Tübingen: J. C. B. Mohr (Paul Siebeck), 1923. English translation: *Light from the Ancient East: The New Testament Illustrated by Recently Discovered Texts of the Graeco-Roman World.* Translated by Lionel R. M. Strachan. New York: George H. Doran, 1927.

———. *Die neutestamentliche Formel "in Christo Jesu."* Marburg: N. G. Elwert, 1892.

———. *New Light on the New Testament: From Records of the Graeco-Roman Period.* Translated by Lionel R. M. Strachan. Edinburgh: T. & T. Clark, 1908.

———. *The New Testament in the Light of Modern Research: The Haskell Lectures, 1929.* Garden City, N.Y.: Doubleday, Doran, 1929.

———. *Paulus: Eine kultur- und religionsgeschichtliche Skizze.* 2d ed. Tübingen: J. C. B. Mohr (Paul Siebeck), 1925. English translation: *Paul: A Study in Social and Religious History.* Translated by William E. Wilson. 1927. Repr., Harper Torchbooks. New York: Harper & Brothers, 1957.

———. *The Philology of the Greek Bible: Its Present and Future.* London: Hodder and Stoughton, 1908.

———. *The Religion of Jesus and the Faith of Paul: The Selly Oak Lectures, 1923, on the Communion of Jesus with God and the Communion of Paul with Christ.* Translated by William E. Wilson. New York: George H. Doran, 1923.

———. *Die sprachliche Erforschung der griechischen Bibel, ihr gegenwärtiger Stand und ihre Aufgaben.* Vorträge der theologischen Konferenz zu Giessen 12. Giessen: J. Ricker, 1898.

———. *Das Urchristentum und die unteren Schichten.* 2d ed. Göttingen: Vandenhoeck & Ruprecht, 1908.

———. *Die Urgeschichte des Christentums im Lichte der Sprachforschung.* Tübingen: J. C. B. Mohr (Paul Siebeck), 1910.

Grammatical and Lexicographical Research

Blass, Friedrich. *Acta apostolorum sive Lucae ad Theophilum liber alter. Editio philologica apparatu critico, commentario perpetuo, indice verborum illustrata.* Göttingen: Vandenhoeck & Ruprecht, 1895.

———. *Euangelium secundum Lucam sive Lucae ad Theophilum liber prior. Secundum formam quae videtur Romanam.* Leipzig: B. G. Teubner, 1897.

———. *Grammatik des neutestamentlichen Griechisch.* Göttingen: Vandenhoeck & Ruprecht, 1896. English translation: *Grammar of New Testament Greek.* Translated by Henry St. John Thackeray. 2d ed. London: Macmillan, 1905.

———. *Philology of the Gospels.* London, 1898. Repr., Amsterdam: B. R. Grüner, 1969.

———. *Über die Textkritik im Neuen Testament. Ein Vortrag, gehalten auf der theologischen Konferenz in Eisenach am 25. Mai 1904.* Leipzig: A. Deichert (Georg Böhme), 1904.

Buttmann, Alexander. *A Grammar of the New Testament Greek.* Translated by J. H. Thayer. Andover, Mass.: Warren F. Draper, 1873.

Cremer, Hermann. *Biblisch-theologisches Wörterbuch der Neutestamentlichen Gräcität.* 7th ed. Gotha: Friedrich Andreas Perthes, 1893. English translation: *Biblico-Theological Lexicon of New Testament Greek.* Translated by William Urwick. 4th English ed. Edinburgh: T. & T. Clark, 1895.

Grimm, Carl Ludwig Wilibald. *Lexicon graeco-latinum in libros Novi Testamenti.* 2d ed. Leipzig: Arnold, 1878.

Porter, Stanley E., and Jeffrey T. Reed. "Greek Grammar since BDF: A Retrospective and Prospective Analysis." *Filologia Neotestamentaria* 4 (1991): 143–64.

Winer, Georg Benedikt. *A Grammar of the Idiom of the New Testament, Prepared as a Solid Basis for the Interpretation of the New Testament.* 7th edition by Gottlieb Lünemann. Translated by J. Henry Thayer. Andover, Mass.: Warren F. Draper, 1883.

———. *A Treatise on the Grammar of New Testament Greek, Regarded as a Sure Basis for New Testament Exegesis.* Translated by W. F. Moulton. 3d ed. (9th English ed.). Edinburgh: T. & T. Clark, 1882.

Moulton

Primary Sources

Moulton, James Hope. *From Egyptian Rubbish-Heaps.* London: Charles H. Kelly, 1916.

———. *A Grammar of New Testament Greek, Vol. 1: Prolegomena.* 3d ed. Edinburgh: T. & T. Clark, 1908.

Moulton, James Hope, and George Milligan. *The Vocabulary of the Greek Testament: Illustrated from the Papyri and Other Non-Literary Sources.* London: Hodder and Stoughton, 1949.

Secondary Sources

Barrett, C. Kingsley. "Biblical Classics: IV. J. H. Moulton: A Grammar of New Testament Greek: Prolegomena." *Expository Times* 90 (1978): 68–71.

Hemer, C. J. "Towards a New Moulton and Milligan." *Novum Testamentum* 24 (1982): 97–123.

North, J. L. "'I Sought a Colleague': James Hope Moulton, Papyrologist, and Edward Lee Hicks, Epigraphist, 1903–1906." *Bulletin of the John Rylands University Library of Manchester* 79 (1997): 195–206.

Ramsay

Primary Sources

Ramsay, William M. *The Bearing of Recent Discovery on the Trustworthiness of the New Testament.* 4th ed. London: Hodder and Stoughton, 1920.
———. *The Church in the Roman Empire before A.D. 170.* Mansfield College Lectures. New York: G. P. Putnam's Sons, 1893.
———. *The Cities of St. Paul: Their Influence on His Life and Thought: The Cities of Eastern Asia Minor.* London: Hodder and Stoughton, 1907. Repr., Grand Rapids, Mich.: Baker, 1963.
———. *A Historical Commentary on St. Paul's Epistle to the Galatians.* New York: G. P. Putnam's Sons, 1900. Repr., Grand Rapids, Mich.: Baker, 1979.
———. *The Historical Geography of Asia Minor.* Royal Geographical Society, Supplementary Papers 4. London: John Murray, 1890. Repr., Amsterdam: Adolf M. Hakkert, 1962.
———. *The Letters to the Seven Churches of Asia and Their Place in the Plan of the Apocalypse.* London: Hodder and Stoughton, 1904. Repr., Grand Rapids, Mich.: Baker, 1963.
———. *Luke the Physician and Other Studies in the History of Religion.* London: Hodder and Stoughton, 1908. Repr., Grand Rapids, Mich.: Baker, 1956.
———. *Pauline and Other Studies in Early Christian History.* London: Hodder and Stoughton, 1906.
———. *St. Paul the Traveler and the Roman Citizen.* 3d ed. London: Hodder and Stoughton, 1897. Repr., Grand Rapids, Mich.: Baker, 1962.
———. *Was Christ Born at Bethlehem? A Study on the Credibility of St. Luke.* 3d ed. London: Hodder and Stoughton, 1905.

Secondary Sources

Gasque, W. Ward. *Sir William M. Ramsay: Archaeologist and New Testament Scholar: A Survey of His Contribution to the Study of the New Testament.* Baker Studies in Biblical Archaeology. Grand Rapids, Mich.: Baker, 1966.
Howard, Wilbert Francis. "William Mitchell Ramsay: Archaeologist and Historian." *Religion in Life* 8 (1939): 580–90. Repr., pages 138–55 in Wilbert Francis Howard, *The Romance of New Testament Scholarship.* Drew Lectureship in Biography. London: Epworth, 1949.
Yamauchi, Edwin. "Ramsay's Views of Archaeology in Asia Minor Reviewed." Pages 27–40 in *The New Testament Student and His Field; Vol. 5: The New Testament Student.* Edited by John H. Skilton and Curtiss A. Ladley. Phillipsburg, N.J.: Presbyterian and Reformed Publishing, 1982.

Dalman

Primary Sources

Dalman, Gustaf. *Aramäische Dialektproben unter dem Gesichtspunkt neutestamentlicher Studien.* 2d ed. Leipzig: J. C. Hinrichs, 1927.
———. *Aramäisch-neuhebräisches Handwörterbuch zu Targum, Talmud und Midrasch.* 3d ed. Göttingen: Eduard Pfeiffer, 1938.
———. *Arbeit und Sitte in Palästina.* 7 vols. 1927–41. Repr., Hildesheim: Georg Olms, 1964.

———. *Der Gottesname Adonaj und Seine Geschichte.* Studien zur biblischen Theologie. Berlin: H. Reuther, 1889.

———. *Grammatik des jüdisch-palästinischen Aramäisch: Nach den Idiomen des palästinischen Talmud und Midrasch, des Onkelostargum (Cod. Socini 84) und der Jerusalemischen Targume zum Pentateuch.* Leipzig: J. C. Hinrichs, 1894.

———. "Gustaf Dalman." Pages 1–29 in *Die Religionswissenschaft der Gegenwart in Selbstdarstellungen* 4. Edited by Erich Stange. Leipzig: Felix Meiner, 1928.

———. *Jerusalem und sein Gelände.* Schriften des Deutschen Palästina-Instituts 3. Gütersloh: C. Bertelsmann, 1930.

———. *Jesus-Jeshua: Die drei Sprachen Jesu, Jesus in der Synagoge, auf dem Berge, am Kreuz.* Leipzig: J. C. Hinrichs, 1922; English translation: *Jesus-Jeshua: Studies in the Gospels.* Translated by Paul P. Levertoff. London: SPCK, 1929. Repr., New York: KTAV, 1971.

———. *Jesus Christ in the Talmud, Midrash, Zohar and the Liturgy of the Synagogue.* Translated by A. W. Streane. Cambridge: Deighton, Bell, 1893. Repr., New York: Arno, 1973.

———. *Orte und Wege Jesu.* Schriften des Deutschen Palästina-Instituts 1. 3d ed. Beiträge zur Förderung christlicher Theologie 2. Reihe. Gütersloh: C. Bertelsmann, 1924. English translation: *Sacred Sites and Ways: Studies in the Topography of the Gospels.* Translated by Paul P. Levertoff. New York: Macmillan, 1935.

———. *The Words of Jesus: Considered in the Light of Post-Biblical Jewish Writings and the Aramaic Language.* Translated by D. M. Kay. Edinburgh: T. & T. Clark, 1909.

Secondary Sources

Männchen, Julia. *Gustaf Dalman als Palästinawissenschaftler in Jerusalem und Greifswald, 1902–1941.* Abhandlungen des deutschen Palästinavereins, 9/2. Wiesbaden: Harrassowitz, 1993.

Schürer

Primary Sources

Schürer, Emil. *Geschichte des jüdischen Volkes im Zeitalter Jesu Christi.* 3 vols. 3d and 4th ed. Leipzig: J. C. Hinrichs, 1898–1901. English translation: *A History of the Jewish People in the Time of Jesus Christ.* 6 vols. Translated by John Macpherson, Sophia Taylor, Peter Christie. Clark's Foreign Theological Library, New Series, 23, 25, 41, 43. Edinburgh: T. & T. Clark, 1885–96. *A History of the Jewish People in the Time of Jesus.* Edited by Nahum N. Glatzer. New York: Schocken Books, 1961. *The History of the Jewish People in the Age of Jesus Christ (175 B.C.–A.D. 135): A New English Version Revised and Edited by Géza Vermes and Fergus Millar.* Edinburgh: T. & T. Clark, 1973.

———. *Das messianische Selbstbewusstsein Jesu Christi.* Festrede im Namen der Georg-August-Universität zur Akademischen Preisverteilung am X. June MCMIII. Göttingen: Dietrich (W. Fr. Kästner), 1903.

———. *Die Predigt Jesu Christi in ihrem Verhältniss zum Alten Testament und zum Judenthum.* Vortrag gehalten zu Darmstadt am 11. Januar 1882. Darmstadt: Fr. Würtz, 1882.

Secondary Sources

Hengel, Martin. "Der alte und der neue 'Schürer.'" *Journal of Semitic Studies* 35 (1990): 19–72.

Hoenig, Sidney B. "The New Schürer." *Jewish Quarterly Review* 67 (1976): 47–54.
Stern, Menahem. "A New English Schürer." *Journal of Jewish Studies* 25 (1974): 419–24.
Vermes, Géza, and Martin Goodman. "La littérature juive intertestamentaire à la lumière d'un siècle de recherches et de découvertes." Pages 19–39 in *Études sur le judaïsme hellénistique: Congrès de Strasbourg (1983)*. Edited by R. Kuntzmann and J. Schlosser. Paris: Les Éditions du Cerf, 1984.

Charles

Charles, R. H. *The Apocalypse of Baruch: Translated from the Syriac* (London: Adam and Charles Black, 1896).

———. *The Apocrypha and Pseudepigrapha of the Old Testament, with Introductions and Critical and Explanatory Notes to the Several Books.* 2 vols. Oxford: Clarendon Press, 1913.

———. *The Ascension of Isaiah: Translated from the Ethiopic Version, Which, together with the New Greek Fragment, the Latin Version and the Latin Translation of the Slavonic, Is Here Published in Full.* London: Adam and Charles Black, 1900.

———. *The Assumption of Moses: Translated from the Latin Sixth Century MS., the Unemended Text of Which Is Published Herewith, together with the Text in Its Restored and Critically Emended Form.* London: Adam and Charles Black, 1897.

———. *The Book of Enoch: Translated from Professor Dillmann's Ethiopic Text: Emended and Revised in Accordance with Hitherto Uncollated Ethiopic MSS. and with the Gizeh and Other Greek and Latin Fragments Which Are Here Published in Full.* Oxford: Clarendon Press, 1893.

———. *The Book of Jubilees or the Little Genesis: Translated from the Editor's Ethiopic Text.* London: Adam and Charles Black, 1902.

———. *The Book of the Secrets of Enoch: Translated from the Slavonic by W. R. Morfill.* Oxford: Clarendon Press, 1896.

———. *A Critical and Exegetical Commentary on the Revelation of St. John.* 2 vols. International Critical Commentary. Edinburgh: T. & T. Clark, 1920.

———. *A Critical History of the Doctrine of the Future Life: In Israel, in Judaism, and in Christianity; or Hebrew, Jewish, and Christian Eschatology from Pre-Prophetic Times till the Close of the New Testament Canon.* Jowett Lectures, 1898–99. London: Adam and Charles Black, 1899.

———. *The Greek Versions of the Testaments of the Twelve Patriarchs: Edited from Nine MSS together with the Variants of the Armenian and Slavonic Versions and Some Hebrew Fragments.* Oxford: Clarendon Press, 1908.

———. *Lectures on the Apocalypse: The Schweich Lectures, 1919.* London: British Academy, 1922.

———. *Religious Development between the Old and the New Testaments.* Home University Library of Modern Knowledge 88. London: Williams & Norgate, n.d.

———. *Studies in the Apocalypse: Being Lectures Delivered before the University of London.* Edinburgh: T. &. T. Clark, 1913.

Hellenistic Backgrounds

Hatch, Edwin. *Essays in Biblical Greek.* Oxford: Clarendon, 1889.

———. *The Influence of Greek Ideas and Usages upon the Christian Church.* Hibbert Lectures, 1888. Edited by A. M. Fairbairn. London: Williams & Norgate, 1890. Repr., with foreword by Frederick C. Grant. *The Influence of Greek Ideas on Christianity*. Harper Torchbooks/The Cloister Library. New York: Harper & Row, 1957.

———. *The Organization of the Early Christian Churches*. Bampton Lectures, 1880. 3d ed. London: Rivingtons, 1888.

Hatch, Edwin, and Henry A. Redpath. *A Concordance to the Septuagint and Other Greek Versions of the Old Testament (Including the Apocryphal Books)*. 3 vols. Oxford: Clarendon, 1897. Repr., Grand Rapids, Mich.: Baker, 1983. 2d ed. Grand Rapids, Mich.: Baker, 1998.

Heinrici, C. F. Georg. *Das erste Sendschreiben des Apostel Paulus an die Korinther*. Berlin: Wilhelm Hertz, 1880.

———. *Hellenismus und Christentum*. Biblische Zeit- und Streitfragen 5/8. Lichterfelde-Berlin: Edwin Runge, 1909.

———. *Die Hermes-Mystik und das Neue Testament*. Edited by Ernst von Dobschütz. Arbeiten zur Religionsgeschichte des Urchristentums 1/1. Leipzig: J. C. Hinrichs, 1918.

———. *Paulinische Probleme*. Leipzig: Dürr, 1914.

———. *Das zweite Sendschreiben des Apostel Paulus an die Korinther*. Berlin: Wilhelm Hertz, 1887.

Wendland, Paul. "Die christliche Literatur." Revised by Hans Lietzmann. Pages 1–6 in *Einleitung in die Altertumswissenschaft*. Edited by Alfred Gercke and Eduard Norden 1/5. Leipzig: B. G. Teubner, 1923.

———. *Die hellenistisch-römische Kultur in ihren Beziehungen zu Judentum und Christentum. Die urchristliche Literaturformen*. 3/4 ed. Handbuch zum Neuen Testament 1, 3/4. Tübingen: J. C. B. Mohr (Paul Siebeck), 1912.

———. *Ein Wort des Heraklit im Neue Testament*. Sitzungsberichte der königlich preussischen Akademie der Wissenschaften zu Berlin. Berlin: Georg Reimer, 1898.

Pfleiderer

Pfleiderer, Otto. *Das Christusbild des urchristlichen Glaubens in religionsgeschichtlicher Beleuchtung*. Berlin: Georg Reimer, 1903. English translation: *The Early Christian Conception of Christ: Its Significance and Value in the History of Religion*. London: Williams & Norgate, 1905.

———. *Die Entstehung des Christentums*. Munich: J. F. Lehmann, 1905. English translation: *Christian Origins*. Translated by Daniel A. Huebsch. New York: B. W. Huebsch, 1906.

———. *Die Entwicklung des Christentums*. Munich: J. F. Lehmann, 1907. English translation: *The Development of Christianity*. Translated by Daniel A. Huebsch. London: T. Fisher Unwin, 1910.

———. *The Influence of the Apostle Paul on the Development of Christianity*. Hibbert Lectures, 1885. Translated by J. Frederick Smith. New York: Charles Scribner's Sons, 1885.

———. *Der Paulinismus: Ein Beitrag zur Geschichte der urchristlichen Theologie*. 2d ed. Leipzig: O. R. Reisland, 1890. English translation of 1st (1873) ed.: *Paulinism: A Contribution to the History of Primitive Christian Theology*. Translated by Edward Peters. 2 vols. Theological Translation Fund. London: Williams & Norgate, 1877.

———. *Das Urchristenthum, seine Schriften und Lehren, in geschichtlichem Zusammenhang*. 2d ed. Berlin: Georg Reimer, 1902. English translation: *Primitive Christian-*

ity: *Its Writings and Teachings in Their Historical Connections*. Translated by W. Montgomery. Edited by W. D. Morrison. 4 vols. Theological Translation Library 22, 26, 27, 31. London: Williams & Norgate, 1906–11.

———. *Die Vorbereitung des Christentums in der griechischen Philosophie*. 2 ed. Religionsgeschichtliche Volksbücher 3/1. Tübingen: J. C. B. Mohr (Paul Siebeck), 1912.

6. METHODOLOGICAL DEVELOPMENTS

Weiss

Primary Sources

Weiss, Johannes. *Das älteste Evangelium: Ein Beitrag zum Verständnis des Markus-Evangelium und der ältesten evangelischen Überlieferung*. Göttingen: Vandenhoeck & Ruprecht, 1903.

———. *Die Aufgaben der Neutestamentlichen Wissenschaft in der Gegenwart*. Göttingen: Vandenhoeck & Ruprecht, 1908.

———. *Beiträge zur Paulinischen Rhetorik*. Göttingen: Vandenhoeck & Ruprecht, 1897.

———. *Christus: Die Anfänge des Dogmas*. Religionsgeschichtliche Volksbücher 1. Reihe; 18/19. Heft. Tübingen: J. C. B. Mohr (Paul Siebeck), 1909. English translation: *Christ: The Beginnings of Dogma*. Translated by V. D. Davis. London: Philip Green, 1911.

———. *Der erste Korintherbrief*. Kritisch-exegetischer Kommentar über das Neue Testament (Meyer-Kommentar) 9. Göttingen: Vandenhoeck & Ruprecht, 1910.

———. *Die Idee des Reiches Gottes in der Theologie*. Vorträge der theologischen Konferenz zu Giessen 16. Giessen: J. Ricker (Alfred Töpelmann), 1901.

———. *Jesus im Glauben des Urchristentums*. Tübingen: J. C. B. Mohr (Paul Siebeck), 1910.

———. *Jesus von Nazareth: Mythus oder Geschichte?: Eine Auseinandersetzung mit Kalthoff, Drews, Jensen*. Vorträge, gehalten auf dem Theologischen Ferienkurs in Berlin am 31. März und 1. April 1910. Tübingen: J. C. B. Mohr (Paul Siebeck), 1910.

———. *Die Nachfolge Christi und die Predigt der Gegenwart*. Göttingen: Vandenhoeck & Ruprecht, 1895.

———. *Die Offenbarung des Johannes: Ein Beitrag zur Literatur- und Religionsgeschichte*. Forschungen zur Religion und Literatur des Alten und Neuen Testaments 3. Göttingen: Vandenhoeck & Ruprecht, 1904.

———. *Paulus und Jesus*. Berlin: Reuther & Reichard, 1909. English translation: *Paul and Jesus*. Translated by H. J. Chaytor. Harper's Library of Living Thought. London: Harper & Brothers, 1909.

———. *Die Predigt Jesus vom Reiche Gottes*. Göttingen: Vandenhoeck & Ruprecht, 1892. English translation: *Jesus' Proclamation of the Kingdom of God*. Translated by Richard H. Hiers and D. Larrimore Holland. Lives of Jesus Series. Philadelphia: Fortress Press, 1971. 2d ed., 1900. 3d., edited by Ferdinand Hahn. Göttingen: Vandenhoeck & Ruprecht, 1964.

———. *Ueber die Absicht und den literarischen Charakter der Apostelgeschichte*. Göttingen: Vandenhoeck & Ruprecht, 1897.

———. *Das Urchristentum*. Göttingen: Vandenhoeck & Ruprecht, 1914. English translation: *Earliest Christianity: A History of the Period A.D. 30–150*. Edited by Frederick C. Grant. 2 vols. New York: Harper & Brothers, 1959.

Secondary Sources

Lannert, Berthold. *Die Wiederentdeckung der neutestamentlichen Eschatologie durch Johannes Weiss.* Texte und Arbeiten zum neutestamentlichen Zeitalter 3. Tübingen: A. Francke, 1989.

Morgan, Robert. "From Reimarus to Sanders: The Kingdom of God, Jesus, and the Judaisms of His Day." Pages 80–139 in *The Kingdom of God and Human Society: Essays by Members of the Scripture, Theology and Society Group.* Edited by Robin Barbour. Edinburgh: T. & T. Clark, 1993.

Prümm, Karl. "Johannes Weiss als Darsteller und religionsgeschichtlicher Erklärer der Paulinischen Botschaft." *Biblica* 40 (1959): 815–36.

Regner, Friedemann. "Johannes Weiss: Die Predigt Jesu vom Reiche Gottes: Gegen eine theologiegeschichtliche fable convenue." *Zeitschrift für Kirchengeschichte* 84 (1973): 82–92.

Schäfer, Rolf. "Das Reich Gottes bei Albrecht Ritschl und Johannes Weiss." *Zeitschrift für Theologie und Kirche* 61 (1964): 68–88.

Schmithals, Walter. "Johannes Weiss als Wegbereiter der Formgeschichte." *Zeitschrift für Theologie und Kirche* 80 (1983): 389–410.

Schweitzer

Primary Sources

Schweitzer, Albert. *Das Abendmahl im Zusammenhang mit dem Leben Jesu und der Geschichte des Urchristentums.* 2 vols. 2d ed. Tübingen: J. C. B. Mohr (Paul Siebeck), 1929.
Vol. 1: *Das Abendmahlsproblem auf Grund der wissenschaftlichen Forschung des 19. Jahrhunderts und der historischen Berichte.* English translation: *The Problem of the Lord's Supper according to the Scholarly Research of the Nineteenth Century and the Historical Accounts. Volume 1: The Lord's Supper in Relation to the Life of Jesus and the History of the Early Church.* Translated by A. J. Mattill Jr. Edited by John Reumann. Macon, Ga.: Mercer University Press, 1982.
Vol. 2. *Das Messianitäts- und Leidensgeheimnis: Eine Skizze des Lebens Jesus.* English translation: *The Mystery of the Kingdom of God: The Secret of Jesus' Messiahship and Passion.* Translated by Walter Lowrie. New York: Macmillan, 1960.

———. *Aus meinem Leben und Denken.* Leipzig: F. Meiner, 1931. English translation: *Out of My Life and Thought: An Autobiography.* Translated by A. B. Lemke. New York: Henry Holt, 1990.

———. "The Conception of the Kingdom of God in the Transformation of Eschatology." Pages 87–117 in E. N. Mozley, *The Theology of Albert Schweitzer for Christian Inquirers.* New York: Macmillan, 1951.

———. *Geschichte der paulinischen Forschung von der Reformation bis auf die Gegenwart.* Tübingen: J. C. B. Mohr (Paul Siebeck), 1911. English translation: *Paul and His Interpreters: A Critical History.* Translated by W. Montgomery. New York: Schocken Books, 1964.

———. *Die Mystik des Apostels Paulus.* Tübingen: J. C. B. Mohr (Paul Siebeck), 1930. English translation: *The Mysticism of Paul the Apostle.* Translated by W. Montgomery. New York: Henry Holt and Co., 1931. Repr., New York: Seabury, 1968. Repr. with Foreword by Jaroslav Pelikan. Albert Schweitzer Library. Baltimore: Johns Hopkins University Press, 1998.

———. *Reich Gottes und Christentum.* Edited by Ulrich Luz, Ulrich Neuenschwander, and Johann Zürcher. Albert Schweitzer: Werke aus dem Nachlass. Munich: C. H. Beck, 1995.

———. *Reich Gottes und Christentum.* Edited by Ulrich Neuenschwander. Tübingen: J. C. B. Mohr (Paul Siebeck), 1967; English translation: *The Kingdom of God and Primitive Christianity.* Translated by L. A. Garrard. New York: Seabury, 1968.

———. *Von Reimarus zu Wrede: Eine Geschichte der Leben-Jesu-Forschung.* Tübingen: J. C. B. Mohr (Paul Siebeck), 1906. English translation: *The Quest of the Historical Jesus: A Critical Study of Its Progress from Reimarus to Wrede.* Translated by W. Montgomery. New York: Macmillan, 1957. Repr., Albert Schweitzer Library. Baltimore: Johns Hopkins University Press, 1998. 2d ed. *Geschichte der Leben-Jesu-Forschung.* Tübingen: J. C. B. Mohr (Paul Siebeck), 1913. *The Quest of the Historical Jesus: Complete Edition.* Edited by John Bowden. London: SCM, 2000.

Secondary Sources

Barrett, C. K. "Albert Schweitzer and the New Testament: A Lecture Given in Atlanta on 10th April 1975 as Part of the Albert Schweitzer Centenary Celebration." *Expository Times* 87 (1975): 4–10.

Dungan, David. "Albert Schweitzer's Disillusionment with the Historical Reconstruction of the Life of Jesus." *Perkins (School of Theology) Journal* 29 (1976): 27–48.

Grässer, Erich. *Albert Schweitzer als Theologe.* Beiträge zur historischen Theologie 60. Tübingen: J. C. B. Mohr (Paul Siebeck), 1979.

Kümmel, Werner Georg. "Albert Schweitzer als Jesus-Paulusforscher." Pages 1–11 in *Heilsgeschehen und Geschichte: Vol. 2, Gesammelte Aufsätze 1965–1977.* Edited by Erich Grässer and Otto Merk. Marburger Theologische Studien 16. Marburg: N. G. Elwert, 1978.

———. "Albert Schweitzer als Paulusforscher." Pages 269–89 in *Rechtfertigung: Festschrift für Ernst Käsemann zum 70. Geburtstag.* Edited by Johannes Friedrich, Wolfgang Pöhlmann, and Peter Stuhlmacher. Tübingen: J. C. B. Mohr (Paul Siebeck), 1976.

———. "Die 'Konsequente Eschatologie' Albert Schweitzers im Urteil der Zeitgenossen." Pages 328–39 in *Heilsgeschehen und Geschichte: Gesammelte Aufsätze 1933–1964.* Edited by Erich Grässer, Otto Merk, and Adolf Fritz. Marburger Theologische Studien 3. Marburg: N. G. Elwert, 1965.

Nicol, Iain G. "Schweitzer's Jesus: A Psychology of the Heroic Will." *Expository Times* 86 (1974): 52–55.

Pleitner, Henning. *Das Ende der liberalen Hermeneutik am Beispiel Albert Schweitzers.* Texte und Arbeiten zum neutestamentlichen Zeitalter. Tübingen: A. Francke, 1992.

Reumann, John. "'The Problem of the Lord's Supper' as Matrix for Albert Schweitzer's 'Quest of the Historical Jesus.'" *New Testament Studies* 27 (1981): 475–85.

Thiselton, Anthony C. "Biblical Classics: VI. Schweitzer's Interpretation of Paul." *Expository Times* 90 (1979): 132–37.

Wilder, Amos. "Albert Schweitzer and the New Testament in the Perspective of Today." Pages 348–62 in *In Albert Schweitzer's Realms: A Symposium.* Edited by A. A. Roback. Cambridge, Mass.: Sci-Art, 1962.

History of Religion

Baumgartner, Walter. "Zum 100. Geburtstag von Hermann Gunkel." Pages 1–18 in *Supplements to Vetus Testamentum* 9. Congress Volume. Leiden: E. J. Brill, 1963.

Bovon, François. "Hermann Gunkel, historien de la religion et exégète des genres littéraires." Pages 86–97 in *Exégèsis: Problèmes de méthode et exercices de lecture (Genèse 22 et Luc 15)*. Edited by François Bovon and Grégoire Rouiller. Bibliothèque théologique. Neuchâtel: Delachaux & Niestlé, 1975. English Ed.: "Hermann Gunkel: Historian of Religion and Exegete of Literary Genres." In *Exegesis: Problems of Method and Exercises in Reading*. Edited by F. Bovon and G. Rouiller. Translated by D. G. Miller. Pittsburgh Theological Monograph Series 21. Pittsburg: Pickwick, 1978.

Burkitt, F. C. *Church and Gnosis: A Study of Christian Thought and Speculation in the Second Century.* Cambridge: Cambridge University Press, 1932.

Colpe, Carsten. *Die religionsgeschichtliche Schule: Darstellung und Kritik ihres Bildes vom gnostischen Erlösermythus.* Forschungen zur Religion und Literatur des Alten und Neuen Testaments 78. Göttingen: Vandenhoeck & Ruprecht, 1961.

Coppes, Leonard J. "An Introduction to the Hermeneutic of Hermann Gunkel." *Westminster Theological Journal* 32 (1970): 148–78.

Cumont, Franz. *The Oriental Religions in Roman Paganism.* With an Introductory Essay by Grant Showerman. Chicago: Open Court, 1911.

Eichhorn, Albert. *Das Abendmahl im Neuen Testament.* Hefte zur "Christlichen Welt" 36. Leipzig: J. C. B. Mohr (Paul Siebeck), 1898.

Frye, Richard Nelson. "Reitzenstein and Qumran Revisited by an Iranian." *Harvard Theological Review* 55 (1962): 261–68.

Gressmann, Hugo. *Albert Eichhorn und Die Religionsgeschichtliche Schule.* Göttingen: Vandenhoeck & Ruprecht, 1914.

Gunkel, Hermann. The 'Historical Movement' in the Study of Religion." *Expository Times* 38 (1926–27): 532–36.

———. *Zum religionsgeschichtlichen Verständnis des Neuen Testaments.* 3d ed. Forschungen zur Religion und Literatur des Alten und Neuen Testaments 1. Göttingen: Vandenhoeck & Ruprecht, 1930.

———. *Schöpfung und Chaos in Urzeit und Endzeit: Eine religionsgeschichtliche Untersuchung über Gen 1 und Ap Joh 12.* Göttingen: Vandenhoeck & Ruprecht, 1895.

Heitmüller, W. *Taufe und Abendmahl bei Paulus: Darstellung und religionsgeschichtliche Beleuchtung.* Göttingen: Vandenhoeck & Ruprecht, 1903.

Ittel, Gehard Wolfgang. "Die Hauptgedanken der Religionsgeschichtliche Schule." *Zeitschrift für Religions- und Geistesgeschichte* 10 (1958): 61–78.

Kelley, William V. "Albert Eichhorn and the History-of-Religion School." *Methodist Review* 99 (1917): 470–73.

Klatt, Werner. *Hermann Gunkel: Zu seiner Theologie der Religionsgeschichte und zur Entstehung der formgeschichtlichen Methode.* Forschungen zur Religion und Literatur des Alten und Neuen Testaments 100. Göttingen: Vandenhoeck & Ruprecht, 1969.

Lüdemann, Gerd. "Die Religionsgeschichtliche Schule." Pages 325–61 in *Theologie in Göttingen: Eine Vorlesungsreihe.* Edited by Bernd Moeller. Göttinger Universitätsschriften A, 1. Göttingen: Vandenhoeck & Ruprecht, 1987.

Lüdemann, Gerd, and Martin Schröder. *Die Religonsgeshichtliche Schule: Ein Dokumentation.* Göttingen: Vandenhoeck & Ruprecht, 1987.

Müller, Karlheinz. "Die religionsgeschichtliche Methode: Erwägungen zu ihrem Verständnis und zur Praxis ihrer Vollzüge an neutestamentlichen Texten." *Biblische Zeitschrift* 29 (1985): 161–92.
Reitzenstein, Richard. *Die hellenistischen Mysterienreligionen: Nach ihren Grundgedanken und Wirkungen.* 3d ed. 1927. Repr., Stuttgart: B. G. Teubner, 1956. English translation: *Hellenistic Mystery-Religions: Their Basic Ideas and Significance.* Translated by John E. Steely. Pittsburgh: Pickwick, 1987.
———. *Das iranische Erlösungsmysterium: Religionsgeschichtliche Untersuchungen.* Bonn: A. Marcus & W. Weber, 1921.
———. *Poimandres: Studien zur griechisch-ägyptischen und frühchristlichen Literatur.* Leipzig: B. G. Teubner, 1904.
Rollmann, Hans. "William Wrede, Albert Eichhorn, and the 'Old Quest' of the Historical Jesus." Pages 79–99 in *Self-Definition and Self-Discovery in Early Christianity: A Study in Changing Horizons, Essays in Appreciation of Ben F. Meyer.* Edited by David J. Hawkin and Tom Robinson. Studies in the Bible and Early Christianity 26. Lewiston: Edwin Mellen, 1990.
———. "Zwei Briefe Hermann Gunkels an Adolf Jülicher zur religionsgeschichtlichen und formgeschichtlichen Methode." *Zeitschrift für Theologie und Kirche* 78 (1981): 276–88.
Sänger, Dieter. "Phänomenologie oder Geschichte? Methodische Anmerkungen zur religionsgeschichtlichen Schule." *Zeitschrift für Religions- und Geitesgeschichte* 32 (1980): 13–27.
Weinel, Heinrich. *Biblische Theologie des Neuen Testaments: Die Religion Jesu und des Urchristentums.* 4th ed. Grundriss der theologischen Wissenschaften 3/2. Tübingen: J. C. B. Mohr (Paul Siebeck), 1928.
———. *Ist das "liberale" Jesusbild widerlegt? Eine Antwort an seine "positiven" und seine radikalen Gegner mit besonderer Rücksicht auf A. Drews, Die Christusmythe.* Tübingen: J. C. B. Mohr (Paul Siebeck), 1910.
———. *Paulus: Der Mensch und sein Werk: Die Anfänge des Christentums, der Kirche und des Dogmas.* 2d ed. Lebensfragen. Tübingen: J. C. B. Mohr (Paul Siebeck), 1915. English translation of 1st (1904) ed.: *St. Paul: The Man and His Work.* Translated by G. A. Bienemann. Edited by W. D. Morrison. Theological Translation Library 21. New York: G. P. Putnam's Sons, 1906.
Wernle, Paul. *Die Anfänge unserer Religion.* 2d ed. Tübingen and Leipzig: J. C. B. Mohr (Paul Siebeck), 1904. English translation: *The Beginnings of Christianity.* Translated by G. A. Bienemann. Edited by W. D. Morrison. 2 vols. Theological Translation Library 15, 17. New York: G. P. Putnam's Sons, 1903–4.
———. *Jesus und Paulus: Antithesen zu Boussets Kyrios Christos.* Tübingen: J. C. B. Mohr (Paul Siebeck), 1915.
———. *Die synoptische Frage.* Freiburg i. Br.: J. C. B. Mohr (Paul Siebeck), 1899.
Yamauchi, Edwin M. *Pre-Christian Gnosticism: A Survey of the Proposed Evidences.* Grand Rapids, Mich.: Eerdmanns, 1973.

Bousset

Primary Sources

Bousset, Wilhelm. *Der Antichrist in der Überlieferung des Judentums, des neuen Testaments und der alten Kirche: Ein Beitrag zur Auslegung der Apocalypse.* Göttingen: Vandenhoeck & Ruprecht, 1895. Repr., Hildesheim: Georg Olms, 1983. English translation: *The Antichrist Legend: A Chapter in Christian and Jewish Folklore.* Translated by A. H. Keane. London: Hutchinson, 1896. Repr., with Introduction by David Frankfurter. American Academy of Religion Texts and Translations Series 24. Atlanta: Scholars Press, 1999.

———. *Die Bedeutung der Person Jesu für den Glauben: Historische und rationale Grundlage des Glaubens.* Sonderausgabe aus dem Protokoll des 5. Weltkongresses für Freies Christentum und Religiösen Fortschritt, Berlin 1910. Berlin-Schöneberg: Protestantischer Schriftenvertrieb, 1910.

———. *Hauptprobleme der Gnosis.* Forschungen zur Religion und Literatur des Alten und Neuen Testaments 10. Göttingen: Vandenhoeck & Ruprecht, 1907.

———. *Die Himmelreise der Seele. Archiv für Religionswissenschaft* 4 (1901): 229–73. Repr., Darmstadt: Wissenschaftliche Buchgesellschaft, 1960.

———. *Jesu Predigt in ihrem Gegensatz zum Judentum: Ein religionsgeschichtlicher Vergleich.* Göttingen: Vandenhoeck & Ruprecht, 1892.

———. *Jesus.* 4th ed. Religionsgeschichtliche Volksbücher. 1. Reihe; 2/3. Heft. Tübingen: J. C. B. Mohr (Paul Siebeck), 1922. English translation: *Jesus.* Translated by Janet Penrose Trevelyan. Edited by W. D. Morrison. London: Williams & Norgate, 1906.

———. *Jesus der Herr: Nachträge und Auseinandersetzungen zu Kyrios Christos.* Forschungen zur Religion und Literatur des Alten und Neuen Testaments 25. Göttingen: Vandenhoeck & Ruprecht, 1916.

———. *Die jüdische Apokalyptik: ihre religionsgeschichtliche Herkunft und ihre Bedeutung für das Neue Testament.* Berlin: Reuther & Reichard, 1903.

———. *Kyrios Christos: Geschichte des Christusglaubens von den Anfängen des Christentums bis Irenaeus.* 5th ed. Göttingen: Vandenhoeck & Ruprecht, 1965. English translation: *Kyrios Christos: A History of the Belief in Christ from the Beginnings of Christianity to Irenaeus.* Translated by John E. Steely. Nashville: Abingdon Press, 1970.

———. *Die Offenbarung Johannis.* Kritsch-exegetischer Kommentar über das Neue Testament (Meyer-Kommentar). 6th ed., 1906. Repr., Göttingen: Vandenhoeck & Ruprecht, 1966.

———. *Die Religion des Judentums im neutestamentlichen Zeitalter.* 2d ed. Berlin: Reuther & Reichard, 1906. 3d ed., Hugo Gressmann. 4th repr. ed. with foreword by Eduard Lohse. Handbuch zum Neuen Testament 21. Tübingen: J. C. B. Mohr (Paul Siebeck), 1966.

———. *Religionsgeschichtliche Studien: Aufsätze zur Religionsgeschichte des hellenistischen Zeitalters.* Edited by Anthonie F. Verheule. Novum Testamentum Supplements 50. Leiden: E. J. Brill, 1979.

———. *Unser Gottesglaube.* Religionsgeschichtliche Volksbücher. 5. Reihe; 6. Heft. Tübingen: J. C. B. Mohr (Paul Siebeck), 1908; English translation: *The Faith of a Modern Protestant.* Translated by F. B. Low. New York: Charles Scribner's Sons, 1909.

———. *Das Wesen der Religion: Dargestellt an ihrer Geschichte.* 4th ed. Lebensfragen 28. Tübingen: J. C. B. Mohr (Paul Siebeck), 1920. English translation: *What Is Religion?* Translated by F. B. Low. London: T. Fisher Unwin, 1907.

Secondary Sources

Harnack, Adolf. "Rezension über: Wilhelm Bousset, Hauptprobleme der Gnosis." Pages 231–37 in *Gnosis und Gnostizismus.* Edited by Kurt Rudolph. Darmstadt: Wissenschaftliche Buchgesellschaft, 1975.

Hurtado, Larry W. "New Testament Christology: A Critique of Bousset's Influence." *Theological Studies* 40 (1979): 306–17.
Perles, Felix. *Bousset's Religion des Judentums im neutestamentlichen Zeitalter: kritisch untersucht*. Berlin: Wolf Peiser, 1903.
Perrin, Norman. "Reflections on the Publication in English of Bousset's *Kyrios Christos*." *Expository Times* 83 (1971): 340–42.

Jewish Research

Bowler, Maurice Gerald. *Claude Montefiore and Christianity*. Brown Judaic Studies 157. Atlanta: Scholars Press, 1988.
Heschel, Susannah. *Abraham Geiger and the Jewish Jesus*. Chicago Studies in the History of Judaism. Chicago: University of Chicago Press, 1998.
Klausner, Joseph. *From Jesus to Paul*. Translated by William F. Stinespring. New York: Macmillan, 1943.
———. *Jesus of Nazareth: His Life, Times and Teaching*. Translated by Herbert Danby. New York: Macmillan, 1925. Repr., Boston: Beacon, 1964.
———. *The Messianic Idea in Israel: From Its Beginning to the Completion of the Mishnah*. Translated by W. F. Stinespring. New York: Macmillan, 1955.
Kümmel, Werner Georg. "Jesus und Paulus: Zu Joseph Klausners Darstellung des Urchristentums." Pages 81–106 in *Heilsgeschehen und Geschichte: Gesammelte Aufsätze 1933–1964*. Edited by Erich Grässer, Otto Merk, and Adolf Fritz. Marburg: N. G. Elwert, 1965.
Montefiore, C. G. *Judaism and St. Paul: Two Essays*. London: Max Goschen, 1914. Repr., New York: Arno, 1973.
———. *Liberal Judaism: An Essay*. London: Macmillan, 1903.
———. *Rabbinic Literature and Gospel Teachings*. London: Macmillan, 1930.
———. *Some Elements of the Religious Teaching of Jesus: According to the Synoptic Gospels*. Jowett Lectures, 1910. London: Macmillan, 1910.
———. "The Spirit of Judaism." Pages 35–81 in *The Beginnings of Christianity: Part I: The Acts of the Apostles*. Edited by F. J. Foakes Jackson and Kirsopp Lake. London: Macmillan, 1939.
———. *The Synoptic Gospels: An Introduction and a Commentary*. 2d ed. 2 vols. London: Macmillan, 1927.
Tal, Uriel. *Christians and Jews in Germany: Religion, Politics and Ideology in the Second Reich, 1870–1914*. Translated by Noah Jonathan Jacobs. Ithaca, N.Y.: Cornell University Press, 1975.

Gospel Research in England

Allen, Willoughby C. *A Critical and Exegetical Commentary on the Gospel According to S. Matthew*. 2d ed. International Critical Commentary. Edinburgh: T. & T. Clark, 1907.
Bethune-Baker, J. F., et al. "Francis Crawford Burkitt." *Journal of Theological Studies* 36 (1935): 225–54.
Burkitt, Francis Crawford. *Christian Beginnings: Three Lectures*. London: University of London Press, 1924.
———. *The Earliest Sources for the Life of Jesus*. Modern Religious Problems. London: Constable, 1910.
———. *The Gospel History and Its Transmission*. 3d ed. Edinburgh: T. & T. Clark, 1911.

———. *Jesus Christ: An Historical Outline*. London: Blackie & Son, 1932.
———. *Two Lectures on the Gospels*. London: Macmillan, 1901.
Chapman, Mark D. "The Socratic Subversion of Tradition: William Sanday and Theology, 1900–1922." *Journal of Theological Studies* 45 (1994): 94–116.
Hawkins, John C. *Horae Synopticae: Contributions to the Study of the Synoptic Problem*. 2d ed. 1909. Repr., Oxford: Clarendon Press, 1968.
Rushbrooke, W. G. *Synopticon: An Exposition of the Common Matter of the Synoptic Gospels*. London: Macmillan, 1880.
Sanday, William. *The Authorship and Historical Character of the Fourth Gospel: Considered in Reference to the Contents of the Gospel Itself: A Critical Essay*. London: Macmillan, 1872.
———. *Christologies Ancient and Modern*. Oxford: Clarendon Press, 1910.
———. *The Criticism of the Fourth Gospel: Eight Lectures on the Morse Foundation, Delivered in the Union Seminary, New York in October and November, 1904*. New York: Charles Scribner's Sons, 1923.
———. *Eight Lectures on the Early History and Origin of the Doctrine of Biblical Inspiration*. London: Longmans, Green, 1893.
———. *An Examination of Harnack's 'What Is Christianity?': A Paper Read before the Tutors' Association on October 24, 1901*. London: Longmans, Green, and Co., 1901.
———. *Inspiration: Eight Lectures on the Early History and Origin of the Doctrine of Biblical Inspiration*. Bampton Lectures. London and New York: Longmans, Green, and Co., 1893.
———. *The Life of Christ in Recent Research*. Oxford: Clarendon Press, 1907.
———. *Sacred Sites of the Gospels: With Illustrations, Maps and Plans*. Oxford: Clarendon Press, 1903.
———, ed. *Studies in the Synoptic Problem: By Members of the University of Oxford*. Oxford: Clarendon Press, 1911.
Sanday, William, and Arthur C. Headlam. *A Critical and Exegetical Commentary on the Epistle to the Romans*. 5th ed. International Critical Commentary. Edinburgh: T. & T. Clark, 1902.
Sanday, W., F. G. Kenyon, F. C. Burkitt, F. H. Chase, A. C. Headlam, and J. H. Bernard. *Criticism of the New Testament: St. Margaret's Lectures*. London: John Murray, 1902.
Streeter, Burnett Hillman. *The Four Gospels: A Study of Origins: Treating of the Manuscript Tradition, Sources, Authorship, and Dates*. London: Macmillan, 1956.
———. *The Primitive Church: Studied with Special Reference to the Origins of the Christian Ministry*. New York: Macmillan, 1929.

Form Criticism

Primary Sources

Bultmann, Rudolf. *Die Erforschung der synoptischen Evangelien*. 3d ed. Aus der Welt der Religion 1. Berlin: Alfred Töpelmann, 1960. Repr., pages 1–41 in *Glauben und Verstehen: Gesammelte Aufsätze* 4. Tübingen: J. C. B. Mohr (Paul Siebeck), 1965. English translation: "The Study of the Synoptic Gospels." Pages 5–76 in *Form Criticism: Two Essays on New Testament Research*. Translated by Frederick C. Grant. Harper Torchbooks. New York: Harper & Brothers, 1962.
———. *Exegetica: Aufsätze zur Erforschung des Neuen Testaments*. Edited by Erich Dinkler. Tübingen: J. C. B. Mohr (Paul Siebeck), 1967.
———. *Die Geschichte der synoptischen Tradition*. 3d ed. Forschungen zur Religion und

Literatur des Alten und Neuen Testaments 29. Göttingen: Vandenhoeck & Ruprecht, 1957. English translation: *The History of the Synoptic Tradition.* Translated by John Marsh. New York: Harper & Row, 1963.

———. "The New Approach to the Synoptic Problem." *Journal of Religion* 6 (1926): 337–62. Repr., pages 35–54 in *Existence and Faith: Shorter Writings of Rudolf Bultmann.* Edited by Schubert M. Ogden. Living Age Books. New York: Meridian Books, 1960.

———. *Der Stil der paulinischen Predigt und die kynisch-stoische Diatribe.* Göttingen: Vandenhoeck & Ruprecht, 1910.

———. *Das Urchristentum im Rahmen der antiken Religionen.* 2d ed. Erasmus-Bibliothek. Zurich: Artemis, 1954. English translation: *Primitive Christianity in Its Contemporary Setting.* Translated by R. H. Fuller. Living Age Books. New York: Meridian Books, 1957.

Dibelius, Martin. *Aufsätze zur Apostelgeschichte.* Edited by Heinrich Greeven. Forschungen zur Religion und Literatur des Alten und Neuen Testaments 60. Göttingen: Vandenhoeck & Ruprecht, 1953. English translation: *Studies in the Acts of the Apostles.* Edited by Heinrich Greeven. Translated by Mary Ling. New York: Charles Scribner's Sons, 1956.

———. *Botschaft und Geschichte: Gesammelte Aufsätze: 1. Zur Evangelienforschung; 2. Zum Urchristentum und zur hellenistischen Religionsgeschichte.* Edited by Günther Bornkamm and Heinz Kraft. Tübingen: J. C. B. Mohr (Paul Siebeck), 1953, 1956.

———. *Die Botschaft von Jesus Christus: Die alte Überlieferung der Gemeinde in Geschichten, Sprüchen und Reden.* Tübingen: J. C. B. Mohr (Paul Siebeck), 1935. English translation: *The Message of Jesus Christ: The Tradition of the Early Christian Communities.* Translated by Frederick C. Grant. International Library of Christian Knowledge. New York: Charles Scribner's Sons, 1939.

———. *Die Briefe des Apostels Paulus: II Die neun kleinen Briefe.* Handbuch zum Neuen Testament. Tübingen: J. C. B. Mohr (Paul Siebeck), 1913. *An die Thessalonischer I II. An die Philipper.* 3d ed. Handbuch zum Neuen Testament. Tübingen: J. C. B. Mohr, 1937.

———. *Der Brief des Jakobus.* 10th ed. Edited by Heinrich Greeven. Kritisch-exegetischer Kommentar über das Neue Testament (Meyer Kommentar). Göttingen: Vandenhoeck & Ruprecht, 1959. English translation: *A Commentary on the Epistle of James.* Translated by Michael A. Williams. Hermeneia. Philadelphia: Fortress Press, 1976.

———. *Die Formgeschichte des Evangeliums: Dritte, durchgesehene Auflage mit einem Nachtrag von Gerhard Iber.* Edited by Günther Bornkamm. Tübingen: J. C. B. Mohr (Paul Siebeck), 1959. English translation: *From Tradition to Gospel.* Translated by Bertram Lee Woolf. Scribner Library. New York: Charles Scribner's Sons, n.d.

———. *Die Geisterwelt im Glauben des Paulus.* Göttingen: Vandenhoeck & Ruprecht, 1909.

———. *Geschichte der urchristlichen Literatur: I Evangelien und Apokalypsen; II Apostolisches und Nachapostolisches.* Sammlung Göschen 934, 935. Berlin: Walter de Gruyter, 1926. English translation: *A Fresh Approach to the New Testament and Early Christian Literature.* International Library of Christian Knowledge. New York: Charles Scribner's Sons, 1936.

———. *Geschichtliche und übergeschichtliche Religion im Christentum.* Göttingen: Vandenhoeck & Ruprecht, 1925. Repr., *Evangelium und Welt.* Göttingen: Vandenhoeck & Ruprecht, 1929.

―――. *Gospel Criticism and Christology*. London: Ivor Nicholson & Watson, 1935. German translation: "Evangelienkritik und Christologie." Pages 293–358 in *Botschaft und Geschichte: Gesammelte Aufsätze*, vol. 1. Edited by Günther Bornkamm. Tübingen: J. C. B. Mohr (Paul Siebeck), 1952.

―――. "Die Isisweihe bei Apuleius und verwandte Initiations-Riten." Pages 30–79 in *Botschaft und Geschichte: Gesammelte Aufsätze: 2. Zum Urchristentum und zur hellenistischen Religionsgeschichte*. Edited by Günther Bornkamm with Heinz Kraft. Tübingen: J. C. B. Mohr (Paul Siebeck), 1956. English translation: "The Isis Initiation in Apuleius and Related Initiatory Rites." Pages 61–121 in *Conflict at Colossae: A Problem in the Interpretation of Early Christianity Illustrated by Selected Modern Studies*. Edited and translated by Fred O. Francis and Wayne A. Meeks. Sources for Biblical Study 4. Missoula, Mont.: Society of Biblical Literature, 1973.

―――. *Jesus*. 3d ed. with *Nachtrag* by Werner Georg Kümmel. Sammlung Göschen 1130. Berlin: Walter de Gruyter, 1960. English translation: *Jesus*. Translated by Charles B. Hedrick and Frederick C. Grant. Philadelphia: Westminster, 1949.

―――. "Martin Dibelius: Zeit und Arbeit." Pages 1–37 in *Die Religionswissenschaft der Gegenwart in Selbstdarstellungen* 5. Edited by Erich Stange. Leipzig: Felix Meiner, 1929.

―――. *Paulus*. Sammlung Göschen 1160. Berlin: Walter de Gruyter, 1950. English translation: *Paul*. Edited by Werner Georg Kümmel. Translated by Frank Clarke. Philadelphia: Westminster, 1957.

―――. *The Sermon on the Mount*. New York: Charles Scribner's Sons, 1940. German translation: "Die Bergpredigt." Pages 79–174 in *Botschaft und Geschichte: Gesammelte Aufsätze*, vol. 1. Edited by Günther Bornkamm. Tübingen: J. C. B. Mohr (Paul Siebeck), 1953.

Schmidt, Karl Ludwig. "Formgeschichte." In *Religion in Geschichte und Gegenwart*. 2d ed. 2:638–40.

―――. "Jesus Christus." In *Religion in Geschichte und Gegenwart*. 2d ed. 3:110–51. English translation: "Jesus Christ." Pages 93–168 in *Twentieth Century Theology in the Making: I Themes of Biblical Theology*. Edited by Jaroslav Pelikan. Translated by R. A. Wilson. London: William Collins Sons, 1969.

―――. *Die Judenfrage im Lichte der Kapitel 9–11 des Römerbriefes*. Theologische Studien 13. Zollikon-Zurich: Evangelischer Verlag, 1942.

―――. "Die literarische Eigenart der Leidensgeschichte Jesu." Pages 17–20 in *Redaktion und Theologie des Passionsberichtes nach den Synoptikern*. Edited by Meinrad Limbeck. Wege der Forschung 481. Darmstadt: Wissenschaftliche Buchgesellschaft, 1981.

―――. *Neues Testament-Judentum-Kirche: Kleine Schriften*. Edited by Gerhard Sauter. Munich: Chr. Kaiser, 1981.

―――. *Der Rahmen der Geschichte Jesu: literarkritische Untersuchungen zur ältesten Jesusüberlieferung*. Berlin: Trowitzsch & Sohn, 1919.

―――. "Die Stellung der Evangelien in der allgemeinen Literaturgeschichte." Pages 50–134 in ΕΥΧΑΡΙΣΤΗΡΙΟΝ: *Studien zur Religion und Literatur des Alten und Neuen Testaments: Hermann Gunkel zum 60. Geburtstage, dem 23. Mai 1922*. Edited by Hans Schmidt. Forschungen zur Religion und Literatur des Alten und Neuen Testaments 36. Göttingen: Vandenhoeck & Ruprecht, 1923. Repr., pages 37–130 in Karl Ludwig Schmidt, *Neues Testament, Judentum, Kirche: Kleine Schriften*. Edited by Gerhard Sauter. Munich: Chr. Kaiser, 1981. English translation: *The Place of the Gospels in the General History of Literature.* Translated by Byron R. McCane. Columbia, S.C.: University of South Carolina Press, 2002.

Secondary Sources

Blank, Reiner. *Analyse und Kritik der formgeschichtlichen Arbeiten von Martin Dibelius und Rudolf Bultmann.* Theologische Dissertationen 16. Basel: Friedrich Reinhardt Kommissionsverlag, 1981.

Büchsel, Friedrich. *Die Hauptfragen der Synoptikerkritik: Eine Auseinandersetzung mit R. Bultmann, M. Dibelius und ihren Vorgängern.* Beiträge zur Förderung christlicher Theologie 40/6. Gütersloh: C. Bertelsmann, 1939.

Buss, Martin J. *Biblical Form Criticism in Its Context.* Journal for the Study of the Old Testament: Supplement Series 294. Sheffield: Sheffield Academic Press, 1999.

De Valerio, Karolina. *Altes Testament und Judentum im Frühwerk Rudolf Bultmanns.* Beihefte zur neutestamentlichen Wissenschaft 71. Berlin: Walter de Gruyter, 1994.

Dodd, C. H. "The Framework of the Gospel Narrative." Pages 1–11 in *New Testament Studies.* Manchester: Manchester University Press, 1953.

Evang, Martin. *Rudolf Bultmann in seiner Frühzeit.* Beiträge zur historischen Theologie 74. Tübingen: J. C. B. Mohr (Paul Siebeck), 1988.

Fascher, Erich. *Die formgeschichtliche Methode: Eine Darstellung und Kritik: Zugleich ein Beitrag zur Geschichte des synoptischen Problems.* Beihefte zur neutestamentlichen Wissenschaft. Giessen: Alfred Töpelmann, 1924.

Grobel, Kendrick. *Formgeschichte und synoptische Quellenanalyse.* Forschungen zur Religion und Literatur des Alten und Neuen Testaments 53. Göttingen: Vandenhoeck & Ruprecht, 1937.

Koehler, Ludwig. *Das formgeschichtliche Problem des Neuen Testaments.* Sammlung gemeinverständlicher Vorträge und Schriften aus dem Gebiet der Theologie und Religionsgeschichte 127. Tübingen: J. C. B. Mohr (Paul Siebeck), 1927.

Koester, Helmut. "Early Christianity from the Perspective of the History of Religions: Rudolf Bultmann's Contribution." Pages 59–74 in *Bultmann, Retrospect and Prospect: The Centenary Symposium at Wellesley.* Edited by Edward C. Hobbs. Harvard Theological Studies 35. Philadelphia: Fortress Press, 1985.

Kümmel, Werner Georg. "Martin Dibelius als Theologe." *Theologische Literaturzeitung* 74 (1949): 129–40. Repr., pages 192–206 in *Heilsgeschehen und Geschichte: Gesammelte Aufsätze, 1933–1964.* Edited by Erich Grässer, Otto Merk, and Adolf Fritz. Marburger Theologische Studien 3. Marburg: N. G. Elwert, 1965.

Lührmann, Dieter. "Rudolf Bultmann and the History of Religion School." Pages 3–14 in *Text and Logos: The Humanistic Interpretation of the New Testament.* Edited by Theodore W. Jennings Jr. Society of Biblical Literature Homage Series. Atlanta, Ga.: Scholars Press, 1990.

Marlé, René. *Bultmann et l'interprétation du Nouveau Testament.* Théologie: Études publiées sous la direction de la faculté S. J. de Lyon-Fourvière. Aubier: Éditions Montaigne, 1956.

McGinley, Laurence J. *Form-Criticism of the Synoptic Healing Narratives: A Study in the Theories of Martin Dibelius and Rudolf Bultmann.* Woodstock, Md.: Woodstock College Press, 1944.

McKnight, Edgar V. *What Is Form Criticism?* Guides to Biblical Scholarship: New Testament Series. Philadelphia: Fortress Press, 1969.

Meagher, John C. "The Implications for Theology of a Shift from the K. L. Schmidt Hypothesis of the Literary Uniqueness of the Gospels." Pages 203–33 in *Colloquy on New Testament Studies: A Time for Reappraisal and Fresh Approaches.* Edited by Bruce Corley. Macon, Ga.: Mercer University Press, 1983.

Merk, Otto. "Aus (unveröffentlichten) Aufzeichnungen Rudolf Bultmanns zur Synoptikerforschung." Pages 195–207 in *Jesu Rede von Gott und ihre Nachgeschichte im frühen Christentum: Beiträge zur Verkündigung Jesu und zum Kerygma der Kirche: Festschrift für Willi Marxsen zum 70. Geburtstag.* Edited by Dietrich-Alex Koch, Gerhard Sellin, and Andreas Lindemann. Gütersloh: Gütersloher Verlagshaus (Gerd Mohn), 1989.

Mühling, Andreas. *Karl Ludwig Schmidt: "Und Wissenschaft ist Leben."* Arbeiten zur Kirchengeschichte. Berlin: Walter de Gruyter, 1997.

Schick, Eduard. *Formgeschichte und Synoptikerexegese: Eine kritische Untersuchung über die Möglichkeit und die Grenzen der formgeschichtlichen Methode.* Neutestamentliche Abhandlungen. Bd. 18; Heft 2–3. Münster: Aschendorffsche Verlagsbuchhandlung, 1940.

Simonsen, Hejne. "Zur Frage der grundlegenden Problematik in form- und redaktionsgeschichtlicher Evangelienforschung." *Studia theologica* 27 (1972): 1–23.

Stowers, Stanley Kent. *The Diatribe and Paul's Letter to the Romans.* Society of Biblical Literature Dissertation Series 57. Chico, Calif.: Scholars Press, 1981.

7. THE ADVANCE OF AMERICAN NEW TESTAMENT RESEARCH

General Works

Hatch, Nathan O., and Mark A. Noll. *The Bible in America: Essays in Cultural History.* New York: Oxford University Press, 1982.

Hutchison, William R. *The Modern Impulse in American Protestantism.* Cambridge: Harvard University Press, 1976.

Marsden, George M. *Fundamentalism and American Culture: The Shaping of Twentieth-Century Evangelicalism: 1870–1925.* New York: Oxford University Press, 1980.

Noll, Mark A. *Between Faith and Criticism: Evangelicals, Scholarship, and the Bible in America.* Society of Biblical Literature Confessional Perspectives Series. San Francisco: Harper & Row, 1986.

Orlinsky, Harry M., and Robert Bratcher. *A History of Bible Translation and the North American Contribution.* Society of Biblical Literature Biblical Scholarship in North America. Atlanta: Scholars Press, 1991.

Sandeen, Ernest R. *The Origins of Fundamentalism: Toward a Historical Interpretation.* Facet Books: Historical Series, 10. Philadelphia: Fortress Press, 1968.

Saunders, Ernest W. *Searching the Scriptures: A History of the Society of Biblical Literature, 1880–1980.* Society of Biblical Literature Biblical Scholarship in North America 8. Chico, Calif.: Scholars Press, 1982.

Szasz, Ferenc Morton. *The Divided Mind of Protestant America, 1880–1930.* Alabama: University of Alabama Press, 1982.

Briggs

Primary Sources

Briggs, Charles Augustus. *The Bible, the Church and the Reason: The Three Great Foundations of Divine Authority*. New York: Charles Scribner's Sons, 1892.
———. *Biblical Study: Its Principles, Methods and History, together with a Catalogue of Books of Reference*. New York: Charles Scribner's Sons, 1883.
———. *The Ethical Teaching of Jesus*. New York: Charles Scribner's Sons, 1904.
———. *General Introduction to the Study of Holy Scripture: Principles, Methods, History, and Results of Its Several Departments and of the Whole*. New York: Charles Scribner's Sons, 1899.
———. *Inaugural Address and Defense, 1891/1893*. Religion in America. New York: Arno, 1972.
———. *The Messiah of the Apostles*. New York: Charles Scribner's Sons, 1895.
———. *The Messiah of the Gospels*. New York: Charles Scribner's Sons, 1894.
———. *Messianic Prophecy: The Prediction of the Fulfilment of Redemption through the Messiah: A Critical Study of the Messianic Passages of the Old Testament in the Order of Their Development*. 7th ed. New York: Charles Scribner's Sons, 1898.
———. *New Light on the Life of Jesus*. New York: Charles Scribner's Sons, 1904.

Secondary Sources

Hatch, Carl E. *The Charles A. Briggs Heresy Trial: Prologue to Twentieth-Century Liberal Protestantism*. New York: Exposition, 1969.
Hill, Doug. "Charles Augustus Briggs, Modernism, and the Rise of Biblical Scholarship in Nineteenth-Century America." Pages 71–104 in *The Bible and the American Myth: A Symposium of the Bible and Constructions of Meaning*. Edited by Vincent L. Wimbush. Studies in American Biblical Hermeneutics 16. Macon, Ga.: Mercer University Press, 1999.
Massa, Mark S. *Charles Augustus Briggs and the Crisis of Historical Criticism*. Harvard Dissertations in Religion 25. Minneapolis: Fortress Press, 1990.
Rogers, Max Gray. "Charles Augustus Briggs: Heresy at Union." Pages 89–147 in *American Religious Heretics: Formal and Informal Trials*. Edited by George H. Shriver. Nashville: Abingdon, 1966.
Sawyer, M. James. *Charles Augustus Briggs and Tensions in Late Nineteenth-Century Theology*. Lewiston: Mellen University Press, 1994.

Moffatt

Moffatt, James. *The Approach to the New Testament*. Hibbert Lectures, 1921. 4th ed. London: Hodder and Stoughton, 1922.
———. *A Critical and Exegetical Commentary on the Epistle to the Hebrews*. International Critical Commentary. Edinburgh: T. & T. Clark, 1924.
———. *The First Epistle of Paul to the Corinthians*. Moffatt New Testament Commentary. New York: Harper & Brothers, 1938.
———. "The First and Second Epistles of Paul the Apostle to the Thessalonians." Pages 41–54 in *The Expositor's Greek Testament*, vol. 4. Edited by W. Robertson Nicoll. Grand Rapids, Mich.: Eerdmans, 1910.
———. *The First Five Centuries of the Church*. London Theological Library. New York: Abingdon-Cokesbury, 1938.

———. *The General Epistles: James, Peter, and Judas.* Moffatt New Testament Commentary. New York: Harper & Brothers, 1928.

———. *The Historical New Testament: Being the Literature of the New Testament Arranged in the Order of Its Literary Growth and according to the Dates of the Documents; A New Translation: Edited with Prolegomena, Historical Tables, Critical Notes, and an Appendix.* 2d ed. Edinburgh: T. & T. Clark, 1901.

———. *An Introduction to the Literature of the New Testament.* 3d ed. International Theological Library. Edinburgh: T. & T. Clark, 1918.

———. *Jesus Christ the Same: The Shaffer Lectures for 1940 in the Divinity School of Yale University.* New York: Abingdon-Cokesbury, 1940.

———. *Love in the New Testament.* London: Hodder and Stoughton, 1929.

———. *Paul and Paulinism.* Modern Religious Problems. Boston: Pilgrim, 1910.

———. "The Revelation of St. John the Divine." Pages 279–494 in *The Expositor's Greek Testament*, vol. 5. Edited by W. Robertson Nicoll. Grand Rapids, Mich.: Eerdmans, 1910.

———. *The Theology of the Gospels.* Studies in Theology. New York: Charles Scribner's Sons, 1920.

Stevens

Stevens, George Barker. *The Christian Doctrine of Salvation.* International Theological Library. New York: Charles Scribner's Sons, 1911.

———. *The Johannine Theology: A Study of the Doctrinal Contents of the Gospel and Epistles of the Apostle John.* Rev. ed. New York: Charles Scribner's Sons, 1904.

———. *The Pauline Theology: A Study of the Origin and Correlation of the Doctrinal Teachings of the Apostle Paul.* Rev. ed. New York: Charles Scribner's Sons, 1897.

———. *The Theology of the New Testament.* 2d ed., 1906. Repr., International Theological Library. New York: Charles Scribner's Sons, 1946.

Bacon

Primary Sources

Bacon, Benjamin Wisner. *The Apostolic Message: A Historical Inquiry.* New York: Century, 1925.

———. *The Beginnings of Gospel Story: A Historico-Critical Inquiry into the Sources and Structure of the Gospel according to Mark, with Expository Notes upon the Text, for English Readers.* The Modern Commentary. New Haven: Yale University Press, 1909.

———. "Enter the Higher Criticism." Pages 1–50 in *Contemporary American Theology: Theological Autobiographies*, vol. 1. Edited by Vergilius Ferm. New York: Round Table, 1932.

———. *The Fourth Gospel in Research and Debate: A Series of Essays on Problems concerning the Origin and Value of the Anonymous Writings Attributed to the Apostle John.* New York: Moffat, Yard, 1910.

———. *The Gospel of the Hellenists.* Edited by Carl H. Kraeling. New York: Henry Holt, 1933.

———. *The Gospel of Mark: Its Composition and Date.* New Haven: Yale University Press, 1925.

———. *An Introduction to the New Testament.* New Testament Handbooks. New York: Macmillan, 1902.

———. *Is Mark a Roman Gospel?* Harvard Theological Studies 7. Cambridge: Harvard University Press, 1919.
———. *Jesus the Son of God or Primitive Christology: Three Essays and a Discussion.* New Haven: Yale University Press, 1911.
———. *The Making of the New Testament.* Home University Library. New York: Henry Holt, 1912.
———. *The Sermon on the Mount: Its Literary Structure and Didactic Purpose.* New York: Macmillan, 1902.
———. *The Story of Jesus and the Beginnings of the Church: A Valuation of the Synoptic Record for History and for Religion.* New York: Century, 1927.
———. *Studies in Matthew.* New York: Henry Holt, 1930.

Secondary Sources

Harrisville, Roy A. *Benjamin Wisner Bacon: Pioneer in American Biblical Criticism.* Society of Biblical Literature Studies in American Biblical Scholarship 2; Schools and Scholars 2. Missoula, Mont.: Scholars Press, 1976.
Smith, D. Moody. "B. W. Bacon on John and Mark." *Perspectives in Religious Studies* 8 (1981): 201–18.

Chicago School

Arnold, Charles Harvey. *Near the Edge of Battle: A Short History of the Divinity School and the "Chicago School of Theology."* Chicago: Divinity School Association, University of Chicago, 1966.
Funk, Robert W. "The Watershed of the American Biblical Tradition: The Chicago School, First Phase, 1892–1920." *Journal of Biblical Literature* 95 (1976): 4–22.
Olbricht, Thomas H. "New Testament Studies at the University of Chicago: The First Decade 1892–1902." *Restoration Quarterly* 22 (1979): 84–99.
Peden, Creighton. *The Chicago School: Voices in Liberal Religious Thought.* Bristol, Ind.: Wyndham Hall, 1987.
Peden, W. Creighton, and Jerome A. Stone, eds. *The Chicago School of Theology: Pioneers in Religious Inquiry: Vol. 1. The Early Chicago School, 1906–1959.* Studies in American Religion 66a. Lewiston: Edwin Mellen, 1996.
Rylaarsdam, J. Coert. "Introduction: The Chicago School—And After." Pages 1–16 in *Transitions in Biblical Scholarship.* Edited by J. Coert Rylaarsdam. Chicago: University of Chicago Press, 1968.

Burton

Burton, Ernest DeWitt. *Christianity and the Modern World: Papers and Addresses.* Edited by Harold R. Willoughby. Chicago: University of Chicago Press, 1927.
———. *A Critical and Exegetical Commentary on the Epistle to the Galatians.* International Critical Commentary. Edinburgh: T. & T. Clark, 1921.
———. "The Function of Interpretation in Relation to Theology." *American Journal of Theology* 2 (1898): 52–79.
———. *A Handbook of the Life of the Apostle Paul: An Outline for Classroom and Private Study.* Chicago: University of Chicago Press, 1906.
———. *A Harmony of the Synoptic Gospels in Greek.* Chicago: University of Chicago Press, 1920.

———. *New Testament Word Studies*. Edited by Harold R. Willoughby. Chicago: University of Chicago Press, 1927.
———. "The Present Problems of New Testament Study," *American Journal of Theology* 9 (1905): 201–37.
———. *The Records and Letters of the Apostolic Age: The New Testament Acts, Epistles, and Revelation in the Version of 1881 Arranged for Historical Study*. New York: International Committee of Young Men's Christian Associations, 1895.
———. *A Short Introduction to the Gospels*. Revised edition by Harold R. Willoughby. Chicago: University of Chicago Press, 1926.
———. *Some Principles of Literary Criticism and Their Application to the Synoptic Problem*. University of Chicago Decennial Publications 5. Chicago: University of Chicago Press, 1904.
———. *A Source Book for the Study of the Teaching of Jesus in its Historical Relationships*. University of Chicago Publications in Religious Education: Handbooks of Ethics and Religion. Chicago: University of Chicago Press, 1923.
———. *Syntax of the Moods and Tenses in New Testament Greek*. 3d ed. Chicago: University of Chicago Press, 1898.
Burton, Ernest DeWitt, and Edgar Johnson Goodspeed. *A Harmony of the Synoptic Gospels for Historical and Critical Study*. New York: Charles Scribner's Sons, 1917.
Burton, Ernest DeWitt, and Shailer Mathews. *Constructive Studies in the Life of Christ: An Aid to Historical Study and a Condensed Commentary on the Gospels*. Rev. ed. Chicago: University of Chicago Press, 1901.
Burton, Ernest DeWitt, John Merlin, Powis Smith and Gerald Birney Smith. *Biblical Ideas of Atonement: Their History and Significance*. Chicago: University of Chicago Press, 1909.
Stevens, Wm. Arnold, and Ernest DeWitt Burton. *A Harmony of the Gospels for Historical Study: An Analytical Synopsis of the Four Gospels*. 3d ed. New York: Charles Scribner's Sons, 1904.

Mathews

Primary Sources

Mathews, Shailer. *The Atonement and the Social Process*. New York: Macmillan, 1930.
———. *The Faith of Modernism*. New York: Macmillan, 1925.
———. *The Gospel and the Modern Man*. New York: Macmillan, 1910.
———. *A History of New Testament Times in Palestine: 175 B.C.–70 A.D.* Rev. ed. New Testament Handbooks. New York: Macmillan, 1910.
———. *Jesus on Social Institutions*. Edited by Kenneth Cauthen. Lives of Jesus Series. Philadelphia: Fortress Press, 1971.
———. *The Messianic Hope in the New Testament*. Decennial Publications of the University of Chicago. Chicago: University of Chicago Press, 1905.
———. *New Faith for Old: An Autobiography*. New York: Macmillan, 1936.
———. *The Social Gospel*. Philadelphia: Griffith & Rowland Press, 1910.
———. *The Social Teaching of Jesus: An Essay in Christian Sociology*. New York: Macmillan, 1897.

Secondary Sources

Lindsey, William D. *Shailer Mathews's Lives of Jesus: The Search for a Theological Foundation for the Social Gospel*. Albany: State University of New York Press, 1997.

———. "Shailer Mathews on Doctrinal Development: Parallels between American Protestant Modernism and European Roman Catholic Modernism." *American Journal of Theology and Philosophy* 11 (1990): 115–32.

———. "'Somebody, Somehow, Somewhere, and Somewhen': Shailer Mathews and the Socio-Historical Interpretation of Doctrine." *American Journal of Theology & Philosophy* 20 (1999): 191–215.

Case

Primary Sources

Case, Shirley Jackson. *The Christian Philosophy of History*. Chicago: University of Chicago Press, 1943.

———. "Education in Liberalism." Pages 107–25 in *Contemporary American Theology: Theological Autobiographies*, vol 1. Edited by Vergilius Ferm. New York: Round Table, 1932.

———. *The Evolution of Early Christianity: A Genetic Study of First-Century Christianity in Relation to Its Religious Environment*. Chicago: University of Chicago Press, 1914.

———. *Experience with the Supernatural in Early Christian Times*. New York: Century, 1929.

———. *The Historicity of Jesus: A Criticism of the Contention That Jesus Never Lived, a Statement of the Evidence for His Existence, an Estimate of His Relation to Christianity*. Chicago: University of Chicago Press, 1912.

———. *Jesus: A New Biography*. Chicago: University of Chicago Press, 1927.

———. *Jesus through the Centuries*. Chicago: University of Chicago Press, 1932.

———. *Makers of Christianity: From Jesus to Charlemagne*. New York: Henry Holt, 1934.

———. *The Millennial Hope*. Chicago: University of Chicago Press, 1918.

———. *The Origins of Christian Supernaturalism*. Chicago: University of Chicago Press, 1946.

———. *The Revelation of John: A Historical Interpretation*. Chicago: University of Chicago Press, 1919.

———. *The Social Origins of Christianity*. Chicago: University of Chicago Press, 1923.

———. *The Social Triumph of the Ancient Church*. New York: Harper & Brothers, 1933.

Secondary Sources

Hynes, William J. *Shirley Jackson Case and the Chicago School: The Socio-Historical Method*. Society of Biblical Literature Biblical Scholarship in North America 5. Chico, Calif.: Scholars Press, 1981.

McCown, C. C. "Shirley Jackson Case's Contribution to the Theory of Sociohistorical Interpretation." *Journal of Religion* 29 (1949): 15–29.

Schubert, Paul. "Shirley Jackson Case, Historian of Early Christianity: An Appraisal." *Journal of Religion* 29 (1949): 30–46.

Goodspeed

Primary Sources

Goodspeed, Edgar J. *The Apocrypha: An American Translation*. Chicago: University of Chicago Press, 1938.

———. *The Formation of the New Testament*. Chicago: University of Chicago Press, 1926.

———. *A History of Early Christian Literature.* Chicago: University of Chicago Press, 1942.
———. *An Introduction to the New Testament.* Chicago: University of Chicago Press, 1937.
———. *A Life of Jesus.* Harper Torchbooks. New York: Harper & Brothers, 1956.
———. *As I Remember.* New York: Harper & Brothers, 1953.
———. *The Making of the English New Testament.* Chicago: University of Chicago Press, 1925.
———. *Matthew: Apostle and Evangelist.* Philadelphia: John C. Winston, 1959.
———. *The Meaning of Ephesians.* Chicago: University of Chicago Press, 1933.
———. *New Chapters in New Testament Study.* Chicago: University of Chicago Press, 1937.
———. *New Solutions of New Testament Problems.* Chicago: University of Chicago Press, 1927.
———. *The New Testament: An American Translation.* Chicago: University of Chicago Press, 1923.
———. *Paul.* Philadelphia: John C. Winston, 1947.
———. *Problems of New Testament Translation.* Chicago: University of Chicago Press, 1945.
———. *The Story of the New Testament.* 2d ed. Chicago: University of Chicago Press, 1929.
———. *The Twelve: The Story of Christ's Apostles.* Philadelphia: John C. Winston, 1957.

Secondary Sources

Cobb, James Harrel, and Louis B. Jennings. *A Biography and Bibliography of Edgar Johnson Goodspeed.* Chicago: University of Chicago Press, 1948.
Cook, James I. *Edgar Johnson Goodspeed: Articulate Scholar.* Society of Biblical Literature Biblical Scholarship in North America 4. Chico, Calif.: Scholars Press, 1981.

Women

Andrews, Mary Edith. *The Ethical Teaching of Paul: A Study in Origin.* Chapel Hill: University of North Carolina Press, 1934.
Bass, Dorothy C. "Women's Studies and Biblical Studies: An Historical Perspective." *Journal for the Study of the Old Testament* 22 (1982): 6–12.
Brown, Antoinette L. "Exegesis of I Corinthians, XIV, 34, 35; and I Timothy, II, 11, 12." *Oberlin Quarterly* 4 (1849): 358–73.
Demers, Patricia. *Women as Interpreters of the Bible.* New York: Paulist, 1992.
Dowd, Sharyn. "Helen Barrett Montgomery's *Centenary Translation* of the New Testament: Characteristics and Influences." *Perspectives in Religious Studies* 19 (1992): 133–50.
Gifford, Carolyn De Swarte. "American Women and the Bible: The Nature of Woman as a Hermeneutical Issue." Pages 11–33 in *Feminist Perspectives on Biblical Scholarship.* Edited by Adela Yarbro Collins. Society of Biblical Literature Biblical Scholarship in North America. Chico, Calif.: Scholars Press, 1985.
Hill, Suzan E. "The Woman's Bible: Reformulating Tradition." *Radical Religion* 3 (1977): 23–30.
Lake, Kirsopp, and Silva Lake. *An Introduction to the New Testament.* London: Christophers, 1938.

Lake, Silva. *Family Π and the Codex Alexandrinus: The Text according to Mark.* Studies and Documents 5. London: Christophers, 1937.
Lyman, Mary Redington Ely. *The Fourth Gospel and the Life of To-Day.* New York: Macmillan, 1931.
———. *Jesus.* Hazen Books on Religion. New York: Association Press, 1937.
———. *Knowledge of God in Johannine Thought.* New York: Macmillan, 1925.
Montgomery, Helen Barrett. *Centenary Translation: The New Testament in Modern English.* Philadelphia: Judson, 1924.
Oden, Amy, ed. *In Her Words: Women's Writings in the History of Christian Thought.* Nashville: Abingdon, 1994.
Page, Ruth. "Elizabeth Cady Stanton's *The Woman's Bible.*" Pages 16–23 in *Feminist Theology: A Reader.* Edited by Ann Loades. London: SPCK, 1990.
Sampson, Emily Walter. "'More Than Any Man Has Ever Done': Julia Smith's Search for the Meaning of God's Word." *Bible Review* 14 (1998): 41–45, 54–55.
Selvidge, Marla J. *Notorious Voices: Feminist Biblical Interpretation, 1500–1920.* New York: Continuum, 1996.
Shaw, Susan J. *A Religious History of Julia Evelina Smith's 1876 Translation of the Holy Bible: Doing More Than Any Man Has Ever Done.* San Francisco: Mellen Research University Press, 1993.
Smith, Julia E. *The Holy Bible: Containing the Old and New Testaments; Literally Translated from the Original Tongues.* Hartford: American, 1876.
Smylie, James H. "*The Woman's Bible* and the Spiritual Crisis." *Soundings* 59 (1976).
Stanton, Elizabeth Cady. *The Woman's Bible: Parts I and II.* 1895, 1898. Repr. in the series American Women: Images and Realities. New York: Arno, 1972.
Stern, Madeleine B. "The First Feminist Bible: The 'Alderney' Edition, 1876." *Quarterly Journal of the Library of Congress* 34 (1977): 23–31.
Stevenson-Moessner, Jeanne. "Elizabeth Cady Stanton, Reformer to Revolutionary: A Theological Trajectory." *Journal of the American Academy of Religion* 62 (1994): 673–89.
Todd, Anne. "The Woman's Bible: 100 Years Ahead of Its Time?" *Daughters of Sarah* 21 (1995): 47–51.

Warfield

Primary Sources

Warfield, Benjamin B. *Acts and Pastoral Epistles: Timothy, Titus, and Philemon.* The Temple Bible. London: J. M. Dent, 1902.
———. *Biblical and Theological Studies.* Edited by Samuel C. Craig. The Benjamin B. Warfield Collection. Philadelphia: Presbyterian and Reformed Publishing, 1968.
———. *Christology and Criticism.* New York: Oxford University Press, 1929.
———. *The Inspiration and Authority of the Bible.* Edited by Samuel G. Craig. The Benjamin B. Warfield Collection. Phillipsburg, N.J.: Presbyterian and Reformed Publishing, 1948.
———. *An Introduction to the Textual Criticism of the New Testament.* Theological Educator. 3d ed. London: Hodder and Stoughton, 1890.
———. *The Person and Work of Christ.* Edited by Samuel G. Craig. The Benjamin B. Warfield Collection. Philadelphia: Presbyterian and Reformed Publishing, 1950.
———. *Selected Shorter Writings: B. B. Warfield.* Edited by John E. Meeter. 2 vols. Phillipsburg, N.J.: Presbyterian and Reformed Publishing., 1970, 1973.

———. *The Works of Benjamin B. Warfield.* 10 vols. 1927–32. Repr., Grand Rapids, Mich.: Baker, 1981.

Secondary Sources

Gerstner, John H. "Warfield's Case for Biblical Inerrancy." Pages 115–42 in *God's Inerrant Word: An International Symposium on the Trustworthiness of Scripture.* Edited by John Warwick Montgomery. Minneapolis: Bethany Fellowship, 1973.
Letis, Theodore P. "B. B. Warfield, Common-Sense Philosophy and Biblical Criticism." *American Presbyterians: Journal of Presbyterian History* 69 (1991): 175–90.
Noll, Mark A., ed. *The Princeton Theology, 1812–1921: Scripture, Science, Theological Method from Archibald Alexander to Benjamin Breckinridge Warfield.* Grand Rapids, Mich.: Baker, 1983.
Parsons, Mike. "Warfield and Scripture." *Churchman* 91 (1977): 198–220.
Silva, Moisés. "Old Princeton, Westminster, and Innerrancy." *Westminster Theological Journal* 50 (1988): 65–80.

Machen

Primary Sources

Machen, J. Gresham. *The Christian Faith in the Modern World.* New York: Macmillan, 1936.
———. "Christianity in Conflict." Pages 245–74 in *Contemporary American Theology: Theological Autobiographies* 1. Edited by Vergilius Ferm. New York: Round Table, 1932.
———. *Christianity and Liberalism.* Grand Rapids, Mich.: Eerdmans, 1946.
———. *New Testament Greek for Beginners.* New York: Macmillan, 1923.
———. *The Origin of Paul's Religion.* Grand Rapids, Mich.: Eerdmans, 1946.
———. *The Virgin Birth of Christ.* 2d ed. New York: Harper & Brothers, 1932.
———. *What Is Faith?* New York: Macmillan, 1925.

Secondary Sources

Hart, D. G. *Defending the Faith: J. Gresham Machen and the Crisis of Conservative Protestantism in Modern America.* Baltimore: Johns Hopkins University Press, 1994.
———. "Fundamentalism, Inerrancy, and the Biblical Scholarship of J. Gresham Machen." *Journal of Presbyterian History* 75 (1997): 13–28.
———. "When Is a Fundamentalist a Modernist? J. Gresham Machen, Cultural Modernism, and Conservative Protestantism." *Journal of the American Academy of Religion* 65 (1997): 605–33.
Marsden, George M. "J. Gresham Machen, History, and Truth." *Westminster Theological Journal* 42 (1979): 157–75.
———. "Understanding J. Gresham Machen." Pages 182–201 in *Understanding Fundamentalism and Evangelicalism.* Grand Rapids, Mich.: Eerdmans, 1991.
Russell, C. Allyn. "J. Gresham Machen: Scholarly Fundamentalist." Pages 135–61 in *Voices of American Fundamentalism: Seven Biographical Studies.* Philadelphia: Westminster, 1976.
Stonehouse, Ned B. *J. Gresham Machen: A Biographical Memoir.* Grand Rapids, Mich.: Eerdmans, 1954.
Story, Cullen I. K. "J. Gresham Machen: Apologist and Exegete." *Princeton Seminary Bulletin* 2 (1979): 91–103.

8. CONSERVATIVE ALTERNATIVES ON THE CONTINENT

von Dobschütz

von Dobschütz, Ernst. *Das apostolische Zeitalter.* Religionsgeschichtliche Volksbücher 1/9. Halle, Gebauer-Schwetschke, 1904. English translation: *The Apostolic Age.* Translated by F. L. Pogson. Boston: American Unitarian Association, 1910.

———. *Probleme des apostolischen Zeitalters.* Leipzig: J. C. Hinrichs, 1904.

———. *Die urchristlichen Gemeinden: Sittengeschichtliche Bilder.* Leipzig: J. C. Hinrichs, 1902. English translation: *Christian Life in the Primitive Church.* Translated by George Bremner. Edited by W. D. Morrison. London: Williams & Norgate, 1904.

Feine

Feine, Paul. *Der Apostel Paulus: Das Ringen um das geschichtliche Verständnis des Paulus.* Beiträge zur Förderung christlicher Theologie 2/12. Gütersloh: C. Bertelsmann, 1927.

———. *Das Christentum Jesu und das Christentum der Apostel in ihrer Abgrenzung gegen die Religionsgeschichte.* Christentum und Zeitgeist 1. Stuttgart: Max Kielmann, 1904.

———. *Einleitung in das Neue Testament.* 3d ed. Evangelisch-Theologische Bibliothek. Leipzig: Quelle & Meyer, 1923.

———. *Paulus als Theologe.* Biblische Zeit- und Streitfragen. Lichterfelde-Berlin: Edwin Runge, 1906. English translation: *St. Paul as a Theologian.* 2 vols. Foreign Religious Series. New York: Eaton & Mains, 1908.

———. *Die Religion des Neuen Testaments.* Evangelisch-Theologische Bibliothek. Leipzig: Quelle & Meyer, 1921.

———. *Theologie des Neuen Testaments.* 8th ed. Berlin: Evangelische Verlagsanstalt, 1953.

Zahn

Primary Sources

Zahn, Theodor. *Das apostolische Symbol: Eine Skizze seiner Geschichte und eine Prüfung seines Inhalts.* Erlangen: A. Deichert (Georg Böhme), 1893. English translation: *The Apostles' Creed: A Sketch of Its History and an Examination of Its Contents.* Translated by C. S. Burn and A. E. Burn. London: Hodder and Stoughton, 1899.

———. *Die bleibende Bedeutung des neutestamentlichen Kanons.* Leipzig: A. Deichert (Georg Böhme), 1898.

———. *Der Brief des Paulus an die Galater.* 3d ed. Friedrich Hauck. Kommentar zum Neuen Testament 9. Leipzig: A. Deichert (Werner Scholl), 1922. Repr., Wuppertal: R. Brockhaus, 1990.

———. *Der Brief des Paulus an die Römer.* 1st and 2d ed. Kommentar zum Neuen Testament 6. Leipzig: A. Deichert (Georg Böhme), 1910.

———. *Einleitung in das Neue Testament.* 2 vols. Leipzig: A. Deichert (Georg Böhme), 1897, 1899. Repr., Wuppertal: R. Brockhaus, 1994. English translation: *Introduction to the New Testament.* Translated by Fellows and Scholars of Hartford Theological Seminary. Edited by Melancthon Williams Jacobus. 2d ed. 3 vols. in 1. New York: Charles Scribner's Sons, 1917.

———. *Das Evangelium des Johannes.* 5th and 6th ed. Kommentar zum Neuen Testament 4. Leipzig: A. Deichert (Werner Scholl), 1921. Repr., Wuppertal: R. Brockhaus, 1983.

———. *Das Evangelium des Lucas*. 3d and 4th ed. Kommentar zum Neuen Testament 3. Leipzig: A. Deichert (Werner Scholl), 1913. Repr., Wuppertal: R. Brockhaus, 1988.

———. *Das Evangelium des Matthäus*. Kommentar zum Neuen Testament 1. Leipzig: A. Deichert (Georg Böhme), 1903. Repr., Wuppertal: R. Brockhaus, 1984.

———. *Grundriss der Einleitung in das Neue Testament*. Leipzig: A. Deichert (Werner Scholl), 1928.

———. *Grundriss der Geschichte des Apostolischen Zeitalters*. Leipzig: A. Deichert (Werner Scholl), 1929.

———. *Grundriss der Geschichte des Lebens Jesu*. Leipzig: A. Deichert (Werner Scholl), 1928.

———. *Grundriss der Geschichte des Neutestamentlichen Kanons: Eine Ergänzung zu der Einleitung in das Neue Testament*. 2d ed. Leipzig: A. Deichert (Georg Böhme), 1904. Repr., Wuppertal: R. Brockhaus, 1985.

———. "Mein Werdegang und meine Lebensarbeit." Pages 221–48 in *Die Religionswissenschaft der Gegenwart in Selbstdarstellungen* 1. Edited by Erich Stange. Leipzig: Felix Meiner, 1925.

———. *Skizzen aus dem Leben der Alten Kirche*. 2d ed. Erlangen and Leipzig: A. Deichert (Georg Böhme), 1898.

Secondary Sources

Swarat, Uwe. *Alte Kirche und Neues Testament: Theodor Zahn als Patristiker*. Theologische Verlagsgemeinschaft. Wuppertal: R. Brockhaus, 1991.

Schlatter

Primary Sources

Schlatter, Adolf. "Atheistische Methoden in der Theologie." Beiträge zur Förderung christlicher Theologie 9 (1905) 5:229–50. Repr., pages 134–50 in Adolf Schlatter, *Zur Theologie des Neuen Testament und zur Dogmatik: Kleine Schriften*. Edited by Ulrich Luck. Munich: Chr. Kaiser, 1969. English translation: "Atheistic Methods in Theology." Translated by David R. Bauer. Pages 211–25 in Werner Neuer, *Adolf Schlatter: A Biography of Germany's Premier Biblical Theologian*. Grand Rapids, Mich.: Baker, 1996.

———. *Das christliche Dogma*. Stuttgart: Calwer, 1923.

———. *Einleitung in die Bibel*. 4th ed. Stuttgart: Calwer, 1923.

———. *Erläuterung zum Neuen Testament*. Stuttgart: Calwer, 1922–1923. Repr., 1987.

———. *Die Geschichte des Christus*. 2d ed. Stuttgart: Calwer, 1923. Repr., 1984. English translation: *The History of the Christ: The Foundation for New Testament Theology*. Translated by Andreas J. Köstenberger. Grand Rapids, Mich.: Baker, 1997.

———. *Die Geschichte der ersten Christenheit*. 2d ed. Beiträge zur Förderung christlicher Theologie. Gütersloh: C. Bertelsmann, 1926. Repr., Stuttgart, 1983. English translation: *The Church in the New Testament Period*. Translated by Paul P. Levertoff. London: SPCK, 1955.

———. *Der Glaube im Neuen Testament*. 6th ed. Stuttgart: Calwer, 1982.

———. *Gottes Gerechtigkeit: Ein Kommentar zum Römerbrief*. Stuttgart: Calwer, 1935. Repr., 1991. English translation: *Romans: The Righteousness of God*. Translated by Siegfried S. Schatzmann. Peabody, Mass: Hendrickson, 1995.

———. *Die Theologie der Apostel*. 2d ed. Stuttgart: Calwer, 1922. English translation:

The Theology of the Apostles: The Development of New Testament Theology. Translated by Andreas J. Köstenberger. Grand Rapids, Mich.: Baker, 1999.

———. "Die Theologie des Neuen Testaments und die Dogmatik." Beiträge zur Förderung christlicher Theologie 13 (1909): 2:7–82. Repr. in Adolf Schlatter, *Zur Theologie des Neuen Testaments und zur Dogmatik: Kleine Schriften,* edited by Ulrich Luck, 203–72. Munich: Chr. Kaiser, 1969. English translation: "The Theology of the New Testament and Dogmatics." Pages 117–66 in *The Nature of New Testament Theology: The Contribution of William Wrede and Adolf Schlatter.* Edited by Robert Morgan. Studies in Biblical Theology, Second Series 25. Naperville, Ill.: Alec R. Allenson, 1973.

Schlatter, Theodor, ed. *Adolf Schlatters Rückblick auf seine Lebensarbeit: Zu seinem hundertsten Geburtstag.* Gütersloh: C. Bertelsmann, 1952.

Secondary Sources

Bailer, Albert. *Das systematische Prinzip in der Theologie Adolf Schlatters.* Arbeiten zur Theologie 2/12. Stuttgart: Calwer, 1968.

Bittner, Wolfgang J. "Methodische Grundentscheide in der exegetischen Arbeit Adolf Schlatters am Beispiel seiner Schriften zum Johannes-Evangelium. Pages 113–17 in *Die Aktualität der Theologie Adolf Schlatters.* Edited by Klaus Bockmühl. Giessen: Brunnen, 1988.

Dintaman, Stephen F. *Creative Grace: Faith and History in the Theology of Adolf Schlatter.* American University Studies 7; Theology and Religion 153. New York: Peter Lang, 1993.

Egg, Gottfried. *Adolf Schlatters kritische Position gezeigt an seiner Matthäusinterpretation.* Arbeiten zur Theologie 2/14. Stuttgart: Calwer, 1968.

Güting, Eberhard. "Zu den Voraussetzungen des systematischen Denkens Adolf Schlatters." *Neue Zeitschrift für systematische Theologie und Religionsphilosophie* 15 (1973): 132–47.

Stuhlmacher, Peter. "Adolf Schlatter's Interpretation of Scripture." *New Testament Studies* 24 (1978): 433–46.

———. "Adolf Schlatter als Paulusausleger—ein Versuch," *Theologische Beiträge* 20 (1989): 176–90.

Lagrange

Primary Sources

Lagrange, Marie-Joseph. *L'Évangile de Jésus-Christ (avec la synopse évangélique,* translated by C. Lavergne). Études bibliques. Paris: J. Gabalda. 1954. English translation: *The Gospel of Jesus Christ.* Translated by Members of the English Dominican Province. 2 vols. Westminster, Md.: Newman Press, 1958.

———. *Évangile selon saint Jean.* 7th ed. Études bibliques. Paris: J. Gabalda, 1948.

———. *Évangile selon saint Luc.* 8th ed. Études bibliques. Paris: J. Gabalda, 1948.

———. *Évangile selon saint Marc.* 4th ed. Études bibliques. Paris: J. Gabalda, 1947.

———. *Évangile selon saint Matthieu.* 8th ed. Études bibliques. Paris: J. Gabalda, 1948.

———. *Introduction à l'étude du Nouveau Testament: Première partie: Histoire ancienne du canon du Nouveau Testament.* 2d ed. Études bibliques. Paris: J. Gabalda, 1933.

———. *Introduction à l'étude du Nouveau Testament: Deuxième partie: Critique textuelle. II La critique rationnelle.* 2d ed. Études bibliques. Paris: J. Gabalda, 1935.

———. *Introduction à l'étude du Nouveau Testament: Quatrième partie: Critique historique. I Les mystères: l'Orphisme.* Études bibliques. Paris: J. Gabalda, 1937.
———. *Le judaïsme avant Jésus-Christ.* 3d ed. Études bibliques. Paris: J. Gabalda, 1931.
———. *Le messianisme chez les Juifs.* Études bibliques. Paris: J. Gabalda, 1909.
———. *La méthode historique, surtout à propos de l'Ancien Testament.* Études bibliques. Paris: V. Lecoffre, 1903. English translation: *Historical Criticism and the Old Testament.* Translated by Edward Myers. London: Catholic Truth Society, 1905.
———. *Père Lagrange: Personal Reflections and Memoirs.* Translated by Henry Wansbrough. New York: Paulist, 1985.
———. *Saint Paul: Épître aux Galates.* 2d ed. Études bibliques. Paris: J. Gabalda, 1925.
———. *Saint Paul: Épître aux Romains.* 4th ed. Études bibliques. Paris: J. Gabalda, 1950.
———. *Le sens du christianisme d'après l'exégèse allemande.* Études bibliques. Paris: J. Gabalda, 1918. English translation: *The Meaning of Christianity according to Luther and His Followers in Germany.* Translated by W. S. Reilly. New York: Longmans, Green, 1920.

Secondary Sources

Braun, F.-M. *L'œuvre du Père Lagrange: étude et bibliographie.* Fribourg: Éditions de l'Imprimerie St-Paul, 1943. English translation: *The Work of Père Lagrange.* Translated by Richard T. A. Murphy. Milwaukee: Bruce, 1963.
Kourie, C. E. T. "Leading Lights in Twentieth Century Roman Catholic Biblical Scholarship: Marie-Joseph Lagrange (1855–1938)." *Theologia Evangelica* 24/3 (September 1991): 37–43.
Montagnes, Bernard. *Le Père Lagrange (1855–1938): L'exégèse catholique dans la crise moderniste.* Paris: Cerf, 1995.
Murphy, Richard T. A., ed. *Lagrange and Biblical Renewal.* Aquinas Institute Studies 1. Chicago: Priory, 1966.
———, trans. *Père Lagrange and the Scriptures.* Milwaukee: Bruce, 1946.
Murphy-O'Connor, Jerome. *The École Biblique and the New Testament: A Century of Scholarship (1890–1990).* Novum Testamentum et Orbis Antiquus. Göttingen: Vandenhoeck & Ruprecht, 1990.
Refoulé, François. "La méthode historico-critique et le Père Lagrange." *Revue des Sciences Philosophiques et Théologiques* 76 (1992): 553–87.
Schroeder, Francis J. "Père Lagrange: Record and Teaching in Inspiration." *Catholic Biblical Quarterly* 20 (1958): 206–17.

9. THE REFINING OF HISTORICAL CRITICISM

Continuing Discovery and Research in Text Criticism

Bensly, Robert L., J. Rendel Harris, and F. Crawford Burkitt. *The Four Gospels in Syriac: Transcribed from the Sinaitic Palimpsest, with an Introduction by Agnes Smith Lewis.* Cambridge: University Press, 1894.
Foakes Jackson, F. J., and Kirsopp Lake, eds. *The Beginnings of Christianity, Part I: The Acts of the Apostles.* 5 vols. London: Macmillan, 1920–33. Repr. vols. 4 and 5. Limited Editions Library. Grand Rapids, Mich.: Baker, 1966.
Harris, J. Rendel, ed. *Biblical Fragments from Mount Sinai.* London: C. J. Clay and Sons, 1890.

———. *Codex Bezae: A Study of the So-called Western Text of the New Testament.* Texts and Studies 2/1. Cambridge: University Press, 1891.
———. *The Codex Sangallensis (Δ): A Study in the Text of the Old Latin Gospels.* London: C. J. Clay and Sons, 1891.
———. *The Diatessaron of Tatian: A Preliminary Study.* London: C. J. Clay and Sons, 1890.
———. *Further Researches into the History of the Ferrar-Group.* London: C. J. Clay and Sons, 1900.
———. *New Testament Autographs.* Supplement to *American Journal of Philology* 12. Baltimore: Isaac Friedenwald, n.d.
———. *On the Origin of the Ferrar-Group: A Lecture on the Genealogical Relations of New Testament MSS. Delivered at Mansfield College, Oxford, on Nov. 6th, 1893.* London: C. J. Clay and Sons, 1893.
———. *The Origin of the Prologue to St John's Gospel.* Cambridge: University Press, 1917.
———. *Side-Lights on New Testament Research: Seven Lectures Delivered in 1908, at Regent's Park College, London.* Angus Lectureship. London: Kingsgate Press, 1908.
———. *Stichometry.* London: C. J. Clay and Sons, 1893.
———. *The Teaching of the Apostles, Newly Edited, with Facsimile Text and a Commentary: From the MS. of the Holy Sepulchre, Jerusalem.* London: C. J. Clay and Sons, 1887.
———. *The Twelve Apostles.* Cambridge: W. Heffer & Sons, 1927.
———, with the assistance of Vacher Burch. *Testimonies.* 2 vols. Cambridge: University Press, 1916, 1920.
Kenyon, Frederic G., ed. *The Chester Beatty Biblical Papyri: Descriptions and Texts of Twelve Manuscripts on Papyrus of the Greek Bible.* I–III. London: Emery Walker Limited, 1933–36.
———. *The Codex Alexandrinus: New Testament and Celementine Epistles.* London: British Museum, 1909.
———. *Handbook to the Textual Criticism of the New Testament.* 2d ed. London: Macmillan, 1926.
———. *Our Bible and the Ancient Manuscripts.* 4th ed. New York: Harper & Brothers, 1938.
———. *Recent Developments in the Textual Criticism of the Greek Bible.* Schweich Lectures 1932. London: British Academy, 1933.
Lake, Kirsopp. *Codex 1 of the Gospels and Its Allies.* Texts and Studies 7/3. Cambridge: University Press, 1902.
———. *The Earlier Epistles of St. Paul: Their Motive and Origin.* London: Rivingtons, 1911.
———. *The Historical Evidence for the Resurrection of Jesus Christ.* Crown Theological Library 21. London: Williams & Norgate, 1907.
———. *The Text of the New Testament.* 6th rev. ed. by Silva New. Oxford Church Text Books. London: Rivingtons, 1928.
———, ed. *Codex Sinaiticus Petropolitanus: The New Testament, the Epistle of Barnabas and the Shepherd of Hermas.* Oxford: Clarendon Press, 1911.
Lake, Kirsopp, and Robert P. Blake, "The Text of the Gospels and the Koridethi Codex." *Harvard Theological Review* 16 (1923): 267–86.
Lake, Kirsopp, Robert P. Blake, and Silva New. "The Caesarean Text of the Gospels of Mark." *Harvard Theological Review* 21 (1928): 208–404.

Lake, Kirsopp, and Silva New, eds. *Six Collations of New Testament Manuscripts.* Harvard Theological Studies 17. Cambridge: Harvard University Press, 1932.
von Soden, Hermann Freiherr. *Hebräerbrief, Briefe des Petrus, Jakobus, Judas.* 3d ed. Hand-Commentar zum Neuen Testament, 3.2. Tübingen and Leipzig: J. C. B. Mohr (Paul Siebeck), 1899.

———. *Die Schriften des Neuen Testaments in ihrer ältesten erreichbaren Textgestalt auf Grund ihrer Textgeschichte.* I. Teil: Untersuchungen; I. Abteilung: Die Textzeugen; II. Abteilung: Die Textformen: A. Die Evangelien; B. Der Apostolos mit Apokalypse. II. Teil: Text mit Apparat. 2d ed. Göttingen: Vandenhoeck & Ruprecht, 1911, 1913.

———. *Urchristliche Literaturgeschichte (Die Schriften des Neuen Testaments).* Berlin: Alexander Duncker, 1905. English translation: *The History of Early Christian Literature: The Writings of the New Testament.* Translated by J. R. Wilkinson. Edited by W. D. Morrison. CTL 13. London: Williams & Norgate; New York: G. P. Putnam's Sons, 1906.

———. *Die wichtigsten Fragen im Leben Jesu.* 2d ed. Berlin: Alexander Duncker, 1907.

New Testament Grammar and Lexicography

Primary Sources

Bauer, Walter. *Griechisch-Deutsches Wörterbuch zu den Schriften des Neuen Testaments und der übrigen urchristlichen Literatur.* 4th ed. Berlin: Alfred Töplemann, 1952. English translation: *A Greek-English Lexicon of the New Testament and Other Early Christian Literature.* Translated by William F. Arndt and F. Wilbur Gingrich. Chicago: University of Chicago Press; Cambridge: University Press, 1957. 2d ed. revised and edited by F. Wilbur Gingrich and Frederick W. Danker from Walter Bauer's 5th edition, 1958. Chicago: University of Chicago Press, 1979. 6th German edition: *Griechisch-Deutsches Wörterbuch zu den Schriften des Neuen Testaments und der frühchristlichen Literatur.* Edited by Kurt and Barbara Aland. Berlin: Walter de Gruyter, 1988. 3d English edition. Edited by F. W. Danker. Chicago: University of Chicago Press, 2000.

Robertson, Archibald Thomas. *A Grammar of the Greek New Testament in the Light of Historical Research.* New York: George H. Doran, 1914.

———. *A Harmony of the Gospels for Students of the Life of Christ: Based on the Broadus Harmony in the Revised Version.* New York: Harper & Brothers, 1922.

———. *An Introduction to the Textual Criticism of the New Testament.* Nashville: Broadman Press, 1925.

———. *Luke the Historian in the Light of Research.* Edinburgh: T. & T. Clark, 1920.

———. *The Pharisees and Jesus.* The Stone Lectures for 1915–16, Delivered at the Princeton Theological Seminary. New York: Charles Scribner's Sons, 1920.

———. *A Short Grammar of the Greek New Testament: For Students Familiar with the Elements of Greek.* New York: George H. Doran, 1908.

———. *Word Pictures in the New Testament.* 6 vols. New York: Harper & Brothers, 1930–33.

Secondary Sources

Gingrich, F. Wilbur. "The Contributions of Professor Walter Bauer to New Testament Lexicography." *New Testament Studies* 9 (1962–63): 3–10.

McKnight, Edgar V. "A. T. Robertson." Pages 93–104 in *Bible Interpreters of the Twentieth Century: A Selection of Evangelical Voices*. Edited by Walter A. Elwell and J. D. Weaver. Grand Rapids, Mich.: Baker, 1999.

Research in Jewish Backgrounds

Golling, Ralf, and Peter von der Osten-Sacken, eds. *Hermann L. Strack und das Institutum Judaicum in Berlin*. Studien zu Kirche und Israel 17. Berlin: Institut Kirche und Judentum, 1996.

Moore, George Foot. *The Birth and Growth of Religion*. Morse Lectures of 1922. New York: Charles Scribner's Sons, 1924.

———. "Christian Writers on Judaism." *Harvard Theological Review* 14 (1921): 197–254.

———. *History of Religions*. 2 vols. International Theological Library. 1913, 1919–20. Repr., New York: Charles Scribner's Sons, 1949.

———. *Judaism in the First Centuries of the Christian Era: The Age of the Tannaim*. 3 vols. Cambridge: Harvard University Press, 1927, 1930.

Smith, Morton. "The Work of George Foot Moore." *Harvard Library Bulletin* 15 (1967): 169–79.

Strack, Hermann L. *Einleitung in Talmud und Midras*. 5th ed. Munich: C. H. Beck, 1930. English translation: *Introduction to the Talmud and Midrash*. Philadelphia: Jewish Publication Society, 1931. Repr., New York: Meridian Books, 1959.

———. *Grammatik des Biblisch-Armäischen mit den nach Handschriften berichtigten Texten und einem Wörterbuch*. 4th ed. Leipzig: J. C. Hinrichs, 1905.

———. *Das Wesen des Judentums: Vortrag gehalten auf der Internationalen Konferenz für Judenmission zu Amsterdam*. Schriften des Institutum Judaicum, 36. Leipzig: J. C. Hinrichs, 1906.

Strack, Hermann L., and Paul Billerbeck. *Kommentar zum Neuen Testament aus Talmud und Midrasch*. 4 vols. Munich: C. H. Beck, 1922–28.

Strange, James Riley. "G. F. Moore and E. E. Urbach Revisited." Pages 141–59 in *The Annual of Rabbinic Judaism: Ancient, Medieval, and Modern*. Edited by Alan J. Avery-Peck, William Scott Green, Jacob Neusner. Vol. 2. Leiden: Brill, 1999.

Research in Hellenism

Kennedy, H. A. A. *Philo's Contribution to Religion*. London: Hodder and Stoughton, 1919.

———. *St. Paul and the Mystery-Religions*. London: Hodder and Stoughton, 1913.

———. *St Paul's Conceptions of the Last Things*. Cunningham Lectures. 2d ed. London: Hodder and Stoughton, 1904.

———. *Sources of New Testament Greek, or the Influence of the Septuagint on the Vocabulary of the New Testament*. Edinburgh: T. & T. Clark, 1895.

———. *The Theology of the Epistles*. New York: Charles Scribner's Sons, 1920.

Nock, Arthur Darby. *Conversion: The Old and the New in Religion from Alexander the Great to Augustine of Hippo*. Oxford: Clarendon, 1933.

———. *Early Gentile Christianity and Its Hellenistic Background*. Harper Torchbooks / The Cloister Library. New York: Harper & Row, 1964.

———. *St. Paul*. 1938. Repr., Harper Torchbooks / The Cloister Library. New York: Harper & Row, 1963.

Stewart, Zeph, ed. *Arthur Darby Nock: Essays on Religion and the Ancient World*. 2 vols. Cambridge: Harvard University Press, 1972.

Lietzmann

Primary Sources

Lietzmann, Hans. *An die Galater.* 3d ed. Handbuch zum Neuen Testament 10. Tübingen: J. C. B. Mohr (Paul Siebeck), 1932.

———. *Geschichte der alten Kirche.* 4 vols. Berlin: Walter de Gruyter, 1932–44. English translation: *I The Beginnings of the Christian Church; II The Founding of the Church Universal; III From Constantine to Julian; IV The Era of the Church Fathers.* Translated by Bertram Lee Woolf. 2d ed. New York: Charles Scribner's Sons, 1949–52.

———. *Kleine Schriften.* 3 vols. Edited by Kurt Aland and Kommission für spätantike Religionsgeschichte. Texte und Untersuchungen 67, 68, 74. Berlin: Akademie-Verlag, 1958–62.

———. *An die Korinther I. II.* 4th ed. Werner Georg Kümmel. Handbuch zum Neuen Testament 9. Tübingen: J. C. B. Mohr (Paul Siebeck), 1949.

———. *Der Menschensohn: Ein Beitrag zur neutestamentlichen Theologie.* Freiburg i. Br.: J. C. B. Mohr (Paul Siebeck), 1896.

———. *Messe und Herrenmahl: Eine Studie zur Geschichte der Liturgie.* 3d ed. Arbeiten zur Kirchengeschichte 8. Berlin: Walter de Gruyter, 1955. English translation: *Mass and Lord's Supper: A Study in the History of the Liturgy.* Translated by Dorothea H. G. Reeve. Introduction and Supplementary Essay by Robert Douglas Richardson. Leiden: E. J. Brill, 1953–79.

———. *Petrus und Paulus in Rom: Liturgische und archäologische Studien.* Bonn: A. Marcus und E. Weber, 1915.

———. *An die Römer.* 4th ed. Handbuch zum Neuen Testament 8. Tübingen: J. C. B. Mohr (Paul Siebeck), 1933.

———. *Der Weltheiland: Einer Jenaer Rosenvorlesung mit Anmerkungen.* Bonn: A. Marcus und E. Weber, 1909.

———. *Wie wurden die Bücher des Neuen Testaments heilige Schrift? Fünf Vorträge* Lebensfragen 21. Tübingen: J. C. B. Mohr (Paul Siebeck), 1907. Repr., *Kleine Schriften, II Studien zum Neuen Testament,* edited by Kurt Aland, 15–98. Texte und Untersuchungen 68. Berlin: Akademie-Verlag, 1958.

Huck, Albert. *Synopse der drei ersten Evangelien.* 9th ed. Hans Lietzmann. Tübingen: J. C. B. Mohr (Paul Siebeck), 1936. English translation: *A Synopsis of the First Three Gospels.* Translated by Frank Leslie Cross. Tübingen: J. C. B. Mohr (Paul Siebeck), 1936.

Secondary Sources

Higgins, A. J. B. "Important and Influential Foreign Books: H. Lietzmann's 'Mass and Lord's Supper' (Messe und Herrenmahl)," *Expository Times* 65 (1953–54): 333–36.

Wyrwa, Dietmar. "Hans Lietzmanns theologisches Verständnis der Kirchengeschichte." Pages 387–418 in *450 Jahre Evangelische Theologie in Berlin.* Edited by Gerhard Besier and Christof Gestrich. Göttingen: Vandenhoeck & Ruprecht, 1989.

Goguel

Goguel, Maurice. *L'Église primitive.* Paris: Payot, 1947. English translation: *The Primitive Church.* Translated by H. C. Snape. New York: Macmillan, 1964.

———. *L'Eucharistie: des origines à Justin Martyr.* La Roche-sur-Yon: Imprimerie Centrale de l'Ouest, 1910.

———. *L'Évangile de Marc et ses rapports avec ceux de Matthieu et de Luc: essai d'une introduction critique à l'étude du second évangile.* Bibliothèque de l'École des Hautes Études, Sciences religieuses. Paris: Ernest Leroux, 1909.

———. *La foi à la résurrection de Jésus dans le christianisme primitif: étude d'histoire et de psychologie religieuses.* Bibliothèque des Hautes Études, Sciences religieuses 47. Paris: Librairie Ernest Leroux, 1933.

———. *Introduction au Nouveau Testament.* 4 vols. Bibliothèque historique des religions. Paris: Ernest Leroux, 1922–26.

———. *Jésus de Nazareth: mythe ou histoire?* Paris: Payot, 1925. English translation: *Jesus the Nazarene: Myth or History?* Translated by Frederick Stevens. New York: D. Appleton, 1926.

———. *La naissance du christianisme.* Paris: Payot, 1946. English translation: *The Birth of Christianity.* Translated by H. C. Snape. New York: Macmillan, 1954.

———. *La notion johannique de l'Esprit et ses antécédents historiques.* Étude de théologie biblique. Paris: Fischbacher, 1902.

———. *Les sources du récit johannique de la passion.* La Roche-sur-Yon: Imprimerie Centrale de l'Ouest, 1910.

———. *La vie de Jésus.* Paris: Payot, 1932. English translation: *The Life of Jesus.* Translated by Olive Wyon. New York: Macmillan, 1933. Repr., *Jesus and the Origins of Christianity.* 2 vols. Harper Torchbooks / The Cloister Library. New York: Harper & Brothers, 1960.

W. Bauer

Primary Sources

Bauer, Walter. *Der Apostolos der Syrer in der Zeit von der Mitte des vierten Jahrhunderts bis zur Spaltung der Syrischen Kirche.* Giessen: J. Ricker (Alfred Töpelmann), 1903.

———. *Das Johannesevangelium.* 3d ed. Handbuch zum Neuen Testament 6. Tübingen: J. C. B. Mohr (Paul Siebeck), 1933.

———. *Das Leben Jesu: Im Zeitalter der neutestamentlichen Apokryphen.* Darmstadt: Wissenschaftliche Buchgesellschaft, 1967.

———. *Rechtgläubigkeit und Ketzerei im ältesten Christentum.* 2d ed. Georg Strecker. Beiträge zur historischen Theologie 10. Tübingen: J. C. B. Mohr (Paul Siebeck), 1964. English translation: *Orthodoxy and Heresy in Earliest Christianity.* Edited by Robert A. Kraft and Gerhard Krodel. Philadelphia: Fortress Press, 1971.

Secondary Sources

Betz, Hans Dieter. "Orthodoxy and Heresy in Primitive Christianity." *Interpretation* 19 (1965): 299–311.

Desjardins, Michel. "Bauer and Beyond: On Recent Scholarly Discussions of Αἵρεσις in the Early Christian Era." *Second Century* 8 (1991): 65–82.

Fascher, Erich. "Walter Bauer als Kommentator." *New Testament Studies* 9 (1962–1963): 23–38.

Robinson, Thomas A. *The Bauer Thesis Examined: The Geography of Heresy in the Early Church.* Lewiston: Edwin Mellen, 1988.

Schneemelcher, Wilhelm. "Walter Bauer als Kirchenhistoriker." *New Testament Studies* 9 (1962–63): 11–22.

Strecker, Georg. "Walter Bauer—Exegete, Philologe und Historiker." *Novum Testamentum* 20 (1978): 75–80.

Windisch

Primary Sources

Windisch, Hans. *Die Frömmigkeit Philos und ihre Bedeutung für das Christentum: Eine religionsgeschichtliche Studie.* Leipzig: J. C. Hinrichs, 1909.

———. *Der Hebräerbrief.* 2d ed. Handbuch zum Neuen Testament 14. Tübingen: J. C. B. Mohr (Paul Siebeck), 1931.

———. *Johannes und die Synoptiker: Wollte der vierte Evangelist die älteren Evangelien ergänzen order ersetzen?* Untersuchungen zum Neuen Testament 12. Leipzig: J. C. Hinrichs, 1926.

———. *Die katholischen Briefe.* 3d ed. Edited by Herbert Preisker. Handbuch zum Neuen Testament 15. Tübingen: J. C. B. Mohr (Paul Siebeck), 1951.

———. *Der messianische Krieg und das Urchristentum.* Tübingen: J. C. B. Mohr (Paul Siebeck), 1909.

———. *Paulus und Christus: Ein biblisch-religionsgeschichtlicher Vergleich.* Untersuchungen zum Neuen Testament 24. Leipzig: J. C. Hinrichs, 1934.

———. *Der Sinn der Bergpredigt: Ein Beitrag zum geschichtlichen Verständnis der Evangelien und zum Problem der richtigen Exegese.* 2d ed. Untersuchungen zum Neuen Testament 16. Leipzig: J. C. Hinrichs, 1937. English translation: *The Meaning of the Sermon on the Mount: A Contribution to the Historical Understanding of the Gospels and to the Problem of Their True Exegesis.* Translated by S. MacLean Gilmour. Philadelphia: Westminster, 1950.

———. *The Spirit-Paraclete in the Fourth Gospel.* Translated by James W. Cox. Facet Books: Biblical Series 20. Philadelphia: Fortress Press, 1968.

———. *Taufe und Sünde im ältesten Christentum bis auf Origenes: Ein Beitrag zur altchristlichen Dogmengeschichte.* Tübingen: J. C. B. Mohr (Paul Siebeck), 1908.

———. *Der zweite Korintherbrief.* 9th ed. Kritisch-exegetischer Kommentar über das Neue Testament (Meyer-Kommentar). 1924. Repr., Göttingen: Vandenhoeck & Ruprecht, 1970.

Secondary Sources

Beijer, Erik. "Hans Windisch und seine Bedeutung für die neutestamentliche Wissenschaft." *Zeitschrift für die neutestamentliche Wissenschaft und die Kunde der ältesten Kirche* 48 (1957): 22–49.

de Jonge, Marinus. "Hans Windisch als Neutestamentler an der Universität Leiden (1914–1929)." Pages 47–65 in *Texte und Geschichte: Facetten theologischen Arbeitens aus dem Freundes- und Schülerkreis Dieter Lührmann zum 60. Geburtstag.* Edited by Stefan Maser and Egbert Schlarb. Marburger Theologische Studien 50. Marburg: N. G. Elwert, 1999).

Prümm, Karl. "Zur Früh- und Spätform der religionsgeschichtlichen Christus Deutung von H. Windisch." *Biblica* 42 (1961): 391–422; 43 (1962): 22–56.

Lohmeyer

Primary Sources

Lohmeyer, Ernst. *Von Begriff der religiösen Gemeinschaft: Eine problemgeschichtliche Untersuchung über die Grundlagen des Urchristentums.* Wissenschaftliche Grundfragen 3. Leipzig: B. G. Teubner, 1925.

———. *Die Briefe an die Philipper, an die Kolosser und an Philemon.* 11th ed. Kritisch-exegetischer Kommentar über das Neue Testament (Meyer-Kommentar) 9. Göttingen: Vandenhoeck & Ruprecht, 1956.

———. *Das Evangelium des Markus.* 15th ed. Kritisch-exegetischer Kommentar über das Neue Testament (Meyer-Kommentar) 1/2. Göttingen: Vandenhoeck & Ruprecht, 1959.

———. *Galiläa und Jerusalem.* Forschungen zur Religion und Literatur des Alten und Neuen Testaments 52. Göttingen: Vandenhoeck & Ruprecht, 1936.

———. *Gottesknecht und Davidsohn.* 2d ed. Forschungen zur Religion und Literatur des Alten und Neuen Testaments 61. Göttingen: Vandenhoeck & Ruprecht, 1953.

———. *Grundlagen paulinischer Theologie.* Beiträge zur historischen Theologie 1. Tübingen: J. C. B. Mohr (Paul Siebeck), 1929.

———. *Kultus und Evangelium.* Göttingen: Vandenhoeck & Ruprecht, 1942. English translation: *Lord of the Temple: A Study of the Relation between Cult and Gospel.* Translated by Stewart Todd. Richmond, Va.: John Knox, 1962.

———. *Kyrios Jesus: Eine Untersuchung zu Phil. 2:5-11.* Sitzungsberichte der heidelberger Akademie der Wissenschaften (1927/28) 4. Heidelberg: Carl Winter, 1928.

———. *Die Offenbarung des Johannes.* 2d ed. Handbuch zum Neuen Testament 16. Tübingen: J. C. B. Mohr (Paul Siebeck), 1953.

Secondary Sources

Brown, Colin. "Ernst Lohmeyer's *Kyrios Jesus.*" Pages 6–42 in *Where Christology Began: Essays on Philippians 2.* Edited by Ralph P. Martin and Brian J. Dodd. Louisville: Westminster John Knox, 1998.

Esking, Erik. *Glaube und Geschichte in der theologischen Exegese Ernst Lohmeyers: Zugleich ein Beitrag zur Geschichte der neutestamentlichen Interpretation.* Acta seminarii neotestamentici upsaliensis 18. Lund: Gleerups, 1951.

Otto, Wolfgang, ed. *Freiheit in der Gebundenheit: Zur Erinnerung an den Theologen Ernst Lohmeyer anlässlich seines 100. Geburtstages.* Göttingen: Vandenhoeck & Ruprecht, 1990.

Index of Subjects

Acts of the Apostles, 49, 59, 67, 68, 98, 100, 104, 110, 116–17, 121, 129–30, 131–32, 140–41, 147, 155, 161, 168, 185, 192–93, 218, 225, 277, 295, 324–28, 325, 326, 347, 355, 370, 409–10, 430, 445, 475
Adam, 7, 9, 26, 35, 47, 108–9, 120, 334
Allegory, 8, 94, 140, 158–59, 162, 284, 443, 448
Andover, 4, 5, 21–22, 24, 28, 31, 422
Anti-Christ, 10, 248. *See also* Apocalyptic
Anti-Judaism, 58, 200–204, 206, 245–47, 254–56, 260, 281–82, 355, 377, 417–18, 422, 424, 428, 458
Antioch, 33, 49, 51, 64, 130, 142, 181, 192, 193, 266, 326, 355, 392, 399, 450, 453
Apocalypse. *See* Revelation, book of
Apocalyptic, 27, 97, 194, 206–7, 214, 218, 222–37, 241, 244–45, 315, 365, 387, 468–69, 473. *See also* Eschatology
Apocrypha
 OT, 203, 205–6, 220, 246–47, 259, 420, 425
 Wisdom of Solomon, 70, 205
 NT, 129, 218, 329, 445, 451–52, 454
Apologetics, 10, 36, 45, 76, 140–42, 162, 168, 170–71, 189–95, 204, 284–85, 302, 303, 344, 351, 353–54, 393, 424
Apostolic decree, 90, 97, 101, 129–30, 131, 192, 209, 268, 355, 437, 441. *See also* Acts of the Apostles
Apostolic fathers, 71–73, 76, 83, 251, 436, 456
 1 Clement, 71–72, 76, 142, 327, 436, 439, 453
 Ignatius, 71–73, 76, 218, 327, 436
 Polycarp, 71–72, 76, 218, 327
 Didache, 48, 129, 368, 402, 435, 439
Aramaic, 21, 79, 104, 130, 131, 153, 166, 197–98, 218, 262, 295, 300, 326, 370, 372, 388–89, 390, 418, 421, 438, 464
Archeology, 177–78, 190–91, 195, 434, 438–38
Ascension, 49, 168, 248, 407, 449
Asia Minor, 103, 113, 141, 143, 160, 169, 189–94, 239, 248, 320, 362, 410, 437, 445, 453
Atonement, 41–42, 67–68, 86, 91–92, 105, 107, 111, 124–25, 316–17, 350, 382–83, 426, 433. *See also* Redemption; Salvation
Authority, biblical, 7–8, 19–20, 22–23, 27, 28, 39, 74, 102, 263, 290, 294, 331, 345–47, 375–76, 378–79. *See also* Theology

INDEX OF SUBJECTS

Authorship of NT Documents. *See* Introduction

Backgrounds (historical setting). *See* Hellenism; Judaism
Baptism, 40, 50, 119, 229, 236, 242, 250, 365, 366, 432, 450, 456. *See also* Sacraments
Basel, 139, 251, 270, 367, 374
Berlin, 20, 28, 32, 44, 85, 86, 101, 111, 123, 138, 156, 179, 199, 210, 214, 223, 252, 253, 254, 270, 273, 280, 289, 311, 323, 362, 364, 367, 374, 398, 415, 417, 419, 434, 462
Bishops. *See* Ministry, early Christian
Bonn, 86, 87, 242, 251, 252, 270, 338, 434
Breslau, 145, 210, 223, 240, 254, 280, 301, 362, 364, 415, 462–63

Caesarea, 24, 95, 265, 265–66, 268, 405, 409, 445
Caesarean text. *See* Text criticism
Calvinism, 4, 6–10, 11, 31–33, 37, 38, 344, 352, 353
Cambridge, 54–56, 60, 66, 187, 267, 293, 401, 429
Canon, 76–77, 95–96, 127–28, 132–33, 135, 142–43, 162, 165–66, 263, 324, 346–47, 368–69, 391–92, 435–36
Catholic Epistles, 52, 61, 103, 110, 117, 147, 161, 180, 295, 297, 338, 368, 370, 378, 392, 395, 461, 462
    James, 62, 90, 92, 95, 108, 278–79, 299, 369, 378, 392, 441
    1 Peter, 61–62, 90, 98, 103, 108, 117, 129, 161, 190–91, 192, 277, 292, 295, 299–300, 303, 325, 326, 368, 370, 381
    2 Peter, 59, 77, 95, 103, 117, 161, 263, 292, 295, 346, 364, 370, 378, 436
    Jude, 19, 95, 103, 117, 204, 299, 370
Census (of Luke 2), 48, 194, 201, 372
Chicago, 44, 305–6, 311, 317, 323, 338, 339, 341

Chicago School, 305–30, 338–39, 473
Christology, 7, 22, 36, 40–41, 44–46, 70, 79, 81–82, 88, 109, 118–19, 120, 124–25, 149–50, 215, 228, 240, 249–51, 260, 348–50, 379–81, 389, 463–66, 468. *See also* Logos; Theology: New Testament
Chronology, 141, 271, 292, 447–48
Church, doctrine of, 129, 372, 450–51. *See also* Early Christianity, history of; Ministry, early Christian
Commentaries, 24–27, 34–36, 46, 66–70, 77–82, 93–94, 104–5, 118–19, 207–9, 255–56, 278–79, 296–97, 335–37, 382–83, 410, 419–22, 475
    Études bibliques, 388–91
    Handbuch zum Neuen Testament (HNT), 278, 436–38, 454–55, 461–62, 467–69
    Hermeneia, 278, 279
    International Critical Commentary (ICC), 207, 293, 296–97, 309, 423
    Kommentar zum Neuen Testament (KNT) 371–73
    Meyer Kommentar (KEK), 104, 226–27, 248–49, 278–9, 371, 460–61, 466–67
    Moffatt New Testament Commentary (MNTC), 297
Conservative scholars, 4, 10, 341–59, 361–9, 473. *See also* Fundamentalism
Corinth, 36, 97, 113, 114, 133, 152, 181, 193, 210, 266, 297, 324, 326, 339, 363, 369, 382, 394, 437, 441, 445, 453
Creation, 7–8, 10, 17, 33, 54–55, 57, 70, 79, 238, 357, 375, 381. *See also* God, doctrine of
Crucifixion, 30, 41–42, 58, 91–92, 259, 380–81. *See also*, Life of Jesus; Passion narrative

Dennison University, 306, 323

Early Christianity, history of, xv, 47–52, 70–73, 89–91, 93–101, 113,

INDEX OF SUBJECTS

Early Christianity, history of (*continued*) 125–28, 216–19, 227–29, 251–52, 268–69, 318–21, 362–63, 379, 433–55, 476

École Biblique, 384–85

Enoch, Book of., 26, 203, 204, 205, 206, 209, 438, 476. *See also* Pseudepigrapha

Enlightenment, xiii, 3, 4, 10, 15, 47, 55, 138, 156, 172, 376, 385, 455, 469. *See also* Science (*Wissenschaft*)

Ephesus, 50, 78, 80, 95, 101, 103, 133, 146, 178, 179, 181, 182, 193, 194, 209, 227, 266, 295, 304, 308, 324–28, 340, 347, 370, 379, 394, 438, 445

Epistles. *See* Catholic Epistles; John, Epistles of; Pauline Epistles; Pastoral Epistles

Erlangen, 123, 186, 199, 241, 243, 367, 462

Eschatology, 10, 120–21, 171, 204–9, 245–46, 262, 381, 427–28, 433, 460–61, 468–69. *See also* Apocalyptic

Essence of Christianity, 74, 87, 106, 125, 128, 164, 243–44, 263, 272, 319, 344

Ethics, 91, 120, 157, 206, 217, 228–29, 231–32, 237, 278, 339, 362–63, 383, 450–51, 456, 458–59

Eucharist. *See* Last Supper; Lord's Supper

Eusebius, 96, 408

Exegesis. *See* Commentaries; Methods of Interpretation

Faith, 7, 376–77, 382, 392. *See also* Justification, doctrine of; Theology

Form criticism, xiv, 146, 158, 168, 226, 229, 319, 238, 269–86, 321–32, 472–73

Fundamentalism, 312, 342–43, 352–53

Galilee, 15, 29–30, 46, 130, 161, 167, 201, 277–78, 292, 322, 407, 447–48, 449, 464–66, 467

Geography, 28–31, 189–91, 198–99, 472

German biblical scholarship, xv, 5, 16, 17–18, 20–21, 24, 27, 35, 47, 55, 60, 99, 171, 178, 189, 264, 453–54, 455–70

Giessen, 123, 199, 238, 240, 243, 252, 270, 280

Glasgow, 188, 189, 293

Gnosticism, 14, 52, 59, 70, 90, 95, 114, 115, 119–20, 123, 127–28, 132, 169, 171, 211, 218, 219, 240–41, 242, 247, 269, 282, 304, 318, 339–40, 378, 381, 430, 436, 442, 453, 454, 461, 467

God, doctrine of, 7, 11, 41, 42, 91, 246, 254, 426. *See also* Theology

Gospels, 13–15, 57–58, 74–76, 99–100, 110, 146–47, 152–55, 166–68, 249–50, 255–56, 261–69, 265–66, 267–68, 276–77, 292, 302–5, 309–11, 324, 390–91, 425, 435

Matthew, 18, 46, 51, 76, 86, 95, 100, 102, 103, 104, 115, 130, 132, 154, 161, 166, 167, 195, 255, 256, 261–62, 267, 291, 304–5, 356–57, 364, 370, 371–72, 381, 389, 390, 403, 420–21, 467

Mark, 51, 76, 86, 95, 100, 102–3, 115–16, 148–49, 151,153–54, 161, 166, 172, 225–26, 231, 255–56, 262, 265, 267, 271, 275, 276, 284–85, 292, 295, 301–3, 321, 338, 370, 378, 388, 405, 444, 466–67

Luke, 51, 76, 89, 102, 115, 130, 132, 154, 159, 167–68, 185, 255, 261, 262, 266, 276, 285, 356, 370, 372, 388–89

John (the Fourth Gospel), 18, 26, 61, 77–80, 94, 98–99, 100, 101, 107, 113, 117, 118, 136, 143, 148, 154–55, 161, 168–69, 219, 250, 263–64, 265–66, 281, 292–93, 303–4, 311, 327, 340–41, 370, 372–73, 389–90, 441–42, 444–45, 450, 454–55, 456–57

INDEX OF SUBJECTS 541

Göttingen, 20, 87, 93, 138, 145, 151, 189, 199, 210, 222, 223, 238, 240, 241, 242, 243, 251, 351, 364, 367, 415
Grammar, 24, 184–85, 186–88, 196, 208, 307–8, 354, 412–14. *See also* Language; Linguistics
Greifswald, 151, 185, 196, 242, 374, 419, 462
Griesbach hypothesis, 18, 59, 105–6, 122

Halle, 28, 31, 32, 44, 86, 93, 101, 151, 184, 210, 238, 241, 362, 364, 456
Harvard, 4, 5, 6, 10–12, 16, 20, 31, 38, 41, 301, 406, 422, 423, 429
Hebrews, Epistle to the, 9, 24–25, 52, 59, 80–82, 90, 95, 98, 103, 113, 115, 134, 142–43, 160, 184–85, 296–97, 368, 370, 441, 461–62
Heidelberg, 86, 111–12, 179, 199, 223, 257, 273, 462
Hellenism, 180–83, 190, 203, 209–220, 235, 236, 239–41, 282, 318, 340–41, 355–56, 362–63, 379, 428–33, 460–62
Hellenistic Judaism. *See* Hellenism; Judaism
Hermetic literature, 240, 340, 430, 454, 461. *See also* Hellenism; Gnosticism
Hermeneutics, xv, 5, 28, 37–42, 235, 315–16, 474. *See also* Methods of interpretation
Heresy, 61, 70, 163–72, 288, 290, 352, 452–54
Higher criticism. *See* Historical criticism; Introduction
Historical criticism (grammatico-historical method), xiv, xv, 11, 12, 15, 23, 52, 83, 92, 96, 108, 144, 156–62, 172–73, 229, 286, 290–91, 294, 306–7, 353–54, 371, 375–76, 385–87, 434–35, 437, 440, 448, 455–70, 471, 473, 476–77
History, philosophy (theology) of, 124–25, 139–40, 190, 214, 301, 318, 374–75, 434, 442, 463, 468–69, 474

History of religion *(Religionsgeschichte)*, 145, 165, 180–81, 214–15, 222, 223, 229, 235–36, 238–53, 264, 268, 269, 280–82, 318, 340, 362–66, 376, 387, 392–93, 394, 397, 407, 428–29, 430, 442, 443, 436–37, 443, 455, 456, 459–60, 463, 464, 470, 471–72
Holy Land (Palestine), 29–31, 198–99, 384, 440
Holy Spirit. *See* Spirit

Idealism (and Hegelianism), 16, 47, 52, 73, 152, 214, 301, 463. *See also* Philosophy
ἱλαστήριον, 26, 34, 47, 92, 105, 382, 391, 438
Incarnation, 41, 43, 51, 61, 66, 69, 73–74, 79, 83, 84, 98, 179, 261, 267, 269, 304, 358, 431. *See also* Christology
Inerrancy, xiii, 37, 289, 290, 298, 342, 346–47, 348, 351, 353, 354, 360, 378–79, 393, 394, 473. *See also* Infallibility; Inspiration
Infallibility, 8, 12, 17, 19, 28, 33, 39, 61, 74, 75, 83, 86, 172, 166, 254, 290, 343, 345, 385–86. *See also* Inerrancy
Inspiration, 8, 17, 19, 20, 22, 33, 37, 75, 77, 83, 86, 88, 146–47, 166, 172, 205, 245, 263, 290, 298, 331, 336, 345–47, 351, 354, 360, 375, 378, 385, 394, 473 *See also* Infallibility; Inerrancy
Integrity (of NT documents). *See* Introduction
Introduction (historical setting of NT documents), 17–18, 94–95, 103–4, 113–16, 146, 160–62, 294–95, 301–2, 326–27, 364, 369–71, 377–79, 391–93, 398, 443–46, 474–75
Irenaeus, 13, 251, 303, 392, 399, 403, 435, 436

Jena, 139, 185, 214, 252, 270, 364, 434
Jerusalem, 29–30, 52, 67, 80, 107, 192, 193, 196, 198–99, 201–2, 228, 257,

Jerusalem (*continued*)
    258, 363, 365, 384–85, 447, 449, 464–66
Jerusalem conference (council), 50, 68, 90, 97, 101, 129, 131, 192, 308, 355, 410, 437, 450
Jesus, 18–19, 89, 94, 135–36, 143–44, 170, 228, 231–35, 244–45, 252, 256, 257–60, 292–93, 316
    ethics of, 4, 15, 293
    historical, 48, 99, 100, 117, 150–51, 215, 232–34, 249, 255, 264, 275, 287, 321, 348–49, 356, 364, 365, 375–76, 379–81, 446, 463, 476
    life of, 14–15, 18, 40, 44–46, 56–58, 105–8, 166–67, 268, 271–73, 277–78, 329–30, 341, 390, 446–48, 452, 459–60, 466, 475–76
    religion of, 125, 126, 152, 156–57, 183, 224–25, 301, 322–23
    teachings of, 14, 17, 90, 91, 113, 119, 196–97, 259, 276, 283–84, 313–14, 331, 337. *See also* Parables; Sermon on the Mount
Jewish Christianity, 67, 68, 89–91, 97, 141, 149, 308, 362, 391, 449, 464. *See also* Judaism; Judaizers
John
    Epistles of, 6, 75, 80, 92
    Gospel of. *See* Gospels
    Theology of, 51, 78, 109, 121, 127, 150, 340–41, 379. *See also* Theology: New Testament
John, Apostle (Son of Zebedee), 26, 50, 68, 78, 80, 88, 106, 264, 336, 362, 364, 370–71, 390, 441, 444–45, 469
John the Baptist, 89, 150, 234, 292, 241, 447
John, the Elder, 208, 248, 266, 276, 277, 304, 327, 338, 362, 371, 445
Judaism, 18, 97, 101, 113, 128, 132, 150, 152, 168, 199–209, 211, 239, 245–47, 253–60, 358, 387, 417–28, 440, 449–50, 472. *See also* Anti-Judaism; Jewish Christianity
Judaizers, 36, 67, 71, 95, 97, 101, 103, 114, 149, 160, 193, 266, 308, 335, 391. *See also* Jewish Christianity; Opponents (of Paul)
Justification, doctrine of, 35, 49, 88, 90, 91–92, 98, 150, 152, 236, 355, 364–65. *See also* Atonement; Faith; Redemption; Salvation
Justin Martyr, 13, 77, 324, 368, 424, 436

Kiel, 199, 210, 367, 456
Kingdom of God, 91, 97, 100, 106–7, 119, 152, 166–67, 183, 197, 206–7, 218, 224–25, 236, 258, 272, 298, 313–15, 318, 322, 341, 366, 380, 388, 390–91, 440, 447–48, 456. *See also* Apocalyptic; Eschatology; Teaching of Jesus
Kyrios, 249–51, 252, 352, 432, 464. *See also* Christology

Language, 38–39, 80, 151, 178–83, 184–89, 413–14, 416. *See also* Linguistics; Philology
Last Supper, 6, 58, 107, 198, 303, 452. *See also* Lord's Supper; Passover
Lazarus, raising of, 30, 57, 107, 169, 263
Legalism, 92, 200, 202, 243–44, 428. *See also* Anti-Judaism; Judaizers
Leiden, 401, 406, 455
Leipzig, 123, 138, 145, 195–96, 199, 210, 238, 241, 242, 243, 273, 306, 343, 362, 417, 419, 455, 462
Lexicography, xv, 185–86, 188–89, 291, 415–17. *See also* Language; Linguistics; Philology
Liberalism, 37, 85–136, 200, 219–20, 223, 234, 243, 251, 253, 317–18, 353, 391, 442–43, 462, 473. *See also* Modernism
Linguistics, 195–97, 212, 298, 308, 332, 340, 471. *See also* Grammar; Language
Literary analysis, 276–78, 280–81, 464, 468. See also Form criticism
Literature, NT as, 141–42, 227–28, 271–72, 275, 276–77

INDEX OF SUBJECTS

Logia. See Q source
Logos, 22, 51, 66, 70, 79, 118, 121, 128, 185, 189, 203, 214, 219, 272, 281, 340, 366, 381, 390, 421, 454, 464. *See also* Christology
London, 31, 56, 73, 254, 267
Lord's Supper, 50, 103, 119, 229, 230–32, 236, 237, 241–43, 421, 432, 439–40, 443. *See also* Last Supper
Lower criticism. *See* Text criticism

Mandaeans, 240–41, 281, 454, 461. *See also* Gnosticism; Redeemer myth
Manuscripts. *See* Text criticism
Marburg, 123, 151, 156, 179, 210, 223, 242, 270, 280, 351, 415, 442
Marcion, 89, 95, 127–28, 132–33, 327, 368, 392, 436, 442, 453, 460
Mary, mother of Jesus, 103, 121, 194, 198, 313, 357–58, 370, 389, 452
Medical language, 51, 130, 194–95. *See also* Acts of the Apostles; Gospels: Luke
Mercersburg, 43–44
Messiah, 18, 48, 107, 116, 117, 157, 232, 233–34, 248, 258, 291–92, 314–16, 349, 387, 398, 421, 432, 440, 448, 456
  Messianic secret, 103, 116, 147–49, 245, 249, 254, 264, 466–67
  See also Son of Man
Methods of interpretation, 8, 19, 22, 26, 33–34, 221–87. *See also* Hermeneutics
Ministry, early Christian, 69–70, 212, 266, 450. *See also* Early Chistianity, history of.
Millennium, 10, 27, 319–20. *See also* Apocalyptic; Eschatology
Miracles, 19, 31, 40, 57, 100, 106, 123, 193, 275–76, 292–93, 375, 380, 430–31, 440, 455. *See also* Lazarus, raising of; Supernatural; Virgin birth
Mission, early Christian, 128–29, 431–32
Modernism, 163, 312–13, 342–43, 384–85. *See also* Liberalism
Mystery religions (Hellenistic cults), 170, 210–11, 218, 239, 240, 274, 318–19, 365, 393, 429, 431–32, 437, 462. *See also* Hellenism
Mysticism, 94, 98–99, 127, 157, 169, 182–83, 208, 230, 234, 236, 250, 252, 339
Myth, 167, 169–70, 216, 238–39, 248–49, 250, 285, 463. *See also* Hellenism

National Association of Biblical Instructors, 338–39
National Socialism, 270, 273, 434, 462
Natural theology, 3, 12, 15, 39–40, 307, 321. *See also* Enlightenment; Rationalism; Science *(Wissenschaft)*
Neo-orthodoxy, 312, 318
Newton Theological Institution, 306, 311

Old Testament (Hebrew Bible), 19, 21, 36, 41, 59, 78, 127, 238–39, 243, 246, 350, 436, 442, 453
  Genesis, 9, 33, 238
  Deuteronomy, 207
  Judges, 422
  Ezra. 418, 424
  Nehemiah, 424
  Psalms, 246, 256, 346
  Isaiah, 19, 36, 226, 232, 379, 464, 466, 467, 476
  Jeremiah, 372
  Ezekiel, 26
  Daniel, 26, 109, 117, 169, 203, 418, 438
  See also Pentateuch; Septuagint
Ontology. *See* Philosophy
Opponents (of Paul), 92, 114, 226, 274, 391, 432–33, 441, 467. *See also* Gnosticism, Judaizers
Oral tradition. *See* Form Criticism
Original sin, 4, 7, 8, 26, 40, 358–59. *See also* Adam
Orthodoxy, 86, 87, 102, 123, 452–54. *See also* Conservative scholars
Oxford, 55, 56, 73, 82, 177, 189, 190, 204, 212, 254, 261–263, 265, 293, 301, 406

Papacy, 10, 163–64, 384–85. *See also* Roman Catholicism
Papyri, 177, 180, 181, 183, 397, 411, 437. *See also* Language; Text criticism
Papias, 75, 76, 102, 153, 161, 268, 295, 302–3, 326–27, 370, 371, 402, 435
Parables, 158–59, 166, 224, 256, 275–76, 284, 388. *See also*, Gospels; Jesus: teachings of
Paris, 32, 93, 164, 230, 384, 442
Passion narrative, 232, 271, 275, 284, 448. *See also* Crucifixion
Passover, 58, 107, 198, 380, 421, 439, 443. *See also* Last Supper
Pastoral Epistles, 49, 59, 103, 108–9, 111, 114–15, 121, 160–61, 347, 364, 369–70, 378, 441
   1 Timothy, 88, 114, 278, 347, 369–70
   2 Timothy, 95, 114, 278, 347, 370
   Titus, 95, 114, 347, 369–70, 278
Paul, 89, 94, 142, 143–44, 149–50, 182, 235–37, 240, 252–53, 257, 259–60, 336–37, 347, 354–56, 365–66, 391, 407, 423, 429, 432–33, 439, 441, 445, 449, 453, 456, 459–60, 465
   life of, 49, 192–93, 250, 274, 315–16, 329, 430, 433–38
   theology of, 51, 90, 98, 100–1, 108–9, 113, 120–21, 126, 216–17, 227–29, 339, 364–65, 381–82, 428, 463. *See also* Theology: New Testament
Pauline Epistles, 34, 94–95, 103, 110, 111, 114, 133–34, 146, 160, 292, 294, 323–28, 378, 411, 432–33, 445
   Romans, 25–26, 34–35, 47, 62, 67, 101, 104–5, 170–71, 373, 382, 391, 437–38,
   1 Corinthians, 25, 36, 226–227, 297, 437, 445
   2 Corinthians, 36, 160, 437, 460–61
   Galatians, 67–68, 191–92, 227, 308–9, 373, 391, 437
   Ephesians, 35–36, 114, 160, 278, 324–28
   Philippians, 59, 68–69, 378, 463–64, 467, 469
   Colossians, 70, 114, 278, 325–27
   1 Thessalonians, 59, 278, 347, 369
   2 Thessalonians, 59, 278, 347, 369
   Philemon, 70, 182, 278, 325, 328, 467
Pentateuch, 58, 93, 151, 182, 336. *See also* Old Testament
Peter, 49, 68, 80, 90, 104, 115, 134, 142, 192, 267, 300, 303, 321, 407, 437, 438–39, 449, 450, 453
   Confession of, 107, 116, 117, 148, 154, 166, 232, 258, 372, 388, 447–48, 450
   Epistles of. *See* Catholic Epistles
Pharisees, 202–3, 255, 257–58, 293, 315, 322, 377, 424, 427. *See also* Judaism; Legalism
Philo, 121, 185, 203, 210, 214, 340, 366, 381, 387, 429, 461. *See also* Hellenism; Judaism
Philology, xv, 23–24, 376–77, 413, 464. *See also* Grammar; Language; Linguistics
Philosophy, 16, 47, 52, 87, 96, 124, 138, 139–40, 210–11, 213–15, 230, 243, 460
Piety, 31, 43, 52, 53, 135, 156, 294, 306, 394–95
Presbyterian Church, 31, 290, 335, 342, 352
Presbyters. *See* Ministry, early Christian
Presuppositions, xv, 89, 92, 234, 237, 337, 393, 470. *See also* Philosohpy; Theology
Princeton, 4, 5, 6, 31–32, 43, 289, 341–43, 344, 351–52
Princeton theology, 31–37, 289, 341–59
Prisca (Priscilla), 134–35, 334
Prophecy, 7, 31, 457. *See also* Messiah
Protestantism, xv, 44, 127. *See also* Reformation
Proto–Luke, 266, 473. *See also* Synoptic Problem

INDEX OF SUBJECTS

Pseudepigrapha, 205–6, 247, 425. *See also* Apocrypha, OT
Pseudonymous writings. *See* Introduction

Q source, 102, 130–31, 166, 195, 197, 256, 261–62, 265–66, 405, 444. *See also* Source criticism; Synoptic problem

Rabbinic literature, 198, 204, 210 247, 417–22. *See also*, Judaism
Rationalism, 3, 10, 12, 30, 93, 96, 144, 171, 234, 359, 374, 387, 455, *See also* Enlightenment
Redeemer myth, 211, 217, 218, 236, 240–41, 247, 252, 281–82, 365, 432. *See also* Gnosticism; Mandaeans
Received text. *See* Text criticism
Reformation, 23, 87, 96, 104, 127, 140, 231, 387. *See also* Protestantism
Redemption, 34, 36, 350, 373, 391. *See also* Atonement; Salvation
Resurrection, 49, 74, 86, 107–8, 123, 134, 148, 168, 170, 245, 249, 259, 268, 284, 354, 362, 381, 406–7, 441, 448–49, 452, 464–65. *See also* Eschatology, Jesus, life of
Revelation, xiii, 6, 8, 22–23, 39, 87, 93, 112, 124, 272–73, 294, 296, 307, 345, 425–27, 435. *See also* Inspiration
Revelation, Book of, 6, 9–10, 19, 26–27, 50, 51, 52, 59, 61, 62, 73–74, 79, 88, 90, 95, 97, 103, 109–10, 117, 155, 161, 169, 194, 207–9, 219, 225, 238–39, 246–47, 248–49, 300, 320, 347, 371, 381, 450, 453, 467–69
Revised version, 82, 186, 334. *See also* Translation
Righteousness of God. *See* God, doctrine of; Justification, doctrine of
Roman Catholicism, xv, 27, 44, 85–86, 112, 163–65, 171, 384–93. *See also* Papacy
Rome, 25, 68, 85, 95, 103, 109, 113, 115, 119, 132, 147, 160, 185, 192–93, 210, 227, 239, 266, 302–3, 347, 369, 379, 404, 434, 438–39, 450, 453

Sacraments, 241–43, 432. *See also* Baptism; Last Supper
Salvation, 7, 183, 313, 426–27. *See also* Atonement; Justification, doctrine of; Redemption
Science *(Wissenschaft)*, xiii, 32–33, 60–61, 85–86, 96, 137, 344, 396
Scottish common sense philosophy, 7, 31, 38, 344, 353
Septuagint (LXX), 78, 180, 184, 203, 212, 296, 350, 416. *See also* Old Testament
Sermon on the Mount, 57, 213, 256, 457–59. *See also* Jesus, teachings of
Silvanus, 295, 370
Sitz im Leben. See Form Criticism
Society of Biblical Literature, 44, 337–38
Sociological interpretation, 179–83, 190, 198–99, 221, 311–23, 340, 423, 473. *See also* Methods of interpretation
Son of Man, 45, 97, 104, 109, 117, 119, 153, 197, 206–7, 217–18, 224, 232, 241, 245, 246, 249–50, 258–59, 272, 278, 298, 302, 314, 322, 380, 383, 388, 438, 448, 464, 465–67, 476. *See also* Christology; Messiah
Source criticism, 115–16, 130–31, 153, 155, 166, 208, 267–68, 304. *See also* Form Criticism; Synoptic problem
Spirit, 7, 31, 33, 75, 121, 236, 298, 336, 345, 366, 392, 431, 432, 443, 451, 466
St. Catherine's Monastery, 29, 177, 402–3
Stoicism, 210, 211, 213, 215, 216–17, 280–81, 339, 390, 431. *See also* Hellenism
Strasbourg, 93, 112, 230, 240, 362, 415
Suffering servant. *See* Christology, Messiah
Supernatural, 6, 39–40, 55, 66, 320–21, 344. *See also* Miracles

Synoptic Problem, 13–14, 24, 51, 55, 59, 75–76, 89, 93, 95, 100, 102–3, 115, 116, 122, 161, 251, 255, 261–62, 265–66, 295, 302, 309–10, 348, 364, 370, 378, 389, 390, 440, 444. *See also* Gospels; Source criticism

Syriac, 21, 72, 177–78, 399, 402–3, 404, 406, 408. *See also* Text criticism

Talmud. *See* Rabbinic literature
Testimonies, 268, 405–6
Text criticism, xv, 28, 62–65, 83–84, 93–94, 96, 109–11, 162, 265, 338, 392, 397–411, 437–38, 471
Theology, 6–7, 22, 39, 73–74, 87–88, 140, 186, 374–75
  biblical, xiv, 10, 88, 91–92, 96, 97–99, 290, 348–50, 457–59
  New Testament, xv, 108–9, 119–21, 145, 160, 252, 297–98, 299–300, 366, 379–82, 475
  See also Natural Theology; Philosophy
Tradition, 144, 151–56, 166–67, 173, 241, 242, 248–49, 253, 270, 282–85, 302, 322, 368–69, 394, 439, 446–47, 448–49, 452, 454. See also Canon; Early Christianity, history of; Form criticism
Transcendentalism, 12, 15–20. *See also* Unitarians
Translation, 82, 94, 96, 292–93, 295–96, 328–29, 332–35. *See also* Language
Trinity, 7, 10–11, 12–13, 15, 22, 133, 354. See also Christology; God, doctrine of; Spirit

Tübingen, 43, 87, 99, 179, 213, 242, 273, 280, 374, 398, 462
Tübingen school, 49, 55, 58–59, 67, 86, 102, 116–17, 123, 139, 233, 303
Two-document hypothesis. *See* Synoptic Problem

Union Theological Seminary (New York), 28, 44, 264, 289–98, 330, 339–40, 341–43, 422
Unitarians, 4, 5, 10–20, 21, 38, 40
Urmarcus, 95, 100, 115, 116, 295, 364. *See* also Source criticism; Synoptic problem

Virgin birth, 36, 41, 86, 123, 132, 337, 348–48, 356–59, 367, 379. *See also* Miracles

"We-sections," 104, 116, 130, 131, 141, 147, 193, 260, 261. *See also* Acts of the Apostles
Western text. *See* Text criticism
Westminster Confession, 21, 28
Woman's Bible, The, 335–37
Women, 50, 134, 227, 268, 314, 330–41, 474
World War I, 178, 196, 207–8, 220, 270, 283, 288, 314, 320, 342, 361, 396, 401–2, 456, 462
World War II, xiv, 396, 455, 474, 476

Yale, 4, 5, 6, 21, 31, 37, 40, 294, 299–305, 317, 323, 330, 341, 422

Index of Names

(Italic type indicates pages on which the main discussion of a person is found.)

Abbott, T. K., 404
Abel, F. -M., 484
Adamson, W. R., 37
Adcock, F. E., 269
Adolf, Kurt, 421
Agnew, J. H., 186
Ahlstrom, Sydney, 5, 479
Aland, Barbara, 65, 400, 401, 410, 416, 532
Aland, Kurt, 65, 123, 129, 151, 400, 401, 410, 416, 434, 435, 495, 532, 534
Albrecht, R. C., 15
Alexander, Archibald, 31, 32, 343, 480, 484, 485, 526
Allen, W. C., 261, 262, 513
Alt, Albrecht, 484
Anderson, J. G. C., 190
Andrews, Mary E., *338–39*, 341, 525
Anselm of Canterbury, 316
Anthony, Susan B., 337
Aquinas, Thomas, 384, 385, 530
Arndt, W. F., 416, 533
Arnold, C. H., 305, 306, 311, 317, 521
Augustine of Hippo, 126, 127, 290, 316, 431, 533
Avery-Peck, A. J., 428, 533

Bacon, Benjamin W., 264, 299, *300–5*, 317, 331, 359, 520–21
Bacon, Leonard, 331

Bailer, Albert, 374, 375, 529
Bailey, C. E., 178
Baillie, John, 429
Bainton, R. H., 37, 299, 300, 301, 480
Baird, William, xviii, 11, 21
Bammel, Ernst, 124, 152, 496
Bancroft, George, 20–21
Bandstra, A. J., 367
Banner, Lois W., 335
Barbour, Robin, 223, 508
Barnard, L. W., 71, 488
Barnes, H. A., 37, 38
Barnett, W. R., 88
Barrett, C. K., 55, 71, 77, 188, 231, 488, 489, 502, 509
Barth, Karl, xiv, 87, 123, 318, 338
Barton, John, 222, 390, 479
Bass, Dorothy C., 335, 337, 525
Bauer, David R., 374, 528
Bauer, Walter, xv, 111, 118, 119, 412, *415–17*, 433, 436, *451–55*, 469, 470, 471, 473, 532, 535
Baumgartner, Walter, 238, 510
Baur, F. C., 14, 16, 43, 44, 47, 49, 55, 58–59, 66, 68, 71, 72, 86, 87, 89, 90–91, 92, 97, 99, 123, 140, 143, 145, 214, 216, 218, 219, 301, 352, 365, 387, 424, 433, 469, 476, 488, 490
Baynes, N. H., 269
Beare, Francis W., 149, 498

547

Beatty, A. Chester, 392, 411, 469, 471, 531
Beck, J. T., 374
Beecher, Lyman, 331
Behm, Johannes, 364
Beijer, Erik, 455, 537
Bell, Gertrude L., 191
Bellinzoni, A. J., Jr., 265
Bengel, J. A., 398
Bensly, R. L., 178, 267, 403, 530
Berger, Klaus, 286
Bergson, Henri, 443
Bernard, J. H., 267, 515
Bernoulli, C. Albrecht, 139, 143–44, 496
Besier, Gerhard, 434, 534
Best, E., 293
Bethune-Baker, J. F., 267, 513
Betz, Hans Dieter, 153, 453, 535
Bewer, J. A., 28, 29, 484
Beza, Theodore, 403
Bianchi, Ugo, 222, 241
Bienemann, G. A., 251, 253, 511
Bierma, L. D., 127, 495
Billerbeck, Paul, 417, *419–422*, 428, 472, 533
Bismarck, Otto von, 85–86, 123
Bittner, W. J., 376, 529
Black, J. S., 158, 490, 499
Blake, R. P., 397, 408, 409, 531
Blanchamp, Henry, 417
Blank, Reiner, 285, 517
Blass, Friedrich, xvii, *184–85*, 220, 370, 389, 412, 471, 473, 502
Blayney, Benjamin, 329
Blondel, Maurice, 163
Bockmuehl, Marcus, 418
Bockmühl, Klaus, 376, 530
Boers, Hendrikus, 222
Bonhoeffer, Dietrich, 122
Bopp, F., 413
Bornkamm, Günther, 273, 274, 467, 516, 517
Bornkamm, Heinrich, 434
Borsch, Frederick H., 486
Bousset, Wilhelm, 162, 222, 226, *243–251*, 252, 264, 280, 286, 352, 355, 365, 424, 436, 472, 475, 499, 511, 512, 513
Bovon, François, 152, 154, 238, 499, 510
Bowden, John, 233, 509
Bowden, H. W., 486
Bowler, M. G., 254, 513
Boynton, R. W., 163, 500
Braaten, Carl E., 272
Brändle, Rudolf, 140, 142, 497
Bratcher, Robert, 333, 334, 518
Braun, F. -M., 384, 530
Bray, Gerald, 478
Bremner, George, 363, 486, 527
Bricker, G. M., 48, 486
Briggs, Charles Augustus, 207, *289–93*, 298, 360, 519–20
Brind, Moses, 257
Brinton, Crane, 429, 430
Bromily, Geoffrey W., xx
Brown, Antoinette (A. B. Blackwell), 332, 524
Brown, Colin, 223, 463, 537
Brown, Francis, 291
Brown, Jerry W., 21, 23, 29, 37, 480
Browning, Elizabeth B., 16
Brugmann, K., 413
Buchanan, Neil, 125, 495
Büchsel, Friedrich, 269, 285, 517
Buckminster, J. S., 20
Bultmann, Rudolf, xiv, 123, 151, 168, 223, 269, 270, 280–286, 287, 319, 338, 339, 434, 462, 473, 479, 496, 514, 515, 517
Burch, Vacher, 405, 531
Burckhardt, Jakob, 374
Burgon, J. W., 65, 82, 488
Buri, Fritz, 112
Burke, Ronald, 164, 500
Burkett, Delbert, 478
Burkitt, F. C., 178, 223, 254, 261, *267–69*, 403, 474, 510, 513, 514, 530
Burn, A. E., 368, 527
Burn, C. S., 368, 527
Burton, Ernest DeWitt, 305, *306–11*, 317, 330, 359, 474, 475, 521, 522
Bushnell, Horace, 5, 10, *37–42*, 53, 475, 485

INDEX OF NAMES

Bushnell, Katharine C., 335
Buss, Martin J., 269, 270, 517
Buttmann, Alexander, *184*, 185, 186, 502
Buttmann, Philip, 29, 184, 186
Buttolph, Philip, 278

Cadbury, H. J., xiv, 410
Calhoun, R. L., 300
Calvin, John, 4, 6, 290
Campbell, Alexander, 5, 6
Campbell, Jerry D., 46, 480
Canney, M. A., 135
Caquot, André, 93, 206, 491
Carlyle, Thomas, 16, 243
Case, Shirely Jackson, 123, 305, 306, *317–23*, 330, 328, 338, 473, 475, 523
Casey, R. P., 406
Cassels, W. R., 55, 487
Causse, A., 93, 491
Cauthen, Kenneth, 311, 316, 522
Cazden, Elizabeth, 332
Chable, E. R., 11, 21, 480
Chadwick, Henry, 73, 429, 430
Chadwick, J. W., 15
Chai, Leon, 6
Chamberlain, Ava, 8, 481
Channing, W. E., 11, 22, 483
Chapman, M. D., 264, 514
Charles, M. P., 269
Charles, R. H., 199, *204–9*, 220, 472, 475, 505–6
Charlesworth, James H., 206
Chase, F. H., 267, 515
Chauncy, Charles, 11
Chaytor, H. J., 223, 507
Cheney, Mary Bushnell, 37, 38
Cherry, Conrad, 6, 8, 38, 480, 481
Cheyne, T. K., 158, 499
Chilton, Bruce, 263, 265
Chrisope, T. A., 352
Christensen, R. L., 289
Christie, Peter, 200, 504
Church, F. F., 4
Clarke, Frank, 274, 517
Clayton, Joseph, 73, 74
Cobb, J. H., 323, 524
Coffin, H. S., 289

Cohen, Lucy, 254
Cohen, Shaye J. D., 128, 204
Coleridge, Samuel Taylor, 37, 38, 55, 351
Collins, Adela Yarbro, 287, 331, 524
Collins, Robert E., 482
Colpe, Carsten, 241, 510
Colwell, E. C., 65, 488
Commager, H. S., 15, 16, 482
Comte, A, 138
Conforti, J. A., 6
Conser, W. H., Jr., 480
Conzelmann, Hans, 278
Cook, James I., 323, 524
Cook, S. A., 269
Coppes, L. J., 238, 510
Corley, Bruce, 272, 518
Cotton, John, 6
Couchoud, P. L., 446
Cox, J. W., 455, 536
Craig, S. G., 343, 344, 345, 525
Craik, G. M., 135
Cremer, Hermann, *185*, 502
Crosby, D. A., 38, 485
Cross, Barbara M., 37
Cross, Frank Leslie, 261, 435, 534
Cross, Frank M., Jr., 429
Cullmann, Oscar, 270, 442, 443, 462
Cumont, Franz, 222, *239*, 510

D'Arcy, C. F., 204
Dahl, Nils A., 152, 499
Dale, R. W., 94, 96, 491
Dalman, Gustaf, *195–99*, 220, 472, 476, 503, 504
Danby, Herbert, 253, 258, 513
Danhof, R. J., 32, 484
Danker, Frederick W., 416, 533
Dare, Joseph, 141, 496
Darwin, Charles, xiii, 54, 61
Davey, F. N., 77
Davidson, A. J. K., 103, 492–93
Davidson, Anne J., 58
Davidson, Samuel, *58–59*, 487
Davies, Ina M., 61
Davis, V. D., 225, 507
Dawes, Gregory W., 478
Day, J., 195

De Valerio, Karolina, 280, 282, 517
de Jonge, Marinus, 455, 536
de Wette, W. M. L., 17, 140, 482
de Zwaan, J., xiv
Dearman, J. A., 28
Debrunner, Albert, xvii, 184, 412
Deegan, D. L., 87
Deissmann, Adolf, *178–83*, 185, 187, 188–89, 220, 413, 429, 471, 501–2
Delbrück, B., 413
Delitzsch, Franz, 195
Demarest, Bruce, 33, 484
Demers, Patricia, 331, 525
Deschner, John, 47, 486
Desjardins, Michel, 453, 535
Dibelius, Martin, 168, 269, 270, *273–79*, 280, 283, 285, 319, 436, 453–54, 457, 462, 473, 475, 515–17
Dibelius, Otto, 123
Dickerson, P. L., 262
Dietrich, W. S., 164, 501
Dietrick, Ellen B., 336
Dillmann, August, 505
Dinkler, Erich, 281, 514
Dintaman, S. F., 374, 529
Dirks, J. E., 16, 18, 482
Dodd, Brian J., 463, 537
Dodd, C. H., xiv, 271, 517
Dodds, E. R., 429, 430
Donaldson, Marceline, 122
Dörbertin, Winfried, 122, 496
Dorner, Isaac, 289
Dowd, Sharyn, 334, 335, 524
Doxapatrius, Nilus, 404
Drews, Arthur, 252, 321, 507
Driver, S. R., 207, 291
Duchêsne, Louis, 163
Duguid, J. E., 492
Duke, James O., xix, 38, 480, 485
Duling, Dennis C., 478
Dungan, D. L., 112, 235, 265, 478, 509
Dunn, James D. G., 66, 351, 422
Dwight, Timothy, 21

Eaton, David, 492
Ebbeke, O. G., 186
Eberlein, Hermann-Peter, 138, 497
Eden, G. R., 66

Edersheim, Alfred, 56, 487
Edwards, David L., 54, 486
Edwards, James R., 462
Edwards, Jonathan, xiv, xv, 4, 5, *6–10*, 21, 36, 42, 53, 299, 480, 481
Edwards, R. L., 37
Egg, Gottfried, 374, 529
Eichhorn, Albert, 146, 222, *241–42*, 472, 498, 510, 511
Eichhorn, Johann Gottfried, 21
Eliot, Catherine, 11
Eliot, George (Mary Anne Evans), 55, 330
Ellicott, J. C., 82
Elliger, W., 123
Elliot-Binns, L. E., 54, 62, 486–87
Ellis, Ieuan, 212
Elwell, W. A., xvii, 373, 412, 533
Ely, Mary Redington (M. R. E. Lyman), *339–41*, 474, 475, 525
Emerson, Ralph Waldo, 12, 16, 482
Emmelius, Johann-Christoph, 139, 140, 141, 497
Epp, E. J., 410
Erlemann, Kurt, 162
Ernesti, J. A., 23, 96, 483
Esking, Erik, 463, 469. 537
Estienne, Robert, 392
Evang, Martin, 280, 517
Evans, Mary Anne. *See* Eliot, George
Everett, Edward, 20, 21
Ewald, H., 16

Fairbairn, A. M., 56, 212, 505
Farmer, William R., 112, 262, 494
Farrar, Frederic W., *56–58*, 487
Fascher, Erich, 269, 285, 319, 454, 517, 535
Fay, F. R., 47, 486
Fee, Gordon D., 410
Feine, Paul, 361, 362, *364–66*, 376, 393, 394, 395, 472, 474, 476, 527
Ferm, Vergilius, 300, 317, 351, 520, 521, 523, 526
Ferrar, W. H., 404
Festugière, A. -J., 430
Feuerbach, Ludwig, 138
Fiebig, Paul, 162

INDEX OF NAMES

Fitzgerald, Edward, 230
Fitzmyer, Joseph A., 406
Foakes Jackson, F. J., 254, 268, 293, 409, 430, 513, 530
Fosdick, Harry Emerson, 342–43
Foster, A. Haire, 204
Foster, F. H., 7, 480
Frame, J. E., 293
France, Anatole, 446
Francis, Fred O., 274, 516
Francis, Saint, 143
Frankfurter, David, 248, 512
Frerichs, Ernest S., 4, 333, 480
Fridrichsen, A., xiv
Friedrich, G., xx
Friedrich, Johannes, 235, 509
Fries, J. F., 243
Frischmuth, Gertrud, 179
Fritz, Adolf, 232, 260, 273, 509, 513, 517
Fröhlich, Karlfried, 442, 462
Frothingham, O. B., 15
Frye, R. N., 241, 510
Fuller, Reginald H., 281, 515
Funk, Robert W., xvii, 305, 306, 412, 521

Gage, Matilda J., 336
Gardener, Helen, 336
Garrard, L. A., 235, 509
Garrett, J. L., 122
Garvie, A. E., 87
Gasque, W. Ward, 131, 140, 189, 478, 503
Gathercole, S. J., 233
Geden, A. S., 187
Geiger, Abraham, *253–54*, 513
Geikie, J. C., 56
Gercke, Alfred, 211, 506
Gerstner, John H., 7, 8, 9, 33, 345, 481, 484, 526
Gesenius, Wilhelm, 37, 291
Gestrich, Christof, 434, 534
Gfroerer, Friedrich, 424
Gibbs, Willard, 37
Gibson, Margaret Dunlop, 177–78, 330, 403
Gieseler, J. C. L., 13, 75

Gifford, Carolyn D. S., 331, 524
Gill, Everett, 412, 414
Gilmour, S. MacLean, 122, 139, 457, 479, 536
Giltner, J. H., 21, 483
Gingrich, F. W., 415, 416, 532
Gladstone, W. E., 56
Glasson, T. F., 237
Glatzer, Nahum N., 200, 504
Glick, G. W., 122, 123, 124, 125, 496
Gloede, Günter, 179
Glover, Willis B., 478
Godet, F. L., 444
Goen, C. C., 10
Goguel, Maurice, 165, 433, **442–51**, 469, 474, 475, 500, 534–35
Golling, Ralf, 417, 533
Gollwitzer, Helmut, 112, 494
Goodman, Martin, 200, 505
Goodspeed, Edgar J., xv, 123, 305, 306, 311, **323–30**, 338, 359, 414, 473, 475, 522, 523–24
Goodspeed, T. W., 306, 307
Gore, Charles, 83, 486
Gossip, A. J., 293
Gouldner, Michael, 262
Gracie, D. M., 135
Graetz, Heinrich, 254
Graf, F. W., 252
Graham, S. R., 43
Granquist, Mark, 23, 483
Grant, F. C., xiv, 82, 212, 227, 273, 275, 282, 506, 507, 514, 515, 516
Grant, Robert, 478
Grässer, Erich, 156, 230, 231, 232, 260, 273, 509, 513, 517
Green, W. S., 428, 533
Greeven, Heinrich, 277, 278, 279, 515, 516
Gregory, C. R., 101, 110, 399, 400, 486, 493
Greig, J. C. G., 147, 497
Grenfell, B. P., 177
Greschat, Martin, xxi, 478
Gressmann, Hugo, 241, 245, 510, 512
Griesbach, J. J., 18, 20, 59, 105, 106, 122, 392
Grieve, Alexander, 180

Griffioen, A. J., 43
Griffith, Elizabeth, 335
Grimké, Angelina, 331
Grimké, Sarah, 331
Grimm, C. L. W., *185–86*, 502
Gringrich, F. W., 415, 416–17, 532
Grobel, Kendrick, 269, 517
Grusin, Richard A., 480
Guelzo, A. C., 6
Guignebert, Charles, 165, 442, 443, 500
Gunkel, Hermann, 222, *238–39*, 248, 270, 272, 280, 286, 365, 510, 511, 516
Güting, Eberhard, 374, 529

Habich, R. D., 12, 482
Hahn, A., 29, 94, 483
Hahn, Ferdinand, 507
Hall, D. R., 271
Hamstra, Sam, Jr., 43
Handlin, Lilian, 11, 482
Handlin, Oscar, 335
Handy, Robert T., 28, 289, 480
Hanna, William, 56
Hanson, R. D., 58
Harnack, Adolf von, xvi, 71, 87, 101, *122–35*, 136, 145, 149, 164–65, 185, 195, 199, 200, 212, 216, 243, 247, 263, 269, 317, 334, 368, 409, 434, 451, 460, 473, 475, 476, 494–96, 512, 514
Harnack, Axel von, 133
Harnack, Theodosius, 122, 123
Harnisch, Wolfgang, 158, 162, 499
Harper, William Rainey, 305–6, 323
Harris, J. Rendel, 178, 205, 267, 397, *401–6*, 408, 469, 471, 473, 530–31
Harrisville, Roy A., 300, 352, 478, 521
Hart, D. G., 351, 352, 353, 354, 527
Harwood, Annie, 94, 96, 491
Hasert, C. A., 122
Hatch, Carl E., 519
Hatch, Edwin, 209, *212–13*, 220, 472, 505
Hatch, N. O., 8, 342, 481, 518
Hatch, S. C., 212
Hauck, Friedrich, 373, 527

Haufe, Günter, 463
Hawkin, D. J., 146, 241, 498, 511
Hawkins, J. C., *261–62*, 514
Hayes, John H., xv, xviii
Headlam, A. C., 265, 267, 514
Hedrick, Charles B., 273, 516
Hefner, Philip, 87, 89, 490, 491
Hegel, G. W. F., 47, 463
Hegler, Alfred, 99
Heidegger, Martin, 280
Heiler, Friedrich, 163
Heinrici, C. F. G., 179, *210*, 211, 212, 235, 460, 506
Heitmüller, Wilhelm, 83, 222, 226, 241, *242–43*, 365, 472, 499, 510
Hemer, Colin J., 188, 502
Hengel, Martin, 200, 504
Hennecke, Edgar, 451, 452
Henry, Martin, 138, 142
Herbst, Jurgen, 21, 480
Herder, Johann Gottfried, 96, 351
Héring, Jean, 112
Herrmann, Wilhelm, 135, 351, 442
Heschel, Susannah, 253, 513
Hicks, E. L., 188, 502
Hiers, Richard H., 224, 507
Higgins, A. J. B., 440, 534
Higginson, T. W., 18, 482
Hill, Doug, 289, 519
Hill, Harvey, 164, 500
Hill, James S., 146, 497
Hill, Suzan E., 335, 524
Hirsch, Emanuel, 102, 152, 213, 478
Hitchcock, R. D., 28
Hobbs, E. C., 280, 338, 517
Hodge, Alexander A., 32, 34, 289
Hodge, Charles, 5, 10, 26, *31–37*, 47, 53, 289, 342, 343, 344, 471, 473, 475, 484–85
Hoenig, Sidney B., 200, 203, 505
Hoffecker, W. A., 32, 343, 485
Hofmann, J. C. K. von, 367
Holbrook, C. A., 9, 481
Holland, D. L., 224, 507
Holtzmann, Heinrich J., *111–22*, 131, 136, 162, 230, 233, 264, 295, 365, 398, 473, 474, 475, 476, 493–94
Home, Christopher, 164, 500

INDEX OF NAMES 553

Hönigswald, Richard, 463
Hope, J. W., 105, 492
Hope, M. G., 105, 492
Horne, T. H., 58
Horsley, G. H. R., 187, 188
Hort, Arthur F., 60, 61
Hort, F. A. J., xvi, 54, **60–65**, 66, 67, 73, 74, 77, 82–84, 110, 311, 346, 392, 397, 398, 401, 402, 406, 408, 471, 487–88, 489
Horton, Walter, 341
Hoskyns, E. C., 77
Houghton, E. L., 94, 491
Houtin, Albert, 163, 165
Howard, W. F., 179, 188, 189, 195, 204, 478, 503
Howe, L. T., 47, 486
Huck, Albert, 261, 435, 534
Huebsch, D. A., 214, 219, 507
Hunt, A. S., 177
Hunter, David, 95, 491
Hurd, John C., 149, 498
Hurst, J. G., 47, 486
Hurtado, Larry W., 251, 513
Hurth, Elisabeth, 479
Hutchison, W. R., 342, 518
Hynes, W. J., 306, 317, 523

Ice, J. L., 230
Ingersoll, Mrs. Robert, 336
Ittel, G. W., 222, 510

Jacks, L. P., 169, 171, 500
Jackson, S. M., xix
Jacob, Ed., 93, 491
Jacob, Walter, 253, 257
Jacobs, N. J., 253, 513
Jacobus, M. W., 369, 527
Jacquier, E., 444
James, M. R., 452
Jamison, A. L., 5, 480
Jantsch, Johanna, 124, 496
Jefferson, Thomas, 4
Jennings, Louis B., 323, 524
Jennings, T. W., Jr., 280, 517
Jensen, P., 507
Jeremias, Joachim, 419, 421
Jodock, Darrell, 87

Johnson, David W., 48
Johnson, William A., 40, 485
Johnstone, William, 151
Jones, Alan H., 165, 442, 500
Jones, Maurice, 479
Jowett, Benjamin, 254
Jülicher, Adolf, 119, 123, *156–62*, 166, 172, 238, 280, 474, 476, 499–500, 511

Kabisch, Richard, 235
Kähler, Martin, 272
Kaiser, Jochen-Christoph, 156
Kaltenborn, Carl-Jürgen, 122
Kalthoff, Albert, 507
Kant, I., 54, 87, 93, 230, 374, 487
Kantzenbach, F. W., 368
Käsemann, Ernst, 235, 352, 478, 509
Kautsky, Karl, 456
Kautzsch, E. F., 418
Kay, D. M., 197, 504
Kaye, B. N., 66, 71, 488
Keane, A. H., 248, 512
Kee, Howard Clark, 122, 139, 364, 479
Keil, K. A. G., 23, 483
Keim, Theodor, 233
Kelley, W. V., 213, 241, 510
Kennedy, H. A. A., *429*, 533
Kent, C. F., 299
Kenyon, Frederic G., 267, 405, *410–11*, 469, 471, 514, 531
Kenyon, Kathleen, 410
Kessler, Edward, 254
Kiehl, E. H., 367
King, Philip J., 28
Kinzig, Wolfram, 122
Kittel, Gerhard, xx, 273, 376
Klais, D. S., 5, 6, 480
Klatt, Werner, 238, 510
Klauck, Hans-Josef, 156
Klausner, Joseph, 253, 254, *257–60*, 286, 472, 476, 513
Kloppenborg Verbin, John S., 115, 212, 479
Klostermann, Erich, 436, 456
Knight, Douglas A., 152, 499
Knopf, Rudolf, 435
Knox, John, 325, 326, 327

Koch, D.-A., 518
Koehler, Ludwig, 269, 285, 517
Koenigs, Elise, 398
Koester, Helmut, 128, 280, 517
Köstenberger, A. J., 379, 381, 383, 528, 529
Kourie, C. E. T., 384, 530
Kraeling, C. H., 304, 521
Kraft, Heinz, 274, 515, 516
Kraft, Robert A., 204, 452, 453, 535
Krauth, C. P., 5
Krodel, Gerhard, 452, 535
Krüger, Friedrich, 400
Kuist, H. T., 77, 489
Kümmel, Werner Georg, 122, 139, 156, 231, 232, 235, 260, 273, 274, 364, 437, 479, 509, 513, 516, 517, 534
Kuntzmann, R., 200, 505

Ladley, C. A., 195, 503
Lagrange, Marie-Joseph, 167, *384–93*, 394, 395, 472, 473, 529–30
Lahutsky, Nadia M., 167, 388
Lake, Agnes K., 406
Lake, Gerard K., 406
Lake, Helen, 408
Lake, Kirsopp, 65, 254, 267, 268, 293, 338, 397, 401, 404, *406–10*, 430, 469, 471, 513, 524, 530, 531, 532
Lake, Silva (Mrs. Robert New; Mrs. Kirsopp Lake), 65, *338*, 397, 401, 406, 409, 471, 474, 524, 525, 531, 532
Lange, Dietz, 87
Lange, J. P., 46, 47, 485, 486
Langton, D. R., 254
Lannert, Berthold, 223, 508
Lantero, Ermine H., 338
Larsson, Tord, 78, 118
Latourette, Kenneth S., 479
Laurence, David, 7, 481
Lavergne, C., 390, 529
Le Clerc, J., 29
Lee, Sang Hyun, 6
Lee, William, 33
Lemke, A. B., 230, 508
Leo XIII, 163, 384, 385
Lerner, Gerda, 331
Lessing, Gotthold E., 123, 151, 429

Letis, T. P., 346, 526
Leuze, Reinhard, 213
Levertoff, P. P., 198, 379, 504, 526
Lewis, Agnes Smith, *177–78*, 205, 330, 403, 408, 471, 530
Lewis, G. R., 33, 484
Liddon, H. P., 73
Lidzbarski, Mark, 240
Lietzmann, Hans, 179, 210, 211, 261, 278, 433, *434–42*, 444, 451, 454, 466, 470, 476, 506, 534–35
Lightfoot, J. B., 54, 60, 61, *66–73*, 77, 82–84, 471, 488–89
Lightfoot, John, 66
Limbeck, Meinrad, 271, 516
Lindars, Barnabas, 479
Lindemann, Andreas, 518
Lindsey, William D., 311, 312, 313, 314, 522
Ling, Mary, 277, 515
Lipsius, R. A., 118
Loades, Ann, 335, 525
Lock, Walter, 263
Locke, J., 3, 6, 7, 12, 16, 31, 38
Lods, Adolf, 442
Loetscher, L. A., 289
Logan, S. T., Jr., 481
Lohmeyer, Ernst, 436, 455, *462–69*, 470, 473, 475, 476, 536–37
Lohse, Eduard, 245, 513
Loisy, Alfred, *163–72*, 172, 173, 385, 388, 442, 443. 473, 500–1
Longfield, B. J., 351
Lotz, D. W., 87, 88, 91, 486
Low, F. B., 243, 244, 512
Lowrie, Walter, 231, 508
Luck, Ulrich, 374, 528
Lüdemann, Gerd, 222, 510
Luehrs, R. B., 140, 497
Lührmann, Dieter, 280, 455, 466, 517, 536
Lummis, Edward, 149, 497
Lünemann, Gottlieb, 186–87, 502
Luther, M., 85, 87, 127, 290, 386, 387, 391, 445, 530
Luz, Ulrich, 235, 509
Lyman, M. R. E. *See* Ely, Mary Redington

INDEX OF NAMES 555

Macaulay, A. B., 490
MacDonald, F. C., 66
Machen, J. Gresham, 33, 341, 343, *351–59*, 359–60, 473, 484, 526
Mackintosh, H. R., 490
Mackintosh, Robert, 86
Macmillan, Alexander, 60, 74
Macpherson, John, 200, 504
Magnin, Étienne, 387
Major, H. D. A., 129, 204, 205, 406, 495
Männchen, Julia, 195, 504
Manson, T. W., xiv
Manson, William, xiv
Marlé, René, 280, 517
Marsden, G. M., 342, 352, 518, 526
Marsh, Clive, 88, 89, 490
Marsh, H., 55
Marsh, John, 282, 515
Martin, Abbé, 404
Martin, Ralph P., 463, 537
Marxsen, Willi, 518
Maser, Stefan, 455, 537
Massa, M. S., 289, 519
Masson, E., 186
Mathews, Shailer, 305, 306, *311–17*, 319, 330, 342, 359, 473, 522, 523
Mattill, A. J., Jr., 230, 364, 508
Mayhew, Jonathan, 11
McCane, B. R., 272, 517
McCasland, Selby V., 329
McClymond, M. J., 6
McCown, C. C., 317, 523
McCulloh, G. W., 88, 490
McGiffert, A. C., Jr., 6
McGinley, L. J., 285, 517
McKim, Donald K., xviii, 343, 479
McKnight, Edgar V., 269, 412, 517, 533
Meagher, John C., 272, 518
Meeks, Wayne A., 274, 516
Meeter, J. E., 343, 525
Meijboom, H. U., 115
Meijering, E. P., 124, 496
Mell, Ulrich, 156, 158, 159, 500
Mencken, H. L., 353
Merk, A., 392
Merk, Otto, 156, 231, 232, 260, 273, 509, 513, 517, 518
Merrifield, Fred, 309

Metzger, Bruce M., 110, 368, 398, 401, 409, 410, 486
Meurer, Siegfried, 151
Meyer, B. F., 241, 511
Meyer, Eduard, 124, 496
Meyer, H. A. W., 35, 104, 105, 226, 248, 278, 363, 371, 460, 466
Michaéli, Frank, 442
Mill, J., 96
Millar, Fergus, 200, 504
Millar, James, 100, 491
Miller, Donald G., 152, 499, 510
Miller, G. T., 5, 480
Miller, Perry, 6, 16, 482
Miller, Samuel, 31
Milligan, George, 188–89, 220, 471, 502
Milton, John, 3
Mingana, Alphonse, 403
Minocchi, Salvatore, 163
Mitchell, E. K., 126, 496
Mitton, C. L., 448
Moeller, Bernd, 151, 222, 510
Moessner, David P., 270
Moffatt, James, 128, 287, *293–98*, 301, 326, 359, 474, 476, 495, 519, 520
Montagnes, Bernard, 384, 530
Montefiore, Claude G, 253, *254–57*, 260, 286, 472, 475, 513
Montgomery, Helen Barrett, *334–35*, 474, 524, 525
Montgomery, John W., 345, 526
Montgomery, W., 101, 147, 149, 216, 232–33, 235, 236, 507, 508, 509
Moore, George Foot, 203–4, 246–47, 417, *422–28*, 470, 472, 533–34
Moran, V. G., 164, 501
Morfill, W. R., 506
Morgan, John H., 122
Morgan, Robert, 56, 145, 222, 261, 374, 375, 479, 487, 497, 498, 508, 509, 529
Morrison, W. D., 216, 244, 251, 253, 363, 398, 507, 511, 512, 527, 532
Morus, S. F. N., 23, 483
Mott, Lucretia C., 331
Moulton, James H., *186–89*, 220, 402, 413, 429, 471, 502

Moulton, W. Fiddian, 187
Moulton, William F., 186–187, 188, 502
Mozley, E. N., 235, 508
Mueller, David L., 87
Mueller, William A., 122, 123
Mühling, Andreas, 270, 518
Muller, Karl, 134
Müller, Hans-Peter, 238
Müller, Karlheinz, 222, 511
Mullin, R. B., 40
Murphy, Richard T. A., 384, 385, 387, 530
Murphy-O'Conner, J., 384, 530
Murray, I. H., 6
Myers, Edward, 385, 530

Neander, A., 44, 47
Neill, Stephen, 479
Neuenschwander, Ulrich, 235, 509
Neuer, Werner, 373, 374, 528
Neusner, Jacob, 428, 533
Neville, Graham, 61
Nevin, John W., 43
New, Silva. *See* Lake, Silva
Newburgh, Charles, 253
Newcome, W., 29
Newsome, David, 73, 489
Nichols, J. H., 43, 486
Nickelsburg, George W. E., 204
Nicol, I. G., 235, 509
Nicole, Roger, 351
Nicoll, W. Robertson, 56, 297, 429, 520
Niebuhr, H. Richard, 300
Niebuhr, Reinhold, 300
Nietzsche, Friedrich, 138, 139, 230
Niewyk, D. L., 115, 251, 479
Nigg, Walter, 138
Nock, Athur Darby, 428, *429–33*, 470, 472, 533
Noll, Mark A., 31, 32, 33, 342, 343, 344, 345, 480, 484, 485, 518, 526
Norden, Eduard, 168, 211, 270, 506
North, J. L., 188, 502
Norton, Andrews, 5, 10, *11–15*, 16, 20, 24, 51, 53, 471, 481, 482, 483

O'Neill, J. C., 123, 151, 479
Oden, Amy, 331, 335, 525
Ogden, Schubert, 280, 282, 515
Olbricht, T. H., 5, 6, 33, 305, 485, 521
Olofsson, Folke, 73, 489
Orlinsky, Harry M., 333, 334, 519
Osten-Sacken, Peter von der, 417, 533
Ott, H., 196
Otto, Wolfgang, 462, 463, 466, 537
Outler, Albert C., 47, 486
Overbeck, Franz, *138–44*, 150, 156, 162, 172, 173, 272, 473, 475, 496–97

Pack, Frank, 65
Page, Ruth, 335, 525
Pals, D. L., 56, 458, 487
Parker, Theodore, 5, 10, 12, *15–20*, 38, 53, 471, 474, 482
Parsons, Mike, 345, 526
Patrick, G. A., 60, 61, 65, 488
Patton, F. L., 343
Patton, William, 29, 483
Pauck, Wilhelm, 122, 124
Peabody, D. B., 112, 122, 494
Peake, A. S., 187
Pearson, Birger A., 128
Peden, W. Creighton, 305, 521
Pelikan, Jaroslav, 236, 272, 508, 516
Penzel, Klaus, 43, 44, 47, 48, 82, 486
Perles, Felix, 246, 513
Perlitt, Lothar, 152
Perrin, Norman, 249, 513
Peter, Niklaus, 139, 496
Peters, Edward, 216, 506
Petrie, Flinders, 177
Pfeiffer, Arnold, 138, 497
Pfisterer, Karl Dietrich, 7, 481
Pfleiderer, Otto, 54, 156, 179, 209, *213–20*, 220, 235, 475, 476, 487, 506
Phillips, C. A., 401
Picht, Werner, 230
Pick, Bernhard, 185
Pius IX, 163
Pius X, 163, 164, 385
Plantz, Samuel, 213
Pleitner, Henning, 235, 509

INDEX OF NAMES

Plummer, Alfred, 207, 291
Pogson, F. L., 129, 363, 495, 527
Pöhlmann, Wolfgang, 235, 509
Porter, F. C., 300, 317, 428
Porter, Stanley E., 184, 502
Poulat, Émile, 163
Pranger, G. K., 43
Preisker, H., 462, 536
Preuschen, Erwin, 415, 436
Prior, J. G., 163
Prümm, Karl, 227, 460, 508, 536

Rade, Martin, 280
Radermacher, Ludwig, 436,
Ramsay, William M., *189–95*, 201, 220, 472, 474, 475, 503
Ramsey, Paul, 6
Ratté, John, 163
Rawlinson, A. E. J., 431
Reardon, B. M. G., 163
Redpath, H. A., 212, 505, 506
Reed, J. T., 184, 502
Reeve, Dorothea H. G., 439, 534
Refoulé, François, 385, 530
Regner, Friedemann, 224, 508
Rehkopf, Friedrich, 412
Reibnitz, Barbara von, 139, 143, 496
Reicke, Bo, 115
Reid, W. Stanford, 352
Reilly, W. S., 386, 530
Reimarus, H. S., 101, 138, 147, 222, 232, 233, 508, 509
Reitzenstein, Richard, 222, 239, *240–41*, 247, 339, 365, 510, 511
Renan, Ernst, 45, 93, 164, 443
Rese, Martin, 140
Reumann, John, 230, 231, 455, 509, 510
Reuss, Eduard, *93–99*, 122, 136, 475, 491–92
Reventlow, H. G., 112, 494
Rhodes, E. F., 65, 400
Richards, P. H., 66, 488
Richardson, Peter, 149, 498
Richardson, Robert D., 439, 440, 534
Riches, J. K., 479
Richmond, James, 87
Riddle, M. B., 47, 486

Rieff, Philip, 126, 495
Ringleben, Joachim, 87, 91, 152, 491
Ritschl, Albrecht, 37, *86–92*, 93, 99, 111, 122, 124, 135, 136, 145, 200, 216, 223, 224, 225, 243, 490–91, 508
Ritschl, Otto, 86, 87
Roback, A. A., 509
Robertson, A. T., *412–14*, 416, 470, 471, 532, 533
Robinson, David, 11
Robinson, Edward, 5, 10, 20, 24, *28–31*, 53, 289, 290, 291, 472, 483–84
Robinson, Fred N., 429
Robinson, Thomas A., 453, 535
Robinson, Tom, 146, 241, 498, 511
Robinson, William C., Jr., 147, 498
Roche, O. I. A., 4
Rockefeller, J. D., 306, 323
Rogers, Jack B., 343, 479
Rogers, Max G., 289, 519
Rogerson, John, 479
Rollmann, Hans, 111, 145, 146, 149, 238, 241, 498, 511
Ropes, J. H., 410
Rouiller, Grégoire, 152, 238, 499, 510
Rowland, Christopher, 479
Rudolph, Kurt, 247, 512
Rumscheidt, Martin, 122
Rupp, E. G., 62, 488
Rushbrooke, W. G., 261, 514
Russel, C. Allyn, 351, 526
Russel, G. W. E., 73
Rylaarsdam, J. Coert, 65, 305, 306, 488, 521

Sabatier, Auguste, 230, 443
Sampson, Emily W., 332, 525
Sanday, William, 60, 212, 261, 262, *263–64*, 267, 474, 475, 514
Sandeen, E. R., 4, 342, 480, 518
Sanders, E. P., 122, 222, 282, 422, 494, 508
Sanders, F. K., 299
Sanders, James A., 28
Sandmel, Samuel, 422
Sänger, Dieter, 241, 511

Sartiaux, Félix, 163, 165
Saunders, Ernest W., 337, 518
Saunders, T. B., 125, 495, 496
Sauter, Gerhard, 270, 516
Sawyer, M. J., 290, 519
Scanlin, H. P., 333
Schafer, T. A., 8, 481
Schäfer, Rolf, 87, 224, 491, 508
Schaff, David S., 43
Schaff, Philip, 5, 10, *43–52*, 53, 82, 289, 485, 486
Schatzmann, S. S., 382, 528
Schechter, Solomon, 254
Scheick, W. J., 6, 9, 10
Schick, Eduard, 269, 285, 518
Schlarb, Egbert, 455, 536
Schlatter, Adolf, 145, 367, *373–83*, 393, 394, 395, 473, 474, 475, 476, 497, 528–29
Schlatter, Theodor, 373, 376
Schleiermacher, Friedrich, 86, 87, 93, 231, 233
Schlosser, J., 200, 505
Schmauch, Werner, 467
Schmidt, Daryl D., 235
Schmidt, Hans, 272, 516
Schmidt, Johann Michael, 243
Schmidt, Karl Ludwig, 269, *270–73*, 275, 284, 292, 319, 472, 516, 518
Schmiedel, P. W., 118
Schmithals, Walter, 226, 508
Schneemelcher, Wilhelm, 434, 451–52, 535
Schodde, G. H., 109, 493
Scholder, Klaus, 89, 490
Schopenhauer, A., 230
Schorsch, Ismar, 254
Schreiber, Johannes, 498
Schröder, Martin, 222, 510
Schroeder, Francis, 530
Schubert, Paul, 317, 318, 523
Schulhof, J. M., 81
Schürer, Emil, *199–204*, 220, 424, 472, 476, 504–5
Schüssler Fiorenza, E., 122
Schwaiger, Georg, 156
Schwarz, Hans, 91
Schweitzer, Albert, 101, 112, 122, 147, 149, 222, *229–37*, 242, 264, 286, 363, 365, 387, 473, 475, 476, 508–9
Scott, Bernard Brandon, 164, 500
Scott, E. F., 293
Scott, Thomas, 58
Scrivener, F. H. A., 65
Seaver, George, 230
Seeley, J. R., 56, 487
Sellin, Gerhard, 518
Selvidge, Marla J., 331, 332, 335, 525
Semeria, Giovanni, 163
Semler, J. S., 96
Shaw, Susan J., 332, 525
Shogren, G. S., 347
Showerman, Grant, 239, 510
Shriver, G. H., 43, 44, 289, 519
Silva, Moisés, 347, 526
Simms, P. M., 333, 334, 480
Simon, Marcel, 442
Simons, Eduard, 112, 119, 493
Simonsen, Hejne, 518
Skilton, J. H., 195, 503
Small, Albion W., 311
Smend, Rudolf, 151, 152, 434
Smith, Abby, 332, 333
Smith, D. Moody, 303, 521
Smith, David L., 38, 485
Smith, E., 29, 483, 484
Smith, Gerald Birney, 309, 522
Smith, Henry B., 28
Smith, J. Frederick, 54, 216, 487, 506
Smith, J. M. Powis, 309, 328–29, 522
Smith, James W., 5, 480
Smith, John E., 6, 7, 481
Smith, Julia Evelina, *332–34*, 474, 525
Smith, Louise P. 338
Smith, Morton, 422, 428, 533
Smith, W. Robertson, 151, 289
Smith, William, 77, 489
Smylie, J. H., 32, 335, 525
Snape, H. C., 442, 448, 450, 534, 535
Sohm, Rudolf, 129
Spencer, Herbert, 55
Spengler, Oswald, 396
Spinoza, B., 352
Stalker, James, 56
Stange, Erich, xx, 479, 499, 501, 504, 516, 528

INDEX OF NAMES

Stanton, Elizabeth Cady, 331, *335–37*, 525
Stanton, Henry B., 331
Steck, K. G., 112, 494
Steely, John E., 127, 240, 249, 495, 511, 512
Stegemann, Ekkehard W., 139, 140, 142, 496, 497
Stein, S. J., 8, 9, 10, 26, 481
Stemberger, G., 418
Stendahl, Krister, 429
Stephens, B. M., 22, 483
Stern, Madeleine B., 332, 525
Stern, Manahem, 200, 203, 505
Stevens, Frederick, 446, 535
Stevens, George B., 37, *299–300*, 520
Stevens, Wm. A., 311, 522
Stevenson-Moessner, Jeanne, 335, 525
Stewart, J. B., 4
Stewart, Zeph, 429, 430, 431, 533, 534
Stinespring, William F., 30, 257, 260, 484, 513
Stoldt, Hans-Herbert, 115, 122, 251, 479
Stone, J. A., 305, 521
Stonehouse, Ned B., 351, 526
Story, Cullen I. K., 354, 526
Stout, H. S., 8, 481
Stowers, Stanley K., 281, 518
Strachan, L. R. M., 179, 181, 501
Strack, Hermann L., *417–22*, 470, 472, 533
Strange, J. R., 428, 533
Strauss, D. F., 14, 18, 45, 55, 115, 144, 232, 233, 330, 387, 482
Streane, A. W., 196, 504
Strecker, Georg, 111, 146, 415, 452, 453, 454, 535, 536
Streeter, B. H., 261, 262, *265–66*, 287, 409, 473, 474, 514
Stuart, Moses, 5, 10, 20, *21–27*, 28, 29, 33, 34, 35, 37, 47, 51, 52, 53, 186, 299, 422, 471, 474, 475, 483
Stuhlmacher, Peter, 235, 376, 382, 509, 529
Stupperich, Robert, 373
Sullivan, W. L., 163
Sundberg, Albert C., Jr., 406

Sundberg, Walter, 352, 478
Swarat, Uwe, 367, 528
Swing, Albert T., 87, 490
Swing, Alice M., 87, 490
Sykes, S. W., 56, 261, 487
Szasz, F. M., 342, 518

Tal, Uriel, 253, 513
Talar, C. J. T., 164
Tayler, J. J., 55
Taylor, Nathaniel, 4, 37, 38
Taylor, Sophia, 200, 504
Taylor, Vincent, xiv, 147, 498
Thackeray, H. St. John, 184, 502
Thayer, J. H., 184, 186, 187, 502
Thiselton, A. C., 235, 509
Tholuck, A., 16, 44
Thornhill, Alan, 265
Timmer, John, 153, 499
Tindal, Matthew, 17
Tischendorf, C., 96, 110, 410
Todd, Anne, 335, 525
Todd, Stewart, 465, 537
Torrey, C. C., 325
Toulouse, M. G., xix, 480
Tracy, David, 478
Trantham, Henry, 122
Traub, Hellmut, 112, 494
Treloar, G. R., 66, 489
Trench, R. C., 82
Trevelyan, Janet Penrose, 244, 512
Trocmé, Etienne, 111
Troeltsch, Ernst, 122, 156
Tuckett, Christopher M., 147, 262, 498
Turnbull, R. G., 7, 481
Turner, H. E. W., 453
Turner, James, 11, 482
Turretin, François, 31
Turvasi, Francesco, 164, 501
Tyndale, William, 77, 329, 333
Tyrrell, George, 163
Tyson, Joseph B., 131, 377

Urbach, E. E., 428, 533
Urwich, William, 185, 502

Van Dusen, H. P., 341

Van Til, Cornelius, 345
Vardaman, E. J., 122
Vatke, Wilhelm, 152
Verheule, A. F., 243, 247, 512
Vermes, Géza, 200, 504, 505
Vielhauer, Philipp, 140, 270, 497
Vincent, J. M., 93, 94, 97, 491
Vincent, L.-H., 384
Vincent, M. R., 293
von Dobschütz, Ernst, *362–63*, 366, 376, 393, 394, 456, 472, 506, 527
von Hügel, Friedrich, 111, 163, 254
von Ranke, L., 434
von Soden, Hermann, 118, 397, *398–401*, 469, 471, 532

Walker, James, 11
Walker, Peter, 60
Walther, C. F. W., 5
Wansbrough, Henry, 384, 530
Ward, Janet P., 160, 499
Ward, Marcus, 187
Ware, Henry, 10, 11, 21
Warfield, Benjamin B., 31, 32, 33, 34, 289, 341–42, *343–51*, 353, 354, 359, 473, 480, 484, 485, 525, 526
Warren, E. W., 5
Weaver, Walter P., 479
Weaver. J. D., xvii, 478, 533
Weber, Ferdinand, 424
Weber, Georg, 113, 493
Weber, Timothy P., 342
Weder, Hans, 200
Weigle, Luther, 294
Weinel, Heinrich, 222, 251, *252–53*, 511
Weiss, Bernhard, *101–11*, 122, 136, 156, 179, 223, 233, 471, 475, 492–93
Weiss, Johannes, 87, 162, 222, *223–29*, 233, 242, 264, 280, 286, 363, 365, 387, 460, 473, 474, 475, 476, 491, 507–8
Weiss, John, 15, 18
Weizsäcker, Carl, 93, *99–101*, 122, 136, 179, 475, 491
Welch, Claude, 479
Weld, Theodore D., 4–5, 331

Wellhausen, Julius, *151–56*, 157, 159, 172, 162, 476, 498–99
Wells, D. F., 32, 343, 352
Wells, Jonathan, 33, 485
Wendland, Paul, 209, *210–11*, 220, 339, 472, 506
Wentz, R. E., 43
Wernle, Paul, 222, *251–52*, 476, 511
Westcott, Arthur, 62, 73, 74, 78, 489
Westcott, B. F., 54, 60, 61, 62–65, 66, 67, *73–82*, 82–84, 110, 311, 346, 392, 397, 398, 401–2, 406, 408, 471, 474, 487, 488, 489
Wettstein, J. J., 399
Weyer-Menkhoff, Stephan, 87, 91, 491
Weymouth, R. F., 296
Whiston, William, 11
Whitby, Daniel, 11
Wiefel, Wolfgang, 149
Wiener, Max, 253
Wilder, Amos, 509
Wilke, C. G., 122, 185
Wilkinson, J. R., 130, 131, 132, 398, 494, 495, 532
Willard, Frances E., 337
Williams, George H., 11, 480
Williams, Jay G., 28, 228, 484
Williams, Michael A., 279, 515
Willis, Wendell, 229
Willoughby, H. R., 307, 308, 311, 521, 522
Wilson, John E., 139
Wilson, R. A., 272, 516
Wilson, R. McL., 452
Wilson, William E., 182, 183, 501
Wimbush, Vincent L., 289, 519
Windelband, W., 230
Windisch, Hans, 436, *455–62*, 463, 466, 470, 472, 536
Winer, G. B., 24, 29, 186, 187, 188, 502
Wolf, Ernst, 112, 494
Wolfes, Matthias, 273
Wonneberger, Reinhard, 238
Wood, J. T., 178
Woolf, B. L., 274, 440, 516, 535
Woolley, Mary E., 337
Wrede, William, 87, 101, 102, 117,

INDEX OF NAMES

144–51, 156, 157, 162, 172, 173, 222, 228, 232, 233–34, 241, 249, 264, 270, 274, 287, 355, 364, 365, 372, 374, 472, 476, 497–98, 509, 511, 529
Wright, Conrad E., 11, 480, 482
Wright, Tom, 479
Wright, William A., 77, 489
Wycliffe, J., 333
Wyon, Olive, 123, 446, 535
Wyrwa, Dietmar, 434, 534

Yamauchi, E. M.. 195, 241, 503, 511
Yarbro, Adela. *See* Collins, Adela Yarbro

Yarbrough, R. W., 21, 373, 383
Yeomans, E. E., 48, 486
Yrigoyen, Charles, Jr., 48, 486

Zahn, Theodor, *367–73*, 389, 392, 394, 395, 473, 474, 527–28
Zahn-Harnack, Agnes von, 122, 124, 133, 496
Zeller, E., 122, 141, 496
Zöpffel, R., 112
Zürcher, Johann, 235, 509

Index of Scripture

OLD TESTAMENT

Genesis
1	238, 510
1:1	79, 118
1:3	118
8:6-7	333
15:6	279
22	152, 154, 499

Leviticus
19:18	420

Deuteronomy
10:19	420
21:23	68

Psalms
88:27	70

Isaiah
7:14	132, 358
40–66	291

Daniel
7:1-7	209
7:13-14	45

APOCRYPHA

Wisdom of Solomon
9:15	460

NEW TESTAMENT

Matthew
1:16	356–57
4:10	154
4:11	167
5:43	420
5:43-48	256
6:34	283
8:28	104, 106
10:23	232
10:27	199
13	403
15:21-28	14
15:22-28	134
16:13	64
16:13-20	104

INDEX OF SCRIPTURE

16:13-28	372	14:51-52	103	1:2-5	79
16:18	46, 450	14:52	267	1:3	118, 373, 390
23	458	14:61-64	232	1:4	118
23:15	420	15:40	78	1:6-13	79
24:32-33	159	16:7	464	1:6	90
26:28	107	16:9-20	51, 110, 400, 402	1:14-18	79
27:56	78			1:51	455
28:16-20	464			2:4	455
28:19	13	**Luke**		3:6	9
		1–2	356	4:35-36	155
Mark		1	356	4:37-38	155
1:2	405	1:5—2:52	356	6:17	31
2:1-12	255, 275	2:1-5	194, 201, 372	6:24	31
2:1-5	283			6:46	22
2:4	199	2:1	48	7:53—8:11	107, 400, 402
2:23	328	3:23	154		
3:1-5	283	4:13	167	8:58	45
3:31-35	388	4:29-30	30	10:1-18	334
4	303	5:39	373	10:19-30	334
4:11-12	158	9:22	465	10:30	45
4:11	148	9:51—18:34	295	10:34-35	346
5:2	106	10:29-37	159	11:25	117, 169
5:36	376	10:34	198	11:26	117
6:1-6	283	10:38-42	169	11:39	117
6:34	283	11:20	284	14:1—18:1	155
6:53	31	11:47-51	8	14:5-6	61
7:1-23	256	12:3	199	14:28	349
7:24-30	14	15	152, 154, 499	14:30-31	155
8:1-10	167			18:1-3	155
8:22-26	275	15:11-32	154, 159, 499	18:36	456
8:27—9:1	466			19:20	332
8:27-33	232	18:2-7	275–76	19:23	199
8:27-30	388	18:33	465	19:25	78
8:27-29	467	21:29-31	159	20:1-2	80
8:27	104, 154	21:33	16	20:3-10	80
8:30-33	467	21:38	402	20:11-18	266
8:31	117	22:43	167	20:14-18	80
8:33	154	23:34	402	20:31	143
9:2-8	232	24:7, 21, 46	465	21	110, 169, 263–64, 295, 304, 327, 370, 445, 465
12:35-37	117, 149	24:26	421		
13	303	24:38-39	328		
13:28-29	159	24:39	347, 351	21:1-22	266
13:32	349			21:7	465
14:24	107, 231	**John**			
14:25	231	1–20	465	**Acts**	
14:28	464	1:1	2, 22, 118, 390	1–15	325
14:36	421			1	131
14:42-43	155, 267	1:1-18	79	1:9-11	168

(Acts *continued*)
1:18-19	334
2	131, 148
3:1—5:6	131
3:7	130
4:13	321
5:17-42	131
5:37	194
6:1—8:4	131
6:3-6	69
6:3	167
8:1	49
8:5-40	131
9:8-9	373
9:26-30	67
9:31	465
9:31—11:18	131
11:19-30	131
11:29	192
11:30	268
12:1-23	131
12:25—15:13	131
13:4—21:18	277
13:6-12	430
13:46	193
15	101, 192, 268, 355, 409
15:23-29	90, 97, 192, 209, 355, 437, 441
15:29	129
16:1-6	308
16:10	193
16:17	193
17	270
18:22	193
19:11	193
21:22-26	132
21:25	129
22:3	365
22:17	192
23:1-10	132
26:4	365

Romans
1–16	62
1:1—16:23	445
1–7	488
1	148
1:1-7	349
1:17	25
1:18—8:39	382
2:14	159
3:21-31	34, 382, 438
3:21-30	391
3:21-26	333, 334
3:22	382
3:24-25	373
3:24	34, 391
3:25	26, 47, 92, 105, 382–83, 391
3:27—4:25	171
5	109
5:12-21	26, 35
5:12	26, 35, 47
5:13-17	35
5:14	8
5:18-19	26, 35
7	9
7:18	9
8	9
8:3	349
12:1—15:13	383
14	25
14:12	189
15:19	465
16	25, 59, 101, 103, 146, 182, 294–95, 326, 369, 438
16:1-20	160
16:24	438
16:25-27	134

1 Corinthians
1:10-17	297
1:10-12	437
1:18—3:4	226
1:18-25	226
3:11	46
5:9	294
6:3-13	171
9:9	198
10:4	36
10:16	242
10:21	437
11:23	439
11:23-26	242
14:33-36	227
14:34	334
14:34-35	118, 332, 335, 524
15	436, 461
15:3-8	134
15:5-8	465
15:24-28	12
15:42-57	351
15:50	121, 347, 367
15:52-54	461

2 Corinthians
1–9	294, 460
5	433, 461
5:1-10	460-61
5:1	460
5:2	461
5:4	461
5:14	92
5:16	228, 365
5:17-18	42
5:21	67
6:14—7:1	294
10–13	114, 294, 432–33, 460
10:7	437
12	171
12:2	247
12:7	192

Galatians
1	67, 391
1:2	192
1:11-12	309
1:15-17	67
1:15	373, 391
1:16	373
1:18-24	67
2	129, 142, 268, 355
2:1-10	192, 437
2:9	437
2:11-21	192
3:1	365, 416

INDEX OF SCRIPTURE

3:13	67, 309	**2 Thessalonians**		**1 John**	
4:4	357	2:2-12	228	1:1	80
4:13	192			5:7	400
5:11-12	296	**1 Timothy**			
		2:8-15	118	**Revelation**	
Ephesians		2:11-12	332, 524	1–13	208
1:1	35, 324	2:11-15	333–34	1–5	27
1:4	35	5:18	198	1	208
2:20	46, 325			1:4	325
		2 Timothy		2	208
Philippians		3:16	346	2:1-7	209
1:1	69			2:6	209
2	469	**Philemon**		2:14	209
2:5-11	463–64, 537	22	25	3:18	461
2:5-9	349	**Hebrews**		6–11	27
2:6	69	1:1-4	297	11:8	27
2:6-11	464	1:3	22	12–19	27
2:6-7	22	2:9	25	12–14	248
2:8-11	25	8	81	12	238, 252
2:11	466	8:1-6	81	12:1-17	248
2:24	25	9:4	9	13	209
4:4	328	9:22	41	13:1-10	209
4:18	69	13:18-19	25	13:1	27, 320
				13:4	209
Colossians		**James**		13:11	27, 320
1:15-17	70	2:14-26	279	14–22	208
1:16	390			16:12	10
4:16	325	**1 Peter**		17:10,11	225
		3:19	402	20:1-22:5	27
1 Thessalonians		5:13	302	21:14	325
4	461			22:2	209
5:23	217	**2 Peter**			
		1:19-21	346